ENCYCLOPEDIA OF

FOODS

HEALTHY RECIPES

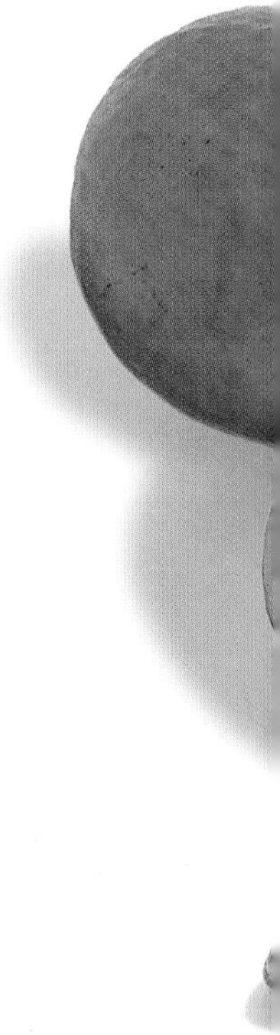

ENCYCLOPEDIA OF

FOODS

HEALTHY RECIPES

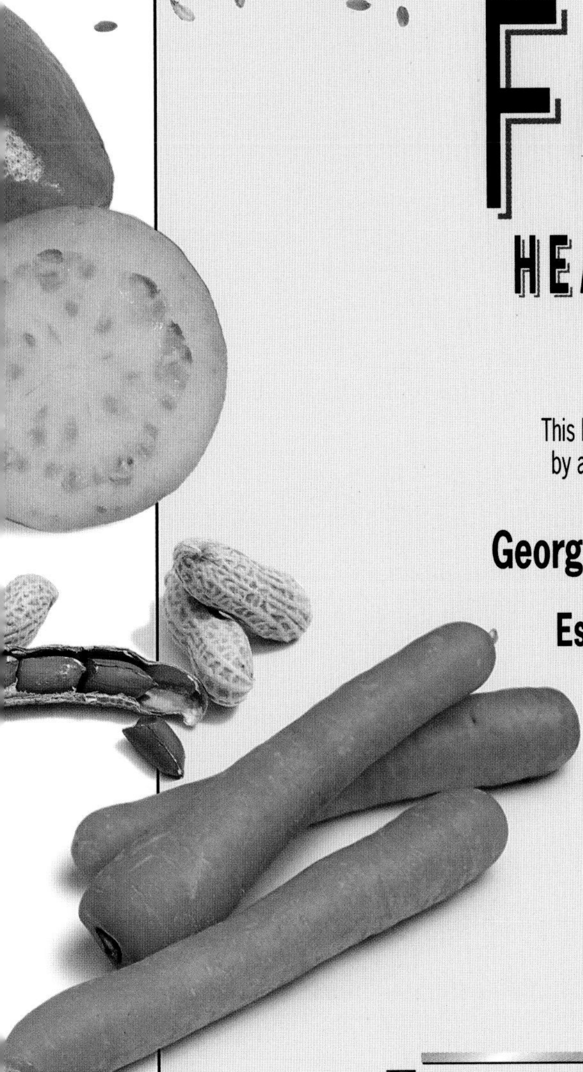

This book of Healthy Recipes has been prepared by a team of experts in dietetics and nutrition, under the medical direction of

George D. Pamplona-Roger, M.D.

and the contribution of

Ester Malaxetxebarria, M.D.

3

EDUCATION AND HEALTH LIBRARY

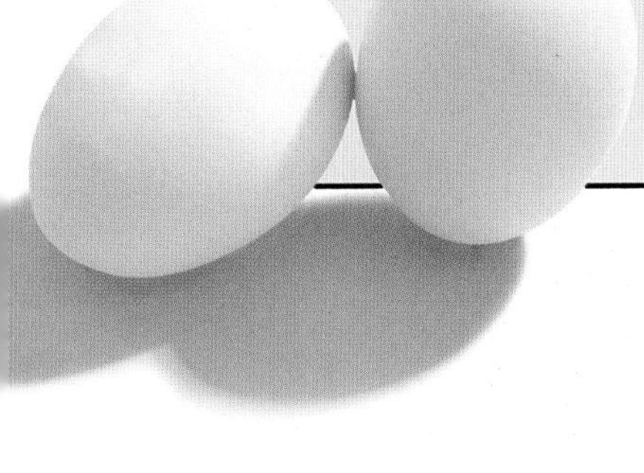

editorial safeliz

Education and Health Library

Encyclopedia of Foods and Their Healing Power

EDITORIAL TEAM

General Manager CÉSAR MAYA MONTES
Administration SERGIO MATO RHINER
Research & Development GEORGE D. PAMPLONA-ROGER
International Marketing ELISABETH SANGÜESA ABENIA
Publishing Manager LEONARDO ESTEBAN RAVIER
Production & Logistics MARTÍN GONZÁLEZ HUELMO

Edition RAQUEL CARMONA, MÓNICA DÍAZ, LUIS GONZÁLEZ SORIANO, JUAN F. SÁNCHEZ PEÑAS
Layout, Design & Photography ISAAC CHÍA MAYOLAS, JOSÉ Mª WEINDL, JAVIER ZANUY PASCUAL

Translation Annette Melgosa

Pradillo, 6 – Polígono Industrial La Mina
E-28770 Colmenar Viejo, Madrid, Spain
tel. [+34] 918 459 877 – fax [+34] 918 459 865
admin@safeliz.com – www.safeliz.com

Legal Deposit: V-4966-2006
ISBN: 978-84-7208-345-5 (Complete work)
978-84-7208-348-6 (Volume 3)

This ENCYCLOPEDIA is distributed in USA and Canada by
Review and Herald Publishing Association
55 W. Oak Ridge Drive, Hagerstown, Maryland 21701, USA
tel. [+1] 301-393-3000
email: hhes@rhpa.org

PRINTED IN THE UNITED STATES OF AMERICA

Disclaimer: It is the wish of the author and the publisher that the contents of this work be of value in orienting and informing our readers concerning the nutritional, preventive, curative and culinary value of foods and recipes. Although the recommendations and information given are appropriate in most cases, they are of a general nature and cannot take into account the specific circumstances of individual situations. The information given in this book is not intended to take the place of professional medical care either in diagnosing or treating medical conditions. Do not attempt self-diagnosis or self-treatment without consulting a qualified medical professional. Some foods and products may cause allergic reactions in sensitive persons. Neither the publisher nor the author can assume responsibility for problems arising from the inappropriate use of foods or recipes by readers.

To the Reader

What we eat is fundamental to our health. We nourish our bodies with proteins, carbohydrates, lipids, vitamins, minerals and water; essential elements for sustaining life. But furthermore, every kind of food in the state that nature provides it is enriched with innumerable precious substances, endowed with regulating and medicinal properties that improve our health, prevent illness and are essential factors on the road to curing many ailments.

Why not extract everything that we think is necessary from food, then concentrate and compress it and take it comfortably as pills or biscuits that are easy to keep, transport and store? Many have tried to do so, but it seems that this will never be achieved. Who decides what is useful in food and what is no good? Criteria change as knowledge broadens, thus what we scorned in years gone by, for example roughage (which is removed from white bread), is today taken as a product for curing constipation and preventing cancer of the colon, amongst just some of its properties. If food were reduced down to pills, we would always leave something by the wayside. If we ever managed to find out the full benefit every last particle, we would understand that everything the Creator provided for us to eat proves useful and totally necessary.

How to go from theory to practice? How to take advantage of the benefits described in the other two volumes that comprise this work? How to serve up healthy food that is accepted by all those sitting around the dining table? This third volume, with the same lay out as the rest of the work, will help us to introduce novel foods into our diet or healthy ways of preparing those familiar friends.

On other occasions the opposite will occur: Readers will approach this work by starting with this volume, moved by their taste for culinary arts, by their search for new flavours (sometimes unknown, pure, natural flavours) or by the desire to experiment with simple ways of preparing foods that respect their curative properties. From this eminently practical and tasty volume readers will then pass on to the previous two, where they will discover the benefits of the foods used in these recipes will bring to their health.

I hope readers will enjoy every dish as much as I have in compiling, adapting and savouring the recipes we have presented here.

Dr. Ester Malaxechevarría
Doctor and Health Promoter

General Plan

VOLUME ONE

Part One: The Science of Foods

To the Reader ... 5
General Plan of the Work ... 6
Index of Diseases ... 8
Index of Foods ... 10
How to Use this Book ... 14
Prologue ... 19

1. Foods for Humans ... 22
2. Fruits ... 30
3. Nuts ... 52
4. Cereals and Grains ... 60
5. Legumes ... 78
6. Vegetables ... 92
7. Oils and Margarine ... 112
8. Seaweed ... 128
9. Mushrooms ... 136
10. Honey, Sugar and Chemical Sweeteners ... 158
11. Milk and Dairy Products ... 180
12. Eggs ... 218
13. Fish and Shellfish ... 230
14. Meat ... 262
15. Condiments and Spices ... 334
16. Nutritional Supplements ... 348
17. Beverages ... 362
18. The Components of Foods ... 382

Appendix: Table of the Composition of Foods ... 412
Bibliography ... 423

VOLUME TWO

Part Two: The Healing Power of Foods

Testimony ... 5
General Plan of the Work ... 6
Index of Diseases ... 8
Index of Foods ... 10
How to use this Book ... 14
Table of RDA (Recommended Dietary Allowance) ... 17

19. Foods for the Eyes ... 22
20. Foods for the Nervous System ... 30
21. Foods for the Heart ... 52
22. Foods for the Arteries ... 82
23. Foods for the Blood ... 118
24. Foods for the Respiratory System ... 138
25. Foods for the Digestive System ... 150
26. Foods for the Liver and Gallbladder ... 168
27. Foods for the Stomach ... 182
28. Foods for the Intestine ... 206
29. Foods for the Urinary Tract ... 242
30. Foods for the Reproductive System ... 260
31. Foods for Metabolism ... 278
32. Foods for the Musculoskeletal System ... 312
33. Foods for the Skin ... 330
34. Foods for Infectious Diseases ... 348
35. Foods and Cancer ... 368
36. Foods throughout Life ... 378
37. Getting the Most out of Foods ... 388

Bibliography ... 404
Source of Illustrations ... 416
Common Abbreviations and Acronyms ... 417
Index of Food Names in other Languages ... 419
General Alphabetical Index ... 425

of the Work

VOLUME THREE

Part Three: The Healthy Kitchen

To the Reader 5
Index of Recipes by Organs and Functions 8
Description of Pages, Tables and Boxes 14

38. Counsels for a Healthy Kitchen 20
39. A Healthy and Attractive Table 32
40. Basic Recipes 40
41. Dressings, Sauces and Hors d'oeuvres 54
42. Transitional Recipes 78

Dressings, Sauces and Hors d'oeuvres, Ch. 41

Part Four: Recipes that Prevent and Heal

43. Recipes for the Eyes 128
44. Recipes for the Nervous System 142
45. Recipes for the Heart 160
46. Recipes for the Arteries 180
47. Recipes for the Blood 202
48. Recipes for the Respiratory System 214
49. Recipes for the Liver and Gallbladder 226
50. Recipes for the Stomach 238
51. Recipes for the Intestine 256
52. Recipes for the Urinary Tract 274
53. Recipes for the Reproductive System 294
54. Recipes for Metabolism 306
55. Recipes for the Musculoskeletal System 328
56. Recipes for the Skin 344
57. Recipes for Infectious Diseases 356
58. Recipes for Cancer Prevention 368

Average Weights per Fruit and Vegetable Piece 386
Usual Volumes and Weights in the Kitchen 388
English Synonyms and Equivalents 390
Recipe Index by Ingredients 392
Recipe Index by Course 396
Index of Recipes 398
Source of Illustrations 399

Recipes for the Eyes, Ch. 43

Recipes for the Musculoskeletal System, Ch. 55

Recipes for the Skin, Ch. 56

Index of Recipes by Organs and Functions

Vol./Page

Eyes (Chapter 43)

Apricot Shake . . . 3/141
Carrot Cake . . . 3/125
Cream of Pumpkin . . . 3/134
Filled Cucumbers . . . 3/348
Mango Custard . . . 3/354
Melon and Orange Juice . . . 3/367
Potatoes and Spinach . . . 3/138
Quinoa Risotto . . . 3/136
Rice with Carrots . . . 3/133
Rice with Spinach . . . 3/192
Spaghetti with Spinach . . . 3/210
Spinach Croquettes . . . 3/213
Spinach Salad . . . 3/132
Spinach Shake . . . 3/140

Nervous System (Chapter 44)

Almond Cookies . . . 3/155
Almond Croquettes . . . 3/151
Almond Soup . . . 3/146
Aromatic Linden . . . 3/159
Cashew Stew . . . 3/150
Cereal Bars . . . 3/174
Cherimoya and Orange Shake . 3/178
Chickpea Salad . . . 3/186
Chickpea Stew . . . 3/148
Coconut Balls . . . 3/339
Cream of Avocado . . . 3/351
Falafel Patties . . . 3/198
Granola . . . 3/156
Muesli . . . 3/175
Oat Medallions . . . 3/122
Oatmeal . . . 3/154
Oats Soup . . . 3/147
Pasta Bow Salad . . . 3/165
Pasta Bows with Chickpeas 3/149
Refreshing Tea . . . 3/254
Sesame Chips . . . 3/304
Tropical Shake . . . 3/158
Vegetable Hamburgers . . . 3/152
Zucchini Salad . . . 3/185

Vol./Page

Heart (Chapter 45)

Almond Milk . . . 3/342
Andalusian Gazpacho . . . 3/360
Aromatic Linden . . . 3/159
Artichoke Soup . . . 3/231
Autumn Rice . . . 3/168
Baked Apples . . . 3/268
Baked Potatoes . . . 3/251
Banana Shake . . . 3/179
Banana Soup . . . 3/188
Beans and Rice . . . 3/320
Boiled Marinated Gluten . . . 3/90
Boiled Vegetables . . . 3/223
Broccoli Bake . . . 3/336
Cabbage Rolls . . . 3/101
Cashew Stew . . . 3/150
Catalonian Fava Beans . . . 3/209
Cereal Bars . . . 3/174
Cherimoya and Orange Shake . . . 3/178
Christmas Red Cabbage . . . 3/248
Couscous with Vegetables . . . 3/322
Cream of Banana . . . 3/252
Cream of Zucchini . . . 3/246
Eggplant Pie . . . 3/289
Falafel Patties . . . 3/198
Fettuccini with Green Beans . . 3/283
Fettuccini with Green Sauce . . 3/335
Fruit Salad . . . 3/200
Garden Pasta . . . 3/334
Grecian Green Beans . . . 3/288
Hot Marinated Gluten . . . 3/89
Kombu Paella . . . 3/318
Leek, Potato and Pumpkin Stew . . . 3/281
Mango Custard . . . 3/354
Mangu/Fufu (Plantain) . . . 3/172
Mexican Meat Analogs . . . 3/88
Mexican Salad . . . 3/260
Mixed Vegetables . . . 3/166
Mung Bean Stew . . . 3/315
Muesli . . . 3/175
Nut Hamburgers . . . 3/171
Oat Soup . . . 3/147

Vol./Page

Oriental Salad . . . 3/164
Party Melon . . . 3/176
Pasta Bow Salad . . . 3/165
Peach Bavarian . . . 3/173
Pinto Beans . . . 3/353
Portuguese Beans . . . 3/324
Potato Salad . . . 3/245
Potato Stew . . . 3/190
Potatoes with Peas . . . 3/169
Rice Hamburgers . . . 3/170
Rice with Artichokes . . . 3/234
Rice with Carrots . . . 3/133
Rice with Cauliflower . . . 3/282
Rice with Pumpkin . . . 3/193
Rice with Spinach . . . 3/192
Rye Bread . . . 3/194
Sangria (non-alcoholic) . . . 3/327
Sautéed Marinated Gluten . . . 3/91
Soy Milk . . . 3/305
Spring Salad . . . 3/312
Sprouts Salad . . . 3/244
Strawberry Delight . . . 3/177
Stuffed Artichokes . . . 3/286
Stuffed Avocados . . . 3/207
Stuffed Tomatoes . . . 3/300
Sweet Corn Drink . . . 3/293
Tabulé . . . 3/261
Three-colored Purée . . . 3/377
Tropical Fruit Salad . . . 3/253
Tropical Shake . . . 3/158
Vegetable Hamburgers . . . 3/152
Vegetable Paella . . . 3/86
Vegetable Pie . . . 3/104
Vegetable Purée . . . 3/361
Vegetable Rice . . . 3/266
Vegetable Turnovers . . . 3/106
Yam with Tomato . . . 3/191

Arteries (Chapter 46)

Almond Milk . . . 3/342
Andalusian Gazpacho . . . 3/360
Aromatic Linden . . . 3/159
Artichoke Cannelloni . . . 3/100

The recipes in bold print form part of the chapter pertaining to the listed organ or function.

See also the recipe indexes that are given at the end of this volume, pages 392, 396, 398.

	Vol./Page
Autumn Rice	3/168
Avocado Shake	**3/201**
Baked Apples	3/268
Baked Potatoes	3/251
Baked Tomatoes	3/364
Banana Shake	3/179
Banana Soup	**3/188**
Beans and Rice	3/320
Beans with Spinach	3/352
Boiled Vegetables	3/223
Broccoli Bake	3/336
Carrot Croquettes	3/112
Catalonian Fava Beans	3/209
Cereal Bars	3/174
Cereal Soup	3/314
Cherimoya and Orange Shake	3/178
Chickpea Salad	**3/186**
Chickpea Stew	3/148
Chinese Stir-Fry	3/116
Christmas Red Cabbage	3/248
Couscous with Vegetables	3/322
Cream of Banana	3/252
Cream of Onion	3/220
Cream of Pumpkin	3/134
Cream of Zucchini	3/246
Eggplant Pie	3/289
Falafel Patties	**3/198**
Fettuccini with Green Sauce	3/335
Fruit Salad	**3/200**
Garden Pasta	3/334
Garlic Eggplant	3/279
Garlic Soup	3/374
Grecian Green Beans	3/288
Grilled Vegetables	**3/189**
Hot Marinated Gluten	3/89
Italian-style Macaroni	3/84
Kumbu Paella	3/318
Leek, Potato and Pumpkin Stew	3/281
Mangu/Fufu (Plantain)	3/172
Mangu/Fufu (Plantain)	3/172
Mexican Meat Analogs	3/88
Mexican Salad	3/260
Mixed Vegetables	3/166

	Vol./Page
Mung Bean Stew	3/315
Muesli	3/175
Mushroom and Garlic Scrambled Eggs	3/119
Mushroom Lasagna	3/110
Oat Soup	3/147
Onion Sausages	3/96
Oriental Salad	3/164
Party Melon	3/176
Pasta Bow Salad	3/165
Peach Bavarian	3/173
Persimmon Shake	3/270
Pinto Beans	3/353
Portuguese Beans	3/324
Potato Salad	3/245
Potato Stew	**3/190**
Potatoes and Mushrooms	3/83
Potatoes with Peas	3/169
Rainbow Salad	**3/184**
Red and White Salad	3/372
Rice Crackers	**3/196**
Rice Pudding	**3/199**
Rice Salad	3/380
Rice with Artichokes	3/234
Rice with Carrots	3/133
Rice with Cauliflower	3/282
Rice with Pumpkin	**3/193**
Rice with Spinach	**3/192**
Roasted Vegetables	3/384
Rye Bread	**3/194**
Salted Soy Sprouts	3/265
Sangria (non-alcoholic)	3/327
Sauerkraut and Carrots	3/264
Soy Milk	3/305
Spinach Lasagna	3/108
Spring Rolls	3/102
Spring Salad	3/312
Sprouts Salad	3/244
Strawberry Delight	3/177
Stuffed Artichokes	3/286
Stuffed Avocados	3/207
Stuffed Eggplant	3/120
Stuffed Tomatoes	3/300
Sweet Corn Drink	3/293

	Vol./Page
Tabulé	3/261
Three-colored Purée	3/377
Tofu Salad	3/299
Tomato and Vegetable Stew	3/212
Tropical Shake	3/158
Vegetable Hamburgers	3/152
Vegetable Juice	3/385
Vegetable Paella	3/86
Vegetable Pie	3/104
Vegetable Rice	3/266
Vegetable Turnovers	3/106
Violet Salad	3/373
Yam with Tomato	**3/191**
Zucchini Salad	**3/185**

Blood (chapter 47)

Avocado Shake	3/201
Beans with Spinach	3/352
Catalonian Fava Beans	**3/209**
Filled Cucumbers	3/348
Lentil Stew	3/321
Lentils and Rice	**3/211**
Pasta Bow Salad	3/165
Pasta with Chard	3/82
Persimmon Shake	3/270
Pinto Beans	3/353
Potatoes and Spinach	3/138
River Salad	**3/206**
Seed Salad	3/298
Spaghetti with Spinach	**3/210**
Spanish Bouillon	3/332
Spinach Croquettes	**3/213**
Spinach Shake	3/140
Stuffed Avocados	**3/207**
Tomato and Vegetable Stew	**3/212**
Turnip Greens and Potatoes	**3/208**
Violet Salad	3/373

Respiratory System (chapter 48)

Apricot Shake	3/141
Belgian Endive Salad	3/230

Index of Recipes by Organs and Functions (continued)

Vol./Page

Boiled Vegetables 3/223
Borage and Potatoes 3/362
Cabbage Salad 3/219
Cream of Onion 3/220
Garlic Soup 3/374
Leek Pie 3/338
Leeks with Mayonnaise . . . 3/222
Onion and Pepper Pizza . . . 3/224
Onion Sausages 3/96
Orange with Honey 3/366
Potato Stew 3/221
Sautéed Marinated Gluten 3/91
Stewed Figs and Pears 3/225
Sweet Cassava Salad 3/218

LIVER AND GALLBLADDER (CHAPTER 49)

Artichoke Cannelloni 3/100
Artichoke Soup 3/231
Belgian Endive Salad 3/230
Cardoons in Almond Sauce. 3/232
Carrot and Apple Juice 3/355
Grilled Vegetables 3/189
Italian-style Artichokes 3/236
Potato Stew. 3/190
Refreshing Tea 3/254
Rice with Artichokes. 3/234
River Salad 3/206
Stuffed Artichokes 3/286
Sweet Cassava Salad 3/218
Tamarind Drink 3/237
Vegetable Rice 3/266

STOMACH (CHAPTER 50)

Aromatic Linden 3/159
Asparagus Fondant 3/284
Autumn Cabbage 3/376
Baked Potatoes 3/251
Belgian Endive Salad 3/230
Cabbage Salad 3/219
Cabbage Soup. 3/375
Cabbage Varieties 3/378
Cereal Soup. 3/314

Vol./Page

Chard with Potatoes
and Pumpkin 3/263
Chinese Salad 3/243
Christmas Red Cabbage. . . 3/248
Chufa Milk 3/272
Corn Platter. 3/247
Cream of Banana. 3/252
Cream of Leeks 3/262
Cream of Pumpkin 3/134
Cream of Zucchini 3/246
Crunchy Fennel 3/242
Garlic Eggplant 3/279
Italian-style Artichokes 3/236
Leek, Potato
and Pumpkin Stew 3/281
Oat Soup. 3/147
Oatmeal 3/154
Oven Potatoes 3/250
Pineapple Water. 3/255
Pomegranate Drink. 3/271
Potato Salad 3/245
Potatoes and Almonds 3/333
Potatoes with Peas. 3/169
Quinoa Risotto 3/136
Refreshing Tea. 3/254
Rice Milk 3/273
Rice Pudding 3/199
Rice with Pumpkin 3/193
Salted Soy Sprouts. 3/265
Sprouts Salad 3/244
Stuffed Peppers. 3/382
Three-colored Purée 3/377
Tropical Fruit Salad 3/253
Vegetable Purée. 3/361
Yam with Tomato 3/191

INTESTINE (CHAPTER 51)

Almond Soup 3/146
Andalusian Asparagus. 3/349
Aromatic Linden. 3/159
Asparagus Fondant 3/284
Asparagus Salad 3/278
Autumn Cabbage 3/376

Vol./Page

Avocado Shake 3/201
Baked Apples. 3/268
Beans and Rice 3/320
Cabbage Soup. 3/375
Cabbage Varieties 3/378
Carrot and Apple Juice 3/355
Cashew Stew. 3/150
Cereal Soup. 3/314
Chard with Potatoes
and Pumpkin 3/263
Chinese Salad 3/243
Christmas Red Cabbage 3/248
Corn Platter. 3/247
Couscous with Vegetables . . . 3/322
Cream of Banana 3/252
Cream of Leeks 3/262
Cream of Zucchini 3/246
Crunchy Fennel 3/242
Falafel Patties 3/198
Granola 3/156
Leek Pie 3/338
Leek, Potato
and Pumpkin Stew 3/281
Leeks with Mayonnaise 3/222
Lentils and Rice 3/211
Mangu/Fufu (Plantain) 3/172
Mexican Salad 3/260
Mixed Vegetables 3/166
Oat Medallions 3/122
Oat Soup. 3/147
Oatmeal 3/154
Pasta Bows with Chickpeas. . . 3/149
Persimmon Shake 3/270
Pomegranate Drink 3/271
Potatoes and Almonds 3/333
Potatoes with Peas. 3/169
Quinoa Risotto 3/136
Red and White Salad. 3/372
Refreshing Tea 3/254
Rice Crackers 3/196
Rice Milk 3/273
Rice Pudding 3/199
Rice with Artichokes. 3/234
Rice with Carrots 3/133

The recipes in bold print form part of the chapter pertaining to the listed organ or function.

See also the recipe indexes that are given at the end of this volume, pages 392, 396, 398.

Vol./Page

Rice with Pumpkin 3/193
Roasted Vegetables 3/384
Rye Bread 3/194
Salted Soy Sprouts. 3/265
Sauerkraut and Carrots . . . 3/264
Seed Salad 3/298
Soy Milk 3/305
Spinach Lasagna 3/108
Sprouts Salad 3/244
Stewed Figs and Pears 3/225
Stuffed Peppers 3/382
Sweet Balls 3/269
Sweet Corn Drink 3/293
Tabulé 3/261
Tamarind Drink. 3/237
Tiger Nut Horchata 3/272
Three-colored Purée 3/377
Vegetable Paella. 3/86
Vegetable Pie. 3/104
Vegetable Purée. 3/361
Vegetable Rice. 3/266
Watermelon Shake 3/292

URINARY SYSTEM (CHAPTER 52)

Andalusian Asparagus. 3/349
Artichoke Cannelloni. 3/100
Artichoke Soup 3/231
Asparagus Fondant 3/284
Asparagus Salad 3/278
Baked Potatoes 3/251
Banana Soup 3/188
Borage and Potatoes 3/362
Celery Pie 3/290
'Cordon Bleu' Eggplants 3/121
Cream of Asparagus. 3/350
Cream of Banana 3/252
Cream of Leeks 3/262
Cream of Pumpkin 3/134
Eggplant Pie 3/289
Fettuccini with Green Beans 3/283
Garlic Eggplants 3/279
Grecian Green Beans 3/288
Hazelnut Milk. 3/291

Vol./Page

Italian-style Artichokes 3/236
Leek, Potato and Pumpkin Stew 3/281
Leeks with Mayonnaise. 3/222
Melon and Orange Juice 3/367
Party Melon 3/176
Pineapple Water. 3/255
Rainbow Salad 3/184
Rice with Artichokes. 3/234
Rice with Cauliflower 3/282
Sangria (non-alcoholic) 3/327
Stewed Figs and Pears 3/225
Stuffed Artichokes 3/286
Stuffed Eggplant 3/120
Stuffed Kohlrabi 3/337
Sweet Corn Drink. 3/293
Vichyssoise 3/280
Watermelon Shake. 3/292
Winter Log. 3/340

REPRODUCTIVE SYSTEM (CHAPTER 53)

Cashew Stew. 3/150
Cereal Bars 3/174
Chinese Noodles 3/316
Mung Bean Stew 3/315
Rice Hamburgers 3/170
Rice Pudding 3/199
Sardinian Adzuki 3/302
Seed Salad 3/298
Sesame Chips 3/304
Soy Croquettes 3/326
Soy Milk 3/305
Soybean Stew 3/381
Stuffed Peppers. 3/382
Stuffed Tomatoes. 3/300
Tofu Salad 3/299
Vegetable Turnovers. 3/106
Vegetarian Tamale. 3/301

METABOLISM (CHAPTER 54)

Almond Cookies. 3/155
Andalusian Asparagus. 3/349

Vol./Page

Artichoke Soup 3/231
Asparagus Fondant 3/284
Baked Tomatoes 3/364
Banana Casserole 3/124
Beans and Rice 3/320
Beans with Spinach 3/352
Belgian Endive Salad 3/230
Boiled Vegetables. 3/223
Borage and Potatoes 3/362
Cabbage Rolls 3/101
Cardoons in Almond Sauce . . . 3/232
Carrot Cake. 3/125
Celery Pie 3/290
Cereal Soup. 3/314
Chard with Potatoes and Pumpkin 3/263
Chickpea Salad 3/186
Chickpea Stew. 3/148
Chinese Noodles 3/316
Coconut Balls. 3/339
Couscous with Vegetables . 3/322
Cream of Avocado 3/351
Cream of Mushroom 3/313
Eggplant Pie 3/289
Granola 3/156
Grecian Green Beans 3/288
Grilled Vegetables 3/189
Hazelnut Milk 3/291
Italian-style Artichokes 3/236
Kombu Paella 3/318
Lentil Stew. 3/321
Lentils and Rice 3/211
Mexican Salad 3/260
Millet Croquettes 3/111
Mixed Vegetables. 3/166
Mung Bean Stew 3/315
Mushroom Lasagna 3/110
Nut Hamburgers. 3/171
Nut Loaf 3/94
Oat Medallions 3/122
Onion and Pepper Pizza 3/224
Onion Sausages. 3/96
Oranges with Honey 3/366
Oven Potatoes 3/250

Index of Recipes by Organs and Functions (continued)

Vol./Page

Pasta Bows and Mushrooms . . 3/85
Pasta Bows with Chickpeas. . . 3/149
Peach Bavarian 3/173
Portuguese Beans 3/324
Potato Stew. 3/221
Potatoes and Almonds 3/333
Potatoes and Spinach. 3/138
Red and White Salad. 3/372
River Salad 3/206
Rye Bread 3/194
Sangria (non-alcoholic) . . . 3/327
Sautéed Marinated Gluten 3/91
Soy Croquettes 3/326
Soy Hamburgers 3/117
Soybean Stew 3/381
Spaghetti with Spinach 3/210
Spanish Bouillon. 3/332
Spanish Omelet 3/114
Spinach Croquettes 3/213
Spinach Lasagna 3/108
Spinach Shake 3/140
Spring Rolls 3/102
Spring Salad 3/312
Stuffed Kohlrabi 3/337
Sweet Balls 3/269
Sweet Corn Drink 3/293
Tabulé 3/261
Tomato and Vegetable Stew . . 3/212
Turnip Greens and Potatoes . . 3/208
Vegetable Cannelloni 3/98
Vegetable Hamburgers 3/152
Vegetable Pie. 3/104
Vegetable Purée. 3/361
Vegetarian Sausages and Drumsticks 3/92
Vichyssoise 3/280
Violet Salad 3/373
Watermelon Shake 3/292
Winter Log. 3/340
Zucchini Salad 3/185

Locomotion System (chapter 55)

Almond Milk. 3/342

Vol./Page

Boiled Marinated Gluten 3/90
Broccoli Bake 3/336
Cabbage Soup. 3/375
Cardoons in Almond Sauce . . . 3/232
Cashew Stew. 3/150
Cherimoya and Orange Drink. . 3/178
Chinese Noodles 3/316
Coconut Balls. 3/339
Coconut Milk 3/343
Fettuccine with Green Sauce. 3/335
Garden Pasta. 3/334
Leek Pie 3/338
Mexican Meat Analogs 3/88
Museli 3/175
Pasta with Chard 3/82
Potatoes and Almonds 3/333
Rice Crackers 3/196
Sardinian Adzuki. 3/302
Sauerkraut and Carrots. 3/264
Soybean Stew 3/381
Spanish Bouillon 3/332
Spring Rolls 3/102
Stuffed Kohlrabi. 3/337
Tofu Salad 3/299
Tropical Shake 3/158
Turnip Greens and Potatoes . . 3/208
Vegetable Cannelloni 3/98
Vegetable Turnovers. 3/106
Vichyssoise 3/280
Winter Log. 3/340

Skin (chapter 56)

Almond Milk. 3/342
Andalusian Asparagus 3/349
Apricot Shake 3/141
Beans with Spinach 3/352
Carrot and Apple Juice. . . . 3/355
Carrot Cake. 3/125
Carrot Croquettes 3/112
Coconut Milk 3/343
Cream of Asparagus 3/350
Cream of Avocado 3/351

Vol./Page

Filled Cucumbers. 3/348
Mango Custard 3/354
Pinto Beans 3/353
Portuguese Beans 3/324
Spinach Salad 3/132
Tropical Fruit Salad. 3/253
Vegetarian Tamale 3/301

Infections (chapter 57)

Andalusian Gazpacho. 3/360
Apricot Shake 3/141
Autumn Rice 3/168
Baked Tomatoes 3/364
Borage and Potatoes 3/362
Cherimoya and Orange Shake . 3/178
Melon and Orange Juice . . 3/367
Oranges with Honey. 3/366
Party Melon 3/176
Tropical Fruit Salad. 3/253
Vegetable Juice 3/385
Vegetable Purée 3/361

Cancer (chapter 58)

Andalusian Gazpacho 3/360
Autumn Cabbage 3/376
Autumn Rice 3/168
Avocado Shake 3/201
Baked Tomatoes 3/364
Boiled Marinated Gluten 3/90
Broccoli Bake 3/336
Cabbage Rolls 3/101
Cabbage Soup 3/375
Cabbage Varieties 3/378
Carrot Croquettes 3/112
Catalonian Fava Beans 3/209
Chickpea Salad 3/186
Chinese Noodles 3/316
Chinese Salad 3/243
Christmas Red Cabbage 3/248
'Cordon Bleu' Eggplant 3/121
Cream of Onion 3/220
Cream of Pumpkin 3/134

The recipes in bold print form part of the chapter pertaining to the listed organ or function.

See also the recipe indexes that are given at the end of this volume, pages 392, 396, 398.

	Vol./Page
Eggplant Pie	3/289
Fruit Salad	3/200
Garden Pasta	3/334
Garlic Soup	**3/374**
Grilled Vegetables	3/189
Mango Custard	3/354
Melon and Orange Juice	3/367
Mexican Meat Analogs	3/88
Mexican Salad	3/260
Mixed Vegetables	3/166
Mung Bean Stew	3/315
Mushroom and Garlic Scrambled Eggs	3/119
Onion and Pepper Pizza	3/224
Onion Sausages	3/96
Oranges with Honey	3/366
Oven Potatoes	3/250
Party Melon	3/176
Potatoes and Mushrooms	3/83
Quinoa Risotto	3/136
Rainbow Salad	3/184
Red and White Salad	**3/372**
Rice Crackers	3/196
Rice Hamburgers	3/170
Rice Pudding	3/199
Rice Salad	**3/380**
Rice with Cauliflower	3/282
Roasted Vegetables	**3/384**
Salted Soy Sprouts	3/265
Sardinian Adzuki	3/302
Soy Croquettes	3/326
Soy Hamburgers	3/117
Soy Milk	3/305
Soybean Stew	**3/381**
Spinach Salad	3/132
Spring Rolls	3/102
Stuffed Eggplant	3/120
Stuffed Peppers	**3/382**
Stuffed Tomatoes	3/300
Three-colored Purée	**3/377**
Tomato and Vegetable Stew	3/212
Tropical Fruit Salad	3/253
Vegetable Juice	**3/385**
Vegetable Paella	3/86
Vegetable Rice	3/266
Violet Salad	**3/373**

Pregnancy and Lactation

	Vol./Page
Almond Cookies	3/155
Almond Milk	3/342
Beans and Rice	3/320
Broccoli Bake	3/336
Catalonian Fava Beans	3/209
Chickpea Stew	3/148
Coconut Balls	3/339
Couscous with Vegetables	3/322
Crunchy Fennel	3/242
Granola	3/156
Lentil Stew	3/321
Lentils and Rice	3/211
Nut Loaf	3/94
Oat Medallions	3/122
Oranges with Honey	3/366
Pasta Bows with Chickpeas	3/149
Peach Bavarian	3/173
Persimmon Shake	3/270
Potatoes and Almonds	3/333
Potatoes and Spinach	3/138
Sardinian Adzuki	3/302
Sautéed Marinated Gluten	3/91
Soy Croquettes	3/326
Soybean Stew	3/381
Spinach Croquettes	3/213
Spinach Salad	3/132
Spinach Shake	3/140
Vegetable Hamburgers	3/152
Vegetarian Sausages and Drumsticks	3/92
Vegetarian Tamale	3/301
Winter Log	3/340

Strength

	Vol./Page
Almond Cookies	3/155
Almond Croquettes	3/151
Beans with Spinach	3/352
Cereal Bars	3/174
Coconut Balls	3/339
Granola	3/156
Italian-style Macaroni	3/84
Millet Croquettes	3/111
Mushroom and Garlic Scrambled Eggs	3/119
Mushroom Lasagna	3/110
Nut Hamburgers	3/171
Pasta Bows with Chickpeas	3/149
Pasta with Chard	3/82
Peach Bavarian	3/173
Sardinian Adzuki	3/302
Soy Croquettes	3/326
Spaghetti with Spinach	3/210
Spanish Omelet	3/114
Spinach Croquettes	3/213
Spinach Lasagna	3/108
Stuffed Eggs	3/118
Sweet Balls	3/269
Vegetable Cannelloni	3/98
Vegetarian Sausages and Drumsticks	3/92
Winter Log	3/340

Explanation of pages, tables and boxes in this
Encyclopedia of Foods and Their Healing Power

Color-coded bar to identify each section of the Encyclopedia

Chapter number

Captions and annotations

Title of chapter

Summary of the subjects discussed in this chapter with page numbers.

Main text

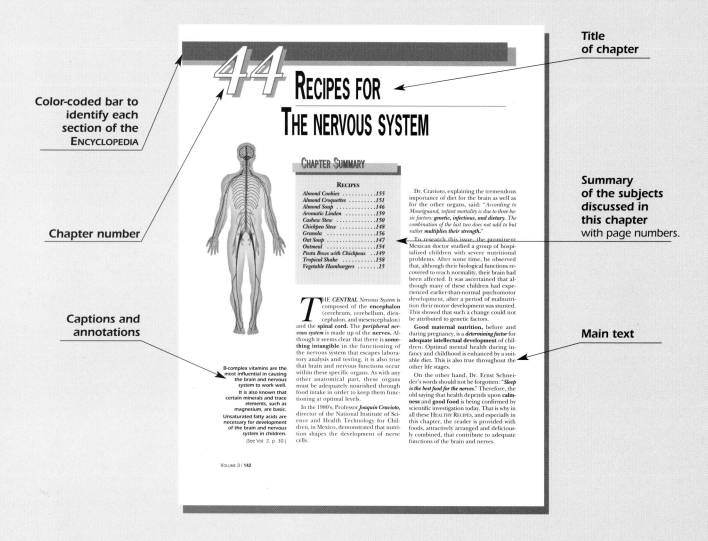

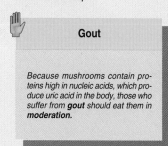

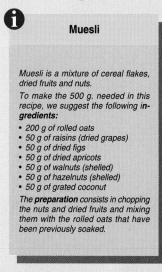

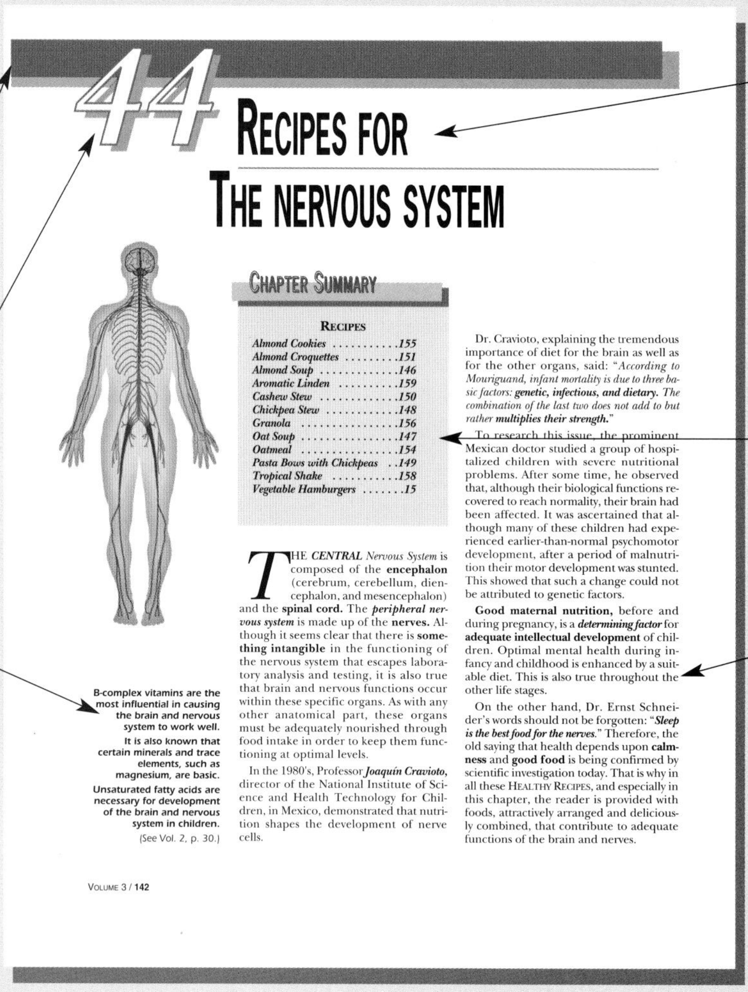

44

RECIPES FOR THE NERVOUS SYSTEM

CHAPTER SUMMARY

RECIPES

Almond Cookies *155*
Almond Croquettes *151*
Almond Soup *146*
Aromatic Linden *159*
Cashew Stew *150*
Chickpea Stew *148*
Granola *156*
Oat Soup *147*
Oatmeal *154*
Pasta Bows with Chickpeas . .*149*
Tropical Shake *158*
Vegetable Hamburgers *15*

B-complex vitamins are the most influential in causing the brain and nervous system to work well.

It is also known that certain minerals and trace elements, such as magnesium, are basic.

Unsaturated fatty acids are necessary for development of the brain and nervous system in children.

(See Vol. 2, p. 30.)

THE *CENTRAL Nervous System* is composed of the **encephalon** (cerebrum, cerebellum, diencephalon, and mesencephalon) and the **spinal cord.** The ***peripheral nervous system*** is made up of the **nerves.** Although it seems clear that there is **something intangible** in the functioning of the nervous system that escapes laboratory analysis and testing, it is also true that brain and nervous functions occur within these specific organs. As with any other anatomical part, these organs must be adequately nourished through food intake in order to keep them functioning at optimal levels.

In the 1980's, Professor ***Joaquín Cravioto,*** director of the National Institute of Science and Health Technology for Children, in Mexico, demonstrated that nutrition shapes the development of nerve cells.

Dr. Cravioto, explaining the tremendous importance of diet for the brain as well as for the other organs, said: "*According to Mouriguand, infant mortality is due to three basic factors: **genetic, infectious, and dietary.** The combination of the last two does not add to but rather **multiplies their strength.***"

To research this issue, the prominent Mexican doctor studied a group of hospitalized children with severe nutritional problems. After some time, he observed that, although their biological functions recovered to reach normality, their brain had been affected. It was ascertained that although many of these children had experienced earlier-than-normal psychomotor development, after a period of malnutrition their motor development was stunted. This showed that such a change could not be attributed to genetic factors.

Good maternal nutrition, before and during pregnancy, is a ***determining factor*** for **adequate intellectual development** of children. Optimal mental health during infancy and childhood is enhanced by a suitable diet. This is also true throughout the other life stages.

On the other hand, Dr. Ernst Schneider's words should not be forgotten: "***Sleep is the best food for the nerves.***" Therefore, the old saying that health depends upon **calmness** and **good food** is being confirmed by scientific investigation today. That is why in all these HEALTHY RECIPES, and especially in this chapter, the reader is provided with foods, attractively arranged and deliciously combined, that contribute to adequate functions of the brain and nerves.

VOLUME 3 / **142**

Warning box
Gives advice and warnings about the recipe.

Gout

*Because mushrooms contain proteins high in nucleic acids, which produce uric acid in the body, those who suffer from **gout** should eat them in **moderation.***

Information box
Gives additional information on the recipe or of general interest.

Muesli

Muesli is a mixture of cereal flakes, dried fruits and nuts.

*To make the 500 g. needed in this recipe, we suggest the following **ingredients:***

- *200 g of rolled oats*
- *50 g of raisins (dried grapes)*
- *50 g of dried figs*
- *50 g of dried apricots*
- *50 g of walnuts (shelled)*
- *50 g of hazelnuts (shelled)*
- *50 g of grated coconut*

*The **preparation** consists in chopping the nuts and dried fruits and mixing them with the rolled oats that have been previously soaked.*

Volume   Page number

Explanation of the menu pages

Type of menu
At the beginning of each chapter (from chapter 43 on) at least two pages appear with three suggested menus especially good for each organ or system.

Arrangement of the menu
It is made up of three meals: **breakfast, lunch** and **supper.** A healthy adult can skip supper if the other two meals provide enough variety and nutritional balance. The dishes or foods that are suggested are all described in more detail in the pages of this ENCYCLOPEDIA OF FOODS AND THEIR HEALING POWER or in some cases in EMP ("Encyclopedia of Medicinal Plants").

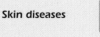

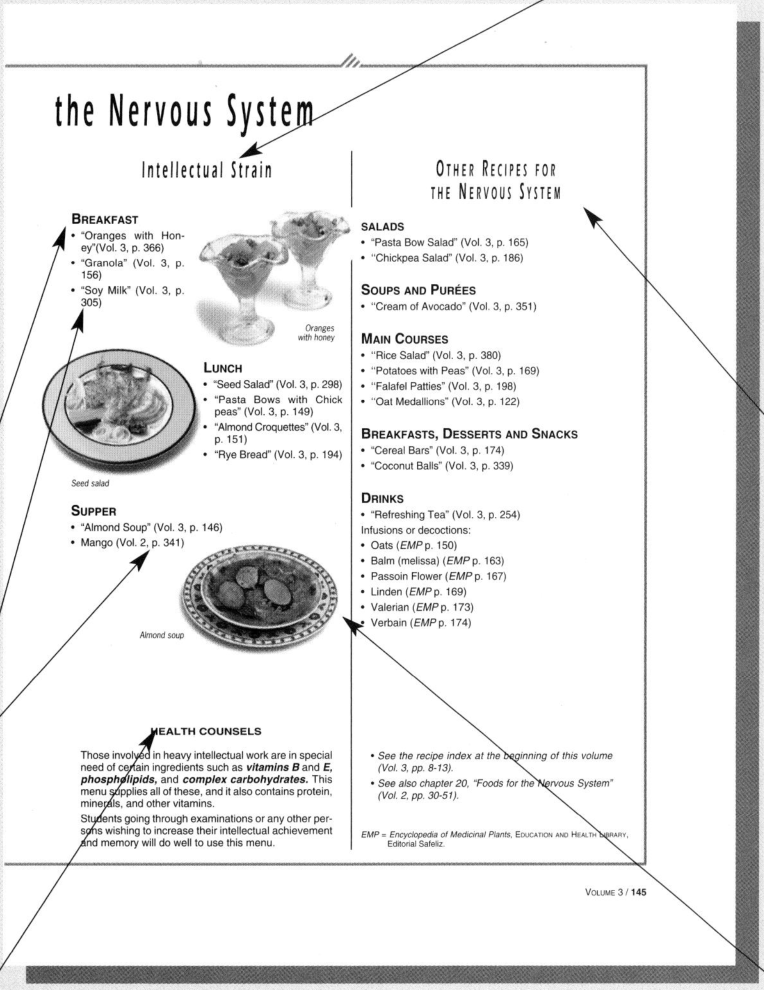

the Nervous System

Intellectual Strain

BREAKFAST
- "Oranges with Honey"(Vol. 3, p. 366)
- "Granola" (Vol. 3, p. 156)
- "Soy Milk" (Vol. 3, p. 305)

Oranges with honey

LUNCH
- "Seed Salad" (Vol. 3, p. 298)
- "Pasta Bows with Chick peas" (Vol. 3, p. 149)
- "Almond Croquettes" (Vol. 3, p. 151)
- "Rye Bread" (Vol. 3, p. 194)

Seed salad

SUPPER
- "Almond Soup" (Vol. 3, p. 146)
- Mango (Vol. 2, p. 341)

Almond soup

HEALTH COUNSELS

Those involved in heavy intellectual work are in special need of certain ingredients such as ***vitamins B*** and ***E, phospholipids,*** and ***complex carbohydrates.*** This menu supplies all of these, and it also contains protein, minerals, and other vitamins.

Students going through examinations or any other persons wishing to increase their intellectual achievement and memory will do well to use this menu.

OTHER RECIPES FOR THE NERVOUS SYSTEM

SALADS
- "Pasta Bow Salad" (Vol. 3, p. 165)
- "Chickpea Salad" (Vol. 3, p. 186)

SOUPS AND PURÉES
- "Cream of Avocado" (Vol. 3, p. 351)

MAIN COURSES
- "Rice Salad" (Vol. 3, p. 380)
- "Potatoes with Peas" (Vol. 3, p. 169)
- "Falafel Patties" (Vol. 3, p. 198)
- "Oat Medallions" (Vol. 3, p. 122)

BREAKFASTS, DESSERTS AND SNACKS
- "Cereal Bars" (Vol. 3, p. 174)
- "Coconut Balls" (Vol. 3, p. 339)

DRINKS
- "Refreshing Tea" (Vol. 3, p. 254)

Infusions or decoctions:
- Oats (*EMP* p. 150)
- Balm (melissa) (*EMP* p. 163)
- Passoin Flower (*EMP* p. 167)
- Linden (*EMP* p. 169)
- Valerian (*EMP* p. 173)
- Verbain (*EMP* p. 174)

- *See the recipe index at the beginning of this volume (Vol. 3, pp. 8-13).*
- *See also chapter 20, "Foods for the Nervous System" (Vol. 2, pp. 30-51).*

EMP = Encyclopedia of Medicinal Plants, EDUCATION AND HEALTH LIBRARY, Editorial Safeliz.

VOLUME 3 / **145**

Varying the menus
Each menu is a model of an ideal diet for one day. If you wish to follow the menus during several consecutive days, it is wise to modify them by substituting one or more of the dishes for other similar recipes. This column gives some options.

Volume and page number where the recommended recipe or description of food may be found.

"Health Counsels"
The health **benefits** obtained from following the menu are described here along with the **diseases** or **ailments** for which the menu is most **useful.**

Photograph of one of the dishes
For each menu, a photograph shows one of the recommended dishes.

Meanings of the medical icons used in this work

Eye diseases	Blood disorders	Diseases of the intestines	Diseases of the locomotion system	Pregnancy and lactation
Diseases of the nervous system	Lung diseases	Diseases of the urinary system	Skin diseases	Exhaustion and asthenia
Heart diseases	Liver and gallbladder diseases	Diseases of the reproductive system	Infectious diseases	
Diseases of the arteries	Diseases of the stomach	Metabolic diseases	Cancer	

Explanation of the recipe pages

"Preparation time":
HOURS : MINUTES
Time necessary to prepare the **ingredients:** peel, wash, slice, chop... This represents, in general terms, step of "Preparation". It **does not include time** for **soaking,** nor does it include ingredients that are, in themselves, **recipes** (white sauce, marinated gluten...) or vegetable **gravies.**

"Cooking time":
HOURS : MINUTES
Time needed **to make** the recipe. This can include simultaneous processes such as beating, frying, sautéing, boiling, baking... This refers, in general terms, to step À under "Preparation". This **does not include** time for **steeping** or **soaking.**

Number and title of the chapter

Icon for the organ or system that most benefits from this recipe
(see Vol. 2, p. 16).

Icons for other organs or systems that can also benefit from this recipe
(see Vol. 2, p. 16).

"Preparation" of the recipe
Detailed description of the preparation process.

Photographs showing how to make the recipe
These photographs demonstrate some of the important steps in the recipe.

Name of the recipe
Within each chapter, recipes follow a culinary order: first come the **salads,** then the **first and second courses,** and finally the **desserts and drinks.**

"Ingredients"
Normally these are for **four servings.** First the **main** ingredients are given and later the **added** ingredients.
The sign ≅ means "around"

"Additional Ingredients"
One can **do without** these or **vary** the amount indicated. None of these, including **oil*** and **salt****, have been used to calculate the **caloric and nutritional value** of each serving.

"The Chef Suggests"
Suggestions and culinary tricks that help to make the **dish more tasty.** Those who need to follow a **strict diet** should only use these suggestions **with caution.**

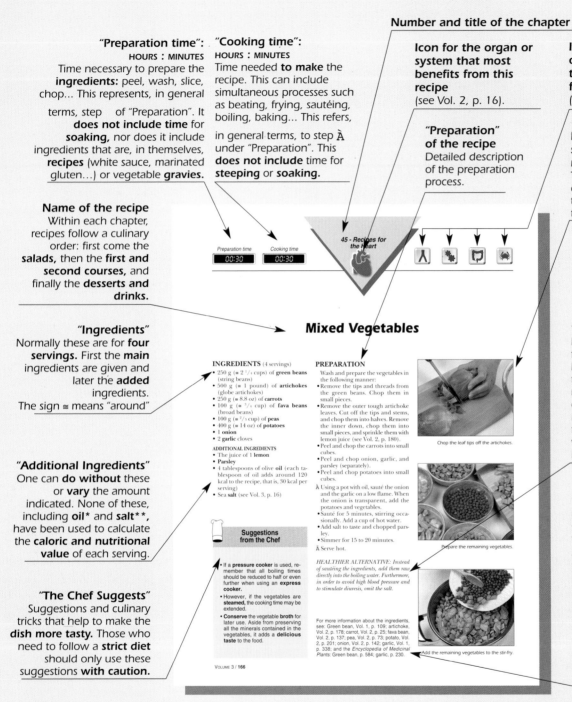

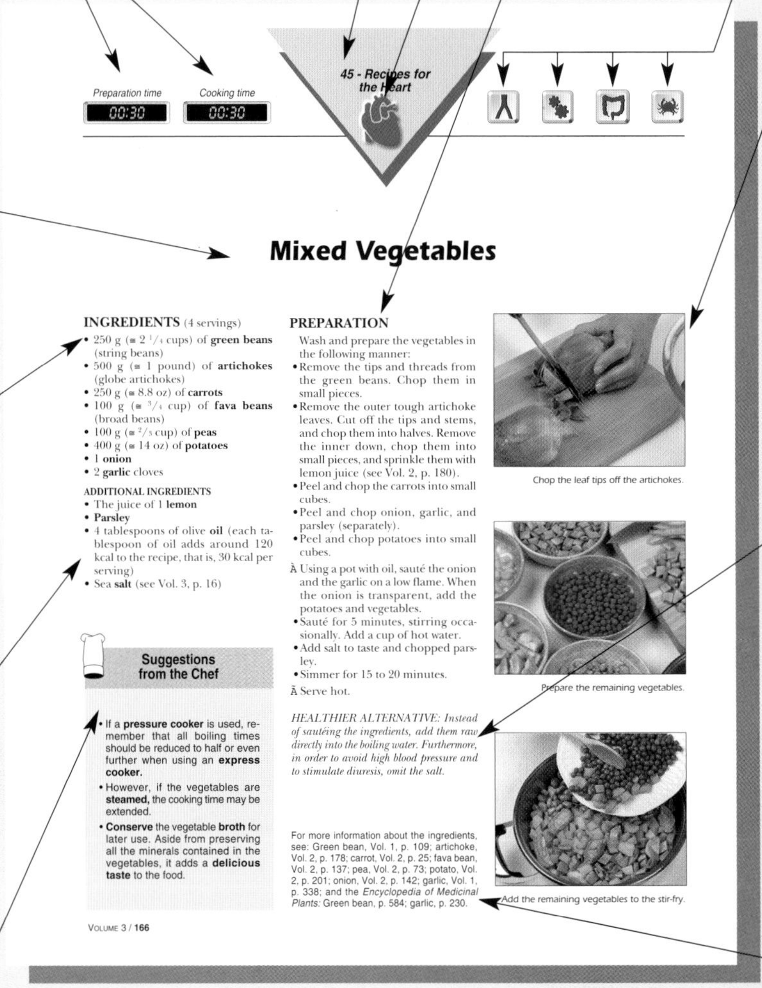

Preparation time
00:30
Cooking time
00:30
45 - Recipes for the Heart
Mixed Vegetables
INGREDIENTS (4 servings)
• 250 g (≅ 2 1/4 cups) of green beans (string beans)
• 500 g (≅ 1 pound) of artichokes (globe artichokes)
• 250 g (≅ 8.8 oz) of carrots
• 100 g (≅ 3/4 cup) of fava beans (broad beans)
• 100 g (≅ 2/3 cup) of peas
• 400 g (≅ 14 oz) of potatoes
• 1 onion
• 2 garlic cloves
ADDITIONAL INGREDIENTS
• The juice of 1 lemon
• Parsley
• 4 tablespoons of olive oil (each tablespoon of oil adds around 120 kcal to the recipe, that is, 30 kcal per serving)
• Sea salt (see Vol. 3, p. 16)
Suggestions from the Chef
• If a pressure cooker is used, remember that all boiling times should be reduced to half or even further when using an express cooker.
• However, if the vegetables are steamed, the cooking time may be extended.
• Conserve the vegetable broth for later use. Aside from preserving all the minerals contained in the vegetables, it adds a delicious taste to the food.
PREPARATION
Wash and prepare the vegetables in the following manner:
• Remove the tips and threads from the green beans. Chop them in small pieces.
• Remove the outer tough artichoke leaves. Cut off the tips and stems, and chop them into halves. Remove the inner down, chop them into small pieces, and sprinkle them with lemon juice (see Vol. 2, p. 180).
• Peel and chop the carrots into small cubes.
• Peel and chop onion, garlic, and parsley (separately).
• Peel and chop potatoes into small cubes.
À Using a pot with oil, sauté the onion and the garlic on a low flame. When the onion is transparent, add the potatoes and vegetables.
• Sauté for 5 minutes, stirring occasionally. Add a cup of hot water.
• Add salt to taste and chopped parsley.
• Simmer for 15 to 20 minutes.
Ã Serve hot.
HEALTHIER ALTERNATIVE: Instead of sautéing the ingredients, add them raw directly into the boiling water. Furthermore, in order to avoid high blood pressure and to stimulate diuresis, omit the salt.
For more information about the ingredients, see: Green bean, Vol. 1, p. 109; artichoke, Vol. 2, p. 178; carrot, Vol. 2, p. 25; fava bean, Vol. 2, p. 137; pea, Vol. 2, p. 73; potato, Vol. 2, p. 201; onion, Vol. 2, p. 142; garlic, Vol. 1, p. 338; and the Encyclopedia of Medicinal Plants: Green bean, p. 584; garlic, p. 230.
Chop the leaf tips off the artichokes.
Prepare the remaining vegetables.
Add the remaining vegetables to the stir-fry.
VOLUME 3 / 166

"Healthier option"
For those who need to follow a **stricter** or **healthier diet,** or for those who wish to **reduce** the **calorie content** of a recipe. Normally suggestions focus on how to **do without** certain ingredients.

"For more information about the ingredients..."
This shows the volume and page numbers of this ENCYCLOPEDIA OF FOODS AND THEIR HEALING POWER, or the page numbers of "Encyclopedia of Medicinal Plants," where the **properties of the ingredients** used in the recipe are shown.

* Oil

Those who wish to **monitor** their **calorie intake** should bear in mind that to the number of calories listed in the "Nutritional value per serving" they must add calories for the **oil used** (around 120 kcal per tablespoon, or, 30 kcal per serving if the recipe is for four servings).

In the example that is given on this page, **each serving** contains **194 kcal** (calories) **without** counting the **added oil.** If, for example, **3 tablespoons** of oil were added to this recipe, each serving would contain:

$$\mathbf{194} + \frac{\mathbf{120}\ \text{kcal}\ \mathbf{x\ 3}\ \text{tablespoons}}{\mathbf{4}\ \text{servings}} \cong \mathbf{194} + (\mathbf{30}\ \text{kcal}\ \mathbf{x\ 3}\ \text{tablespoons}) \cong \mathbf{284}\ \text{kcal}$$

All oils contain a similar caloric value. We recommend **olive oil** because of its therapeutic and culinary properties (see Vol. 1, pp. 124-127).

** Added Salt

Sodium, from which common table salt is derived (sodium chloride = NaCl), added to each recipe is not shown in the graphs "Nutritional value per serving" (see Vol. 3, p. 17). Those who need to control their dietary intake of sodium should bear in mind that:

- **1.25 g of salt** (a pinch) covers the RDA (Recommended Dietary Allowance) of sodium for an adult.
- **6 g of salt** (a level teaspoon) is the estimated safe daily dietary intake, that is, one should not use more than this amount per day (see Vol. 1, p. 346).

Explanation of the recipe pages

Photograph of the recipe when ready to serve
In order for this work to be esthetically pleasing, some dishes may show the ingredients in a different proportion than that indicated in the instructions. In addition to this, in some cases, which will be evident, additional products have been added to the photograph for decorative purposes.

Section of the ENCYCLOPEDIA

Title of the ENCYCLOPEDIA

Logo of the ENCYCLOPEDIA
The background color corresponds to the section.

"Nutritional value"
Normally in this chart the value is **per serving,** but, when necessary, it is given for **100 g.** A serving is **generally a fourth** of the total amount of the completed recipe. Of course, depending on the needs or characteristics of the individual, the amount for one serving can be increased or decreased.

Energy (calories)
The amount of energy that serves as a base when calculating the length of the bar (blue), is **2,000 kcal** (calories), or the equivalent **8,368 kj** (jules), which is the **daily amount** needed by an **average person** (see Vol. 1, p. 385).

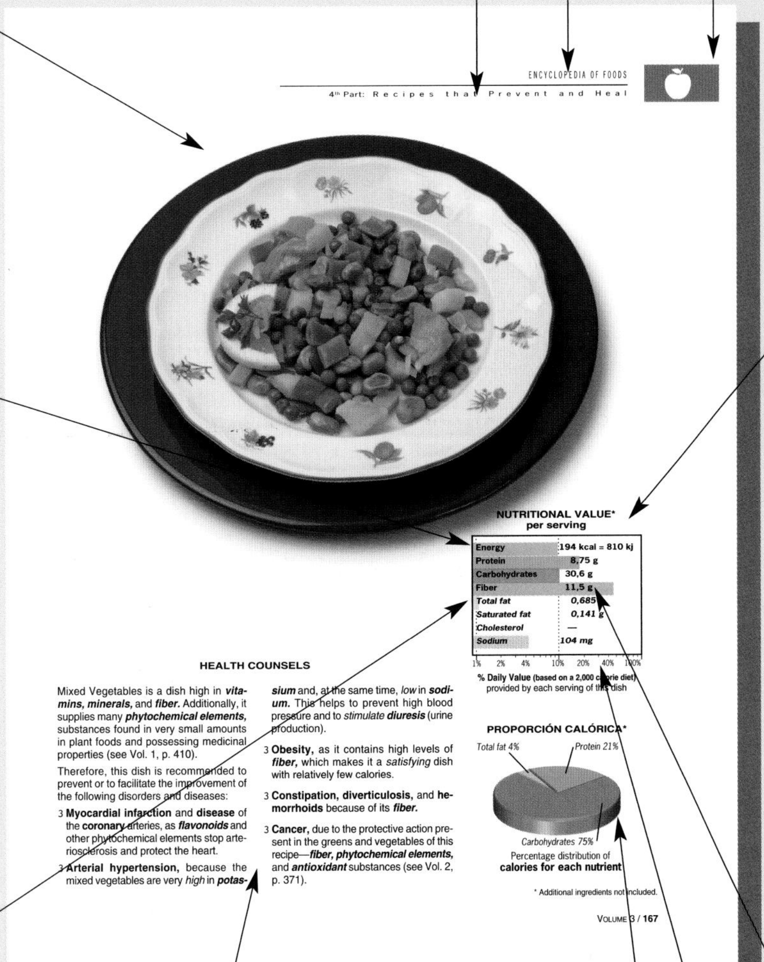
ENCYCLOPEDIA OF FOODS
4th Part: Recipes that Prevent and Heal
NUTRITIONAL VALUE* per serving
Energy 194 kcal = 810 kj
Protein 8,75 g
Carbohydrates 30,6 g
Fiber 11,5 g
Total fat 0,685
Saturated fat 0,141 g
Cholesterol —
Sodium 104 mg
1% 2% 4% 10% 20% 40% 100%
% Daily Value (based on a 2,000 calorie diet) provided by each serving of this dish
HEALTH COUNSELS
Mixed Vegetables is a dish high in vitamins, minerals, and fiber. Additionally, it supplies many phytochemical elements, substances found in very small amounts in plant foods and possessing medicinal properties (see Vol. 1, p. 410).
Therefore, this dish is recommended to prevent or to facilitate the improvement of the following disorders and diseases:
Myocardial infarction and disease of the coronary arteries, as flavonoids and other phytochemical elements stop arteriosclerosis and protect the heart.
Arterial hypertension, because the mixed vegetables are very high in potassium and, at the same time, low in sodium. This helps to prevent high blood pressure and to stimulate diuresis (urine production).
Obesity, as it contains high levels of fiber, which makes it a satisfying dish with relatively few calories.
Constipation, diverticulosis, and hemorrhoids because of its fiber.
Cancer, due to the protective action present in the greens and vegetables of this recipe—fiber, phytochemical elements, and antioxidant substances (see Vol. 2, p. 371).
PROPORCIÓN CALÓRICA*
Total fat 4%
Protein 21%
Carbohydrates 75%
Percentage distribution of calories for each nutrient
* Additional ingredients not included.
VOLUME 3 / 167

Fat/Cholesterol/Sodium
For **total fat, saturated fat, cholesterol** and **sodium,** the **SDI** (estimated safe daily dietary intake)is given, that is, the maximum amount **per day above which one should never go.** To differentiate these nutrients, they appear in cursive letters (italic).

For **sodium,** only what is contained in the ingredients is measured, **not what is added** in the form of **salt** in the "Added ingredients" (see Vol. 3, p. 16).

RDA / SDI
The length of the bars indicate the **percentage** (%) of the **RDA** (recommended daily allowance) or of the **SDI** (estimated safe daily dietary intake) for an adult male that is contained in the recipe (see Vol. 1, pp. 16, 384).

For example, in this chart you can see that a serving provides 11.5 g of fiber (**total amount**), which represents almost 50% of the RDA for an adult male (**relative amount** indicated by the green bar). The RDA for fiber is 25 g, so 11.5 g covers exactly 46%.

"Health Counsels"
This section describes the **beneficial effects** of this recipe on one's health. Noted are the **organs or systems** that **benefit the most** as a result of the preventive and curative powers of each of the ingredients that form part of the recipe. The **nutritional and culinary values** are also given.

"Caloric Proportion" Graph
This shows the proportion of calories for the recipe that come from protein, carbohydrates and fat. The ideal proportion for the total amount of food eaten in a day is shown in Vol. 2, p. 393.

Logarithmic Scale
This scale presents proportional concepts in a non-proportional way (see Vol. 1, p. 16).

Volume **Page number**

Index of Chapters

Volume 3

PAGE

38. Counsels for a Healthy Kitchen 20
39. A Healthy and Attractive Table 32
40. Base Recipes 40
41. Dressings, Sauces, and Hors d'oeuvres 54
42. Transition Recipes 78

ENCYCLOPEDIA OF

FOODS

HEALTHY RECIPES

THIRD PART

The Healthy Kitchen

To sit down at the table should never represent a burden. Foods should be presented in such a way that they please both sight and palate.

Ruth Kunz-Bircher

Current administrator of the dietetic school of her father, Dr. Max Bircher-Benner, in Switzerland.

38 Counsels for a Healthy Kitchen

Chapter Summary

Advantages of cooking 24
"Au Gratin" 28
Baking/Roasting 28
Blanching 29
Boiling 29
Chopping 23
Chopping foods 23
Contamination by the cooking utensils 25
Cooking 23
Cooking foods, how the foods are affected 26
Cooking foods, ways of 28
Cooking with a double-boiler 31
Fried foods 23
Frying 30
Hot pots 30
Hygiene 23
Inconveniences of cooking 25
Mediterranean diet 21
Microwaves 31
Pressure-cooking 31
Sautéing 30
Simmering 29
Slow Simmer 30
Steaming 31
Stew 30
The healthy kitchen 22
Vitamin Loss 24

The way of preparing and cooking foods affects their nutritional properties and healing power; the simpler the processing is, the better such properties are preserved.

THE KITCHEN can be compared to a chemical laboratory in which foods are processed in various ways. Fire, the symbol of transformation, and, by extension, **heat,** is *the most important physical agent* among those within the kitchen that act upon foods.

But in addition to heat, other physical agents in the kitchen, such as **cold, electromagnetic radiation,** or **blending** act upon food products. Other processes used daily in the kitchen are *physicochemical,* like **steeping, soaking, sedimentation** (the formation of sediments), or **emulsion** (for example, the beating of mayonnaise).

All these physicochemical processes transform and alter foods to a greater or lesser degree. In *some aspects,* this process **benefits** the foods because by cooking them, they are ***more easily digested, they taste better, and pathological germs are eliminated*** (see Vol. 3, p. 24, ***"Benefits of Cooking"***).

However, in *other aspects,* processing of foods in the kitchen ends in **unfavorable** and **damaging** results for human health (see Vol. 3, p. 25, ***"Problems with Cooking"***). This is due primarily to the action of intense heat that ***partially destroys the vitamins, enzymes, and other active substances naturally endowed with healing or preventive powers.*** Cooking meats and meat derivatives at high temperatures produces cancerous substances (see Vol. 1, p. 276), especially if placed directly on the fire.

In this chapter, we present the general principals of healthy cooking. The objective is to manipulate and process foods in such a way that:

- One obtains the **health benefits,** while at the same time,
- **Losses** in **nutritional value** and **healing properties** *are reduced to a minimum.*

The Mediterranean Diet

The recipes presented in this volume represent a practical application of the Mediterranean diet. All recipes meet most of the criteria that define this type of diet, for example:

- *Abundant use* of **cereals, fruits, vegetables, garden greens, nuts, and seeds.**
- *Major role* of dishes based on **raw foods,** such as salads and fresh fruit desserts.
- Use of **olive oil, garlic,** and **lemon** as the main dressings.
- *Reduced use* of **milk, dairy** products, and **eggs.**

Besides all this, the recipes of this work avoid the use of **meat, fish,** and all their derivatives.

This type of diet can be presented in an **attractive** and **tasty** way, as can be demonstrated by the recipes in the following chapters; furthermore, it is proven to be the *most successful* diet for **preserving health.**

The Healthy

Vegetable Foods

- The *more foods of vegetable origin* are used in the kitchen, and the *less processed* they are, the healthier our meals will be.
- Fruits, nuts, seeds, cereals, legumes, and vegetables *form* the **basis** of a healthy diet.

Know How To Shop

The **first rule** for a healthy kitchen is to shop wisely by only including healthy foods and products in your purchases.

The choice of foods is an **important** act that holds *consequences* for ***individual health*** and for ***ecology*** and the ***environment*** (see Vol. 2, p. 390).

Sugar

- *Reduce* consumption of **white sugar,** use honey, molasses (cane honey), or brown sugar instead (see chapter 10, Vol. 1, p. 158).
- *Reduce* or *avoid* the recipes in which sugar is combined with eggs or milk, because these combinations cause **digestive fermentation.** Besides, because *none* of the three ingredients contain ***fiber,*** they contribute to **constipation** and **arteriosclerosis.**

Whole Grain Products

- *Whenever possible,* use whole products: for example, whole bread and pasta, instead of refined foods; or, brown rice rather than white.

Oils

- Vegetable oils (sunflower seed, soybean, corn, grape seed, etc.), and especially **olive oil,** are *much* **healthier** than fats of animal origin such as suet or lard, butter, and even margarine (see Vol. 1, pp. 112-127).

Dressings

- **Salt:** Use *as little as possible,* especially in cool climates. ***Sea salt,*** rather than ***refined salt,*** contains more minerals. In some places far from the sea, it is useful to use ***iodized salt.***
- **Lemon:** It is preferable to vinegar (see Vol. 1, p. 338).
- **Garlic:** Substitutes with advantage hot spices (see Vol. 1, p. 338).
- **Aromatic herbs:** They are preferable to spices (see Vol. 1, p. 342).

Kitchen

Kitchen Utensils

- **Choose** your kitchen utensils carefully (see Vol. 3, p. 25).
- **Avoid** those that contain lead (such as those made of enameled earthenware) or aluminum.
- Stainless steel, glass, and porcelain are the **most inert** materials and the ones that interact less with the foods.

Hygiene

- **Wash your hands well** before handling foods.
- Maintain **absolute cleanliness** with your utensils and kitchen surfaces. This is *especially important* when handling **meat products,** since they tend to be contaminated by bacteria (see Vol. 1, p. 302).

Cooking

- *Avoid* **overheating,** that is, exposing food to heat for too long.
- *Do not* **brown** or **burn** foods.

In the crust that forms through browning, an ***important loss of vitamins and other nutrients*** occurs. Besides, ***cancerous substances can form*** in the crust.

Chopping

- The *more* a food is *chopped,* the *greater the surface* that is left exposed to the action of oxygen, of the enzymes released by the tearing of the cells, and of germs found in the environment.
- In this way, slicing and chopping *encourages oxidation and destruction of nutrients* (more intense in vegetables and greens), along with the contamination and bacterial proliferation (more important in meat).
- ***Use*** chopped or sliced greens or vegetables ***immediately.***

Balance Between Raw and Cooked Foods

- Cook only those foods that need it.
- *Compensate* for **cooked foods** by eating a considerable amount of **raw** ones at the same time (counsel of Bircher-Benner).

After Cooking

- *Avoid reheating* foods or *keeping them hot* for prolonged periods before eating them, because many ***vitamins*** and ***enzymes*** *are lost.*

Frying

- *Avoid* fried and barbecued foods, especially when dealing with meats (see Vol. 1, pp. 122-123; 274-279).

Advantages of Cooking

- It makes some foods more **digestible.**
- *Destroys* **pathological germs** that could be found in foods. This makes food consumption more secure from a microbiological point of view.
- *Disarms* certain **toxic substances** that are present in some foods, for example:
  - Inhibitors of (**proteases**), **lecithin,** and **hemagglutinins** that are found in legumes such as soybeans (see Vol. 2, p. 274).
  - **Solanine** from immature potatoes or eggplant (see Vol. 2, p. 203).
  - **Hydrocyanic acid** of Cassava (see Vol. 1, p. 108).
- It makes some foods more attractive and tasty, improving taste, smell, and texture.

Approximate loss of vitamins through cooking foods

Vitamins	% Loss	
Provitamin and Vitamin A	10%-15%	Frying and cooking are the processes that produce *greatest* **loss.**
Vitamin B_1	15%-50%	Boiling in water is the form of cooking that produces *more* **losses.**
Vitamin B_2	4%-30%	Frying and roasting, in which high temperatures are used, *favor* the **destruction** of these vitamins.
Vitamin B_6	10%-50%	
Vitamin B_{12}	5%-15%	
Niacin	10%-40%	
Folic Acid	20%-50%	
Vitamin C	15%-90%	This is the *most* **sensitive** vitamin to the action of heat.

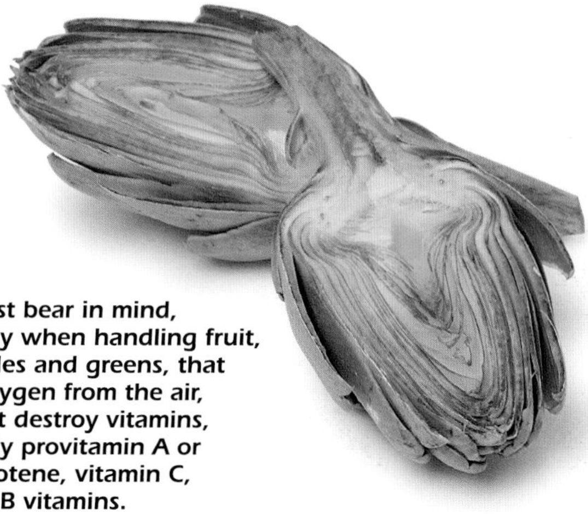

One must bear in mind, especially when handling fruit, vegetables and greens, that light, oxygen from the air, and heat destroy vitamins, especially provitamin A or beta-carotene, vitamin C, and the B vitamins.

Inconveniences of Cooking

- **Loss of Nutrients:**
  - **Vitamins:** especially **C, A,** and the **folates.**
  - **Minerals:** because they are water soluble, a part of them passes into the boiling water. Boiled foods are ***impoverished in minerals,*** while the water in which they were cooked is enriched.
  - **Proteins:** They are denaturalized, but, in general, they do not lose their nutritional value. Varying proportions of certain amino acids, such as lysine, are *lost* when certain foods like bread, potatoes, or nuts are toasted forming a discolored crust.
  - **Carbohydrates:** These are the nutrients that *best resist* heat, although when the heat is *excessive,* they carbonize and lose their **nutritional value.**
  - **Fats:** They resist heat fairly well, but if the temperature is very elevated, ***a part of the fat oxidizes and changes into toxic or harmful substances.*** For example, this is the case with **acrolein** formed through frying at high temperatures. Besides, they form **'trans' fatty acids** that favor an increase in levels of **cholesterol** and **arteriosclerosis.**
- **Loss of enzymes:** Cereals and germinated legumes, as well as fruits and raw vegetables in their natural state contain enzymes in their cells. When eaten, these enzymes help digestion and perform different beneficial functions in the body although these are not well known yet. The ***heat of cooking inactivates these enzymes and stops the curative*** and ***preventive powers*** of the foods.
- **Loss of the hardness of the foods,** which, by being *softer,* require *less effort to chew.* This brings with it, on one hand, a *weakening* of the **teeth** and **jaws,** and on the other hand *less* **salivation** of the foods.
- **Formation of carcinogenic elements** by cooking meat and its derivatives at high temperatures (see Vol. 1, p. 276).
- **Contamination** during cooking **by the materials** of which the utensils are made which can partially dissolve and pass into the foods that are being cooked. This is how certain materials used in the kitchen react with different foods:
  - **Glass:** This, along with ceramic, is the *most inert* material used in the kitchen. It does *not interact* with foods, and does *not release* any substance that can pass to the foods.
  - **Iron and copper:** Utensils release small amounts of these metals, which can be **toxic.** To reduce this risk, one should prevent them from entering into direct contact with acid products such as citric fruit juices, tomato, or vinegar.
  - **Aluminum:** It is *quite unstable* and loses a certain amount in the foods. It is **inadvisable** as a material for cooking. Although there are no conclusive studies, it is suspected that an excess of aluminum in foods can *be* toxic to the **nervous system.**
  - **Stainless steel:** This is one of the *most stable* materials, although very acidic foods can cause this material to lose small amounts of nickel, one of the metals that make up the alloy.
  - **Earthenware:** One should dispose of any items of earthenware that are ***internally covered with brilliant enamel*** because the enamel contains **lead,** which is easily released and can cause **chronic poisoning.**
  - **Teflon:** This is one of the substances used to cover the inside of non-stick pans. Its use is safe as long as you *do not go above* **300 degrees centigrade** in frying, and you *avoid* **scratches.** The substances released when Teflon is scratched with a scouring pad or with a metal object can be carcinogenic.

Glass

Iron

Aluminum

Stainless Steel

Earthenware

Teflon

How Cooking

Overall, we can say that cooking is beneficial for foods of animal origin, whereas it presents more inconveniences than advantages for fruit, nuts, and some greens.

Legumes

Dried legumes (lentils, beans, chickpeas, etc.) should ***always be cooked*** before eating. The cooking process destroys the toxic substances that may be present. Cooking also makes them easier to digest (see Vol. 1, p. 83).

Tender legumes such as broad beans and peas ***can be eaten raw*** in moderate amounts.

Eggs

An old belief exists that raw eggs provide more nutrition than cooked ones. However, cooked eggs carry several advantages over raw:

- They are **easier to digest,** since their proteins, predigested by the action of heat, are **easier to assimilate.**
- They are more nutritious, because one can take advantage of all the vitamins. A protein called ***avidin,*** which is present in raw eggs, *prevents the absorption* of the vitamin factor ***biotin*** (see Vol. 1, p. 221).
- They are **safer** from the standpoint of hygiene because heat *destroys the pathogenic germs* such as **salmonella** that may be present.

Hard-boiled eggs *are better* than **fried** or **soft-boiled** ones (in these, the cooking time is insufficient).

Meats and Fish

Raw meats and fish carry a *high risk* of **food infections** due to the frequency with which they are contaminated by germs.

On the other hand, *when heated too much,* especially on the grill or in the frying pan, **cancer-producing substances** may form. This phenomenon occurs more often in meats and meat products (see Vol. 1, pp. 274-279).

Affects Foods

Fruits

In general, they should be eaten **raw,** since this is the best way to take advantage of their healthy and medicinal properties.

Heat destroys a significant portion of their vitamins; if cooking happens in a liquid medium, some minerals *dissolve in the water.*

Only when ill patients suffer from a **weak digestive system,** can it be justified to boil or bake apples, plums, loquats, or other fruits.

Nuts and Seeds

Toasting or *frying* nuts and seeds increases their taste but *destroys* a large part of ***Vitamin*** B_1. Besides, they can be **harder to digest.**

Cereals

Although they can be eaten raw, cereals are *more easily digested* when **cooked** or even leavened, as occurs with bread.

Germinated cereal **sprouts** *may be eaten* **raw** in order to take advantage of the *large amount* of ***vitamins*** and ***enzymes*** found within them (see Vol. 1, p. 86).

Vegetables

Cooking helps their digestion but *destroys* some ***vitamins,*** especially ***C,*** as well as ***enzymes. Minerals*** *dissolve* in boiling water (see Vol. 1, p. 99).

For this reason, vegetables should be eaten **raw** or **blanched** whenever possible.

However, some vegetables ***should always be cooked*** before eating because in their ***raw*** state they may be **hard to digest** or even **poisonous.**

- **Potatoes** and **eggplant:** when raw they may contain ***solanine*** (poisonous alkaloid), especially if they are not ripe.
- **Mushrooms:** it is better to cook them in order to avoid the risk of ***cancer-causing*** agents that may be present (see Vol. 2, p. 294).
- **Sweet Cassava:** this root, in its raw state, contains a ***toxic substance*** that disappears when cooked (see Vol. 1, p. 108).

Baked or oven-grilled vegetables take on an enjoyable flavor. No mineral loss occurs as it does with boiling. There is little loss of vitamins if one avoids too much heat.

Ways of

Cooking Without Liquid

Barbecued: Cooking at a **high temperature** on a grate placed at a certain *distance* from the center of heat (hot coals).

Grilled: Cooking at a **high temperature** on a hot grilling iron which receives the heat *directly* from the heat source: electric, gas, or coals.

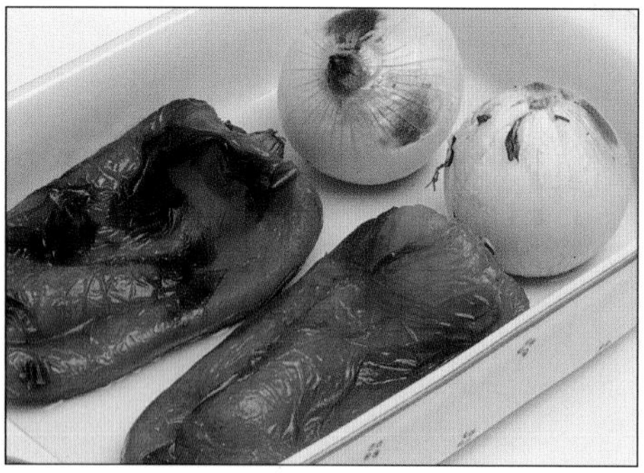

Oven-baked: Cooking at **different temperatures** done within an enclosure (oven). Radiation or convection transfers the heat.

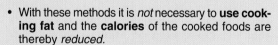

Browning: A finish given to a casserole that gives the top a toasted appearance.

Advantages

- With these methods it is *not* necessary to **use cooking fat** and the **calories** of the cooked foods are thereby *reduced.*
- The foods *do not lose* **nutrients** through dilution because they are not immersed in water.
- The **flavors** of the foods are *enhanced.*

Disadvantages

- In general, with these methods, **temperatures reach very high levels** thus *destroying* many ***vitamins*** and ***active properties*** of the vegetables.
- In the case of meat or fish, barbecuing can *produce* **cancer-causing agents** (see Vol. 1, p. 278).
- Some ***proteins*** and ***carbohydrates*** are *destroyed* in the toasted crust that forms on the surface of foods cooked in this way. The result is a *reduction* in **nutritional value.**

Cooking Foods (1)

Cooking in Liquid

Boiling: *Complete* cooking by immersion in water or broth. At the *beginning* of the cooking process the liquid can be **cold, hot,** or **boiling.**

Blanching: *Partial* cooking of food for a *short period* through exposure to the thermal action of **boiling water.**

Simmering: *Complete* cooking of a food in liquid whose temperature is *just below* **boiling** point.

Advantages

- The cooking temperature reached in a liquid medium is lower than that of barbecuing or frying. This is because as long as the water is boiling at normal atmospheric pressure, it never goes above 100 degrees centigrade. In this way, ***vitamins*** and ***other nutrients*** are *altered less.*
- The food does *not soak in oil,* thus making it more easily **digestible** than when fried. In addition, the **fat** that may be part of the food *does not decompose* from high temperatures as it does in roasting. This also helps to make boiled foods more digestible than roasted or fried ones.

Disadvantages

- *Loss* of nutrients into the water, especially ***minerals.*** This inconvenience can be overcome by saving the water for later use.

Ways of

Cooking with Fat

Disadvantages

- **Loss of nutrients** (especially vitamins) due to the high temperatures reached (between 160 and 200 degrees centigrade, or even more). This loss is less important in a sauté than with frying.
- **Unfavorable changes** in the oil (see Vol. 1, p. 122).
- **Soaking in oil,** which increases the number of calories in fried foods. This soaking can be reduced if foods are put into the pan once the oil is hot so that they form an outer crust that isolates the interior of the food.
- **Formation of cancer-causing substances,** especially when frying meat (see Vol. 1, p. 123).

Stir Frying: *Complete* or *partial* cooking of foods in oil at a high temperature but for a short time.

Deep Fried: *Complete* cooking of a food in a fat medium at **high temperatures.** With this method a *golden crust* develops.

Advantages

- The foods acquire a *stronger* **flavor.**
- Stir-fry: causes *fewer inconveniences* than frying since it is a *quick process* and the foods *absorb less* oil.

Cooking in a mixed medium

The ***advantages*** and ***disadvantages*** of these cooking methods are the result of combining those of cooking in oil with those of cooking with water (see Vol. 3, pp. 29, 30).

Slow cooking: *Complete* cooking of a food in a fat medium to which a *little water* is added. Cooking is done over a **low fire** and the food is served with the cooking liquid.

Sautéing: *Complete* or *partial* cooking of foods in such a way that the foods **do not change color.** Cooking is done on a **low fire** with *very little* fat and with the juices of the food itself.

Light Frying: Similar to the previous process except that in this case, the foods **acquire a golden tone.**

Stewed: *Complete* cooking of a food in an *equal mixture of oil and water.* The ingredients have been *sautéed* first or, if not, they will be at the end of the process.

Cooking Foods (and 2)

Other Cooking Methods

High pressure: This is done in **special pots** that have airtight lids and that produce steam at high pressure in order to create an ***internal temperature of 105-120 degrees centigrade.***

- **Advantages:** The cooking time is reduced considerably. Although the temperature is somewhat higher than in a traditional pot, the destruction of vitamins is less since the food is submitted to heat during less time.

Steaming: This method uses a pot similar to the previous one with a slightly smaller basket. Some water is placed in the pot, but it should not reach the bottom of the basket; the food is placed in the basket and is ***cooked by the steam produced by the boiling water.***

- **Advantages:** Because the food is cooked with steam and not water or oil, the *loss* of ***nutrients*** through dilution and overheating is *reduced.* Additionally, the ***flavor*** and ***texture*** of the foods are preserved.

Cooking in a double boiler: The container that holds the food is placed within another recipient in which a minimum amount of water is placed. In this way, the heat does *not act directly* upon the recipient that holds the food ***but through the water surrounding it.***

- **Advantages:** Recommended for delicate foods such as fruit. Cooking happens in a slow and even way with moderate *loss* of ***nutrients.***

Baking in aluminum foil: The food is wrapped in aluminum foil that has been lightly greased (and with the matte side ready to protect the food), or in bags of appropriate material. In this way the foods cook in their own juices without the need to add water or fat.

- **Advantages:** Because a metallic layer protects the food, direct contact with the heat source is avoided. In this way vitamins and other nutrients are protected.

Microwaves: Foods are cooked at a **high temperature** without coming into contact with a heat source. There are no serious proofs that this method is harmful to foods or health.

- **Advantages:** The food is cooked from the inside out in a uniform way; there is no nutritional loss through dilution; the taste is generally preserved along with the food properties including its nutritional value.

Without water: In order to cook in this way, a **special pot** is needed. The base of the pot diffuses the heat and the lid closes perfectly. The foods ***cook due to the water already contained within them.*** This method is very appropriate for vegetables.

- **Advantages:** The *loss* of ***minerals*** and the destruction of vitamins are *reduced* to a *minimum* thus making it unnecessary to use oil or salt in order to add flavor.

39 A HEALTHY AND ATTRACTIVE TABLE

CHAPTER SUMMARY

A Healthy Meal 38
Correct Behavior at the Table 36
Crystal and Napkins 35
Food Compatibility............ 38
How to Serve the Different Dishes . 37
Particularly Healthy Foods...... 38
Seating of the Guests.......... 36
Table Settings................ 34
Use of Cutlery 37

HAVING PREPARED dishes that are healthy and tasty, it is now time to serve and eat the food. Although it may not seem obvious, the table setting also influences our health.

If the foods we eat as part of these healthy recipes are to exert their full preventive and curative effect, they should be presented and consumed appropriately.

While it is true that the foods we eat and the way they are cooked are important, the following factors also influence our health:

- Our **attitude** when we eat; that is, do we exhibit a happy spirit or are we stressed and worried;
- **Where** we are served, whether on an unattractive, carelessly-laid table or in a neat, orderly environment;
- **When** we eat, in an unplanned manner or while under pressure, or in a timely and regular pattern;
- Also, with **whom** we eat.

All these factors physiologically influence the way in which our body digests and assimilates food.

Do Not Eat Between Meals

The presentation of the table along with where and when the meal is eaten hold special **physiological significance.** Between one meal and the next, the **digestive organs** must *recuperate* from the work performed. *Five hours* is the ideal resting time necessary between meals to prevent digestive overload that can negatively affect general health.

A Healthy Table

Besides what has already been said, this simple advice also helps produce good digestion and health:

- Establish and follow a regular meal **schedule.**
- Avoid foods that are too **hot** or **cold.**
- *Adjust the menu to* **those partaking** of the meal, bearing in mind such factors as physical or intellectual occupation, periods of growth, pregnancy and old age, difficulty in chewing, etc.
- **Dress** the foods in a tasty manner while *avoiding* **chemical additives** (such as glutamate and *artificial coloring*) or **irritating spices.** Be *careful* with **salt** (it is preferable to use sea salt) and *use* only **vegetable oils** in moderation.

The Table

A properly set table that is decorative and well lit, when combined with happy diners and a healthy, natural, and balanced menu can turn a simple meal into an unforgettable celebration.

The Place

Whether or not the meal celebration takes place at home or elsewhere, one should make sure the location is as tastefully decorated and well-lit as possible, with enough space to accommodate the service staff (should there be any) and the guests, who should be able to walk around with reasonable ease. Wherever possible, the meal should take place close to the kitchen, never on a different floor.

If possible, the appetizers and after-dinner drinks should be served in a location other than the dining room. If this is not possible, then plates, cutlery and glasses should be removed before serving the hot drinks.

The Table and Tablecloth

The **table,** *preferably* ***round*** or ***oval*** (square and rectangular are used less in order to avoid separating those persons seated at the ends), should not seat more than **twelve guests;** this allows better communication without isolating those at the ends.

It is better to leave at least 60 cm. but never more than 80 cm. of **space** between each guest.

The tablecloth seems more elegant if it is **light** in **color,** plain or made of lace.

To protect the table from possible spills and burn marks, place a well-fitting, waterproof table pad under the tablecloth.

If using a lace tablecloth, place a soft-colored **linen** underneath so the color can show through.

Only if there is *great friendship* with the guests, rather than a formal relationship, can **individual place mats** be used.

The China and Cutlery

The **plates** are placed in front of the guest. Two plates are generally used: one flat and a second **deeper** dish on top. If the menu contains *hors d'oeuvres* or other similar appetizers, one would put a third, smaller plate in the top position.

Setting

The **lower plate,** or presentation plate, always enriches the table, even if its function is merely decorative. It is situated at the edge of the table or approximately 2 centimeters in from the edge.

The **cutlery** is placed by **order of use.** The **spoon** is placed to the right of the plate, and the **knife** is placed next to it on its left. The spoon is placed with the bowl-like side facing up and the sharpened edge of the knife must face the plate.

The fork or **forks** are placed to the left of the plate.

If several similar pieces of cutlery are present, that is, one for each dish on the menu, the one furthermost from the plate is used first.

At formal celebrations, serve the **dessert cutlery** with the dessert. In less formal situations, they can be placed on the table from the beginning. They lie in front of the plates with the spoon handle to the right and that of the fork to the left.

If we need to put down our cutlery during the meal, to drink for example, we should place them on the plate forming an angle, the fork to the left with the tips facing down and the knife to the right with the blade facing the dinner guest.

When we finish eating, the cutlery (knife and fork) is placed on the plate, to the right, lying parallel to each other; the fork with the teeth facing upwards and closest to the guest, the knife (to the right of the fork) with the blade facing the guest. In this way the service staff perceive that we have finished with the plate.

The Crystal and the Napkins

The **glasses** and **stemware** vary in number according to the drinks on offer. If only using one, place it slightly to the right of the plate.

If planning to serve several drinks, the simplest way to place the stemware is from smallest to largest and from right to left; in this way the drinks can easily be served from the right.

The large goblet is for water, the following, by size, is for fruit juice; if there are bubbly drinks (champagne style) preferably without alcohol, they should be poured into the tall, thin goblet, and the liquors, also without alcohol, in the smaller goblet.

Never fill the cups to the rim.

The **napkin** is folded in a simple manner and placed on the plate or to the left of it; however, depending on the custom, in some places the folding of the napkin can become an art form.

When seated at the table, and before beginning to eat, the napkin should be opened and placed on the lap. It should always be used before each drink in order to avoid leaving a mark on the glass as well as after drinking to dry the lips.

The Bread

The bread, individual or in slices, is placed to the left of the plate on a small tray or in several baskets distributed along the table. Different kinds of bread can be served but they should always be within reach of all the guests.

Bread is broken by hand (never with a knife), one small piece at a time and only enough to fit in the mouth.

It is considered incorrect to use the bread to help manipulate the food or to soak up sauces no matter how appetizing they may be.

Decoration

Decorations add a touch of good taste if there is sufficient space on the table and if they harmonize with the table setting. Flowers, porcelain figurines, a fruit basket or a centerpiece, will give your table a touch of distinction; do not forget that the decorations should never interfere with visual contact between guests.

Concerning candelabra on the table, a tasteful practice is to light the candles at the supper once all the guests are seated. The candlelight should be accompanied by electric light since candlelight alone creates an atmosphere that is too intimate or somber.

Correct Behavior

The rules of etiquette and courtesy, which are sometimes unduly disregarded, provide a clear example of exquisite behavior, elegance and education.

A luncheon, a formal supper, or a dinner engagement, requires the **knowledge** and **use** of a series of ***rules,*** for the hosts as well as the guests. The following advice can serve as a starting point for greater knowledge later on, or at least, to provide us with the assurance that we know how to behave correctly.

Seating of the Guests

There are two principal ways of seating the guests:

- **Anglo-Saxon:** The seating of the guests follows a system known as ***Cartesian*** in which the **place of honor** (reserved for those persons whom you wish to *honor,* for the *oldest* guest or for the host) is at either end of the table. The *most important* male guest is seated to the right of the place of honor and the male guest second in importance is seated on the left-hand side. The same holds true for the second host with the *most important* female guest seated to the right and the second-most important female guest to the left. The rest of the guests are seated in *order of importance,* always *alternating* a gentleman with a lady. If there are no ***categories*** involved, the seating is arranged by ***age.***
- **French:** The hosts are seated facing each other in the center of the table. The guests are seated clockwise following the same rules as in the Anglo-Saxon way.

The hostess may seat herself in the place closest to the kitchen in order to control the serving of the food.

Other points to bear in mind at the time of seating the guests are the following:

- Seating the remaining guests is done in such a way as to increase the establishment of **new friendships** among them.
- *Avoid* seating **married couples** together (unless they are in their first year of marriage). Also avoid placing **work colleagues** or **good friends** together in order to make sure that no one is left out.
- Be tactful and *do not seat guests together* who have so little in common that it becomes *difficult to maintain a conversation;* avoid seating people together who may be in *conflict.*

If you have a considerable number of guests, you can place ***handwritten*** name **cards** leaning on the glasses.

Correct Posture

Once seated, it is important to maintain an adequate posture. You should be *comfortable* but not too *relaxed.* You should **never rest** a part of your body on the table, **nor** should you sit **rigidly** against the back of your chair. *Elbows* should ***not*** rest on the table, but *forearms* **may;** the arms are kept **close** to the body.

at the Table

How to Serve the Different Dishes

There are also **two principal ways** to serve the food: ***French*** and ***Anglo-Saxon.***

- The **French** way stipulates that the female guest of honor be served first; afterwards, and in order of importance, serve the rest of the female guests. Finally, after serving all the male guests, the hosts are served.

  The guests may begin to eat once *everyone* is served and *never before* the hostess indicates so.

  Serve the plates from the **left** and *remove* them from the **right.** This process takes place after *everyone finishes:* remove the used plate and replace it with a clean one. *Never* **pile** dirty plates, with cutlery and leftover food, on the table. Nor should one take the plates of several guests simultaneously.

- If serving the **Anglo-Saxon** way, begin with the hostess; the rest of the guests are served in the same order as in the French option; the waiter holds the tray to the left of the guest when serving. If not using service staff, place trays of food on the table so everyone can serve him or herself. If some foods are too far away, the guest should *never reach his or her arms across the table.* Rather, ask those closest to the tray to pass it. The correct way to transfer food from the trays to the plate is with the *fork* and *spoon held* with one hand in the *form of pincers.* If you cannot do this easily, then hold the fork with the left hand and the spoon with the right.

Other types of service exist:

- **English with *service table:*** the waiter presents the tray on the left and immediately places it on the *serving table* (a small table with an alcohol warming lamp to keep the food hot). The waiter serves the food on a plate that is setting on the same *service table.* The empty plate is removed from the right and the full plate is also served on the right.
- **Russian,** characterized by the use of special serving trolleys, and where large pieces of meat are cooked to the taste of the client.
- **American,** characterized by the buffet where each guest serves him or herself as much as he or she wants.
- **Food served from the kitchen:** food is served in the kitchen and brought to the guest on the plate; this type of service is of a lesser category.

Use of Cutlery

Cutlery has its specific form according to the type of food for which it is designed, its place on the table, and its proper use:

- When solid food needs to be cut, hold the **fork** in the **left** hand and the **knife** with the **right;** cut the food **piece by piece** as you go along, without shifting the utensils to the other hand. The knife also helps to fix the food on the fork, but it should ***never*** *be raised to the mouth.*
- If there is no food to cut, the **fork** is held with the **right** hand.
- Some foods, like eggs and omelets, can be eaten using just the fork.
- Some foods need *special* treatment with cutlery. This is the case with **spaghetti;** holding the **fork** in the **right** hand, pinch the spaghetti and then roll it with the help of the **spoon,** which is held in the **left** hand.

Other Points

- Dinner guests must maintain a **courteous relationship** at all times with the hosts and the other guests.
- It is important to **confirm** your ***acceptance*** of the invitation immediately or to communicate your ***inability to attend the event,*** always expressing appreciation for the honor shown you by the invitation.
- Once seated at the table, do ***not begin*** to eat until everyone is served and the hosts begin.
- Once the food is in the mouth, **chew** it with the ***mouth closed,*** and when the food is *very hot* you must **never *blow*** on it. Rather, take small amounts from the edges.
- If it is necessary to **remove** some **piece of food from the mouth,** deposit it discreetly on the fork and leave it on the edge of the plate or on the small plates provided for this purpose, if such should exist. With olive or cherry **pits** or with other similar items, deposit them in the hand almost closed as a fist and do the same as in the previous example.
- If we wish to **talk,** do not forget that the ***mouth*** must be ***empty;*** the same holds true when wishing to drink.
- It is courteous to maintain an adequate rhythm between the food and the conversation in line with the other guests. If one guest eats more slowly than the rest, one of the hosts will serve him or herself a little more in order to accompany the guest.

A Healthy

Making food and eating it requires time and attitudes that we do not always recognize. Taste and eating habits have evolved but perhaps it would be useful to consider whether the way we eat is the best way.

Sitting at the table in a **happy frame of mind** with a **desire** to partake of the food may be more important or at least as important for your health as eating healthy foods.

To receive benefit from the foods we eat, we should keep negative emotions such as **depression, sadness, anxiety,** and **hurry** *away* from the table. If this is not possible, it is better to *skip* the meal because it will hurt the body more than it will help.

Create a Pleasant Atmosphere

Relaxing music and **pleasant,** unhurried **conversation** help to produce good digestion. It is the privilege of the ***hosts*** to *guide* the conversation into positive topics and to keep it moving.

The **type** and **variety** of the **food** and the **way it is presented** holds a relevant and important place at the meal because this is the main part of the meal.

Particularly Healthy Foods

A **healthy meal** should be made up of ***grains, legumes, vegetables, fruits,*** and ***nuts.*** The ideal is that the table is provided with the appropriate vegetables from each locale, climate and season.

A ***healthy*** meal **begins** with a plate of ***raw vegetables*** in the form of a salad. This improves the digestion due to the vitamins, minerals and phytochemical elements that it provides. It also helps to prevent thirst. If the meal *begins* with **cooked foods,** the body interprets it as an ***attack*** and produces an ***increase in white blood cells*** in the blood (digestive leukocytosis, see Vol. 1, p. 98). This does not happen if, as stated earlier, we begin with a salad.

Foods ought to be prepared in a ***simple manner*** and *presented* in an ***attractive*** and appetizing ***way.*** The sensation of food that is appealing is passed to the nervous system by the senses and, consciously and unconsciously, it positively influences the digestive processes.

Variety in the foods eaten is achieved through the *different meals* of the day and of the week, not within one meal. A large variety of foods in the same meal produces ***undesirable reactions to the digestive processes*** and can cause disease.

Food Compatibility

Although much has been written about **food compatibility,** and although it is not easy to arrive at agreement, we offer the following advice:

- Do not eat more than **three or four different dishes** in one meal.
- *Avoid* eating **fruits and vegetables together** as much as possible, as well as mixing **milk and sugar,** or **milk, eggs, and sugar.**
- Observe your own body to understand its reaction to different foods and food combinations. In this way you can avoid repeating foods that do not suit you.
- If you do use a food that is suspect, eat only a small amount and chew it well.

Meal

The Drinks

Convention dictates that food is accompanied with a drink, but drinking liquids during the meal is ***not*** the ***healthiest*** habit because it *harms* **digestive processes.** The ideal is to ***avoid drinking*** until at least two hours after having eaten and thirty minutes before the next meal. In this way the body is well *hydrated* and the digestive organs can provide an abundance of digestive juices without the person feeling the least sensation of thirst.

The *best drink* will always be **water. Fruit** and **vegetable** juices, raw and freshly squeezed, provide an ideal appetizer when taken *thirty minutes* before eating.

Appropriate Amounts in Food Consumption

We must bear in mind that, no matter how healthy the foods we eat, *eating in excess can ruin* the meal. The ability of the digestive organs to process foods becomes ***saturated,*** digestion ***slows,*** and ***fermentation*** and ***decay*** begin. These processes release gas and irritating substances. One should *never* reach the point of saturation. It is better to take a little and repeat later than to serve too much and feel obliged to finish it.

Hosts should ***never force*** their guests to take second servings ***nor*** should they ***serve more*** than that indicated by the guest, no matter how proud they are of the cuisine being served.

It is helpful if the guests are *informed* of the **complete menu** at the beginning of the meal. This helps them to *regulate their appetites* in a reasonable way from the start to the end of the meal. It avoids the danger that they satisfy their hunger with the first dish thinking that there is nothing more or that they eat less because they expect an imagined delicious dessert and remain hungry.

Appetizers

Frequently, **appetizers** are served to the guests in the few moments before the main meal. Appetizers may be made up of ***drinks*** and ***foods in small amounts*** served on toothpicks or as canapés. These are eaten before guests are seated at the table while waiting for everyone to arrive or while final preparations continue in the kitchen.

Appetizers also serve a **social function** because while they are being eaten, the guests mingle and establish relationships.

Some celebrations are made up of only these types of foods. In this case, they are placed on *many trays and served on a large, buffet-style table* in plentiful amounts. If served by waiters, the guests may partake freely from the trays when they come around.

They are appropriate for certain kinds of events such as garden parties and, in general, where one wishes to create a relaxed atmosphere where guests feel free to mingle with each other.

It is said that **appetizers** help to open the appetite. To ensure that they are **healthy,** bear in mind the following advice:

- Use healthy products as ingredients.
- Appetizers only make sense within the context of a meal.
- Remember the other advice given.

40 Base Recipes

Chapter Summary

Recipes

Arabian Pita Bread 47
Crepes 42
Fresh Italian Pasta 48
Marinated Gluten 52
Marinated Gluten with Vegetables 53
Mexican Corn Tortillas 44
Mexican Wheat Tortillas 45
Pie Crust 43
Whole Bread 46

The base ingredients of the base recipes are grains, the true foundation of nutrition. From a health point of view, whole flour is best. (Unless specified, the flour used in these recipes is wheat.)

THE 'BASE RECIPES' receive this name because they represent the base or foundation for making many dishes and recipes. Many of the recipes in this work, found in the chapters of the fourth section (Vol. 3, p. 126) need these base recipes for their completion.

The base recipes represent a challenge for those who wish to enter the world of the culinary art. By taking a look at the recipes in this chapter, experienced cooks will be able to imagine the delicious dishes that can be created when using these recipes as the base.

The base recipes are probably also ***the first*** that all cooks should learn to make. In fact, those who are learning to cook should take special care to master these recipes. This requires an in-depth understanding of the processes of kneading, raising, and baking. If the dough or pasta that forms part of the basic recipe does not turn out well, the rest of the dish is spoiled; good dough or pasta is what makes the dish a success.

The Foundation of Nutrition

The base recipes are also called this way because their main ingredient is cereal **flour,** and cereals form the ***base*** of **human nutrition,** as they provide a good proportion of ***carbohydrates*** and ***proteins,*** which are not easy to get from other foods.

Besides, when the **flour** with which these base recipes are made is **whole,** it also provides other nutrients that are present in bran and in the germ of the grain (see Vol. 1, p. 64):

- ***Fiber,*** necessary for healthy functioning of the large intestine;
- ***Essential fatty acids;***
- ***Vitamins,*** especially those of the ***B*** complex and ***E;*** and
- ***Minerals*** such as ***phosphorus, magnesium, iron,*** and ***calcium.***

This means that from the nutritional and dietary points of view it is *definitely preferable* to prepare these basic recipes with **whole flour.**

Cereal **flour,** although a first-rate food, has one limitation from the nutritional point of view: the ***proteins*** are ***not*** **complete.** However, it is easy to **supplement** them and thereby enrich their nutritional value. This is accomplished simply by combining the dough or the pasta with other protein sources such as **legumes** or **milk products** (see Vol. 1, p. 70).

Crepes (183 kcal/100 g = 52 kcal/oz)

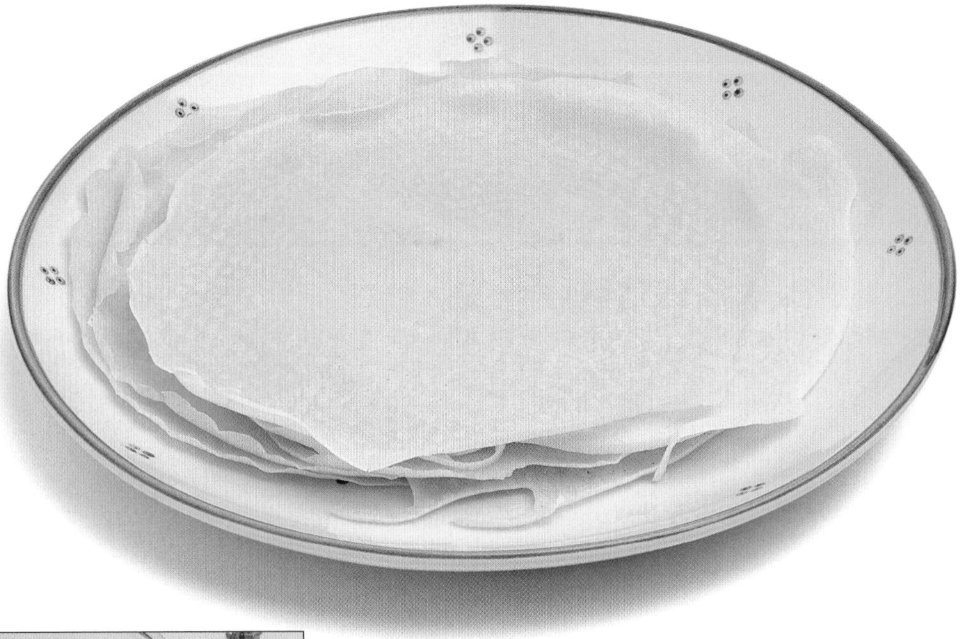

Main ingredients of crepes.

Mix all ingredients.

Flip the crepe with a spatula.

INGREDIENTS

- 125 g (≅ 1cup) wheat **flour**
- 1 **egg**
- 125 ml (≅ 1/2 cup) **milk**
- 2 tablespoons sunflower seed **oil**
- 125 ml (≅ 1/2 cup) **water**
- 1/2 teaspoon sea **salt** (see Vol. 3, p. 16)

PREPARATION

- Beat the egg.
- Mix all the ingredients and let them set for 1 or 2 hours.
- When the time is up, lightly stir the mixture.
- Put a pan with a few drops of oil on the fire and add 3 tablespoons of the mixture so that it covers the bottom of the pan.
- Turn the crepe with a spatula until both sides are golden.
- Repeat the process until the mixture is finished.

HEALTHIER ALTERNATIVE: Instead of cow's milk, you can use soy milk (see Vol. 3, p. 305) and you can do without the egg; if so, add a little more liquid and bear in mind that the crepe will lose some of its elasticity.

Pie Crust (384 kcal/100 g = 109 kcal/oz)

INGREDIENTS

- 250 g (≅ 2 cups) whole wheat **flour**
- 125 g (4.4 oz) vegetable **margarine**
- 1 **egg**
- 3 tablespoons **milk**
- Sea **salt** (see Vol. 3, p. 16)

PREPARATION

- Put the flour and salt in a bowl.
- Add the margarine using your fingertips to dissolve it.
- Once the margarine is dissolved, add the egg and milk little by little.
- Mix the ingredients carefully and quickly.
- Once the dough is done, let it set in the refrigerator for 30 minutes.
- With the help of a rolling pin, roll out the dough until it is 5 mm thick.
- Cut circles of the appropriate size to cover the selected pan.
- Once the dough is placed in the pie pan, pinch it with a fork and bake it in an oven at 180°C for 10 or 15 minutes. If over baked, it will break more easily and will have a sour flavor.
- The crust can be filled with various types of vegetables or cold purées.

Allow the dough to set for 30 minutes.

Place the dough in the pie pan.

Mexican Corn Tortillas

(201 kcal/100 g = 57 kcal/oz)

Add the water little by little.

INGREDIENTS

- 1 kg (≅ 2 pounds) **corn flour**
- **Water** (the quantity is not specified because it is never exact; it will depend upon the humidity level of the flour, its texture, as well as environmental levels of humidity, etc.)
- Sea **salt** (see Vol. 3, p. 16)

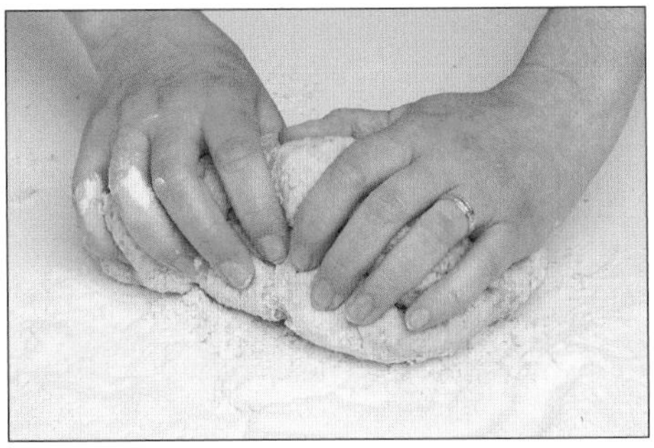

Knead on a floured surface.

PREPARATION

- Put the flour and the salt in a bowl and add water while mixing until it forms into a compact dough that does not stick to the hands.
- Take a portion of the dough and roll into a small ball. Place it between two sheets of Saran (plastic) wrap; using a rolling pin or a wooden press on the upper piece of plastic, roll the dough until it is very fine and circular.
- Place a pan or a griddle iron on the fire and place the tortilla on it. Flip so that both sides are golden; repeat the process until the dough is used up.
- They should be eaten right away.

Mexican Wheat Tortillas

(221 kcal/100 g = 63 kcal/oz)

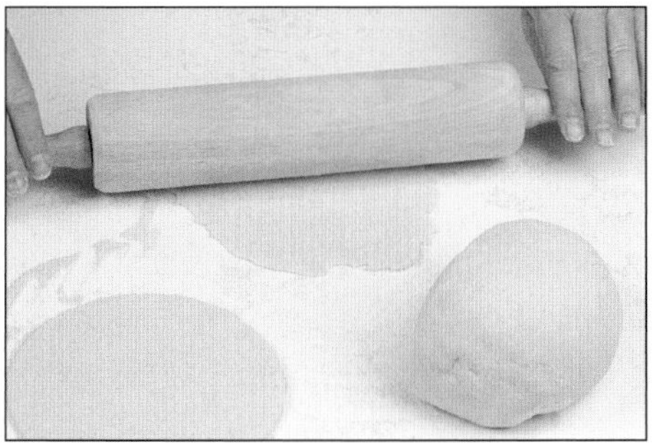

With the help of a rolling pin, stretch the dough.

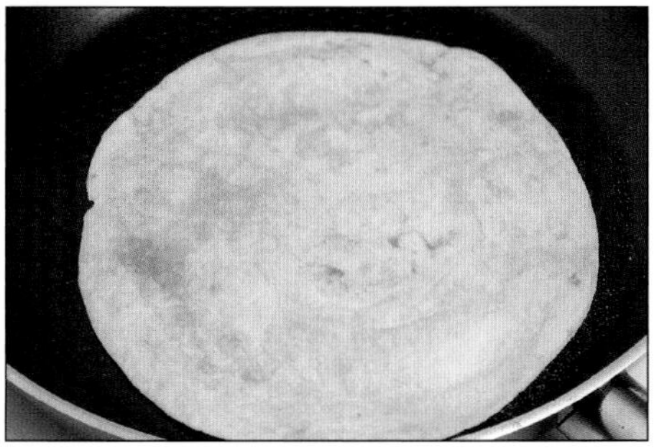

Cook the tortilla on both sides until golden.

INGREDIENTS

- 1 kg (≅ 2 pounds) **whole** wheat **flour**
- 100 ml (≅ 7 tablespoons) olive **oil**
- **Water** (the quantity is not specified because it is never exact; it will depend upon the humidity level of the flour, its texture, as well as environmental levels of humidity, etc.)
- Sea **salt** (see Vol. 3, p. 16)

PREPARATION

- Mix the flour and salt in a bowl. Add the oil and water and mix everything until achieving a compact dough that does not stick to the hands.
- Roll the dough into small balls and allow them to set for 5 or 10 minutes.
- Roll out each ball with a rolling pin until it is as flat and circular as possible.
- Place a pan or a griddle iron on the fire and cook each tortilla until golden on each side.

Whole Bread

(233 kcal/100 g = 66 kcal/oz)

INGREDIENTS

- 1 kg (≅ 2 pounds) **whole** wheat **flour**
- 500 g (≅ 4 cups) **white flour** (with a high gluten content)
- 60 g (≅ 2 oz) dry **yeast**
- 6 tablespoons **olive oil**
- 1 liter (≅ 1 quart) **water**
- Sea **salt** (see Vol. 3, p. 16)

PREPARATION

- Dissolve the yeast in a little lukewarm water.
- Put the flour in a large bowl. Make a hole in the center and add the salt and the dissolved yeast.
- Add the oil and mix well; begin to knead with one hand while adding the lukewarm water with the other; knead well with both hands for 10 minutes or more.
- Cover the bowl containing the dough with a clean cloth; allow it to set in a warm place away from currents of air for one hour (the dough must double in size).
- Divide the dough into six pieces and form into the desired shapes: bars, rolls…. Cover each piece and allow them to set for another hour in a warm and protected place until it doubles in size once more.
- Grease the oven pan with a little oil and place the bread on the pan.
- Put the pan in an oven that is previously heated to 220°C. Bake until you can insert a fork and it comes out clean (without dough attached).

Dissolve the yeast with lukewarm water.

Shape the dough into traditional or round bars.

Arabian Pita Bread

(231 kcal/100 g = 65 kcal/oz)

INGREDIENTS

- 350 g (≅ 3 cups) **whole** wheat **flour**
- 150 g (≅ 1 1/4 cups) **white flour** (with a high gluten content)
- 20 g (≅ 0.7 oz) dry **yeast**
- 350 ml (≅ 1 1/2 cups) **water**
- 2 tablespoons olive **oil**
- Sea **salt** (see Vol. 3, p. 16) (a pinch)

Add the oil and mix well.

Shape the dough into a ball.

PREPARATION

- For the mixture and kneading, follow the instructions given for whole bread (see Vol. 3, p. 46).
- After allowing the dough to rise, knead for 2 more minutes and divide into 10 portions. Form into balls; flatten each to 3 mm of thickness with a rolling pin.
- Allow to set, covered with a kitchen towel for 20 minutes; then put them on an oven pan that has been previously greased. The pan should be preheated (in this way the bread will separate in the middle).
- Put the tray into a preheated oven at 250 degrees centigrade; bake until the loaves are golden; this process can also be done on a hot iron; turn over during the baking process so the loaves are evenly baked on both sides.
- Once the process is finished and the bread is cool or is ready to be eaten, slice the loaves in half. This allows you to serve them filled with many combinations of vegetables, sauces, hamburgers, etc. (see Vol. 3, pp. 170, 171, 117, 152, 198).

Fresh Italian Pasta (348 kcal/100 g = 99 kcal/oz)

Making fresh pasta is an art form, but with interest and practice we can all learn how to do it. Pasta that is handmade from the beginning to the end offers all the guarantees sought by the consumer and it has a flavor and quality that cannot be equaled.

INGREDIENTS

- 200 g (≅ 1 1/2 cups) **whole** wheat **flour**
- 200 g (≅ 1 1/2 cups) **white** wheat **flour**
- 2 tablespoons olive **oil**
- 100 ml (≅ 3/8 cup) **water**
- Sea **salt** (see Vol. 3, p. 16) (a pinch)

How to Make and Stretch the Dough

- Place the two types of flour on a counter at room temperature (not a counter made of marble). Arrange into the shape of a crown.
- In the center of the crown, put the remaining ingredients.
- With much care, little by little, mix the flour into the center of the crown. Do not break the wall of flour, as this will release the oil and the water.
- Rapidly, and with two hands, begin to work the dough until all ingredients are completely mixed.
- Knead the dough, adding flour if it is necessary (the dough should be moist but not sticky), until it reaches the proper consistency. To knead the dough correctly, hold it with one hand and stretch it with the other; gather it into a ball and repeat as many times as necessary; the process will be finished when the dough is elastic and does not stick to the hands.
- To stretch the dough by hand you will need a rolling pin. Starting at the bottom and moving out toward the exterior, you roll the dough onto the rolling pin and then unroll it. Repeat this process until you have a sheet of dough. Leave it on a kitchen towel until it dries.
- If you make the pasta with a machine, change the position of the rollers on the grooves making sure that none of them skip as this will ruin the texture of the pasta.

1. Make a crown with the two flours.

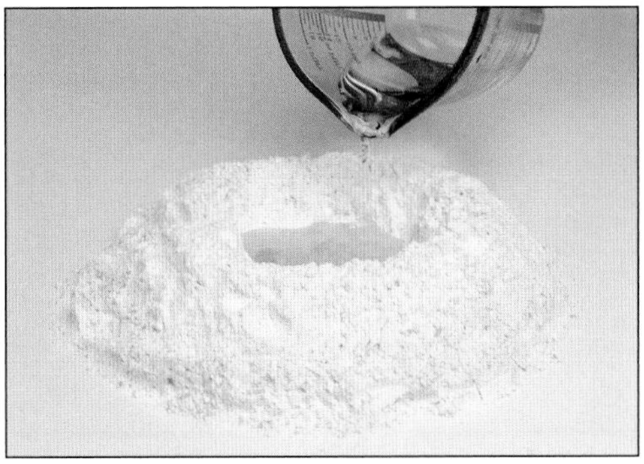

2. Pour the lukewarm water and oil into the hole in the middle of the crown.

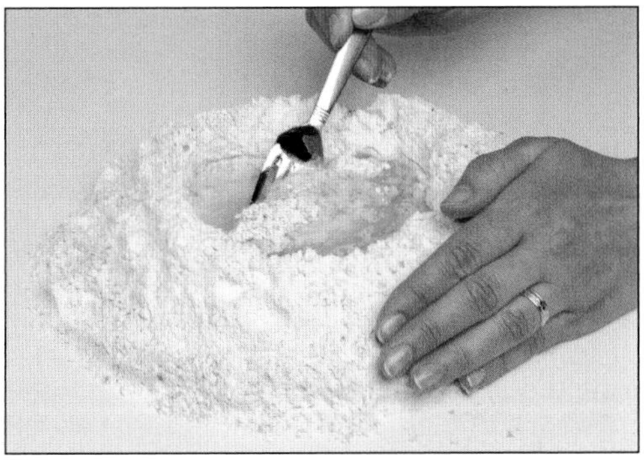

3. Mix the ingredients well while making sure not to break the wall of the crown.

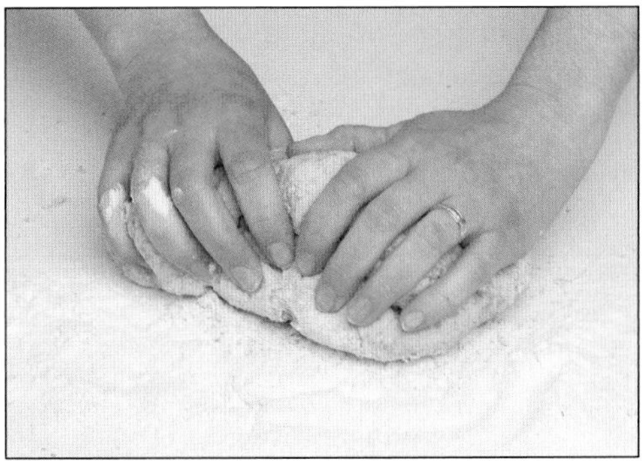

4. Rapidly mix all ingredients.

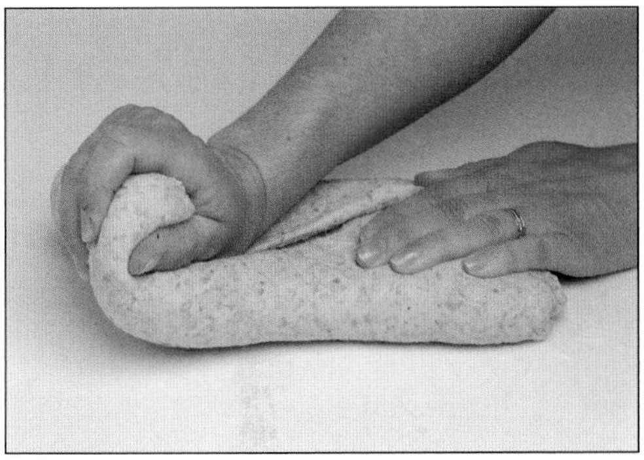

5. Hold the dough with one hand and stretch it with the other.

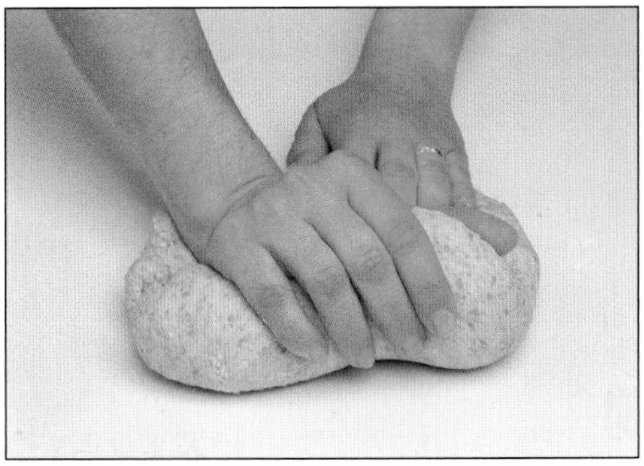

6. Gather up the dough and roll into a ball.

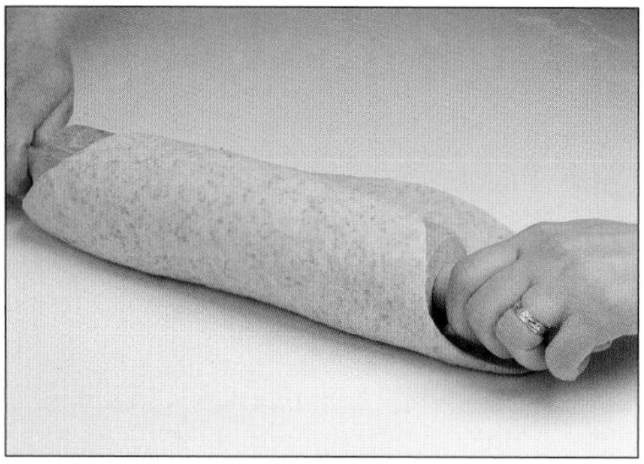

7. With the help of a rolling pin, roll out the dough.

8. Stretching the dough can also be done in the machine.

■ ■ ■

How to Color and Cut the Pasta

- To make colored pasta, simply add the appropriate ingredients to the dough before kneading. If you wish to obtain the following color:
  - **Yellow:** Add three eggs to the center of the flour crown where they will be beaten lightly.
  - **Red:** In this case, add to the dough three tablespoons of tomato sauce.
  - **Green:** Boil 125 g of spinach and drain it well and then blend; add to the flour and proceed with the kneading.
  - **Purple:** In this case, use 125 g of boiled, mashed red beet.
  - **Brown:** Use 125 g of bitter cocoa to give a special touch to the pasta.
- To cut the pasta by hand, roll up the sheet of dough into a flat roll 5 cm across. With a knife cut the pasta roll into strips of the desired width. Unroll the strips.
- If we cut the dough with a serrated knife or cutter into squares 4 cm long on each side, we can paste them together and tie them in the center to make pasta bows or **farfalle.**
- If we cut the pasta with a machine, we will roll the pasta until reaching the last groove and then we will put the sheet of pasta through the cutters of the machine.

If you want the pasta to be more nutritious, simply add egg.

Tomato sauce adds a nice red color to the pasta.

Colored pasta can be made into many shapes.

How to Shape and Fill Pasta

- If we exclude **tortellini** and **cappelletti** (which require special dexterity), filled pasta is easy to make and you do not need any special ability. The only problem that could occur would be that the pasta is too dry. To prevent this, wrap the dough in Saran (plastic) wrap when you are not working with it.
- To make **tortelloni,** cut two strips 10 cm wide. Put the filling along the strip leaving a space of 5 cm between. Cover with another strip of pasta. Using wet fingers, join the borders, seal them and cut them into small rectangular pieces.
- **Raviolini** are similar to tortelloni. We need a circular mold 5 cm in diameter to cut the pasta. Each circle is filled, doubled over in the center and closed.
- **Pansoti** begin with a square piece of pasta (5 cm on each side) that is filled and then doubled over diagonally creating a triangular shape.
- **Cappelletti** are made from pansoti; once the pansoti are formed, the two furthermost corners are joined to form a miter-like shape.
- **Tortellini** are made from a circle of 5 cm in diameter. The filling is placed inside. Then the circle is doubled over in the middle and the extremes are joined.

Tortellini

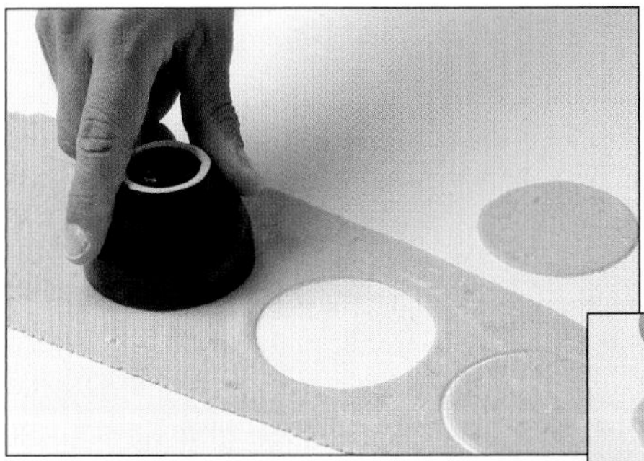

1. Cut circles five centimeters in diameter.

2. Fill each circle.

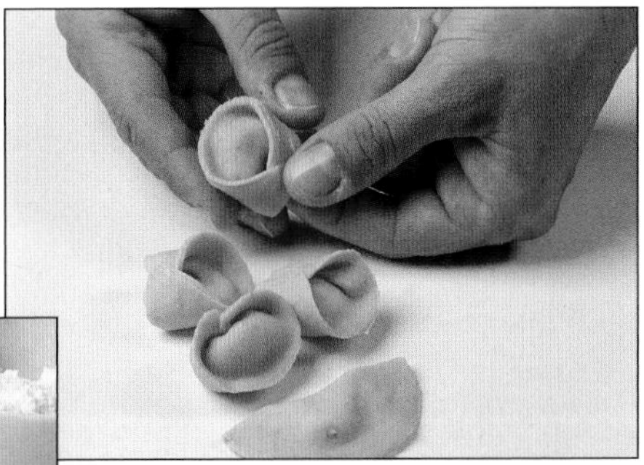

3. Fold the circles over in the middle and, using wet fingers, seal the edges.

Tortelloni

1. To make tortelloni, place some filling along the strip every 5 cm.

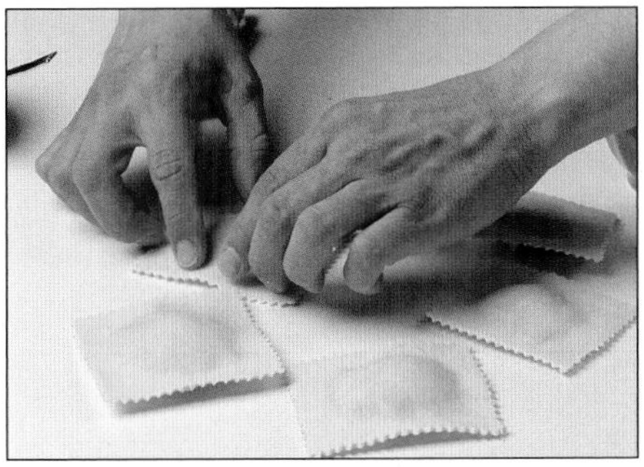

2. Covering with another strip closes tortelloni.

Seitan or Marinated Gluten (156 kcal/100 g = 44 kcal/oz)

INGREDIENTS

- 250 g (≅ 8.8 oz) **gluten flour**
- 2 1/2 liters (≅ 2 1/2 quarts) **vegetable broth** (without salt)
- **Soy sauce** (each tablespoon of this sauce adds 8 kcal and 857 mg of sodium to the recipe; see Vol. 3, p. 16)

Seitan is the name given to gluten made from wheat and boiled in vegetable broth with soy sauce.

Gluten is first extracted from wheat flour (it must be a wheat flour **high in gluten**). The process consists in mixing the flour with a small amount of water or vegetable broth, enough to form a ball that is kneaded and then left to set in a bowl covered with lukewarm water. After some time, the dough is washed alternately in cold and hot water. With this washing, the starch and bran are removed. When the water in which the dough is washed runs completely clear, what remains is gluten. Cook on a slow fire during 60 minutes in the vegetable broth and soy sauce.

Nowadays, if you have, as in our case, **gluten flour** (gluten in powder form), the process of kneading and washing described above is avoided. This also allows you to include other ingredients (in this case, legumes) before adding the water. In this way seitan, enriched both in taste and in nutritional value, is achieved.

1. Mix the glutenous flour with two cups of vegetable broth and shape the dough into the form of a cylinder or a ball.

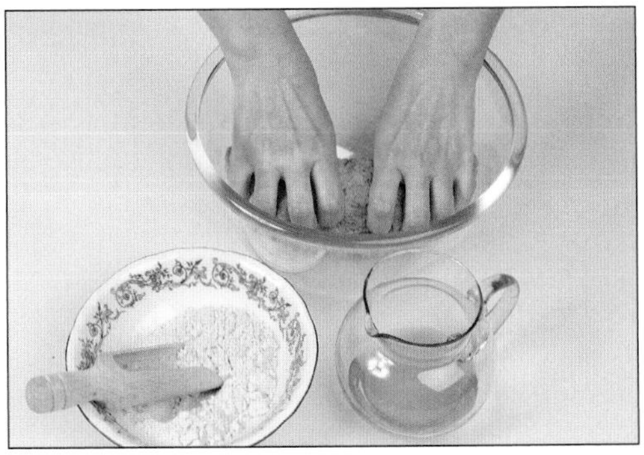

2. Combine the rest of the broth with the soy sauce and place in a pot. Add the washed dough. Cook for 1 hour. Strain the seitan and prepare it according to the chosen recipe.

Vegetable Seitan (158 kcal/100 g = 45 kcal/oz)

The texture of seitan is similar to that of meat. But because it is a grain-based product, it does ***not*** contain ***cholesterol or saturated fat,*** nor does it possess the other inconveniences of meat or its derivatives.

Proteins from seitan are *supplemented* with those of **legumes** so that the combination provides all the amino acids the body needs.

INGREDIENTS

- 250 g (≅ 8.8 oz) **gluten flour**
- 300 g (≅ 5.3 oz) boiled **legumes** (beans, soybeans, chickpeas, lentils…)
- 2 liters (≅ 2 quarts) **vegetable broth** (without salt)
- **Soy sauce** (each tablespoon of this sauce adds 8 kcal and 857 mg of sodium to the recipe; see Vol. 3, p. 16)

1. Discard the broth from the legumes, if there is any. Make a fine purée out of the legumes. Mix into the glutenous flour.

2. Shape the dough into a cylinder or into 2 balls.

   Combine the vegetable broth and the soy sauce into a pot; when boiling, add the gluten. Cook for 1 hour. Drain the seitan and prepare according to the chosen recipe.

41 DRESSINGS, SAUCES AND HORS D'OEUVRES

CHAPTER SUMMARY

RECIPES

Canapés .68
Cooking Without Cheese 73
Cooking Without Egg 76
Dressings 57
International Sauces and Dressings .60
Kebabs 74
Mayonnaise Spreads 58
Nut Butters 65
Other Sauces 64
Special Complementary Dishes 70
Spreads .66
Tomato Sauces 62
Vegetarian Kebabs 75
Vinaigrettes 56
White Sauces 59

The dressings, sauces, and hors d'oeuvres described in this chapter are both tasty and healthy. They enhance the natural flavors of the foods while at the same time providing vitamins, minerals and other nutrients that stimulate the appetite and help the digestive processes.

DRESSINGS, sauces, and hors d'oeuvres form a group of **complementary** foods whose *main purpose* is to make foods ***more* tasty** and **appetizing.**

For the palate accustomed to strong flavors from processed foods, healthy recipes made primarily from plant-based foods can seem unappetizing. Consequently, when modifying eating habits is a voluntary decision or a necessity dictated by health reasons, sauces and dressings play an important role in making healthy foods more attractive to the eye and to the palate.

Educating the appetite to appreciate more natural products and subtle flavors is a slow and progressive process that can be made easier with the help of the suggestions in this chapter.

Tasty and Healthy

Using dressings and sauces to make the transition to a healthy diet more enjoyable makes sense only if these dressings or sauces cause no harm to one's health. It serves no purpose to eat healthy foods while dressing them with harmful products.

That is why in this work we have tried to *combine* **taste** with **health,** although this may seem to be a contradiction in terminology. Common belief seems to indicate that if something is tasty it cannot be healthy and vice versa; that is, if it is healthy, it cannot be tasty.

However, as we show in the following pages, the plant kingdom provides enough variety for us to make vinaigrettes, dressings, mayonnaise, sauces, nut butters, and spreads that provide delicious flavor to food while supporting a healthy lifestyle. Most of these dressings are made from an **olive oil** base. This is the king of oils, as it provides the most preventive and curative properties (see other healthy oils in Vol. 1, pp. 112-127).

In addition to making the recipes in this encyclopedia tastier, these dressings and sauces provide ***vitamins*** and ***minerals, fatty acids,*** and other nutrients of great biological value. Many of them also contain ***phytochemical*** elements (see Vol. 1, p. 410) that help to prevent and cure common human diseases and conditions.

Vinaigrettes

Traditional vinaigrette is a cold sauce made from a base of oil, onion, and vinegar. The alternatives suggested below draw their natural and healthy acidity from lemon juice. Lemons provide vitamins, stimulate the appetite, help in the absorption of iron, and ease digestion. The dressings provided here are perfect for salads, vegetables, and legumes.

Lemon Vinaigrette

(78 kcal per tablespoon)

- 1/2 small **onion**
- 1 clove **garlic**
- 1 branch of **peppermint**
- 2 tablespoons of **lemon** juice
- 110 ml (≅ 8 tablespoons) olive **oil**
- Sea **salt** (see Vol. 3, p. 16)

Beat all the ingredients (once washed and chopped) with a hand-held blender until the mixture is fine and well mixed.

Oregano Vinaigrette

(82 kcal per tablespoon)

- 1/2 teaspoon **oregano**
- 2 tablespoons **brewer's yeast**
- 1 crushed **garlic** clove
- A pinch ground **cumin**
- 1/2 teaspoon sweet **mustard sauce**
- 1 **lemon** (juice)
- 100 ml (≅ 7 tablespoons) olive **oil**
- Sea **salt** (see Vol. 3, p. 16)

Mix all the ingredients.

Soy Sweet-and-Sour Sauce (28 kcal per tablespoon)

- 3 tablespoons soy sauce (857 mg of sodium per tablespoon; see Vol. 3, p. 16)
- 3 tablespoons **lemon** juice
- 1 tablespoon **honey**
- 1 tablespoon sesame seed **oil**
- Sea **salt** (see Vol. 3, p. 16)

Mix all the ingredients.

Sweet-and-Sour Sauce from Seeds

(81 kcal per tablespoon)

- 1/2 teaspoon **fennel seeds**
- 1/2 teaspoon **coriander seeds**
- 1 clove **garlic**
- 1 tablespoon **honey**
- 3 tablespoons **lemon** juice
- 6 tablespoons olive **oil**
- Sea **salt** (see Vol. 3, p. 16)

Mash in a mortar the seeds, the garlic clove, and the salt; mix with the lemon juice, honey, and oil.

Dressings

We now offer a series of cold dressings to accompany plant-based foods, either raw or cooked. The ingredients used add color and taste and will enliven the appearance of the foods as well as their taste. In addition, they contain healthy substances that add to the nutritional and preventive qualities of the food that they accompany. We want to highlight the fact that all provide protection against cancer due to the inclusion of certain ingredients such as soybeans, beets, tomato, pepper, and yogurt.

Radish Dressing

(39 kcal per tablespoon)

- 150 g (≅ $^2/_3$ cup) of **soybean mayonnaise** (Vol. 3, p. 58)
- 1 tablespoon of grated **radish**
- $^1/_2$ **lemon** (juice)
- 150 g of creamy **tofu,** natural yogurt, or cream
- Sea **salt** (see Vol. 3, p. 16)

Beat the radish, the lemon juice, and the tofu. Mix in the mayonnaise carefully, using a fork.

Beet Dressing

(19 kcal per tablespoon)

- 2 grated **carrots**
- 1 boiled **beet**
- 100 g (≅ 4 oz) of creamy **tofu,** natural yogurt, or quark
- 50 ml (≅ 4 tablespoons) of olive **oil**
- **Parsley** (or coriander)
- Sea **salt** (see Vol. 3, p. 16)

Beat all the ingredients, except the oil, which will be progressively added at the end in order to obtain a creamy sauce.

Andalusian Dressing (24 kcal per tablespoon)

- 100 g (≅ 2/3 cup) of **soybean mayonnaise** (Vol. 3, p. 58)
- 1 ripe, blended **tomato**
- 1 **sweet red pepper,** peeled and finely chopped
- 50 g (≅ 1.75 oz) of pitted **green olives,** finely chopped

Mix all the ingredients well. This sauce is a good dressing for salads or pasta. It can also be used when making canapés.

Iranian Dressing (22 kcal per tablespoon)

- 2 natural **yogurts**
- 2 tablespoons of **lemon** juice
- 1 tablespoon of fresh chopped **peppermint**
- 2 tablespoons of **sultanas** (raisins without seeds)
- 2 tablespoons of sesame seed **oil**
- Sea **salt** (see Vol. 3, p. 16)

Mix all the ingredients. This is a good dressing to accompany salads or rice.

Mayonnaise

Mayonnaise is traditionally made by beating an egg yolk and then adding raw oil, drop by drop, in order to achieve a smooth mixture. Electric mixers allow us to use a whole egg and to mix all the ingredients at the same time. One of the inconveniences of traditional mayonnaise is the transmission of gastrointestinal infections through contaminated eggs, among other things (see Vol. 1, p. 225). We therefore give alternatives that are healthy for the heart and that do not contain egg. These tasty dressings are easy to prepare and, as in the case of soy mayonnaise, they taste similar to traditional recipes.

Soybean Mayonnaise

(79 kcal per tablespoon)

- 100 ml (≅ $^{3}/_{8}$ cup) of **soy milk** (Vol. 3, Pg. 305)
- 200 ml (≅ 1 cup) of **oil** (half-and-half olive and sunflower)
- 1 clove of chopped garlic
- $^{1}/_{2}$ **lemon** (juice)
- Sea **salt** (see Vol. 3, p. 16)

Put the ingredients in the container of the blender in the order listed and blend on slow speed until the ingredients mix together to form the consistency of mayonnaise. It is convenient that all ingredients are at room temperature when ready to use.

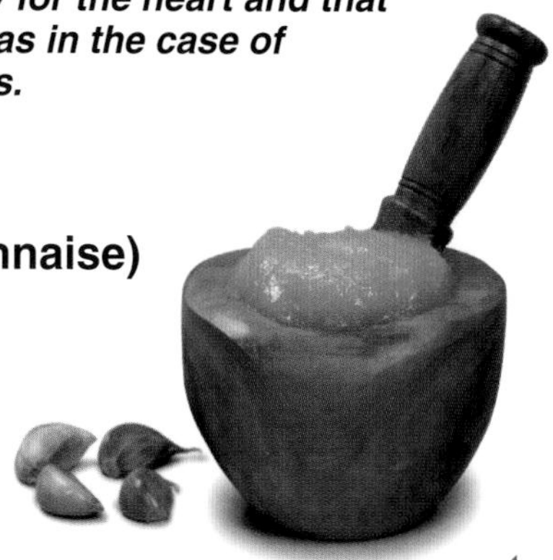

Alioli (Garlic Mayonnaise)

(68 kcal per tablespoon)

- 6 cloves of **garlic**
- $^{1}/_{2}$ litre of virgin **olive oil**
- Sea **salt** (see Vol. 3, p. 16)

Put the pealed garlic and salt in a mortar. Mash the garlic till the paste is well mixed. Add the oil, almost drop by drop, stirring always in the same direction, in order to obtain a creamy sauce, so that even if you turn upside down the mortar the paste will not fall. A few drops of lemon juice are added at the end.

The alioli curdles very easily. In order to avoid it, just add some bread crumb of the same size as the mashed garlic cloves dipped in water and vinegar.

Yogurt Mayonnaise

(73 kcal per tablespoon)

- 100 g of natural **yogurt**
- 100 g of virgin **olive oil**
- 100 g of **corn oil**
- **Coriander, Chives** and **Tarragon**
- Sea **salt** (see Vol. 3, p. 16)

Put the ingredients in the container of the blender in the order listed. Introduce the hand blender completely in the container and without moving it, beat on maximum speed till all ingredients are well mixed. From this moment on the hand blender can be moved up and down.

Vegetable Mayonnaise

(26 kcal per tablespoon)

- 1 boiled **potato**
- 2 boiled **carrots**
- 1 clove of mashed **garlic**
- **Parsley**
- $^{1}/_{2}$ **lemon** (juice)
- 4 tablespoons of olive **oil**
- Sea **salt** (see Vol. 3, p. 16)

Blend all the ingredients until a creamy mixture with the consistency of normal mayonnaise is obtained.

White Sauces

White sauces derive their name from their color. Among them, béchamel is the queen. It was invented in France in the 17th Century by the Marquis of Béchamel. The original recipe contained flour, dairy cream, and butter. Since then it has evolved substantially and the cream and butter, high in saturated fats, which are harmful to the cardiovascular system, have been substituted with other lighter and healthier ingredients such as oil and milk. The latter can be skim or plant-based.

Béchamel (18 kcal per tablespoon)

- 30 g (≅ 1/4 cup) of wheat **flour**
- 1/2 liter (≅ 1/2 quart) of dairy or soybean **milk**
- 3 tablespoons of olive **oil**
- Sea **salt** (see Vol. 3, p. 16)

Heat the oil in a frying pan, and lightly brown the flour; add the cold milk while stirring constantly. Add in the salt and boil on a slow fire for 10 minutes while continuing to stir. You can also add a pinch of nutmeg.

Béchamel with Onion (15 kcal per tablespoon)

- The **same ingredients** as in the previous recipe, adding
- 1 small **onion**

Sauté the chopped onion in the frying pan; when it is golden, add the flour and continue the process according to the previous recipe. Use the hand blender to blend the sauce.

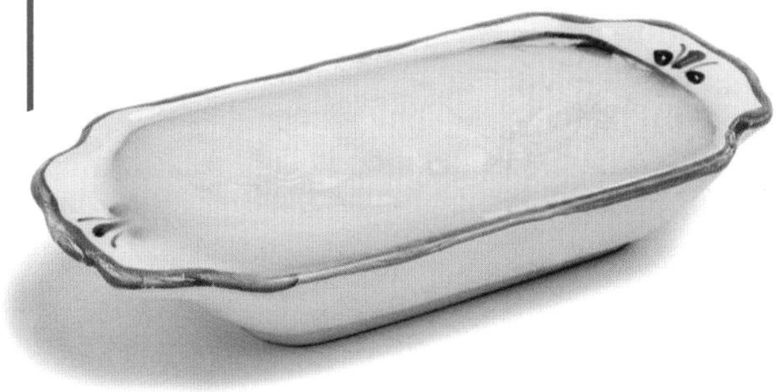

White Sauce (12 kcal per tablespoon)

This sauce is different from traditional béchamel sauce in that it uses **vegetable broth** instead of milk. Flour can also be substituted with **boiled potato.**

Follow the same process as with the traditional béchamel.

Seasoned White Sauce

(11 kcal per tablespoon)

- 1 small **onion**
- 1 small **sweet pepper**
- 1 clove of **garlic**
- **Parsley**
- 1 tablespoon of wheat **flour**
- 350 ml (≅ 1 1/2 cup) of **water**
- Sea **salt** (see Vol. 3, p. 16)
- 2 tablespoons of olive **oil**

Heat the oil in a frying pan, and sauté the chopped vegetables. When the onion is golden, add the flour and continue to sauté for two more minutes, stirring constantly. Add in the cold water and the salt and stir to avoid lumps. Boil for 10 minutes. Strain.

International Sauces and Dressings

The world of sauces is inexhaustible with each culture developing their own and adapting those of others. We therefore present, among others, pesto and bolognaise from Italy, salsiki from Greece, and tahini and sesame sauce from the Far East. All of these provide nutrients and essential elements for maintaining life and preserving health.

Bolognaise (9 kcal per tablespoon)

- $^{1}/_{2}$ kg (≅ 1 pound) of mature, crushed **tomatoes**
- 1 chopped **onion**
- 1 clove of crushed **garlic**
- 100 g (≅ 1 $^{1}/_{2}$ cups) of sliced **mushrooms**
- 100 ml (≅ $^{3}/_{8}$ cup) of **vegetable broth** (without salt)
- 30 g (≅ 1 oz) **texturized soy protein,** dried and finely chopped, or of seitán (gluten), or mashed tofu
- **Parsley**
- **Basil**
- **Oregano**
- 2 tablespoons of olive **oil**
- Sea **salt** (see Vol. 3, p. 16)

Soak the dried soy protein in the vegetable broth for 30 minutes. Sauté the garlic, onion, and soy protein in a pot for 10 minutes, stirring occasionally; add the mushrooms and after 5 more minutes add the remaining ingredients and continue to cook for 30 minutes.

Herb (47 kcal per tablespoon)

- 100 g (≅ 3.5 oz) of **spinach** (tender leaves)
- 2 teaspoons of mixed **anise** and **fennel seeds**
- 4 tablespoons of chopped **chives**
- 4 tablespoons of chopped **parsley** (or coriander)
- 2 tablespoons of chopped **estragon**
- 1 tablespoon of **lemon** juice
- 200 ml (≅ $^{3}/_{4}$ cup) of **vegetable broth** (without salt)
- 250 ml (≅ 1 $^{1}/_{8}$ cups) of olive **oil**
- Sea **salt** (see Vol. 3, p. 16)

Boil the seeds in the vegetable broth for 5 minutes (if the seeds are toasted and chopped previously, they will soak up more flavor). Allow to cool and strain. With the hand blender, make a mayonnaise-style mixture using the broth and the remaining ingredients. This sauce can be served cold or hot (heat in a double pan).

Sesame (60 kcal per tablespoon)

- 2 tablespoons of **tahini** (Vol. 3, p. 61)
- 1 tablespoon of sweet **paprika** (powder)
- 2 tablespoons of **lemon** juice
- 2 tablespoons of **soy sauce** (857 mg of sodium per tablespoon; see Vol. 3, p. 16)
- 2 tablespoons of sesame seed **oil**

Mix all the ingredients. Among other uses, this dressing is ideal for salads and vegetables.

Pesto

(58 kcal per tablespoon)

- 100 g (≅ 3.5 oz) of fresh **basil**
- 4 cloves of crushed **garlic**
- 50 g (≅ 1.75 oz) of peeled **pine nuts**
- 100 g (≅ $^{1}/_{2}$ cup) of fresh **cheese,** natural yogurt, or creamy tofu
- 8 tablespoons of olive **oil**
- Sea **salt** (see Vol. 3, p. 16)

Mix everything with the help of the hand blender, adding the oil at the end. In the traditional Pesto sauce, grated Parmesan cheese is used instead of fresh cheese (with fewer calories). A variation of this sauce consists in using chives instead of garlic.

This sauce goes very well with pasta or with fresh tomatoes. It makes a tasty canapé when spread on toast.

Orange (8 kcal per tablespoon)

- The peel of an **orange** cut into thin slices
- The juice of one **orange**
- Grated **ginger** (a pinch)
- 100 ml (≅ 3/8 cup) of **water**
- 1 teaspoon of cornstarch (very fine corn flour)

Dilute the cornstarch in the orange juice; boil the orange peel and the ginger in the water for 10 minutes. Strain and save the orange skin for decoration. Bring the water to a boil again, add the orange juice little by little, and boil for 3 more minutes, stirring continually. It is served cold and accompanies foods made of seitan, texturized soy protein products, or with "Nut Loaf" (see Vol. 3, p. 94).

Salsiki (13 kcal per tablespoon)

- 3 natural, skimmed **yogurts** or 400 g (≅ 14 oz) of quark cheese
- 1 small **cucumber,** peeled and chopped
- 1 clove of crushed **garlic**
- 1 teaspoon of **capers**
- 1 teaspoon of fresh **peppermint,** parsley or coriander leaves
- 2 tablespoons of olive **oil**
- Sea **salt** (see Vol. 3, p. 16)

Mix all the ingredients with the hand blender. Decorate with chopped chives.

Mediterranean (57 kcal per tablespoon)

- 50 g (≅ 1.75 oz) of toasted **almonds,** peeled and chopped
- 20 g (≅ 1/6 cup) of toasted **hazelnuts,** peeled and chopped
- 1 head of roasted **garlic**
- 2 roasted **tomatoes**
- 2 **hot peppers,** soaked in water (or two roasted peppers)
- 1 slice of **bread** soaked in water
- 1 teaspoon of **paprika** (powder)
- 1 teaspoon of **lemon** juice
- 350 ml (≅ 1 2/3 cup) of olive **oil**
- Sea **salt** (see Vol. 3, p. 16)

The garlic and tomato should be peeled and the meat of the hot pepper should be scraped with a knife. Mix all the ingredients with the hand blender until achieving the consistency of mayonnaise. This is ideal for grilled vegetables or pasta.

Tahini (103 kcal per tablespoon)

- 100 g (≅ 3.5 oz) of toasted **sesame** seeds
- 5 tablespoons of sesame seed **oil**
- Sea **salt** (see Vol. 3, p. 16)
- A little **water**

In a mortar, mash the sesame seeds and the salt. Add the oil and stir. Finally, add the water very slowly until achieving the consistency of dried fruit butters.

Tomato

The tomato, always present in the kitchen and at the table, is particularly versatile. It cannot be substituted in its fresh state where it is used as a base ingredient in salads. Nor can it be substituted in its preserved state where it forms part of many sauces that are used to accompany various recipes and gives them color and flavor. Lycopene, the pigment that gives the tomato its red color and the properties of which are especially visible in sauces, is a powerful antioxidant that protects against cancer (see Vol. 2, pp. 276, 394). Thanks to the vitamins, minerals, and antioxidants that it contains, the tomato helps to fortify the immune system and protects the arteries against the negative effects of cholesterol. It also helps to clean away impurities in the blood.

Traditional (9 kcal per tablespoon)

- 1 kg (≅ 2 pounds) of ripe **tomatoes**
- 500 g (≅ 1 pound) of **onions**
- 4 tablespoons of olive **oil**
- Sea **salt** (see Vol. 3, p. 16)

Peel the onions. Wash and chop them and sauté until golden. Add the tomato. Cook on a medium fire for 20 minutes from the time that the liquid from the tomatoes begins to boil. During this time, stir occasionally. Run it through a strainer before serving. If you wish to put less onion, the sauce will be redder, but it may need a teaspoon of sugar to counteract the acidity of the tomato.

Tomato Specialty (9 kcal per tablespoon)

- 1 kg (≅ 2 pounds) of **tomatoes**
- 1 **carrot**
- 1 **onion**
- 1 stalk of **celery**
- 4 tablespoons of olive **oil**
- Sea **salt** (see Vol. 3, p. 16)

Peel and chop the onion and the carrot; sauté until the onion is golden. Add the cleaned and chopped celery and a few minutes later the tomato. Continue the process as indicated in the Traditional Tomato Sauce. You can achieve a unique flavor by adding almonds, garlic, or aromatic herbs.

Sauces

Natural (15 kcal per tablespoon)

- 1/2 kg (≅ 1 pound) of ripe **tomatoes**
- 1 **spring onion**
- 1 clove of **garlic**
- Chopped **parsley**
- 1/2 **lemon** (juice)
- 4 tablespoons of olive **oil**
- Sea **salt** (see Vol. 3, p. 16)

Wash, peel, and chop all of the vegetables. Liquify them with the hand blender by adding them little by little. Add the oil last so that the sauce mixes well. This is a variation of "Andalusian Gazpacho" (see Vol. 3, p. 360).

Red (7 kcal per tablespoon)

- 2 large, ripe **tomatoes,** liquefied
- 2 **red sweet peppers,** grilled and peeled
- 1 clove of crushed **garlic**
- A pinch of **paprika** (powder)
- 2 tablespoons of olive **oil**
- Sea **salt** (see Vol. 3, p. 16)

Liquefy the ingredients with the hand blender until you achieve a homogenous mixture. If you wish, you can give a different touch to the recipe by adding chili or spicy paprika. This is a good accompanying sauce for salads. It can also be used as a sandwich spread.

Chopped (11 kcal per tablespoon)

- 2 **tomatoes**
- 1 **onion**
- **Coriander**
- 2 tablespoons of olive **oil**
- Sea **salt** (see Vol. 3, p. 16)

Chop all the ingredients and mix together. This is a good accompaniment for tacos, Mexican tortillas, and in general for any pasta or legume that you wish to eat cold.

Other Sauces

In a healthy diet, sauces and other accompanying items carry special importance because they revive the daily foods, avoid monotony, and enrich and complement their nutritional value. In this regard, we advise that a food high in calories be combined with a lighter sauce that adds vitamins and minerals and vice versa.

Green (9 kcal per tablespoon)

- 1/2 small **onion**
- 1 tablespoon of wheat **flour**
- 1 clove of crushed **garlic**
- Generous portion of **parsley,** chopped fine
- 1 tablespoon of olive **oil**
- 250 ml (≅ 1 cup) of **water**
- Sea **salt** (see Vol. 3, p. 16)

Sauté the chopped onion in a frying pan; when it is golden, add the flour and stir for 2 minutes; add the garlic, parsley, salt, and water, and then boil on a low fire for 10 minutes while continuing to stir. A light sauce will result. You can add other aromatic herbs such as chervil, dill, chives, etc., to vary the flavor.

Vegetable (22 kcal per tablespoon)

- 100 g of **spinach,** lettuce (dark leaves), broccoli, or zucchini with the skin
- 1 small **spring onion**
- 2 **carrots**
- 1 small **potato**
- 2 tablespoons of **hazelnut butter** (Vol. 3, p. 65)
- 2 cloves of crushed **garlic**
- **Parsley**
- 1/2 liter (≅ 1/2 quart) of **water**
- 150 ml (≅ 2/3 cup) of olive **oil**
- Sea **salt** (see Vol. 3, p. 16)

Clean and boil the vegetables; once tender, blend all the ingredients with a hand mixer until the sauce is light and creamy.

Mushroom (7 kcal per tablespoon)

- 200 g (≅ 7 oz) of sliced **mushrooms** (white mushrooms)
- 1 medium chopped **onion**
- 1 clove of crushed **garlic**
- 2 tablespoons of olive **oil**
- 2 teaspoons of **cornstarch** (fine corn flour)
- 2 tablespoons of **soy sauce** (857 mg of sodium per tablespoon; see Vol. 3, p. 16)
- 1/2 liter (≅ 1/2 quart) of **vegetable broth** (without salt)

Sauté the garlic and the onion; when the onion is golden, remove and then sauté the mushroom. Make a light cream with part of the vegetable broth, the oil, the soy sauce, the mushrooms, the onion, and the garlic. Put the cream on the fire and add the cold, diluted cornstarch to the rest of the broth. Boil for 8 minutes. Serve hot and decorate with a sliced mushroom.

This sauce goes well with rice, pasta, or dishes made of soy protein or seitan.

Almond Cream Sauce

(20 kcal per tablespoon)

- 2 tablespoons of raw grated **almonds**
- 2 tablespoons of wheat **flour**
- 400 ml (≅ 1 2/3 cups) of **almond milk**, cow's milk, or soy milk (beverage)
- 2 tablespoons of olive **oil**
- Sea **salt** (see Vol. 3, p. 16)

Heat the oil in a frying pan, brown the almonds and remove from the fire; in the same oil, brown the flour and add the cold milk and salt. Boil on a low flame for 10 minutes. Stir constantly throughout the process and, just before turning off the fire, add the almonds.

Nut Butters

Nut butters are rich in minerals, vitamins (including Vitamin E) and in trace elements. They are also a privileged source of unsaturated fatty acids. Their use is recommended to help the nervous system function better throughout growth periods, pregnancy, and lactation. When they substitute other products that are high in saturated fats, such as butter or sausage, they reduce the level of cholesterol in the blood.

Hazelnut (101 kcal per tablespoon)

- 250 g (≅ 8.8 oz) of peeled and toasted **hazelnuts**
- 3 tablespoons of corn germ **oil**

Chop the hazelnuts and grind them with the blender. Add the oil and blend until a fine and homogenous butter results. Keep in a glass jar.

When spread on bread along with honey, jam, banana, or dried fruits it is delicious; it can also be used as the base for "Hazelnut Milk" (see Vol. 3, p. 291).

Almond

(95 kcal per tablespoon)

- 250 g (≅ 8.8 oz) of peeled and toasted **almonds**
- 3 tablespoons of corn germ **oil**

Chop in the same way as in the preparation of the hazelnut butter. Fried almonds may also be used; if they are salted, wash with water and allow to drain.

Walnut

(53 kcal per tablespoon)

- 100 g (≅ 3.5 oz) of blended fresh **cheese** or tofu
- 40 g (≅ 3/8 cup) of shelled **walnuts**
- 1 clove of **garlic**
- Sea **salt** (see Vol. 3, p. 16)

Grind the nuts, crush the garlic, and mix in the cheese. Add the salt and mix well. Keep in the refrigerator.

Chestnut (28 kcal per tablespoon)

- 150 g (≅ 2.6 oz) of boiled and peeled **chestnuts**
- 100 g (≅ 3.5 oz) of **tofu** or fresh cheese
- 50 g (≅ 1/2 cup) of **cashews**
- 2 tablespoons of **brewer's yeast**
- 1 baked **onion**
- 1 clove of **garlic,** baked
- **Coriander, thyme, cloves**
- 1 tablespoon of peanut **oil**
- **Soy sauce** (857 mg of sodium per tablespoon; see Vol. 3, p. 16)

Mix all the ingredients with the blender until achieving a paste. Keep in the refrigerator.

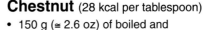

Peanut (92 kcal per tablespoon)

- 250 g (≅ 8.8 oz) of peeled and toasted **peanuts**
- 3 tablespoons of corn germ **oil**

Prepare in the same way as with hazelnut butter.

Spreads

Spreads are eaten on bread, either in the form of a canapé, a sandwich or to accompany another dish. Although sandwich spreads are generally high in fat and calories, these spreads differ in that they have no cholesterol and do not contain other toxic substances that are present in meat-based pâtés or sandwich spreads *(see Vol. 1, p. 327).*

Lupine

(57 kcal per tablespoon)

- 100 g (≅ 3.5 oz) of lupine bean **flour** or 150 g (≅ 2.6 oz) of boiled and peeled lupine beans
- 1 tablespoon of **hazelnut butter** (Vol. 3, p. 65)
- 1 tablespoon of fat-free natural **yogurt**
- Sea **salt** (see Vol. 3, p. 16)

Make a smooth and homogenous cream with the help of the hand blender, mixing all the ingredients. Keep in the refrigerator.

Tofu and Fine Herbs

(39 kcal per tablespoon)

- 100 g (≅ 3.5 oz) of creamy **tofu**
- 1 clove of **garlic**
- **Parsley**
- **Basil** and **coriander**
- 2 tablespoons of **oil**
- Sea **salt** (see Vol. 3, p. 16)
- **Sweet paprika,** powder (optional)

Make a smooth and homogenous cream with the help of the hand blender, mixing all the ingredients. Keep in the refrigerator.

Mushroom (31 kcal per tablespoon)

- 250 g (≅ 3 cups) of **mushrooms** (white mushrooms; other types of mushrooms may also be used)
- 2 cloves of chopped **garlic**
- 50 g (≅ 1.75 oz) of **vegetable margarine**
- 20 g (≅ 1/2 cup) of shredded **bread**
- Chopped **parsley**
- 2 tablespoons of olive **oil**
- Sea **salt** (see Vol. 3, p. 16)

Sauté all the ingredients in a frying pan, grind with the help of the hand mixer and allow to cool before storing in a container.

Spicy Vegetable Spread (63 kcal per tablespoon)

- 240 g (≅ 8.5 oz) of **texturized soy protein,** soaked in vegetable broth (110 g dried)
- 50 g (≅ 1.75 oz) of raw, peeled **almonds** (other nuts may be used)
- 50 g (≅ 1/3 cup) of peeled **sunflower seeds** (other seeds may be used)
- 4 crushed cloves of **garlic**
- 1 tablespoon of **sweet paprika,** powder
- 1 teaspoon of **hot pepper,** powder
- 1 tablespoon of **oregano**
- 8 tablespoons of olive **oil**
- Sea **salt** (see Vol. 3, p. 16)

Mix the soy protein, the oil, the spices, salt and garlic, and blend as fine as you wish. Crush the almonds with the rolling pin making sure that they do not disintegrate into powder and add to the mix along with the sunflower seeds. Mix together and keep in the refrigerator in a covered container.

Olive (vegetarian caviar)

(18 kcal per tablespoon)

- 250 g (≅ 8.8 oz) of **black olives**
- 2 crushed cloves of **garlic**

Soak the olives overnight if they are very dry or salty. Drain and pit. Blend them along with the garlic with the help of the hand blender until the mixture is creamy in texture.

A more creamy consistency can be obtained by adding creamy tofu, quark cheese, or fresh cheese spread with a little olive oil.

Hummus (41 kcal per tablespoon)

- 300 g of boiled **chickpeas** (150 g [3/4 cup] dried)
- 2 tablespoons of **Tahini** (Vol. 3, p. 61)
- 2 cloves of crushed **garlic**
- 1 teaspoon of **ground cumin**
- 1 branch of chopped **parsley**
- 1/2 teaspoon of **hot pepper**
- 1/2 **lemon** (juice)
- 3 tablespoons of olive **oil**
- Sea **salt** (see Vol. 3, p. 16)

Mix all the ingredients until achieving a fine spread. Keep it in a container in the refrigerator. Sesame seeds may be added. To make the mixture creamier, add a tablespoon of fat-free natural yogurt or light tofu.

Guacamole (36 kcal per tablespoon)

- 1 ripe **avocado**
- 1 tablespoon of **lemon** juice
- 1 pinch of **celery salt**
- 1/4 de kg (≅ 1/2 pound) of **spring onions** or 1/2 **onion**

Peel the avocado and remove the stone. Chop the Welsh onions. Mix all the ingredients with a hand blender until the spread is smooth. Keep the guacamole in a container in the refrigerator.

Lentil (15 kcal per tablespoon)

- 90 g of boiled **lentils** (50 g [≅ 1/4 cup] dried)
- 1 chopped **onion**
- 1 grated **carrot**
- 1 branch of **celery,** chopped fine
- **Marjoram**
- **Chives**
- 2 tablespoons of olive **oil**
- Herbal **salt** (see Vol. 3, p. 16)

Sauté the onion, carrot, and celery. Add the lentils and make everything into a purée. If the lentils are shelled, the spread will be smoother.

Canapés

Canapés, artistically decorated and carefully laid out on a tray, add a touch of joy, color, and variety to any celebration. Because the ingredients are many, it is good to avoid excess in the number of products eaten, as this can cause digestive problems and food incompatibilities.

Lettuce and Hearts of Palm (24 units)

(28 kcal per unit)

- 3 leaves of **lettuce,** chopped fine
- 2 stems of **hearts of palm,** cut into round slices
- 2 **radishes,** cut into thin round slices
- 6 slices from a loaf of **bread**
- **Garlic** powder
- 3 tablespoons of **soy mayonnais**e (Vol. 3, p. 58)
- Sea **salt** (see Vol. 3, p. 16)

Mix the lettuce with the mayonnaise and the garlic powder and spread the mixture on the bread. Decorate with the heart of palm and the radish, and, just before serving, add the salt.

Cheese and Red Pepper (24 units)

(45 kcal per unit)

- 6 slices from a loaf of **bread**
- 250 g (1 cup) of **fresh cheese** or tofu
- 1 **sweet** red **pepper,** grilled and chopped fine
- 3 tablespoons of **soy mayonnaise** (Vol. 3, p. 58)
- 24 pitted black **olives**
- Sea **salt** (see Vol. 3, p. 16)

Mash the cheese with a fork and add a little mayonnaise, the pepper, and the salt. Spread on the bread and decorate with the black olives.

Cucumber and Onion (24 units)

(27 kcal per unit)

- 1 **cucumber** cut into round slices
- 1 **spring onion** peeled and chopped
- 6 slices from a loaf of **bread**
- **Oregano**
- **Parsley**
- 3 tablespoons of **soy mayonnaise** (Vol. 3, p. 58)
- Sea **salt** (see Vol. 3, p. 16)

Soak the cucumber and the Welsh onion in the oil to which the aromatic herbs have been added. Spread mayonnaise on the bread, and add a slice of cucumber, a little more mayonnaise, and, finally, the Welsh onion. Add salt before serving. These canapés may also be decorated with crumbs of hard-boiled egg yolk.

Zucchini (24 units)

(27 kcal per unit)

- 1 **zucchini,** in round slices and grilled
- 3 tablespoons of **traditional tomato sauce** (Vol. 3, p. 62)
- 6 slices from a loaf of **bread**
- **Parsley,** finely chopped
- 3 tablespoons of **soy mayonnaise** (Vol. 3, p. 58)
- Sea **salt** (see Vol. 3, p. 16)

Mix the mayonnaise and the parsley and spread this mixture on the canapés; place a slice of zucchini on top of each canapé and cover with a little tomato sauce. A little chopped parsley or dill may also be used for decoration.

Asparagus and Egg (24 units)

(44 kcal per unit)

- 4 hard-boiled **eggs** (boil for 12 minutes)
- 6 boiled green **asparagus**
- 3 tablespoons of **soy mayonnaise** (Vol. 3, p. 58)
- 1 **sweet** red **pepper,** grilled and chopped into thin slices
- 6 slices from a loaf of **bread**

Spread the mayonnaise on the bread, peel the eggs and mash them; add the mashed egg to the canapé and add a little more mayonnaise. Decorate with a piece of asparagus and a slice of pepper. The salt should be added at the moment of serving. The canapés spoil and lose freshness if it is added earlier.

Artichoke (24 units) (33 kcal per unit)

- 6 boiled **artichoke** hearts
- 3 tablespoons of **soy mayonnaise** (Vol. 3, p. 58)
- 6 slices from a loaf of **bread**
- 1 **sweet** red **pepper,** grilled and chopped into thin slices
- 6 boiled green **asparagus stalks**

Mash the artichoke, mix it with the mayonnaise and spread the paste on the bread. Decorate with a piece of asparagus and a piece of pepper.

Mushroom (24 units) (33 kcal per unit)

- 150 g (≅ 2 cups) of **mushrooms** (white mushrooms), washed, sliced, sprinkled with lemon juice and scalded in boiling water
- 1 clove of crushed **garlic**
- 1 tablespoon of **coriander**
- 1 tablespoon of olive **oil**
- 3 tablespoons of **soy mayonnaise** (Vol. 3, p. 58)
- 6 slices from a loaf of **bread** (individual pastries can also be used, as shown in the photograph)
- Sea **salt** (see Vol. 3, p. 16)

Soak the mushrooms in the oil to which has been added the garlic, coriander, and salt. Spread the mayonnaise over the canapés and cover with mushrooms. One way to decorate these canapés is with slices of red pepper.

Curried Rice (24 units)

(47 kcal per unit)

- 100 g (≅ 1/4 cup) of boiled **rice**
- 3 tablespoons of **soy mayonnaise** (Vol. 3, p. 58)
- 6 slices from a loaf of **bread**
- 8 **artichoke** stems, boiled and cut into three pieces
- 1 teaspoon of teaspoon of curry

Mix the rice with the mayonnaise and the curry, and place on top of the bread. Decorate with a piece of the artichoke stem.

Special Complementary Dishes (1)

We present three dishes based on the Mexican tortilla, which can serve as inspiration for other recipes. The only things needed are imagination at the time of combining them with other foods and a good appetite at the time of serving them. Cheese is not necessary, and can be substituted by other products such as avocado or tofu.

Nachos (4 servings)

(391 kcal per serving)

- 8 **Mexican** corn **tortillas** (Vol. 3, p. 44)
- 250 g (≅ 8.8 oz) of **chopped** tomato sauce (Vol. 3, p. 63)
- 200 g (≅ 7 oz) of melting **cheese**
- 4 tablespoons of olive **oil**

Break the Mexican tortilla into pieces and fry in hot oil; drain and allow to cool. Mix the sauce, the grated cheese, and the Mexican tortilla and place in the oven under the 'grill' until the cheese is melted.

Quesadillas (4 servings)

(299 kcal per serving)

- 8 **Mexican** wheat **tortillas** (Vol. 3, p. 45)
- 250 g (≅ 8.8 oz) of **chopped** tomato sauce (Vol. 3, p. 63)
- 200 g (≅ 7 oz) of melting **cheese**

Put cheese and sauce in each tortilla. Wrap. Brush on a tablespoon of olive oil and heat in the frying pan or in the oven until the cheese melts.

Tacos (4 servings)

(336 kcal per serving)

- 12 **Mexican** corn **tortillas** (Vol. 3, p. 44)
- 200 g of **vegetarian** minced **meat**
- 200 g (≅ 1 cup) of fresh **cheese** or tofu
- 200 g (≅ 7 oz) of **chopped** tomato sauce (use half of the quantity given in Vol. 3, p. 63)
- 4 chopped **lettuce** leaves

Fill the tortillas with a mixture of the vegetarian mincemeat, the cheese, the chopped tomato sauce and the lettuce.

Tomato Bread (4 servings)

(210 kcal per serving)

- 4 slices of French **bread**
- 2 ripe **tomatoes**
- 2 tablespoons of olive **oil**
- Sea **salt** (see Vol. 3, p. 16)

Slice the tomatoes in half and rub each slice of bread with half a tomato; add a little oil and salt. This style of eating bread is typical in the Catalan region of Spain. It seems that in this way, they managed to soften the hard bread that was several days old. Today, even with fresh bread, we can benefit from this custom and its variations (grated tomato, slices of tomato...), by using it as the basis for any sandwich, or simply as is.

Garlic Bread (4 servings)

(192 kcal per serving)

- 4 slices of French **bread**
- 1 clove of **garlic**
- Chopped **parsley**
- 2 tablespoons of olive **oil**

Toast the bread in the oven, in the toaster, or dry it by placing it in a 150°C oven; in this way it will dry out slowly. In a dry climate, dried bread can last several days. Rub the bread with the garlic, sprinkle with parsley, and add a few drops of oil. This kind of bread can be used as the base for sandwich spreads, canapés or to accompany a meal.

Tropical Salad Pastries (24 units)

(98 kcal per unit)

- 24 individual **pastries**
- 150 g (≅ 5.3 oz) of grated **carrot**
- 150 g (≅ 5.3 oz) of grated **celery**
- 150 g (≅ 1 cup) of chopped **pineapple**
- 2 tablespoons of **soy mayonnaise** (Vol. 3, p. 58)
- 100 g (≅ 3.5 oz) of chopped **walnuts**

Mix all the ingredients and fill each pastry. Decorate with ground walnuts.

Complementary Dishes (and 2)

(28 kcal per unit)

Garden "Fish"

(24 units)

- 250 g (≅ 1 cup) of boiled **green beans**
- 250 g (≅ 2 cups) of **onion** rings
- **Batter** (Vol. 3, p. 76)
- Olive **oil**

Take two or three green beans, coat them with batter in the same way as the onion rings, and fry in hot oil. These can also be done in the oven.

(50 kcal per unit)

Cheese Balls (24 units)

(45 kcal per unit)

- 250 g (≅ 1 cup) of **fresh cheese**
- **Celery,** chopped fine
- 24 slices from a small loaf of toasted **bread**
- Olive **oil**
- Sea **salt** (see Vol. 3, p. 16)

Mash the cheese; add the salt, and a few drops of oil. Form balls of cheese by hand, coat with chopped celery, and place on top of the toast.

Canoes (24 units)

(32 kcal per unit)

- 6 wide and tender stalks of **celery**
- 250 g (≅ 1 cup) of **fresh cheese** or tofu
- 20 chopped **black olives**
- 3 tablespoons of **soy mayonnaise** (Vol. 3, p. 58)
- 1 **sweet** red **pepper,** grilled and sliced into thin strips
- 1 **lemon** (juice)

Clean the celery stalks and remove the fibrous strings. Cut the stalks into sections 4-5 cm in length and soak in the lemon juice. Make a mixture with the cheese, mayonnaise, olives, and salt. Fill each stalk with this mixture and decorate with a slice of red pepper.

Cooking Without Cheese

Whatever the reason may be for eliminating cheese from our diet, either permanently or occasionally, we do not necessarily have to do without the dishes that use cheese as the main ingredient. We give you three substitute recipes for cheese that not only resemble cheese in their taste and texture, but also provide calcium, proteins, vitamins and minerals in similar or higher amounts to those of real cheese.

Alternative to Parmesan Cheese

(71 kcal per tablespoon)

- 50 g (≅ 1.75 oz) of **brewer's yeast**
- 75 g (≅ 3/4 cup) of raw, peeled **almonds**
- Sea **salt** (see Vol. 3, p. 16)

Put all the ingredients in the food processor until they are ground into a fine powder. Keep in the refrigerator and use in the same way as Parmesan cheese.

Alternative to Cheese Sauce (9 kcal per tablespoon)

- 1 medium, chopped **potato**
- 1 small **carrot,** peeled and chopped
- 1 small **onion,** peeled and chopped into four pieces
- 1 clove of peeled **garlic**
- 250 ml (≅ 1 cup) of **water**
- 125 g (≅ 1/2 cup) of **tofu**
- 50 g (≅ 1.75 oz) of **brewer's yeast**

Boil the vegetables until they are very soft. Drain. Use the tofu, salt, brewer's yeast, and the vegetables to make a cream. It should be thick, so slowly add only the necessary water or vegetable broth at the end. This is a good complement to vegetable dishes.

"Au Gratin" Without Cheese

(48 kcal per tablespoon)

- 100 g (≅ 2 cups) of **bread** crumbs
- 100 g (≅ 3.5 oz) of mashed **tofu**
- 2 tablespoons of **brewer's yeast**
- 1 tablespoon of **ground almonds**
- 1 tablespoon of olive **oil**
- Sea **salt** (see Vol. 3, p. 16)

Mix all the ingredients. Sprinkle over the desired recipe and place under the grill to melt.

Vegetarian

Kebabs, of Arab origin, are made from chopped, skewered foods that are grilled. They are accompanied by a variety of sauces in which they are later dipped. The kebabs that we offer here, unlike those made from meat, contain no cholesterol and provide vitamins and minerals in greater quantities than the traditional meat kebabs. To better absorb the iron in these kebabs, it is advisable to use dressings made with lemon juice.

Mushroom (4 units)

(22 kcal per unit)

- 8 **cherry tomatoes**
- 8 small **mushrooms** (white)
- 4 **Welsh onions**
- 1 sweet **green bell pepper**

Thread the ingredients on a skewer in alternating fashion until the skewer is full. Cook under the grill and serve accompanied with a sauce (see Vol. 3, p. 56).

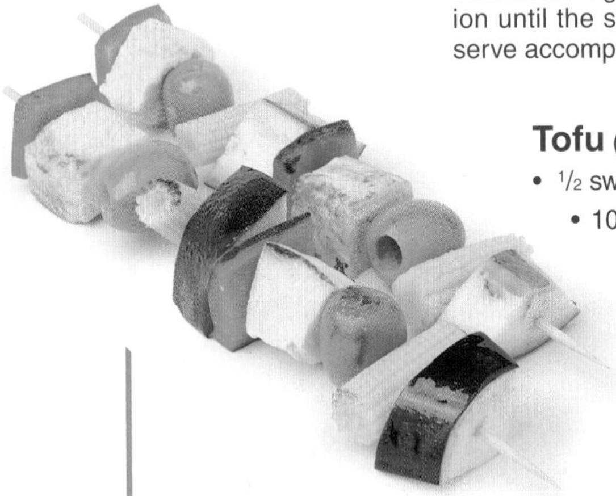

Tofu (4 units) (67 kcal per unit)

- 1/2 sweet **red pepper**
- 100 g (≅ 3.5 oz) of **tofu**
- 4 small **cobs** of young corn
- 8 pitted **green olives**
- 1/2 small **eggplant**

Cut the tofu into squares and place in the freezer overnight. Thaw, drain, and soak the tofu for 30 minutes in a mixture of olive oil, sweet paprika (powder), garlic, and salt. Thread the ingredients on a skewer in alternate form until the skewer is full. Grill and serve with a sauce (see Vol. 3, p. 56).

Vegetarian Sausage

(4 units) (91 kcal per unit)

- 1/2 small **zucchini**
- 1 medium **carrot**
- 2 vegetarian **sausages**
- 1 small **spring onion**
- 8 **snow peas** (or bean pods)

Alternate on the skewer until full, grill, and serve accompanied by a sauce (see Vol. 3, p. 56).

Soy or Meat Analog (4 units)

(74 kcal per unit)

- 100 g (≅ 3.5 oz) of **soy or meat analog**
- 1 sweet **green bell pepper**
- 12 **cherry tomatoes**

Soak the meat analog in a mixture of olive oil, curry, onion and salt. Alternate the ingredients until the skewer is full; cook and serve with a sauce (see Vol. 3, pp. 60, 61).

Kebabs

Kebabs can also be made with products such as fruits and vegetables. The possibilities vary and only the imagination mixed with a little good taste can limit the combinations.

Banana (4 units)

(107 kcal per unit)

- 100 g (≅ 3.5 oz) of **vegetarian meat**
- 1 **plantain** (cooking banana)

Chop the vegetarian meat and plantain and thread alternately on the sticks. Grill and serve accompanied with a sauce (see Vol. 3, pp. 60, 61). Serve hot.

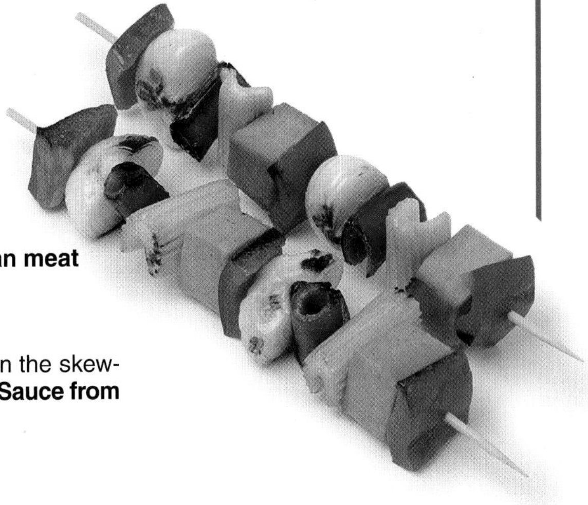

Celery (4 units)

(111 kcal per unit)

- 1 sweet **red pepper**
- 1 sweet **green bell pepper**
- 100 g (≅ 3.5 oz) of **vegetarian meat**
- 2 stalks of **celery**
- 4 **Welsh onions**

Thread in alternating fashion on the skewer. Serve with **Sweet-and-Sour Sauce from Seeds** (see Vol. 3, p. 56).

Sweet-and-Sour (4 units) (67 kcal per unit)

- 1 **tangerine**
- 100 g (≅ 2/3 cup) of **pineapple**
- 12 **grapes**
- 1/2 **Belgian endive**
- 100 g (≅ 3.5 oz) of **fresh cheese** or tofu

Thread the ingredients in an alternating manner until the skewer is full. Serve with **Sweet-and-Sour Sauce from Seeds** (see Vol. 3, p. 56).

Fresh Cheese (4 units)

(50 kcal per unit)

- 100 g (≅ 3.5 oz) of **fresh cheese** (tofu may also be used)
- 8 **strawberries**
- 1/2 **apple**
- 1/2 **peach**

Thread the ingredients in alternating fashion on the stick until it is full. Serve with syrup, sugarcane syrup, or chocolate *fondant.*

Egg is used in the kitchen to bind the ingredients and to give a smooth texture to many recipes. However, egg contains cholesterol, which some individuals cannot tolerate. This does not mean that we cannot enjoy recipes that use eggs as one of their ingredients. Some countries produce egg substitutes. Here we propose several egg alternatives.

Batter (12 kcal per tablespoon)

- 200 ml (≅ 4/5 cup) of **soy milk** (beverage; see Vol. 3, p. 305)
- 1 heaped tablespoon of **wheat flour**
- 1 level tablespoon of **soy flour**
- 1 clove of crushed **garlic**
- 1 tablespoon of **brewer's yeast**
- Chopped **parsley**
- Sea **salt** (see Vol. 3, p. 16)

Mix all the ingredients with a hand blender. The batter should be thick enough to stick to the food that is to be coated.

Spanish Omelet (4 servings) (363 kcal per serving)

- 1 kg (≅ 2 pounds) of **potatoes**
- 1 large, chopped **onion**
- 2 sweet **red peppers,** grilled and chopped
- 150 ml (≅ 2/3 cup) of **rice milk** (Vol. 3, p. 273)
- 2 tablespoons of **rice flour**
- A few threads of **saffron** (toast, dissolve, and mix with the milk). This is optional; its purpose is to give a yellow color to the omelet
- 4 tablespoons of olive **oil**
- Sea **salt** (see Vol. 3, p. 16)

Sauté the onion in the oil. The potato may be fried (though this will require more oil) or boiled. Cut into small slices or mash. Mix with the onion (once drained of the oil), the pepper, the salt and the milk (into which the flour has been dissolved). Place the frying pan with a tablespoon of oil on the heat source. Add the mixture and proceed with the recipe for "Spanish Omelet" (see Vol. 3, p. 114).

Instead of "Rice Milk" you can also use a thick **béchamel sauce** (see Vol. 3, p. 59).

Without Egg

Muffins (238 kcal/100g = 67 kcal/oz)

- 50 g (≅ 1.75 oz) of **bran**
- 100 g (≅ 2/3 cup) of **raisins** (dried)
- 150 g (≅ 1 1/4 cup) of **whole flour**
- 150 g (≅ 1 1/4 cup) of **wheat flour**
- 180 g (≅ 6.4 oz) of **sugarcane syrup** or molasses
- 350 ml (≅ 1 1/2 cup) of **soy milk**
- 50 g (≅ 1.75 oz) of chopped **walnuts**
- 10 g (≅ 0.35 oz) of chemical **yeast**

Mix all the ingredients and form into a mass that is not too compact. Using molds that have been previously greased, put a little of the mixture into each mold. Introduce into a 180°C oven for 15 minutes.

Sweet Walnut Rolls

(422 kcal/100g = 120 kcal/oz)

- 500 g (≅ 4 cups) of **whole flour**
- 200 ml (≅ 1 cup) of olive **oil**
- 200 g (≅ 7 oz) of chopped **walnuts**
- 4 tablespoons of **honey**
- 200 ml (≅ 4/5 cup) of **water**
- Sea **salt** (see Vol. 3, p. 16)

Beat the oil, salt and water and mix with the flour. Knead until the mixture no longer sticks to the hands. Roll out the dough with a rolling pin, fold over and roll again 3 to 5 times. Taking small amounts of the dough, form them into thin pancakes and fill with a mixture of the chopped walnuts and honey. Close the pancakes, forming a package, and bake or fry. Decorate with honey or powdered sugar.

42 TRANSITION RECIPES

CHAPTER SUMMARY

RECIPES

Artichoke Cannelloni 100
Banana Casserole 124
Boiled Marinated Gluten 90
Cabbage Rolls 101
Carrot Cake 125
Carrot Croquettes 112
Chinese Stir-Fry 116
'Cordon Bleu' Eggplant 121
Hot Marinated Gluten 89
Italian-style Macaroni 84
Mexican Meat Analogs 88
Millet Croquettes 111
Mushroom and Young Garlic Scrambled Eggs 119
Mushroom Lasagna 110
Nut Loaf 94
Oat Medallions 122
Onion Sausages 96
Pasta Bows and Mushrooms ...85
Pasta with Chard 82
Potatoes and Mushrooms 83
Sautéed Marinated Gluten 91
Soy Hamburgers 117
Spanish Omelet 114
Spinach Lasagna 108
Spring Rolls 102
Stuffed Eggplant 120
Stuffed Eggs 118
Vegetable Cannelloni 98
Vegetable Paella 86
Vegetable Pie 104
Vegetable Turnovers 106
Vegetarian Sausages and Drumsticks 92

Adapting to a healthier and less meat-based diet is not only necessary from the physiological perspective, but also from the psychological viewpoint.

It is therefore important to follow a transition diet for a period, using some of the recipes included in this chapter.

CHANGING *from* an **omnivorous diet,** which takes in "a bit of everything," ***to a* healing** and **preventive diet,** *should be done* ***progressively.*** It is recommended to set aside a period of adaptation, where the organism phases out certain foods and, at the same time, gets used to others.

Meat and meat products, **fried food, spices,** excessive **fat,** and of **refined products,** should ***gradually*** *be substituted by* a variety of **fruits, nuts, whole grains, legumes, greens** and **vegetables** ***prepared in a simple way.***

This **adaptation period** toward a healthier diet should be slow. For some, this change may be effected in a few weeks. For others, however, the process may take longer.

The recipes presented in this chapter are particularly useful to facilitate the transition from a meat-based diet to a diet composed of plant foods.

Through their looks, taste, and satisfying effect, these transition recipes replace their meat equivalents, as well as a number of very refined products. As far as nutritional value, these recipes are comparable or superior to those prepared with meat.

Many recipes in this chapter include **eggs** and/or **milk** among their ingredients. This makes the transition from a meat-based diet to a healthier diet made up of plant foods easier. However, in Part 4 (Vol. 3, p. 126) of this encyclopedia practically all recipes are strictly vegetarian, in order to take maximum advantage of the healing and preventive powers of fruits and vegetables.

Transition

Menu A

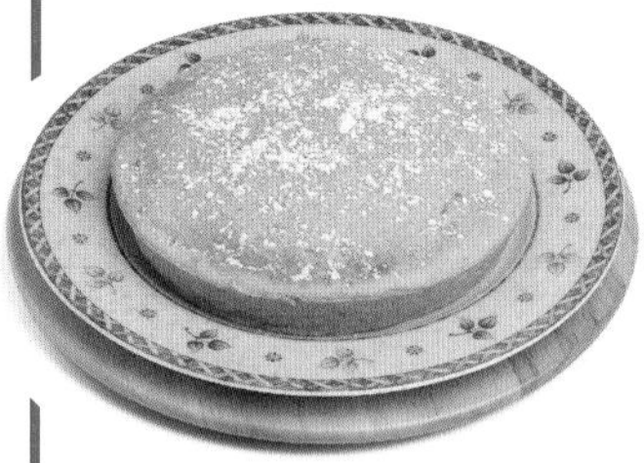

Carrot Cake

Breakfast

- Fruit (Vol. 1, p. 30)
- "Carrot Cake" (Vol. 3, p. 125)
- Milk (Vol. 1, p. 182)

Lunch

Vegetable Cannelloni

- Lettuce, Tomato, Cucumber, Carrot, and Onion Salad (Vol. 2, pp. 45, 275, 339, 25, 142)
- "Portuguese Beans" (Vol. 3, p. 324)
- "Vegetable Cannelloni" (Vol. 3, p. 98)
- "Whole Bread" (Vol. 3, p. 46, Vol. 1, p. 72)

Supper

Potatoes and Mushrooms

- Tomato and Garlic Salad (Vol. 2, p. 275; Vol. 1, p. 338)
- "Potatoes and Mushrooms" (Vol. 3, p. 83)
- 'Cordon Bleu' Eggplant (Vol. 3, p. 121)

'Cordon Bleu' Eggplant

Menu B

Peanut Butter

Breakfast

- Fruit (Vol. 1, p. 30)
- "Whole Bread" with "Peanut Butter" and Honey (Vol. 3, pp. 46, 65; Vol. 1, pp. 72, 160)
- Skimmed Milk (Vol. 1, p. 182)

Lunch

Chinese Stir-Fry

- "Seed Salad" (Vol. 3, p. 298)
- "Chinese Stir-Fry" (Vol. 3, p. 116)
- "Millet Croquettes" (Vol. 3, p. 111)
- "Whole Bread" (Vol. 3, p. 46; Vol. 1, p. 72)

Supper

Millet Croquettes

- "Asparagus Salad" (Vol. 3, p. 278)
- "Pasta with Chard" (Vol. 3, p. 82))
- 'Bio' Yogurt (Vol. 1, p. 202)

Pasta with Chard

Menus

Menu C

Breakfast

- Freshly squeezed Orange Juice (Vol. 2, p. 360)
- Fruit (Vol. 1, p. 30)
- "Bircher-muesli" (Vol. 3, p. 175)

Bircher-muesli

Lunch

- Carrot and Tomato Juice (Vol. 2, pp. 25, 275)
- "Mexican Salad" (Vol. 3, p. 260)
- "Vegetable Paella" (Vol. 3, p. 86)
- Nuts (Vol. 1, p. 52)
- "Rye Bread" (Vol. 3, p. 194)

Mexican Salad

Vegetable Paella

Supper

- "Cream of Zucchini" (Vol. 3, p. 246)
- Fruit (Vol. 1, p. 30)
- "Whole Bread" Toast (Vol. 3, p. 46, Vol. 1, p. 72)

Cream of Zucchini

HEALTH COUNSELS

These menus are designed to *ease the transition* from an **omnivorous** diet to a **healthier, *plant*-**based diet. In order to make the transition smoother, these recipes include dairy products and eggs.

These recipes, through their looks and satisfying effect, are similar to their corresponding meat-based preparations. However, they have an *advantage*—very *low* or *zero* ***cholesterol,*** and are *low* in ***saturated fat.***

From the nutritional viewpoint, these dishes do not have anything to be desired from their equivalent recipes prepared with meat, shellfish, and fish:

- Combined ***plant proteins*** supply *all* the ***amino acids*** needed by our organism (see Vol. 1, p. 386).
- ***Plant fat*** is in general much *healthier* than animal fat.
- ***Complex carbohydrates*** are only found in **plant food.** That is why these menus provide an excellent source of such nutrients.
- ***Antioxidant vitamins*** and other preventive and healing substances are found *almost exclusively* in food of **vegetable** origin, so these dishes supply them abundantly.

Therefore, these are nutritious and healthy menus that contribute to prevent many illnesses of our civilization that originate from a heavy use of meat, fish, shellfish, and their derivatives.

Preparation time 00:20

Cooking time 00:20

Pasta with Chard

INGREDIENTS (4 servings)

- 150 g (≅ 5 oz) **shell macaroni**
- 300 g (≅ 10.6 oz) **chard**
- 1 teaspoon **corn flour**
- 1 **garlic** clove
- 1 **egg**
- 1 liter **vegetable broth** (unsalted)

ADDITIONAL INGREDIENTS

- 3 tablespoons olive **oil** (each tablespoon of oil adds around 120 kcal to the recipe, that is, 30 kcal per serving)
- Sea **salt** (see Vol. 3, p. 16)

PREPARATION

❶ Peel, wash, and chop the chard.
- Peel and grind the garlic.
- Beat the egg together with the ground garlic, the corn flour, and two tablespoons of vegetable broth.

❷ Steam the chard.
- Pour the vegetable broth into a pot and add the pasta when it begins boiling. Stir occasionally to prevent sticking.
- Add the beaten egg, the oil and salt to taste in the middle of the boiling process. Finally, add the chard.

❸ When the pasta is al dente (firm to the bite), serve hot in a soup dish.

HEALTHIER ALTERNATIVE: It may be prepared without egg.

For more information about the ingredients, see: Pasta, Vol. 1, p. 74; chard, Vol. 2, p. 297; corn flour, Vol. 1, p. 69; garlic, Vol. 1, p. 338; egg, Vol. 1, p. 218; and the *Encyclopedia of Medicinal Plants:* Garlic, p. 230.

HEALTH COUNSELS

This soup made of pasta and greens, and garnished with egg, is *nutritious* and *easy to digest* and can advantageously substitute those dishes made up of pasta and meat. It supplies:

✓ ***Carbohydrates*** and ***calories,*** coming especially from pasta.

✓ ***Vegetable protein,*** coming from pasta and corn, whose biological principles increase when combined with egg.

✓ ***Minerals,*** including the ***iron*** supplied by chard.

✓ *Hardly any **cholesterol** and **fat.***

This is therefore a recommended dish for its nutritional value and, at the same time, makes the transition to a vegetarian diet easy.

NUTRITIONAL VALUE* per serving

Energy	182 kcal = 763 kj
Protein	8.21 g
Carbohydrates	28.8 g
Fiber	3.87 g
Total fat	*2.20 g*
Saturated fat	*0.564 g*
Cholesterol	*63.8 mg*
Sodium	*173 mg*

1% 2% 4% 10% 20% 40% 100%

% Daily Value (based on a 2,000 calorie diet) provided by each serving of this dish

CALORIC PROPORTION*

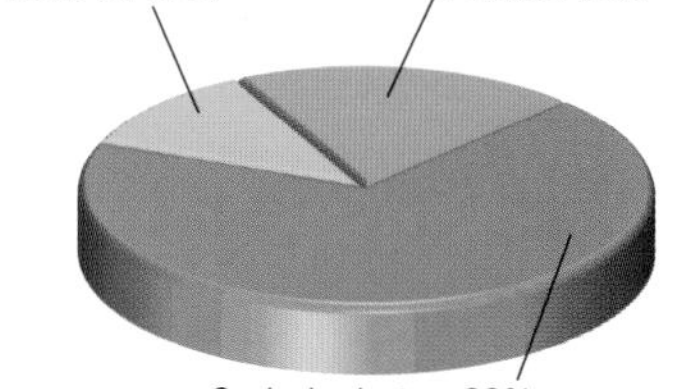

Percentage distribution of **calories for each nutrient**

*Additional ingredients not included.

Preparation time 00:25

Cooking time 00:30

Potatoes and Mushrooms

INGREDIENTS (4 servings)

- 1 kg (≅ 2 pounds) **potatoes**
- 250 g (≅ 8.8 oz) **mushrooms**
- 1 sweet **red pepper**
- 1 **carrot**
- 1 **onion**
- 1 **tomato**
- 2 **garlic** cloves
- 1 1/2 liters (≅ 1 1/2 quarts) **vegetable broth** (unsalted)

ADDITIONAL INGREDIENTS

- 2 **laurel** leaves
- 1/2 teaspoon sweet **paprika**
- 4 tablespoons olive **oil** (each tablespoon of oil adds around 120 kcal to the recipe, that is, 30 kcal per serving)
- Sea **salt** (see Vol. 3, p. 16)

PREPARATION

❶Peel, wash and chop the potatoes and the carrots.
- Using a knife, cut off all impurities that may be found in the mushrooms. Wash them in abundant water and chop them.
- Peel and chop the onion and garlic.
- Clean the pepper from seeds, wash and cut into strips.
- Peel and crush the tomato.

❷Heat the oil in a pot and sauté the vegetables, mushrooms, and laurel leaves for a few minutes.
- When the sauté takes color, add the potatoes and paprika. Stir and cover with the vegetable broth. Boil until the potatoes are tender. Add the salt shortly before the boiling process is over.

❸Serve hot.

HEALTHIER ALTERNATIVE: Instead of sautéing the ingredients, add them raw to the boiling vegetable broth.

For more information about the ingredients, see: Potato, Vol. 2, p. 201; mushroom, Vol. 1, p.152; pepper, Vol. 2, p. 198; carrot, Vol. 2, p. 25; onion, Vol. 2, p. 142; tomato, Vol. 2, p. 275; garlic, Vol. 1, p. 338; and the *Encyclopedia of Medicinal Plants:* Garlic, p. 230.

HEALTH COUNSELS

This tasty potato stew allows one to forget the meat in the transition process from an omnivorous to a healthier diet.

Mushrooms supply high quality ***protein,*** which completes the nutritional properties of potatoes. Peppers, carrots, and tomatoes are *high* in ***carotene*** and ***antioxidant carotenoids,*** which protect us from **cancer** and **arteriosclerosis.**

Garlic and olive oil top up the healthy attributes of this dish, which unlike other similar ones prepared with animal products, is ***cholesterol****-free* and *low* in ***saturated fat.***

NUTRITIONAL VALUE* per serving

Energy	227 kcal = 950 kj
Protein	7.05 g
Carbohydrates	44.3g
Fiber	7.09 g
Total fat	*0.816 g*
Saturated fat	*0.140 g*
Cholesterol	—
Sodium	*30.1 mg*

1% 2% 4% 10% 20% 40% 100%

% Daily Value (based on a 2,000 calorie diet) provided by each serving of this dish

CALORIC PROPORTION*

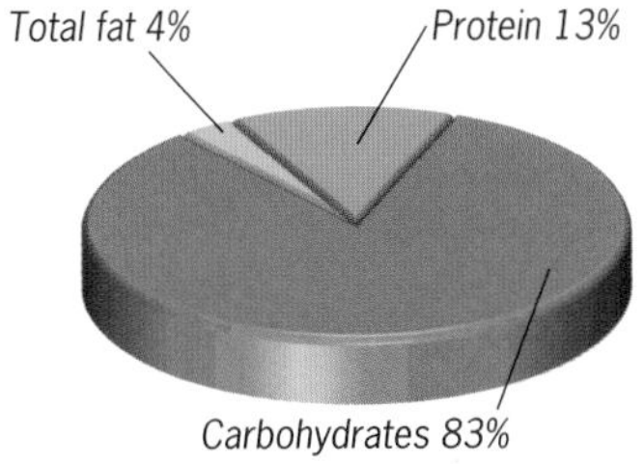

Percentage distribution of **calories for each nutrient**

*Additional ingredients not included.

Preparation time 00:10 | Cooking time 00:30

Italian-style Macaroni

INGREDIENTS (4 servings)

- 250 g (≅ 8.8 oz) **whole macaroni** (pasta)
- 150 g (≅ 5.3 oz) **vegetarian meat analog** (available in health food stores or it may be prepared–see Vol. 3, p. 52)
- **Traditional Tomato Sauce** (Vol. 3, p. 62)
- 50 g (≅ 1.75 oz) shredded tender **cheese**
- 1 **onion**

ADDITIONAL INGREDIENTS

- 1/2 teaspoon sweet **paprika**
- 4 tablespoons olive **oil** (each tablespoon of oil adds around 120 kcal to the recipe, that is, 30 kcal per serving)
- Sea **salt** (see Vol. 3, p. 16)

PREPARATION

❶ Peel and chop the onion.
- Chop the vegetarian meat analog.

❷ Boil the macaroni in abundant water with salt and drain when they are *al dente* (firm to the bite).
- Heat the oil in a frying pan and sauté the onion. When transparent, add the paprika and the vegetarian meat. Stir and add the tomato sauce. Keep cooking for an additional 5 minutes.
- Add the drained macaroni and part of the shredded cheese. Mix well and keep cooking for another 5 minutes.
- Place the sautéed macaroni in an oven dish, sprinkle the remaining shredded cheese and grill until the cheese is melted.

❸ Serve hot.

HEALTHIER ALTERNATIVE: Instead of sautéing the ingredients steam them or boil them in the tomato sauce. (To grill without cheese, see Vol. 3, p. 73.)

For more information about the ingredients, see: Pasta, Vol. 1, p. 74; vegetarian meat analogs, Vol. 1, p. 332; tomato, Vol. 2, p. 275; cheese, Vol. 1, p. 206; onion, Vol. 2, p. 142.

HEALTH COUNSELS

This pasta dish, garnished with cheese and vegetarian meat, makes a *good source* of ***calories*** and ***protein.*** The combination of the pasta's protein together with the soybeans in the vegetarian meat analogs supplies all the ***amino acids*** required by our organism.

It is a nutritious dish that helps in the transition toward a healthier diet, with the following advantages:

✓ It *hardly* contains ***cholesterol*** (just what is found in cheese).

✓ It is a *low-**fat*** dish, especially low in ***saturated fat,*** which is the most injurious to the arteries.

✓ It is prepared with olive oil and other vegetable oils, much healthier than butter or other animal fats.

NUTRITIONAL VALUE* per serving

Energy	406 kcal = 1.699 kj
Protein	18.1 g
Carbohydrates	52.6 g
Fiber	3.84 g
Total fat	*12.7 g*
Saturated fat	*3.37 g*
Cholesterol	*5.75 mg*
Sodium	*388 mg*

1% 2% 4% 10% 20% 40% 100%

% Daily Value (based on a 2,000 calorie diet) provided by each serving of this dish

CALORIC PROPORTION*

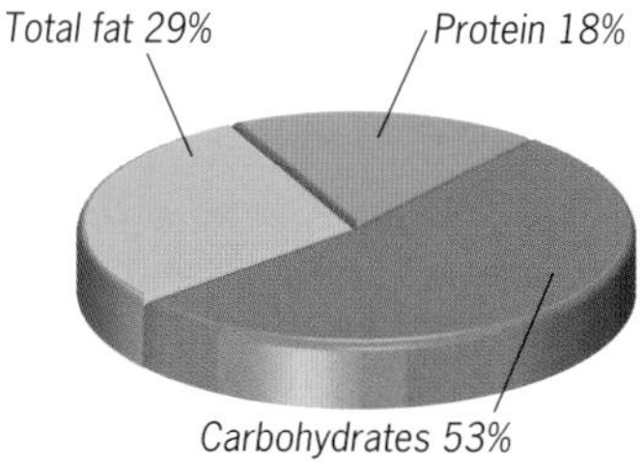

Percentage distribution of **calories for each nutrient**

* Additional ingredients not included.

Preparation time 00:15 | Cooking time 00:20

Pasta Bows and Mushrooms

INGREDIENTS (4 servings)

- 300 g (≅ 10.6 oz) **pasta bows**
- 350 g (≅ 12.3 oz) **mushrooms**
- 2 **garlic** cloves

ADDITIONAL INGREDIENTS

- **Parsley**
- **Basil**
- 4 tablespoons olive **oil** (each tablespoon of oil adds around 120 kcal to the recipe, that is, 30 kcal per serving)
- Sea **salt** (see Vol. 3, p. 16)

PREPARATION

❶ With the help of a knife, cut off all the possible impurities from the mushrooms. Wash them in abundant water and chop them into large chunks.
- Peel and chop the garlic.
- Chop parsley and basil.

❷ Boil the pasta in plenty of water with salt. Drain when the pasta bows are al dente (firm to the bite).
- Heat oil in a frying pan and sauté the garlic and herbs with a pinch of salt.
- Add the mushrooms. Cover to avoid losing their juices and simmer until they are tender.
- Arrange the pasta in a serving dish and pour the mushrooms with their sauce over it.

❸ Serve immediately.

HEALTHIER ALTERNATIVE: Instead of sautéing the garlic and the potherbs, add them raw to the mushrooms.

For more information about the ingredients, see: Pasta, Vol. 1, p. 74; mushroom, Vol. 1, p.152; garlic, Vol. 1, p. 338; and the *Encyclopedia of Medicinal Plants:* Garlic, p. 230.

Suggestions from the Chef

- Mushrooms may be substituted by textured soy protein or vegetarian meat analog.

HEALTH COUNSELS

This pasta dish is nutritious and tasty. It serves as a superior substitute to other similar dishes made with meat. Mushrooms are very well tolerated by diabetics, and they supply plenty of trace minerals.

In addition, this is a ***cholesterol****-free* dish with *very little* ***saturated fat,*** supplying high quality ***protein*** from mushrooms and combining with pasta very well.

NUTRITIONAL VALUE* per serving

Energy	301 kcal = 1,260 kj
Protein	11.3 g
Carbohydrates	57.7 g
Fiber	2.76 g
Total fat	*1.52 g*
Saturated fat	*0.213 g*
Cholesterol	—
Sodium	*8.76 mg*

1% 2% 4% 10% 20% 40% 100%

% Daily Value (based on a 2,000 calorie diet) provided by each serving of this dish

CALORIC PROPORTION*

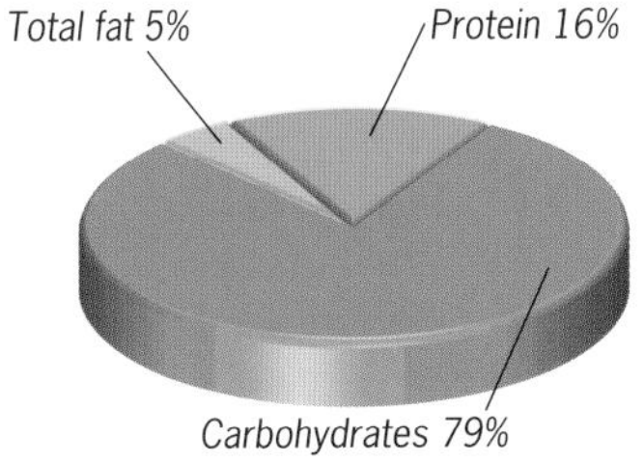

Percentage distribution of **calories for each nutrient**

* Additional ingredients not included.

Vegetable Paella

INGREDIENTS (4 servings)

- 350 g (≅ 1 3/4 cups) **rice**
- 3 **artichokes** (globe artichokes)
- 1 sweet **red pepper**
- 250 g (≅ 8.8 oz) **mushrooms**
- 100 g (≅ 1.75 oz) boiled **Lima beans** (a variety of flat, large, white bean)
- 150 g (≅ 3.5 oz) **green beans**
- 100 g **peas**
- 1 **tomato**
- 2 **garlic** cloves
- 800 ml (≅ 3 1/3 cups) **water** or unsalted **vegetable broth**

ADDITIONAL INGREDIENTS

- **Parsley**
- 1 teaspoon sweet **paprika**
- A few **saffron** stigmas
- The juice of one **lemon**
- 8 tablespoons olive **oil** (each tablespoon of oil adds around 120 kcal to the recipe, that is, 30 kcal per serving)
- Sea **salt** (see Vol. 3, p. 16)

PREPARATION

❶ Wash the vegetables thoroughly.

- Remove the outer, tough leaves of the artichokes and cut off their leaf tips and stems. Chop them into 4 or 6 pieces each and coat them with lemon juice to avoid darkening.
- Cut the pepper into strips and slice the mushrooms.
- Cut off the ends of the green beans and remove their threads. Chop and wash.
- Peel the garlic cloves and grind them in a mortar together with the parsley.
- Crush the tomato.

❷ Heat the oil in the "paellera" (large, flat, double-handled pan) and sauté the Lima beans, peas, and green beans.

- Sauté the artichokes and the pepper in a separate pan and set aside for final decoration.
- When the green beans are tender, add the tomato and paprika. Let the tomato juice evaporate through cooking.
- Add the rice and sauté for about 3 minutes. Add the boiling vegetable broth, the salt, and the contents of the mortar and the saffron. Stir in order to distribute all the ingredients uniformly and keep a rapid boiling for an additional 5 minutes. Reduce the flame so that it may simmer equally across the entire surface.
- Turn the fire off when the rice is ready (dried and fluffy).
- Let it rest for an additional 5 minutes.

❸ Serve in the "paellera" decorated with the artichokes, red pepper strips, and lemon slices.

HEALTHIER ALTERNATIVE: Instead of sautéing the ingredients steam them slightly or boil them in the vegetable broth. Whole rice may be used, as it is a healthier option, but its flavor and preparation are different.

Suggestions from the Chef

- Another **typical** way to prepare paella is adding the broth to the sauté and allowing it to boil together with the vegetables. The rice is added later. Using this system makes the loss of water more difficult to calculate.
- To decorate, two **hard-boiled eggs** may be added arranging them on top in slices or quarters.

Sauté the vegetables in the "paellera" (special pan for making paella).

Add the rice and sauté it lightly.

Lastly, add the vegetable broth.

For more information about the ingredients, see: Rice, Vol. 2, p. 225; artichoke, Vol. 2, p. 178; pepper, Vol. 2, p. 198; mushroom, Vol. 2, p. 294; bean, Vol. 2, p. 343; green bean, Vol. 1, p. 109; pea, Vol. 2, p. 73; tomato, Vol. 2, p. 275; garlic, Vol. 1, p. 338; and the *Encyclopedia of Medicinal Plants:* Green bean, p. 584; garlic, p. 230.

HEALTH COUNSELS

This typical dish originally from the eastern region of Spain constitutes a perfect sample of the so-called Mediterranean diet. It has rice as its base, and it is accompanied by a variety of vegetables and legumes.

Vegetable paella offers a *healthier* alternative to the traditional paella prepared with meat or shellfish. This is due to the following:

✓ It is ***cholesterol****-free*, and contains *little* ***saturated fat,*** which makes it ideal for the **cardiovascular system.**

✓ It is *high* in ***fiber,*** especially if prepared with whole rice. This contributes to *regulate* the **bowel movement,** and to *prevent* **cholelithiasis, diverticulosis,** and **cancer of the colon.**

✓ It is *high* in ***vitamins*** and ***phytochemical elements, which*** possess *antioxidant* and *preventive* effects from **deteriorating diseases** and **premature aging.** This is because this paella contains more vegetables and legumes than the conventional paella.

Vegetable paella may be as tasty or even tastier than that prepared with animal products. Due to this and to its nutritional and preventive properties, it is a fundamental dish in the transition diet for those wishing to take extra care of their health.

NUTRITIONAL VALUE* per serving

Energy	446 kcal = 1.864 kj
Protein	13.9 g
Carbohydrates	87.2 g
Fiber	8.89 g
Total fat	*1.31 g*
Saturated fat	*0.353 g*
Cholesterol	—
Sodium	*56.2 mg*

1% 2% 4% 10% 20% 40% 100%

% Daily Value (based on a 2,000 calorie diet) provided by each serving of this dish

CALORIC PROPORTION*

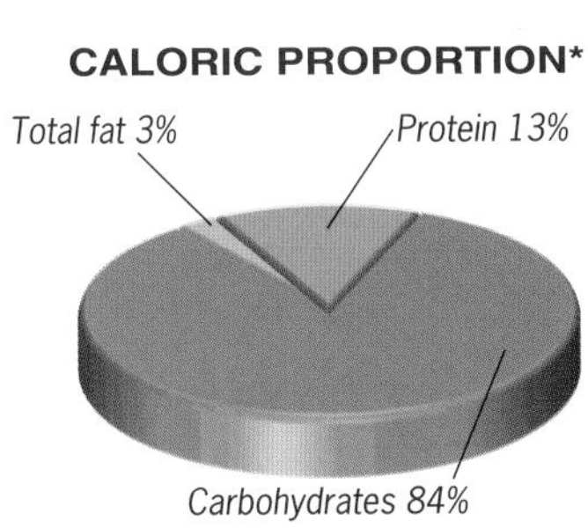

Percentage distribution of
calories for each nutrient

* Additional ingredients not included.

Preparation time 00:20

Cooking time 00:30

Mexican Meat Analogs

INGREDIENTS (4 serving)

- 120 g (≅ 4.2 oz) dehydrated **textured soy protein** (or gluten, see Vol. 3, p. 53)
- 500 g (≅ 1 pound) **potatoes**
- 4 **tomatoes**
- 6 sweet **green peppers**
- 1 **onion**
- 50 g pitted **olives**
- 25 g (≅ 1 oz) **capers**
- 2 **garlic** cloves
- $^1/_2$ liter (≅ $^1/_2$ quart) unsalted **vegetable broth**

ADDITIONAL INGREDIENTS

- 1 tablespoon **coriander** or **parsley**
- 7 tablespoons olive **oil** (each tablespoon of oil adds around 120 kcal to the recipe, that is, 30 kcal per serving)
- Sea **salt** (see Vol. 3, p. 16)

PREPARATION

❶ Soak the textured soy protein in the vegetable broth for a few minutes.
- Peel, wash, and chop the potatoes into small cubes.
- Peel and crush the tomato.
- Wash, remove the seeds, and chop the pepper.
- Peel and grind the garlic and slice the onion.

❷ Boil the potatoes and peppers for 20 minutes. Drain.
- In a pot, sauté the onion until it becomes transparent. Add the potherbs. Stir and add the tomato, garlic, olives, capers, peppers, and finally the textured soy protein. Continue cooking for 10 minutes and add the potatoes. Cook for an additional 10 minutes.

❸ Serve hot.

HEALTHIER ALTERNATIVE: Steam the onion instead of sautéing it.

For more information about the ingredients, see: Soy protein, Vol. 1, p. 89; potato, Vol. 2, p. 201; tomato, Vol. 2, p. 275; pepper, Vol. 2, p. 198; onion, Vol. 2, p. 142; olive, Vol. 2, p. 165; caper, Vol. 1, p. 342; garlic, Vol. 1, p. 338; and the *Encyclopedia of Medicinal Plants:* Garlic, p. 230.

HEALTH COUNSELS

In this Mexican recipe, soy protein replaces meat. This replacement has the advantage of being ***cholesterol**-free* and of containing *very little **fat.*** Soy protein's biological properties are *equal or superior* to that of meat protein. Furthermore, its taste, if prepared adequately, as indicated in this recipe, satisfies the most demanding palates.

Peppers, tomatoes, onions, garlic, and the remaining vegetables, add to the *beneficial* properties of this dish upon the **heart, blood circulation,** and the **bones** (thanks to soybeans' ***isoflavones***). In addition, the dish is effective in **cancer** *prevention.*

NUTRITIONAL VALUE* per serving

Energy	336 kcal = 1.406 kj
Protein	31.9 g
Carbohydrates	38.7 g
Fiber	8.49 g
Total fat	*6.31 g*
Saturated fat	*1.03 g*
Cholesterol	—
Sodium	445 mg

1% 2% 4% 10% 20% 40% 100% 500%

% Daily Value (based on a 2,000 calorie diet) provided by each serving of this dish

CALORIC PROPORTION*

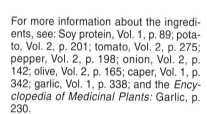

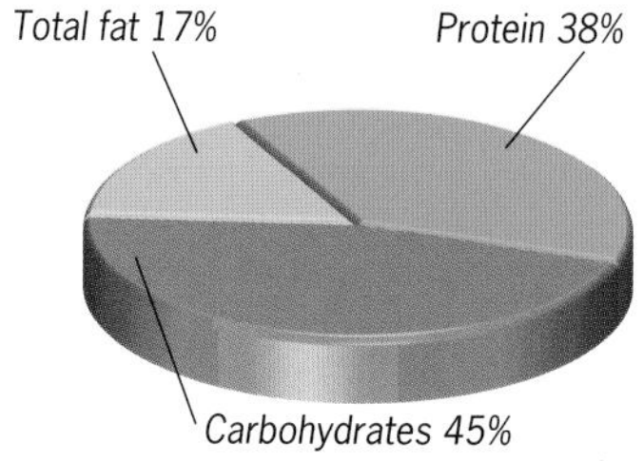

Percentage distribution of **calories for each nutrient**

* Additional ingredients not included.

Preparation time 00:15

Cooking time 00:20

Hot Marinated Gluten

INGREDIENTS (4 servings)

- 250 g (≅ 8.8 oz) **gluten** (Vol. 3, p. 52)
- 4 **onions**
- 4 dried sweet **red peppers**
- 300 g (≅ 10.6 oz) **Traditional Tomato Sauce** (Vol. 3, p. 62)

ADDITIONAL INGREDIENTS

- 1 **hot chili** or **cayenne pepper** (optional)
- 4 tablespoons olive **oil** (each tablespoon of oil adds around 120 kcal to the recipe, that is, 30 kcal per serving)
- Sea **salt** (see Vol. 3, p. 16)

PREPARATION

❶ Soak the dried peppers in cold water for one hour or boil for a few minutes.
- Peel and chop the onion.
- Chop the gluten.

❷ Heat the oil in a frying pan and sauté the onion until it becomes transparent.
- Blend the onion and the pepper with an electric blender.
- Place in a pot the pepper sauce, the gluten, and the tomato sauce. Add the salt and stir. Cook on a medium flame for about 10 minutes until the flavors are mixed.

❸ Serve hot.

HEALTHIER ALTERNATIVE: Instead of sautéing the onion, steam it using a non-stick frying pan.

For more information about the ingredients, see: Gluten, Vol. 2, p. 307; onion, Vol. 2, p. 142; pepper, Vol. 2, p. 198; tomato, Vol. 2, p. 275.

HEALTH COUNSELS

Gluten is the protein of wheat and it has a soft and elastic consistency that reminds one of cow's tripe. However, this recipe prepared with gluten possesses many healthy advantages over that meat. It is highly recommended for those seeking a transition diet toward healthier eating habits:

✓ It is ***cholesterol**-free.*

✓ Contains very *little* ***saturated fat.***

✓ It *does not contain* **contaminants** and **unhealthy substances,** usually present in animal organs.

NUTRITIONAL VALUE* per serving

Energy	217 kcal = 905 kj
Protein	19.4 g
Carbohydrates	20.6 g
Fiber	5.40 g
Total fat	*5.24 g*
Saturated fat	*0.548 g*
Cholesterol	—
Sodium	*11.5 mg*

1% 2% 4% 10% 20% 40% 100%

% Daily Value (based on a 2,000 calorie diet) provided by each serving of this dish

CALORIC PROPORTION*

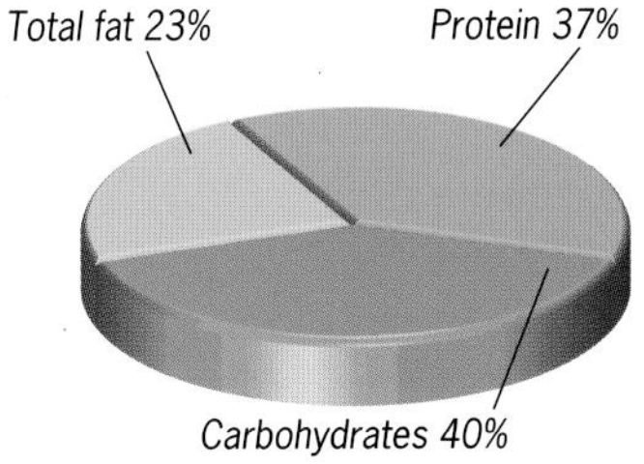

Percentage distribution of **calories for each nutrient**

* Additional ingredients not included.

Preparation time 00:20

Cooking time 00:30

Boiled Marinated Gluten

INGREDIENTS (4 servings)

- 250 g (≅ 8.8 oz) **marinated gluten with vegetables** (Vol. 3, p. 53)
- 1 **onion**
- 1 sweet **green pepper**
- 1 **eggplant** (optional)
- 1 **carrot**
- 2 **garlic** cloves
- 100 ml ($^3/_8$ cup) **apple juice**

ADDITIONAL INGREDIENTS

- 1 tablespoon of **potherbs** (parsley, oregano, thyme...)
- 2 tablespoons olive **oil** (each tablespoon of oil adds around 120 kcal to the recipe, that is, 30 kcal per serving)
- Sea **salt** (see Vol. 3, p. 16)

PREPARATION

❶ Peel and chop the onion and garlic.
- Peel and cut the carrot into strips. Remove the pepper seeds and cut them into strips.
- Slice the gluten.

❷ Heat the oil in a frying pan and sauté the vegetables for 2 minutes. Stir occasionally.
- Add the gluten slices and continue sautéing for an additional 2 or 3 minutes.
- Add the apple juice, the salt, and the potherbs. Add water until the gluten is covered and boil on a medium flame for at least 15 minutes with the lid on.

❸ Serve hot.

HEALTHIER ALTERNATIVE: Instead of sautéing the ingredients, steam them. When finished, dress them with the apple juice and the potherbs.

For more information about the ingredients, see: Gluten, Vol. 2, p. 307; onion, Vol. 2, p. 142; pepper, Vol. 2, p. 198; eggplant, Vol. 2, p. 256; carrot, Vol. 2, p. 25; garlic, Vol. 1, p. 338; apple juice, Vol. 1, p. 368; and the *Encyclopedia of Medicinal Plants:* Garlic, p. 230.

HEALTH COUNSELS

Gluten, the main ingredient in this recipe, is **wheat flour *protein.*** Although it is not a complete protein, its nutritional value increases when it is combined with other plant or animal proteins in the same meal or even on the same day.

Gluten and soybean are the types of protein most commonly used in the preparation of the so-called **vegetarian meat.** This resembles the texture found in meat, without its many drawbacks, and has the advantage of being ***cholesterol-free*** and containing *little* ***fat.***

This gluten recipe is appropriate in a transition diet, as a partial meat substitute. It is healthy because it nourishes and, at the same time, *prevents* **heart** disease, **rheumatism,** and even **cancer.**

NUTRITIONAL VALUE* per serving

Energy	164 kcal = 686 kj
Protein	14.7 g
Carbohydrates	18.6 g
Fiber	5.74 g
Total fat	*1.88 g*
Saturated fat	*0.137 g*
Cholesterol	—
Sodium	*15.5 mg*

1% 2% 4% 10% 20% 40% 100%

% Daily Value (based on a 2,000 calorie diet) provided by each serving of this dish

CALORIC PROPORTION*

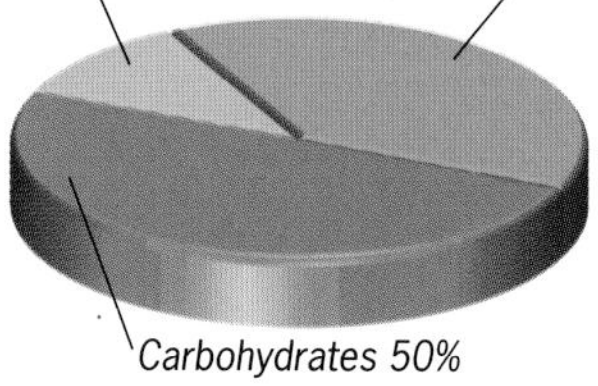

Percentage distribution of **calories for each nutrient**

* Additional ingredients not included.

Preparation time 00:20

Cooking time 00:20

Sautéed Marinated Gluten

INGREDIENTS (4 servings)

- 250 g (≅ 8.8 oz) **marinated gluten with vegetables** (Vol. 3, p. 53)
- 2 **onions**
- 2 sweet **red peppers**
- 2 sweet **green peppers**
- 2 **tomatoes**
- 1 **garlic** clove

ADDITIONAL INGREDIENTS

- 5 tablespoons olive **oil** (each tablespoon of oil adds around 120 kcal to the recipe, that is, 30 kcal per serving)
- Sea **salt** (see Vol. 3, p. 16)

PREPARATION

❶ Peel the onions, tomatoes, and garlic. Clean the peppers from seeds. Chop all vegetables.

- Chop the gluten into cubes, slightly larger than the rest of the ingredients.

❷ Heat three tablespoons of oil in a frying pan and sauté the onion and the gluten. When the onion starts taking color, add the salt and the garlic. Remove from heat and arrange it in a serving dish.

- Heat the remaining oil and sauté the peppers. When they start turning golden, add the tomato and a pinch of salt.
- Once the tomato juices are evaporated, remove from the heat and add it to the serving dish that contains the gluten sauté.

❸ Serve hot.

HEALTHIER ALTERNATIVE: Steam the ingredients instead of sautéing them.

For more information about the ingredients, see: Gluten, Vol. 2, p. 307; onion, Vol. 2, p. 142; pepper, Vol. 2, p. 198; tomato, Vol. 2, p. 275; garlic, Vol. 1, p. 338; and the *Encyclopedia of Medicinal Plants:* Garlic, p. 230.

HEALTH COUNSELS

This gluten dish, in addition to wheat protein, also includes legume purée. Both of them are the ingredients for marinated gluten with vegetables. Wheat protein is supplemented with legume protein, resulting in ***complete protein.***

This is therefore a very nutritious dish, which supplies high-quality protein. This is why it is *recommended* to enhance the growth and physical development of **children** and **adolescents.** Besides, it is good for **pregnant women, nursing mothers,** and **convalescing patients.**

Furthermore, this dish includes pepper, tomato, and onion, which possess *healing powers,* especially to the **heart,** the **arteries,** the **respiratory system,** and the **prostate.**

Therefore, this recipe advantageously substitutes similar dishes prepared with meat, as, in addition to the properties described above, it is ***cholesterol-free,*** and ***low fat.***

NUTRITIONAL VALUE* per serving

Energy	175 kcal = 732 kj
Protein	15.5 g
Carbohydrates	20.2 g
Fiber	6.24 g
Total fat	*2.20 g*
Saturated fat	*0.173 g*
Cholesterol	—
Sodium	*15.1 mg*

1% 2% 4% 10% 20% 40% 100%

% Daily Value (based on a 2,000 calorie diet) provided by each serving of this dish

CALORIC PROPORTION*

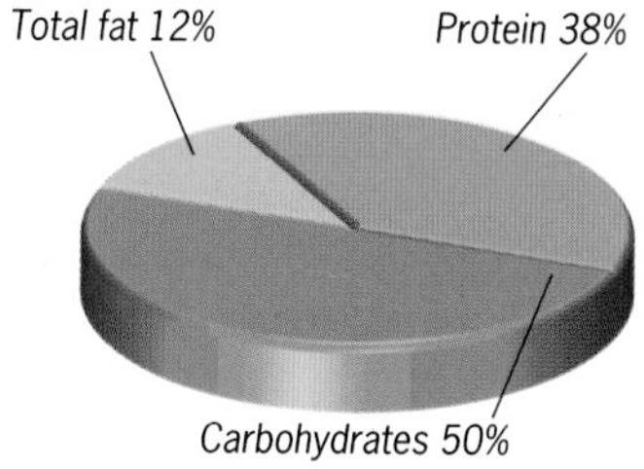

Percentage distribution of **calories for each nutrient**

* Additional ingredients not included.

Preparation time 00:30

Cooking time 0 1:00

Vegetarian Sausages and Drumsticks

INGREDIENTS

- 500 g (≅ 1 pound) **gluten** (without boiling) (Vol. 3, p. 52)
- 2 **eggs**
- 80 g **flour**
- 50 g **bread** crumbs
- 2 **garlic** cloves
- 2 liters unsalted **vegetable broth**

ADDITIONAL INGREDIENTS

- **Parsley**
- **Dill**
- Sea **salt** (see Vol. 3, p. 16)

PREPARATION

❶ Peel and grind in a mortar the garlic together with the salt and the potherbs.
- Beat the eggs and mix with the ground ingredients and the flour. Let it rest.
- Shape part of the gluten into sausages and wrap them one by one in aluminum or transparent plastic wrap without tightening too much.
- Shape the remaining gluten to resemble chicken drumsticks. Do this around wooden sticks such as those used in kebabs.

❷ In the vegetable broth, boil the sausages and the drumsticks for 30 minutes.
- Remove the sausages from their wrappings and set aside for later use as they are to be garnished with a sauce or as part of a stew.
- Remove the drumsticks from the pot and drain the excess water.
- Coat the drumsticks with egg and breadcrumbs. Bake until they are golden.

❸ Serve immediately.

For more information about the ingredients, see: Gluten, Vol. 2, p. 307; egg, Vol. 1, p.218; flour, Vol. 1, p. 68; bread, Vol. 1, p. 70; garlic, Vol. 1, p. 338; and the *Encyclopedia of Medicinal Plants:* Garlic, p. 230.

Wrap the sausages in aluminum foil.

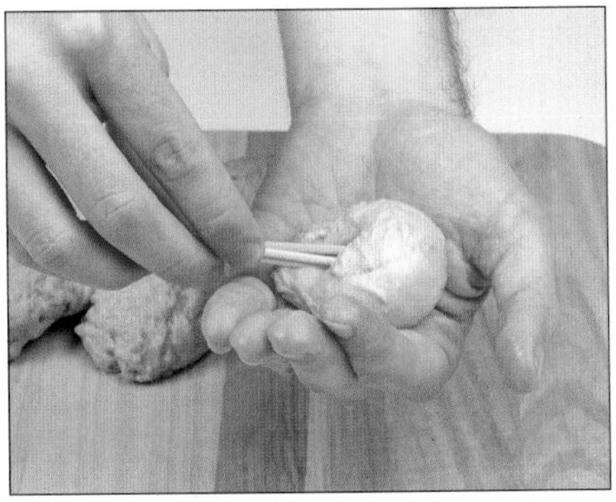

Introduce the sticks in the gluten.

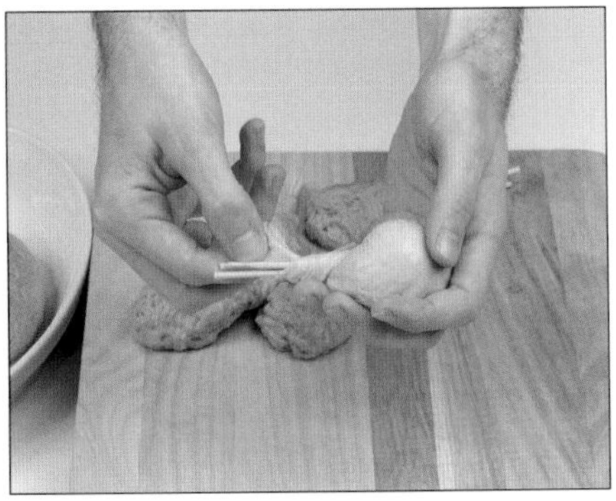

Shape the gluten in the shape of chicken drumsticks.

Gluten-sensitive Enteropathy

*The use of foods containing gluten, such as wheat flour and the flour of other cereals, bread, and other similar recipes included here, may cause digestive disorders in persons who are **sensitive** to this protein. This disorder is known as **celiac disease** in childhood and as **non-tropical sprue** in adulthood.*

NUTRITIONAL VALUE*
per 100 g

Energy	191 kcal = 797 kj
Protein	21.4 g
Carbohydrates	16.9 g
Fiber	1.70 g
Total fat	*3.71 g*
Saturated fat	*0.639 g*
Cholesterol	*66.9 mg*
Sodium	*21.3 mg*

1% 2% 4% 10% 20% 40% 100%

% Daily Value (based on a 2,000 calorie diet) provided by each 100 g of this dish

HEALTH COUNSELS

Gluten is wheat protein that, eaten by itself, results in an incomplete protein. However, combined with egg, as shown in this recipe, the deficiency is compensated through the amino acid **lysine.**

This is, therefore, a very nutritious dish, which mainly supplies high-quality ***protein,*** as well as other nutrients coming from the egg.

Although the recipe contains a certain amount of cholesterol from eggs, the dish is free from the drawbacks of meat (see Vol. 1, p. 300). Therefore, this is a recommended recipe for the **transition diet** toward healthier eating habits based on vegetables.

It is also recommended when there is a higher demand for protein, such as the **growth stages, pregnancy, lactation,** and **convalescence** from weakening diseases.

Suggestions from the Chef

These vegetarian sausages and drumsticks may be frozen after cooking for later use. Or else, keep them for a few days covered with soy sauce in an airtight glass jar in the refrigerator.

CALORIC PROPORTION*

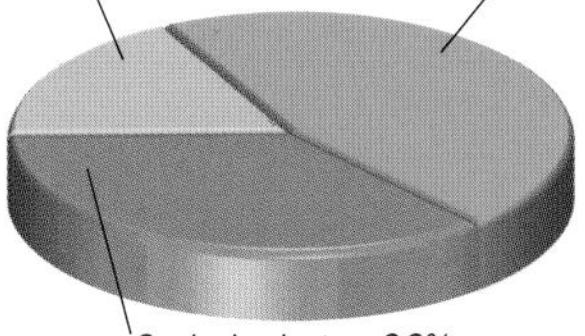

Percentage distribution of
calories for each nutrient

* Additional ingredients not included.

Nut Loaf

INGREDIENTS (6 servings)

- 150 g (≅ 1 1/4 cups) minced **walnuts**
- 120 g (≅ 4.2 oz) shredded **fresh cheese**
- 2 **onions**
- 3 **eggs**
- 250 g (≅ 8.8 oz) **carrots**
- 200 g (≅ 4 cups) **bread** crumbs
- 5 **garlic** cloves

ADDITIONAL INGREDIENTS

- 4 tablespoons olive **oil** (each tablespoon of oil adds around 120 kcal to the recipe, that is, 30 kcal per serving)
- 1 concentrated **vegetable stock** cube (unsalted)
- **Parsley**
- 1 teaspoon **oregano**
- 1 teaspoon **sweet paprika**
- Sea **salt** (see Vol. 3, p. 16)

For more information about the ingredients, see: Walnut, Vol. 2, p. 64; fresh cheese, Vol. 1, p. 212; onion, Vol. 2, p. 142; egg, Vol. 1, p. 218; carrot, Vol. 2, p. 25; bread, Vol. 1, p. 70; garlic, Vol. 1, p. 338; and the *Encyclopedia of Medicinal Plants: Garlic,* p. 230.

Suggestions from the Chef

"Orange sauce" makes up a good complement to this dish (see Vol. 3, p. 61).

PREPARATION

❶ Beat the eggs, chop one onion, the garlic cloves, and parsley.
- Mix the walnuts, cheese, bread crumbs, paprika, and half the vegetable stock cube (ground) together with the eggs, chopped onion, 3 garlic cloves, and parsley. Knead until it becomes packed. Shape as a cylinder, wrap with cloth and tie up the extremes.
- Peel and chop the other onion and the carrots.

❷ Heat the oil in a frying pan and sauté the onion, carrots, and the remaining two garlic cloves.
- Place the loaf in a pot. Add the sautéed ingredients and the remaining half of the stock cube. Add water to raise the level, but not to cover the loaf completely.
- Simmer for 30 minutes.
- Remove the loaf, untie it, and slice it thinly.
- Blend the leftover broth to obtain a thin sauce with which to garnish the loaf.

❸ Serve hot, accompanied by sweet red peppers or other raw or roasted vegetables.

HEALTHIER ALTERNATIVE: Discard the egg yolks, substitute cheese with tofu, and steam the vegetables instead of sautéing them.

Mix all ingredients well.

Form a cylinder-like shape with the dough.

Wrap the loaf with cloth
and tie up with cooking thread.

NUTRITIONAL VALUE*
per serving

Energy	435 kcal = 1.818 kj
Protein	16.5 g
Carbohydrates	35.2 g
Fiber	4.26 g
Total fat	*24.7 g*
Saturated fat	*5.69 g*
Cholesterol	*137 mg*
Sodium	*133 mg*

1% 2% 4% 10% 20% 40% 100%

% Daily Value (based on a 2,000 calorie diet)
provided by each serving of this dish

HEALTH COUNSELS

This dish constitutes a true concentrate of nutrients, which matches and even surpasses in nutritional value and taste other similar dishes made from meat. Together walnuts, cheese, and eggs supply *more* high-***biological*** value ***protein, minerals,*** and ***vitamins*** than meat, which, for example, lacks calcium.

Although this recipe includes a certain amount of cholesterol, it is free from other problems found in meat—risk of contaminating bacteria, presence of carcinogenic substances, and the decalcifying effect (see Vol. 1, p. 300).

The walnuts included in this recipe *enrich* the dish with essential ***fatty acids,*** which protect against excessive cholesterol. Furthermore, carrots, onions, and garlic also protect from the undesirable effects of cholesterol.

This is a suitable dish for those who require high-calorie and nutritional food (**children, adolescents, physical workers, sportsmen, women who are pregnant** or **nursing,** etc.). Furthermore, it is beneficial to those wishing to follow a transition diet to reduce their intake of animal products progressively.

CALORIC PROPORTION*

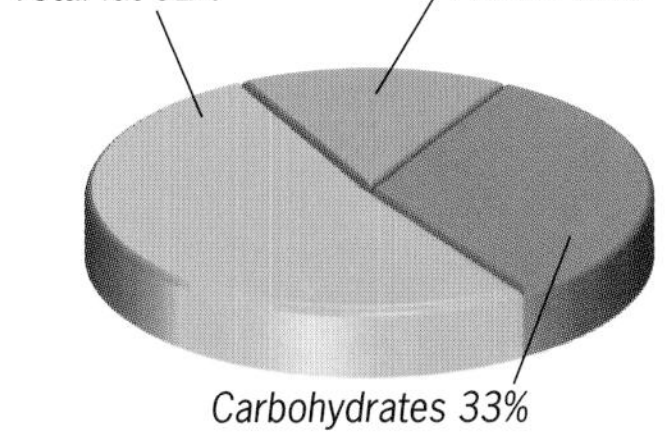

Percentage distribution of
calories for each nutrient

* Additional ingredients not included.

Onion Sausages

INGREDIENTS

- 20 kg (≅ 40 pounds) **onions**
- 200 g (≅ 7 oz) shelled **pine nuts** (pine kernels)
- 250 ml (≅ 18 tablespoons) of olive **oil**

ADDITIONAL INGREDIENTS

- 40 g (≅ 1.4 oz) **anise**
- 50 g (≅ 1.75 oz) **sweet paprika**
- 20 g (≅ 0.7 oz) **oregano**
- 20 g (≅ 0.7 oz) **cinnamon powder**
- 80 g (≅ 2.8 oz) **salt** (see Vol. 3, p. 16)

* * *

- 8 meters of **intestine** (synthetic)
- Cooking **thread**

Suggestions from the Chef

- Variations may include rice and leek, but to avoid rice becoming moldy it is necessary to add a greater proportion of fat to the mixture or to store the sausages in oil or frozen.
- If a packing device is not available, store the mixture in glass jars with sealing lids and boil in a **double boiler** for 20 minutes in order to sterilize and preserve the contents. Use as a spread.
- The dry husk of the onion and garlic can be easily removed if soaked in water for a few minutes.

PREPARATION

❶ Peel the onions.
- Soak the intestine in water.

❷ Boil the onions until they are tender. Drain the water by applying weight on top. Grind.
- Roast the anise seeds and grind them.
- Fry the pine nuts in 4 tablespoons of oil.
- Mix all the ingredients, including the remaining oil.
- Stuff the mixture and tie up along the line at regular intervals.
- Keep the sausages in hot water (not boiling) for 10 minutes.

❸ Drain the sausages and hang them to dry. Once dried they are ready to use.

For more information about the ingredients, see: Onion, Vol. 2, p. 142; pine nut, Vol. 2, p. 47; olive oil, Vol. 1, p. 118; and the *Encyclopedia of Medicinal Plants:* Anise, p. 465.

Onion is the principal ingredient of this recipe.

Mix all ingredients well.

Stuff the mixture into the synthetic intestine.

NUTRITIONAL VALUE* per 100 g

Nutrient	Amount
Energy	264 kcal = 1,105 kj
Protein	6.25 g
Carbohydrates	33.9 g
Fiber	9.34 g
Total fat	*9.13 g*
Saturated fat	*1.31 g*
Cholesterol	—
Sodium	*18.2 mg*

1% 2% 4% 10% 20% 40% 100%

% Daily Value (based on a 2,000 calorie diet) provided by each 100 g of this dish

HEALTH COUNSELS

Sausages include meat as their principal ingredient and represent a very serious hazard to our health (see Vol. 1, pp. 324-326). On the contrary, these vegetarian sausages exert a beneficial effect, and they are free from the problems associated to meat sausages. Specifically:

✓They are completely ***cholesterol**-free*, and contain *little* ***saturated fat,*** facts that make them good to *prevent* **arteriosclerosis** and **coronary diseases.**

✓Although they contain a certain amount of oil, these sausages contain *fewer* ***calories*** than animal sausages. Furthermore, the calories that they do contain come from a healthy vegetable oil, and not from lard or animal fat.

✓They do not have *any* **risk of contaminating bacteria** as is common in ordinary sausages.

✓Their use *prevents* the risk of **cancer,** as opposed to meat sausages.

Therefore, these onion sausages replace traditional cold cuts and have many healthy advantages. In addition, they are useful for a transition diet toward healthier eating habits.

The healing powers of onions upon the **respiratory system,** the **metabolism,** and **blood circulation,** make these vegetable sausages of even greater dietary value.

CALORIC PROPORTION*

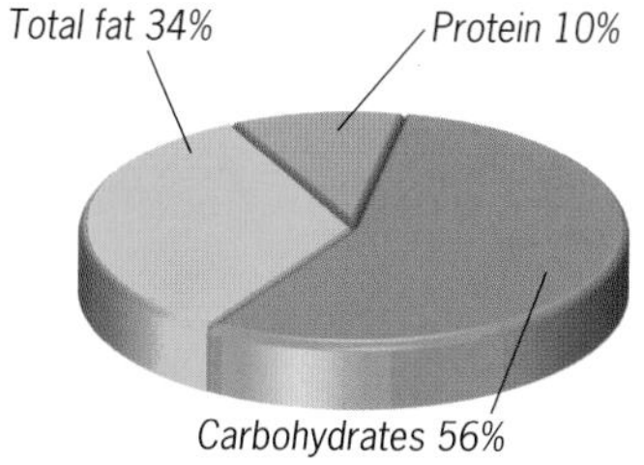

Percentage distribution of **calories for each nutrient**

* Additional ingredients not included.

Preparation time 00:20 Cooking time 00:50

42 - Transition Recipes

Vegetable Cannelloni

INGREDIENTS (6 servings)

- 18 **cannelloni**
- 500 g (≅ 1 pound) **mushrooms**
- 270 g (≅ 9.5 oz) **vegetarian meat analogs** (you may use the commercially available vegetarian meat or gluten (see Vol. 3, p. 52)
- 1 **eggplant**
- 1 **onion**
- 50 g (≅ 1/2 cup) ground **almonds**
- 50 g (≅ 2 oz) ground **pine nuts** (pine kernels)
- **White** Sauce (Vol. 3, p. 59)
- 50 g (≅ 1.75 oz) of grated **cheese**

ADDITIONAL INGREDIENTS

- 5 tablespoons olive **oil** (each tablespoon of oil adds around 120 kcal to the recipe, that is, 30 kcal per serving)
- Sea **salt** (see Vol. 3, p. 16)

Suggestion from the Chef

- Cannelloni can be prepared on the previous day. Consequently, a **lighter white sauce** may be used.
- They also can be frozen for later use.
- They are removed from the freezer a few hours in advance. Then grated **cheese** is sprinkled over the cannelloni and placed in the oven to **grill.**

PREPARATION

❶ Peel, wash, and chop into small chunks the eggplant, mushrooms, and onion.
- Shred the vegetarian meat.

❷ Heat the oil in a frying pan and sauté the onion. When it is transparent, add the mushrooms, the eggplant, and the vegetarian meat. Sauté for a few more minutes.
- Remove from heat and grind.
- Add the ground almonds and pine nuts to the mixture. Let rest.
- Prepare the cannelloni following the manufacturer's directions (soaking, cooking, etc.).
- Lay the filling over the cannelloni. Wrap them and place them in an oven dish. Cover with white sauce and sprinkle the cheese. Grill.

❸ Serve hot.

HEALTHIER ALTERNATIVE: Steam the ingredients instead of sautéing them. White sauce may also be prepared using vegetable milk and can be grilled without cheese (see Vol. 3, pp. 59, 73).

For more information about the ingredients, see: Pasta, Vol. 1, p. 74; mushroom, Vol. 1, p. 152; meat analogs, Vol. 1, p. 332; eggplant, Vol. 2, p. 256; onion, Vol. 2, p. 142; almond, Vol. 2, p. 48; pine nut, Vol. 2, p. 47; cheese, Vol. 1, p. 206.

Chop the ingredients according to the directions.

Prepare the cannelloni.

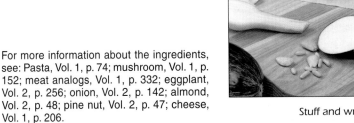

Stuff and wrap the cannelloni.

NUTRITIONAL VALUE* per serving

Energy	415 kcal = 1,737 kj
Protein	19.2 g
Carbohydrates	27.1 g
Fiber	6.80 g
Total fat	*25.2 g*
Saturated fat	*4.68 g*
Cholesterol	*9.50 mg*
Sodium	*486 mg*

1% 2% 4% 10% 20% 40% 100%

% Daily Value (based on a 2,000 calorie diet) provided by each serving of this dish

CALORIC PROPORTION*

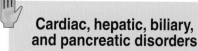

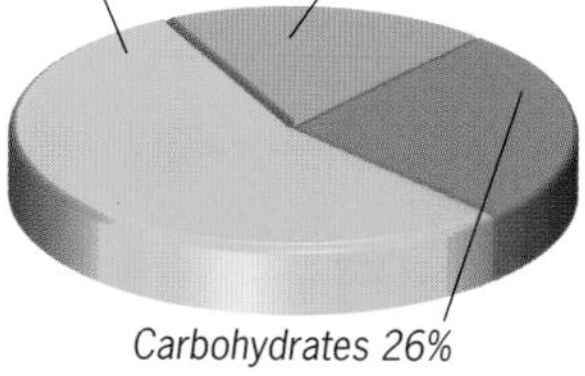

Percentage distribution of
calories for each nutrient

HEALTH COUNSELS

This is a tasty, nutritious, and high-calorie dish. It substitutes other cannelloni recipes prepared with meat, as it *hardly* supplies ***cholesterol.*** Although it contains fat, the fat is ***unsaturated*** and of vegetable origin, coming mainly from almonds, pine nuts, and oil.

Sportsmen and **women,** those carrying out **intensive physical labor,** and those in need of gaining a few kilos of weight, would especially benefit from this dish, which is packed with ***nutrients*** of *high biological value.*

Its use *prevents* **osteoporosis,** as it is *high* in ***calcium*** and in other ***minerals*** that contribute to the formation of bone structure, especially coming from almonds and cheese. Furthermore, soybeans' ***isoflavones*** *fixate* calcium into the bones.

Cardiac, hepatic, biliary, and pancreatic disorders

*In case of **dyspepsia, hypochlorhydria, pancreas, liver, or gallbladder alterations,** it is recommended to reduce this recipe's fat content, removing partially or totally the oil and the cheese.*

* Additional ingredients not included.

Preparation time 00:15

Cooking time 00:50

Artichoke Cannelloni

INGREDIENTS (6 servings)

- 18 **cannelloni**
- 300 g (≅ 10.6 oz) **artichokes**
- 50 g (≅ 1.75 oz) shelled **pine nuts** (pine kernels)
- 1 **onion**
- 1 **garlic** clove
- 50 g (≅ 1.75 oz) grated **fresh cheese**
- 500 g (≅ 1 pound) **white sauce** (Vol. 3, p. 59)

ADDITIONAL INGREDIENTS

- 5 tablespoons olive **oil** (each tablespoon of oil adds around 120 kcal to the recipe, that is, 30 kcal per serving)
- Sea **salt** (see Vol. 3, p. 16)

PREPARATION

❶ Remove the outer tough leaves and stems of the artichokes–leave only the tender leaves and the core.

- Peel, wash, and chop the garlic and onion.

❷ Boil the artichokes until they are tender.

- Heat the oil in a frying pan and sauté the onion and the garlic. When the onion is transparent, add the chopped artichokes, pine nuts, and salt. Keep cooking everything for a few more minutes.
- Prepare the cannelloni following the manufacturer's directions.
- Fill the cannelloni with the previously prepared filling. Place them in an oven dish, cover with white sauce and sprinkle with grated cheese. Grill.

❸ Serve hot.

HEALTHIER ALTERNATIVE: Steam the ingredients instead of sautéing them.

For more information about the ingredients, see: Pasta, Vol. 1 p. 74; artichoke, Vol. 2 p. 178; pine nut, Vol. 2 p. 47; onion, Vol. 2 p. 142; garlic, Vol. 1 p. 338; fresh cheese, Vol. 1 p. 212; and the *Encyclopedia of Medicinal Plants:* garlic, p. 230.

HEALTH COUNSELS

Artichoke cannelloni are comparable in taste to those prepared with meat and they are, of course, superior due to their beneficial effects upon our health. They are not only *low* in ***cholesterol*** and in ***saturated fat,*** but their ***fiber*** content is also *higher.* They contain *fewer* **calories** and are *easier* to *digest.*

If this were not enough, these cannelloni contain healthy ingredients, such as artichoke and pine nuts. Artichokes help with the *functioning* of the **liver, gallbladder,** and **kidneys,** apart from being able to *reduce* the level of **cholesterol.** Pine nuts supply unsaturated ***fatty acids,*** which *reduce* the level of **cholesterol.** They also contain ***protein, vitamins,*** and ***minerals.***

NUTRITIONAL VALUE* per serving

Energy	228 kcal = 952 kj
Protein	7.62 g
Carbohydrates	20.5 g
Fiber	4.00 g
Total fat	*11.8 g*
Saturated fat	2.66 g
Cholesterol	*3.83 mg*
Sodium	*67.8 mg*

1% 2% 4% 10% 20% 40% 100%

% Daily Value (based on a 2,000 calorie diet) provided by each serving of this dish

CALORIC PROPORTION*

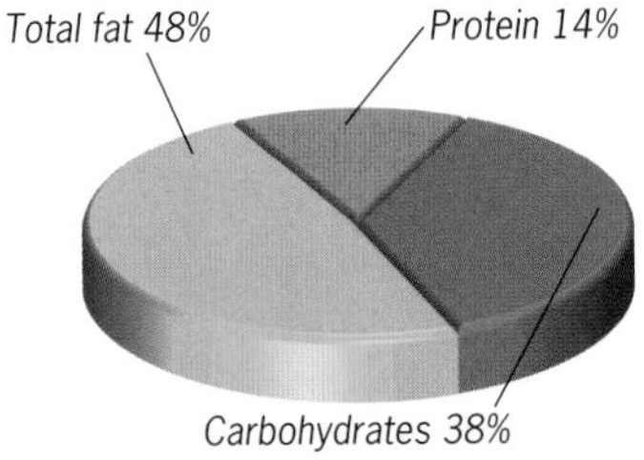

Percentage distribution of **calories for each nutrient**

* Additional ingredients not included.

Preparation time 00:15 | Cooking time 00:30

Cabbage Rolls

INGREDIENTS (4 servings)

- 8 large white **cabbage** leaves
- 200 g (≅ 3.5 oz) boiled **whole rice**
- 150 g (≅ 5.3 oz) chopped **Marinated Gluten with Vegetables** (Vol. 3, p. 53)
- 80 g (≅ 2.8 oz) shelled **walnuts**
- 1 **onion**
- 1 **garlic** clove

ADDITIONAL INGREDIENTS

- **Traditional Tomato Sauce** (Vol. 3, p. 62) (each tablespoon of this sauce adds 9 kcal to the recipe, that is, around 2 kcal per serving)
- 3 tablespoons olive **oil** (each tablespoon of oil adds around 120 kcal to the recipe, that is, 30 kcal per serving)
- Sea **salt** (see Vol. 3, p. 16)

PREPARATION

❶ Peel and chop fine the onion and garlic.
- Chop the gluten and walnuts.

❷ Boil the cabbage for 7 minutes.
- Drain the leaves, remove the toughest parts around the central stem and lay them on a cloth.
- Heat the oil in a frying pan and sauté the onion and the garlic. When the onion is transparent, add the rice, gluten, walnuts, and salt. Stir lightly and continue cooking for an additional 5 minutes.
- Place two tablespoons of the mixture in the center of each cabbage leaf. Make a package by wrapping the filling with each cabbage leaf. Arrange the packages face down in a pot.
- Pour the tomato sauce over them and cook for 10 minutes.

❸ Serve hot.

HEALTHIER ALTERNATIVE: Steam the ingredients instead of sautéing them.

For more information about the ingredients, see: Cabbage, Vol. 2, p. 191; rice, Vol. 2, p. 225; meat analogs, Vol. 1, p. 332; onion, Vol. 2, p. 142; garlic, Vol. 1, p. 338; walnut, Vol. 2, p. 64; and the *Encyclopedia of Medicinal Plants:* Garlic, p. 230.

HEALTH COUNSELS

These delicious little cabbage packages are very nutritious, as they supply:

✓ ***Carbohydrates*** and ***fiber*** from whole rice.

✓ ***Protein*** from the gluten and the walnuts.

✓ ***Healthy fat*** from walnuts and from olive oil.

✓ ***Vitamins,*** especially ***B-complex*** coming from whole rice and from walnuts.

✓ ***Minerals*** and ***trace minerals,*** such as ***zinc*** from meat analogs and walnuts.

Therefore, this is a healthy dish, which also contributes to **development** in children and adolescents. Besides, those wishing to *protect* their **heart** and *reduce* the risk of **cancer** will especially benefit from this dish.

NUTRITIONAL VALUE* per serving

Energy	275 kcal = 1,151 kj
Protein	13.1 g
Carbohydrates	22.7 g
Fiber	5.17 g
Total fat	*14.0 g*
Saturated fat	*1.28 g*
Cholesterol	—
Sodium	*15.8 mg*

1% 2% 4% 10% 20% 40% 100%

% Daily Value (based on a 2,000 calorie diet) provided by each serving of this dish

CALORIC PROPORTION*

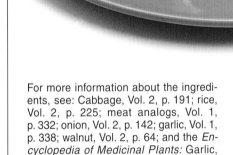

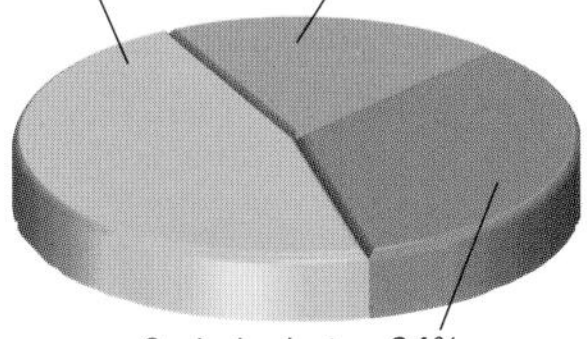

Percentage distribution of **calories for each nutrient**

* Additional ingredients not included.

Spring Rolls

INGREDIENTS (4 servings)

- 200 g (≅ 7 oz) **soybean sprouts**
- 2 **onions**
- 100 g (≅ 3.5 oz) **textured soy protein**
- 1 **zucchini**
- 2 **carrots**
- 300 g (≅ 2 1/3 cups) **wheat flour**
- 1 **egg**
- 250 ml (≅ 1 cup) unsalted **vegetable broth**

ADDITIONAL INGREDIENTS

- 1 tablespoon olive **oil** (each tablespoon of oil adds around 120 kcal to the recipe, that is, 30 kcal per serving)
- 1 tablespoon **soy sauce** (each tablespoon of this sauce adds 8 kcal and 857 mg of sodium to the recipe, that is, around 2 kcal and around 214 mg of sodium per serving)
- 1/2 teaspoon **brown sugar** (soft sugar)
- 1 teaspoon sea **salt** (see Vol. 3, p. 16)

For more information about the ingredients, see: Soybean sprouts, Vol. 1, p. 86; onion, Vol. 2, p.142; textured soy protein, Vol. 1, p. 89; zucchini, Vol. 2, p. 159; carrot, Vol. 2, p. 25; flour, Vol. 1, p. 68; egg, Vol. 1, p. 218.

PREPARATION

❶ Mix the flour, egg, and vegetable broth to obtain a slightly thinner batter than for crepes (see Vol. 3, p. 42).
- Mix the soy sauce, sugar, and salt. Set aside.
- Peel, wash, and cut into thin strips the onion, zucchini, and carrot.
- Soak in water the textured soy protein (use same volume of water as soy protein).

❷ Steam the vegetables together with the soybean sprouts and the soaked soy protein until they are tender. Heat the soy sauce and mix together with the vegetables. Set aside—this will be the filling.
- Heat a little oil in a non-sticky frying pan. Pour a small portion of the batter already prepared. Spread over the pan bottom and turn it over to form a thin wafer.
- Place a tablespoon of filling in the center of wafer, fold each side and roll.
- When all the little rolls are packed, place them in a 220°C oven until they are golden.

❸ Serve hot with "Soy Sweet-and-Sour Sauce" (see Vol. 3, p. 56).

Mix together the soy sauce, sugar, and salt.

Chop the vegetables.

Wrap the filling with the wafers.

HEALTH COUNSELS

These soybean Spring Rolls are very tasty and healthy. They supply *high biological value* ***protein*** from the soybean sprouts, soy protein, and egg. In addition, they supply ***carbohydrates*** from flour, as well as ***minerals*** and ***vitamins*** from the vegetables.

Unlike the spring rolls prepared with meat, these contain *little* ***fat,*** especially saturated fat, which is the most injurious to the arteries. In addition, they contain ***isoflavones,*** a type of phytoestrogen found in soybeans. They facilitate the storage of ***calcium*** in the **bones,** bring *balance* to the **hormonal system,** *avoid* **arteriosclerosis** and *prevent* **cancer** (see Vol. 2, pp. 267-268).

This is, therefore, a highly recommended dish in the transition diet where meat and other animal products are progressively substituted by healthier food of vegetable origin.

Suggestions from the Chef

- Spring Rolls can be **fried,** but their fat content and caloric proportion increase.
- They may be garnished with **salad** or a recipe where **rice** is the main ingredient.
- In specialty food stores, there are dehydrated rice **wafers** that only need slight soaking before cooking.
- Springs Rolls may be **frozen** for later use. Prepare them following the instructions and place them in the freezer (without baking). To use them, simply move them directly from the freezer onto a baking tray and into the oven. There is no need of thawing.

NUTRITIONAL VALUE* per serving

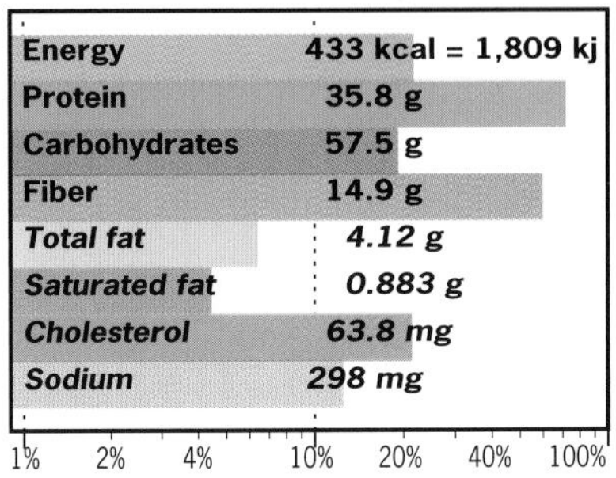
Energy 433 kcal = 1,809 kj
Protein 35.8 g
Carbohydrates 57.5 g
Fiber 14.9 g
Total fat 4.12 g
Saturated fat 0.883 g
Cholesterol 63.8 mg
Sodium 298 mg
1% 2% 4% 10% 20% 40% 100%

% Daily Value (based on a 2,000 calorie diet) provided by each serving of this dish

CALORIC PROPORTION*

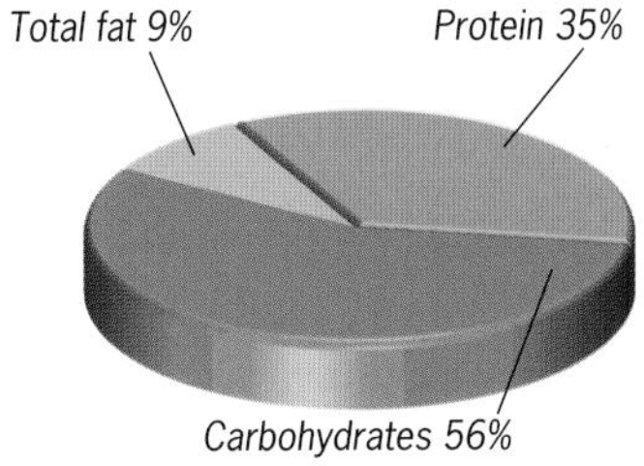
Total fat 9%
Protein 35%
Carbohydrates 56%

Percentage distribution of **calories for each nutrient**

* Additional ingredients not included.

Vegetable Pie

INGREDIENTS

- 200 g (≅ 7 oz) **mushrooms**
- 200 g (≅ 7 oz) **carrots**
- 2 sweet **red peppers**
- 150 g (≅ 5.3 oz) **chard**
- 150 g (≅ 1 1/3 cups) **green beans** (string beans)
- 2 **tomatoes**
- 1 **onion**
- 9 tablespoons olive **oil**
- 400 g (≅ 2 1/3 cups) **whole flour**
- 1 tablespoon **brewer's yeast**
- 100 ml (≅ 3/8 cups) **water**
- 100 ml (≅ 3/8 cups) **milk**
- 1 teaspoon **sweet paprika**

ADDITIONAL INGREDIENTS

- Sea **salt** (see Vol. 3, p. 16)

PREPARATION

❶Clean and chop the mushrooms, chard, and peppers.
- Peel and chop the carrots, tomatoes, and onion.
- Cut off the tips and remove the threads from the green beans. Chop them.

❷Boil the chard, carrots, and green beans.
- Heat 3 tablespoons of oil in a frying pan and sauté the onion. When it is transparent, add the peppers and, five minutes later, add the mushrooms. Finally, add the tomatoes and keep cooking until the vegetable juices have evaporated.
- Mix the sauté with the boiled vegetables and the filling is ready.
- Mix the salt and flour. Make a hole in the middle and pour in the water and the remaining oil. Knead until the dough becomes elastic and does not stick.
- Divide the dough into two parts, one slightly bigger than the other.
- Spread the larger portion over a round, ovenproof piecrust dish, leaving the dough jut out about 2 cm from the edge. Prick it with a fork. Place the filling onto the crust and cover with the other portion of dough. Wet the border of the lower dough and fold it over the upper dough, thus sealing the pie. Prick the dough with a fork several times and decorate the pie with dough strips.
- Place the pie in a preheated, 220°C oven. Bake for 30 minutes.

❸It may be served immediately or cold. This dish lends itself to be taken on a trip or a picnic.

HEALTHIER ALTERNATIVE: Instead of sautéing the ingredients, bake or steam them.

Add the water and the oil to the flour.

Divide the dough into two parts, one slightly bigger than the other.

With the greater portion, spread over the pie dish.

Place the filling in the pie.

Cover the filling with the remaining dough.

For more information about the ingredients, see: Mushrooms, Vol. 1, p. 152; carrot, Vol. 2, p. 25; pepper, Vol. 2, p. 198; chard, Vol. 2, p. 297; green bean, Vol. 1, p. 109; tomato, Vol. 2, p. 275; onion, Vol. 2, p. 142; oil, Vol. 1, p. 112; flour, Vol. 1, p. 68; and the *Encyclopedia of Medicinal Plants:* Green beans, p. 584.

NUTRITIONAL VALUE*
per 100 g

Energy	132 kcal = 554 kj
Protein	4.00 g
Carbohydrates	15.4 g
Fiber	4.06 g
Total fat	*5.26 g*
Saturated fat	*0.81 g*
Cholesterol	*0.68 mg*
Sodium	*25.3 mg*

1% 2% 4% 10% 20% 40% 100%

% Daily Value (based on a 2,000 calorie diet) provided by each 100 g of this dish

HEALTH COUNSELS

This Vegetable Pie possesses several advantages compared to those prepared with meat. First, it is cholesterol-free and its fat content is very low. In addition, it contains fewer calories, which helps to prevent obesity. And, above all, thanks to the vegetables included, it is healthier than meat pies, particularly for:

✓The **heart** and the **circulatory system,** thanks to the ***vitamins,*** and ***antioxidant phytochemical elements*** from carrots, peppers, chard, and other vegetables.

✓The **intestine,** as all the vegetables included in this pie supply ***fiber,*** which *regulates* the **bowel movement** and *prevents* **constipation.**

✓The *prevention* of **obesity,** as this is a nutritious and satisfying dish, which at the same time supplies a moderate number of ***calories.***

✓**Cancer** *prevention,* due to the **protecting** and *antioxidant* effect of ***flavonoids' beta-carotene*** (provitamin A), and other healthy components found in this pie's vegetables.

The Vegetable Pie substitutes those prepared with meat in the framework of a transition diet toward a healthier lifestyle.

CALORIC PROPORTION*

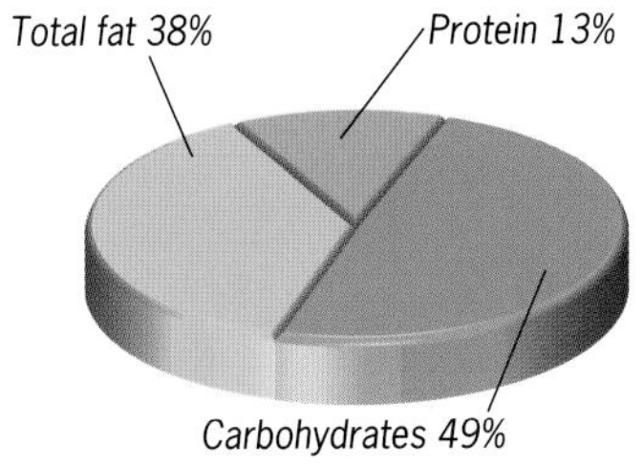

Percentage distribution of
calories for each nutrient

* Additional ingredients not included.

Preparation time 00:15

Cooking time 00:45

Vegetable Turnovers

INGREDIENTS (6 servings)

- Pie **crust dough** (Vol. 3, p. 104)
- 200 g (≅ 7 oz) **tofu**
- 1 **onion**
- 1 sweet **green pepper**
- 1 sweet **red pepper**
- 100 g (≅ 3.5 oz) .pitted **green olives**
- 100 g (≅ 3.5 oz) **Traditional Tomato Sauce** (Vol. 3, p. 62)

ADDITIONAL INGREDIENTS

- 3 tablespoons olive **oil** (each tablespoon of oil adds around 120 kcal to the recipe, that is, 30 kcal per serving)
- Sea **salt** (see Vol. 3, p. 16)

For more information about the ingredients, see: Tofu, Vol. 1, p. 88; onion, Vol. 2, p. 142; pepper, Vol. 2, p. 198; olive, Vol. 2, p. 165; tomato, Vol. 2, p. 275; garlic, Vol. 1, p. 338; and the *Encyclopedia of Medicinal Plants:* Garlic, p. 230.

Suggestions from the Chef

Hard-boiled egg or sweet corn may be used instead of tofu.

PREPARATION

❶Wash, clean, and chop the onion and peppers.

- Chop the olives and the tofu.

❷Heat the oil in a frying pan and sauté the onion and the peppers.

- When they are tender, add the olives and the tofu. Stir and finally add the tomato sauce.
- Using a rolling pin, spread the dough over a floured board and cut circles of about 12 cm diameter.
- Place in the center of each circle a small amount of filling. Fold each circle by half to form a half-moon shape. Join the borders to seal the turnovers.
- Place the turnovers on a slightly greased oven tray and bake for 20 minutes at 180°C.

❸Serve hot.

HEALTHIER ALTERNATIVE: Instead of sautéing the ingredients, steam them.

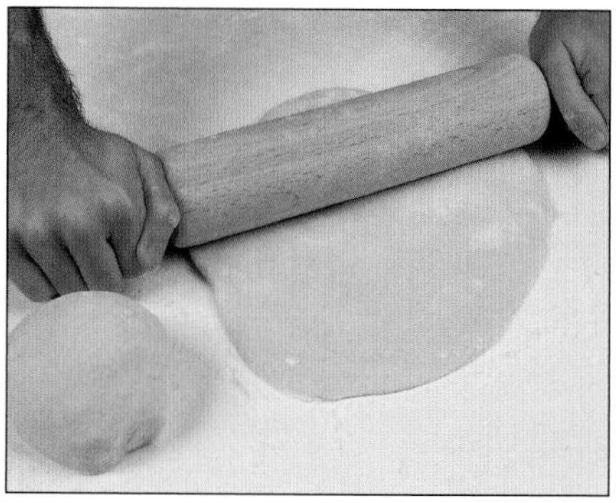

Spread the dough using a rolling pin.

Cut out the dough into circles.

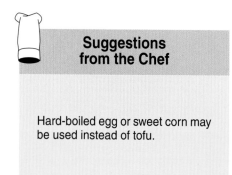

Place a small portion of filling in the center of each circle.

NUTRITIONAL VALUE*
per serving

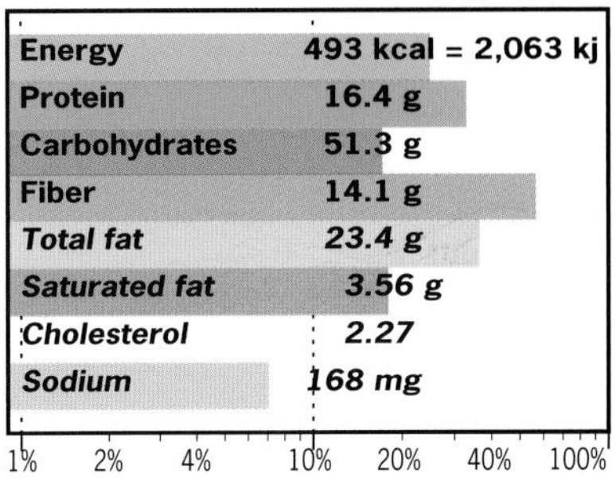
Energy 493 kcal = 2,063 kj
Protein 16.4 g
Carbohydrates 51.3 g
Fiber 14.1 g
Total fat 23.4 g
Saturated fat 3.56 g
Cholesterol 2.27
Sodium 168 mg
1% 2% 4% 10% 20% 40% 100%

% Daily Value (based on a 2,000 calorie diet) provided by each serving of this dish

HEALTH COUNSELS

Turnovers are a reduced pie. The filling, mainly made up of tofu (soy "cheese") used in these turnovers, makes the dish very healthy, nutritious, and suitable for a transition diet toward one based on vegetables.

Tofu mainly supplies high-quality ***protein,*** as well as ***calcium, iron,*** and other ***minerals.*** Furthermore, it contains ***isoflavones,*** a type of phytoestrogens or vegetable hormones endowed with outstanding preventive effects upon the **heart,** the **arteries,** the musculoskeletal system, and the reproductive organs (see Vol. 1, p. 411).

The vegetables that accompany tofu in these turnovers supply **vitamins, minerals,** and ***phytochemicals, which*** multiply the beneficial effects of tofu.

This is especially favorable for the *prevention* of **cholesterol** excess, **coronary disease, stroke, osteoporosis,** and **cancer,** due to the properties of its ingredients.

In addition, this recipe is appropriate for the diet of **youth, pregnant women, nursing women, convalescing patients,** and all those requiring a supply of high-quality nutrients, prepared in an attractive and delicious way.

CALORIC PROPORTION*

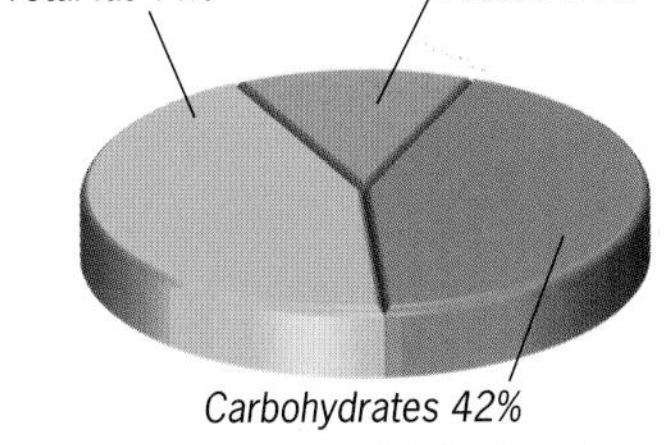
Total fat 44%
Protein 14%
Carbohydrates 42%

Percentage distribution of
calories for each nutrient

* Additional ingredients not included.

Preparation time 00:15

Cooking time 01:00

Spinach Lasagna

INGREDIENTS (6 servings)

- 6 **lasagna shells**
- 750 g (≅ 26.5 oz) **spinach**
- 150 g (≅ 5.3 oz) **gluten** (Vol. 3, p. 52) or vegetarian meat analogs
- 100 g **vegetable spread**
- 150 g (≅ 5.3 oz) **Traditional Tomato Sauce** (Vol. 3, p. 62)
- 50 g (≅ 1.75 oz) of ground **walnuts**
- 1 **garlic** clove
- 250 g (≅ 8.8 oz) of **white sauce** (Vol. 3, p. 59)
- 100 g (≅ 3.5 oz) of shredded **fresh cheese**

ADDITIONAL INGREDIENTS

- 4 tablespoons olive **oil** (each tablespoon of oil adds around 120 kcal to the recipe, that is, 30 kcal per serving)
- Sea **salt** (see Vol. 3, p. 16)

PREPARATION

❶Wash and chop the spinach.
- Peel and chop the garlic.
- Chop the gluten.

❷Heat the oil in a frying pan and sauté the spinach, garlic, and gluten.
- Add the tomato sauce, vegetable spread, walnuts, and salt. Stir.
- Prepare the lasagna shells following the manufacturer's directions.
- In a slightly greased oven dish, place two lasagna shells, side by side. Spread over a layer of filling. Alternate another two lasagna shells with another filling layer. Finish with two lasagna shells.
- Cover with the white sauce and sprinkle with cheese.
- Bake for 45 minutes.

❸Serve hot.

HEALTHIER ALTERNATIVE: Steam the ingredients instead of sautéing them. Prepare the white sauce using vegetable milk and grill without cheese (see Vol. 3, p. 73).

As a healthier alternative, steam the spinach.

Sauté the ingredients.

Place the layers of lasagna shells and filling alternately.

For more information about the ingredients, see: Pasta, Vol. 1, p. 74; spinach, Vol. 2, p. 28; gluten, Vol. 2, p. 307; tomato, Vol. 2, p. 275; walnut, Vol. 2, p. 64; garlic, Vol. 1, p. 338; cheese, Vol. 1, p. 206; and the *Encyclopedia of Medicinal Plants:* Garlic, p. 230.

NUTRITIONAL VALUE*
per serving

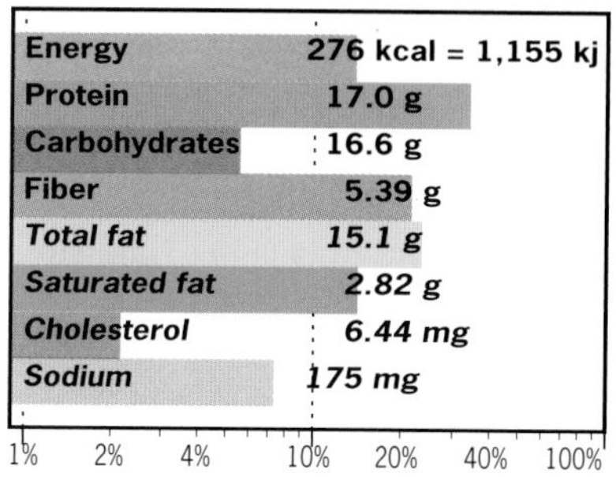
Energy 276 kcal = 1,155 kj
Protein 17.0 g
Carbohydrates 16.6 g
Fiber 5.39 g
Total fat 15.1 g
Saturated fat 2.82 g
Cholesterol 6.44 mg
Sodium 175 mg
1% 2% 4% 10% 20% 40% 100%

% Daily Value (based on a 2,000 calorie diet) provided by each serving of this dish

HEALTH COUNSELS

The base of this dish is pasta (lasagna), accompanied by spinach and the other ingredients. This lasagna matches or surpasses meat lasagna in terms of looks, flavor and nutritional value. Besides, it offers a number of healthy advantages due to:

✓**Being** *high* in ***fiber,*** which *prevents* constipation and *avoids* an *excess* of **cholesterol.**

✓Being *low* in ***saturated fat*** and ***cholesterol,*** which makes it helpful to keep the **arteries** and **blood circulation** in good health.

✓Its supply of unsaturated essential ***fatty acids*** coming from soybeans and nuts.

In general, this dish is very nutritious and high in calories, which supply energy and necessary nutrients for the organism, such as ***iron*** in spinach, ***calcium*** in fresh cheese, and ***zinc*** in walnut.

Spinach and walnut lasagna is an ideal dish for those wishing to follow a transition diet toward a healthier lifestyle. It is highly recommended for those who carry out **intense physical work, children** and **youth** during growth periods, the **malnourished** and those with tendency to suffer from **anemia.**

CALORIC PROPORTION*

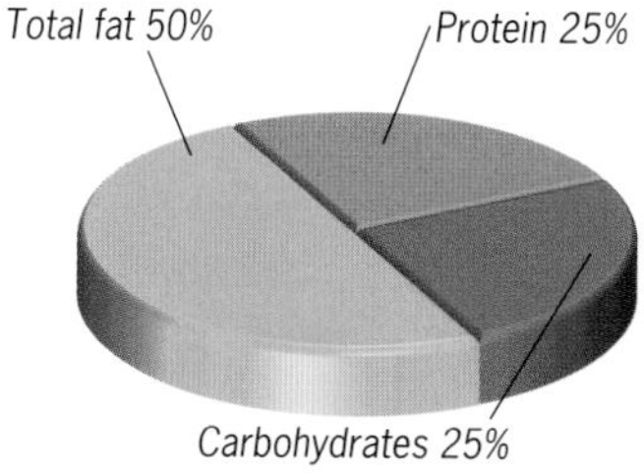
Total fat 50%
Protein 25%
Carbohydrates 25%

Percentage distribution of
calories for each nutrient

* Additional ingredients not included.

Preparation time 00:20

Cooking time 00:50

Mushroom Lasagna

INGREDIENTS (6 servings)

- 6 **lasagna shells**
- 200 g (≅ 7 oz) **mushrooms**
- 200 g (≅ 7 oz) **elm oyster or oyster mushrooms**
- 100 g (≅ 2/3 cup) **peas**
- 2 **eggs**
- 1 **onion**
- 2 **garlic** cloves
- 50 g (≅ 1.75 oz) shredded **mild cheese**
- 150 g (≅ 5.3 oz) **Traditional Tomato Sauce** (Vol. 3, p. 62)

ADDITIONAL INGREDIENTS

- **Parsley**
- 4 tablespoons olive **oil** (each tablespoon of oil adds around 120 kcal to the recipe, that is, 30 kcal per serving)
- Sea **salt** (see Vol. 3, p. 16)

PREPARATION

❶ Clean, wash, and chop all the mushrooms.
- Peel and chop the onion and garlic.
- Wash and chop the parsley.
- Prepare the lasagna shells following the manufacturer's directions.

❷ Boil the eggs for 12 minutes. Boil the peas separately.
- Heat the oil in a frying pan and sauté the onion. When the onion is transparent, add all the mushrooms and salt and sauté for 10 minutes. Add the garlic and parsley and cook for an additional 2 minutes.
- Remove from the stove and add the peas and the chopped eggs. Mix well.
- In an oven dish, lay alternatively, lasagna shells, mushrooms, and tomato sauce. Top with a layer of lasagna shells.
- Sprinkle with the shredded cheese and grill until the surface becomes golden and brown.

❸ Serve hot.

HEALTHIER ALTERNATIVE: Instead of sautéing the mushrooms, bake them or grill them. (To grill without cheese, see Vol. 3, p. 73.)

For more information about the ingredients, see: Pasta, Vol. 1, p. 74; mushroom, Vol. 2, p. 294; elm oyster mushroom, Vol. 1, p. 156; pea, Vol. 2, p. 73; egg, Vol. 1, p. 218; onion, Vol. 2, p. 142; garlic, Vol. 1, p. 338; cheese, Vol. 1, p. 206; tomato, Vol. 2, p. 275; and the *Encyclopedia of Medicinal Plants:* Garlic, p. 230.

HEALTH COUNSELS

This mushroom lasagna offers good amounts of ***protein*** and ***calories,*** and a *moderate* supply of ***fat*** and ***cholesterol.***

Protein from mushrooms has the advantage of not being accompanied by fat as meat and meat products. The protein nutritional value of mushrooms is enhanced when combined with eggs and cheese protein, in spite of being used in small amounts, such as in this recipe.

Besides, mushrooms and peas supply ***vitamins*** and ***minerals,*** which enrich the nutritional value of this dish.

NUTRITIONAL VALUE* per serving

Energy	215 kcal = 898 kj
Protein	9.92 g
Carbohydrates	30.1 g
Fiber	5.09 g
Total fat	*5.52 g*
Saturated fat	*2.11 g*
Cholesterol	*88.8 mg*
Sodium	*64.6 mg*

1% 2% 4% 10% 20% 40% 100%

% Daily Value (based on a 2,000 calorie diet) provided by each serving of this dish

CALORIC PROPORTION*

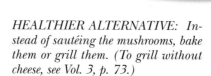

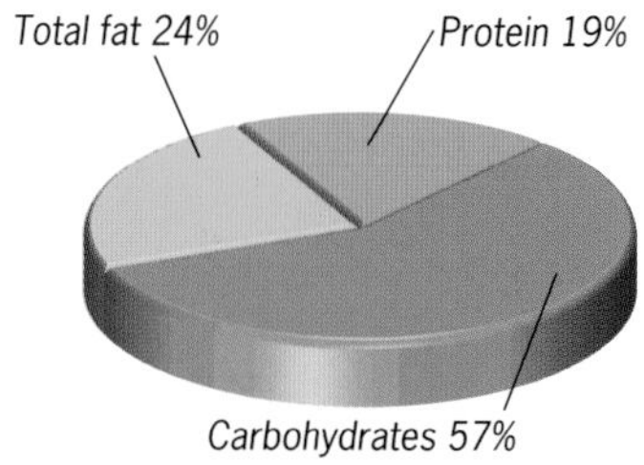

Percentage distribution of **calories for each nutrient**

* Additional ingredients not included.

Preparation time 00:10 | Cooking time 01:00

Millet Croquettes

INGREDIENTS (4 servings)

- 50 g (≅ 1/4 cup) husked **millet**
- 1 **onion**
- 50 g (≅ 3/8 cup) **whole flour**
- 300 ml (≅ 1 1/4 cup) **milk**
- 1 **egg**
- 50 g (≅ 1 cup) **bread** crumbs

ADDITIONAL INGREDIENTS

- 3 tablespoons olive **oil** (each tablespoon of oil adds around 120 kcal to the recipe, that is, 30 kcal per serving)
- Sea **salt** (see Vol. 3, p. 16)

PREPARATION

❶ Wash, peel, and shred the onion.

❷ Boil the millet in water with salt for 20 minutes.

- Heat the oil in a frying pan and sauté the onion until it becomes transparent. Add the millet, stir, and keep cooking for an additional 5 minutes. Add the flour and stir for two more minutes.
- Remove the frying pan from the stove. Add the milk (cold) little by little. Stir continuously to avoid the formation of lumps.
- Return to the stove. Add the salt, and keep cooking until it thickens and becomes unstuck from the pan surface.
- Pour into a large dish and let cool.
- When the dough is cold, take spoonfuls and shape in the form of croquettes. Roll in the beaten egg and the breadcrumbs. Bake for about 20 minutes in a 220°C oven until the croquettes take on a golden color.

❸ Serve hot.

HEALTHIER ALTERNATIVE: Instead of sautéing the onion, steam it. Slightly toast the flour and use vegetable milk. (To roll the croquettes without egg, see Vol. 3, p. 76.)

For more information about the ingredients, see: Millet, Vol. 1, p. 76; onion, Vol. 2, p. 142; flour, Vol. 1, p. 68; milk, Vol. 1, p. 182; egg, Vol. 1, p. 218.

HEALTH COUNSELS

Millet is a very nutritious cereal containing more ***protein*** than wheat, rice, or corn. In this recipe, millet and wheat proteins are combined with those of milk and egg, increasing the biological value of the dish.

These croquettes have the advantage of supplying protein and ***calories*** that are *easy* to digest, with a *good proportion* of ***fiber*** from whole wheat. They are *low* in ***cholesterol*** and in ***saturated fat,*** quite appropriate for **children, youth, sports enthusiasts,** and **physical laborers.**

NUTRITIONAL VALUE* per serving

Energy	222 kcal = 927 kj
Protein	9.43 g
Carbohydrates	30.6 g
Fiber	3.56 g
Total fat	*5.50 g*
Saturated fat	*2.32 g*
Cholesterol	*73.6 mg*
Sodium	*58.7 mg*

1% 2% 4% 10% 20% 40% 100%

% Daily Value (based on a 2,000 calorie diet) provided by each serving of this dish

CALORIC PROPORTION*

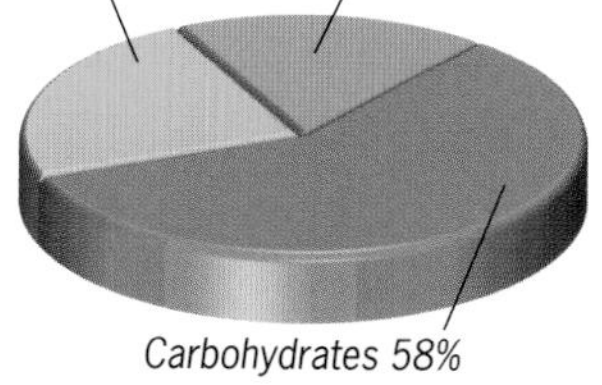

Percentage distribution of **calories for each nutrient**

* Additional ingredients not included.

Preparation time 00:15

Cooking time 00:50

Carrot Croquettes

INGREDIENTS (4 servings)

- 250 g (≅ 2 cups) **carrots**
- 1 **onion**
- 50 g (≅ 3/8 cup) **whole flour**
- 300 ml (≅ 1 1/4 cup) **milk**
- 1 **egg**
- 50 g (≅ 1 cup) **bread** crumbs

ADDITIONAL INGREDIENTS

- 3 tablespoons olive **oil** (each tablespoon of oil adds around 120 kcal to the recipe, that is, 30 kcal per serving)
- Sea **salt** (see Vol. 3, p. 16)

PREPARATION

1. Wash, peel, and shred the onion and carrots.
2. Heat the oil in a frying pan and sauté the onion until it becomes transparent. Add the carrots and cook for 5 additional minutes. Add the flour and stir for two more minutes. Remove from the stove.
   - While removed from the fire, add the cold milk little by little and stir constantly to avoid the formation of lumps. Return to the stove. Add the salt, and keep cooking until it thickens and becomes unstuck from the pan surface.
   - Pour into a large dish and let cool.
   - When the dough is cold, take spoonfuls and shape into the form of croquettes.
   - Roll in the beaten egg and the breadcrumbs.
   - Bake in a 220°C oven until the croquettes take on a golden color.
3. Serve hot.

HEALTHIER ALTERNATIVE: Instead of sautéing the carrots and the onion, steam them. Slightly toast the flour and use vegetable milk. (To roll the croquettes without egg, see Vol. 3, p. 76.)

For more information about the ingredients, see: Carrot, Vol. 2, p. 25; onion, Vol. 2, p. 142; flour, Vol. 1, p. 68; milk, Vol. 1, p. 182; egg, Vol. 1, p. 218.

When the onion becomes transparent, add the shredded carrots.

Add the flour after a few minutes.

Add the milk and stir with a wooden spoon.

Let the dough cool.

Suggestions from the Chef

They may be deep-fried. When done, place on soaking paper to rid excess oil.

HEALTH COUNSELS

Croquettes are a dish enjoyed by everyone, especially children and older people. These croquettes, prepared with carrot, offer significant health benefits over those prepared with meat or fish.

First, these croquettes contain *very little* ***saturated fat.*** Second, they provide a *good source* of ***beta-carotene*** (provitamin A) and ***fiber*** from carrots.

Beta-carotene is essential for healthy skin and mucosae. Furthermore, it is an *antioxidant* able to *slow* premature **aging** and to *protect from* **arteriosclerosis** and **cancer.**

Those who need to control their **cholesterol** levels should prepare these croquettes with vegetable milk and without eggs.

Beta-carotene

Beta-carotene *or* ***provitamin A*** *is a vegetable pigment of orange or yellow color. That is the reason why vegetables that produce it are of these colors. The organism transforms this substance into* ***vitamin A*** *as needed so there is* ***no risk*** *of an* ***overdose.***

It is not so with vitamin A found in animal products (especially in liver) and in pharmaceutical supplements. There is a risk of ***hypervitaminosis A*** *(vitamin A toxicity,* *see Vol. 1, p. 389**) when using these products.*

NUTRITIONAL VALUE*
per serving

Energy	**201 kcal = 841 kj**
Protein	**8.69 g**
Carbohydrates	**27.0 g**
Fiber	**4.38 g**
Total fat	***5.10 g***
Saturated fat	***2.25 g***
Cholesterol	***74.0 mg***
Sodium	***79.9 mg***

1% 2% 4% 10% 20% 40% 100%

% Daily Value (based on a 2,000 calorie diet) provided by each serving of this dish

CALORIC PROPORTION*

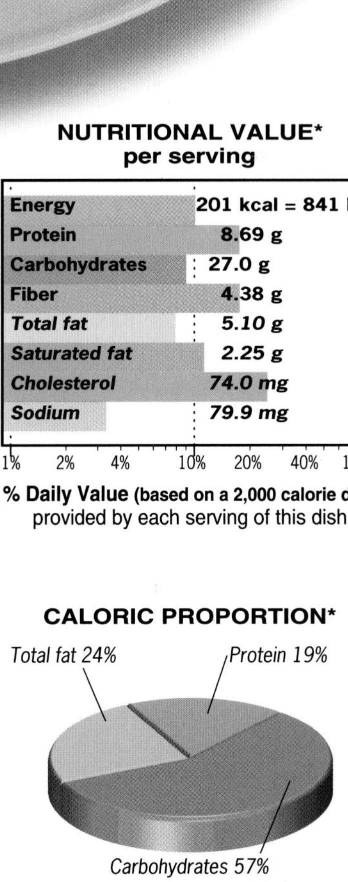

Percentage distribution of
calories for each nutrient

* Additional ingredients not included.

Preparation time 00:15 | Cooking time 00:30

Spanish Omelet

INGREDIENTS (4 servings)

- 500 g (≅ 1 pound) **potatoes**
- 3 **eggs**
- 1 **onion**

ADDITIONAL INGREDIENTS

- 5 tablespoons olive **oil** (each tablespoon of oil adds around 120 kcal to the recipe, that is, 30 kcal per serving)
- Sea **salt** (see Vol. 3, p. 16)

For more information about the ingredients, see: Potato, Vol. 2, p. 201; egg, Vol. 1, p. 218; onion, Vol. 2, p. 142.

PREPARATION

❶ Peel, wash, and chop the potatoes into thin slices.
- Peel and chop the onion.

❷ Heat 3 tablespoons of oil in a frying pan and fry the potatoes on a low flame. After turning them twice, add the onion and the salt. Stir occasionally until they become golden and tender.
- Beat the eggs in a deep bowl. Add the fried potatoes and onion and mix well.
- Heat the remaining oil in a frying pan. Pour the mixture into the pan when the oil is warm. Keep a high flame to cook the egg, and then reduce to the minimum. At this time it is very important not to stir, but to shake the frying pan to prevent the omelet from sticking (use a non-stick frying pan). Turn the omelet over so it becomes golden on both sides.

❸ Serve hot.

HEALTHIER ALTERNATIVE: In order to make this omelet without eggs, see Vol. 3, p. 76.

Cut potatoes into thin slices.

Fry potatoes and onions on a low flame.

Cook the omelet on both sides.

Suggestions from the Chef

If some of the potatoes are substituted by zucchini, the result will be a smoother and creamier omelet.

NUTRITIONAL VALUE*
per serving

Energy	**160 kcal = 670 kj**
Protein	**8.13 g**
Carbohydrates	**19.5 g**
Fiber	**2.28 g**
Total fat	***4.67 g***
Saturated fat	***1.43 g***
Cholesterol	***191 mg***
Sodium	***63.8 mg***

1% 2% 4% 10% 20% 40% 100%

% Daily Value (based on a 2,000 calorie diet)
provided by each serving of this dish

HEALTH COUNSELS

This typical Spanish dish is very appropriate for picnics and excursions. It supplies some ***calories*** and ***carbohydrates*** from potatoes, and high-quality ***protein*** from both eggs and potatoes. It also supplies ***vitamins A, B*** (including ***B12***), ***D,*** and ***E.***

Those with a tendency to high levels of **cholesterol** or those prone to **arteriosclerosis** should be *cautious* when using this dish, as it is not recommendable for them to have more than two eggs a week. However, this potato omelet is generally less adverse for health than meat, especially red meat and sausage.

Children, adolescents, sportsmen and **active persons** in general can *best tolerate* eggs and take better advantage of their nutritional properties.

As the main ingredients in Spanish Omelet are eggs and potatoes, which are easy to digest and assimilate, the dish is appropriate for those with a delicate **digestive system, malnourished** individuals, or people **convalescing** from weakening diseases or from surgery.

CALORIC PROPORTION*

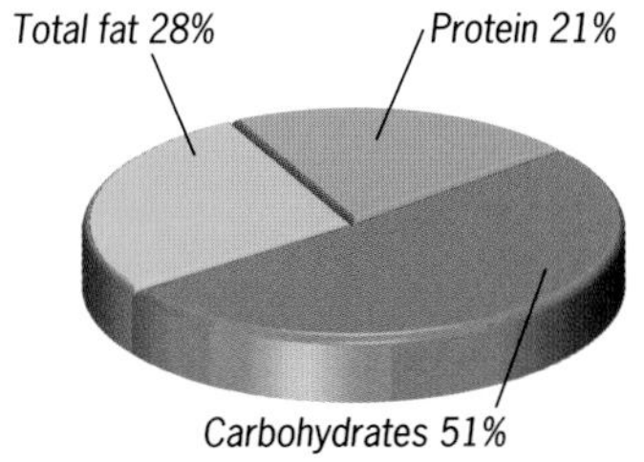

Percentage distribution of
calories for each nutrient

* Additional ingredients not included.

Preparation time 00:15 | Cooking time 00:40

Chinese Stir-Fry

INGREDIENTS (4 servings)

- 500 g (≅ 1 pound) **soybean sprouts**
- 50 g (≅ 1.75 oz) dried **shiitake mushrooms**
- 200 g (≅ 7 oz) **Marinated Gluten with Vegetables** (Vol. 3, p. 53)
- 8 **garlic** cloves
- 1 **carrot**
- 1 tablespoon **corn flour**
- 1/2 liter (≅ 1/2 quart) unsalted **vegetable broth**

ADDITIONAL INGREDIENTS

- **Ginger**
- 3 tablespoons of **soy sauce** (each tablespoon of this sauce adds 8 kcal and 857 mg of sodium to the recipe, that is, around 2 kcal and 214 mg of sodium per serving)
- The juice of 1/2 **lemon**
- 2 tablespoons of sesame or olive **oil** (each tablespoon of oil adds around 120 kcal to the recipe, that is, 30 kcal per serving)
- Sea **salt** (see Vol. 3, p. 16)

PREPARATION

❶ Soak the mushrooms in warm water for 15 minutes. Wash them and chop them.

- Peel and chop very fine the garlic and carrot, together with the ginger and gluten.

❷ If the soybean sprouts are fresh, they may be scalded.

- Heat the oil in a pot, and stir-fry the garlic and ginger. Add the mushrooms, stir, and add the marinated gluten, soybean sprouts, vegetable broth, and salt. Reduce the flame, cover, and simmer for 20 minutes. Stir occasionally.
- Lastly, add the carrot, a tablespoon of soy sauce, and the corn flour. Stir until it thickens.

❸ Serve immediately while hot.

HEALTHIER ALTERNATIVE: : Instead of sautéing the ingredients, add them raw to the boiling vegetable broth.

For more information about the ingredients, see: Soybean sprouts, Vol. 1, p. 86; shiitake mushrooms, Vol. 1, p. 151; gluten Vol. 2, p. 307; garlic, Vol. 1, p. 338; carrot, Vol. 2, p. 25; corn flour, Vol. 1, p. 69; and the *Encyclopedia of Medicinal Plants: Garlic,* p. 230.

HEALTH COUNSELS

This typical Chinese dish, made from soybean sprouts, mushrooms, and gluten, supplies a proportion of ***protein*** similar to that of meat. Besides, it contains ***carbohydrates*** and ***unsaturated fat,*** which help in the *reduction* of **cholesterol** levels. Soybean sprouts are rich in minerals, ***iron*** among them, as well as ***enzymes*** that make digestion easy.

Therefore, this Chinese Stir-Fry substitutes meat advantageously and it is very adequate for the time of transition to a healthier diet.

NUTRITIONAL VALUE* per serving

Energy	191 kcal = 800 kj
Protein	16.5 g
Carbohydrates	25.9 g
Fiber	6.65 g
Total fat	*1.81 g*
Saturated fat	*0.186 g*
Cholesterol	—
Sodium	*21.5 mg*

1% 2% 4% 10% 20% 40% 100%

% Daily Value (based on a 2,000 calorie diet) provided by each serving of this dish

CALORIC PROPORTION*

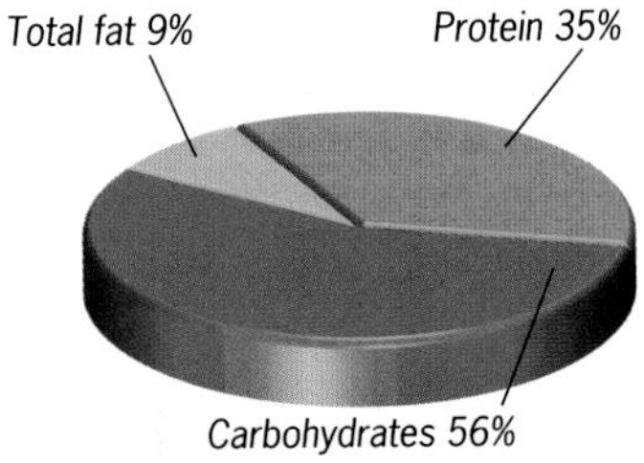

Percentage distribution of **calories for each nutrient**

* Additional ingredients not included.

Preparation time 00:10

Cooking time 00:30

Soy Hamburgers

INGREDIENTS (4 servings)

- 60 g (≅ 2 oz) **textured soy protein** (dried)
- 1 **onion**
- 1 **garlic** clove
- 1 tablespoon **bread** crumbs
- 1 tablespoon **corn flour**
- 1/2 liter (≅ 1/2 quart) of unsalted **vegetable broth**
- 1 **egg**

ADDITIONAL INGREDIENTS

- **Parsley**
- Sea **salt** (see Vol. 3, p. 16)

PREPARATION

❶ Soak the textured soy protein in the vegetable broth for 10 minutes.
- Peel and chop the onion and garlic, as well as the parsley (previously washed).
- Beat the egg.

❷ Combine all the ingredients.
- Knead and divide up into portions to be shaped as hamburgers.
- Place the hamburgers on an oven tray and bake at 220°C until they are golden on both sides. Turn once.

❸ Serve hot. They can be garnished with fresh tomatoes and potatoes.

For more information about the ingredients, see: Textured soy protein, Vol. 1, p. 89; onion, Vol. 2, p.142; garlic, Vol. 1, p. 338; egg, Vol. 1, p. 218; bread, Vol. 1, p. 70; and the *Encyclopedia of Medicinal Plants:* Garlic, p. 230.

HEALTH COUNSELS

Soy Hamburgers are notable for their wealth in high-quality protein, coming especially from soybean and egg.

Soy Hamburgers are endowed with many more advantages than their corresponding meat counterparts (see Vol. 1, p. 316). The first ones replace and even surpass the second ones in both nutritional value and taste. Unlike meat hamburgers, soy hamburgers:

✓ Are *low fat,* especially in saturated fat and ***cholesterol.***

✓ Are *free* from ***contaminating bacteria,*** which may be present in ground meat.

✓ Protect against **cancer,** unlike meat hamburgers that favor it.

Soy Hamburgers are especially adequate for **children, young people,** as well as anyone requiring a **significant supply of protein.**

NUTRITIONAL VALUE* per serving

Energy	110 kcal = 462 kj
Protein	15.1 g
Carbohydrates	7.16 g
Fiber	1.95 g
Total fat	*2.34 g*
Saturated fat	*0.591 g*
Cholesterol	*63.8 mg*
Sodium	*171 mg*

1% 2% 4% 10% 20% 40% 100%

% Daily Value (based on a 2,000 calorie diet) provided by each serving of this dish

CALORIC PROPORTION*

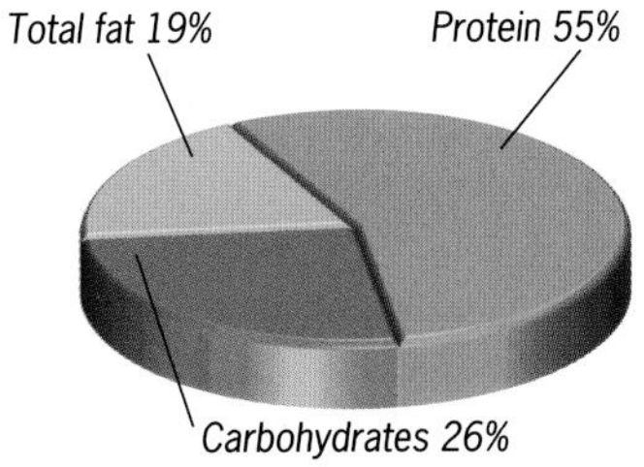

Percentage distribution of **calories for each nutrient**

* Additional ingredients not included.

Preparation time: - - - -

Cooking time: 00:50

Stuffed Eggs

INGREDIENTS (4 servings)

- 4 **eggs**
- 1 **eggplant**
- 5 tablespoons of **Traditional Mayonnaise** (Vol. 3, p. 58)

ADDITIONAL INGREDIENTS

- Sea **salt** (see Vol. 3, p. 16)

PREPARATION

❶ Boil the eggs for 12 minutes.
- Bake the eggplant in the oven. Let it cool. Peel it and chop it.
- Cut the hard-boiled eggs into halves and remove the yolks.

❷ Mix 1 tablespoon of mayonnaise together with the yolks, eggplant, and salt.
- Stuff the eggs with this mixture and arrange them upside down on a serving dish. Cover them with the remaining mayonnaise.

❸ Serve immediately.

HEALTHIER ALTERNATIVE: Mayonnaise may be prepared with soy milk (see Vol. 3, p. 305) and all or part of the yolks may be discarded.

Salmonellosis

*Eggs provide an **excellent environment** for the production of **germs,** among them, those causing **gastroenteritis** (such as salmonella).*

*To reduce this risk to the minimum, it is recommended to **boil** the eggs thoroughly, **discard** those with a broken shell or stained with feces, and **keep** them refrigerated.*

For more information about the ingredients, see: Egg, Vol. 1, p. 218; eggplant, Vol. 2, p. 256.

NUTRITIONAL VALUE* per serving

Energy	208 kcal = 868 kj
Protein	8.43 g
Carbohydrates	3.57 g
Fiber	1.91 g
Total fat	*17.2 g*
Saturated fat	*3.20 g*
Cholesterol	*255 mg*
Sodium	*78.6 mg*

1% 2% 4% 10% 20% 40% 100%

% Daily Value (based on a 2,000 calorie diet) provided by each serving of this dish

HEALTH COUNSELS

Eggs are *very nutritious* and *easy to digest.* For those *without* a tendency toward **arteriosclerosis,** eggs are an alternative to meat, with fewer health risks. Therefore, their use is appropriate for those wishing to follow a diet of transition to a healthier diet.

CALORIC PROPORTION*

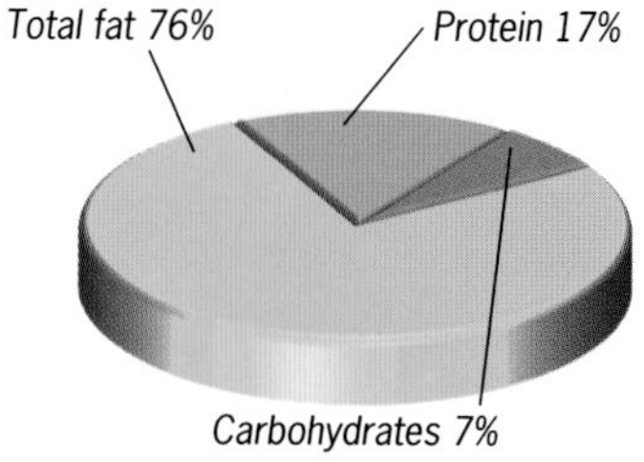

Percentage distribution of **calories for each nutrient**

* Additional ingredients not included.

Preparation time 00:15

Cooking time 00:15

Mushroom and Young Garlic Scrambled Eggs

INGREDIENTS (4 servings)

- 4 **eggs**
- 1 bunch **young garlic** (including leaves)
- 200 g (≅ 7 oz) **mushrooms**

ADDITIONAL INGREDIENTS

- **Parsley**
- 2 tablespoons olive **oil** (each tablespoon of oil adds around 120 kcal to the recipe, that is, 30 kcal per serving)
- Sea **salt** (see Vol. 3, p. 16)

PREPARATION

❶Peel and chop the young garlic.
- Clean and chop the mushrooms.
- Wash and chop the parsley.

❷Heat the oil in a frying pan and sauté the young garlic and mushrooms.
- When they are tender, add the eggs (slightly beaten), salt, and chopped parsley. Stir occasionally and, once the egg is cooked, remove from the stove.

❸Serve hot.

HEALTHIER ALTERNATIVE: Instead of sautéing the young garlic and mushrooms, broil them on a gridiron and either partially or totally discard the egg yolks.

For more information about the ingredients, see: Eggs, Vol. 1, p. 218; garlic, Vol. 1, p. 338; mushrooms, Vol. 1, p. 152; and the *Encyclopedia of Medicinal Plants:* Garlic, p. 230.

HEALTH COUNSELS

This is a dish *high* in ***protein*** from eggs and mushrooms. It contains some ***fat*** from the egg yolks, and a *few* ***carbohydrates.***

Due to its high-protein content, this dish offers advantages over meat since the protein from eggs is of *higher biological quality* and is *better assimilated.* Although eggs include some health risks (see Vol. 1, p. 225), these risks are fewer and smaller that those of meat (see Vol. 1, p. 300).

In addition to protein, mushrooms supply ***B-complex vitamins*** and ***minerals.*** Garlic supplies ***phytochemical elements*** that reduce **cholesterol, blood pressure,** and the risk of **cancer.**

NUTRITIONAL VALUE* per serving

Energy	229 kcal = 958 kj
Protein	13.8 g
Carbohydrates	29.2 g
Fiber	2.29 g
Total fat	*6.61 g*
Saturated fat	*1.96 g*
Cholesterol	*255 mg*
Sodium	*92.0 mg*

1% 2% 4% 10% 20% 40% 100%

% Daily Value (based on a 2,000 calorie diet) provided by each serving of this dish

CALORIC PROPORTION*

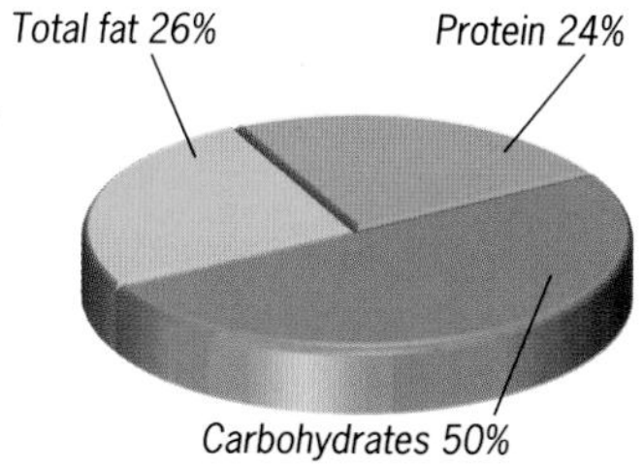

Percentage distribution of **calories for each nutrient**

* Additional ingredients not included.

Preparation time 00:15 | Cooking time 00:45

Stuffed Eggplant

INGREDIENTS (4 servings)

- 4 **eggplants**
- 2 **tomatoes**
- 150 g (≅ 5.3 oz) ground **vegetarian meat analogs** (you may use the commercially available vegetarian meat or gluten, see Vol. 3, p. 52)
- 1 **onion**
- 300 g (≅ 10.6 oz) **White Sauce** (Vol. 3, p. 59)

ADDITIONAL INGREDIENTS

- 3 tablespoons olive **oil** (each tablespoon of oil adds around 120 kcal to the recipe, that is, 30 kcal per serving)
- Sea **salt** (see Vol. 3, p. 16)

PREPARATION

❶Peel and chop the onion and the tomato.
- Empty the eggplant pulp leaving 1/2 cm of thickness around the skin. Arrange them in a baking dish.
- Chop the pulp.

❷Heat the oil in a frying pan and sauté the onion. When it is transparent, add the chopped pulp and tomato.
- When the vegetable fluids have evaporated through the cooking process, add the meat analogs and the salt. Sauté for an additional 3 minutes.
- Stuff the eggplants with the sauté, cover with the white sauce, and bake for 30 minutes in a 220°C preheated oven.

❸Serve hot.

HEALTHIER ALTERNATIVE: Instead of sautéing the ingredients, steam them in their own juices on a low flame.

For more information about the ingredients, see: Eggplant, Vol. 2, p. 256; tomato, Vol. 2, p. 275; meat analogs, Vol. 1, p. 332; onion, Vol. 2, p. 142.

Suggestions from the Chef

The meat analogs can be substituted by **tofu, gluten,** or previously hydrated **textured soy protein.**

Shredded cheese may be added on top of the white sauce (or without white sauce) and melted in the oven.

HEALTH COUNSELS

Baked eggplant, accompanied by gluten and vegetables, makes up a tasty and nutritious dish, which, from the viewpoint of health, substitutes with advantage the equivalent dishes made with meat. For example, it is ***cholesterol-free,*** *low* in saturated fat, and contains ***fiber.***

Eggplant is *diuretic, cleansing,* and *high* in ***fiber.*** Its preventive action against **cancer** multiplies when combined with soy-based vegetarian meat, tomatoes, and olive oil, as in this recipe.

NUTRITIONAL VALUE* per serving

Energy	282 kcal = 1,179 kj
Protein	13.1 g
Carbohydrates	22.7 g
Fiber	11.1 g
Total fat	*13.4 g*
Saturated fat	*2.00 g*
Cholesterol	—
Sodium	*359 mg*

1% 2% 4% 10% 20% 40% 100%

% Daily Value (based on a 2,000 calorie diet) provided by each serving of this dish

CALORIC PROPORTION*

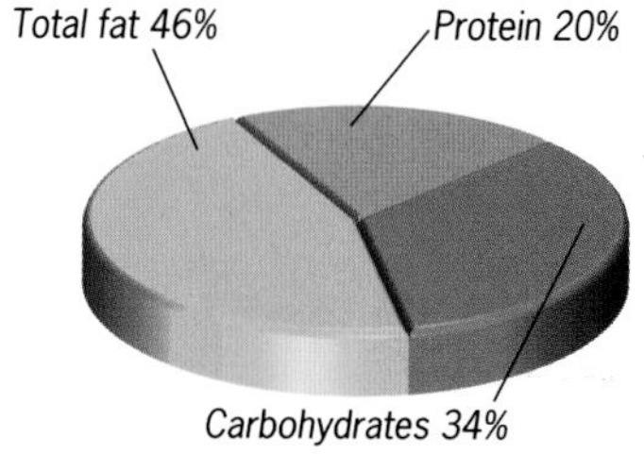

Percentage distribution of **calories for each nutrient**

* Additional ingredients not included.

Preparation time 00:20 Cooking time 00:15

'Cordon Bleu' Eggplant

INGREDIENTS (4 servings)

- 2 **eggplants**
- 8 **tender cheese** slices
- 1 **egg**
- 4 tablespoons **whole flour**
- 25 g (≅ 1/2 cup) **bread** crumbs
- 1 **garlic** clove

ADDITIONAL INGREDIENTS

- 1 **lemon** (rind)
- 6 tablespoons olive **oil** (each tablespoon of oil adds around 120 kcal to the recipe, that is, 30 kcal per serving)
- Sea **salt** (see Vol. 3, p. 16)

PREPARATION

❶ Slice the eggplant and soak in salted water and lemon rind to eliminate any possible bitterness.
- Grind in a mortar the garlic and salt.
- Beat the egg and combine it with the ground mixture and the flour.
- After the soaking is finished, drain the eggplant, place a slice of cheese between two eggplant slices, and roll in beaten egg and bread crumbs.

❷ Heat the oil in a frying pan and fry the breaded eggplant.
- Lay on absorbent paper to eliminate the excess oil.

❸ Serve immediately.

HEALTHIER ALTERNATIVE: Instead of frying the eggplant and cheese, bake. (To batter without egg, see Vol. 3, p. 76.)

For more information about the ingredients, see: Eggplant, Vol. 2, p. 256; cheese, Vol. 1, p. 206; egg, Vol. 1, p. 218; flour, Vol. 1, p. 68; bread, Vol., 1, p. 70; garlic, Vol. 1, p. 338; and the *Encyclopedia of Medicinal Plants:* Garlic, p. 230.

Suggestions from the Chef

The secret of this dish is to serve it immediately, so that it is crunchy outside while tender and creamy inside.

HEALTH COUNSELS

Prepared in this way, eggplants may substitute, as far as nutrition and even taste, a meat steak. Although this recipe contains a *certain* amount of ***cholesterol,*** it is free from the many drawbacks of meat (see Vol. 1, p. 300). It is therefore useful in the context of a transition diet toward a healthier way of eating.

Eggplant has a beneficial effect upon health since it supplies ***fiber,*** facilitates the *functioning* of the **kidneys,** and even *prevents* **cancer.** Cheese in this recipe is a good source of ***calcium,*** and eggs provide ***protein, minerals,*** and ***vitamins.***

NUTRITIONAL VALUE* per serving

Energy	156 kcal = 653 kj
Protein	8.59 g
Carbohydrates	13.9 g
Fiber	3.28 g
Total fat	*6.39 g*
Saturated fat	*3.52 g*
Cholesterol	*73.0*
Sodium	*95.8 mg*

1% 2% 4% 10% 20% 40% 100%

% Daily Value (based on a 2,000 calorie diet) provided by each serving of this dish

CALORIC PROPORTION*

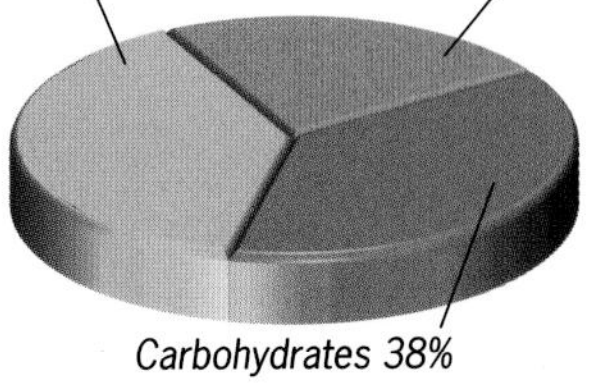

Percentage distribution of **calories for each nutrient**

* Additional ingredients not included.

Oat Medallions

INGREDIENTS (4 servings)

- 100 g (≅ 2/3 cup) **rolled oats**
- 1/2 liter (≅ 1/2 quart) **milk**
- 4 **eggs**
- 100 g (≅ 3.5 oz) **whole flour**
- The juice of 3 **lemons**
- Sea **salt** (see Vol. 3, p. 16)

ADDITIONAL INGREDIENTS

- 12 tablespoons of olive **oil** (each tablespoon of oil adds around 120 kcal to the recipe, that is, 30 kcal per serving)

PREPARATION

❶Soak the rolled oats in the milk for 30 minutes.

❷Boil the eggs for 12 minutes. Peel and chop them.

- Boil the milk and oats for 10 minutes, stirring occasionally to avoid sticking to the pan. After the set time, add the flour and salt and boil for a few more minutes. The result should be a thick, sticky, and manageable dough.
- Turn off the stove. Add the lemon juice, hard-boiled eggs, and stir well.
- Spread the dough over a tray (previously rinsed with cold water) to a 1.5 cm thickness.
- When it has cooled down, cut into 5-cm squares. They may also be triangles, or irregular shapes.
- Roll in the beaten egg and flour and fry in hot oil using a frying pan.

❸Serve garnished with lettuce leaves and lemon slices.

HEALTHIER ALTERNATIVE: Discard the egg yolks and bake instead of frying.

For more information about the ingredients, see: Oats, Vol. 2, p. 41; milk, Vol. 1, p. 182; flour, Vol. 1, p. 68; egg, Vol. 1, p. 218; lemon, Vol. 2, p. 124.

Add the flour and the salt to the boiled rolled oats.

Add the hard-boiled eggs.

Spread the dough and let cool.

Cut the dough into portions.

Cardiovascular Diseases

*Those suffering from a high risk of cardiovascular disease caused by arteriosclerosis, should not use egg yolk in their diets, or **at most,** two **a week** (see Vol. 1, p. 226).*

In these cases, the ideal practice is to use the "HEALTHIER ALTERNATIVE" for this recipe.

NUTRITIONAL VALUE*
per serving

Energy	356 kcal = 1,487 kj
Protein	19.4 g
Carbohydrates	38.0 g
Fiber	5.82 g
Total fat	*12.9 g*
Saturated fat	*4.84 g*
Cholesterol	*272 mg*
Sodium	*139 mg*

1% 2% 4% 10% 20% 40% 100%

% Daily Value (based on a 2,000 calorie diet) provided by each serving of this dish

HEALTH COUNSELS

This is a very complete and nutritional dish, which supplies high-quality ***protein*** from oats, milk, and eggs. It also contains ***carbohydrates, fiber, minerals,*** and ***vitamins.***

Due to its nutritional value, flavor, and satisfying effect, this dish may advantageously substitute other equivalent dishes prepared with meat.

Although it contains ***cholesterol*** coming from the eggs, this recipe is free from the majority of adverse effects of meat (Vol. 1, p. 300). Therefore, it is recommended to those who wish to follow a transition recipe in order to arrive at a plant-based diet. It is also beneficial to those in need of a greater supply of protein, such as **children, adolescents,** as well as **pregnant** and **nursing** women.

Oats supply many benefits to health. Due to its content in ***unsaturated fatty acids, phosphorus, lecithin,*** and ***vitamin B_1,*** this recipe strengthens and balances the ***nervous system.*** Besides, because of its high fiber content, it regulates the **bowel movement.**

CALORIC PROPORTION*

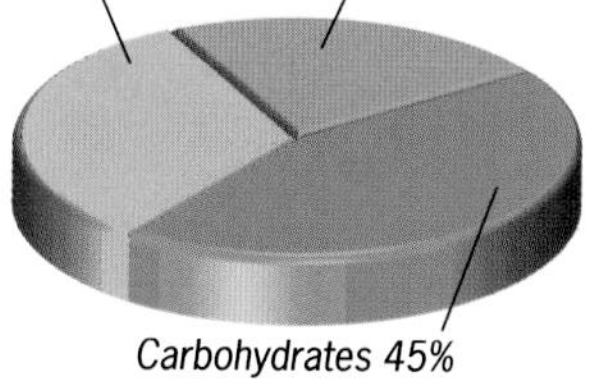

Percentage distribution of
calories for each nutrient

* Additional ingredients not included.

Preparation time 00:15 | Cooking time 0 1:00

Banana Casserole

INGREDIENTS

- 3 **plantains** (cooking bananas)
- 400 g **vegetarian meat analogs** (you may use the commercially available vegetarian meat or gluten, see Vol. 3, p. 52)
- 2 **eggs**
- 250 ml (≅ 1 cup) **milk**
- 1 **onion**
- 2 sweet **green peppers**
- 12 **green olives**
- 100 g (≅ 3.5 oz) grated **tender cheese**
- 6 tablespoons olive **oil**

PREPARATION

❶ Peel and chop the onions and peppers.
- Grind the meat analogs.

❷ Boil the plantains in water until they are tender. Drain and mash. Add the milk and 2 tablespoons of oil to the mashed plantains.
- Boil the eggs for 12 minutes. Cool them in cold water. Peel and chop.
- Using the remaining oil, sauté the meat analogs and add onion, pepper, hard-boiled eggs and green olives. Keep on the stove for an additional 5 minutes.
- Grease an ovenproof casserole. Put a layer of half of the plantain mixture, a layer with the sautéed ingredients, and lastly, a layer of the other half of the plantain.
- Cover with the grated cheese and bake for 30 minutes in a preheated oven at 175°C.

❸ Serve immediately.

HEALTHIER ALTERNATIVE: Instead of sautéing the ingredients, steam them, reduce the amount of oil, and discard the egg yolks.

For more information about the ingredients, see: Plantain, Vol. 2, p. 72; meat analogs, Vol. 1, p. 332; egg. 1, p.218; milk, Vol. 1, p. 182; onion, Vol. 2, p. 142; pepper, Vol. 2, p. 198; olive, Vol. 2, p. 165; cheese, Vol. 1, p. 206.

NUTRITIONAL VALUE per 100 g

Energy	**177 kcal = 739 kj**
Protein	**7.05 g**
Carbohydrates	**10.5 g**
Fiber	**1.65 g**
Total fat	***12.2 g***
Saturated fat	***2.78 g***
Cholesterol	***33.2***
Sodium	***285 mg***

1% 2% 4% 10% 20% 40% 100%

% Daily Value (based on a 2,000 calorie diet) provided by each 100 g of this dish

HEALTH COUNSELS

This is a very nutritious dish containing high-quality ***protein*** from vegetarian meat and eggs. At the same time, it supplies a *limited* amount of ***fat, calories*** and ***cholesterol.*** Those in need of a significant supply of protein who do not wish to use meat or meat products will highly benefit from this dish.

Plantains are used widely in the Central American cuisine. They add ***carbohydrates*** and ***fiber*** to this recipe. These components are missing in the equivalent dishes prepared with meat.

CALORIC PROPORTION

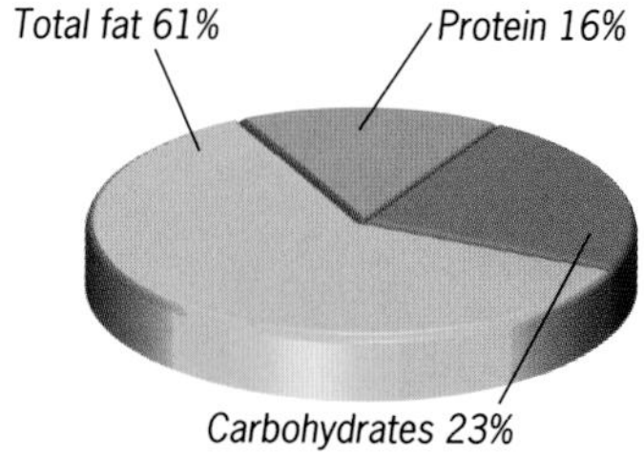

Percentage distribution of **calories for each nutrient**

Carrot Cake

INGREDIENTS

- 1 kg **carrots**
- 150 g (≅ 1 1/4 cup) **white flour**
- 150 g (≅ 1 1/4 cup) **whole flour**
- 4 **eggs**
- 200 g (≅ 1 cup) **brown sugar**
- 1 teaspoon **baking powder**

PREPARATION

❶ Peel the carrots.
- Separate the egg yolks and beat the whites until stiff.

❷ Boil the carrots and mash them.
- Mix the baking powder into the flour.
- Combine all ingredients except the egg whites, which will be added very carefully at the last moment.
- Place the dough into a previously greased baking pan. Bake in a 180°C oven for 40 minutes. Test for doneness by introducing a toothpick and checking that it comes out clean.
- Remove from the pan while hot and let cool.

❸ Serve.

HEALTHIER ALTERNATIVE: Discard the egg yolks, and beat the whites vigorously with a little bit of salt. This technique helps to reduce the amount of baking powder.

For more information about the ingredients, see: Carrot, Vol. 2, p. 25; flour, Vol. 1, p. 68; egg, Vol. 1, p.218; sugar, Vol. 1, p. 170.

HEALTH COUNSELS

This dessert supplies a certain amount of ***protein*** and other nutrients coming mainly from eggs and carrots.

Although this recipe includes a *certain amount* of ***cholesterol,*** it also contains substances that protect the arteries from the adverse effect of this substance. This is the case of ***beta-carotene*** (provitamin A) and ***fiber,*** which come from carrots. This partially compensates for the undesirable effect of eggs.

This dessert is good for those who need a nutritional dish that is delicious and satisfying, without the adverse effects of other high-fat and refined desserts.

NUTRITIONAL VALUE per 100 g

Energy	162 kcal = 677 kj
Protein	4.15 g
Carbohydrates	31.0 g
Fiber	2.85 g
Total fat	1.64 g
Saturated fat	0.459 g
Cholesterol	55.4 mg
Sodium	40.3 mg

1% 2% 4% 10% 20% 40% 100%

% Daily Value (based on a 2,000 calorie diet) provided by each 100 g of this dish

CALORIC PROPORTION*

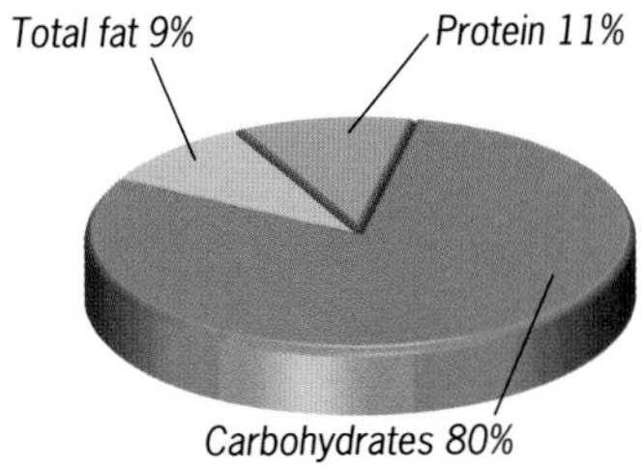

Percentage distribution of **calories for each nutrient**

Chapter Index

Volume 3

PAGE

43. Recipes for the Eyes 128
44. Recipes for the Nervous System 142
45. Recipes for the Heart 160
46. Recipes for the Arteries ... 180
47. Recipes for the Blood 202
48. Recipes for the Respiratory System ... 214
49. Recipes for the Liver and the Gallbladder 226
50. Recipes for the Stomach .. 238
51. Recipes for the Intestine ... 256
52. Recipes for the Urinary System 274
53. Recipes for the Reproductive System .. 294
54. Recipes for Metabolism 306
55. Recipes for the Musculoskeletal System ... 328
56. Recipes for the Skin 344
57. Recipes for the Infections .. 356
58. Recipes to Prevent Cancer . 368

ENCYCLOPEDIA OF

FOODS

HEALTHY RECIPES

PART FOUR

Recipes that Prevent and Heal

*To cook well, to place wholesome food upon
the table in an inviting manner,
requires intelligence and experience.
The one who prepares the food
that is to be placed in the stomach, to be converted
into blood to nourish the system,
occupies a most important and elevated position.*

ELLEN G. WHITE
North American writer and educator (1827-1915)

4

43 RECIPES FOR THE EYES

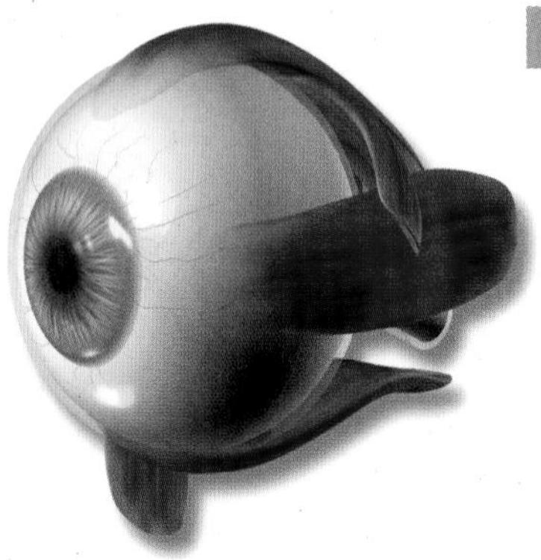

CHAPTER SUMMARY

RECIPES

Apricot Shake *141*
Cream of Pumpkin *134*
Potatoes and Spinach *138*
Quinoa Risotto *136*
Rice with Carrots *133*
Spinach Salad *132*
Spinach Shake *140*

Recipes that promote good visual health should provide antioxidant vitamins A, C, and E (see Vol. 2, p. 22).

ABOUT **fifty percent** of the population in industrialized countries uses **corrective lenses** (spectacles or contact lenses). While it may be true that the use of aids is not always essential, it is certain that a large number of school children lag behind for lack of appropriate corrective lenses. This is a barrier when reading out of textbooks and whiteboards (blackboards).

As with any other human body organ, the eyes need to be appropriately nourished. In the case of the eyes, although they are highly complex, delicate, and their function is fundamental, they do not make many nutritional demands, as indicated before (Vol. 2, p. 22), and they "need very little."

Now, the fact that they need very little does not indicate that the lack of essentials will not affect them. In fact, the opposite is true. Commonly, many people who **change from** a diet ***low in*** **vegetables to one** ***containing more*** report feeling better in all areas:

- They experience an increase in energy and vitality.
- Their skin and hair take on a new shine and their nails become stronger.
- Their digestion becomes easier and intestinal functions are more regular.
- Their night rest improves and becomes more restorative.
- They suffer less from infectious diseases, such as flu and colds.
- Their breath becomes cleaner.
- And **their eyesight improves.**

And this is logical, as nutritional imbalance caused by a deficient diet affects all body organs, and more especially those of a more sensitive nature.

An appropriate diet may also protect against **cataracts** (see Vol. 2, p. 23).

The lack of carotenoids (provitamin A) is especially noticeable in **car drivers** who suffer from so-called **night blindness** and lack of adaptability to changes in light (see Vol. 2, p. 24).

The dishes suggested in this chapter can protect the eyes and sight, and **visual acuity** (see Vol. 2, p. 24) may even improve.

Menus for

Visual Acuity

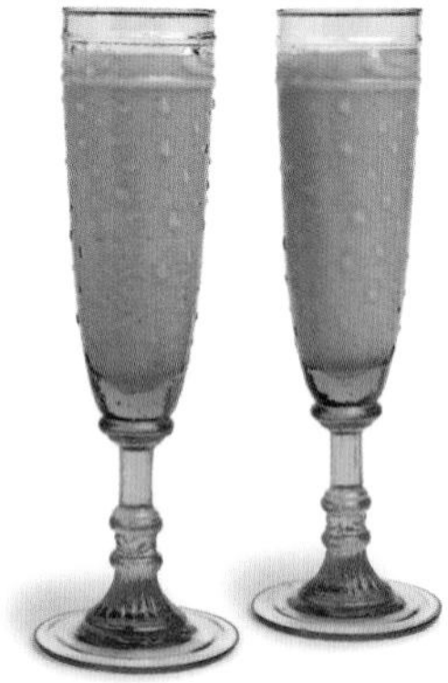

Apricot Shake

BREAKFAST

- "Apricot Shake" (Vol. 3, p. 141)
- "Rye Bread" with blueberry or blackberry jams (Vol. 3, p. 194; Vol. 2, p. 257; Vol. 1, p. 49)

Spinach Salad

LUNCH

- "Cabbage Juice" (Vol. 2, p. 191)
- "Spinach Salad" (Vol. 3, p. 132)
- "Rice with Carrots" (Vol. 3, p. 133)
- "Stuffed Peppers" (Vol. 3, p. 382)
- "Whole Bread" (Vol. 3, Sp. 46; Vol. 1, p. 72)

Cream of Pumpkin

SUPPER

- "Cream of Pumpkin" (Vol. 3, p. 134)
- "Mango Custard" (Vol. 3, p. 354)

HEALTH COUNSELS

This menu is *very rich* in ***vitamin A*** and in vegetable ***antioxidants.*** It helps to keep eyes in good health, to prevent the loss of visual acuity, and to improve one's adaptation to **night vision.**

Virtually all ingredients in this recipe contain ***beta-carotene*** (provitamin A) as well as other ***antioxidant carotenoids,*** which protect the retina and other components of the eye, as well as the skin and mucosae of the entire body.

Macular Degeneration of the Retina

BREAKFAST

- "Spinach Shake" (Vol. 3, p. 140)
- "Carrot Cake" (Vol. 3, p. 125)
- Oranges (Vol. 2, p. 360)
- Wheat germ (Vol. 2, p. 310)

Spinach Shake

LUNCH

- "Filled Cucumbers" (Vol. 3, p. 348)
- "Quinoa Risotto" (Vol. 3, p. 136)
- "Spinach Lasagna" (Vol. 3, p. 108)
- "Whole Bread" (Vol. 3, p. 46; Vol. 1, p. 72)

Quinoa Risotto

SUPPER

- "Potatoes and Spinach" (Vol. 3, p. 138)
- Mango (Vol. 2, p. 341)

Potatoes and Spinach

HEALTH COUNSELS

This menu is high in ***beta-carotene*** (provitamin A) and other vegetable ***carotenoids*** whose *antioxidant* effects are transformed into vitamin A in the organism. Spinach is one of the main ingredients because of its proven action to prevent macular degeneration of the retina, the most common cause of blindness in old persons.

That is why this menu is recommended to those wishing to keep their vision in optimal condition until late in life.

the Eyes

Cataracts, Glaucoma, etc.

BREAKFAST

- "Melon and Orange Juice" (Vol. 3, p. 367)
- "Granola" (Vol. 3, p. 156)
- "Soy Milk" (Vol. 3, p. 305)

Granola

Vegetable Juice

LUNCH

- "Vegetable Juice" (Vol. 3, p. 385)
- "Riviera Salad" (Vol. 3, p. 206)
- "Rice with Spinach" (Vol. 3, p. 192)
- "Carrots Croquettes" (Vol. 3, p. 112)
- "Rye Bread" (Vol. 3, p. 194)

SUPPER

- "Leek, Potato, and Pumpkin Stew" (Vol. 3, p. 281)
- Apricots (Vol. 2, p. 26)

Leek, Potato, and Pumpkin Stew

HEALTH COUNSELS

This menu is designed to contribute to the prevention of several ophthalmological conditions, such as cataracts and glaucoma. It supplies good amounts of ***antioxidant vitamins—A, C,*** and ***E,*** as well as ***type B vitamins*** and ***trace minerals,*** all of which help to keep the eyes in good health.

Besides, this menu *does not contain* ***dairy*** products and is *low* in ***fat.*** These are dietary requirements to prevent the most common ophthalmological conditions.

Other Recipes for the Eyes

SALADS

- In preparing salads, use carrots, spinach, wheat germ, and sunflower seeds as main ingredients (Vol. 2, pp. 25, 28, 105, 310)

SOUPS AND PURÉES

- "Oat Soup" (Vol. 3, p. 147)

MAIN COURSES

- "Spaghetti with Spinach" (Vol. 3, p. 210)
- "Spinach Croquettes" (Vol. 3, p. 213)
- "Rice with Pumpkin" (Vol. 3, p. 193)
- "Chard with Potatoes and Pumpkin" (Vol. 3, p. 263)

BREAKFASTS, DESSERTS, AND SNACKS

- "Oranges with Honey" (Vol. 3, p. 366)
- "Cereal Bars" (Vol. 3, p. 174)

DRINKS

- Spinach juice (Vol. 2, p. 28)
- Carrot juice (Vol. 2, p. 25)
- Orange juice (Vol. 2, p. 360)

Infusions or decoctions:

- Herb Robert (*EMP,* p. 137)
- Cornflower (*EMP,* p. 131)
- Red Eyebright (*EMP,* p. 136)

- *See the recipe index at the beginning of this volume (Vol. 3, pp. 8-13).*
- *See also chapter 19, "Foods for the Eyes" (Vol. 2, pp. 22-29).*

EMP = Encyclopedia of Medicinal Plants, Education and Health Library, Editorial Safeliz.

Preparation time 00:20

Cooking time -- --

Spinach Salad

INGREDIENTS (4 servings)

- 200 g (≅ 7 cups) of **spinach**
- 4 **carrots**
- 100 g (≅ 3.5 oz) of **Savoy cabbage**
- 100 g (≅ 1 cup) of **pumpkin** (squash) pulp
- 8 **radishes**
- 2 tablespoons of **sesame seeds**
- 2 tablespoons of shelled **sunflower seeds**
- 1 tablespoon of **wheat germ**

ADDITIONAL INGREDIENTS

- **Parsley**
- The juice of 1 **lemon**
- 2 tablespoons of olive **oil** (each tablespoon of oil adds around 120 kcal to the recipe, that is, 30 kcal per serving)
- Sea **salt** (see Vol. 3, p. 16)

PREPARATION

❶Peel, wash, and chop each of the raw vegetables and arrange them on a platter with part of the sesame and sunflower seeds.

❷To prepare the dressing, grind the remaining sesame and sunflower seeds in a mortar and add this mixture to the wheat germ, the lemon juice, the olive oil, and the salt.

❸Dress at the time of serving.

For more information about the ingredients, see: Spinach, Vol. 2, p. 28; carrot, Vol. 2, p. 25; Savoy cabbage, Vol. 2, p. 193; pumpkin, Vol. 2, p. 97; radish, Vol. 2, p. 181; sesame, Vol. 1, p. 352; sunflower seeds, Vol. 2, p. 105; wheat germ, Vol. 2, p. 310; and the *Encyclopedia of Medicinal Plants:* Sesame, p. 611.

HEALTH COUNSELS

This Spinach Salad is a pleasant surprise as it allows the discovery of flavors from ingredients that are not normally eaten raw. It is very healthy due to its wealth of ***vitamins, trace minerals,*** and ***phytochemical elements*** that make this dish especially recommended to prevent:

✓**Diseases of the eye,** such as conjunctivitis, cataracts, night blindness, retinal degeneration, and loss of visual acuity. ***Provitamin A*** (beta-carotene) and other ***carotenoids*** that are contained in spinach, carrot, and pumpkin, also contribute to the prevention of abnormal eye conditions.

✓**Skin** disorders, such as **dryness, eczema,** and **dermatitis** in general.

✓**Congenital malformations,** due to its high content in ***folic acid*** and other ***vitamins.*** This salad should be part of the **pregnant woman's** diet.

✓**Cancer,** due to the *antioxidant* action of all these raw vegetables.

NUTRITIONAL VALUE* per serving

Energy	146 kcal = 611 kj
Protein	6.24 g
Carbohydrates	12.7 g
Fiber	7.49 g
Total fat	*6.34 g*
Saturated fat	*0.806 g*
Cholesterol	—
Sodium	*92.9 mg*

1% 2% 4% 10% 20% 40% 100%

% Daily Value (based on a 2,000 calorie diet) provided by each serving of this dish

CALORIC PROPORTION*

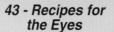

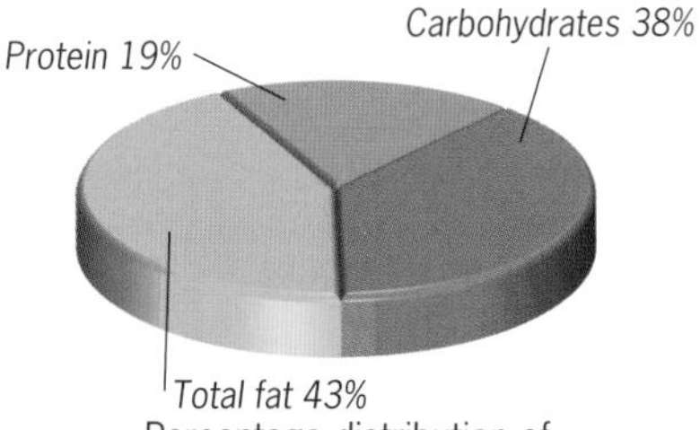

Percentage distribution of
calories for each nutrient

* Additional ingredients not included.

Preparation time: 00:15

Cooking time: 00:35

Rice with Carrots

INGREDIENTS (4 servings)

- 350 g (≅ 12.3 oz) of **whole rice**
- 250 g (≅ 8.8 oz) of **carrots**
- 1 **onion**
- 2 **garlic** cloves
- 800 ml (≅ 3 1/3 cups) of unsalted **vegetable broth**

ADDITIONAL INGREDIENTS

- **Parsley**
- 7 tablespoons of olive **oil** (each tablespoon of oil adds around 120 kcal to the recipe, that is, 30 kcal per serving)
- Sea **salt** (see Vol. 3, p. 16)

PREPARATION

❶ Soak the rice in cold water overnight or for 1 hour in very hot water.

- Peel and chop the carrots into slices and the onion into rings.
- Peel and chop garlic and parsley.

❷ Heat the oil in a large frying pan, and sauté the onion.

- When the onion is transparent, add the carrots.
- Add the drained rice after 3 minutes. Stir.
- In a separate pot, bring the vegetable broth and the salt to a boil.
- Add the boiling broth to the frying pan.
- Add the chopped garlic and parsley. Reduce heat to a minimum. Simmer until the rice is tender, dry, and fluffy (an additional 20-25 minutes).
- Remove from the heat and let rest for 5 minutes before serving.

❸ Serve hot.

HEALTHIER ALTERNATIVE: Instead of sautéing the ingredients, add them raw to the boiling vegetable broth.

HEALTH COUNSELS

This dish adequately combines the *nutritional* and *digestive properties* of rice together with the ***vitamins*** and *softening* effect of carrots. In addition, the vegetable broth enriches this dish with ***mineral salts*** that provide *diuretic* (urine elimination), *blood cleansing* and *alkalinizing* effects.

The use of this dish of rice with carrots effectively contributes to the prevention of the following disorders:

✓ **Vision problems** caused by the lack of ***beta-carotene*** (provitamin A), such as **irritation** of the conjunctiva, dry eyes, and insufficient adaptation to **darkness**.

✓ **Arteriosclerosis** and **myocardial infarction,** thanks to the *protective* action of the ***fiber*** in whole rice and the ***provitamin A*** contained in carrots and garlic. Besides, this is a very *low-**sodium***—if salt is not added—and *low-**saturated-fat*** dish with zero ***cholesterol.***

✓ **Irritable bowel syndrome** and **colitis,** because of the *softening* effect produced by rice and carrots upon the **intestinal *lining.***

For more information about the ingredients, see: Rice, Vol. 2, p. 225; carrot, Vol. 2, p. 25; onion, Vol. 2, p. 142; garlic, Vol. 1, p. 338; and the *Encyclopedia of Medicinal Plants:* Garlic, p. 230.

NUTRITIONAL VALUE* per serving

Energy	362 kcal = 1,515 kj
Protein	7.83 g
Carbohydrates	71.6 g
Fiber	5.59 g
Total fat	*2.54 g*
Saturated fat	*0.500 g*
Cholesterol	*—*
Sodium	*27.0 mg*

1% 2% 4% 10% 20% 40% 100%

% Daily Value (based on a 2,000 calorie diet) provided by each serving of this dish

CALORIC PROPORTION*

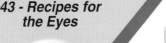

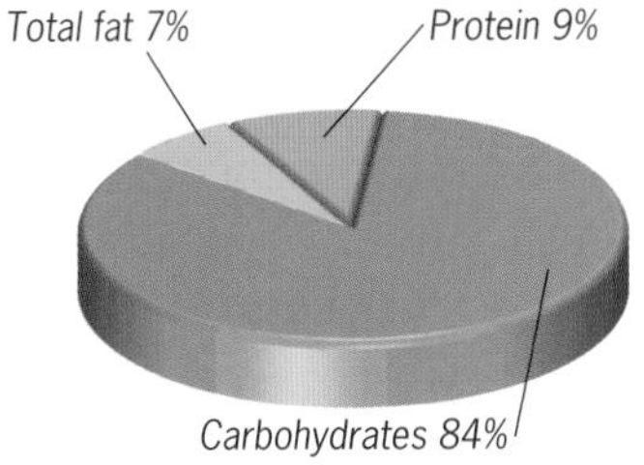

Percentage distribution of **calories for each nutrient**

* Additional ingredients not included.

Preparation time 00:20

Cooking time 00:30

Cream of Pumpkin

INGREDIENTS (4 servings)

- 500 g (≅ 1 pound) of **pumpkin** (squash)
- 300 g (≅ 2 cups) of **potatoes**
- 2 **leeks**
- 1 1/2 liters (≅ 1 1/2 quarts) of **water**

ADDITIONAL INGREDIENTS

- **Chives** to decorate
- 4 tablespoons of olive **oil** (each tablespoon of oil adds around 120 kcal to the recipe, that is, 30 kcal per serving)
- Sea **salt** (see Vol. 3, p. 16)

PREPARATION

❶ To clean the leeks, remove the outer layer and cut the stem lengthwise to reveal possible soil between the leaves. Wash thoroughly with running water while separating the leaves in order to clean any possible dirt from inside.

- Chop the leeks in very thin slices to avoid the presence of long threads when it is time to prepare the cream.
- Peel, wash, and chop the pumpkin and the potatoes into medium-size chunks.

❷ In a pot, bring the water and salt to a boil. Then add the vegetables.

- Boil 20 minutes (or until the vegetables are tender).
- Drain the vegetables and reserve the broth.
- Blend the vegetables to make a purée and dress with the raw olive oil.

❸ Serve hot and decorate with chives.

For more information about the ingredients, see: Pumpkin, Vol. 2, p. 97; potato, Vol. 2, p. 201; leek, Vol. 2, p. 319.

Cut the leek stems lengthwise.

Separate the leaves by holding them apart with your fingers and wash them under the faucet.

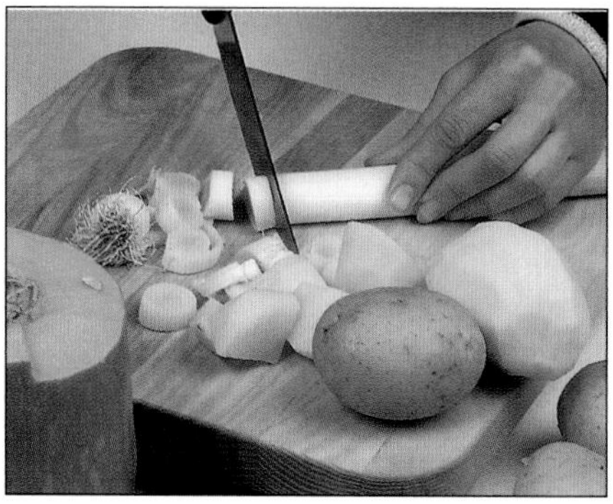

Cut the leek into slices.

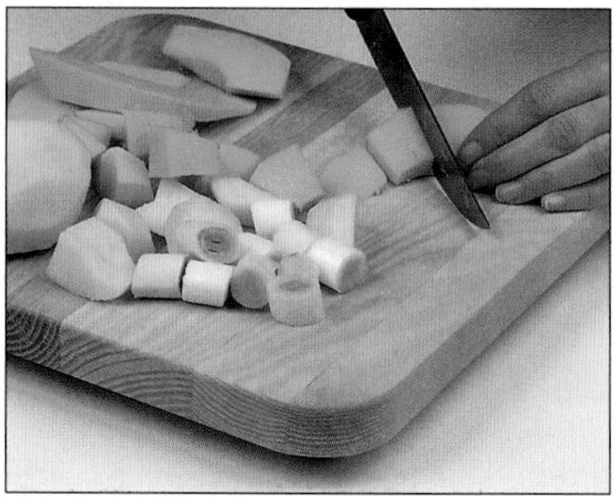

Chop the pumpkin and the potatoes.

Drain the vegetables after boiling.

Suggestions from the Chef

- This Cream of Pumpkin may be served accompanied by a **different color purée**—green, if a spinach purée; red, if a tomato or red pepper purée; or white, if an onion and zucchini purée.
- If a lighter cream is desired, add part of the broth used to boil the vegetables. Freeze the remainder for later use.

NUTRITIONAL VALUE* per serving

Energy	**112 kcal = 466 kj**
Protein	**3.18 g**
Carbohydrates	**23.5 g**
Fiber	**2.59 g**
Total fat	***0.348 g***
Saturated fat	***0.093 g***
Cholesterol	—
Sodium	***17.1 mg***

1% 2% 4% 10% 20% 40% 100%

% Daily Value (based on a 2,000 calorie diet) provided by each serving of this dish

CALORIC PROPORTION*

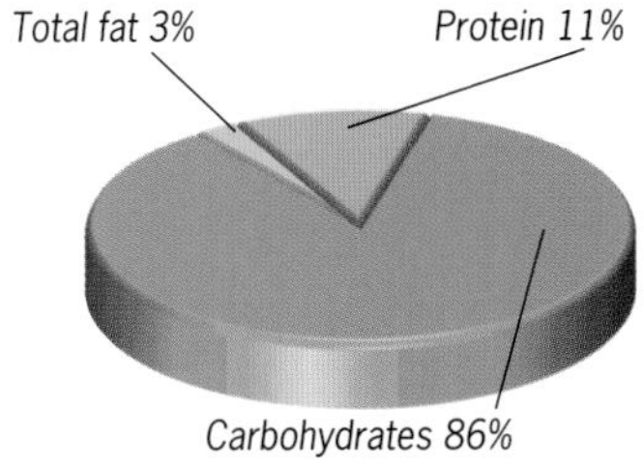

Percentage distribution of **calories for each nutrient**

* Additional ingredients not included.

HEALTH COUNSELS

The three major nutrients of **pumpkins,** the main ingredient in this dish, are beta-**carotene** (provitamin A), **vitamin C,** and **potassium.** All of them exert a beneficial effect upon **vision.** Cream of pumpkin is therefore recommended to prevent the following visual deficiencies:

- ✓**Loss of visual acuity,** both during the day and at night, thanks to beta-carotene (provitamin A) that improves retinal functioning.
- ✓**Cataracts,** because of the *antioxidant* effect of provitamin A and vitamin C, which slows down the process whereby the lens becomes opaque. Potassium contained in pumpkins also contributes to prevent cataracts.

Additionally, Cream of Pumpkin is recommended in these cases:

- ✓**Cancer prevention,** because of ***vitamins A* and *C,*** as well as the vegetable **fiber** found within.
- ✓**Kidney ailments,** for its *low*-**sodium** content and the pumpkin's protein.
- ✓**Prevention** of **arterial circulation** disorders, such as **high blood pressure, arteriosclerosis, apoplexy** attacks (thrombosis and cerebral hemorrhage), and **infarction.** This is because the dish is very *low*-**sodium**—if salt is limited—and also *low* in ***saturated fat,*** with *no* ***cholesterol.*** Besides, the fact that the dish is *high* in ***potassium*** helps to protect the arteries and the heart.
- ✓**Digestive** disorders, because it exerts a *neutralizing* influence when there is an excess of stomach acidity and it has a soft *laxative* effect as well as ability to *protect* the **intestinal *lining.***

Preparation time 00:15
Cooking time 00:25
43 - Recipes for the Eyes

Quinoa Risotto

INGREDIENTS (4 servings)

- 250 g (≅ 1 1/2 cup) of **quinoa**
- 600 g (≅ 21 oz) of **carrots**
- 1 **onion**
- 1 **garlic** clove
- 4 tablespoons of **Traditional Tomato Sauce** (Vol. 3, p. 62)
- 1/2 liter (≅ 1/2 quart) of unsalted **vegetable broth**

ADDITIONAL INGREDIENTS

- **Parsley**
- 4 tablespoons of olive **oil** (each tablespoon of oil adds around 120 kcal to the recipe, that is, 30 kcal per serving)
- Sea **salt** (see Vol. 3, p. 16)

For more information about the ingredients, see: Quinoa, Vol. 1, p. 77; carrot, Vol. 2, p. 25; onion, Vol. 2, p. 142; garlic, Vol. 1, p. 338; tomato, Vol. 2, p. 275; and the *Encyclopedia of Medicinal Plants:* Garlic, p. 230.

PREPARATION

❶ Peel, wash, and chop carrots into slices.
- Chop the onion and the garlic.

❷ Heat oil in a pot, and sauté the onion and the garlic until the onion becomes transparent.
- Add the carrots and stir for a few minutes.
- Add the quinoa seeds. Stir and sauté for 3 additional minutes.
- Add the vegetable broth, tomato sauce, and salt. Simmer for approximately 15 minutes.

❸ Garnish with parsley and serve hot.

HEALTHIER ALTERNATIVE: Instead of sautéing the ingredients, heat the vegetable broth and the tomato sauce. When it begins boiling, add the vegetables, quinoa seeds, and a pinch of salt.

Chop the carrots and the onion. Mince the garlic.

Sauté onion and garlic and add the carrots.

Finally, add the quinoa.

Quinoa

*Quinoa seeds are used **as a cereal.** Outside of the countries where it is grown, it may be found in stores specializing in import foods or health food stores.*

Suggestions from the Chef

Risotto is a typical Italian dish where a creamy touch is desired. If a traditional risotto is desired, quinoa seeds may be substituted for a type of rice that lets out starch without becoming soggy, such as the Italian varieties of round grain—"avorio" and "vialone."

NUTRITIONAL VALUE* per serving

Energy	**324 kcal = 1,354 kj**
Protein	**10.4 g**
Carbohydrates	**53.7 g**
Fiber	**9.08 g**
Total fat	***4.65 g***
Saturated fat	***0.515 g***
Cholesterol	—
Sodium	***68.1 mg***

1% 2% 4% 10% 20% 40% 100%

% Daily Value (based on a 2,000 calorie diet) provided by each serving of this dish

HEALTH COUNSELS

Although sometimes associated with certain types of rice or wheat, **quinoa** is not a true cereal. It is the seed of a **herbaceous plant** from the Chenopodiaceae botanical family, just as chard, spinach, beet, or wormseed.

Quinoa is cultivated in South America, in the Andes area, and it has *equal* or *greater* ***nutritional value*** than true **cereals.** It contains a *higher level* of ***protein*** than wheat or corn, and its ***starch*** is *easily digested* and *assimilated.*

Quinoa is normally consumed as the base ingredient of many dishes, but it is also used ground (as flour) to prepare bread, baby food, or drinks.

In this recipe, quinoa's nutritional properties are combined with the wealth of vitamins in **carrots,** one of the foods highest in ***beta-carotene*** (provitamin A).

For all these reasons, this dish is beneficial to prevent:

- ✓ **Retinal ailments** and **eye conditions,** in general, thanks to the vitamins supplied by carrots.
- ✓ Digestive system disorders such as **gastritis,** stomach **ulcer, colitis,** and **irritable bowel syndrome,** due to the *smoothing* action of both quinoa and carrot.
- ✓ **Cancer,** due to the *preventing* effect of beta-carotene from carrots, as well as the protection offered by garlic and onion.

CALORIC PROPORTION*

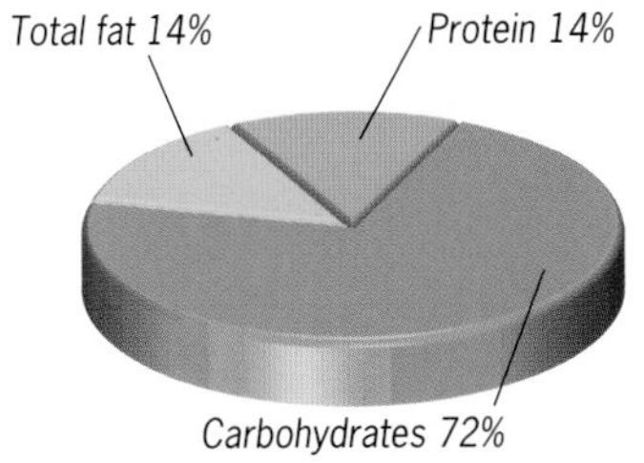

Percentage distribution of
calories for each nutrient

* Additional ingredients not included.

Potatoes and Spinach

INGREDIENTS (4 servings)

- 500 g (≅ 1 pound) of **potatoes**
- 500 g (≅ 1 pound) of **spinach**
- 50 g (≅ 1.75 oz) of shelled **pine nuts** (pine kernels)
- 3 **garlic** cloves

ADDITIONAL INGREDIENTS

- **Parsley**
- $^1/_2$ teaspoon of **potherbs** (dill, basil, tarragon…)
- 7 tablespoons of olive **oil** (each tablespoon of oil adds around 120 kcal to the recipe, that is, 30 kcal per serving)
- Sea **salt** (see Vol. 3, p. 16)

For more information about the ingredients, see: Potato, Vol. 2, p. 201; spinach, Vol. 2, p. 28; pine nut, Vol. 2, p. 47; garlic, Vol. 1, p. 338; and the *Encyclopedia of Medicinal Plants:* Sesame, p. 611; garlic, p. 230.

Oxalic acid

*In certain persons with a hereditary metabolic predisposition, oxalic acid may cause **kidney stones.***

*As **spinach** contains a certain amount of oxalic acid, its use is **not recommended** for those with **predisposition** to develop urinary stones from oxalate.*

PREPARATION

❶Peel and wash the potatoes. If they are small, do not chop them. If big, cut into smaller pieces.
- Wash and chop the spinach.

❷In a frying pan, sauté the spinach in three tablespoons of oil. Cover and reduce heat to the minimum to achieve a slow cooking process.
- When half done, add a finely chopped garlic clove, the pine nuts, and some of the salt. Simmer until the spinach is tender.
- Heat the remaining oil in a pot and add the potatoes and the rest of the salt.
- On a low flame, sauté the potatoes in a covered pot. Stir occasionally.
- When the potatoes begin turning brown, add a finely chopped mixture of the two remaining garlic cloves, parsley, and potherbs. Keep it cooking until the potatoes are golden.

❸Serve immediately, arranging the potatoes around the spinach.

HEALTHIER ALTERNATIVE: Instead of sautéing the spinach and potatoes, steam them. Once cooked, dress them directly on the plate.

Chop the spinach.

Sauté the spinach and add the pine nuts and the garlic halfway through the cooking process.

Fry potatoes lightly on a low flame.

NUTRITIONAL VALUE*
per serving

Energy	192 kcal = 802 kj
Protein	7.38 g
Carbohydrates	19.9 g
Fiber	6.41 g
Total fat	*8.18 g*
Saturated fat	*1.27 g*
Cholesterol	—
Sodium	*115 mg*

1% 2% 4% 10% 20% 40% 100%

% Daily Value (based on a 2,000 calorie diet) provided by each serving of this dish

HEALTH COUNSELS

Spinach contains two vegetable pigments from the ***carotenoid*** group—***lutein*** and ***zeaxanthin,*** which give this vegetable its peculiar color. These pigments are not transformed into vitamin A, as is beta-carotene. However, this does not mean that they perform no function. They act as powerful *antioxidants* to *protect* the **pigmented** cells of the **retina.**

Therefore, its use is recommended to *prevent* **loss of vision** due to macular degeneration or other retinal disorders.

Besides, the potatoes and spinach dish is *very balanced* as far as the caloric proportion supplied in terms of the three energy nutrients—***carbohydrates, fat, and protein.*** This makes it especially suitable for the following conditions:

✓ **Anemia,** thanks to the iron and the folic acid supplied by spinach.

✓ **Pregnancy** and **lactation,** for its nutritional value and for being *high* in ***vitamins*** and ***minerals*** needed during these stages.

✓ During **growth, malnutrition,** and any time there is an increase in nutritional needs. Potatoes, spinach, and pine nuts are beneficial in these cases as they contain ***protein, vitamins,*** and ***minerals.***

CALORIC PROPORTION*

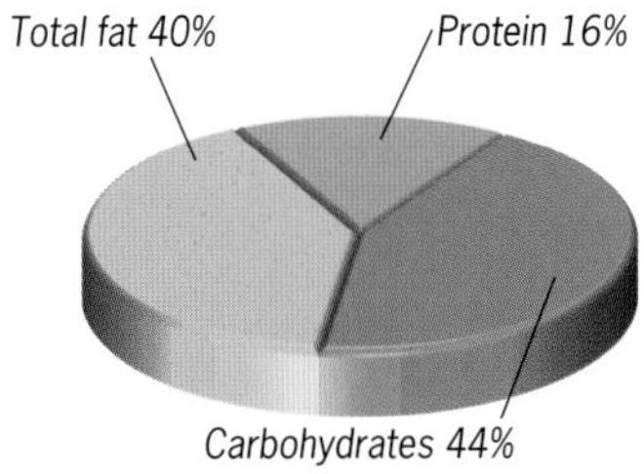

Percentage distribution of
calories for each nutrient

* Additional ingredients not included.

Preparation time 00:15

Cooking time - - - -

Spinach Shake

INGREDIENTS (4 servings)

- 100 g (≅ 3.5 oz) of raw **spinach**
- 2 low-fat **yogurts**
- 1 tablespoon of **honey**
- ½ liter (≅ ½ quart) of **water**

ADDITIONAL INGREDIENTS

- The juice of 1 **lemon**

PREPARATION

❶ Carefully wash and chop the spinach.

❷ Blend the spinach using an electric blender. To facilitate the process, use a container with a little water.

- Add the remaining water, yogurt, and honey. Blend again to obtain a uniform mixture.
- Chill in the refrigerator until it is time to use.

❸ Serve cold, adding a few drops of lemon juice to each glass.

HEALTHIER ALTERNATIVE: Use soy milk instead of yogurt (see Vol. 3, p. 305).

For more information about the ingredients, see: Spinach, Vol. 2, p. 28; yogurt, Vol. 1, p. 201; honey, Vol. 1, p. 160.

HEALTH COUNSELS

Spinach is notable for its levels of ***provitamin A*** (beta-carotene), ***carotenoids*** that provide an *antioxidant* effect, as well as for ***folic acid,*** and minerals such as ***iron.*** Yogurt is a good source of the ***B vitamins,*** including ***B_{12},*** as well as ***calcium.*** For these reasons, this spinach shake is useful in case of:

✓ **Risk** of **visual acuity loss** due to disorders in the retina. Provitamin A and carotenoids found in spinach enhance the **health** of the whole **eye,** from the conjunctiva to the retina.

✓ Automobile **driving,** as its nutrients enhance the **visual** *adaptation* to **darkness** and *increase* **resistance** to **glare.**

✓ Iron deficiency **anemia.**

✓ **Childhood, pregnancy,** and **lactation** (see Vol. 2, pp. 378-387), as this shake supplies *essential nutrients*—such as provitamin A, iron, and calcium—during these stages of life.

NUTRITIONAL VALUE* per serving

Energy	63 kcal = 263 kj
Protein	2.90 g
Carbohydrates	8.25 g
Fiber	0.688 g
Total fat	*2.12 g*
Saturated fat	*1.32 g*
Cholesterol	*7.94 mg*
Sodium	*49.0 mg*

1% 2% 4% 10% 20% 40% 100%

% Daily Value (based on a 2,000 calorie diet) provided by each serving of this shake

CALORIC PROPORTION*

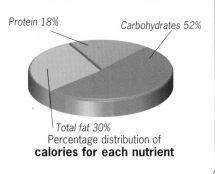

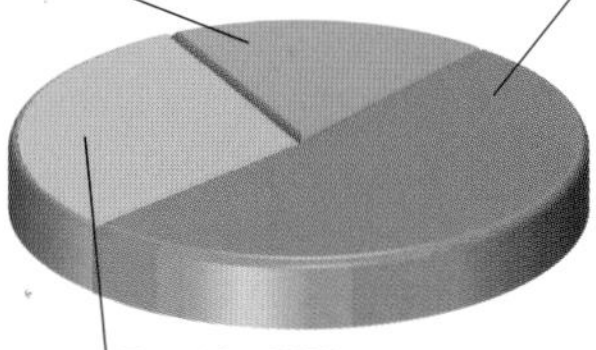

Percentage distribution of **calories for each nutrient**

* Additional ingredients not included.

Preparation time 00:20

Cooking time ----

Apricot Shake

INGREDIENTS (4 servings)

- 250 g (≅ 8.8 oz) of **apricots**
- 2 **bananas**
- 2 tablespoons of **honey**
- 1/2 liter (≅ 1/2 quart) of **hazelnut milk** (Vol. 3, p. 291)

PREPARATION

❶ Wash and pit the apricots.
- Peal and chop the bananas.

❷ Pour the milk and the fruit into the blender. Blend all the ingredients.

❸ Serve cold.

For more information about the ingredients, see: Apricot, Vol. 2, p. 26; banana, Vol. 2, p. 70; honey, Vol. 1, p. 160; hazelnut, Vol. 2, p. 252.

HEALTH COUNSELS

This apricot shake makes a very nutritious and healthy drink. It is *excellent* for **children,** for **sportsmen,** and for any person involved in physical work.

Additionally, due to the beta-carotene from the apricot, it helps to prevent the following disorders:

✓ **Loss** of **vision** due to disorders in the retina, as ***beta-carotene*** (provitamin A) is necessary for good sight.

✓ **Skin** and **mucosae** ailments, including **pharyngitis** and **sinusitis.** ***Provitamin A*** from apricots and the essential ***fatty acids*** from hazelnuts *help* to maintain healthy skin and to *increase* the body's defenses against infection.

NUTRITIONAL VALUE per serving

Energy	**172 kcal = 718 kj**
Protein	**1.37 g**
Carbohydrates	**27.1 g**
Fiber	**3.20 g**
Total fat	***6.27 g***
Saturated fat	***0.539 g***
Cholesterol	—
Sodium	—

1% 2% 4% 10% 20% 40% 100%

% Daily Value (based on a 2,000 calorie diet) provided by each serving of this shake

CALORIC PROPORTION

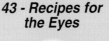

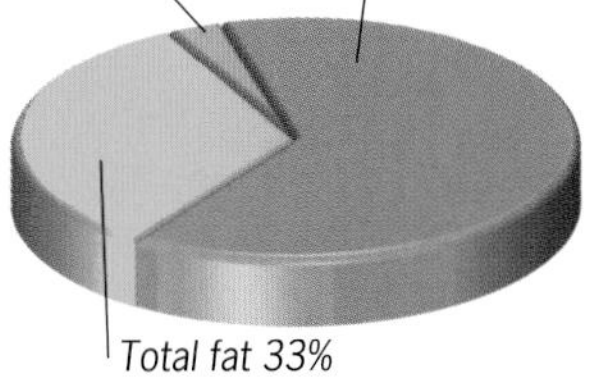

Percentage distribution of **calories for each nutrient**

44 Recipes for the Nervous System

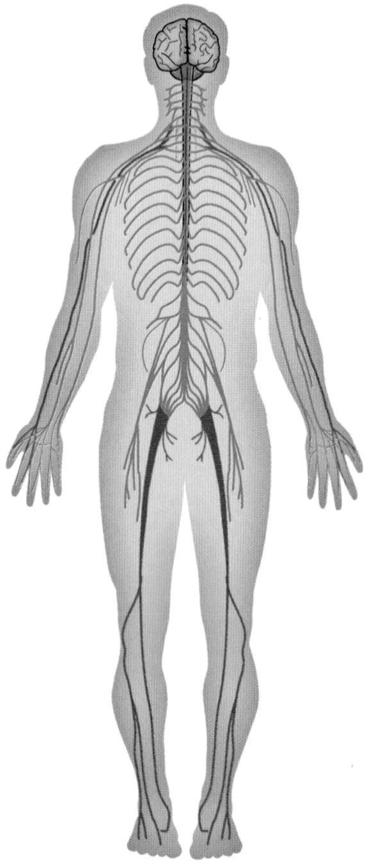

Chapter Summary

Recipes

Almond Cookies 155
Almond Croquettes 151
Almond Soup 146
Aromatic Linden 159
Cashew Stew 150
Chickpea Stew 148
Granola 156
Oat Soup 147
Oatmeal 154
Pasta Bows with Chickpeas 149
Tropical Shake 158
Vegetable Hamburgers 152

B-complex vitamins are the most influential in causing the brain and nervous system to work well.

It is also known that certain minerals and trace elements, such as magnesium, are basic.

Unsaturated fatty acids are necessary for development of the brain and nervous system in children.

(See Vol. 2, p. 30.)

THE ***CENTRAL*** *Nervous System* is composed of the **encephalon** (cerebrum, cerebellum, diencephalon, and mesencephalon) and the **spinal cord.** The ***peripheral nervous system*** is made up of the **nerves.** Although it seems clear that there is **something intangible** in the functioning of the nervous system that escapes laboratory analysis and testing, it is also true that brain and nervous functions occur within these specific organs. As with any other anatomical part, these organs must be adequately nourished through food intake in order to keep them functioning at optimal levels.

In the 1980's, Professor ***Joaquín Cravioto,*** director of the National Institute of Science and Health Technology for Children, in Mexico, demonstrated that nutrition shapes the development of nerve cells.

Dr. Cravioto, explaining the tremendous importance of diet for the brain as well as for the other organs, said: "*According to Mouriguand, infant mortality is due to three basic factors:* ***genetic, infectious, and dietary.*** *The combination of the last two does not add to but rather* ***multiplies their strength.***"

To research this issue, the prominent Mexican doctor studied a group of hospitalized children with severe nutritional problems. After some time, he observed that, although their biological functions recovered to reach normality, their brain had been affected. It was ascertained that although many of these children had experienced earlier-than-normal psychomotor development, after a period of malnutrition their motor development was stunted. This showed that such a change could not be attributed to genetic factors.

Good maternal nutrition, before and during pregnancy, is a ***determining factor*** for **adequate intellectual development** of children. Optimal mental health during infancy and childhood is enhanced by a suitable diet. This is also true throughout the other life stages.

On the other hand, Dr. Ernst Schneider's words should not be forgotten: "***Sleep is the best food for the nerves.***" Therefore, the old saying that health depends upon **calmness** and **good food** is being confirmed by scientific investigation today. That is why in all these Healthy Recipes, and especially in this chapter, the reader is provided with foods, attractively arranged and deliciously combined, that contribute to adequate functions of the brain and nerves.

Menus for

Depression

Bircher-muesli

Breakfast
- "Tropical Shake" (Vol. 3, p. 158)
- "Bircher-Muesli" (Vol. 3, p. 175)

Lunch
- "River Salad" (Vol. 3, p. 206)
- "Cashew Stew" (Vol. 3, p. 150)
- "Vegetable Hamburgers" (Vol. 3, p. 152)
- "Whole Bread" (Vol. 3, p. 46; Vol. 1, p. 72)

Cashew Stew

Supper
- "Almond Cookies" (Vol. 3, p. 155)
- Wheat Germ (Vol. 2, p. 310)
- Aromatic Linden (Vol. 3, p. 159)

Almond Cookies

HEALTH COUNSELS

This is a useful menu for those suffering from depression, as it contains adequate amounts of almonds, whole cereals, and vegetables. Almonds possess a number of characteristics that make them *invigorating* and *balancing* to the **nervous system.**

Muesli, made up of whole cereals, is a very complete food for the nervous system. In combination with the vegetables included in this menu that are *high* in ***vitamins*** and ***minerals,*** it helps the nervous system fight depression.

Stress and Nervousness

Breakfast
- "Cherimoya and Orange Shake" (Vol. 3, p. 178)
- "Oatmeal" (Vol. 3, p. 154)
- "Almond Milk" (Vol. 3, p. 342)
- Wheat Germ (Vol. 2, p. 310)

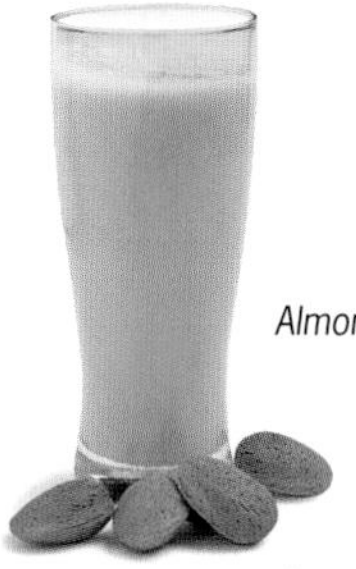
Almond Milk

Lunch
- "Zucchini Salad" (Vol. 3, p. 185)
- "Chickpea Stew" (Vol. 3, p. 148)
- Pine Nuts (Vol. 2, p. 47)
- "Sesame Crepes" (Vol. 3, p. 304; Vol. 1, p. 352)

Chickpea Stew

Supper
- "Oat Soup" (Vol. 3, p. 147)
- "Melon and Orange Juice" with wheat germ (Vol. 2, p. 310; Vol. 3, p. 367)

Oat Soup

HEALTH COUNSELS

This menu contains many ingredients that *stimulate* and *balance* the **nervous system.** Thus, it is able to provide optimal conditions to face **stress** and avoid **nervousness.** It also works well when treating **insomnia.**

Oats, almonds, and chickpeas are the foundation of this menu. All are highly nutritious ingredients for the nervous system. Wheat germ, sesame, nuts, and fresh fruits complete this balanced menu.

the Nervous System

Intellectual Strain

Breakfast

- "Oranges with Honey" (Vol. 3, p. 366)
- "Granola" (Vol. 3, p. 156)
- "Soy Milk" (Vol. 3, p. 305)

Oranges with Honey

Seed Salad

Lunch

- "Seed Salad" (Vol. 3, p. 298)
- "Pasta Bows with Chickpeas" (Vol. 3, p. 149)
- "Almond Croquettes" (Vol. 3, p. 151)
- "Rye Bread" (Vol. 3, p. 194)

Supper

- "Almond Soup" (Vol. 3, p. 146)
- Mango (Vol. 2, p. 341)

Almond Soup

HEALTH COUNSELS

Those involved in heavy intellectual work are in special need of certain ingredients such as ***vitamins B*** and ***E, phospholipids,*** and ***complex carbohydrates.*** This menu supplies all of these, and it also contains protein, minerals, and other vitamins.

Students going through examinations or any other persons wishing to increase their intellectual achievement and memory will do well to use this menu.

Other Recipes for the Nervous System

Salads

- "Pasta Bow Salad" (Vol. 3, p. 165)
- "Chickpea Salad" (Vol. 3, p. 186)

Soups and Purées

- "Cream of Avocado" (Vol. 3, p. 351)

Main Courses

- "Rice Salad" (Vol. 3, p. 380)
- "Potatoes with Peas" (Vol. 3, p. 169)
- "Falafel Patties" (Vol. 3, p. 198)
- "Oat Medallions" (Vol. 3, p. 122)

Breakfasts, Desserts and Snacks

- "Cereal Bars" (Vol. 3, p. 174)
- "Coconut Balls" (Vol. 3, p. 339)

Drinks

- "Refreshing Tea" (Vol. 3, p. 254)

Infusions or decoctions:

- Oats (*EMP* p. 150)
- Balm (melissa) (*EMP* p. 163)
- Passoin Flower (*EMP* p. 167)
- Linden (*EMP* p. 169)
- Valerian (*EMP* p. 173)
- Verbain (*EMP* p. 174)

- *See the recipe index at the beginning of this volume (Vol. 3, pp. 8-13).*
- *See also chapter 20, "Foods for the Nervous System" (Vol. 2, pp. 30-51).*

EMP = *Encyclopedia of Medicinal Plants*, Education and Health Library, Editorial Safeliz.

Preparation time 00:15

Cooking time 00:30

Almond soup

INGREDIENTS (4 servings)

- 100 g (≅ 1 cup) of raw blanched **almonds**
- 75 g (≅ 3/8 cup) of **whole rice**
- 1 **zucchini** (courgette)
- 1 **onion**
- 1 liter (≅ 1 quart) of unsalted **vegetable broth**

ADDITIONAL INGREDIENTS

- 2 **laurel** (bay) leaves
- 1/2 tablespoon of **paprika**
- 3 tablespoons of olive **oil** (each tablespoon of oil adds around 120 kcal to the recipe, that is, 30 kcal per serving)
- Sea **salt** (see Vol. 3, p. 16)

PREPARATION

❶ Grind separately the almonds and rice.
- Peel, wash and chop the onion.
- Wash and slice the zucchini.

❷ Heat oil in a pot, and sauté the onion and the zucchini with a little salt.
- When golden, add the laurel and paprika. Stir and add the vegetable broth.
- At boiling point, add the rice. Let boil for 10 minutes and add the almonds. Boil for an additional 5 to 10 minutes.

❸ Serve hot.

Suggestions from the Chef

- A **mashed hard-boiled egg** may be added to the soup at the time of serving. This adds nutritional value, but it also adds about 250 mg of ***cholesterol*** (62.5 mg per serving).
- Almonds may be **roasted** before they are added to the soup. This enhances flavor.

HEALTHIER ALTERNATIVE: Instead of sautéing the ingredients, add them raw to the boiling vegetable broth and cook for 20 minutes on a medium fire.

For more information about the ingredients, see: Almond, Vol. 2, p. 48; rice, Vol. 2, p. 225; zucchini, Vol. 2, p. 159; onion, Vol. 2, p. 142.

HEALTH COUNSELS

This almond soup is a good source of minerals, especially ***calcium*** and ***potassium,*** which come from almonds and vegetable broth. Besides, the dish supplies high quality ***protein.*** For this reason it is a balanced and nutritious recipe, especially recommended for:

✓ The **nervous system,** due to the ***B*** and ***E vitamins*** and the ***unsaturated fatty acids*** supplied by almonds. Those wishing to prevent **stress, intellectual** and **physical fatigue, depression,** and **nervousness** will find the use of this almond soup quite beneficial.

✓ **Constipation,** due to its *significant* ***fiber*** content.

NUTRITIONAL VALUE* per serving

Energy	236 kcal = 987 kj
Protein	7.38 g
Carbohydrates	19.4 g
Fiber	4.61 g
Total fat	*13.7 g*
Saturated fat	*1.36 g*
Cholesterol	—
Sodium	*6.05 mg*

1% 2% 4% 10% 20% 40% 100%

% Daily Value (based on a 2,000 calorie diet) provided by each serving of this dish

CALORIC PROPORTION*

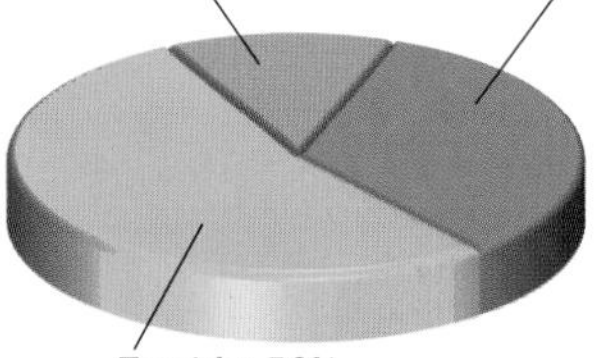

Percentage distribution of **calories for each nutrient**

* Additional ingredients not included.

Preparation time 00:10

Cooking time 00:25

Oat Soup

INGREDIENTS (4 servings)

- 100 g of rolled **oats**
- 50 g of shelled **hazelnuts**
- 2 **garlic** cloves
- $1^1/_4$ liter (≅ $1\ ^1/_4$ quart) of unsalted **vegetable broth**

ADDITIONAL INGREDIENTS

- 3 tablespoons of olive **oil** (each tablespoon of oil adds around 120 kcal to the recipe, that is, 30 kcal per serving)
- Sea **salt** (see Vol. 3, p. 16)

PREPARATION

❶ Peel and chop the garlic.
- Grind the hazelnuts into small chunks but not into meal.

❷ Heat the oil in a frying pan. Sauté the garlic and the oats.
- Add the hazelnuts. Roast them lightly.
- Heat the vegetable broth and salt in a pot. At boiling point add the rolled oats, hazelnuts and garlic.
- Boil for 15 minutes.

❸ Serve hot.

HEALTHIER ALTERNATIVE: Instead of sautéing the ingredients, add them raw to the boiling vegetable broth.

High Blood Pressure

*Persons suffering from high blood pressure should **reduce** the intake of **hazelnuts** as they may raise blood pressure. In such cases, **almonds** or **pine nuts** may be used as a substitute for the **hazelnuts.***

For more information about the ingredients, see: Oats, Vol. 2, p. 41; hazelnut, Vol. 2, p. 252; garlic, Vol. 1, p. 338; and the *Encyclopedia of Medicinal Plants*: Garlic, p. 230.

HEALTH COUNSELS

Oats and **hazelnuts** are the fundamental ingredients of this tasty soup and make it easy to digest, and ideal for:

✓The **nervous system,** due to the sedative effect of oats.

✓The **arteries** and the **heart,** as this dish contains *zero **cholesterol*** and is *very low* in ***sodium***—if salt is not added—and *very low* in **fat.** In addition, the oats supply a substantial amount of ***fiber.***

✓The **digestive system,** due to the ***smoothing*** effect of oats, both upon the stomach and the intestine.

NUTRITIONAL VALUE* per serving

Energy	181 kcal = 755 kj
Protein	6.04 g
Carbohydrates	16.0 g
Fiber	3.48 g
Total fat	*9.57 g*
Saturated fat	*0.882 g*
Cholesterol	—
Sodium	*1.385 mg*

1% 2% 4% 10% 20% 40% 100%

% Daily Value (based on a 2,000 calorie diet) provided by each serving of this dish

CALORIC PROPORTION*

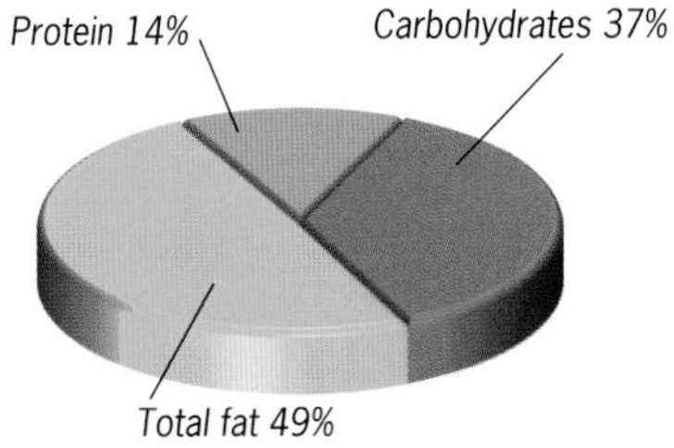

Percentage distribution of **calories for each nutrient**

* Additional ingredients not included.

Preparation time 00:20

Cooking time 01:45

Chickpea Stew

INGREDIENTS (4 servings)

- 300 g (≅ 1 1/2 cups) of **chickpeas** (garbanzo beans)
- 300 g (≅ 10.6 oz) of **chard**
- 250 g (≅ 3 1/3 cups) of **leeks**
- 100 g (≅ 3.5 oz) of **cabbage**
- 100 g (≅ 1 cup) of **green beans** (string beans)
- 1 **carrot**
- 1 **celery** stalk
- 1 sweet **green pepper**
- 1 **onion**
- 1 **tomato**
- 2 **garlic** cloves

ADDITIONAL INGREDIENTS

- 1/2 teaspoon of **paprika**
- 5 tablespoons of olive **oil** (each tablespoon of oil adds around 120 kcal to the recipe, that is, 30 kcal per serving)
- Sea **salt** (see Vol. 3, p. 16)

PREPARATION

❶ Soak the chickpeas overnight in salted hot water.
- Peel, wash, and chop the vegetables.

❷ Heat the water and salt in a pot. When it reaches the boiling point, add the drained chickpeas.
- Heat the oil in a frying pan, and sauté the onion, paprika, garlic, green peppers, and tomato. When the chickpeas are almost tender (after about 1 hour 15 minutes), add the sautéed mixture together with the rest of the vegetables. Boil for an additional 15 minutes.

❸ Serve hot.

For more information about the ingredients, see: Chickpea, Vol. 2, p. 91; chard, Vol. 2, p. 297; leek, Vol. 2, p. 319; cabbage, Vol. 2, p. 191; green bean, Vol. 1, p. 109; carrot, Vol. 2, p. 25; celery, Vol. 2, p. 248; pepper, Vol. 2, p. 198; onion, Vol. 2, p. 142; tomato, Vol. 2, p. 275; garlic, Vol. 1, p. 338; and the *Encyclopedia of Medicinal Plants*: Green bean, p. 584; garlic, p. 230.

HEALTHIER ALTERNATIVE: Instead of sautéing the ingredients, add them directly to the pot at the same time as the chickpeas.

HEALTH COUNSELS

Chickpeas deserve a place of honor in the human diet because of their nutritional and therapeutic properties. Combined with several vegetables, as is done in this stew, their strengthening effect upon the nervous system is enhanced. Additionally, this dish reduces the level of cholesterol and regulates the bowel movement.

For these reasons, chickpea stew is recommended to:

✓ *Strengthen* the **nervous system** when there is stress, depression, inability to concentrate, etc., due to its supply of ***vitamin*** B_1, B_2, B_6, and ***folates.***

✓ *Prevent* **arteriosclerosis,** due to its ***fiber*** content, which reduces **cholesterol.**

✓ **Pregnant women** since it is a dish *high* in ***folates, protein, iron,*** and ***zinc.***

✓ **Diabetic patients,** because it helps to regulate the **glucose** (sugar) level in blood.

NUTRITIONAL VALUE* per serving

Energy	369 kcal = 1,541 kj
Protein	18.7 g
Carbohydrates	46.5 g
Fiber	20.5 g
Total fat	*5.12 g*
Saturated fat	*0.560 g*
Cholesterol	—
Sodium	*218 mg*

1% 2% 4% 10% 20% 40% 100%

% Daily Value (based on a 2,000 calorie diet) provided by each serving of this dish

CALORIC PROPORTION*

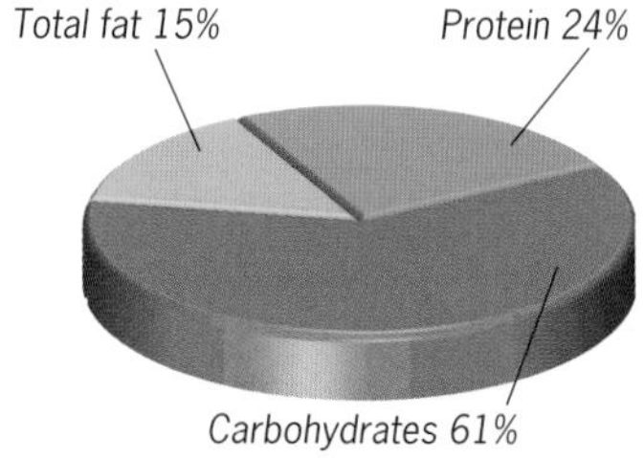

Percentage distribution of **calories for each nutrient**

* Additional ingredients not included.

Preparation time 00:10 | Cooking time 01:45

Pasta Bows with Chickpeas

INGREDIENTS (4 servings)

- 200 g (≅ 7 oz) of **pasta bows**
- 100 g (≅ 1/2 cup) of **chickpeas** (garbanzo beans)
- 1 **onion**
- 1 **carrot**
- 1 **celery** stalk
- 1 **zucchini** (courgette)
- 2 **tomatoes**
- 2 **garlic** cloves

ADDITIONAL INGREDIENTS

- **Potherbs** (peppermint, thyme, coriander…)
- 2 tablespoons of olive **oil** (each tablespoon of oil adds around 120 kcal to the recipe, that is, 30 kcal per serving)
- Sea **salt** (see Vol. 3, p. 16)

PREPARATION

❶ Soak the chickpeas overnight in salted hot water.
- Peel, wash, and chop the vegetables into medium-sized cubes.

❷ Heat plenty of water and salt in a pot. When it reaches the boiling point, add chickpeas and reduce the heat.
- When the chickpeas are almost tender (after about 1 hour 15 minutes), add the vegetables. Cook for a further 15 minutes and add the potherbs, oil, chopped garlic, and pasta.
- Stir so that the pasta does not stick to the pot. When the pasta bows are *al dente* (firm to the bite), turn the stove off.

❸ Serve hot.

For more information about the ingredients, see: Pasta, Vol. 1, p. 74; chickpea, Vol. 2, p. 91; onion, Vol. 2, p. 142; carrot, Vol. 2, p. 25; celery, Vol. 2, p. 248; zucchini, Vol. 2, p. 159; tomato, Vol. 2, p. 275; garlic, Vol. 1, p. 338; and the *Encyclopedia of Medicinal Plants*: Garlic, p. 230.

HEALTHIER ALTERNATIVE: Instead of white pasta (prepared with white flour), use whole pasta.

HEALTH COUNSELS

This cereal-legume combination provides a very nutritious and *highly complete* dish as far as ***protein*** is concerned. Because of this reason and because of the other supplied nutrients (***carbohydrates, type-B vitamins,*** and ***minerals***), its use is very healthy in the following cases:

- ✓ Intellectual and physical **stress, exhaustion, depression,** and **irritability.**
- ✓ **Growth** stages, intense **physical work,** and **sports.**
- ✓ Periods of **pregnancy, lactation** and **convalescence,** as this is a dish *high* in ***folates, iron, zinc,*** and ***B-complex vitamins.***
- ✓ **Constipation,** due to the ***fiber*** content of the chickpeas and vegetables, which is enhanced when using **whole pasta.**

NUTRITIONAL VALUE* per serving

Energy	338 kcal = 1,411 kj
Protein	13.7 g
Carbohydrates	57.1 g
Fiber	9.13 g
Total fat	*2.85 g*
Saturated fat	*0.357 g*
Cholesterol	—
Sodium	*52.1 mg*

1% 2% 4% 10% 20% 40% 100%

% Daily Value (based on a 2,000 calorie diet) provided by each serving of this dish

CALORIC PROPORTION*

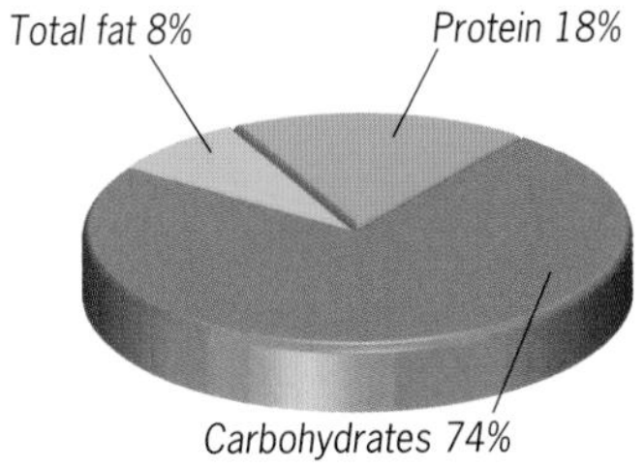

Percentage distribution of **calories for each nutrient**

* Additional ingredients not included.

Preparation time 00:15

Cooking time 00:40

Cashew Stew

INGREDIENTS (4 servings)

- 150 g (≅ 1 cup) of **cashews**
- 150 g (≅ 5.3 oz) of **mushrooms**
- 1 **onion**
- 100 g (≅ 3.5 oz) of **black olives**
- 60 g (≅ 1/2 cup) of **whole flour**
- 250 ml (≅ 1 cup) of **soy milk** (Vol. 3, p. 305)
- 375 ml (≅ 1 1/2 cups) of unsalted **vegetable broth**

ADDITIONAL INGREDIENTS

- 4 tablespoons of olive oil (each tablespoon of oil adds around 120 kcal to the recipe, that is, 30 kcal per serving)
- Sea **salt** (see Vol. 3, p. 16)

PREPARATION

❶ Peel and chop the onion.
- Clean and wash the mushrooms.

❷ Heat the oil in a pot, and sauté the mushrooms and the onion. When they are tender, remove from the pot and set aside.
- In the same oil add the flour and the salt. Stir constantly to avoid lumps.
- Little by little, add the vegetable broth and the milk. Continue stirring.
- At boiling point, add cashews, mushrooms, onion, and olives.
- Simmer for 20 minutes stirring occasionally.

❸ Serve hot.

HEALTHIER ALTERNATIVE: Bake or steam the mushrooms and the onions. Lightly toast the flour in the pan without oil.

For more information about the ingredients, see: Cashew, Vol. 2, p. 40; mushroom, Vol. 2, p. 294; onion, Vol. 2, p. 142; olive, Vol. 2, p. 165; flour, Vol. 1, p. 68; soy milk, Vol. 1, p. 88.

HEALTH COUNSELS

Cashews, onions, and olives are part of this dish and constitute a good source of type-***B vitamins, essential fatty acids,*** and ***minerals,*** such as ***magnesium.*** All these nutrients are necessary for adequate functioning of the nervous system. The cashew stew is especially recommended in the following cases:

✓ Disorders of the **nervous system,** such as **stress** and **depression,** where the use of the aforementioned ingredients is required.

✓ **Magnesium** deficiency, a state that may *cause* or *worsen* muscular **cramps, irritable bowel syndrome, menstrual** discomfort, and **angina pectoris.**

✓ **Diabetes,** thanks to the *anti-diabetic* effect of mushrooms and to the fact that this dish does not cause any increase in the glucose (sugar) level.

NUTRITIONAL VALUE* per serving

Energy	317 kcal = 1,326 kj
Protein	10.4 g
Carbohydrates	23.5 g
Fiber	4.94 g
Total fat	20.3 g
Saturated fat	3.81 g
Cholesterol	—
Sodium	125 mg

1% 2% 4% 10% 20% 40% 100%

% Daily Value (based on a 2,000 calorie diet) provided by each serving of this dish

CALORIC PROPORTION*

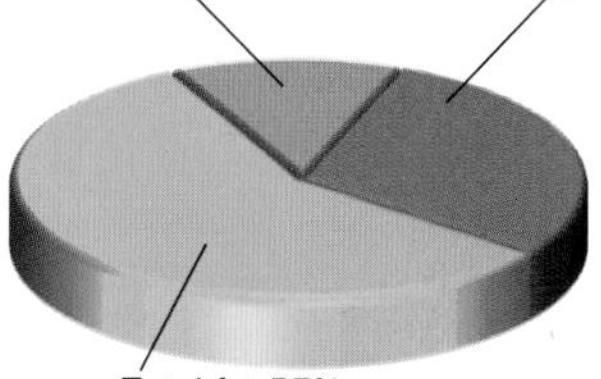

Percentage distribution of **calories for each nutrient**

* Additional ingredients not included.

Preparation time 00:30

Cooking time 00:40

Almond Croquettes

INGREDIENTS (4 servings)

- 100 g (≅ 2/3 cup) of **rolled oats**
- 100 g (≅ 1 cup) of ground blanched raw **almonds**
- 1 small chopped **onion**
- 75 g (≅ 2/3 cup) of **whole flour**
- 300 ml (≅ 1 1/4 cup) of **soy milk** (Vol. 3, p. 305) and half as much unsalted **vegetable broth** at 50%
- 1 **egg**
- 50 g (≅ 1 cup) of **breadcrumbs**

ADDITIONAL INGREDIENTS

- 3 tablespoons of olive **oil** (each tablespoon of oil adds around 120 kcal to the recipe, that is, 30 kcal per serving)
- Sea **salt** (see Vol. 3, p. 16)

PREPARATION

❶ Soak the oats for about half an hour in the mixture of soy milk and vegetable broth. Drain and reserve the extra liquid.

❷ Heat the oil in a frying pan, and sauté the onion until transparent. Add the almonds and the flour. Stir constantly for 2 minutes to avoid the formation of lumps. Add the rolled oats and cook for an additional 2 minutes.

- Remove from heat and little by little add the reserved liquid. Stir constantly. Return the frying pan to the fire, add the salt and simmer. Keep stirring until it thickens and the batter does not stick to the pan. Pour into a dish and let it cool.
- When the dough is thoroughly cold, spoon out portions and shape them into croquettes. Roll in the beaten egg and then in the breadcrumbs. Bake at 220°C until golden throughout.

❸ Serve hot.

For more information about the ingredients, see: Oats, Vol. 2, p. 41, almond, Vol. 2, p. 48; onion, Vol. 2, p. 142; flour, Vol. 1, p. 68; soy milk, Vol. 1, p. 88; egg, Vol. 1, p. 218; bread, Vol. 1, p. 70.

HEALTHIER ALTERNATIVE: Steam or bake the onion; lightly roast the flour and the rolled oats without oil. To roll the croquettes without using egg, see Vol. 3, p. 76.

NUTRITIONAL VALUE* per serving

Energy	412 kcal = 1,721 kj
Protein	17.5 g
Carbohydrates	38.2 g
Fiber	9.28 g
Total fat	*18.8 g*
Saturated fat	*2.39 g*
Cholesterol	*63.8 mg*
Sodium	*33.3 mg*

1% 2% 4% 10% 20% 40% 100%

% Daily Value (based on a 2,000 calorie diet) provided by each serving of this dish

HEALTH COUNSELS

The combination of almonds and oats in this recipe provides ***vitamins, minerals,*** and other ***essential nutrients*** for the **nervous system.**

These croquettes are recommended to those who wish to stimulate their nervous system and their **entire organism,** as well as *improve* their **intellectual performance.**

In case of *high* **cholesterol** or **arteriosclerosis,** these croquettes should be ***avoided,*** as they contain egg.

CALORIC PROPORTION*

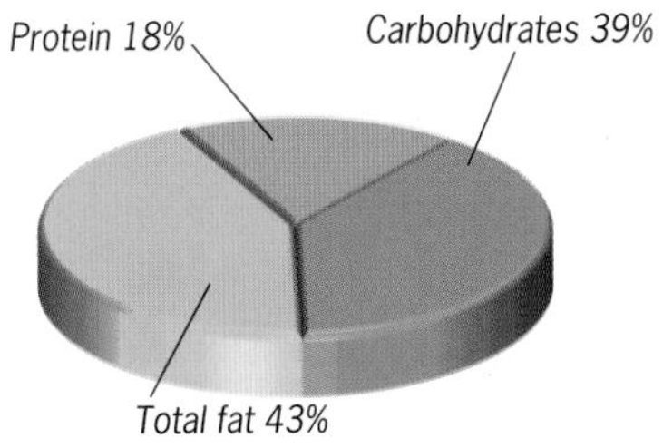

Percentage distribution of **calories for each nutrient**

* Additional ingredients not included.

Preparation time 00:15

Cooking time 00:25

Vegetable Hamburgers

INGREDIENTS (4 servings)

- 60 g (≅ 1/3 cup) of rolled **oats**
- 50 g (≅ 1.75 oz) of shelled **nuts** (almonds, hazelnuts, walnuts...)
- 40 g (1/3 cup) of **wheat germ**
- 1 **zucchini** (courgette)
- 2 **onions**
- 1 **tomato**
- 2 **carrots**
- 1 **garlic** clove
- 50 g (≅ 1 cup) of **bread crumbs**
- 110 ml (≅ 1/2 cup) of unsalted **vegetable broth**
- 2 tablespoons of **whole flour**

ADDITIONAL INGREDIENTS

- 1 tablespoon of **potherbs** (parsley, oregano, thyme...)
- Sea **salt** (see Vol. 3, p. 16)

Suggestions from the Chef

- If the batter is too thin and runny, **flour** may be added.
- The use of potherbs has been mentioned. Additionally, other condiments such as sweet **paprika** may be added.
- Garnished with sesame sticks, lettuce, tomato, and mayonnaise, this dish makes an **excellent snack** for children and grownups.

PREPARATION

❶ Soak rolled oats and wheat germ in the vegetable broth for 30 minutes.

❷ Peel and chop the vegetables.
- Grind the nuts.
- Combine all the ingredients, mix well, and divide up the mixture into equal portions. Shape as hamburgers.
- Arrange the hamburgers in an oven tray and bake in a 220°C oven until they are brown on both sides (turn them over half way through baking).

❸ Serve hot.

HEALTHIER ALTERNATIVE: Instead of only one garlic clove, add several.

For more information about the ingredients, see: Oats, Vol. 2, p. 41; nuts, Vol. 1, p. 52; wheat germ, Vol. 2, p. 310; zucchini, Vol. 2, p. 159; onion, Vol. 2, p. 142; tomato, Vol. 2, p. 275; carrot, Vol. 2, p. 25; garlic, Vol. 1, p. 338; bread, Vol. 1, p. 70; flour, Vol. 1, p. 680; and the *Encyclopedia of Medicinal Plants*: Garlic, p. 230.

Peel and chop the vegetables.

Combine all the ingredients.

Place the hamburgers on an oven tray.

NUTRITIONAL VALUE* per serving

Energy	304 kcal = 1,269 kj
Protein	12.0 g
Carbohydrates	36.9 g
Fiber	9.18 g
Total fat	*9.76 g*
Saturated fat	*1.21 g*
Cholesterol	—
Sodium	*29.7 mg*

1% 2% 4% 10% 20% 40% 100%

% Daily Value (based on a 2,000 calorie diet) provided by each serving of this dish

HEALTH COUNSELS

These hamburgers are both tasty and nutritious due to the cereals, nuts, and vegetables used in their preparation. This dish is recommended in the following cases:

✓Prevention of **nervous system disorders,** as it is very high in the necessary nutrients for adequate functioning—***B-complex vitamins, minerals,*** such as calcium and ***magnesium,*** and ***unsaturated fatty acids***. Nuts, oats, and wheat germ, ingredients used in this dish, supply an excellent nutritional source to strengthen the nervous system.

✓Those carrying out tasks that require **intellectual strain** will benefit from these vegetable hamburgers. These include students, and those fighting **stress, nervousness, anxiety, insomnia,** and **depression.**

✓**Growth stages** (childhood and adolescence), due to the ***protein*** and ***minerals*** supplied by these hamburgers, necessary for development.

✓**Pregnancy** and **lactation,** due to the increased need for essential nutrients provided by many of the ingredients of this dish.

✓Prevention of **arteriosclerosis** and **heart** disease, as these hamburgers are *high* in ***fiber,*** low in ***saturated fat*** and low in ***sodium***—if salt is not added—and contain *zero* ***cholesterol.***

✓**Diabetes,** as most ***carbohydrates*** contained in these hamburgers come from oats and can be tolerated well by diabetic patients.

CALORIC PROPORTION*

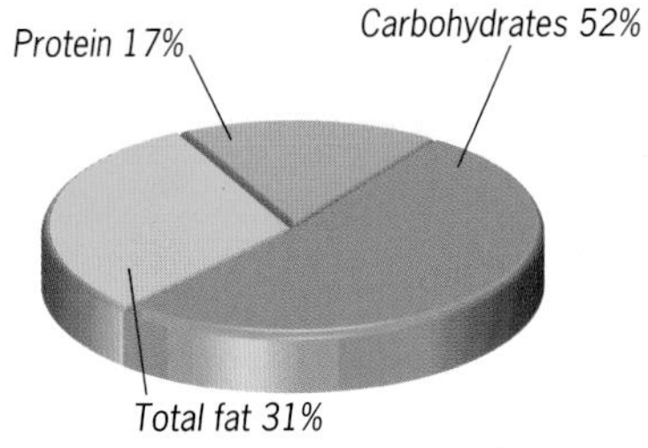

Percentage distribution of
calories for each nutrient

* Additional ingredients not included.

Preparation time 00:10

Cooking time 00:20

Oatmeal

INGREDIENTS (4 servings)

- 200 g (≅ 1 1/5 cups) of **rolled oats**
- 20 **prunes**
- 1 liter (≅ 1 quart) of **water**

ADDITIONAL INGREDIENTS

- Sea **salt** (see Vol. 3, p. 16)

PREPARATION

❶ Pit the prunes.

❷ Boil the rolled oats together with the prunes for about 20 minutes (until thick).

❸ Serve hot in a soup dish.

For more information about the ingredients, see: Oats, Vol. 2, p. 41; prune, Vol. 2, p. 235.

Suggestions from the Chef

- In order to achieve a quicker cooking time, **soak** the rolled oats overnight.
- The water may be substituted by **milk.** Also, 200 ml of **cream** may be added.
- This breakfast may be sweetened with sugar, honey, or molasses. Sprinkle with cinnamon for decoration.

HEALTH COUNSELS

This breakfast supplies ***easy-to-digest energy*** from **oats,** which are among the most nutritional grains, and also from the ***sugar*** in **prunes.**

Oatmeal is recommended to:

✓ *Strengthen* and *balance* the **nervous system,** as ***carbohydrates*** and ***vitamins*** found in oats are an excellent "fuel" for the neurons. Furthermore, oats contain ***avenin,*** a substance with a slight *sedative* effect.

For these reasons, those under **intellectual strain** (such as students during examination times) as well as those suffering from insomnia, nervousness, and **stress** will especially benefit from oatmeal.

✓ *Treat* **constipation,** due to the *laxative* effect of prunes and the *smoothing* action of oats upon the intestinal lining.

✓ *Fight* **stomach** *inflammation,* in cases of **gastritis** or **gastroduodenal ulcer.**

NUTRITIONAL VALUE* per serving

Energy	338 kcal = 1,412 kj
Protein	10.0 g
Carbohydrates	61.2 g
Fiber	9.56 g
Total fat	*3.76 g*
Saturated fat	*0.633 g*
Cholesterol	—
Sodium	*3.40 mg*

1% 2% 4% 10% 20% 40% 100%

% Daily Value (based on a 2,000 calorie diet) provided by each serving of this breakfast

CALORIC PROPORTION*

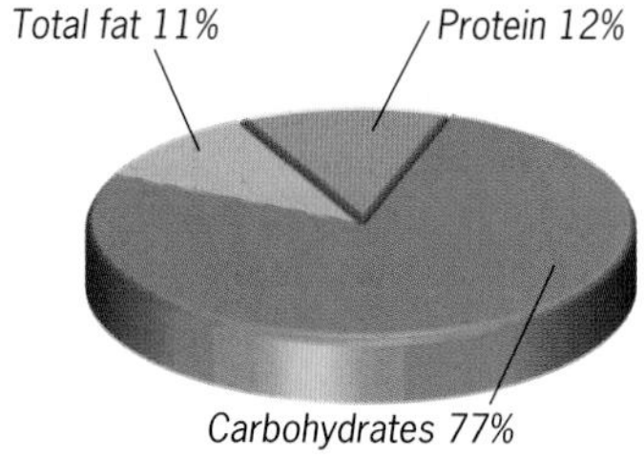

Percentage distribution of **calories for each nutrient**

* Additional ingredients not included.

Preparation time 00:20

Cooking time 00:45

Almond Cookies

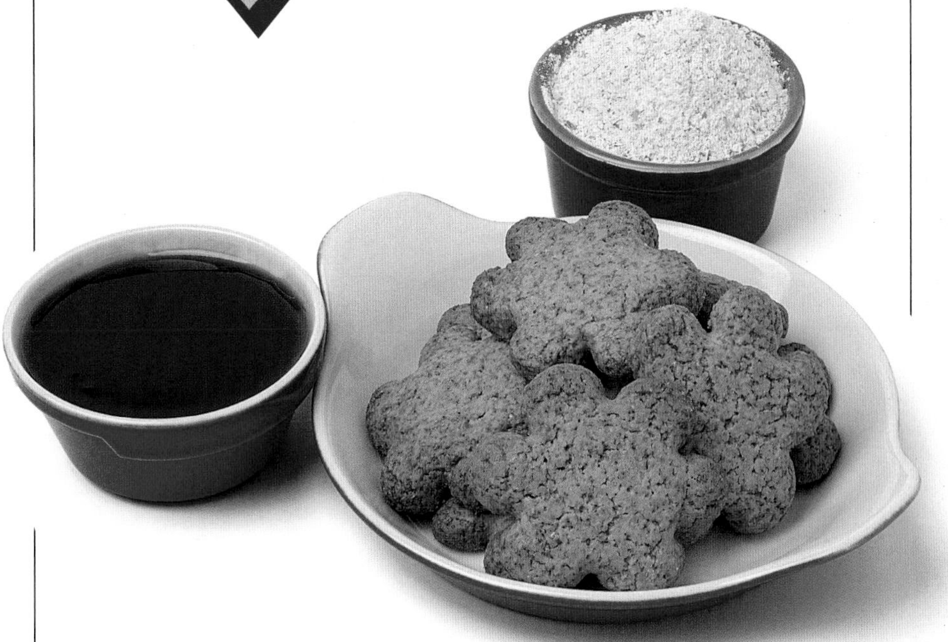

INGREDIENTS

- 300 g (≅ 10.6 oz) of **wheat** grains
- 280 g (≅ 2 1/3 cups) of **whole flour**
- 100 g (≅ 3/4 cup) of **white flour**
- 80 g (≅ 3/4 cup) of raw shredded **almonds**
- 80 g (≅ 1 cup) of shredded **coconut**
- 150 g (≅ 1/2 cup) of **molasses**
- 1 tablespoon of **sesame** seeds
- 1 tablespoon of **green anise** seeds
- 14 tablespoons of seeds **oil**
- 200 ml (≅ 4/5 cup) of **water**

PREPARATION

❶ Grind the wheat grains.

❷ Boil water and anise during 5 minutes and turn the stove off. When the water is lukewarm, add the remaining ingredients and knead until the mixture is smooth.

- Roll the dough to a 5-mm thickness using a rolling pin on a floured surface.
- Cut the dough with cookie cutters or a cup. Lay on a greased baking sheet. Bake in a medium oven until brown on both sides.

❸ Store in an airtight container until it is time to use.

For more information about the ingredients, see: Wheat, Vol. 2, p. 306; flour, Vol. 1, p. 68; almond, Vol. 2, p. 48; coconut, Vol. 2, p. 325; molasses, Vol. 1, p. 160; sesame, Vol. 1, p. 352; oil, Vol. 1, p. 112; and the *Encyclopedia of Medicinal Plants:* Sesame, p. 611; green anise, p. 465.

HEALTH COUNSELS

The ingredients in these cookies supply the basic nutrients for functions of the nervous system. Almonds are high in ***vitamin B*** and ***E,*** and in ***essential fatty acids;*** **sesame** and **molasses** are a good source of ***minerals*** and ***trace minerals;*** and the **seeds oil** also supply essential fatty acids, such as ***linoleic acid.***

Therefore, these cookies are recommended when it is necessary to supply both the **nervous system** and the entire organism with an *additional* dose of ***energy*** and ***nutrients*** that are easy to assimilate:

- ✓**Intellectual strain,** such as that carried out by students during times of exams.
- ✓**Physical strain,** due to intense work or sports competition.
- ✓**Pregnancy** and **lactation.**
- ✓**Thinness** and/or **malnutrition.**

NUTRITIONAL VALUE per 100 g

Energy	444 kcal = 1,857 kj
Protein	8.29 g
Carbohydrates	45.0 g
Fiber	7.57 g
Total fat	*24.4 g*
Saturated fat	*4.86 g*
Cholesterol	—
Sodium	*8.62 mg*

1% 2% 4% 10% 20% 40% 100%

% Daily Value (based on a 2,000 calorie diet) provided by each serving of this dessert

CALORIC PROPORTION

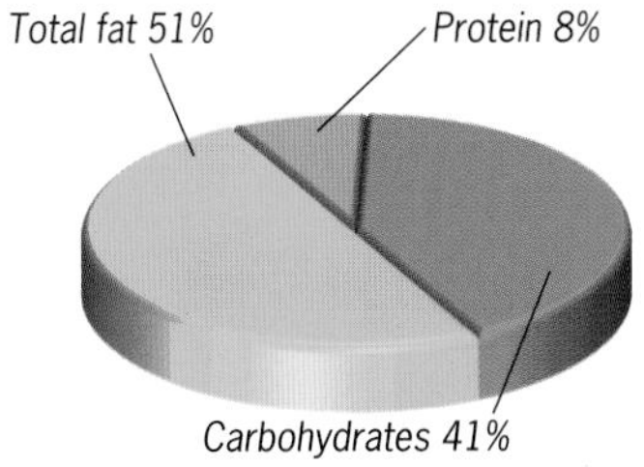

Percentage distribution of **calories for each nutrient**

Granola

INGREDIENTS

- 500 g (≅ 1 pound) of **rolled oats**
- 80 g (≅ 2.8 oz) of ground **walnuts**
- 160 g (≅ 1 cup) of ground **peanuts**
- 160 g (≅ 1 cup) of **brown sugar**
- 100 g (≅ 1 cup) of **wheat germ**
- 125 ml (≅ 1/2 cup) of **water**
- 8 tablespoons of olive **oil**
- 2 tablespoons of **vanilla** powder

PREPARATION

❶ Combine all ingredients and spread the mixture over an oven tray.

❷ Bake in a 180°C oven.

- Stir occasionally. When the water and the oil have been absorbed, turn the oven off and let cool.

❸ Store in an airtight container until it is time to use.

HEALTHIER ALTERNATIVE: Substitute the oil by 200 ml of soy milk (see Vol. 3, p. 305).

Have the ingredients ready.

Combine the dry ingredients.

Pour the water.

Spread the mixture on an oven tray.

Suggestions from the Chef

This recipe may be prepared in various ways. These are a few suggestions:

- **Other** rolled **cereals,** such as corn, rice, barley, rye, millet…
- Different **seeds:** Sunflower, pumpkin, sesame…
- Alternative **nuts:** hazelnuts, almonds, cashews…
- **Dried fruits:** raisins, dried apricots, prunes, dates…
- To sweeten, either honey or molasses may be used. However, decrease the amounts of honey/molasses if dried fruits are used.
- Cream may be substituted for the oil, and milk for water.
- As flavoring, **cinnamon** may be added to vanilla, as well as ground **cardamom** seeds, **anise** seeds, etc.

When using these alternative modifications, bear in mind that they alter this breakfast's nutritional and caloric values.

Celiac Condition

*Oats contain practically no **gliadin,** protein from the gluten that is not tolerated by celiac patients. This breakfast is therefore **compatible** with the diet of celiac patients, as shown by several scientific studies.*

For more information about the ingredients, see: Oats, Vol. 2, p. 41; walnut, Vol. 2, p. 64; peanut, Vol. 2, p. 336; sugar, Vol. 1, p. 170; wheat germ, Vol. 2, p. 310; olive oil, Vol. 1, p. 118.

NUTRITIONAL VALUE per 100 g

Energy	481 kcal = 2,011 kj
Protein	14.3 g
Carbohydrates	44.3 g
Fiber	7.47 g
Total fat	*26.1 g*
Saturated fat	*3.51 g*
Cholesterol	—
Sodium	*10.8 mg*

1% 2% 4% 10% 20% 40% 100%

% Daily Value (based on a 2,000 calorie diet) provided by each serving of this breakfast

HEALTH COUNSELS

Oats are the cereal *richest* in *caloric nutrients* (***protein, carbohydrates,*** and ***fat***) and *non-caloric nutrients* (***vitamins*** and ***minerals***): 100 g of oats contain almost 17 g of easy-to-digest protein that provide all the essential ***amino acids.*** Although oats are comparatively low in ***lysine*** and ***threonine*** (two essential amino acids), peanuts and walnuts contain these substances in adequate proportion. Therefore, this dish supplies a ***complete protein.***

Oats, wheat germ, and walnuts are excellent sources of ***vitamin*** B_1, B_2, and B_6. These are very necessary for good function of the digestive system.

Therefore, granola makes up a balanced and energy-filled breakfast, highly recommended to:

- ✓Keep the **nervous system** at **top** levels of **performance** due to its supply of ***glucose, unsaturated fatty acids, phosphorus, lecithin,*** and ***vitamin*** B_1. All these nutrients help to stimulate intellectual activity, invigorate the brain, and improve adaptation to stress situations.
- ✓Help in **growth** stages, **pregnancy, lactation,** and **sports,** due to the calories and protein supplied by this dish.
- ✓Treat **constipation,** thanks to its ***fiber.***

CALORIC PROPORTION

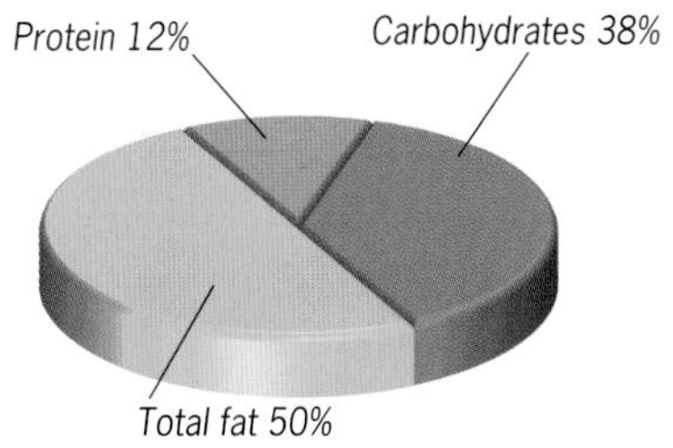

Percentage distribution of
calories for each nutrient

Preparation time: 00:05

Cooking time: - - - -

Tropical Shake

INGREDIENTS (4 servings)

- 1/2 liter (≅ 1/2 quart) of **Almond Milk** (Vol. 3, p. 342)
- 4 **bananas**

PREPARATION

❶ Peel and chop the bananas.
- Place the bananas in a container. Pour the almond milk and mix with an electric blender.

❷ Pour the mixture into individual glasses.

❸ Serve cold.

For more information about the ingredients, see: Almond, Vol. 2, p. 48; banana, Vol. 2, p. 70.

HEALTH COUNSELS

Almonds, the basic ingredient of this shake, are *high* in ***calcium.*** Furthermore, these nuts keep an adequate balance between calcium, ***phosphorus,*** and ***magnesium.*** As for bananas, apart from magnesium, they supply ***potassium, fiber,*** and ***B-complex vitamins.***

For all of the above reasons, this almond and banana shake is beneficial to:

✓ The nervous system, especially when suffering from **stress, intellectual strain, depression,** and **irritability.**

✓ The **musculoskeletal system,** since this shake, apart from its supply of minerals, *helps* the muscles **attach** themselves to the bones. Those wishing to prevent **osteoporosis** and **demineralization** will find this shake helpful.

✓ The arteries and the heart, as this is a *low-**sodium,** high-**potassium,*** **cholesterol**-*free* shake.

NUTRITIONAL VALUE per serving

Energy	131 kcal = 547 kj
Protein	4.20 g
Carbohydrates	23.9 g
Fiber	3.20 g
Total fat	*2.14 g*
Saturated fat	*0.349 g*
Cholesterol	—
Sodium	*4.14 mg*

1% 2% 4% 10% 20% 40% 100%

% Daily Value (based on a 2,000 calorie diet) provided by each serving of this shake

CALORIC PROPORTION

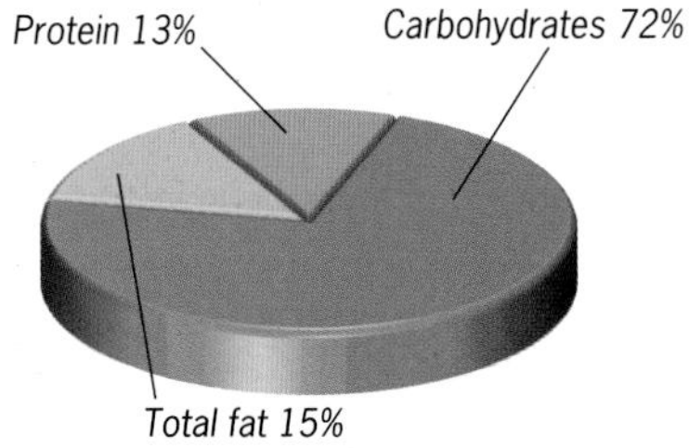

Percentage distribution of **calories for each nutrient**

Preparation time 00:05

Cooking time 00:10

Aromatic Linden

INGREDIENTS

- 4 tablespoons of **linden**
- The juice of one **orange**
- 1 **lemon** rind
- 1/2 liter (≅ 1/2 quart) of **red grape** juice
- 1 **cinnamon** stick
- 1/2 liter (≅ 1/2 quart) of **water**

PREPARATION

❶ Boil the water together with the cinnamon stick and the lemon rind for 3 minutes.

❷ Put the linden in a teapot. Add the boiling water and cover.

- Wait for 5 minutes. Strain off the tea and add orange and grape juice.

❸ Serve hot.

For more information about the ingredients, see: Orange, Vol. 2, p. 360; lemon, Vol. 2, p. 124; grape, Vol. 2, p. 78; and the *Encyclopedia of Medicinal Plants:* Linden, p. 169; cinnamon, p. 442.

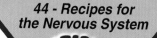

HEALTH COUNSELS

This tea is not only pleasant to drink, but also contains a number of medicinal properties for:

✓The **nervous system,** and it is recommended in case of **nervous agitation, anxiety,** and **insomnia.**

✓The **heart** and the **arteries,** as linden favors *vasodilation* and a slight *hypotension.*

✓The **stomach** and the **intestine,** as cinnamon *whets the appetite* and *helps digestion.* It is especially recommended in cases of **heavy digestion** and **flatulence.**

Suggestions from the Chef

- **Sweeten** with honey, sugar, or molasses. Each tablespoon of honey supplies 67 kcal (1 tablespoon—15-17 ml—is the equivalent to 3 teaspoons—5 ml).
- A cinnamon stick may be used more than once while still preserving the **same aroma.** It is recommended to wash it after use and place it immediately in the freezer for next time.
- A few drops of **lemon** juice may be added to the tea when serving.

45 RECIPES FOR THE HEART

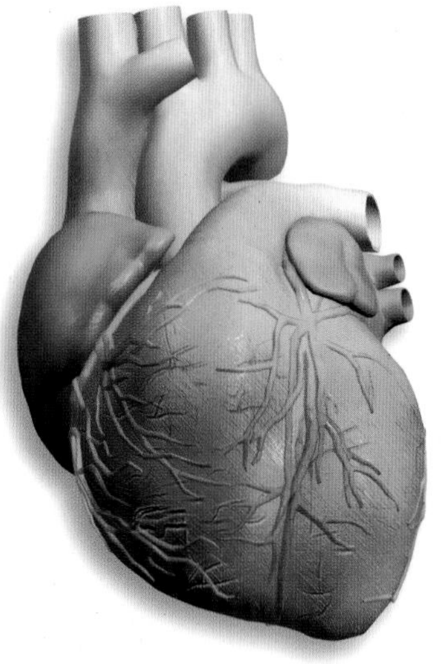

CHAPTER SUMMARY

RECIPES

Autumn Rice *168*
Banana Shake *179*
Bircher-muesli *175*
Cereal Bars *174*
Cherimoya and Orange Shake . . . *178*
Fufú *172*
Mangú/Fufú *172*
Mixed Vegetables *166*
Nut Hamburgers *171*
Oriental Salad *164*
Party Melon *176*
Pasta Bow Salad *165*
Peach Bavarian *173*
Potatoes with Peas *169*
Rice Hamburgers *170*
Strawberry Delight *177*

A HEALTHY HEART FOR LIFE

In our days, most scientific researchers agree with the following dietary guidelines as an effective measure to keep the heart healthy:

- **Reduce or eliminate animal fat from the diet,**
- **Use plenty of vegetables, and**
- **Reduce the use of salt and sugar.**

Additionally, if tobacco, coffee, and alcohol are removed, and moderate, regular physical exercise is practiced, "a good heart for life" can be assured (see Vol. 2, p. 53).

DOCTOR ***Adrian Vander***, a well-recognized expert in natural medicine, says, "the phenomenal muscular work carried out by the heart each day equals the effort of a mason lifting by hand one thousand, two-kilogram bricks up to a ten-meter height."

This gives us an idea of the amount of energy continuously used by this vital, yet small organ—the heart.

The food we eat is the "fuel" that produces this needed energy. Unless we want the engine to start failing or even come to a stop before its time, this "fuel" must be of top quality.

The American Health Association warns that among the causes of cardiac disease are a number of factors closely related to modern lifestyle, such as:

- A greater availability of foods, especially ***animal* fat,**
- **Less physical effort** at work,
- Greater *ease* in **transportation,**
- An increase in the availability and use of **tobacco, alcohol, etc.**

These living conditions are deeply rooted in the lifestyles of many people and social groups.

These HEALTHY RECIPES have been published in order to contribute to a ***better* lifestyle** as far as diet is concerned. A change in habits is so critical that *even* those patients who suffer from a **damaged heart**—through previous heart attacks, for example—but who have modified their lifestyle (diet, exercise, and mental attitude) attain ***greater* vitality** than *before* the attack.

There is no doubt that people enjoying the recipes included in this chapter will experience a stronger heart and a general improvement in their quality of life. In the words of ***Solomon*** the Wise:

"My son, [...] listen closely to my words [...] for they are life to those who find them and health to a man's whole body. ***Above all else, guard your heart, for it is the wellspring of life"*** (Proverbs 4: 20-23).

Menus for

Heart Attack and Angina Pectoris

Walnuts

BREAKFAST

- "Party Melon" (Vol. 3, p. 176)
- "Bircher-Muesli" (Vol. 3, p. 175)
- Walnuts or Cashew nuts (Vol. 2, pp. 64, 40)

LUNCH

- Cabbage Juice (Vol. 2, p. 191)
- "Oriental Salad" (Vol. 3, p. 164)
- "Mixed Vegetables" (Vol. 3, p. 166)
- "Rice Hamburgers" (Vol. 3, p. 170)
- "Whole Bread" (Vol. 3, p.46; Vol. 1, p. 72)

Rice Hamburgers

SUPPER

- "Rye Bread" with "Hummus" (Vol. 3, pp. 194, 67)
- "Strawberry Delight" (Vol. 3, p. 177)

Strawberry Delight

HEALTH COUNSELS

This menu is especially designed to *protect* the **coronary arteries** and to *prevent* **myocardial infarction** (heart attack). It is also useful in the post-infarction rehabilitation phase.

Fruits, whole cereals, legumes, vegetables, and nuts (especially walnuts) prepared in a simple way, make up the best diet to prevent a heart attack and to keep the heart healthy. And these ingredients are precisely the main components of this menu's recipes, which contain *zero* ***cholesterol*** and *very little* ***saturated fat.***

Heart Failure

Cherimoya and Orange Shake

BREAKFAST

- "Cherimoya and Orange Shake" (Vol. 3, p. 178)
- "Cereal Bars" (Vol. 3, p. 174)
- "Soy Milk" (Vol. 3, p. 305)

LUNCH

- Lemon and Grapefruit juice (Vol. 2, pp. 93, 124)
- "Autumn Rice" (Vol. 3, p. 168)
- "Broccoli Bake" (Vol. 3, p. 336)
- "Whole Bread" (Vol. 3, p. 46; Vol. 1, p. 72)
- "Sweet Corn Drink" (Vol. 3, p. 293)

Broccoli Bake

SUPPER

- Cherries (Vol. 2, p. 304)
- "Rye Bread" with "Walnut Buter" (Vol. 3, pp. 194, 65)

Cherries

HEALTH COUNSELS

This menu supplies energy to the heart. At the same time, it contains *large amounts of* ***potassium*** and very *little* ***sodium.*** It also contains *diuretic* foods, such as grapefruit, corn, and cherries. These reduce the blood volume, thus decongesting the circulatory system and helping the heart to work better. All this helps to *prevent* **heart failure** ("tired heart") or to *fight* it when it is present.

the Heart

Arrhythmia

Banana Shake

BREAKFAST
- "Banana Shake" (Vol. 3, p. 179)
- "Peach Bavarian" (Vol. 3, p. 173)
- "Almond Milk" (Vol. 3, p. 342)

Potatoes with Peas

LUNCH
- Carrot and tomato juice (Vol. 2, pp. 25, 275)
- "Red and White Salad" (Vol. 3, p. 372)
- "Potatoes with Peas" (Vol. 3, p. 169)
- "Nut Hamburgers" (Vol. 3, p. 171)
- "Rye Bread" (Vol. 3, p. 194)

SUPPER
- Tomato and onion salad (Vol. 2, pp. 275, 142)
- "Mangú/Fufú" (Vol. 3, p. 172)

Mangú/Fufú

HEALTH COUNSELS

This menu helps to avoid the disorders related to the heartbeat (arrhythmia), as it *lacks stimulating substances,* like ***caffeine*** and ***purine.*** The latter is present in meat and its derivatives.

At the same time, it supplies *good amounts* of ***potassium, magnesium,*** and ***calcium,*** necessary minerals for the heart's rhythmic contraction and relaxation.

Other Recipes for the Heart

SALADS
- "Pasta Bow Salad" (Vol. 3, p. 165)
- "Sprouts Salad" (Vol. 3, p. 244)
- "Mexican Salad" (Vol. 3, p. 260)
- "Spring Salad" (Vol. 3, p. 312)

SOUPS AND PURÉES
- "Andalusian Gazpacho" (Vol. 3, p. 360)
- "Cream of Banana" (Vol. 3, p. 252)
- "Vegetable Purée" (Vol. 3, p. 361)
- "Oat Soup" (Vol. 3, p. 147)

MAIN COURSES
- "Portuguese Beans" (Vol. 3, p. 324)
- "Rice with Cauliflower" (Vol. 3, p. 282)
- "Mung Bean Stew" (Vol. 3, p. 315)
- "Mexican Meat Analogs" (Vol. 3, p. 88)
- "Falafel Patties" (Vol. 3, p. 198)
- "Cashew Stew" (Vol. 3, p. 150)

BREAKFASTS, DESSERTS AND SNACKS
- "Tropical Shake" (Vol. 3, p. 158)
- "Mango Custard" (Vol. 3, p. 354)
- "Tropical Fruit Salad" (Vol. 3, p. 253)

DRINKS
- "Sangria (non-alcoholic)" (Vol. 3, p. 327)
- "Aromatic Linden" (Vol. 3, p. 159)

Infusions or decoctions:
- Hawthorn (*EMP,* p. 219)

- *See the recipe index at the beginning of this volume (Vol. 3, pp. 8-13).*
- *See also chapter 21, "Foods for the Heart" (Vol. 2, pp. 52-81).*

EMP = *Encyclopedia of Medicinal Plants,* Education and Health Library, Editorial Safeliz

Preparation time 00:20

Cooking time 00:35

Oriental Salad

INGREDIENTS (4 servings)

- 100 g (≅ 1/2 cup) of **whole rice**
- 100 g (≅ 1 1/2 cups) of **soybean sprouts**
- 100 g (≅ 3.5 oz) of **mushrooms**
- 1/2 **lettuce**
- 1 **Welsh onion**
- 1 **garlic** clove

ADDITIONAL INGREDIENTS

- **Parsley**
- **Mint**
- **Sesame sauce** (Vol. 3, p. 60) (each tablespoon of this sauce adds 37 kcal and 382 mg of sodium to the recipe, that is, around 9 kcal and 95 mg of sodium per serving)

PREPARATION

❶ Soak the rice in hot water for one hour.
- Wash the mushrooms and slice thin.
- Wash and slice the lettuce and the Welsh onion.
- Peel and chop the garlic, the parsley and the mint.

❷ Scald the mushrooms in boiling water.
- Boil the rice in salted water for 30 minutes. Drain and cool.
- Arrange the ingredients in a salad bowl.

❸ Dress with the sesame sauce and serve.

Gout

*Those who suffer from **gout** should eat mushrooms in moderation. This is because mushrooms contain protein that is high in nucleic acids and that produces **uric acid** in the organism.*

For more information about the ingredients, see: Rice, Vol. 2, p. 225; soybean, Vol. 2, p. 264; mushroom, Vol. 2, p. 294; lettuce, Vol. 2, p. 45; Welsh onion, Vol. 2, p. 144; garlic, Vol. 1, p. 338; and the *Encyclopedia of Medicinal Plants:* Garlic, p. 230.

HEALTHIER ALTERNATIVE: Persons requiring a low-sodium diet may substitute the sesame sauce with a dressing made up of oil and lemon juice.

NUTRITIONAL VALUE* per serving

Energy	**120 kcal = 501 kj**
Protein	**4.34 g**
Carbohydrates	**21.9 g**
Fiber	**2.65 g**
Total fat	***0.983 g***
Saturated fat	***0.184 g***
Cholesterol	—
Sodium	***10.9 mg***

1% 2% 4% 10% 20% 40% 100%

% Daily Value (based on a 2,000 calorie diet) provided by each serving of this dish

HEALTH COUNSELS

All salads whose main ingredients are raw greens and vegetables are **healthy for the heart.** The salad described here combines raw vegetables with boiled whole rice—a good source of ***B-complex vitamins*** and of ***fiber.***

As a result, the salad is rich in foods that protect the heart. Furthermore, due to the whole rice and mushrooms, this salad is particularly nutritious because of its ***energy*** and ***protein*** along with its minimal amount of fat.

This salad is especially beneficial to:

✓ Those requiring a **heart**-*protecting diet.*

✓ Those wishing to *prevent* **arteriosclerosis.**

CALORIC PROPORTION*

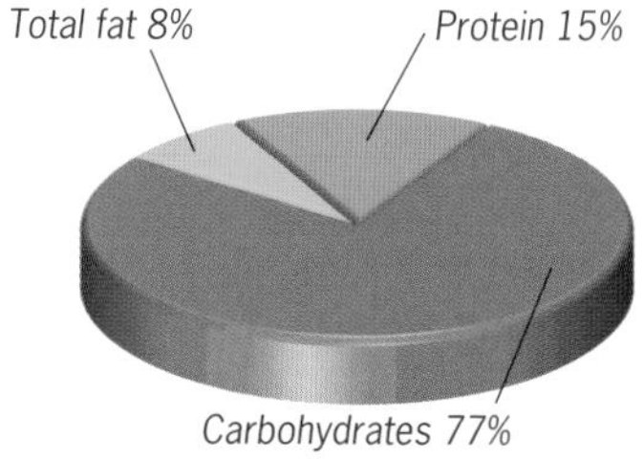

Percentage distribution of **calories for each nutrient**

* Additional ingredients not included.

Preparation time 00:15

Cooking time 00:40

Pasta Bow Salad

INGREDIENTS (4 servings)

- 200 g (≅ 7 oz) of **bow** pasta
- 200 g (≅ 2 cups) of **green beans** (string beans)
- 200 g (≅ 1 1/3 cups) of **peas**
- 1 **avocado**

ADDITIONAL INGREDIENTS

- 4 tablespoons of **lemon vinaigrette** (Vol. 3, p. 56) (each tablespoon of this sauce adds 95 kcal to the recipe, that is, around 23 kcal per serving)
- Sea **salt** (see Vol. 3, p. 16)

PREPARATION

❶ Remove the tips and the side threads in the green beans. Chop and wash the beans.
- Peel and chop the avocado.

❷ In two separate pots, boil green beans (for 20 minutes) and peas (for 5 minutes) in salted water. Drain and reserve the broth.
- Boil the pasta in the water from the vegetables and drain when the pasta is *al dente* (firm to the bite).
- When the pasta, green beans, and peas are cool, combine them in a salad bowl with the avocado.
- Dress with vinaigrette sauce.

❸ Serve cold.

For more information about the ingredients, see: Pasta, Vol. 1, p. 74; green beans, Vol. 1, p. 109; peas, Vol. 2, p. 73; avocado, Vol. 2, p. 108; and the *Encyclopedia of Medicinal Plants:* Green Bean, p. 584.

HEALTH COUNSELS

Pasta Bow Salad contains a combination that makes up a *low*-**fat,** *low*-**sodium**—if no salt is added—and *zero* ***cholesterol*** nutritional dish, especially beneficial to:

✓The **heart** and the **arteries,** due to the *invigorating* effect of green beans upon the heart, the ***antioxidants*** of peas that *prevent* ***arteriosclerosis,*** and the *heart-protecting* qualities of avocados.

✓The **nervous system,** as both avocados and peas are good sources of ***B-complex vitamins.***

✓*Prevent* ***anemia,*** as avocados and peas are relatively *high* in ***iron*** and ***folate,*** which are necessary for the production of red blood cells or erythrocytes.

NUTRITIONAL VALUE* per serving

Energy	300 kcal = 1,255 kj
Protein	10.7 g
Carbohydrates	43.4 g
Fiber	7.16 g
Total fat	*6.79 g*
Saturated fat	*1.07 g*
Cholesterol	—
Sodium	*12.5 mg*

1% 2% 4% 10% 20% 40% 100%

% Daily Value (based on a 2,000 calorie diet) provided by each serving of this dish

CALORIC PROPORTION*

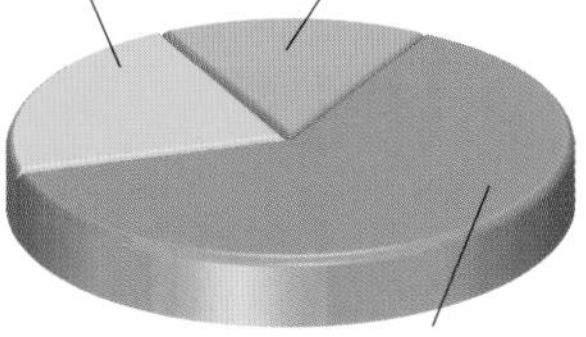

Percentage distribution of **calories for each nutrient**

* Additional ingredients not included.

Preparation time 00:30

Cooking time 00:30

Mixed Vegetables

INGREDIENTS (4 servings)

- 250 g (≅ 2 1/4 cups) of **green beans** (string beans)
- 500 g (≅ 1 pound) of **artichokes** (globe artichokes)
- 250 g (≅ 8.8 oz) of **carrots**
- 100 g (≅ 3/4 cup) of **fava beans** (broad beans)
- 100 g (≅ 2/3 cup) of **peas**
- 400 g (≅ 14 oz) of **potatoes**
- 1 **onion**
- 2 **garlic** cloves

ADDITIONAL INGREDIENTS

- The juice of 1 **lemon**
- **Parsley**
- 4 tablespoons of olive **oil** (each tablespoon of oil adds around 120 kcal to the recipe, that is, 30 kcal per serving)
- Sea **salt** (see Vol. 3, p. 16)

Suggestions from the Chef

- If a **pressure cooker** is used, remember that all boiling times should be reduced to half or even further when using an **express cooker.**
- However, if the vegetables are **steamed,** the cooking time may be extended.
- **Conserve** the vegetable **broth** for later use. Aside from preserving all the minerals contained in the vegetables, it adds a **delicious taste** to the food.

PREPARATION

❶ Wash and prepare the vegetables in the following manner:

- Remove the tips and threads from the green beans. Chop beans into small pieces.
- Remove the outer tough artichoke leaves. Cut off the tips and stems, and chop the artichokes into halves. Remove and discard the inner down. Chop into small pieces, and sprinkle them with lemon juice (see Vol. 2, p. 180).
- Peel and chop the carrots into small cubes.
- Peel and chop onion, garlic, and parsley (separately).
- Peel and chop potatoes into small cubes.

❷ Using a pot with oil, sauté the onion and the garlic on a low flame. When the onion is transparent, add the potatoes and vegetables.

- Sauté for 5 minutes, stirring occasionally. Add a cup of hot water.
- Add salt to taste and chopped parsley.
- Simmer for 15 to 20 minutes.

❸ Serve hot.

HEALTHIER ALTERNATIVE: Instead of sautéing the ingredients, add them raw directly into the boiling water. Furthermore, in order to avoid high blood pressure and to stimulate diuresis, omit the salt.

For more information about the ingredients, see: Green bean, Vol. 1, p. 109; artichoke, Vol. 2, p. 178; carrot, Vol. 2, p. 25; fava bean, Vol. 2, p. 137; pea, Vol. 2, p. 73; potato, Vol. 2, p. 201; onion, Vol. 2, p. 142; garlic, Vol. 1, p. 338; and the *Encyclopedia of Medicinal Plants:* Green bean, p. 584; garlic, p. 230.

Chop the leaf tips off the artichokes.

Prepare the remaining vegetables.

Add the remaining vegetables to the stir-fry.

NUTRITIONAL VALUE*
per serving

Energy	194 kcal = 810 kj
Protein	8.75 g
Carbohydrates	30.6 g
Fiber	11.5 g
Total fat	*0.685 g*
Saturated fat	*0.141 g*
Cholesterol	—
Sodium	*104 mg*

1% 2% 4% 10% 20% 40% 100%

% Daily Value (based on a 2,000 calorie diet) provided by each serving of this dish

HEALTH COUNSELS

Mixed Vegetables is a dish high in ***vitamins, minerals,*** and ***fiber.*** Additionally, it supplies many ***phytochemical elements,*** substances found in very small amounts in plant foods and possessing medicinal properties (see Vol. 1, p. 410).

Therefore, this dish is recommended to prevent or to facilitate the improvement of the following disorders and diseases:

✓ **Myocardial infarction** and **disease** of the **coronary** arteries, as ***flavonoids*** and other phytochemical elements stop arteriosclerosis and protect the heart.

✓ **Arterial hypertension,** because the mixed vegetables are very *high* in ***potassium*** and, at the same time, *low* in ***sodium.*** This helps to prevent high blood pressure and to *stimulate* ***diuresis*** (urine production).

✓ **Obesity,** as this dish contains high levels of ***fiber,*** which makes it *satisfying* with relatively few calories.

✓ **Constipation, diverticulosis,** and **hemorrhoids** because of its ***fiber.***

✓ **Cancer,** due to the protective action present in the greens and vegetables of this recipe—***fiber, phytochemical elements,*** and ***antioxidant*** substances (see Vol. 2, p. 371).

CALORIC PROPORTION*

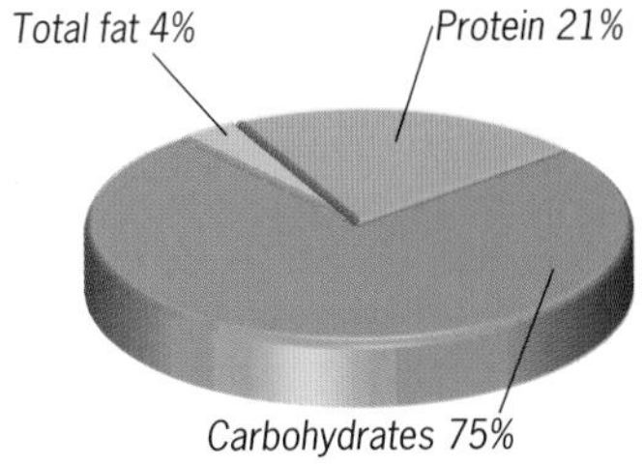

Percentage distribution of
calories for each nutrient

* Additional ingredients not included.

Preparation time 00:20

Cooking time 00:40

Autumn Rice

INGREDIENTS (4 servings)

- 300 g (≅ 1 1/2 cups) of **whole rice**
- 50 g (≅ 1/2 cup) of shelled **walnuts**
- 50 g (≅ 1.75 oz) of shelled **pine nuts** (pine kernels)
- 2 **garlic** cloves
- Unsalted **vegetable broth** (two and one-half times the volume of rice)

ADDITIONAL INGREDIENTS

- 2 tablespoons of olive **oil** (each tablespoon of oil adds around 120 kcal to the recipe, that is, 30 kcal per serving)
- Sea **salt** (see Vol. 3, p. 16)

PREPARATION

❶ Soak the rice in hot water for one hour or overnight in cold water.
- Peel and chop the garlic cloves.
- Chop the walnuts.

❷ Heat the oil in a frying pan, and sauté the garlic. Before they turn brown, add walnuts, pine nuts, boiling vegetable broth, and rice (drained).
- Add salt and simmer for 30 minutes.

❸ Serve hot.

Suggestions from the Chef

- If previously **boiled rice** is available, this dish may be prepared by combining the rice with the oil, raw garlic, and nuts.
- Place it in an oven dish and warm up in a 180°C oven for 10 or 15 minutes.

HEALTHIER ALTERNATIVE: Instead of sautéing the ingredients, add them raw to the boiling vegetable broth.

For more information about the ingredients, see: Rice, Vol. 2, p. 225; walnut, Vol. 2, p. 64; pine nut, Vol. 2, p. 47; garlic, Vol. 1, p. 338; and the *Encyclopedia of Medicinal Plants:* Garlic, p. 230.

HEALTH COUNSELS

Apart from ***carbohydrates,*** whole rice supplies ***fiber*** and ***B-complex vitamins.*** Walnuts and pine nuts are high in essential ***fatty acids, B-complex vitamins,*** and ***minerals.*** The result is a nutritious, *high-**protein*** dish with a moderate number of calories.

Autumn rice is beneficial to those who seek a nutritious dish that is healthy for the heart. It is recommended for:

✓The **heart** and **arteries,** due to the *protecting* properties of rice, walnuts, and garlic upon the *heart.*

✓The **immune system,** due to the ***zinc*** contained in walnuts, which helps the organism to fight **infectious** diseases.

✓**Cancer** *prevention,* due to ***glucosides*** in garlic, ***fiber*** in rice, and ***ellagic acid*** in walnuts, all of which are *anticarcinogenic* substances.

NUTRITIONAL VALUE* per serving

Energy	435 kcal = 1,818 kj
Protein	9.05 g
Carbohydrates	58.3 g
Fiber	4.55 g
Total fat	*17.4 g*
Saturated fat	*2.28 g*
Cholesterol	—
Sodium	*13.8 mg*

1% 2% 4% 10% 20% 40% 100%

% Daily Value (based on a 2,000 calorie diet) provided by each serving of this dish

CALORIC PROPORTION*

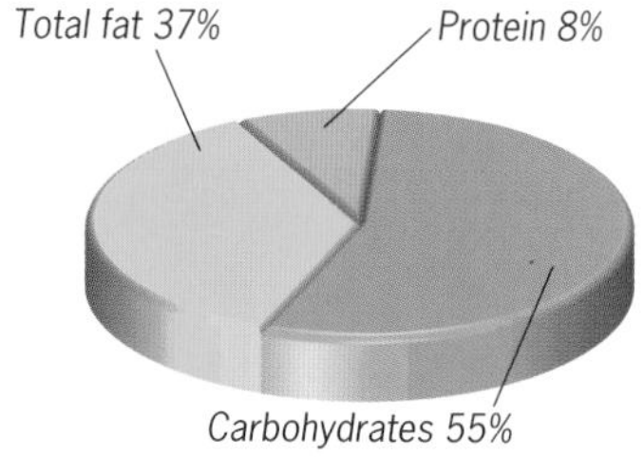

Percentage distribution of **calories for each nutrient**

* Additional ingredients not included.

Preparation time 00:15

Cooking time 00:40

Potatoes with Peas

INGREDIENTS (4 servings)

- 400 g (≅ 14 oz) of **potatoes**
- 400 g (≅ 2 3/4 cups) of **peas**
- 2 **onions**
- 2 **garlic** cloves
- 1 liter of unsalted **vegetable broth**

ADDITIONAL INGREDIENTS

- **Parsley**
- 5 tablespoons of olive **oil** (each tablespoon of oil adds around 120 kcal to the recipe, that is, 30 kcal per serving)
- Sea **salt** (see Vol. 3, p. 16)

PREPARATION

❶ Peel and wash the potatoes and the onions.
- Chop the onions in halves and then into very thin slices.
- Chop garlic and parsley separately.
- Chop the potatoes into thin slices.

❷ Heat the oil in a pot, and sauté the onion and garlic.
- Add the potatoes and sauté for an additional 5 minutes.
- Add boiling vegetable broth until potatoes are covered.
- Add salt.
- Boil for 15-20 minutes (potatoes should be tender and with some broth).
- Add the peas and the parsley 10 minutes before turning the stove off.

❸ Serve hot.

HEALTHIER ALTERNATIVE: Instead of sautéing the ingredients, add them raw to the boiling vegetable broth.

For more information about the ingredients, see: Potato, Vol. 2, p. 201; pea, Vol. 2, p. 73; onion, Vol. 2, p. 142; garlic, Vol. 1, p. 338; and the *Encyclopedia of Medicinal Plants:* Garlic, p. 230.

HEALTH COUNSELS

Potatoes and peas *hardly* contain ***fat*** or ***sodium***—if salt is not added. On the other hand, these ingredients are *high* in ***complex carbohydrates*** and they supply amino acids, which combine to make up *high quality* ***protein.*** Therefore, this dish should not be absent from the diet of those who wish to protect their heart. It is especially recommended:

✓ For the **heart** and the **arteries.** In addition to the aforementioned properties, this dish supplies ***antioxidant*** substances with their ***protective*** *action* upon the coronary arteries. Potatoes, peas, and garlic all contribute to the prevention of **arteriosclerosis, angina pectoris,** and **myocardial infarction.**

✓ For the **stomach** and the **intestine,** as it is easy to digest and potatoes have an *antacid* effect as well as a *relaxing* action. These are the reasons why this dish is quite appropriate to include in the diet of those suffering from **bowel spasms, gastritis,** and **heartburn.**

NUTRITIONAL VALUE* per serving

Energy	**177 kcal = 741 kj**
Protein	**8.14 g**
Carbohydrates	**28.5 g**
Fiber	**7.79 g**
Total fat	***0.615 g***
Saturated fat	***0.114 g***
Cholesterol	—
Sodium	***12.6 mg***

1% 2% 4% 10% 20% 40% 100%

% Daily Value (based on a 2,000 calorie diet) provided by each serving of this dish

CALORIC PROPORTION*

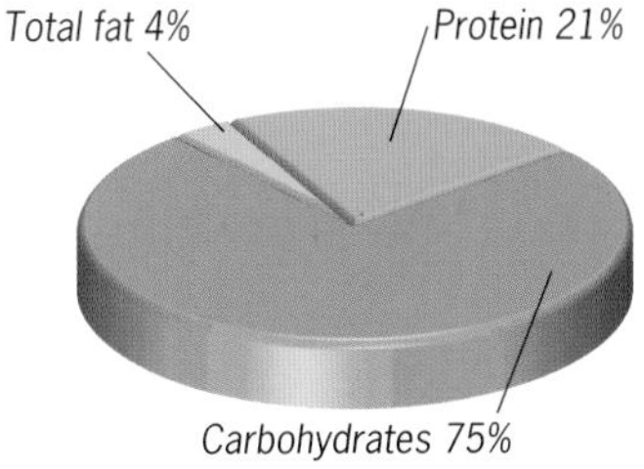

Percentage distribution of **calories for each nutrient**

* Additional ingredients not included.

Preparation time 00:10
Cooking time 01:00

Rice Hamburgers

INGREDIENTS (4 servings)

- 100 g (≅ 1/2 cup) of **whole rice**
- 50 g (≅ 2/3 cup) of ground **walnuts**
- 150 g (≅ 5.3 oz) of **tofu**
- 2 tablespoons of **corn flour**
- 4 tablespoons of **bread** crumbs
- 3 **garlic** cloves

ADDITIONAL INGREDIENTS

- **Potherbs** (parsley, basil, dill...)
- Sea **salt** (see Vol. 3, p. 16)

PREPARATION

❶Soak the rice in hot water for 30 minutes.
- Chop the garlic, the parsley, and the tofu.

❷In a pot, heat water with salt. Boil the rice for 30 minutes.
- Drain it and set aside to cool down.
- Combine the ingredients into dough, divide the mixture up into equal portions, and shape to form hamburgers.
- Place the hamburgers on an oven tray. Bake in a 180°C oven until golden and brown on both sides.

❸Serve hot.

For more information about the ingredients, see: Rice, Vol. 2, p. 225; walnut, Vol. 2, p. 64; tofu, Vol. 1, p. 88; flour, Vol. 1, p. 68; bread, Vol. 1, p. 70; garlic, Vol. 1, p. 338; and the *Encyclopedia of Medicinal Plants:* Garlic, p. 230.

Suggestions from the Chef

These hamburgers may be cooked in different ways: grilled, broiled, barbecued, or fried in oil. This last option is not so healthy for those suffering from the heart.

HEALTH COUNSELS

As opposed to beef hamburgers, these vegetarian hamburgers are very healthy for the heart and, at the same time, they are nutritious and tasty for the young.

Whole rice supplies ***B-complex vitamins*** needed for the heart muscle to carry out its contractions. It also supplies ***fiber,*** useful to "sweep" the bowel and to drag out cholesterol-precursor substances.

Walnuts exert a *favorable* action upon ***cholesterol*** levels, and they are a good source of energy to the heart.

Tofu, a soy-derivative product, is one of the richest in ***isoflavone,*** a substance that *protects* the artery walls and *prevents* ***arteriosclerosis.***

Therefore*,* these hamburgers are recommended to:

✓ *Prevent* **heart** disease, especially those caused by the narrowing of the coronary arteries—angina pectoris and myocardial infarction.

✓ *Reduce* the risk of **cancer,** especially prostate and breast cancers, due to the *protective* effect of tofu.

NUTRITIONAL VALUE* per serving

Energy	264 kcal = 1,101 kj
Protein	8.57 g
Carbohydrates	31.7 g
Fiber	2.90 g
Total fat	*11.0 g*
Saturated fat	*1.25 g*
Cholesterol	—
Sodium	*6.39 mg*

1% 2% 4% 10% 20% 40% 100%

% Daily Value (based on a 2,000 calorie diet) provided by each serving of this dish

CALORIC PROPORTION*

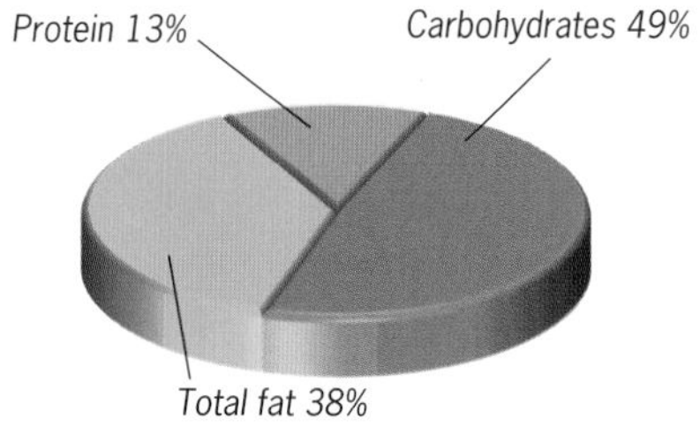

Percentage distribution of
calories for each nutrient

* Additional ingredients not included.

Preparation time 00:15

Cooking time 01:00

Nut Hamburgers

INGREDIENTS (4 servings)

- 250 g (≅ 8.8 oz) of shelled **nuts** (almonds, hazelnuts, walnuts…)
- 125 g (≅ 4.4 oz) of soft **whole bread**
- 1 **onion**
- 1 **garlic** clove
- 1 tablespoon of **brewer's yeast**
- 1 tablespoon of **whole flour**
- 50 g (≅ 1 cup) of **bread crumbs**
- 250 ml (≅ 1 cup) of unsalted **vegetable broth**

ADDITIONAL INGREDIENTS

- **Potherbs** (parsley, oregano, thyme…)
- Ground **cumin**
- 1 tablespoon of olive **oil** (each tablespoon of oil adds around 120 kcal to the recipe, that is, 30 kcal per serving)
- Sea **salt** (see Vol. 3, p. 16)

PREPARATION

❶ Peel and chop the onion and the garlic.
- Grind the nuts.
- Divide the whole bread in small chunks.

❷ Heat the oil in a frying pan, and sauté the onion and garlic.
- When the onion becomes transparent, add the flour and stir for one minute.
- Pour in the (warm) vegetable broth and keep stirring. Boil until it thickens.
- Add the remaining ingredients (except breadcrumbs) and stir a little more.
- Remove from heat and let it cool down.
- Shape the hamburgers with this dough (as thin as possible) and roll them in breadcrumbs.
- Bake the hamburgers in the oven until golden and crunchy on both sides.

❸ Serve hot, garnished with a sauce that is healthy for the heart, such as Almond Cream Sauce (see Vol. 3, p. 64).

For more information about the ingredients, see: Nuts, Vol. 1, p. 52; bread, Vol. 1, p. 70; onion, Vol. 2, p. 142; garlic, Vol. 1, p. 338; brewer's yeast, Vol. 1, p. 358; flour, Vol. 1, p. 68; and the *Encyclopedia of Medicinal Plants:* Garlic, p. 230.

HEALTHIER ALTERNATIVE: Instead of sautéing the onion and the garlic, steam them or roast them, lightly toast the flour, add the broth, and follow the instructions outlined for the preparation of this recipe.

HEALTH COUNSELS

These nut hamburgers are comparable or superior to steak as far as ***vitamins*** (except B_{12} that is absent), ***protein,*** and ***minerals,*** with the advantage of supplying *little* ***saturated fat,*** very *little* **sodium**—if little salt is added—and *zero* ***cholesterol.***

This dish, high in energy and nutrients, is recommended for the following cases:

✓ Persons that carry out **physical work** but who are concerned for their **heart**'s health.

✓ **Children** and **adolescents** in general, especially those who play **sports.**

NUTRITIONAL VALUE* per serving

Energy	527 kcal = 2,202 kj
Protein	18.9 g
Carbohydrates	31.9 g
Fiber	10.8 g
Total fat	*34.9 g*
Saturated fat	*3.57 g*
Cholesterol	—
Sodium	*11.8 mg*

1% 2% 4% 10% 20% 40% 100%

% Daily Value (based on a 2,000 calorie diet) provided by each serving of this dish

CALORIC PROPORTION*

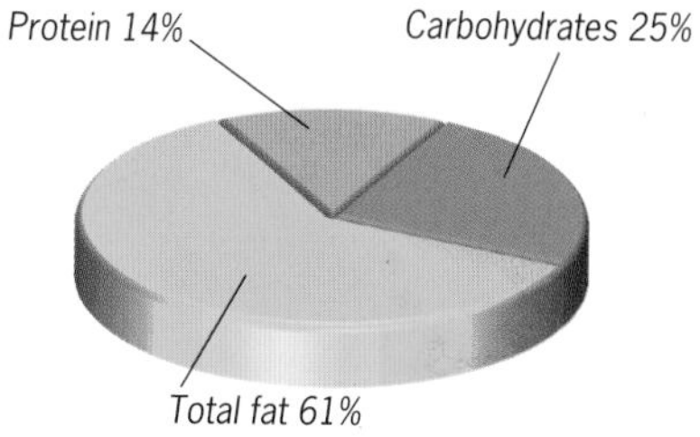

Percentage distribution of **calories for each nutrient**

* Additional ingredients not included.

Preparation time 00:10

Cooking time 00:50

Mangú/Fufú

INGREDIENTS (4 servings)

- 3 **plantains**
- 1 **onion**
- 2 **garlic** cloves

ADDITIONAL INGREDIENTS

- 2 tablespoons of olive **oil** (each tablespoon of oil adds around 120 kcal to the recipe, that is, 30 kcal per serving)
- Sea **salt** (see Vol. 3, p. 16)

PREPARATION

❶ Peel and chop the onion, garlic, and plantains.

❷ Cook the plantains in salted boiling water for 10 minutes.

- Pour in a little cold water to break the boiling and soften the plantains.
- Bring to a second boil and simmer for an additional 20 minutes.
- Remove from heat, drain and mash the plantains.
- Heat the oil in a frying pan and sauté the onion and garlic.
- When the onion is transparent, add the plantains and mash everything to form dough that is consistent.
- Add a little warm water to avoid hardening.

❸ Serve hot.

HEALTHIER ALTERNATIVE: Steam the onion and garlic instead of sautéing them.

For more information about the ingredients, see: Plantain, Vol. 2, p. 72; onion, Vol. 2, p. 142; garlic, Vol. 1, p. 338; and the *Encyclopedia of Medicinal Plants:* Garlic, p. 230.

HEALTH COUNSELS

The ingredients of this recipe, originally from the Caribbean, are especially healthy for the **heart.**

From the nutritional viewpoint, the fufú or mangú is notable for its *low-**fat**, low-**sodium*** content, if little salt is added. It also has a relatively *high-**fiber*** content, and *zero* ***cholesterol.*** All this contributes to a beneficial effect upon the heart.

Additionally, this recipe is recommended to:

✓ Those suffering from **high blood pressure,** due to the *low-**sodium*** content and the garlic effect that stabilizes the arterial pressure.

✓ Those suffering from **intestinal problems,** such as colitis or intestinal flora alterations, due to the *smoothing* effect of plantain and to the *antiseptic* action of garlic and onion. These two ingredients are capable of *fighting* the **pathogen germs** in the bowel.

NUTRITIONAL VALUE* per serving

Energy	**147 kcal = 614 kj**
Protein	**1.99 g**
Carbohydrates	**34.6 g**
Fiber	**3.15 g**
Total fat	*0.464 g*
Saturated fat	*0.163 g*
Cholesterol	—
Sodium	*5.84 mg*

1% 2% 4% 10% 20% 40% 100%

% Daily Value (based on a 2,000 calorie diet) provided by each serving of this dish

CALORIC PROPORTION*

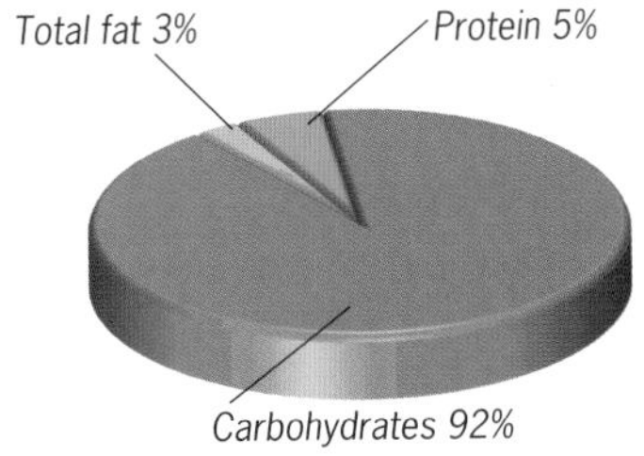

Percentage distribution of **calories for each nutrient**

* Additional ingredients not included.

Preparation time 00:20

Cooking time 00:40

Peach Bavarian

INGREDIENTS (4 servings)

- 2 **peaches** (Persian apples)
- 8 tablespoons of husked **millet**
- 2 tablespoons of **rice flour**
- 2 tablespoons of **brown sugar**
- 2 tablespoons of **honey**
- 1 **orange**
- 1 **lemon**
- 75 ml (≅ 1/3 cup) of **soy milk** (Vol. 3, p. 305)
- **Water** (twice the volume of millet)

ADDITIONAL INGREDIENTS

- Ground **cinnamon**
- Two **vanilla** sticks

PREPARATION

❶ Make a fruit juice using the orange, the lemon, the honey, and a liquefied peach.

❷ In a pot, boil the water with the millet until the water has evaporated.
- Boil the milk and the vanilla for 5 minutes.
- Pour the hot milk onto the millet little by little combining both ingredients very well.
- Turn the stove off and cover to allow the millet to expand.
- Remove the vanilla sticks, mix the millet with the rice flour and half the juice, and pour it into a greased crown-shaped mold. Chill in the refrigerator for 4 hours.

❸ To serve, empty the mold onto an appropriate tray. Pour the remaining juice and sugar and decorate with the remaining peach and cinnamon.

For more information about the ingredients, see: Peach, Vol. 2, p. 75; millet, Vol. 1, p. 76; rice flour, Vol. 1, p. 69; sugar, Vol. 1, p. 170; honey, Vol. 1, p. 160; orange, Vol. 2, p. 360; lemon, Vol. 2, p. 124; soy milk, Vol. 1, p. 88.

HEALTH COUNSELS

Millet has a higher ***protein*** content than wheat and rice, and *hardly* contains ***gluten.*** Together with the citric fruits and the peach, as included in this recipe, it makes a nutritious and tasty dessert that is beneficial to:

✓ The **heart** and the **arteries,** as it has a *very low* content in ***fat*** and in ***sodium,*** with *zero* ***cholesterol.*** Besides, this dessert contains ***flavonoids, beta-carotene*** (provitamin A), and other ***antioxidants*** coming from the fruits in this recipe.

✓ **Growth** stages, **pregnancy, lactation, sports,** and **physical work,** due to the energy supplied by both millet and honey.

✓ The **intestine** and the **stomach,** due to the *smoothing* and *laxative* effects of millet and honey.

NUTRITIONAL VALUE* per serving

Energy	229 kcal = 958 kj
Protein	4.36 g
Carbohydrates	47.2 g
Fiber	4.50 g
Total fat	*1.57 g*
Saturated fat	*0.247 g*
Cholesterol	—
Sodium	*7.57 mg*

1% 2% 4% 10% 20% 40% 100%

% Daily Value (based on a 2,000 calorie diet) provided by each serving of this dessert

CALORIC PROPORTION*

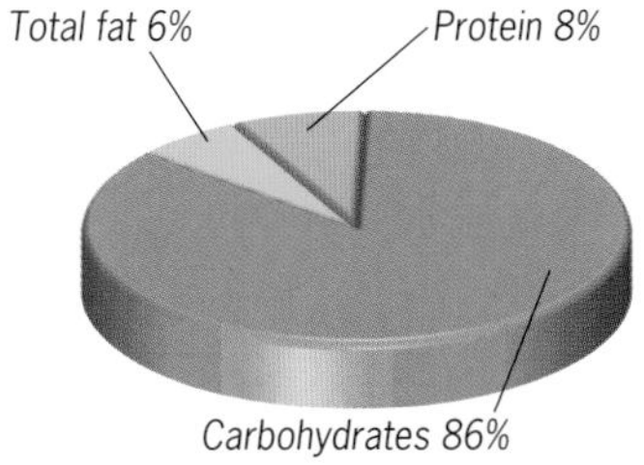

Percentage distribution of **calories for each nutrient**

* Additional ingredients not included.

Preparation time 00:15

Cooking time 00:40

Cereal Bars

INGREDIENTS

- 500 g (≅ 1 pound) of **muesli** (see box below)
- 100 g (≅ 3.5 oz) of toasted **sesame**
- 6 tablespoons of **honey**
- 6 tablespoons of seeds **oil**
- 50 g (1/5 cup) of **water**

PREPARATION

❶ Combine all the ingredients until the mixture becomes uniform.

- Spread it over a previously greased oven tray to make it 1 cm thick.

❷ Bake in a 180°C oven for 35 or 40 minutes until it becomes golden. Remove from the oven. Press strongly using a knife or a wheel to mark the mixture.

- Cool down and break at the marks.

❸ Keep in glass jars until it is time to use.

Muesli

Muesli is a mixture of rolled cereals, dried fruits, and nuts (see next page).

*In order to prepare the 500 g required in this recipe, the following **ingredients** are suggested:*

- *200 g of rolled oats*
- *50 g of raisins*
- *50 g of dried figs*
- *50 g of dried apricots*
- *50 g of shelled walnuts*
- *50 g of shelled hazelnuts*
- *50 g of shredded coconut*

*In order to **prepare** muesli, chop the nuts and the dried fruits and mix in the previously soaked rolled oats.*

For more information about the ingredients, see: Oats, Vol. 2, p. 41; raisins, Vol. 2, p. 81; fig, Vol. 2, p. 145; dried apricot, Vol. 2, p. 27; walnut, Vol. 2, p. 64; hazelnut, Vol. 2, p. 252; coconut, Vol. 2, p. 325; sesame, Vol. 1, p. 352; honey, Vol. 1, p. 160; oil, Vol. 1, p. 112; and the *Encyclopedia of Medicinal Plants:* Sesame, p. 611.

HEALTH COUNSELS

Cereal Bars posses all the advantages of muesli, plus the benefits of sesame seeds. The latter are *very high* in ***unsaturated fatty acids*** and in ***protein*** of high biological value, along with ***lecithin, vitamins, minerals,*** and ***trace elements.*** Cereal bars enjoy the advantage of easy handling and transport, and are very useful to:

✓ *Prevent* **heart** and **artery** diseases.

✓ *Invigorate* the **nervous system.**

✓ *Improve* the health of the **reproductive system,** especially the male reproductive system because of the sesame.

✓ *Supply* ***energy*** and ***nutrients*** in a compact and digestible way.

NUTRITIONAL VALUE per 100 g

Energy	418 kcal = 1,747 kj
Protein	7.95 g
Carbohydrates	37.2 g
Fiber	5.93 g
Total fat	*26.2 g*
Saturated fat	*4.35 g*
Cholesterol	—
Sodium	*6.40 mg*

1% 2% 4% 10% 20% 40% 100%

% Daily Value (based on a 2,000 calorie diet) provided by each 100 g of this breakfast

CALORIC PROPORTION

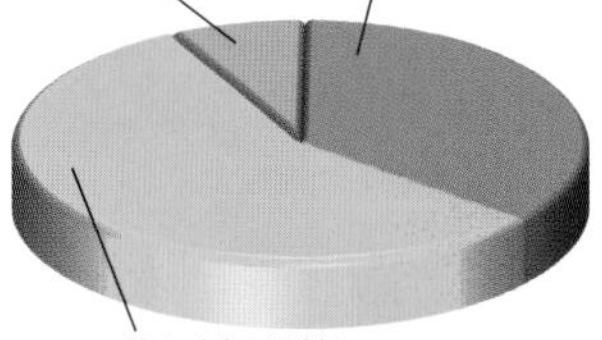

Percentage distribution of **calories for each nutrient**

Preparation time: 00:20

Cooking time: ----

Bircher-Muesli

INGREDIENTS

- 100 g (≅ 2/3 cup) of rolled **oats**
- 30 g (≅ 1 oz) of **raisins**
- 30 g (≅ 1 oz) of **dried figs**
- 30 g (≅ 1 oz) of **dried apricots**
- 50 g (≅ 1/2 cup) of shelled **walnuts**
- 50 g (≅ 1.75 oz) of shelled **hazelnuts**
- 50 g (≅ 2/3 cup) of shredded **coconut**
- 4 **apples**
- 2 **bananas**
- 4 tablespoons of **honey**
- The juice of one **lemon**
- 1/2 liter (≅ 1/2 quart) of **water**
- 1/2 liter (≅ 1/2 quart) of **soy milk** (Vol. 3, p. 305)

PREPARATION

❶ Soak the rolled oats in the water.

- Chop all the dried fruits and nuts and add them to the water with the oats.
- Let rest overnight.

❷ In the morning, before serving the muesli, peel and shred the apples and coat them with the lemon juice.

- Peel and chop the bananas, and add them to the drained apples and oats, nuts, and dried fruits.
- Add the milk and the honey and mix.

❸ It may be served according to taste or season of the year—cold during the warm seasons or warm/hot during the cold seasons.

For more information about the ingredients, see: Oats, Vol. 2, p. 41; raisins, Vol. 2, p. 81; fig, Vol. 2, p. 145; dried apricot, Vol. 2, p. 27; walnut, Vol. 2, p. 64; hazelnut, Vol. 2, p. 252; coconut, Vol. 2, p. 325; apple, Vol. 2, p. 229; banana, Vol. 2, p. 70; honey, Vol. 1, p. 160; soy milk, Vol. 1, p. 88.

HEALTH COUNSELS

Bircher-Muesli is one of the most traditional and healthy ways to prepare the well-known muesli. It makes an excellent breakfast *high* in ***energy*** and in ***nutrients.*** Furthermore, it provides an outstanding protective action on the ***heart*** and the cardiovascular system as it:

✓ *Stimulates* **blood circulation** through the **coronary arteries,** due to the ***flavonoids*** and the ***phytochemical elements*** present in raisins, dried figs, and dried apricots.

✓ *Lowers* the **cholesterol** level in the blood, as the ***fiber*** from oats and dried fruits reduces the intestinal absorption of cholesterol. Additionally, ***fatty acids*** in nuts control its production in the liver.

✓ *Prevents* **coronary spasms,** due to the ***magnesium*** from nuts.

Bircher-muesli is also beneficial for:

✓ The **nervous system,** for its ***B-complex vitamins*** from oats and walnuts.

✓ The **musculoskeletal system,** for its supply of energy for the muscles.

NUTRITIONAL VALUE per 100 g

Energy	**119 kcal = 497 kj**
Protein	**2.56 g**
Carbohydrates	**15.7 g**
Fiber	**2.67 g**
Total fat	***4.90 g***
Saturated fat	***1.14 g***
Cholesterol	—
Sodium	***5.22 mg***

1% 2% 4% 10% 20% 40% 100%

% Daily Value (based on a 2,000 calorie diet) provided by each 100 g of this breakfast

CALORIC PROPORTION

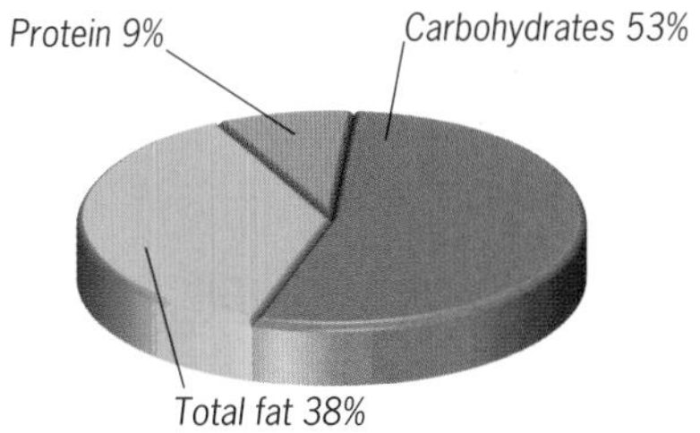

Percentage distribution of **calories for each nutrient**

Preparation time 00:30

Cooking time - - - -

Party Melon

INGREDIENTS (4 servings)

- 2 small **melons**
- 200 g (≅ 1 1/4 cups) of **grapes**
- 2 **bananas**
- 3 **tangerines**
- 1 **orange**
- 100 g (≅ 3.5 oz) of **blackberries (bramble berries)** or **raspberries**
- 50 g (≅ 1.75 oz) of seedless **raisins**
- 250 g (≅ 8.8 oz) of **strawberries**

PREPARATION

❶ Cut the melons into halves and chop off the extremes in order to provide a good base upon which to stand.
- Empty the seeds.
- Scoop out the pulp using a round, melon spoon and set aside.
- Peel and seed the grapes.
- Squeeze the orange and reserve the juice.
- Peel and chop the bananas and coat them with the orange juice.
- Peel and separate the tangerines into segments.
- Wash and clean the remaining fruit.

❷ Place the combined fruits into the melon halves and chill in the refrigerator.

❸ Serve cold.

For more information about the ingredients, see: Melon, Vol. 2, p. 254; grapes, Vol. 2, p. 78; banana, Vol. 2, p. 70; tangerine, Vol. 2, p. 359; orange, Vol. 2, p. 360; blackberry, Vol. 1, p. 49; raspberry, Vol. 1, p. 49; strawberry, Vol. 2, p. 103.

HEALTH COUNSELS

All fruits utilized in this dessert provide an excellent source of ***vitamins, minerals, antioxidants,*** and ***phytochemicals*** that preserve health and protect against illness, especially cardiac disease and cancer.

This is an ideal dessert for those suffering from **heart** disease or for those who decide to maintain a healthy heart. In any case, this is a dessert full of health.

Party Melon is especially recommended in the following cases:

✓ *Prevention* of coronary diseases, such as ***arteriosclerosis*** and ***high blood pressure.*** Besides, it is adequate in the post-infarction diet.

✓ Acute phases of **infectious diseases,** as this dessert supplies very digestible ***sugars*** and ***vitamins,*** which are appropriate in case of fever.

✓ **Cancer** *prevention.*

✓ **Cleansing cures,** due to the *diuretic* effect of fruit upon the kidneys.

NUTRITIONAL VALUE per serving

Energy	**248 kcal = 1,035 kj**
Protein	**4.43 g**
Carbohydrates	**53.0 g**
Fiber	**8.54 g**
Total fat	***1.31 g***
Saturated fat	***0.339 g***
Cholesterol	—
Sodium	***36.3 mg***

1% 2% 4% 10% 20% 40% 100%

% Daily Value (based on a 2,000 calorie diet) provided by each serving of this dessert

CALORIC PROPORTION

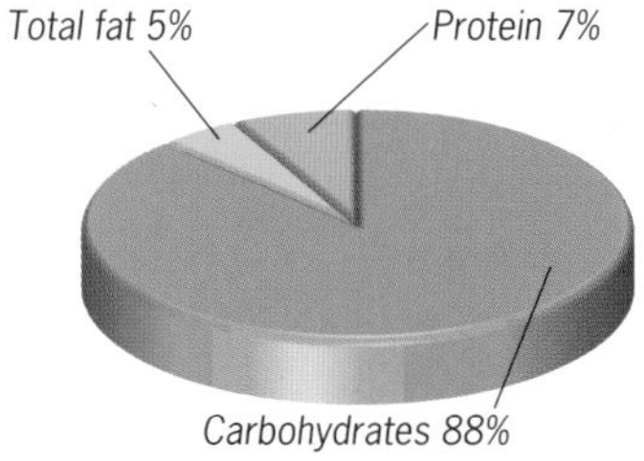

Percentage distribution of **calories for each nutrient**

Preparation time 00:15

Cooking time -- --

Strawberry Delight

INGREDIENTS (4 servings)

- 400 g (≅ 14 oz) of **strawberries**
- 100 g (≅ 1 cup) of shelled **walnuts**
- 4 tablespoons of **honey**
- 2 tablespoons of shelled **sunflower seeds**

PREPARATION

❶ Chop the nuts and grind the sunflower seeds.
- Separate the green section of the strawberries and wash them.
- Either slice them or cut them into halves. Combine them with sunflower seeds, walnuts, and honey.

❷ Arrange the mixture in goblets.

❸ Serve cold.

For more information about the ingredients, see: Strawberry, Vol. 2, p. 103; walnut, Vol. 2, p. 64; honey, Vol. 1, p. 160; sunflower seeds, Vol. 2, p. 105.

HEALTH COUNSELS

Strawberries are among the fruits with the highest antioxidant effect, and therefore they protect against **arteriosclerosis** and **coronary** disease. Together with walnuts, sunflower seeds, and honey, they make a highly recommended dessert for those wanting to keep a strong heart and healthy coronary arteries.

At the same time, this strawberry dessert is both very nutritious and tasty, and is enjoyed by children and grownups.

NUTRITIONAL VALUE per serving

Energy	294 kcal = 1,227 kj
Protein	5.37 g
Carbohydrates	28.8 g
Fiber	3.96 g
Total fat	*18.3 g*
Saturated fat	*1.68 g*
Cholesterol	—
Sodium	*4.60 mg*

1% 2% 4% 10% 20% 40% 100%

% Daily Value (based on a 2,000 calorie diet) provided by each serving of this dessert

CALORIC PROPORTION

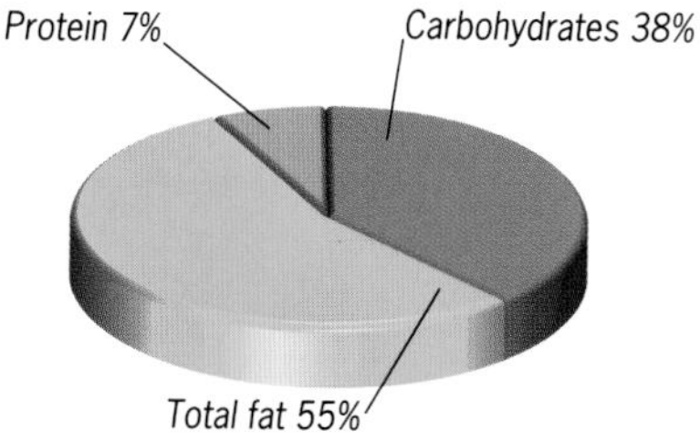

Percentage distribution of **calories for each nutrient**

Suggestions from the Chef

To achieve a **creamier** dessert, add a little hazelnut milk, yogurt (plain or strawberry), cream, etc.

Strawberry Intolerance

*Strawberries may produce **allergic reactions** in **sensitive persons.** Manifestations consist of a rash in the lips or a swollen tongue (glossitis).*

Preparation time 00:20 | Cooking time - - - -

Cherimoya and Orange Shake

INGREDIENTS (4 servings)

- 500 g (≅ 1 pound) of **cherimoyas**
- 4 **oranges**

PREPARATION

❶ Cut the cherimoyas into halves, scoop out the pulp using a spoon and sift it through a vegetables sieve to eliminate the seeds.

• Cut the oranges into halves and squeeze them.

❷ Pour the orange juice and the pulp of the cherimoyas into a suitable container and blend.

❸ Serve cold.

For more information about the ingredients, see: Cherimoya, Vol. 2, p. 59; orange, Vol. 2, p. 360.

Scoop out the pulp of the cherimoya in order to sift it.

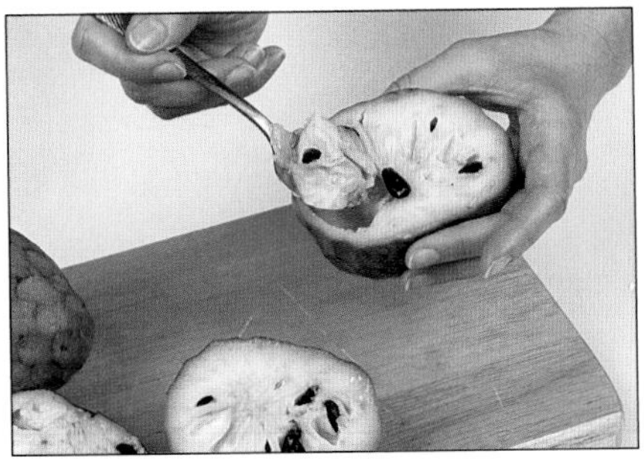

HEALTH COUNSELS

Cherimoya is the fresh fruit highest in ***B-complex vitamins.*** In addition, it contains ***calcium, phosphorus, iron,*** and ***potassium.*** Together with ***vitamin C, beta-carotene*** (provitamin A), and ***calcium*** from oranges, this makes the shake very healthy and aromatic. It is useful for:

✓The **heart** and the **arteries,** due to the *protective* qualities of cherimoyas and oranges.

✓The **immune system,** due to the *immune* and *stimulating* effects of oranges, which are empowered by the ***vitamins*** and ***minerals*** of the cherimoyas.

✓The **nervous system,** especially for **students,** as it supplies ***sugars*** that are immediately available for neurons to use, apart from the already-mentioned ***B-complex vitamins,*** which favor intellectual achievement.

✓The **musculoskeletal system,** as both cherimoyas and oranges are *high* in ***calcium.***

NUTRITIONAL VALUE per serving

Energy	108 kcal = 451 kj
Protein	1.55 g
Carbohydrates	24.7 g
Fiber	2.09 g
Total fat	*0.465 g*
Saturated fat	*0.017 g*
Cholesterol	—
Sodium	*4.76 mg*

1% 2% 4% 10% 20% 40% 100%

% Daily Value (based on a 2,000 calorie diet) provided by each serving of this shake

CALORIC PROPORTION

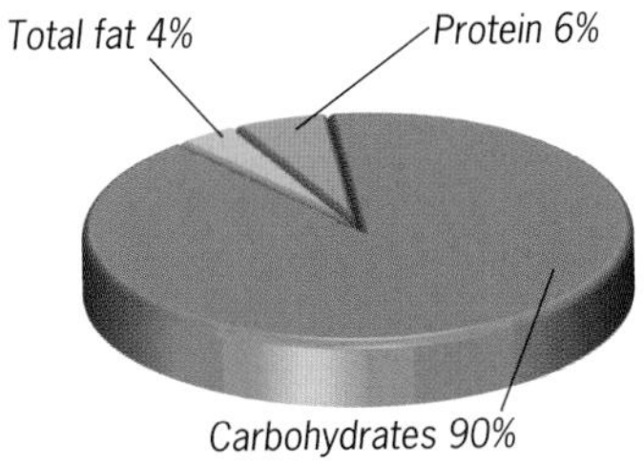

Percentage distribution of **calories for each nutrient**

Preparation time: 00:15

Cooking time: - - - -

Banana Shake

INGREDIENTS (4 servings)

- 2 **bananas**
- 1/2 liter (≅ 1/2 quart) of fresh **orange juice**
- 2 tablespoons of **molasses**
- 250 ml (≅ 1 cup) of water

PREPARATION

❶ Peel and chop the bananas.

❷ Place all the ingredients in a tall container. Blend until a creamy mixture is obtained.

❸ Serve the shake in goblets with crushed ice and use immediately.

For more information about the ingredients, see: Banana, Vol. 2, p. 70; orange, Vol. 2, p. 360; molasses, Vol. 1, p. 175.

Suggestions from the Chef

Water may be substituted with **vegetable milk** (soy, almond, or hazelnut) or with nonfat cow's milk in order to obtain a creamy and nutritious drink with a touch of distinction.

HEALTH COUNSELS

Bananas are *high* in ***potassium*** and ***low*** in ***sodium.*** They are known for their ***B vitamin*** content as well as ***magnesium*** and ***fiber.*** They also contain small amounts of ***serotonin,*** a *vasodilating* substance, which improves blood circulation in the arteries.

The medicinal properties of bananas are empowered by the combination with oranges, *high* in ***vitamin C, beta-carotene*** (provitamin A), and ***flavonoids,*** which exert an *antioxidant* and *thinning* action upon the blood.

Therefore, this banana and orange shake is very helpful to keep a healthy **heart** and to prevent:

- ✓**High blood pressure.**
- ✓Cardiac **arrhythmia.**
- ✓**Infarction**.
- ✓Arterial **arteriosclerosis** and **thrombosis.**

NUTRITIONAL VALUE per serving

Energy	143 kcal = 596 kj
Protein	1.45 g
Carbohydrates	34.1 g
Fiber	1.54 g
Total fat	*0.502 g*
Saturated fat	*0.127 g*
Cholesterol	—
Sodium	*2.28 mg*

1% 2% 4% 10% 20% 40% 100%

% Daily Value (based on a 2,000 calorie diet) provided by each serving of this shake

CALORIC PROPORTION

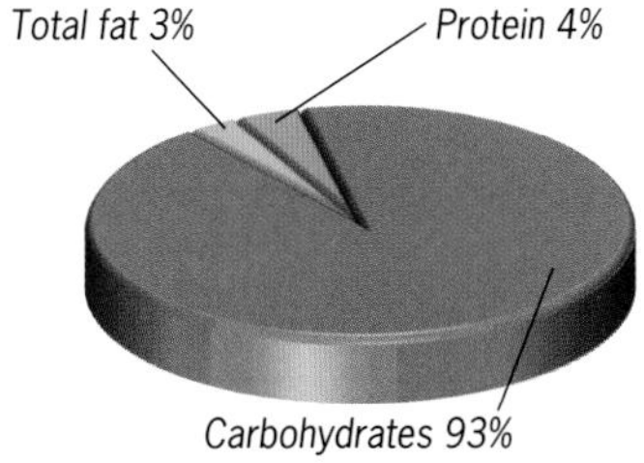

Percentage distribution of **calories for each nutrient**

46

RECIPES FOR THE ARTERIES

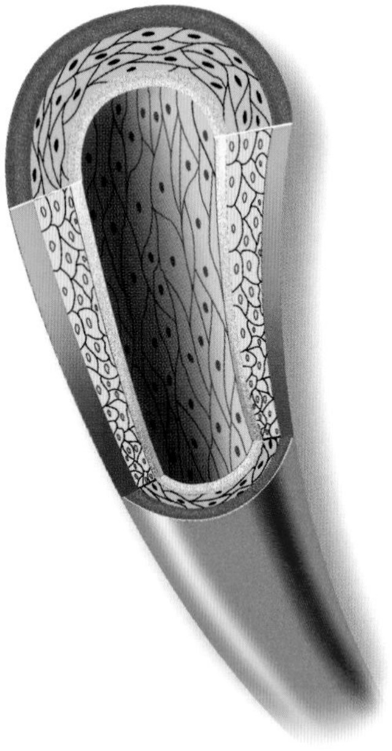

CHAPTER SUMMARY

RECIPES

Avocado Shake *201*
Banana Soup *188*
Chickpea Salad *186*
Falafel Patties *198*
Fruit Salad *200*
Grilled Vegetables *189*
Potato Stew *190*
Rainbow Salad *184*
Rice Crackers *196*
Rice Pudding *199*
Rice with Pumpkin *193*
Rice with Spinach *192*
Rye Bread *194*
Yam with Tomato *191*
Zucchini Salad *185*

There are foods that, adequately prepared, as shown in this chapter, contribute to the good health of the arteries and avoid their deterioration and clotting.

Additionally, it is necessary to keep away from tobacco, prevent high blood pressure, and control the level of cholesterol in order to protect the arteries.

PUMPED by the heart, blood takes oxygen and nutrients via the appropriate ducts—arteries and capillary vessels—to all cells throughout the organism. Erythrocytes or red blood cells carry oxygen, and blood plasma transports nutrients and other vital elements. The elimination of waste substances—carbon dioxide (CO_2) and various substances produced by cellular metabolism—is carried out when blood circulates through the veins on its way to the heart.

It is important that the central pump is in a good working condition and the carrier is in top condition. But it is no less important that the **circulation channels** are kept **clean and clear** so that blood may circulate freely with no obstacles.

Today, it is known that arteries may become clogged or may lose their necessary elasticity due to an unhealthy lifestyle or a poor diet.

Hardening of the arteries (**arteriosclerosis**, Vol. 2, p. 86) is the *most widespread* serious disease in the western world. It is true that arteries undergo a normal hardening process due to age; however, an adequate **lifestyle** may significantly *delay* this process.

It is important to know that arteriosclerosis and **high blood pressure** are the *main* **risk factors** for **myocardial infarction** (Vol. 2, p. 55) and for **cerebral vascular strokes** (Vol. 2, p. 87).

Well Preserved Arteries

The *best* **diet** to keep our arteries in their healthiest condition is *undoubtedly* **vegetarian,** due to its low-sodium content and its zero cholesterol content (see Vol. 2, p. 82-83).

Furthermore, a diet based on vegetables may help arterial **regeneration,** as it reduces cholesterol deposits and improves elasticity.

Therefore, ***"it is never too late to start a healthier diet."*** Besides, a good diet not only helps the entire organism to recover, but also pleases the palate. Health and pleasure—when taste is trained or retrained—do not need to be incompatible when it comes to diet. The following pages are a demonstration of this fact.

Menus for

Arteriosclerosis

BREAKFAST

- "Avocado Shake" (Vol. 3, p. 201)
- "Rice Pudding" (Vol. 3, p. 199)
- Pineapple (Vol. 2, p. 189)

Rice Pudding

Rainbow Salad

LUNCH

- Cabbage juice (Vol. 2, p. 191)
- "Rainbow Salad" (Vol. 3, p. 184)
- "Rice with Pumpkin" (Vol. 3, p. 193)
- "Falafel Patties" (Vol. 3, p. 198)
- "Whole Bread" (Vol. 3, p. 46; Vol. 1, p. 72)

SUPPER

- "Garlic Soup" (Vol. 3, p. 374)
- "Potato Stew" (Vol. 3, p. 190)

Garlic Soup

HEALTH COUNSELS

The ingredients included in this menu *slow down* the development of **arteriosclerosis** (hardening and narrowing of the arteries), and may even reverse it. Vegetables, whole cereals, and especially garlic play an important role in this process.

Antioxidant vitamins (***A, C,*** and ***E***), as well as ***flavonoids*** and other ***phytochemicals*** from the vegetables found in these recipes, also prevent arteriosclerosis.

And, of course, the *absence* of ***cholesterol*** and the *small amounts* of ***saturated fat*** in this menu make it ideal to maintain the arteries in good health.

High Blood Pressure

BREAKFAST

- Grapefruit juice (Vol. 2, p. 93)
- "Party Melon" (Vol. 3, p. 176)
- "Rice Crackers" (Vol. 3, p. 196)
- "Almond Milk" (Vol. 3, p. 342)

Party Melon

LUNCH

- Onion and Celery Juice (Vol. 2, pp. 142, 248)
- "Zucchini Salad" (Vol. 3, p. 185)
- "Rice with Spinach" (Vol. 3, p. 192)
- "Baked Tomatoes" (Vol. 3, p. 364)
- "Whole Bread" (Vol. 3, p. 46)

Rice with Spinach

SUPPER

- Cleansing Broth with Lemon Juice (Vol. 1, p. 369; Vol.2, p. 124)
- "Banana Soup" (Vol. 3, p. 188)
- "Fruit Salad" (Vol. 3, p. 200)

Fruit Salad

HEALTH COUNSELS

In order to fight high blood pressure, these dishes include the combination of ingredients of *diuretic* action (such as melon, vegetables, and cleansing broth) with others *high* in ***potassium*** (such as melon, fruits, and, especially, banana).

The result is a menu that contributes to the *decrease* in **blood pressure figures** at the same time that it *prevents* **arteriosclerosis.**

In order to increase the effectiveness of this menu, it is recommended to *omit* **salt,** especially refined salt.

the Arteries

Circulation

BREAKFAST

- "Cherimoya and Orange Shake" (Vol. 3, p. 178)
- "Bircher-muesli" (Vol. 3, p. 175)
- "Soy Milk" with Wheat Germ (Vol. 3, p. 305; Vol. 2, p. 310)
- Kiwis (Vol. 2, p. 356)

Bircher-muesli

LUNCH

- Carrot Juice (Vol. 2, p. 25)
- "Mexican Salad" (Vol. 3, p. 260)
- Red Cabbage (Vol. 2, p. 193)
- "Yam with Tomato" (Vol. 3, p. 191)
- Walnuts (Vol. 2, p. 64)
- "Rye Bread" (Vol. 3, p. 194)

Yam with Tomato

SUPPER

- Tomato and Garlic Salad (Vol. 2, p. 275; Vol. 1, p. 338)
- "Baked Potatoes" (Vol. 3, p. 251)

Baked Potatoes

HEALTH COUNSELS

This is a good menu to prevent and alleviate a variety of cases of "bad circulation": **chilblains, Raynaud's disease, vascular weakness,** and **insufficient blood circulation** in the head and limbs.

The menu is notable for its supply of ***flavonoids*** and ***antioxidant vitamins,*** necessary for the good working condition of arteries and the capillary vessels.

Other Recipes for the Arteries

Salads

- "Chickpea Salad" (Vol. 3, p. 186)
- "Tofu Salad" (Vol. 3, p. 299)
- "Violet Salad" (Vol. 3, p. 373)
- "Sprouts Salad" (Vol. 3, p. 244)

Soups and Purées

- "Cream of Pumpkin" (Vol. 3, p. 134)
- "Cream of Onion" (Vol. 3, p. 220)

Main Courses

- "Grilled Vegetables" (Vol. 3, p. 189)
- "Vegetable Paella" (Vol. 3, p. 86)
- "Chickpea Stew" (Vol. 3, p. 148)
- "Roasted Vegetables" (Vol. 3, p. 384)
- "Sautéed Soy Sprouts" (Vol. 3, p. 265)
- "Couscous with Vegetables" (Vol. 3, p. 322)

Breakfasts, Desserts and Snacks

- "Tropical Fruit Salad" (Vol. 3, p. 253)
- "Peach Bavarian" (Vol. 3, p. 173)
- "Strawberry Delight" (Vol. 3, p. 177)
- "Cereal Bars" (Vol. 3, p. 174)

Drinks

- "Sangria (non-alcoholic)" (Vol. 3, p. 327)
- "Aromatic Linden" (Vol. 3, p. 159)
- "Banana Shake" (Vol. 3, p. 179)

Infusions or decoctions:

- Milfoil (EMP, p. 691)
- Horsetail (EMP, p. 704)
- Early-flowering Periwinkle (EMP, p. 244)

- *See the recipe index at the beginning of this volume (Vol. 3, pp. 8-13).*
- *See also chapter 22, "Foods for the Arteries" (Vol. 2, pp. 82-117).*

EMP = *Encyclopedia of Medicinal Plants,* Education and Health Library, Editorial Safeliz.

Preparation time: 00:20

Cooking time: - - - -

Rainbow Salad

INGREDIENTS (4 servings)

- 4 **tomatoes**
- 2 **carrots**
- 150 g (≅ 5 oz) of **baby corn**
- 100 g (≅ 3.5 oz) of **watercress**
- 100 g (≅ 3.5 oz) of **red cabbage**
- 100 g (≅ 3.5 oz) of **olives**

ADDITIONAL INGREDIENTS

- 4 tablespoons of olive **oil** (each tablespoon of oil adds around 120 kcal to the recipe, that is, 30 kcal per serving)
- Sea **salt** (see Vol. 3, p. 16)

PREPARATION

❶ Carefully wash the tomatoes, the carrots (previously peeled), the watercress, and the red cabbage.

❷ Chop the tomatoes and other vegetables into medium chunks.
- Arrange vegetables, corn, and olives by color.
- Add oil and salt.

❸ Serve immediately.

For more information about the ingredients, see: Tomato, Vol. 2, p. 275; carrot, Vol. 2, p. 25; corn, Vol. 2, p. 238; watercress, Vol. 2, p. 132; red cabbage, Vol. 2, p. 193; olive, Vol. 2, p. 165.

Suggestions from the chef

This is a **fun** salad for children. They may be told that white light going through raindrops separates into the seven conventional colors of the rainbow: red, orange, yellow, green, blue, indigo, and violet. They should guess which of the seven colors is missing, what was the first rainbow in history, and what was its meaning.

HEALTH COUNSELS

"Eat colorfully" is one of the recommendations given in this Encyclopedia of Foods and Their Healing Power in order to assure the intake of antioxidant substances, thereby protecting the arteries and preventing cancer (see Vol. 2, p. 394).

This Rainbow Salad includes a combination of several types of vegetable pigments which make it especially beneficial for:

✓ The **arteries,** due to the **beta-carotene** (provitamin A) contained in carrots and corn. Beta-carotene along with the other natural pigments included in this salad *slow down* the accumulation of ***cholesterol*** in the arteries.

✓ **Cancer** *prevention,* due to the ***vitamins, minerals, antioxidants,*** and ***phytochemicals*** contained in these raw vegetables (see Vol. 2, p. 370).

✓ The **kidneys,** since the supply of ***protein*** is *very low* in this dish, thus helping the renal function.

NUTRITIONAL VALUE* per serving

Energy	**128 kcal = 533 kj**
Protein	**5.13 g**
Carbohydrates	**19.9 g**
Fiber	**5.79 g**
Total fat	***2.36 g***
Saturated fat	***0.331 g***
Cholesterol	—
Sodium	***171 mg***

1% 2% 4% 10% 20% 40% 100%

% Daily Value **(based on a 2,000 calorie diet)** provided by each serving of this dish

CALORIC PROPORTION*

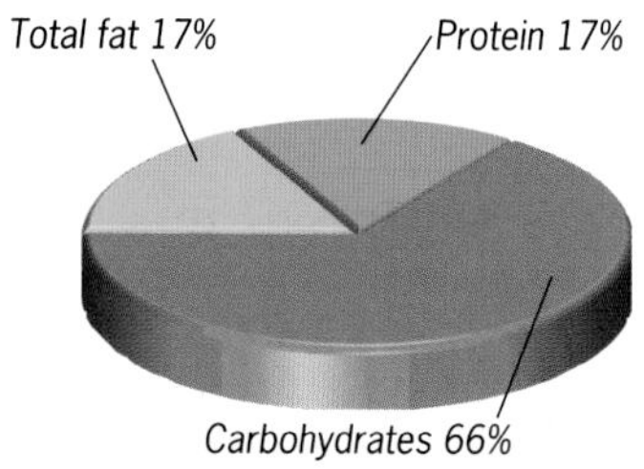

Percentage distribution of **calories for each nutrient**

*Additional ingredients not included.

Preparation time: 00:15

Cooking time: - - - -

Zucchini Salad

INGREDIENTS (4 servings)

- 400 g (≅ 14 oz) of **zucchini** (tender and with small seeds)
- 2 **lettuce** cores (or its equivalent in leaves)
- 1 **garlic** clove

ADDITIONAL INGREDIENTS

- **Parsley**
- **Dill**
- 4 tablespoons of olive **oil** (each tablespoon of oil adds around 120 kcal to the recipe, that is, 30 kcal per serving)
- The juice of one **lemon**
- Sea **salt** (see Vol. 3, p. 16)

PREPARATION

❶ Wash and chop the potherbs (parsley and dill).

- Using a mortar, grind the garlic together with the salt and mix in the lemon juice, herbs, and oil. This makes a delicious dressing.
- Wash, dry and chop the zucchini.
- Wash and slice the lettuce in thin slices.

❷ Marinate the zucchini for 15 minutes in the dressing.

- Arrange the lettuce and the zucchini on individual plates.

❸ Serve immediately.

For more information about the ingredients, see: Zucchini, Vol. 2, p. 159; lettuce, Vol. 2, p. 45; garlic, Vol. 1, p. 338; and the *Encyclopedia of Medicinal Plants:* Garlic, p. 230.

HEALTH COUNSELS

All salads prepared with raw greens and vegetables are good for the arteries. However, this Zucchini Salad is one of the most advisable as it contains *few* ***calories,*** is *low* in ***sodium***—if salt is used moderately—and has a gentle diuretic effect due to the zucchini. Finally, it does *not* contain ***cholesterol.***

Garlic, olive oil, and lemon juice, the components of this salad dressing, strengthen its healing effect upon the arteries.

Therefore, Zucchini Salad is recommended in the following cases:

✓ Arterial **hypertension, arteriosclerosis,** and **coronary** disease.

✓ **Insomnia, nervousness,** and **stress,** due to the gentle *sedative effect* of lettuce.

✓ **Obesity** and **diabetes,** due to the **satisfying effect** of these raw greens and vegetables, and to their *low caloric* content.

NUTRITIONAL VALUE* per serving

Energy	25 kcal = 105 kj
Protein	2.15 g
Carbohydrates	2.53 g
Fiber	2.17 g
Total fat	*0.258 g*
Saturated fat	*0.045 g*
Cholesterol	—
Sodium	*7.66 mg*

1% 2% 4% 10% 20% 40% 100%

% Daily Value (based on a 2,000 calorie diet) provided by each serving of this dish

CALORIC PROPORTION*

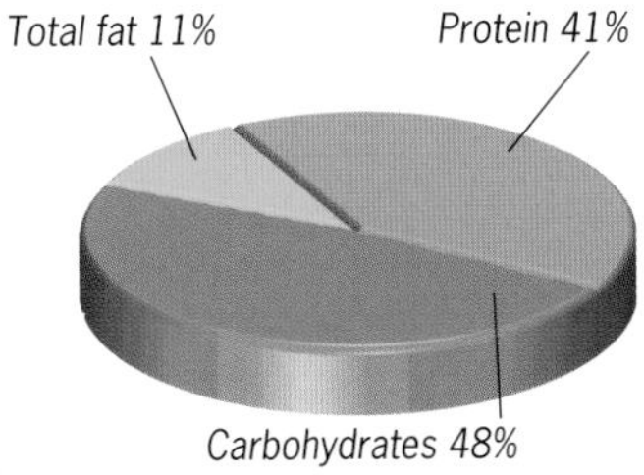

Percentage distribution of **calories for each nutrient**

*Additional ingredients not included.

Preparation time 00:10

Cooking time 01:45

Chickpea Salad

INGREDIENTS (4 servings)

- 100 g (≅ 1/2 cup) of **chickpeas** (garbanzo beans)
- 2 **tomatoes**
- 1 sweet **green pepper**
- 1 **carrot**
- 1 **cucumber**
- 1 **celery** stalk
- 4 **lettuce** leaves

ADDITIONAL INGREDIENTS

- 4 tablespoons of olive **oil** (each tablespoon of oil adds around 120 kcal to the recipe, that is, 30 kcal per serving)
- **Thyme**
- The juice of one **lemon**
- Sea **salt** (see Vol. 3, p. 16)

PREPARATION

❶ Soak the chickpeas overnight in hot water with a little salt.
- Peel, wash, and chop the carrot, the cucumber, and the tomatoes.
- Wash and chop the celery and the pepper.
- Wash the lettuce and set aside.

❷ Prepare a pot with plenty of water and a little salt. When the water is boiling, add the chickpeas.
- Simmer the chickpeas until they are tender. Drain them and let cool.
- Combine all the vegetables (except lettuce) in a container with the cold chickpeas.
- Dress with oil, salt, and lemon juice.

❸ Sprinkle the salad with thyme and serve.

Soak chickpeas.

Drain chickpeas after they are cooked.

Prepare the vegetables.

Suggestions from the Chef

A tablespoon of **soy mayonnaise** (Vol. 3, p. 58) may be used, remembering that this addition changes the amount of calories.

For more information about the ingredients, see: Chickpea, Vol. 2, p. 91; tomato, Vol. 2, p. 275; pepper, Vol. 2, p. 198; carrot, Vol. 2, p. 25; cucumber, Vol. 2, p. 339; celery, Vol. 2, p. 248; lettuce, Vol. 2, p. 45.

NUTRITIONAL VALUE*
per serving

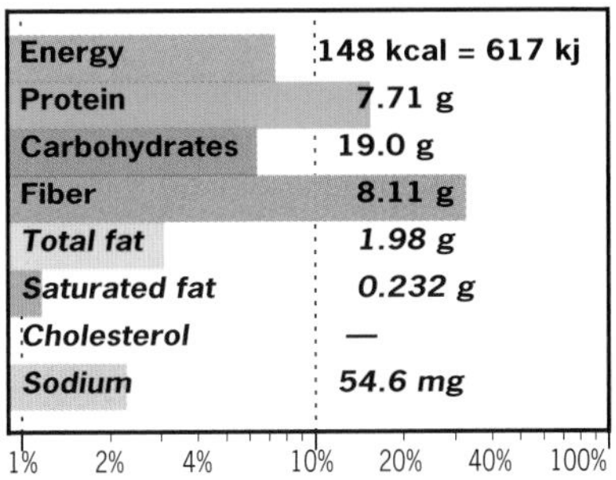
Energy 148 kcal = 617 kj
Protein 7.71 g
Carbohydrates 19.0 g
Fiber 8.11 g
Total fat 1.98 g
Saturated fat 0.232 g
Cholesterol —
Sodium 54.6 mg
1% 2% 4% 10% 20% 40% 100%

% Daily Value (based on a 2,000 calorie diet) provided by each serving of this dish

HEALTH COUNSELS

This salad is made up of **raw vegetables** combined with one **legume—chickpeas.** Both types of food are especially recommended to *avoid* an excess of ***cholesterol*** in the blood and to *keep* the **arteries** healthy.

Chickpea Salad constitutes a *high-**protein*** dish, due to the chickpeas. In addition, it supplies ***fiber*** and vegetable ***antioxidant*** *substances* (***phytochemicals,*** see Vol. 1, p. 410) found both in chickpeas and in vegetables.

This salad is particularly beneficial for:

✓ The **arteries,** as ***fiber, beta-carotene*** (provitamin A), and other ***antioxidants*** found in peppers, tomatoes, and other vegetables, contribute to *control* **cholesterol** and to avoid the *accumulation* of this substance on the artery walls. Therefore, this dish prevents and fights **arteriosclerosis** (hardening of the walls due to cholesterol deposits), **high blood pressure,** and the narrowing of the coronary arteries, which causes **infarction.**

✓ The **nervous system,** thanks to ***folate*** and ***B-complex vitamins*** contained in this salad, especially coming from chickpeas.

✓ **Cancer** *prevention,* especially from the digestive tract, as it is high in fiber and antioxidant substances such as provitamin A from carrots, ***carotenoids*** from tomatoes, and ***vitamin C*** from peppers and tomatoes

✓ The diet of **diabetics** and the **obese,** as it supplies essential nutrients, such as ***protein*** and ***vitamins,*** with few calories (especially if oil is used very sparingly in the dressing). Furthermore, the ***complex carbohydrates*** in chickpeas are tolerated well by diabetic persons.

CALORIC PROPORTION*

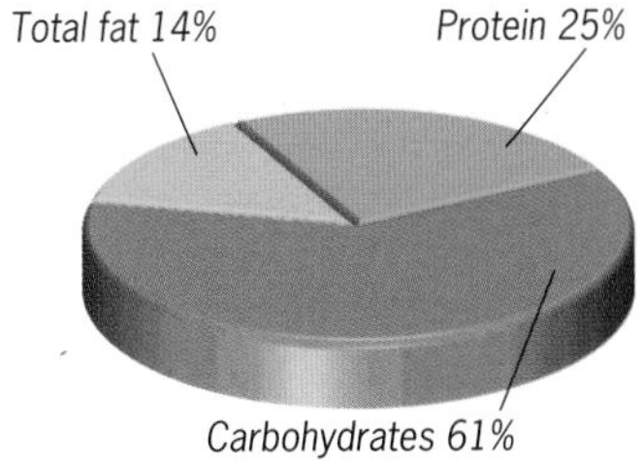
Total fat 14%
Protein 25%
Carbohydrates 61%

Percentage distribution of
calories for each nutrient

*Additional ingredients not included.

Preparation time 00:10

Cooking time 00:30

Banana Soup

INGREDIENTS (4 servings)

- 2 **plantains**
- 40 g (≅ 1/3 cup) of **whole flour**
- 1 **onion**
- 2 **garlic** cloves
- 1 liter of **skimmed milk**
- 1/2 liter (≅ 1/2 quart) of **water**

ADDITIONAL INGREDIENTS

- 2 tablespoons of olive **oil** (each tablespoon of oil adds around 120 kcal to the recipe, that is, 30 kcal per serving)
- The juice of one **lemon**
- Sea **salt** (see Vol. 3, p. 16)

PREPARATION

❶ Peel the plantains and coat them with the lemon juice to avoid darkening when cooking.

- Peel and chop the garlic and the onion.

❷ Boil the plantains in salted water.

- In a frying pan sauté the onion and garlic in oil. Avoid browning. Add the flour and stir for 2 minutes. Add the cold milk. Keep a low flame until the cream boils and thickens.
- Mash the plantains with part of the boiling water and add them to the previous mixture. Simmer for an additional 10 minutes on a very low flame.

❸ Serve hot.

HEALTHIER ALTERNATIVE: Instead of sautéing the onions and garlic, bake them or steam them. Lightly toast the flour before adding it. Substitute the skimmed milk for soy milk or almond milk.

For more information about the ingredients, see: Plantain, Vol. 2, p. 72; flour, Vol. 1, p. 68; onion, Vol. 2, p. 142; garlic, Vol. 1, p. 338; milk, Vol. 1, p. 182; and the *Encyclopedia of Medicinal Plants:* Garlic, p. 230.

HEALTH COUNSELS

Plantains, the main ingredient of this dish, supply *high levels* of ***potassium,*** *low levels* of ***sodium, B-complex vitamins,*** and ***magnesium.*** All these are necessary to *keep* the **arteries** in good health. Additionally, plantains contain small amounts of ***serotonin,*** which has the ability to *dilate* the arteries and to *improve* blood **circulation.**

This plantain soup is *low* in ***fat,*** *low* in ***sodium***—if little salt is added—and contains almost no ***cholesterol.*** All this exerts a strong, favorable effect upon the entire cardiovascular system. It is recommended to those who suffer from or wish to prevent the following illnesses:

✓ Arterial **hypertension,** cardiac **arrhythmia,** and **arteriosclerosis.**

✓ **Myocardial infarction** and other coronary diseases.

✓ **Edema** (excessive accumulation of serous fluid) of circulatory or renal origin.

NUTRITIONAL VALUE* per serving

Energy	226 kcal = 943 kj
Protein	11.4 g
Carbohydrates	42.4 g
Fiber	3.57 g
Total fat	*0.748 g*
Saturated fat	*0.437 g*
Cholesterol	*5.00 mg*
Sodium	*135 mg*

1% 2% 4% 10% 20% 40% 100%

% Daily Value (based on a 2,000 calorie diet) provided by each serving of this dish

CALORIC PROPORTION*

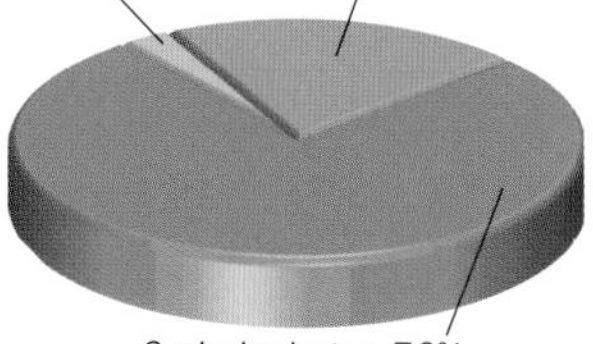

Percentage distribution of **calories for each nutrient**

*Additional ingredients not included.

Preparation time 00:15

Cooking time 00:20

Grilled vegetables

INGREDIENTS (4 servings)

- 500 g (≅ 1 pound) of green asparagus
- 2 **onions**
- 2 sweet **red peppers**
- 1 **zucchini** (courgette)
- 1 **eggplant** (Guinea squash, aubergine)
- 2 **tomatoes**
- 2 **garlic** cloves

ADDITIONAL INGREDIENTS

- 4 tablespoons of olive **oil** (each tablespoon of oil adds around 120 kcal to the recipe, that is, 30 kcal per serving)
- **Parsley**
- **Oregano**
- Sea **salt** (see Vol. 3, p. 16)

PREPARATION

❶ Chop off the tough parts of the asparagus and peel if they are thick.
- Wash and chop the peppers.
- Wash and chop into thick slices the remaining vegetables.
- Using a mortar, grind the garlic, the salt, and the chopped parsley. Once everything is well ground, add the oil.

❷ Place a lightly oiled griddle on the heat. Arrange the onion, eggplant, and asparagus on the griddle.
- After a few minutes—according to taste—add the peppers and the zucchini. Add the tomatoes at the end.

❸ Arrange on a serving plate; pour the dressing mixture over the vegetables and sprinkle with oregano.

For more information about the ingredients, see: Asparagus, Vol. 2, p. 250; onion, Vol. 2, p. 142; pepper, Vol. 2, p. 198; zucchini, Vol. 2, p. 159; eggplant, Vol. 2, p. 256; tomato, Vol. 2, p. 275; garlic, Vol. 1, p. 338; and the *Encyclopedia of Medicinal Plants:* Garlic, p. 230.

HEALTH COUNSELS

The vegetables included in this dish provide a good source of ***vitamins, minerals, fiber,*** and ***antioxidants,*** all of them adding to the health of the arteries. Besides, the dish contains *no* ***cholesterol*** and is very *low* in ***saturated fat*** and in ***sodium***—if salt is used sparingly—substances that cause the artery walls to deteriorate.

The grilling process adds a pleasant flavor to the vegetables and makes them easier to digest than if used raw in salads. At the same time, the loss of nutrients is minimal. All this makes "Grilled Vegetables" a dish especially recommended for the prevention of:

✓ **Arteriosclerosis** and its consequences—thrombosis, infarction, apoplexy, or cerebral stroke.

✓ **Cancer,** due to its ***antioxidants.***

✓ **Obesity,** due to its small supply of calories and fat.

✓ **Liver** and **gallbladder** disorders.

NUTRITIONAL VALUE* per serving

Energy	115 kcal = 482 kj
Protein	5.81 g
Carbohydrates	17.6 g
Fiber	7.91 g
Total fat	*0.949 g*
Saturated fat	*0.163 g*
Cholesterol	—
Sodium	*18.3 mg*

1% 2% 4% 10% 20% 40% 100%

% Daily Value (based on a 2,000 calorie diet) provided by each serving of this dish

CALORIC PROPORTION*

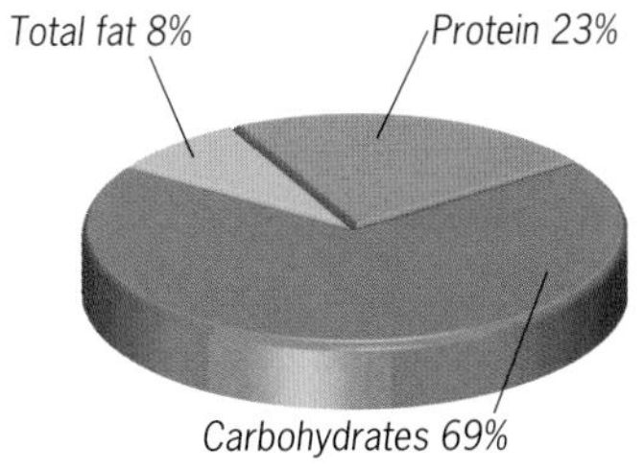

Percentage distribution of **calories for each nutrient**

*Additional ingredients not included.

Preparation time 00:15

Cooking time 00:45

Potato Stew

INGREDIENTS (4 servings)

- 1 kg (≅ 2 pounds) of **potatoes**
- 500 g (≅ 1 pound) **artichokes** (globe artichokes)
- 300 g (≅ 10.5 oz) of **peas**
- 1 **onion**
- 1 sweet **red pepper**
- 4 **garlic** cloves
- 2 liters (≅ 2 quarts) of **water**

ADDITIONAL INGREDIENTS

- 1/2 teaspoon of sweet **paprika**
- 4 tablespoons of olive **oil** (each tablespoon of oil adds around 120 kcal to the recipe, that is, 30 kcal per serving)
- Sea **salt** (see Vol. 3, p. 16)

PREPARATION

❶ Peel, wash and chop the potatoes.

- Chop the stems and outer leaves off the artichokes. Slice them thinly.
- Peel and chop fine the onion, the garlic, and the pepper.

❷ Heat the oil in a pot, and sauté the onion and the pepper.

- When the onion becomes golden, add the potatoes and stir for a few minutes. Add the artichokes and garlic. Simmer for 10 minutes.
- Add paprika and cover with water. When boiling begins, add the peas and the salt.
- Simmer until tender (about 20 additional minutes).

❸ Serve hot.

HEALTHIER ALTERNATIVE: Instead of sautéing the ingredients, add them raw to the boiling water.

For more information about the ingredients, see: Potato, Vol. 2, p. 201; artichoke, Vol. 2, p. 178; pea, Vol. 2, p. 73; onion, Vol. 2, p. 142; pepper, Vol. 2, p. 198; garlic, Vol. 1, p. 338; and the *Encyclopedia of Medicinal Plants:* Garlic, p. 230.

HEALTH COUNSELS

Potato Stew makes up a simple and nutritious dish that is *very healthy* for the cardiovascular system. This is because of its *high* content in ***fiber*** (to *reduce* **cholesterol** and *protect* the **arteries**); in ***potassium*** (to *prevent high blood pressure*); and in ***phytochemical elements*** from peas, garlic, onion, pepper, and artichokes (to *slow down* the aging process of the arteries, known as arteriosclerosis).

Therefore, Potato Stew should not be missing from the diet of those prone to suffer from:

✓ Arterial and heart diseases, especially **high blood pressure, deficient circulation** due to arteriosclerosis, and **infarction.**

✓ Liver conditions, such as **hepatitis, cirrhosis,** and **hepatic failure.** All ingredients, especially artichokes, onions, and garlic, help the good working condition of this organ.

NUTRITIONAL VALUE* per serving

Energy	278 kcal = 1,164 kj
Protein	11.3 g
Carbohydrates	48.6 g
Fiber	11.7 g
Total fat	*0.734 g*
Saturated fat	*0.150 g*
Cholesterol	—
Sodium	*77.2 mg*

1% 2% 4% 10% 20% 40% 100%

% Daily Value (based on a 2,000 calorie diet) provided by each serving of this dish

CALORIC PROPORTION*

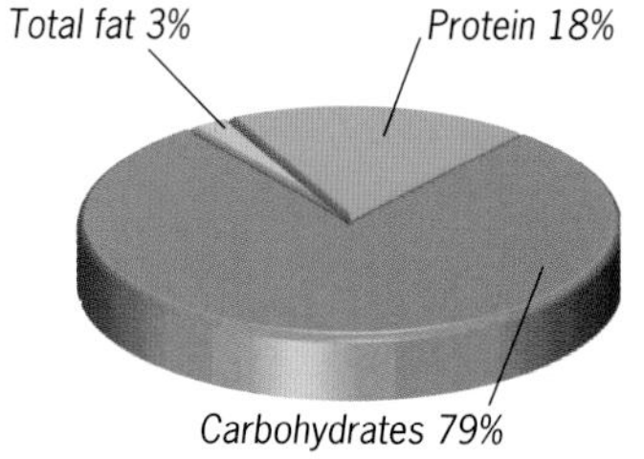

Percentage distribution of **calories for each nutrient**

*Additional ingredients not included.

Preparation time 00:10

Cooking time 00:40

Yam with Tomato

INGREDIENTS (4 servings)

- 750 g (≅ 26.5 oz) of **yam**
- 400 g (≅ 14 oz) of **Tomato Specialty Sauce** (Vol. 3, p. 62)

ADDITIONAL INGREDIENTS

- 3 tablespoons of olive **oil** (each tablespoon of oil adds around 120 kcal to the recipe, that is, 30 kcal per serving)
- Sea **salt** (see Vol. 3, p. 16)

PREPARATION

❶ Peel, wash, and chop the yams.

❷ Prepare the tomato specialty sauce as indicated.

- Boil yams in salted water until they are tender.
- Rinse the yams and sauté them in oil in a frying pan. Add the tomato sauce.
- Cook on a low flame for 10 minutes.

❸ Serve hot.

HEALTHIER ALTERNATIVE: Instead of sautéing the yams, add them already cooked to the tomato sauce.

For more information about the ingredients, see: Yam, Vol. 2, p. 101; tomato, Vol. 2, p. 275.

Raw

*It is not recommended to use raw yams. They contain a **toxin** that may cause **digestive disorders.** This toxin is destroyed by heat when yams are cooked.*

HEALTH COUNSELS

Yams are tubers of tropical origin. They are *high* in ***starch,*** which provides easily absorbed energy. From the healing viewpoint, the most interesting properties are their ability to *reduce* the levels of **triglycerides** in the blood, and to *prevent* **arteriosclerosis.**

With tomatoes and little salt, yams are beneficial to:

✓The **arteries,** especially in case of **insufficient** blood circulation, due to arteriosclerosis.

✓The **heart,** to *prevent* **coronary diseases,** such as infarction.

✓The **stomach,** due to its easy digestion.

NUTRITIONAL VALUE* per serving

Energy	216 kcal = 901 kj
Protein	2.86 g
Carbohydrates	35.1 g
Fiber	6.69 g
Total fat	*4.75 g*
Saturated fat	*0.662 g*
Cholesterol	—
Sodium	*133 mg*

1% 2% 4% 10% 20% 40% 100%

% Daily Value (based on a 2,000 calorie diet) provided by each serving of this dish

CALORIC PROPORTION*

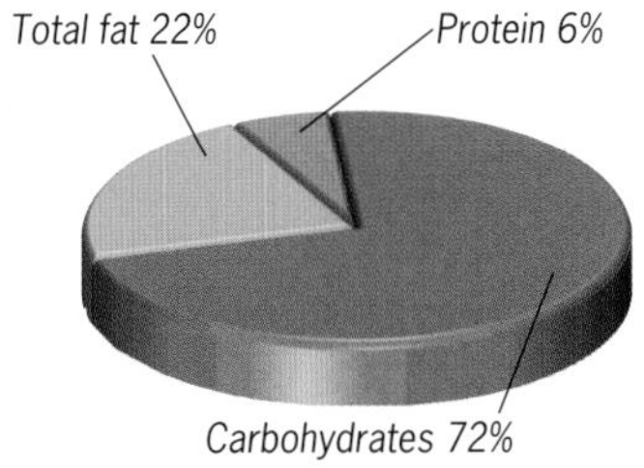

Percentage distribution of **calories for each nutrient**

*Additional ingredients not included.

Preparation time 00:15

Cooking time 00:45

Rice with Spinach

INGREDIENTS (4 servings)

- 300 g (≅ 10.5 oz) of **whole rice**
- 250 g (≅ 8.8 oz) of **spinach**
- 4 **garlic** cloves
- 3/4 liter (≅ 3/4 quart) of unsalted **vegetable broth**

ADDITIONAL INGREDIENTS

- 1/2 teaspoon of **paprika**
- A few **saffron** threads
- 7 tablespoons of olive **oil** (each tablespoon of oil adds around 120 kcal to the recipe, that is, 30 kcal per serving)
- Sea **salt** (see Vol. 3, p. 16)

PREPARATION

❶ Soak the rice in cold water overnight or for one hour in very hot water.

- Wash the spinach with plenty of water. Chop and eliminate the thick and woody stems.
- Peel and chop the garlic.

❷ Heat the oil in a large, flat frying pan.

- Sauté the garlic until it begins to brown. Add the spinach and cook until it loses volume.
- Add the rice (previously drained) and stir.
- Add the boiling vegetable broth and the salt.
- Flavor with paprika and saffron.
- Boil on a high flame for 10 minutes.
- Reduce the flame to the minimum and simmer until the rice is cooked (tender, dry, and fluffy).
- If the broth gets absorbed too quickly, cover the pan for the last few minutes.
- Let rest for 5 minutes.

❸ Serve hot.

HEALTHIER ALTERNATIVE: Instead of sautéing the ingredients, add them raw to the boiling vegetable broth.

For more information about the ingredients, see: Rice, Vol. 2, p. 225; spinach, Vol. 2, p. 28; garlic, Vol. 1, p. 338; and the *Encyclopedia of Medicinal Plants*: Garlic, p. 230.

HEALTH COUNSELS

Rice with Spinach is a nutritious and very healthy dish for the cardiovascular system. To the *beneficial* effect of rice upon the **arteries** (especially if it is whole rice), we should add the *reduction* of **cholesterol** caused by spinach and garlic.

Rice with Spinach is ideal to prevent and fight:

✓ **High blood pressure,** excess of **cholesterol** in the blood, and **arteriosclerosis,** which is the result of both disorders.

✓ **Coronary diseases** such as angina pectoris and myocardial infarction.

✓ **Loss of vision** and **ophthalmological condition** due to lack of ***provitamin A*** (beta-carotene) and ***carotenoids.*** Spinach is very high in these *protective* substances.

NUTRITIONAL VALUE* per serving

Energy	**294 kcal = 1,230 kj**
Protein	**7.79 g**
Carbohydrates	**56.9 g**
Fiber	**4.36 g**
Total fat	***2.26 g***
Saturated fat	***0.442 g***
Cholesterol	—
Sodium	***53.4 mg***

1% 2% 4% 10% 20% 40% 100%

% Daily Value (based on a 2,000 calorie diet) provided by each serving of this dish

CALORIC PROPORTION*

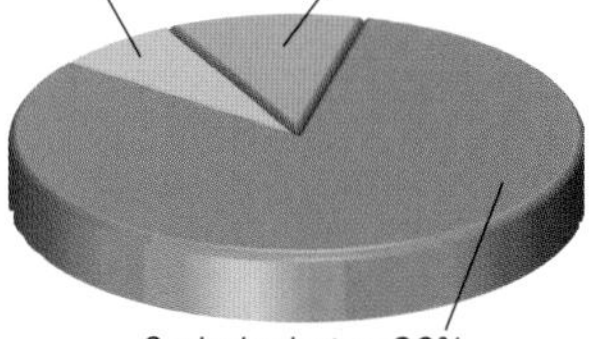

Percentage distribution of **calories for each nutrient**

*Additional ingredients not included.

Preparation time 00:15

Cooking time 00:45

Rice with Pumpkin

INGREDIENTS (4 servings)

- 300 g (≅ 10.5 oz) of **whole rice**
- 100 g (≅ 3.5 oz) of **pumpkin** (squash)
- 1 sweet **red pepper,** baked
- 1 **tomato**
- 1 **onion**
- 1 **dried chile** (hot red pepper—it can be substituted by sweet paprika)
- 4 **garlic** cloves
- 1 liter of **water** or unsalted **vegetable broth**

ADDITIONAL INGREDIENTS

- 7 tablespoons of olive **oil** (each tablespoon of oil adds around 120 kcal to the recipe, that is, 30 kcal per serving)
- Sea **salt** (see Vol. 3, p. 16)

PREPARATION

❶ Soak the rice in cold water overnight or for one hour in hot water.
- Peel and cut the pumpkin into cubes.
- Clean and cut the pepper into strips.
- Peel and chop the onion.

❷ Heat oil in a frying pan.
- Sauté the dried chile and remove.
- Repeat the same process with the garlic and the whole tomato.
- Sauté the onion in the same oil. When it starts getting brown, add the pepper and the pumpkin.
- Using a mortar, grind the dried chile, garlic, and peeled tomato.
- Add this mixture to the pot together with the boiling water (or vegetable broth). Add the rice and the salt.
- Boil on a medium flame, covered, for 30 minutes. If white rice is used, 20 minutes suffice.

❸ Serve hot. The consistency should be somewhat thick and not totally dry.

HEALTHIER ALTERNATIVE: Instead of sautéing the ingredients, add them raw to the boiling vegetable broth.

For more information about the ingredients, see: Rice, Vol. 2, p. 225; pumpkin, Vol. 2, p. 97; pepper, Vol. 2, p. 198; tomato, Vol. 2, p. 275; onion, Vol. 2, p. 142; garlic, Vol. 1, p. 338; and the *Encyclopedia of Medicinal Plants:* Garlic, p. 230.

HEALTH COUNSELS

Rice with Pumpkin is a nutritious dish and very healthy for the arteries and the rest of the cardiovascular system, especially if it is prepared with whole rice and very little salt.

Ingredients are all *very low* in ***sodium*** and ***fat,*** two great enemies of the arteries; furthermore, it does *not* contain ***cholesterol.*** At the same time, the ingredients are *high* in ***potassium*** (a mineral to prevent high blood pressure); in ***beta-carotene*** (provitamin A, antioxidant that protects the artery walls) from the pumpkin; in ***antioxidant carotenoids*** from peppers and tomatoes; and in ***fiber,*** which *reduces* **cholesterol** and *prevents* **arteriosclerosis.**

Therefore, Rice with Pumpkin is especially beneficial to maintain the health of:

✓The **arteries** and the **heart.**

✓The **stomach,** due to the pumpkin's *antacid* and *smoothing* actions.

✓The **intestine,** because of its significant ***fiber*** content.

NUTRITIONAL VALUE* per serving

Energy	**319 kcal = 1,333 kj**
Protein	**7.34 g**
Carbohydrates	**63.4 g**
Fiber	**4.63 g**
Total fat	***2.34 g***
Saturated fat	***0.459 g***
Cholesterol	—
Sodium	***10.5 mg***

1% 2% 4% 10% 20% 40% 100%

% Daily Value (based on a 2,000 calorie diet) provided by each serving of this dish

CALORIC PROPORTION*

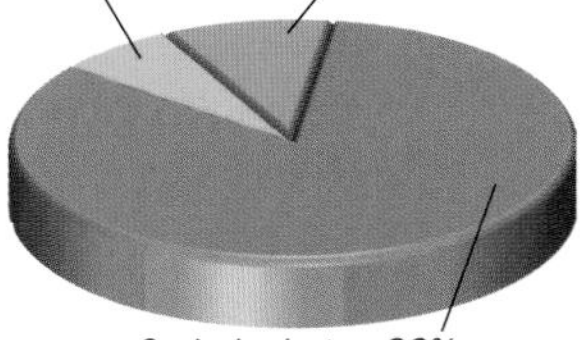

Percentage distribution of **calories for each nutrient**

*Additional ingredients not included.

Preparation time 00:30

Cooking time 00:50

Rye Bread

INGREDIENTS

- 300 g (≅ 2 1/2 cups) of **rye flour**
- 200 g (≅ 1 3/4 cups) of **white flour**
- 250 ml (≅ 1 cup) of lukewarm **water**
- 2 tablespoons of olive **oil**
- 2 teaspoons of active dry **yeast**

ADDITIONAL INGREDIENTS

- Sea **salt** (see Vol. 3, p. 16)

PREPARATION

❶ Dissolve the yeast in the lukewarm water.

- Sieve both flours and mix them well with each other.
- Place the flour mixture in a container, make a hole in the middle and pour in the water with the yeast, salt, and oil.
- Mix all ingredients and knead over a board sprinkled with flour for about 15 minutes until it is not sticky to the hands or to the board. The dough should be consistent and elastic—if pressed with a finger, the dough should go back to the original shape.
- Place the dough into a container covered with a damp cloth. Let it rise in a warm place (20°C – 30°C) for about 1 hour or until it is double in bulk.
- Knead again for 2 additional minutes and place the dough in an oven tray or on a greased baking pan.
- Let it rise again until double in bulk.

❷ Heat the oven at 250°C. Place the dough in the oven and bake until the bread becomes golden.

- To see if it is done, knock the loaf. If the sound is hollow, it is well done. Take it out of the oven. Empty the baking pan after 5 minutes.
- Allow to cool on a grate covered with a piece of cloth.

❸ Serve in slices.

Add the oil and the yeast to the flour mixture.

Once kneading is finished, let the dough rise.

After some time the dough will have doubled in bulk.

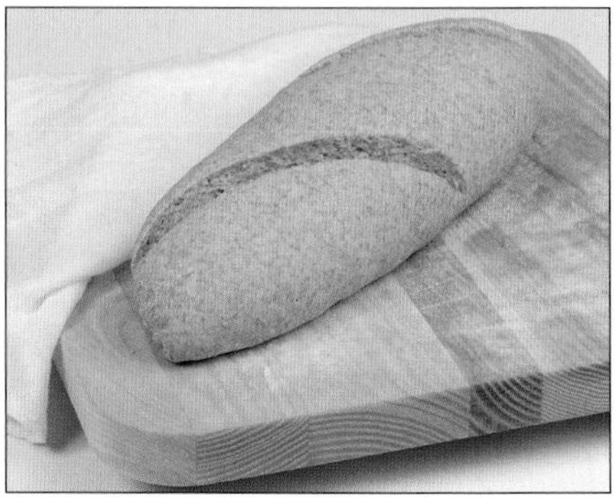

Shape the loaf and make several cuts on the surface.

Suggestions from the Chef

Once cooled, the bread may be cut into slices and placed in the freezer for later use.

For more information about the ingredients, see: Flour, Vol. 1, p. 68; rye, Vol. 2, p. 116, Vol. 1, p. 69; wheat, Vol. 2, p. 306; oil, Vol. 1, p. 112.

High Blood Pressure

Rye bread, like other types of bread, contains a certain amount of ***sodium*** *from the added salt.*

Persons suffering from high blood pressure, on a low-sodium diet, should prepare this bread with ***very little salt****—preferably unrefined sea salt—or no salt at all (see Vol. 1, pp. 346-347, Vol. 3, p. 16).*

NUTRITIONAL VALUE*
per 100 g

Energy	264 kcal = 1,105 kj
Protein	7.06 g
Carbohydrates	42.4 g
Fiber	6.68 g
Total fat	*4.77 g*
Saturated fat	*0.634 g*
Cholesterol	—
Sodium	*2.88 mg*

1% 2% 4% 10% 20% 40% 100%

% Daily Value (based on a 2,000 calorie diet) provided by 100 g of this bread

HEALTH COUNSELS

Rye is a cereal with a similar makeup to wheat but with a *higher* content in ***fiber*** and in ***protein.*** Nevertheless, rye protein contains *less* ***gluten,*** thus making firmer bread.

Rye bread is especially recommended for:

✓The **arteries** and the **heart,** as it causes the artery walls to become more *elastic, reduces* **cholesterol,** *prevents* **high blood pressure,** and *improves* blood **circulation.** This is due to its content in ***fiber,*** in ***antioxidant vitamins*** like ***vitamin E,*** and in ***phytochemicals.***

✓The **intestine,** due to the *laxative* effect of its fiber, which also helps to *prevent* **cancer of colon.**

✓The **diabetic** diet, as the ***carbohydrates*** of rye are assimilated more slowly than those of wheat, thus causing a *lower increase* in the **glucose** (sugar) level in the blood.

CALORIC PROPORTION*

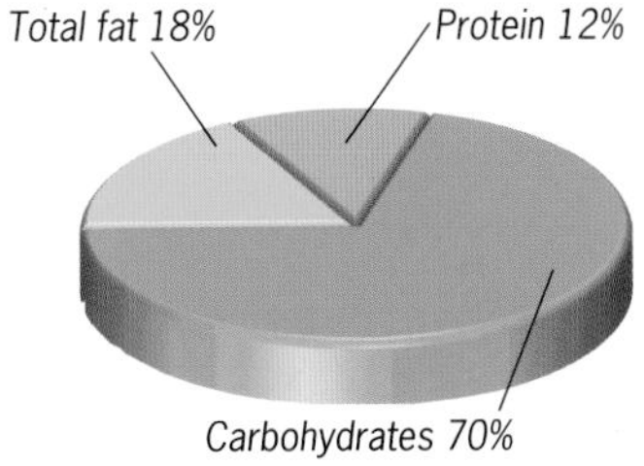

Percentage distribution of
calories for each nutrient

*Additional ingredients not included.

Rice Crackers

INGREDIENTS

- 200 g (≅ 1 cup) of **whole rice**
- 100 g (≅ 1 cup) of ground **raw almonds**
- 50 g (≅ 1/2 cup) of **whole flour**
- 1 **egg** white
- 4 tablespoons of **breadcrumbs**
- 2 tablespoons of olive **oil** (each tablespoon of oil adds around 120 kcal to the recipe, that is, 30 kcal per serving)

ADDITIONAL INGREDIENTS

- Sea **salt** (see Vol. 3, p. 16)

PREPARATION

❶ Soak the rice in hot water for one hour.

❷ Boil the rice in salted water (two and a half times the volume of dry rice). Let it cool down.
- Combine the rice with the remaining ingredients and knead.
- Using a rolling pin, roll the dough into a 5-mm thickness.
- Cut with cookie cutters or with a glass.
- Oil an oven tray and lay out the crackers on the tray.
- Bake in a preheated oven until golden on both sides.

❸ Serve once they are cooled down or keep in an airtight container for later use.

Prepare the necessary ingredients and utensils.

Using a rolling pin, roll the dough into a 5-mm thickness.

For more information about the ingredients, see: Rice, Vol. 2, p. 225; almond, Vol. 2, p. 48; flour, Vol. 1, p. 68; egg, Vol. 1, p. 218; bread, Vol. 1, p. 70.

Celiac Condition

*Persons **unable to tolerate gluten** may substitute the wheat flour and breadcrumbs for the same amount of **corn flour.***

Suggestions from the Chef

These crackers may be used **like bread** as an excellent garnish for salads and vegetables.

Cut the dough with the available cutters.

NUTRITIONAL VALUE*
per 100 g

Energy	424 kcal = 1,774 kj
Protein	11.1 g
Carbohydrates	47.2 g
Fiber	5.47 g
Total fat	*20.0 g*
Saturated fat	*2.37 g*
Cholesterol	—
Sodium	*17.1 mg*

1% 2% 4% 10% 20% 40% 100%

% Daily Value (based on a 2,000 calorie diet) provided by 100 g of this appetizer

CALORIC PROPORTION*

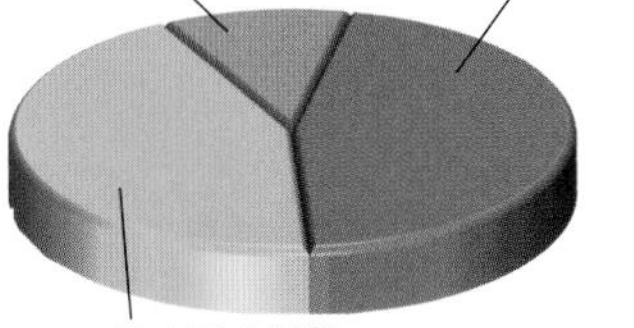

Percentage distribution of **calories for each nutrient**

HEALTH COUNSELS

These crackers, made of rice and almond, are simple to prepare and very nutritious. They can be used as **bread substitutes.** They are especially recommended for the prevention of the following conditions:

✓ **Arteriosclerosis,** coronary diseases, high blood pressure, apoplexy (stroke), and cardiovascular system disorders in general. Low in ***sodium***—if very little salt is used—and in ***saturated fat,*** they help to keep the arteries healthy.

✓ **Constipation** and **cancer of the colon,** as their fiber content is very high.

✓ **Osteoporosis** and **bone demineralization,** as almonds constitute a good source of ***calcium, phosphorus, magnesium*** and other essential minerals for bone formation.

*Additional ingredients not included.

Preparation time 00:25

Cooking time 00:25

Falafel Patties

INGREDIENTS (4 servings)

- 300 g (≅ 1 1/2 cups) of **chickpeas** (boiled)
- 2 **garlic** cloves

ADDITIONAL INGREDIENTS

- **Parsley**
- 1 teaspoon of ground **coriander**
- 1 teaspoon of ground **cumin**
- 1/2 teaspoon of **hot paprika**
- The juice of one **lemon**
- Sea **salt** (see Vol. 3, p. 16)

PREPARATION

❶ Peel the garlic and grind together with the parsley and the salt.

- Mash the chickpeas with a fork or a grinder.
- Combine all the ingredients to obtain a thick purée (add 1 or 2 tablespoons of water if the mixture does not stick together).
- Knead the dough and divide it into portions. Shape into small patties.

❷ Place the patties on a baking tray in a 220°C oven. Bake until golden on both sides. (Turn them over several times during baking.)

❸ Serve hot. They may be garnished with natural zucchini and tomato.

Suggestions from the Chef

Falafel Patties may also be fried. To prepare them in this way, place the patties on absorbent paper immediately after frying in order to eliminate part of the fried oil.

HEALTH COUNSELS

Chickpeas, together with the **potherbs,** are the main ingredients of this eastern hamburger. The healing properties of chickpeas make Falafel Patties especially recommended for:

✓ The **arteries** and the **heart,** as chickpeas contribute to **cholesterol** *reduction.*

✓ The **intestine,** as they are very high in ***fiber.***

✓ The nervous system, due to the B-complex vitamins, including folate, contained in chickpeas.

Zinc

Chickpeas, *as well as soybeans and lentils, are a good source of zinc.*

For each 100 g of chickpeas, there is 3.43 mg of zinc, whereas for each 100 g of meat, the zinc content is only 2.97 mg.

For more information about the ingredients, see: Chickpea, Vol. 2, p. 91; garlic, Vol. 1, p. 338; and the *Encyclopedia of Medicinal Plants:* Garlic, p. 230.

NUTRITIONAL VALUE* per serving

Energy	127 kcal = 533 kj
Protein	6.84 g
Carbohydrates	15.8 g
Fiber	5.76 g
Total fat	*1.96 g*
Saturated fat	*0.204 g*
Cholesterol	—
Sodium	*5.76 mg*

1% 2% 4% 10% 20% 40% 100%

% Daily Value (based on a 2,000 calorie diet) provided by each serving of this dish

CALORIC PROPORTION*

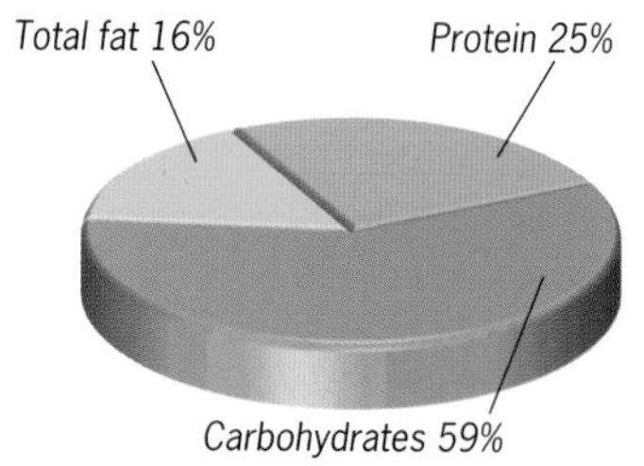

Percentage distribution of **calories for each nutrient**

*Additional ingredients not included.

Preparation time: - - - -

Cooking time: 00:30

Rice Pudding

INGREDIENTS (4 servings)

- 300 g (≅ 2 1/2 cups) of **rice**
- 700 ml (≅ 2 4/5 cups) of **soy milk** (Vol. 3, p. 305)
- 100 g (≅ 1/2 cup) of **brown sugar**
- 1/2 liter (≅ 1/2 quart) of **water**

ADDITIONAL INGREDIENTS

- **Cinnamon** (stick and powder)
- **Lemon rind**
- Sea **salt** (see Vol. 3, p. 16)

PREPARATION

❶ Boil the rice in the water with a little bit of salt for 10 minutes.

❷ Boil the milk with the lemon rind and the cinnamon stick for a few minutes.

- Add the sugar and the rice to the milk.
- Boil for an additional 15 minutes.
- Pour the pudding onto individual serving plates and allow to cool.

❸ Serve cold and sprinkle with cinnamon.

For more information about the ingredients, see: Rice, Vol. 2, p. 225; soy milk, Vol. 1, p. 88; sugar, Vol. 1, p. 170.

Suggestions from the Chef

- Although this dessert is traditionally prepared with cow's milk, it is equally tasty and much healthier if soy milk is used, as indicated in this recipe.
- It may also be prepared with **almond** or **hazelnut milk.**

HEALTH COUNSELS

Prepared with a vegetable milk (such as soy milk), this traditional dessert contains a notable *preventive* effect upon:

✓The **arteries,** due to the ***phytoestrogens*** in the soy that protect the artery walls and *prevent* **arteriosclerosis.** Added to this beneficial effect of Rice Pudding upon the arteries, this dessert is very *low* in ***fat*** and in ***sodium***—if very little salt is used—and contains *zero* **cholesterol** as the milk used in this recipe is of vegetable origin.

✓The reproductive system, as the ***phytoestrogens*** in soy *stabilize* the **menstrual cycle,** *prevent* **prostatic hypertrophia,** and *protect* against breast and prostate **cancer.**

✓The **stomach** and the **intestine,** due to the *protective* action of rice in case of **gastritis** and **colitis.**

NUTRITIONAL VALUE* per serving

Energy	422 kcal = 1,763 kj
Protein	9.77 g
Carbohydrates	84.7 g
Fiber	2.28 g
Total fat	*3.78 g*
Saturated fat	*0.493 g*
Cholesterol	—
Sodium	*31.5 mg*

1% 2% 4% 10% 20% 40% 100%

% Daily Value (based on a 2,000 calorie diet) provided by each serving of this dessert

CALORIC PROPORTION*

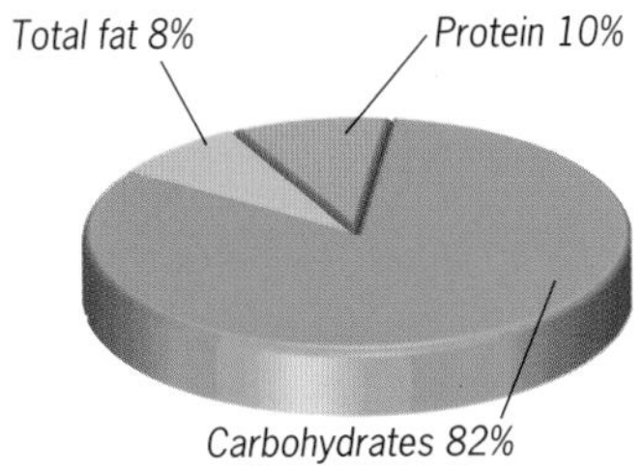

Percentage distribution of **calories for each nutrient**

*Additional ingredients not included.

Preparation time: 00:15

Cooking time: - - - -

Fruit Salad

INGREDIENTS (4 servings)

- 2 **pears**
- 2 **bananas**
- 2 **apples**
- 2 **oranges**
- 2 **peaches**
- 4 slices of **pineapple**
- 250 g (≅ 8.8 oz) **strawberry**

PREPARATION

❶Squeeze the oranges and reserve the juice.

- Peel and chop the remaining fruit.

❷Place the chopped fruit in a deep serving bowl. Add the orange juice.

❸Serve cold. It may be garnished with raisins.

For more information about the ingredients, see: Pear, Vol. 2, p. 112; banana, Vol. 2, p. 70; apple, Vol. 2, p. 229; orange, Vol. 2, p. 360; peach, Vol. 2, p. 75; pineapple, Vol. 2, p. 189; strawberry, Vol. 2, p. 103.

Suggestions from the Chef

Use a tablespoon of **molasses** to sweeten and to add a caramel color and flavor. Those with a sweet tooth will appreciate this.

HEALTH COUNSELS

Fruit, especially in its raw state, supplies many ***antioxidant substances*** that help to keep the arteries in good health thus preventing arteriosclerosis. In this way, the arteries can carry the necessary blood to organs and tissue.

Fruit salad should not be absent from the table of those suffering from or wishing to prevent any of the following:

✓**Circulatory disorders** whose *origin* is **arteriosclerosis:** coronary disease, infarction, apoplexy (stroke).

✓**High blood pressure**, thanks to the *diuretic* effect of fruit and its ***high-potassium*** content, qualities that contribute to stabilize blood pressure.

✓**Cancer,** due to the many ***antioxidants*** and ***anticarcinogenic*** substances found in fruit.

NUTRITIONAL VALUE per serving

Energy	**261 kcal = 1,090 kj**
Protein	**2.69 g**
Carbohydrates	**56.5 g**
Fiber	**9.41 g**
Total fat	***1.65 g***
Saturated fat	***0.222 g***
Cholesterol	—
Sodium	***4.86 mg***

1% 2% 4% 10% 20% 40% 100%

% Daily Value (based on a 2,000 calorie diet) provided by each serving of this dessert

CALORIC PROPORTION

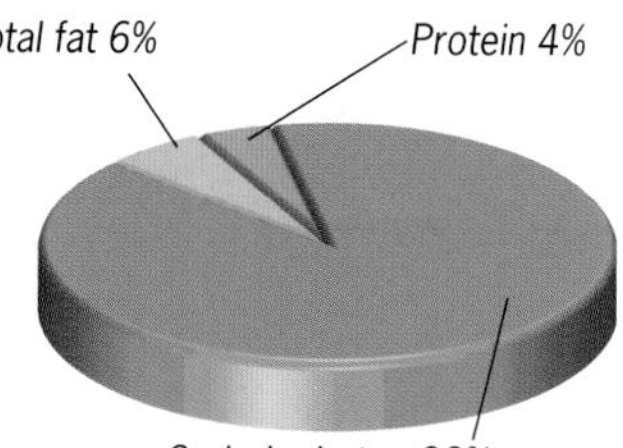

Percentage distribution of **calories for each nutrient**

Preparation time: 00:15

Cooking time: ----

Avocado Shake

INGREDIENTS (4 servings)

- 2 **avocados**
- 2 **apples**
- 200 ml (≅ 4/5 cup) of **almond milk** (Vol. 3, p. 342)
- 2 tablespoons of **honey**

PREPARATION

❶ Peel, empty out the seeds, and chop the apples and the avocados.

❷ Place all the ingredients in a container. Blend until a consistent, lump-free mixture is obtained.

❸ Serve cold.

For more information about the ingredients, see: Avocado, Vol. 2, p. 108; apple, Vol. 2, p. 229; almond milk, Vol. 2, p. 51; honey, Vol. 1, p. 160.

HEALTH COUNSELS

The ingredients of this delicious and nutritious shake are quite appropriate to *reduce* the level of **cholesterol** in the blood, thus avoiding arteriosclerosis and protecting the arteries.

Avocados, in spite of being a *high-**fat*** fruit, have a peculiar hypolipidemic effect (they reduce the amount of lipids in the blood, including cholesterol).

Almonds and **apples** also reduce the levels of cholesterol. Furthermore, almonds supply ***vitamin E,*** which exerts *antioxidant* and *protective* effects upon the arteries.

Therefore, this shake is recommended for the prevention of the following conditions:

✓ High levels of **cholesterol** and **arteriosclerosis.**

✓ **Anemia,** due to the ***iron*** supplied by avocados and apples.

✓ **Constipation, diverticulosis,** and **cancer of the colon,** due to its ***fiber*** content.

NUTRITIONAL VALUE per serving

Energy	**215 kcal = 900 kj**
Protein	**2.91 g**
Carbohydrates	**21.9 g**
Fiber	**6.01 g**
Total fat	***12.4 g***
Saturated fat	***1.93 g***
Cholesterol	—
Sodium	***10.3 mg***

Scale: 1% 2% 4% 10% 20% 40% 100%

% Daily Value (based on a 2,000 calorie diet) provided by each serving of this shake

CALORIC PROPORTION

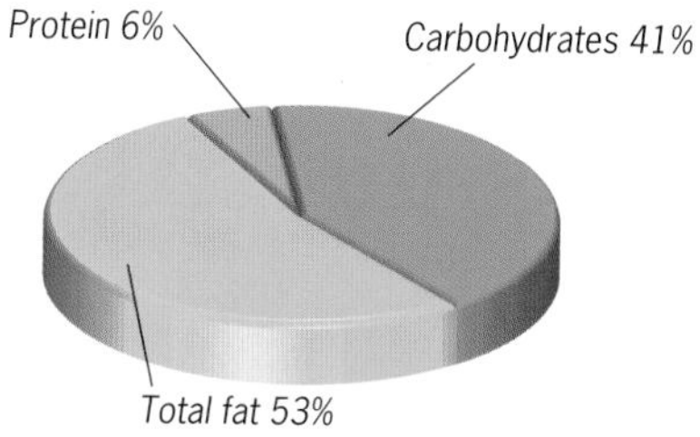

Percentage distribution of **calories for each nutrient**

47 RECIPES FOR THE BLOOD

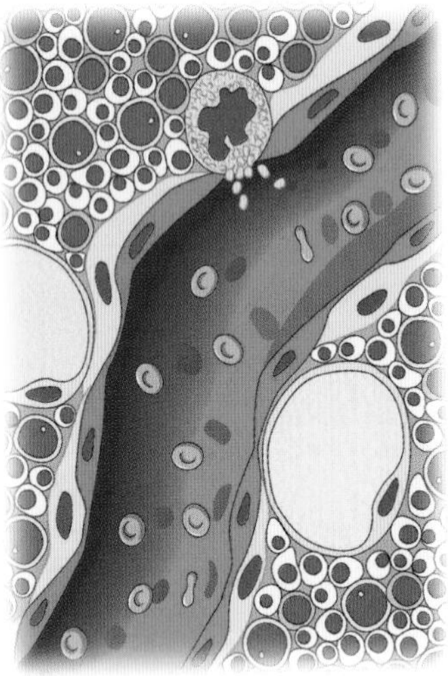

CHAPTER SUMMARY

RECIPES

Catalonian Fava Beans 209
Lentils and Rice 211
River Salad 206
Spaghetti with Spinach 210
Spinach Croquettes 213
Stuffed Avocados 207
Tomato and Vegetable Stew 212
Turnip Greens and Potatoes 208

Blood carries oxygen and nutrients to the cells; additionally, it carries hormones to the various organs that need them. It also transports all the metabolic wastes that are to be eliminated through the urine and respiration.

An adequate diet is essential to keep the blood in good condition.

VIRTUALLY all recipes that are good for the **heart** (see Vol. 3, p. 160) and the **arteries** (see Vol. 3, p. 180) are also recommended for the blood, as both are the principal components of the circulatory system.

Not only does the blood require the necessary pumping force to be able to flow freely, but it also needs an adequate **composition,** including the **pH,** a measure of acidity (see Vol. 2, p. 283). Like the rest of the human body, blood composition changes in order to maintain an optimal balance. This is possible through external input, mainly coming from the digestive tract and respiratory functions.

Science has consistently confirmed the old wives' tale that some types of food *"make **good** blood,"* while others *"make **bad** blood."*

Until recently, it was believed that for our bodies to produce blood it was necessary to eat animal products, such as meat or blood itself.

However, it is now known that ***all*** the *elements* needed to make **good blood** are best obtained from the **plant kingdom** (see Vol. 2, p. 118). That is why the recipes included in this chapter are mainly from plant origin.

To cleanse Our blood

Inherent to the foundations of modern health science is the concept of blood "cleansing" or blood "purification," also referred to as **detoxification** or other similar terms.

Some ingested products or remnants are not completely eliminated through the metabolism (cholesterol, uric acid, toxins, etc.). These make **blood** as well as the **extra-cellular gaps** "dirty" in a similar way as pollution affects lakes and rivers. It is therefore necessary to initiate an **anti-pollution** and **preventive** plan within our own bodies.

One of the advantages of a **diet based on plant food,** aside from supplying all the vital elements for ideal blood preservation, is that it does *not* **contaminate** blood. In addition, such a diet *may* ***help*** **purify** it. One of the best ways to achieve this goal is through **spring cures,** based on fruits or fresh vegetables.

Therefore, the recipes and menus of this chapter, apart from being high in iron, a main component of red blood cells, *help* blood **alkalization** and **"cleansing."**

Menus for

Anemia

Spinach Shake

BREAKFAST

- "Spinach Shake" (Vol. 3, p. 140)
- "Rye Bread" toast with "Mediterranean Tahini" (Vol. 3, pp. 194, 61)
- Pistachios (Vol. 2, p. 135)

LUNCH

- "Seed Salad" (Vol. 3, p. 298)
- "Lentils and Rice" (Vol. 3, p. 211)
- "Spinach Croquettes" (Vol. 3, p. 213)
- "Avocado Shake" (Vol. 3, p. 201)
- Spirulina Tablets (Vol. 1, p. 134)

Lentils and Rice

SUPPER

- "Turnip Greens and Potatoes" (Vol. 3, p. 208)
- "Persimmon Shake" (Vol. 3, p. 270)

Turnip Greens and Potatoes

HEALTH COUNSELS

This menu is especially designed for those who need to recover from anemia or who wish to prevent this ailment. It includes *high-**iron*** food such as spinach, pistachios, and lentils, along with the nutrients that are necessary for blood production, such as ***folic acid*** and several ***trace elements.***

Thrombosis

Soy Milk

BREAKFAST

- "Banana Shake" (Vol. 3, p. 179)
- "Whole Bread" with "Tofu and Herbs Spread" (Vol. 3, pp. 46, 66)
- "Soy Milk" (Vol. 3, p. 305
- Grapes (Vol. 2, p. 78)

LUNCH

- Lemon and Grapefruit Juice (Vol. 2, pp. 124, 93)
- "Andalusian Gazpacho" (Vol. 3, p. 360)
- "Soybean Stew" (Vol. 3, p. 381)
- "Roasted Vegetables" (Vol. 3, p. 384)
- "Rye Bread" (Vol. 3, p. 194)

Roasted Vegetables

SUPPER

- Tomato, Onion, and Garlic Salad (Vol. 2, pp. 275, 142; Vol. 1, p. 338)
- "Cream of Onion" (Vol. 3, p. 220)

Cream of Onion

HEALTH COUNSELS

The ingredients included in this menu are known for their ability to *prevent* ***thrombus*** or clot formation within the arteries, which causes **apoplexy** or **cerebral stroke.** Soy and its derivatives, lemon, onion, and other vegetables *improve blood circulation,* thin the blood, and *reduce the risk* of **arterial thrombosis.**

the Blood

Cleansing

BREAKFAST

- Cleansing Broth with Lemon Juice (Vol. 1, p. 369; Vol. 2, p. 124)
- Melon (Vol. 2, p. 254)
- Grapes (Vol. 2, p. 78)

Grapes

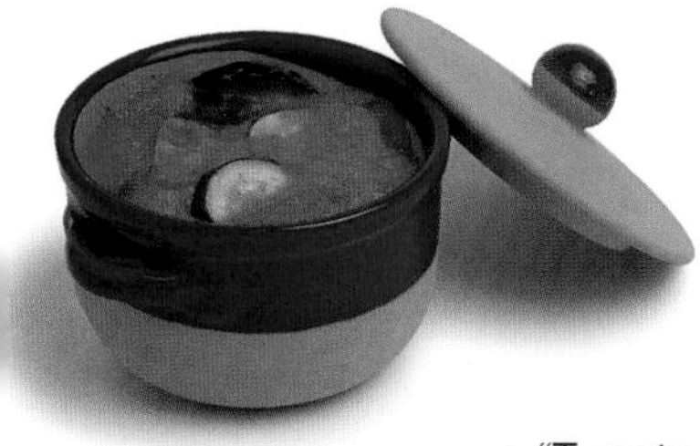

Tomato and Vegetable Stew

LUNCH

- Red Beet Juice (Vol. 2, p. 122)
- "River Salad" (Vol. 3, p. 206)
- "Vegetable Purée" (Vol. 3, p. 361)
- "Tomato and Vegetable Stew" (Vol. 3, p. 212)

SUPPER

- Cleansing Broth with Lemon Juice (Vol. 1, p. 369; Vol. 2, p. 124)
- Celery, Watercress, and Asparagus Salad (Vol. 2, p. 248, 132, 250)
- "Cabbage Varieties" (Vol. 3, p. 378)

Steamed Cauliflower

HEALTH COUNSELS

This menu is ideal for those who wish to follow a **cleansing cure** or a **detoxification cure.** The ingredients facilitate urine production as well as the elimination of waste substances present in the blood. It contributes to alleviate and prevent the development of **allergies,** skin **eczema, obesity, renal complications,** and **chronic disease** in general.

Other Recipes for the Blood

SALADS

- "Stuffed Avocados" (Vol. 3, p. 207)
- "Violet Salad" (Vol. 3, p. 373)
- "Filled Cucumbers" (Vol. 3, p. 348)
- "Pasta Bow Salad" (Vol. 3, p. 165)

SOUPS AND PURÉES

- "Cream of Leek" (Vol. 3, p. 262)
- "Spanish Bouillon" (Vol. 3, p. 332)

MAIN COURSES

- "Rice with Carrots" (Vol. 3, p. 133)
- "Spaghetti with Spinach" (Vol. 3, p. 210)
- "Beans with Spinach" (Vol. 3, p. 352)
- "Catalonian Fava Beans" (Vol. 3, p. 209)
- "Spinach Lasagna" (Vol. 3, p. 108)

BREAKFASTS, DESSERTS AND SNACKS

- "Party Melon" (Vol. 3, p. 176)
- "Cereal Bars" (Vol. 3, p. 174)
- "Oranges with Honey" (Vol. 3, p. 366)

DRINKS

Freshly squeezed juices:

- Grape (Vol. 2, p. 78)
- Lemon (Vol. 2, p. 124)
- Spinach (Vol. 2, p. 28
- Red beet (Vol. 2, p. 122)

Infusions or decoctions:

- Alfalfa (*EMP,* p. 269)
- Knotweed (*EMP,* p. 272)
- Nettle (*EMP,* p. 278)

- *See the recipe index at the beginning of this volume (Vol. 3, pp. 8-13).*
- *See also chapter 23, "Foods for the Blood" (Vol. 2, pp. 118-137).*

EMP = *Encyclopedia of Medicinal Plants,* Education and Health Library, Editorial Safeliz

Preparation time 00:20

Cooking time - - - -

River Salad

INGREDIENTS (4 servings)

- 100 g (≅ 3.5 oz) of **spinach**
- 100 g (≅ 3.5 oz) of **watercress**
- 2 **Belgian endives** (witloofs)

ADDITIONAL INGREDIENTS

- The juice of one **lemon**
- **Potherbs** (mint, basil)
- 4 tablespoons of olive **oil** (each tablespoon of oil adds around 120 kcal to the recipe, that is, 30 kcal per serving)
- Sea **salt** (see Vol. 3, p. 16)

PREPARATION

❶ Wash carefully the spinach, watercress, and Belgian endives.
- Chop the spinach.
- Cut the Belgian endives lengthwise into quarters.

❷ Chop the potherbs and mix with the oil, lemon juice, and salt to make the dressing.
- Arrange the greens in individual plates and dress.

❸ Serve immediately.

For more information about the ingredients, see: Spinach, Vol. 2, p. 28; watercress, Vol. 2, p. 132; Belgian endives, Vol. 2, p. 175.

Suggestions from the Chef

Try a different dressing for this salad—**sweet-and-sour** vinaigrette (see Vol. 3, p. 56).

HEALTH COUNSELS

This River Salad contains a *very low* **calorie count,** especially if oil can be avoided. On the other hand, it is *very high* in ***minerals, trace elements, vitamins,*** and ***phytochemicals,*** which make it particularly beneficial to:

✓The **blood,** due to the cleansing action of raw vegetables which helps to eliminate the metabolic acid residues and "clean" the blood. Furthermore, this salad's ingredients are *high* in **iron,** which is easily absorbed due to the lemon juice.

✓The **liver** and the **gallbladder,** as these vegetables *decongest* the liver and help to eliminate bile. Those suffering from **hepatic disorders, cholelithiasis** (liver stones) or biliary **pancreatitis** will help their condition by including this dish in their diet.

✓**Obesity,** as this salad supplies very few calories and very little fat.

NUTRITIONAL VALUE* per serving

Energy	23 kcal = 96 kj
Protein	1.94 g
Carbohydrates	1.63 g
Fiber	3.18 g
Total fat	*0.188 g*
Saturated fat	*0.039 g*
Cholesterol	—
Sodium	*31.5 mg*

1% 2% 4% 10% 20% 40% 100%

% Daily Value (based on a 2,000 calorie diet) provided by each serving of this dish

CALORIC PROPORTION*

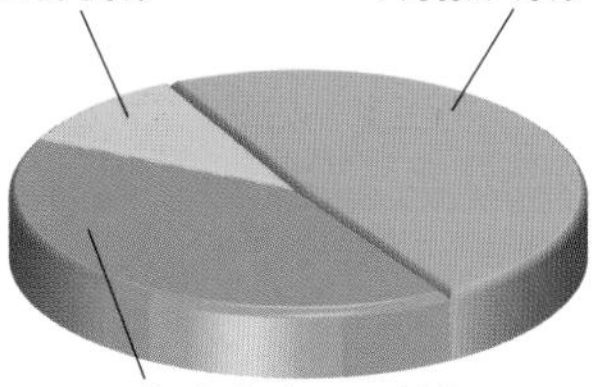

Percentage distribution of **calories for each nutrient**

*Additional ingredients not included.

Preparation time 00:30

Cooking time - - - -

Stuffed Avocados

INGREDIENTS (4 servings)

- 4 **avocados**
- 300 g (≅ 10.6 oz) of **corn**
- 1 **Welsh onion**
- 50 g (≅ 1.75 oz) of pitted **olives**
- 50 g (≅ 1.75 oz) of **capers**
- 1 **celery** stalk

ADDITIONAL INGREDIENTS

- The juice of one **lemon**
- Sea **salt** (see Vol. 3, p. 16)

PREPARATION

❶ Peel, wash, and chop the Welsh onion and celery.

- Chop the olives.

❷ Cut the avocados into halves. Remove the stone and empty part of the pulp (leave at least one centimeter on the rind). Chop and coat with lemon juice to avoid darkening.

- Mix the pulp with the remaining ingredients and add a little bit of salt.
- Spoon the mixture into the avocado shells.

❸ Serve cold.

For more information about the ingredients, see: avocado, Vol. 2, p. 108; corn, Vol. 2, p. 238; Welsh onion, Vol. 2, p. 144; olive, Vol. 2, p. 165; caper, Vol. 1, p. 342; celery, Vol. 2, p. 248.

Suggestions from the Chef

If the avocado stone is big, the filling may be placed in the hole without scooping out any part of the pulp.

HEALTH COUNSELS

There is 1.02 mg of ***iron*** to each 100 g of avocado. This is about half of that found in meat, a significant amount considering that avocado is a plant food. Furthermore, avocados are a good source of ***folic acid*** and ***protein,*** and are highly recommended to those wishing to maintain "good blood."

Corn, Welsh onion, celery, lemon, together with the other accompanying ingredients, supply ***minerals*** and ***vitamins*** which enhance the *antianemic* effect of avocados.

Stuffed avocados constitute a good dish to avoid:

✓ **Anemia** caused by iron deficiency.

✓ *High* **cholesterol** as well as *high* **triglyceride** levels in the blood, due to the *hypolipidic* (i.e., reduces blood's fat content) effect of the avocado.

✓ **Arteriosclerosis** as well as all its consequences, especially myocardial **infarction.**

NUTRITIONAL VALUE* per serving

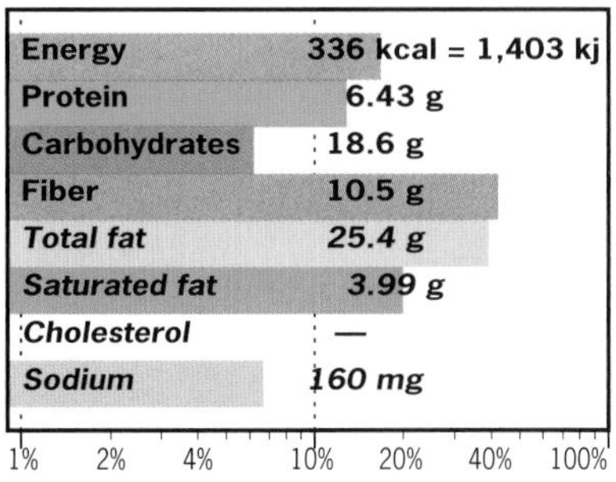
Energy 336 kcal = 1,403 kj
Protein 6.43 g
Carbohydrates 18.6 g
Fiber 10.5 g
Total fat 25.4 g
Saturated fat 3.99 g
Cholesterol —
Sodium 160 mg
1% 2% 4% 10% 20% 40% 100%

% Daily Value (based on a 2,000 calorie diet) provided by each serving of this dish

CALORIC PROPORTION*

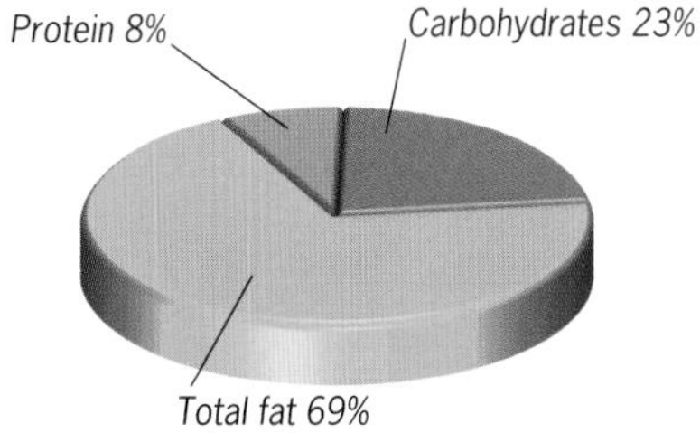
Protein 8%
Carbohydrates 23%
Total fat 69%

Percentage distribution of **calories for each nutrient**

*Additional ingredients not included.

Preparation time 00:15

Cooking time 00:25

Turnip Greens and Potatoes

INGREDIENTS (4 servings)

- 500 g (≅ 1 pound) of **turnip greens**
- 500 g (≅ 1 pound) of **potatoes**
- 250 g (≅ 8.8 oz) of **pumpkin** (squash)

ADDITIONAL INGREDIENTS

- The juice of 1 **lemon**
- 4 tablespoons of olive **oil** (each tablespoon of oil adds around 120 kcal to the recipe, that is, 30 kcal per serving)
- Sea **salt** (see Vol. 3, p. 16)

PREPARATION

❶ Peel, wash, and chop the potatoes and the pumpkin.
- Wash and chop the turnip greens. Peel the stems if they are tough.

❷ Heat water with salt in a pot. When boiling, add the vegetables and boil for 20 minutes.
- Drain and reserve the broth for a different recipe.

❸ Serve hot, dressed with olive oil and lemon juice.

For more information about the ingredients, see: Turnip greens, Vol. 2, p. 321; potato, Vol. 2, p. 201; pumpkin, Vol. 2, p. 97.

HEALTH COUNSELS

Turnip greens are a good source of ***iron, beta-carotene,*** (provitamin A), ***vitamin C,*** and ***folate,*** all of which contribute to blood production. Furthermore, they are *very high* in ***calcium*** and other ***minerals.***

Therefore, this dish with its turnip greens and potatoes is advisable for the prevention of the following ailments:

✓ **Anemia,** due to its wealth in blood-producing ingredients. Additionally, because of the presence of lemon juice, ***iron*** (from turnip greens) is easily *absorbed.*

✓ **Gout** and excess of ***uric acid,*** as this is an ***alkalinizing*** dish. This facilitates the elimination of uric acid together with other waste substances in the kidneys.

✓ **Osteoporosis** and **decalcification** as it is a very *high-**calcium*** dish.

NUTRITIONAL VALUE* per serving

Energy	123 kcal = 515 kj
Protein	4.35 g
Carbohydrates	21.9 g
Fiber	5.80 g
Total fat	*0.515 g*
Saturated fat	*0.134 g*
Cholesterol	—
Sodium	*56.4 mg*

1% 2% 4% 10% 20% 40% 100%

% Daily Value (based on a 2,000 calorie diet) provided by each serving of this dish

CALORIC PROPORTION*

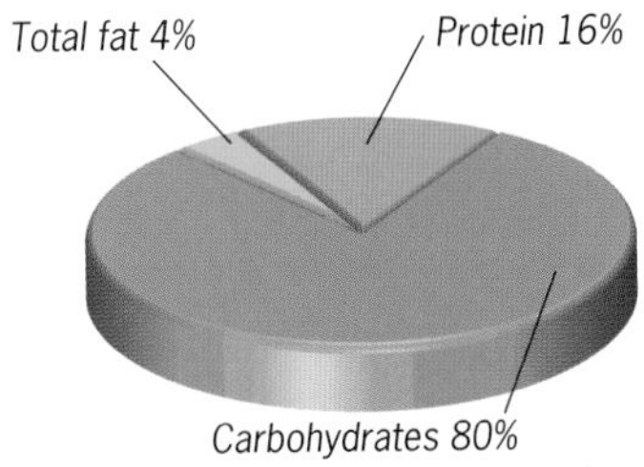

Percentage distribution of **calories for each nutrient**

*Additional ingredients not included.

Preparation time 00:30

Cooking time 00:45

Catalonian Fava Beans

INGREDIENTS (4 servings)

- 1 kg (≅ 2 pounds) of **fava beans** (almost 3 kg if weighed with pod)
- 1 **onion**
- 1 sweet **red pepper**
- 2 **carrots**
- 1 **tomato**
- 150 ml (≅ 2/3 cup) of **water**

ADDITIONAL INGREDIENTS

- **Mint**
- 3 **laurel** leaves
- 4 tablespoons of olive **oil** (each tablespoon of oil adds around 120 kcal to the recipe, that is, 30 kcal per serving)
- Sea **salt** (see Vol. 3, p. 16)

PREPARATION

❶ Separate the beans from their pods.

- Peel and chop the onion, carrot, pepper, and tomato.

❷ Heat the oil in a frying pan, and sauté the onion and pepper; when the onion is transparent, add the tomato.

- Heat the water in a pot. When the water is boiling, add the fava beans, the carrots, and the sautéed vegetables.
- Add salt, mint, and laurel leaves and simmer covered for 30 minutes.
- While simmering, hold the pot by the handles and lid and shake softly in order to stir without smashing the ingredients. Do not uncover.

❸ Serve in a deep dish.

HEALTHIER ALTERNATIVE: Instead of sautéing the ingredients, add them raw to the boiling water.

For more information about the ingredients, see: Fava bean, Vol. 2, p. 137; onion, Vol. 2, p. 142; pepper, Vol. 2, p. 198; carrot, Vol. 2, p. 25; tomato, Vol. 2, p. 275.

HEALTH COUNSELS

Fava beans are quite *high* in ***iron*** (almost as high as meat), as they contain 1.9 mg of this mineral per 100 g. They are also *high* in ***folates,*** nutrients necessary to help our bodies produce good quality **blood.**

In addition, fava beans contain a certain amount of ***vitamin C,*** which helps iron absorption. By adding a few drops of lemon juice, absorption is further enhanced.

Carrots, peppers, and tomatoes supply ***beta-carotene*** (provitamin A) and other ***antioxidant carotenoids*** that are hardly found in fava beans. As a whole, these Catalonian Fava Beans make up a very healthy dish, high in iron, ***protein,*** and antioxidants, especially beneficial to prevent:

✓ **Anemia** caused by iron deficiency.

✓ **Arteriosclerosis** and myocardial **infarction,** because it is high in antioxidants, ***cholesterol-free,*** and very low in ***sodium*** and ***saturated fat.***

✓ **Cancer,** due to the antioxidants that this dish supplies.

NUTRITIONAL VALUE* per serving

Nutrient	Amount
Energy	233 kcal = 975 kj
Protein	15.6 g
Carbohydrates	27.8 g
Fiber	13.8 g
Total fat	*1.87 g*
Saturated fat	*0.400 g*
Cholesterol	—
Sodium	*149 mg*

1% 2% 4% 10% 20% 40% 100% 500%

% Daily Value (based on a 2,000 calorie diet) provided by each serving of this dish

CALORIC PROPORTION*

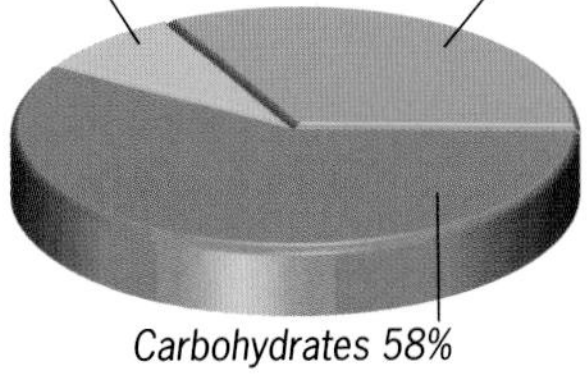

Percentage distribution of **calories for each nutrient**

*Additional ingredients not included.

Preparation time 00:15

Cooking time 00:20

Spaghetti with Spinach

INGREDIENTS (4 servings)

- 250 g (≅ 8.8 oz) of **spaghetti**
- 500 g (≅ 1pound) of **spinach**
- 100 g (≅ 1 cup) of shelled **walnuts**
- 50 g (≅ 1.75 oz) of shelled **pine nuts** (pine kernels)

ADDITIONAL INGREDIENTS

- **White sauce with onion** (Vol. 3, p. 59) (each tablespoon of this sauce adds 15 kcal and 1.3 mg of sodium to the recipe, that is, around 3.7 kcal and 0.32 mg of sodium per serving)
- Sea **salt** (see Vol. 3, p. 16)

PREPARATION

❶ Clean, Wash, and chop the spinach.

❷ Boil the spaghetti in plenty of water with salt. Drain when *al dente* (firm to the bite).

- Boil the spinach in a little water with salt for 5 minutes. Drain.
- In a serving dish, place the spaghetti in a crown shape and cover with the sauce.
- Lay the spinach and nuts in the center.

❸ Serve hot. It may be garnished with raisins.

For more information about the ingredients, see: Spaghetti (pasta), Vol. 1, p. 74; spinach, Vol. 2, p. 28; walnut, Vol. 2, p. 64; pine nut, Vol. 2, p. 47.

HEALTH COUNSELS

Spinach is among the greens *highest* in ***iron,*** an essential mineral in the production of blood. Spinach and nuts, combined together with pasta, supply *high quality* ***protein, essential fatty acids,*** and other nutrients with a high biological value.

Therefore, this dish of spaghetti with spinach is especially beneficial in the following cases:

✓ **Anemia** and **malnutrition.**

✓ Any time there is an increase in nutritional needs, such as during **pregnancy,** the **growth years,** and during times of **convalescence** from debilitating illnesses.

✓ When there is a loss of **visual acuity,** as the carotenoids ***lutein*** and ***zeaxanthin*** from spinach are *antioxidant* and *protective agents* of the retinal cells.

NUTRITIONAL VALUE* per serving

Energy	499 kcal = 2,084 kj
Protein	16.6 g
Carbohydrates	50.6 g
Fiber	7.41 g
Total fat	*24.5 g*
Saturated fat	*2.78 g*
Cholesterol	—
Sodium	*115 mg*

1% 2% 4% 10% 20% 40% 100%

% Daily Value (based on a 2,000 calorie diet) provided by each serving of this dish

CALORIC PROPORTION*

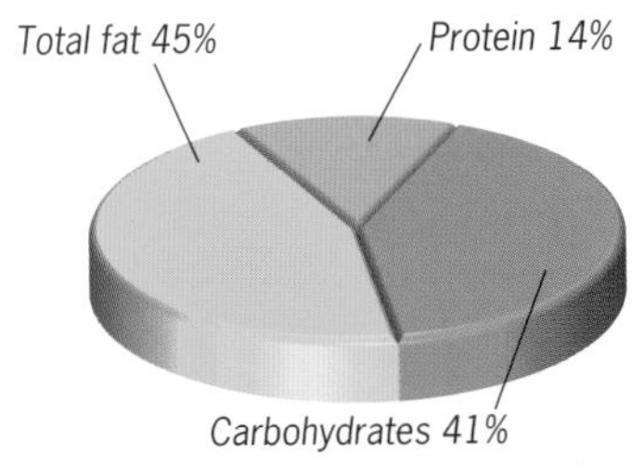

Percentage distribution of **calories for each nutrient**

*Additional ingredients not included.

Preparation time 00:05

Cooking time 00:45

Lentils and Rice

INGREDIENTS (4 servings)

- 200 g (≅ 1 cup) of **lentils**
- 100 g (≅ 1/2 cup) of **whole rice**
- 2 **onions**
- 1 **tomato**
- 1 sweet **green pepper**
- 1 **carrot**
- 50 g (≅ 1.75 oz) of **green olives**

ADDITIONAL INGREDIENTS

- 1 teaspoon of **oregano**
- 4 tablespoons of olive **oil** (each tablespoon of oil adds around 120 kcal to the recipe, that is, 30 kcal per serving)
- Sea **salt** (see Vol. 3, p. 16)

PREPARATION

❶ Soak rice and lentils separately overnight in cold water or for 1 hour in hot water.
- Peel, wash, and chop the vegetables.
- Chop the olives.

❷ Boil the rice and the lentils in a pot with plenty of water.
- Half way through the boiling process, add the vegetables, oregano, oil, and salt.
- Simmer until the stew thickens and it is not too soupy.

❸ Serve hot, garnished with the chopped olives.

For more information about the ingredients, see: Lentils, Vol. 2, p. 127; rice, Vol. 2, p. 225; onion, Vol. 2, p. 142; tomato, Vol. 2, p. 275; pepper, Vol. 2, p. 198; carrot, Vol. 2, p. 25; olive, Vol. 2, p. 165.

HEALTH COUNSELS

Lentils are among the vegetable foods *richest* in ***iron:*** 9 mg per 100 g of raw, edible part of lentils (meat supplies about 2 mg/100 g).

It is true that the iron in lentils, as well as in other vegetables, is absorbed with greater difficulty than that of meat. However, this small disadvantage is compensated for by the great amount of iron supplied by lentils—over four times more than meat.

This stew made up of lentils and rice is especially beneficial in the following cases:

✓**Anemia,** as lentils, aside from iron, supply ***folic acid*** (meat is very poor in this vitamin compound) and ***copper,*** both necessary nutrients in blood formation.

✓**Malnutrition, growth** stages, and **pregnancy** because the ***amino acids*** in lentils, combined with those of rice, supply a high quality, ***complete protein.***

✓**Constipation,** due to the abundant amount of ***fiber*** in this dish.

NUTRITIONAL VALUE* per serving

Energy	**322 kcal = 1,344 kj**
Protein	**17.7 g**
Carbohydrates	**41.2 g**
Fiber	**9.89 g**
Total fat	***2.19 g***
Saturated fat	***0.344 g***
Cholesterol	**—**
Sodium	***76.4 mg***

1% 2% 4% 10% 20% 40% 100%

% Daily Value (based on a 2,000 calorie diet) provided by each serving of this dish

CALORIC PROPORTION*

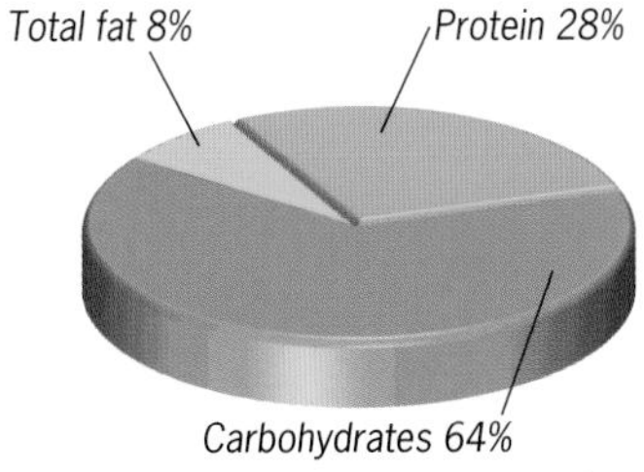

Percentage distribution of **calories for each nutrient**

*Additional ingredients not included.

Preparation time 00:15

Cooking time 00:45

Tomato and Vegetable Stew

INGREDIENTS (4 servings)

- 2 **onions**
- 2 **tomatoes**
- 1 sweet **red pepper**
- 2 sweet **green peppers**
- 1 **zucchini**
- 1 **eggplant** (Guinea squash, aubergine)
- 4 **garlic** cloves

ADDITIONAL INGREDIENTS

- **Parsley**
- 4 tablespoons of olive **oil** (each tablespoon of oil adds around 120 kcal to the recipe, that is, 30 kcal per serving)
- Sea **salt** (see Vol. 3, p. 16)

PREPARATION

❶ Peel and chop the eggplant, zucchini, onions, and garlic.
- Wash and chop the peppers and crush the tomatoes.
- Wash and chop the parsley.

❷ Heat the oil in a pot and lightly sauté the onions and the peppers. Add the garlic, eggplant, zucchini, and lastly, the crushed tomato.
- Add salt and parsley.
- Keep it covered and simmer until the vegetables are tender and the juices have evaporated.

❸ Serve hot.

HEALTHIER ALTERNATIVE: Instead of sautéing the ingredients, mix them raw with the crushed tomato and cook them in their own juice, covered and on a very low flame.

For more information about the ingredients, see: Onion, Vol. 2, p. 142; tomato, Vol. 2, p. 275; pepper, Vol. 2, p. 198; zucchini, Vol. 2, p. 159; eggplant, Vol. 2, p. 256; garlic, Vol. 1, p. 338; and the *Encyclopedia of Medicinal Plants:* Garlic, p. 230.

HEALTH COUNSELS

This dish adequately combines several *alkalinizing* vegetables. It is beneficial for ***cleansing cures*** in order to compensate acidification of the blood caused by a diet rich in cheese, meat, and shellfish.

Furthermore, *all* ***vegetables*** included in this stew are *high* in *antioxidant* ***phytochemicals,*** which *protect* against ***cholesterol*** deposits in the arteries, against **cellular aging,** and against **carcinogenic agents.** This is why the Tomato and Vegetable Stew is especially recommended to avoid:

✓ Acidification of the **blood** caused by an abundant intake of animal products that cause **gout, arthritis, kidney stones, arteriosclerosis,** and other chronic diseases.

✓ **Obesity,** as it supplies few calories and, at the same time, a satisfying effect.

✓ **Cancer,** because of its antioxidant and protective effects.

NUTRITIONAL VALUE* per serving

Energy	**111 kcal = 464 kj**
Protein	**4.28 g**
Carbohydrates	**18.4 g**
Fiber	**6.88 g**
Total fat	***0.867 g***
Saturated fat	***0.136 g***
Cholesterol	—
Sodium	***17.9 mg***

1% 2% 4% 10% 20% 40% 100%

% Daily Value (based on a 2,000 calorie diet) provided by each serving of this dish

CALORIC PROPORTION*

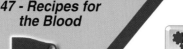

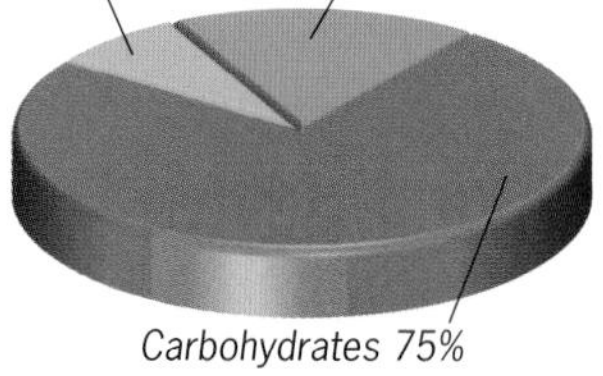

Percentage distribution of **calories for each nutrient**

*Additional ingredients not included.

Preparation time 00:20

Cooking time 00:45

Spinach Croquettes

INGREDIENTS (4 servings)

- 500 g (≅ 1 pound) of **spinach**
- 300 ml (≅ 1 1/4 cups) of **skimmed milk**
- 30 g (≅ 1/4 cup) of **whole flour**
- 50 g (≅ 1.75 oz) of shelled **pine nuts** (pine kernels)
- 1 roasted sweet **red pepper**
- 1 **onion**
- 45 g (1 cup) of **bread crumbs**
- 1 **egg**

ADDITIONAL INGREDIENTS

- 3 tablespoons of olive oil (each tablespoon of oil adds around 120 kcal to the recipe, that is, 30 kcal per serving)
- Sea **salt** (see Vol. 3, p. 16)

PREPARATION

❶ Peel, wash, and shred the onion.
- Wash and chop the spinach.

❷ Simmer the spinach with little water in a covered pot.
- Drain when tender.
- Heat the oil in a frying pan, and sauté the onion until it is transparent. Add flour and stir for 2 minutes. Remove from the heat and add the cold milk little by little while stirring continuously to avoid the formation of lumps. Return the frying pan to the fire, add salt, and keep stirring until the batter thickens.
- Add the spinach, the pine nuts, and the chopped red pepper. When the dough separates from the frying pan, pour it into a dish and let cool.
- Spoon out portions of dough and shape into croquettes.
- Roll in beaten egg and then in breadcrumbs.
- Arrange them onto a tray and bake at 220°C until golden throughout. If you choose to fry them, remember that the fat levels are increased.

❸ Serve hot.

For more information about the ingredients, see: Spinach, Vol. 2, p. 28; milk, Vol. 1, p. 182; flour, Vol. 1, p. 68; pine nut, Vol. 2, p. 47; pepper, Vol. 2, p. 198; onion, Vol. 2, p. 142; bread, Vol. 1, p. 70; egg, Vol. 1, p. 218.

HEALTHIER ALTERNATIVE: Instead of sautéing the onion, bake it or steam it; toast the flour; substitute the skimmed milk with soy milk; and bread without egg (see Vol. 3, p. 76).

HEALTH COUNSELS

Iron, vitamins, phytochemicas, and ***folic acid*** (folate), all from spinach, make this recipe a very appropriate one for those who wish to fight **anemia.**

It is a nutritious, tasty, and fairly energetic recipe. Those who wish to control their **cholesterol** level need to use it sparingly, or omit the egg.

Spinach croquettes are especially recommended for the following cases:

✓ **Anemia,** especially when it is caused by iron deficiency.

✓ **Pregnancy** and **lactation,** because of its content in ***folic acid.***

✓ **Growth** stages, intense **physical activity,** and **sports,** thanks to the ***vitamins*** and ***minerals*** supplied by spinach and pine nuts.

✓ When there is a loss of **visual acuity** due to retinal alterations, because spinach has a *protecting* action.

NUTRITIONAL VALUE* per serving

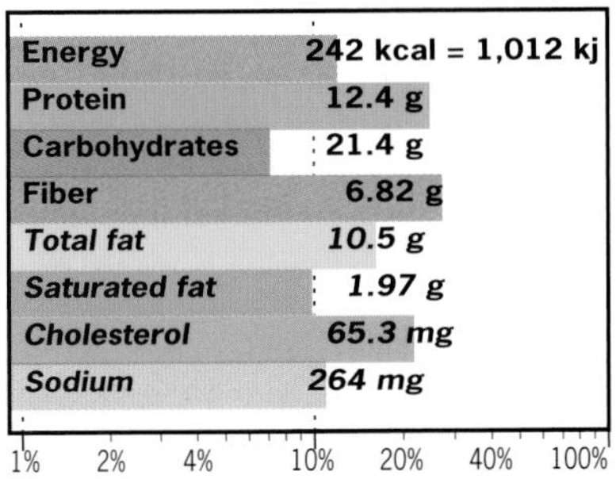
Energy 242 kcal = 1,012 kj
Protein 12.4 g
Carbohydrates 21.4 g
Fiber 6.82 g
Total fat 10.5 g
Saturated fat 1.97 g
Cholesterol 65.3 mg
Sodium 264 mg
1% 2% 4% 10% 20% 40% 100%

% Daily Value (based on a 2,000 calorie diet) provided by each serving of this dish

CALORIC PROPORTION*

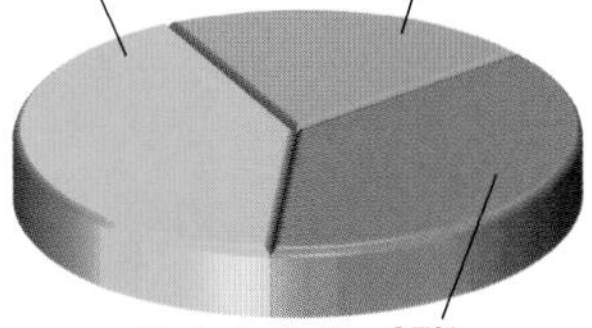
Total fat 41%
Protein 22%
Carbohydrates 37%

Percentage distribution of **calories for each nutrient**

*Additional ingredients not included.

48 Recipes for the Respiratory System

Chapter Summary

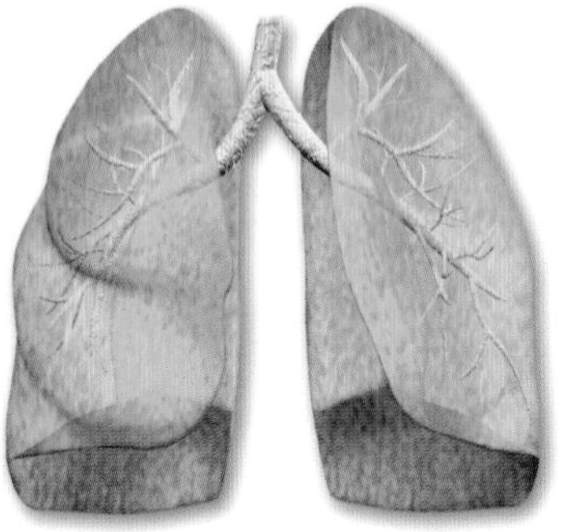

Recipes

Boiled Vegetables 223
Cabbage Salad 219
Cream of Onion 220
Leeks with Mayonnaise 222
Onion and Pepper Pizza 224
Potato Stew 221
Stewed Figs and Pears 225
Sweet Cassava Salad 218

THERE IS nothing as *indispensable* for life as **oxygen.** No human being would be able to survive for more than a few minutes without receiving a sufficient amount of this gas from the atmosphere. Oxygen from the air reaches the blood through the respiratory system: **nose and mouth, larynx, lungs, bronchial tubes, bronchioles,** and **alveoli.**

The respiratory system also has an **excretory function,** eliminating carbon dioxide (CO_2) produced through metabolic combustion as well as other toxic substances.

All our cells, and especially the neurons of the nervous system, require good oxygenation. Hence the importance of healthy lungs and respiratory tract.

Certain foods alter the respiratory system. Others, such as onions, garlic, leeks, radishes, and honey, are excellent medicinal foods for the bronchial tubes and the lungs.

Food intake can affect, for better or for worse, the respiratory function. For example, too much salt, shellfish, and certain preservatives and coloring, among others (see Vol. 2, p. 140), contribute to asthmatic crises and narrow the bronchial tubes, thus making respiration difficult.

On the other hand, **onions, garlic, radishes,** and other vegetables high in essence, produce the opposite effect: dilate the bronchial tubes, facilitate mucus elimination, and improve the air passage through the respiratory ducts. Furthermore, these vegetables produce antiseptic and antibiotic effects, thus facilitating the excretion of germs that often contaminate the respiratory ducts.

Figs and **dates** smooth and protect the membrane lining of the bronchial tubes.

Colorful vegetables, such as carrots, supply beta-carotene (provitamin A) which, together with vitamin C, prevents lung cancer.

The recipes and menus included in this chapter have been designed with these principles in mind. The reader will find the appropriate soups, salads, main dishes, and desserts explained below.

For our respiratory system to work optimally, we must abstain from products—whether food or others—that intoxicate or tax the respiratory system. Likewise, we must use appropriately and consistently those foods that facilitate the healthy function of this system. This is the case of the main ingredients recommended for the recipes found in this chapter.

Menus for

Asthma

Orange Juice

BREAKFAST

- Freshly squeezed Orange Juice with Wheat Germ (Vol. 2, pp. 360, 310)
- "Whole Bread" Toast rubbed with Tomato and Garlic (Vol. 3, p. 46; Vol. 1, pp. 72, 338; Vol. 2, p. 275)
- Bio-Yogurt (Vol. 1, p. 202)

LUNCH

- "Sweet Cassava Salad" (Vol. 3, p. 218)
- "Beans with Spinach" (Vol. 3, p. 352)
- "Onion and Pepper Pizza" (Vol. 3, p. 224)
- "Whole Bread" (Vol. 3, p. 46; Vol. 1, p. 72)

Onion and Pepper Pizza

SUPPER

- Onion, Watercress, and Radish Salad with Wheat Germ (Vol. 2, pp. 142, 132, 181, 310)
- "Oranges with Honey" (Vol. 3, p. 366)

Oranges with Honey

HEALTH COUNSELS

This menu is especially designed for those suffering from asthma and wishing to avoid asthma attacks. In these cases, a natural, **additive-free** diet is required. This diet should also be free from **allergy**-producing foods, such as **dairy products.** Fresh greens and vegetable salads, especially containing onion, prevent and soothe asthma attacks.

Colds, pharyngitis, sinusitis, and bronchitis

BREAKFAST

- "Apricot Shake" (Vol. 3, p. 141)
- Figs and Dates boiled in Milk (Vol. 2, pp. 145, 147; Vol. 1, p. 182)
- Mango (Vol. 2, p. 341)

Mango

LUNCH

- Freshly squeezed Carrot Juice (Vol. 2, p. 25)
- "Cabbage Salad" (Vol. 3, p. 219)
- "Boiled Vegetables" (Vol. 3, p. 223)
- "Leek Pie" (Vol. 3, p. 338)
- "Whole Bread" (Vol. 3, p. 46; Vol. 1, p. 72)

Boiled Vegetables

SUPPER

- "Cream of Onion" (Vol. 3, p. 220)
- "Leeks with Mayonnaise" (Vol. 3, p. 222)
- Lemon Juice with Honey (Vol. 2, p. 124; Vol. 1, p. 160)

Leeks with Mayonnaise

HEALTH COUNSELS

This menu effectively helps to prevent and to heal upper respiratory tract infections. ***Vitamin A*** from apricots, mangoes, and carrots favors *regeneration of mucosae.* The essence contained in leeks and cabbage *fights* **infections.** Figs, dates, and honey have a *pectoral* effect.

the Respiratory System

Tobacco detoxification

Oranges

BREAKFAST

- Oranges, Tangerines, and Melon (Vol. 2, pp. 360, 359, 254)
- "Garlic Bread" with Tomato (Vol. 3, p. 71; Vol. 2, p. 275)
- "Soy milk" with Wheat Germ (Vol. 3, p. 305; Vol. 2, p. 310)

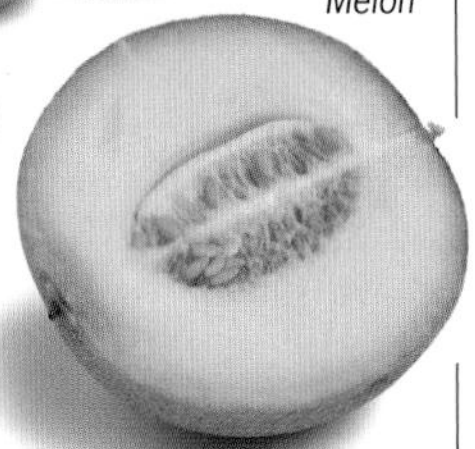
Melon

Belgian Endive Salad

LUNCH

- Carrot and Tomato Juice (Vol. 2, pp. 25, 275)
- "Belgian Endive Salad" (Vol. 3, p. 230)
- "Cabbage Varieties" (Vol. 3, p. 378)
- "Onion Sausages" (Vol. 3, p. 96).
- "Stewed Figs and Pears" (Vol. 3, p. 225)
- "Rye Bread" (Vol. 3, p. 194)

SUPPER

- Kiwis (Vol. 2, p. 356)
- Peaches and Plums (Vol. 2, pp. 75, 233)

Kiwis

HEALTH COUNSELS

This menu helps to *cleanse* the **bronchial tubes** after having given up smoking, and it contributes to the *regeneration* of the **respiratory tract.** Besides, this menu has a high content of ***vitamins A, B,*** and ***C,*** which are especially vital for those who have stopped smoking in order to recover their lost health.

After not having smoked for a few days, a diet containing plenty of fruit and juice is recommended. This menu is ideal to follow after that first stage.

Other Recipes for the Respiratory System

SALADS

- "River Salad" (Vol. 3, p. 206)
- "Rainbow Salad" (Vol. 3, p. 184)
- "Red and White Salad" (Vol. 3, p. 372)

SOUPS AND PURÉES

- "Garlic Soup" (Vol. 3, p. 374)
- "Vegetable Purée" (Vol. 3, p. 361)

MAIN COURSES

- "Borage and Potatoes" (Vol. 3, p. 362)
- "Potato Stew" (Vol. 3, p. 221)
- "Sautéed Marinated Gluten" (Vol. 3, p. 91)

BREAKFASTS, DESSERTS, AND SNACKS

- "Cherimoya and Orange Shake" (Vol. 3, p. 178)
- "Tropical Fruit Salad" (Vol. 3, p. 253)

DRINKS

Freshly squeezed juices:

- Onion (*EMP,* p. 294)
- Cabbage (Vol. 2, p. 191)

Infusions or decoctions:

- Coltsfoot (*EMP,* p. 341)
- High Mallow (*EMP,* p. 511)
- Thyme (*EMP,* p. 769)
- Licorice (*EMP,* p. 308)

- *See the recipe index at the beginning of this volume (Vol. 3, pp. 8-13).*
- *See also chapter 24, "Foods for the Respiratory System" (Vol. 2, pp. 138-149).*

EMP = Encyclopedia of Medicinal Plants, Education and Health Library, Editorial Safeliz.

Preparation time 00:15

Cooking time 00:30

Sweet Cassava Salad

INGREDIENTS (4 servings)

- 500 g (≅ 1 pound) of **sweet cassava** (manioc roots)
- 4 **carrots**
- 2 **red beets**
- 8 **radishes**
- 1 **Welsh onion**

ADDITIONAL INGREDIENTS

- 4 tablespoons of **lemon vinaigrette** (Vol. 3, p. 56) (each tablespoon of this dressing adds 95 kcal to the recipe, that is, around 24 kcal per serving)

PREPARATION

❶ Boil the red beets if they are preferred cooked.
- Peel, wash, and chop the carrots and boiled beets (if they are preferred raw, they may be shredded; the taste is completely different from boiled).
- Wash and slice the radishes.
- Wash and chop the Welsh onion.

❷ Peel and boil the sweet cassava. Slice and arrange on dishes together with the other ingredients.

❸ Dress with the vinaigrette sauce at the time of serving.

Suggestions from the Chef

- Radishes may be presented open like a **flower.** Simply make a cross-shaped cut in the lower part of each radish, soak them in water, and place in the refrigerator for 20 minutes.
- Sweet cassava is a starchy root that may be substituted by potato.

HEALTH COUNSELS

This salad is prepared with true roots—(beets, carrots, and radishes), with a bulb—(Welsh onions), and with a tuber—(sweet cassava or manioc root).

As any other salad, this sweet cassava salad is *high* in ***vitamins, minerals, fiber,*** and ***phytochemical elements*** (see Vol. 1, p. 410) of medicinal effect. Because of these ingredients, this dish is especially recommended for:

✓The **respiratory system,** due to the ***essential oils*** in onions and radishes, which possess *mucolytic* (soften the phlegm), *expectorant,* and *antibiotic actions.* Additionally, the ***beta-carotene*** (provitamin A) from carrots is transformed into ***vitamin A*** which protects the **lining** of the respiratory organs. This roots salad provides support to the treatment of **sinusitis, pharyngitis, bronchitis,** and **bronchial asthma.**

✓The **liver,** because these vegetables detoxify ("clean") this gland and help it to maintain its functionality.

For more information about the ingredients, see: Sweet cassava, Vol. 1, p. 108; carrot, Vol. 2, p. 25; red beet, Vol. 2, p. 122; radish, Vol. 2, p. 181; Welsh onion, Vol. 2, p. 144.

NUTRITIONAL VALUE* per serving

Nutrient	Amount
Energy	204 kcal = 855 kj
Protein	5.78 g
Carbohydrates	38.9 g
Fiber	7.28 g
Total fat	*0.992 g*
Saturated fat	*0.176 g*
Cholesterol	—
Sodium	*107 mg*

1% 2% 4% 10% 20% 40% 100%

% Daily Value (based on a 2,000 calorie diet) provided by each serving of this dish

CALORIC PROPORTION*

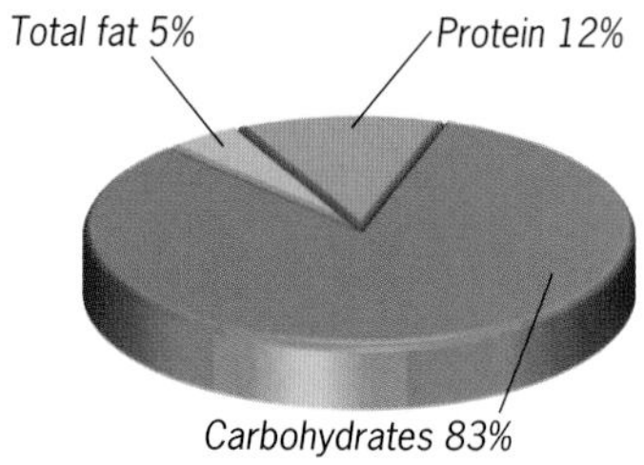

Percentage distribution of **calories for each nutrient**

* Additional ingredients not included.

Preparation time: 00:20 | Cooking time: - - - -

Cabbage Salad

INGREDIENTS (4 servings)

- 400 g (≅ 14 oz) of **cabbage** (central part)
- 4 **Welsh onions**
- 1 **apple**

ADDITIONAL INGREDIENTS

- 1/2 teaspoon of **cumin**
- 4 tablespoons of olive **oil** (each tablespoon of oil adds around 120 kcal to the recipe, that is, 30 kcal per serving)
- The juice of 1 **lemon**
- Sea **salt** (see Vol. 3, p. 16)

PREPARATION

❶ Dispose of the cabbage's outer leaves, remove the central part and chop in fine strips.
- Wash the cabbage with plenty of water and drain. Add salt and let stand.
- Peel and chop the apple and the Welsh onions.

❷ Combine oil, lemon juice, and cumin. Pour this dressing over the Welsh onion and the apple. Add the cabbage. Mix thoroughly and toss to blend the flavors.

❸ Serve.

Suggestions from the Chef

- Instead of lemon juice, mild **vinegar,** such as apple vinegar, may be used.
- To make the Welsh onion **less strong,** chop and soak in water for one hour. If a whole hour is not available, the same effect can be achieved by adding salt and lemon juice (or vinegar) to the soaking water. Rinse before serving.

HEALTH COUNSELS

This salad is easy to prepare in winter, when cabbages are tender and when the respiratory system requires extra protection. As with any other salad, this cabbage salad is *very low* in calories, in ***fat,*** and in ***sodium***—if salt is avoided or used in moderation—and *high* in ***vitamins, minerals, fiber,*** and ***phytochemical elements.*** As with any other salad, it is recommended for those wishing to care of their arteries, their heart, and their shape.

In addition, cabbage salad is beneficial to:

✓The **respiratory system,** as the ***essential sulfured oils*** contained in cabbages and Welsh onions *soften* the respiratory **phlegm** and *help* to *eliminate* it through expectoration. Welsh onions also provide an *antibiotic* effect.

✓The **stomach,** due to the cabbage's *protective* and *sore-healing* effects. Cumin, when added as a condiment, helps to avoid flatulence caused by the cabbage.

For more information about these ingredients see: cabbage, Vol. 2, p. 191; Welsh onion, Vol. 2, p. 144; apple, Vol. 2, p. 229.

NUTRITIONAL VALUE* per serving

Energy	72 kcal = 300 kj
Protein	2.93 g
Carbohydrates	12.6 g
Fiber	4.03 g
Total fat	*0.701 g*
Saturated fat	*0.104 g*
Cholesterol	—
Sodium	*31.3 mg*

1% 2% 4% 10% 20% 40% 100%

% Daily Value (based on a 2,000 calorie diet) provided by each serving of this dish

CALORIC PROPORTION*

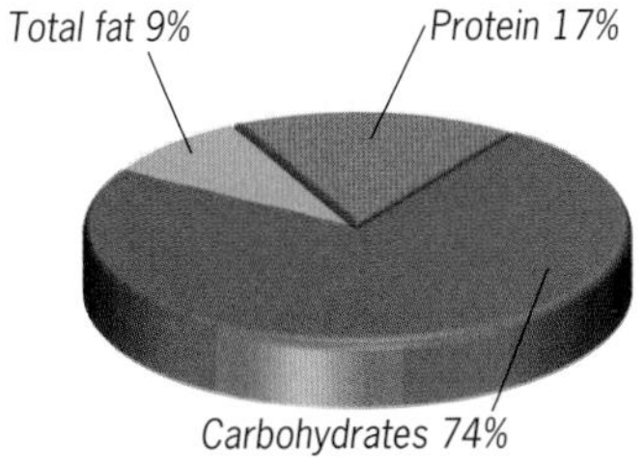

Percentage distribution of **calories for each nutrient**

* Additional ingredients not included.

Preparation time 00:10

Cooking time 00:30

Cream of Onion

INGREDIENTS (4 servings)

- 750 g (≅ 26.5 oz) of **onion**
- 3 tablespoons of Traditional Tomato Sauce (Vol. 3, p. 62)
- 1 liter (≅ 1 quart) of **water**

ADDITIONAL INGREDIENTS

- 3 tablespoons of olive **oil** (each tablespoon of oil adds around 120 kcal to the recipe, that is, 30 kcal per serving)
- Sea **salt** (see Vol. 3, p. 16)

PREPARATION

❶ Peel, wash, and chop the onion.

❷ Heat the water in a pot. Once it is boiling, add the onion, the salt, and the oil. Boil for 15 minutes.

- Blend the onion with an electric blender. Add the tomato sauce, and boil for an additional 5 minutes.

❸ Serve hot.

For more information about the ingredients, see: Onion, Vol. 2, p. 142; tomato, Vol. 2, p. 275.

Suggestions from the Chef

Zucchini and/or potato may be added. It may also be seasoned with different spices.

HEALTH COUNSELS

Onions constitute a true *medicinal food.* When eaten raw, it can cause bad breath. However, boiled onions lose their peculiar odor while preserving a large proportion of their medicinal properties.

This Cream of Onion is especially recommended in the following cases:

✓ **Respiratory system** ailments, such as **bronchitis** and **sinusitis,** due to the *expectorant* and *antibiotic* effects of onion. Tomato's ***carotenoids,*** which account for its red color, also contribute to the good health of the respiratory lining.

✓ **Arteriosclerosis** and **coronary** disease, as onions *protect* against **thrombosis** and *improve* blood **circulation.**

✓ **Cancer** prevention, especially digestive cancer.

NUTRITIONAL VALUE* per serving

Energy	54 kcal = 228 kj
Protein	1.65 g
Carbohydrates	9.68 g
Fiber	2.55 g
Total fat	*0.294 g*
Saturated fat	*0.046 g*
Cholesterol	—
Sodium	*4.33 mg*

1% 2% 4% 10% 20% 40% 100%

% Daily Value (based on a 2,000 calorie diet) provided by each serving of this dish

CALORIC PROPORTION*

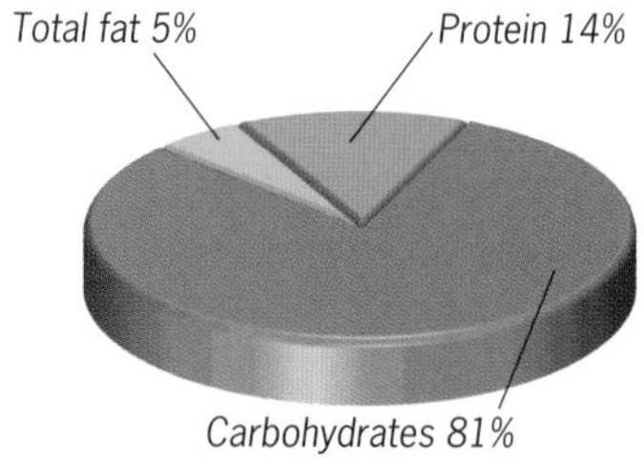

Percentage distribution of **calories for each nutrient**

* Additional ingredients not included.

Preparation time 00:15

Cooking time 00:30

Potato Stew

INGREDIENTS (4 servings)

- 500 g (≅ 1 pound) of **potato**
- 4 **onions**
- $^1/_2$ liter (≅ $^1/_2$ quart) of unsalted **vegetable broth**)

ADDITIONAL INGREDIENTS

- **Sweet paprika**
- **White pepper**
- 4 tablespoons of olive **oil** (each tablespoon of oil adds around 120 kcal to the recipe, that is, 30 kcal per serving)
- **Chives**
- Sea **salt** (see Vol. 3, p. 16)

PREPARATION

❶ Peel, wash, and chop the potatoes.
- Peel and chop the onion.

❷ Heat the oil in a pot, and sauté the onion until it is transparent.
- Add the potatoes and stir.
- Cover the potatoes with the vegetable broth. Add the spices and boil for 20 minutes.

❸ Serve hot.

HEALTHIER ALTERNATIVE: Instead of sautéing the potatoes and onions, add them raw to the boiling vegetable broth.

For more information about the ingredients, see: Potato, Vol. 2, p. 201; onion, Vol. 2, p. 142.

HEALTH COUNSELS

In this simple and healthy stew, the properties of potatoes, onions, and vegetable broth are combined so that the dish is recommended for the following cases:

✓ **Respiratory ailments,** thanks to the *favorable* effect of the onion upon the **bronchial tubes.**

✓ Tendency to **metabolic acidosis** caused by an excess of uric acid, by the kidneys' malfunction, or by a diet predominantly composed of foods of animal origin, such as cheese, meat, or shellfish.

Onions, potatoes, and vegetable broth possess an *alkalinizing* effect and are able to *neutralize* the **excessive acidity** both in blood and tissue. Of course, in order to rectify the acidosis problem, it is necessary to treat the original cause first and then follow an alkalinizing diet based on **vegetables.**

NUTRITIONAL VALUE* per serving

Energy	136 kcal = 568 kj
Protein	3.81 g
Carbohydrates	26.6 g
Fiber	4.30 g
Total fat	*0.340 g*
Saturated fat	*0.065 g*
Cholesterol	—
Sodium	*10.5 mg*

1% 2% 4% 10% 20% 40% 100%

% Daily Value (based on a 2,000 calorie diet) provided by each serving of this dish

CALORIC PROPORTION*

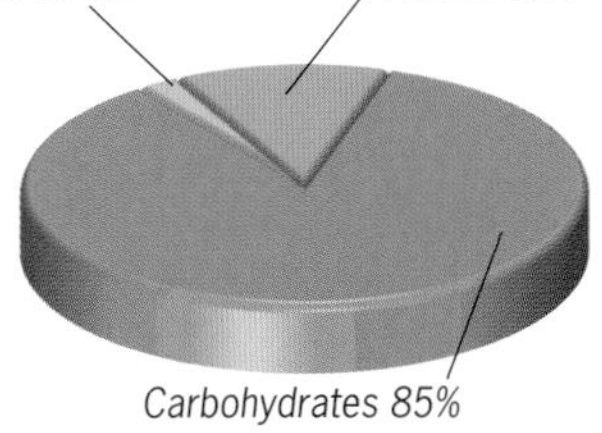

Percentage distribution of **calories for each nutrient**

* Additional ingredients not included.

Preparation time 00:15

Cooking time 00:20

Leeks with Mayonnaise

INGREDIENTS (4 servings)

- 1 kg (≅ 2 pounds) of **leeks**

ADDITIONAL INGREDIENTS

- **Traditional mayonnaise** (Vol. 3, p. 58) (each tablespoon of this sauce adds 82 kcal, that is, around 20 kcal per serving)
- Sea **salt** (see Vol. 3, p. 16)

PREPARATION

❶ Peel the leeks and remove the outer leaves. Wash (see Vol. 3, p. 134).

❷ Boil the leeks in a little water with salt. Drain.

- Prepare the mayonnaise sauce following the instructions given (see Vol. 3, p. 58).

❸ Serve cold or hot, dressed with the traditional mayonnaise. It may be garnished with shredded carrot and radish slices.

HEALTHIER ALTERNATIVE: Substitute the traditional mayonnaise with soy mayonnaise (see Vol. 3, p. 58).

For more information about the ingredients, see: Leek, Vol. 2, p. 319.

NUTRITIONAL VALUE* per serving

Energy	76 kcal = 319 kj
Protein	1.88 g
Carbohydrates	15.4 g
Fiber	2.25 g
Total fat	*0.375 g*
Saturated fat	*0.050 g*
Cholesterol	—
Sodium	*25.0 mg*

1% 2% 4% 10% 20% 40% 100%

% Daily Value (based on a 2,000 calorie diet) provided by each serving of this dish

HEALTH COUNSELS

Leeks contain an essence similar to that of onions that makes respiratory tract phlegm more fluid. Besides, leeks have antibiotic properties, and they are also diuretic and laxative. All this explains the favorable effect of this recipe upon the following cases:

✓ **Sinusitis, bronchitis,** and upper respiratory tract **catarrh.**

✓ **Edema** (serous fluid retention) in tissue caused by malfunctioning of the **kidneys.**

✓ **Constipation** caused by atony or bowel slowness.

CALORIC PROPORTION*

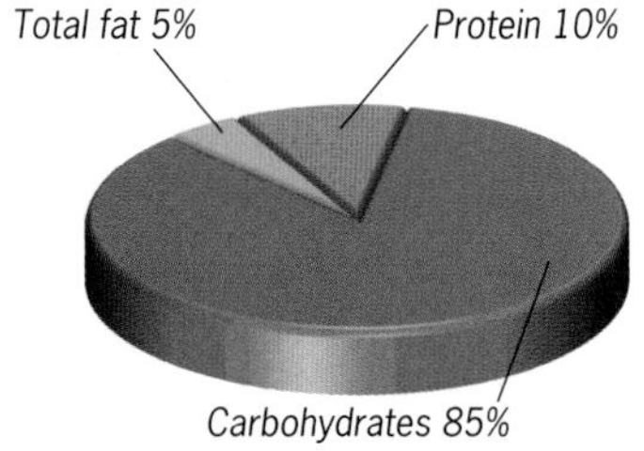

Percentage distribution of **calories for each nutrient**

* Additional ingredients not included.

Preparation time 00:15

Cooking time 00:20

Boiled Vegetables

INGREDIENTS (4 servings)

- 500 g (≅ 1 pound) of **potatoes**
- 500 g (≅ 1 pound) of small **onions**
- 200 g (≅ 1 $^{1}/_{3}$ cups) of **peas**
- 200 g (≅ 7 oz) of **carrots**
- $^{1}/_{2}$ liter (≅ $^{1}/_{2}$ quart) of **water**

ADDITIONAL INGREDIENTS

- 4 tablespoons of olive **oil** (each tablespoon of oil adds around 120 kcal to the recipe, that is, 30 kcal per serving)
- Sea **salt** (see Vol. 3, p. 16)

PREPARATION

❶ Peel, wash and chop the carrots, the small onions, and the potatoes.

❷ Heat the oil in a pot, and sauté the vegetables and the peas.

- Add the water and salt. Simmer, covering with a lid until the vegetables are tender.

❸ Serve hot.

HEALTHIER ALTERNATIVE: Instead of sautéing the ingredients, add them raw to the boiling water. Reduce the flame to the minimum when it starts boiling.

For more information about the ingredients, see: Potato, Vol. 2, p. 201; onion, Vol. 2, p. 142; pea, Vol. 2, p. 73; carrot, Vol. 2, p. 25.

HEALTH COUNSELS

The onions, peas and carrots in this simple and nutritious dish supply ***protein, carbohydrates,*** *very little* ***fat,*** and healthy ***active elements*** for the respiratory system. It is especially recommended for:

✓The **respiratory system,** due to the onions' *balsamic* (smoothing of the respiratory tract) properties. The ***beta-carotene*** (provitamin A) from carrots and ***vitamins B*** and ***C*** from peas, also help to keep the lining of the bronchial tubes healthy.

✓The **arteries** and the **heart,** because this is a ***cholesterol-free*** dish which, in addition, supplies *very little* ***fat*** and ***sodium*** provided that oil and salt are used in moderation.

✓The **metabolism,** as both potatoes and onions produce a significant *alkalinizing* effect, fighting **excess acidity** in the blood, which is associated to many disorders and illnesses.

NUTRITIONAL VALUE* per serving

Energy	173 kcal = 723 kj
Protein	7.08 g
Carbohydrates	30.7 g
Fiber	6.59 g
Total fat	*0.770 g*
Saturated fat	*0.139 g*
Cholesterol	—
Sodium	*41.9 mg*

1% 2% 4% 10% 20% 40% 100%

% Daily Value (based on a 2,000 calorie diet) provided by each serving of this dish

CALORIC PROPORTION*

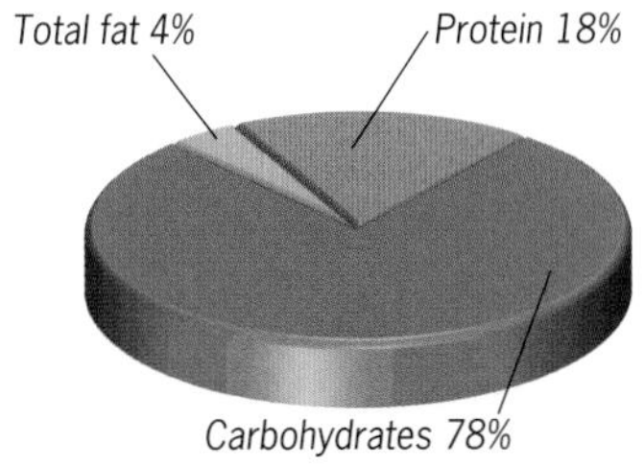

Percentage distribution of **calories for each nutrient**

* Additional ingredients not included.

Preparation time 00:15

Cooking time 00:30

Onion and Pepper Pizza

INGREDIENTS (4 servings)

- 500 g (≅ 1 pound) of **onions**
- 1 **tomato**
- 1 baked sweet **red pepper**
- **Pie dough** (see Vol. 3, p. 104)

ADDITIONAL INGREDIENTS

- 1 tablespoon of **basil**
- 3 tablespoons of olive **oil** (each tablespoon of oil adds around 120 kcal to the recipe, that is, 30 kcal per serving)
- Sea **salt** (see Vol. 3, p. 16)

PREPARATION

❶ Peel and slice the onions very fine.
- Crush the tomato.
- Cut the pepper into wide strips.

❷ Prepare the dough (see Vol. 3, p. 104; use half of the specified amounts), spread the dough on a tray and bake. Remove from the oven before it gets brown.
- Heat the oil in a frying pan, and sauté the onions.
- Spread the tomato, the onions, and the pepper strips over the dough. Sprinkle with basil and grill.

❸ Serve hot.

HEALTHIER ALTERNATIVE: Instead of sautéing the onions, steam or bake them. In this case, they can be baked together with the dough.

Suggestions from the Chef

It may be covered with cheese or with white sauce.

For more information about the ingredients, see: Onion, Vol. 2, p. 142; tomato, Vol. 2, p. 275; pepper, Vol. 2, p. 198; flour, Vol. 1, p. 68.

HEALTH COUNSELS

This delicious onion pizza, garnished with pepper and tomato is very healthy for:

✓ The **respiratory system,** due to the *favorable* effect of onions upon the respiratory tract and to the *antioxidant **carotenoids*** supplied by tomatoes and peppers. It is desirable in the diet of those wishing to prevent **sinusitis, pharyngitis, bronchitis,** and even bronchial **asthma.**

✓ **Cancer** *prevention,* because of the *antioxidant* and *anticarcinogenic* action of onions, peppers, and tomatoes, especially upon the stomach and the colon.

✓ **Children** and **adolescents,** as this tasty onion pizza supplies energy and nutrients.

NUTRITIONAL VALUE* per serving

Energy	363 kcal = 1,517 kj
Protein	8.46 g
Carbohydrates	49.7 g
Fiber	5.86 g
Total fat	*12.7 g*
Saturated fat	*1.73 g*
Cholesterol	—
Sodium	*12.7 mg*

1% 2% 4% 10% 20% 40% 100%

% Daily Value (based on a 2,000 calorie diet) provided by each serving of this dish

CALORIC PROPORTION*

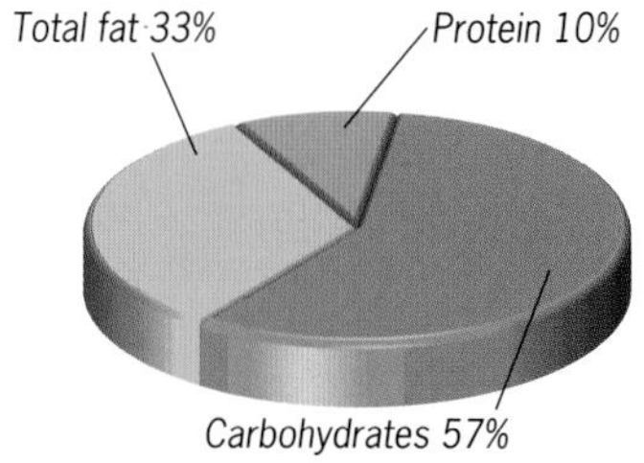

Percentage distribution of **calories for each nutrient**

* Additional ingredients not included.

Preparation time 00:10

Cooking time 00:30

Stewed Figs and Pears

INGREDIENTS (4 servings)

- 8 **pears**
- 8 **figs**
- 50 g (≅ 1.75 oz) **raisins** (preferably seedless)

ADDITIONAL INGREDIENTS

- 1 **cinnamon** stick
- 1/2 **lemon rind**

PREPARATION

❶ Peel the pears and wash the figs.

❷ Place the fruit and the cinnamon in a pot. Cover with water.

- Simmer until the water is reduced and becomes like syrup.
- Remove the lemon rind and the cinnamon.

❸ Serve cold.

For more information about the ingredients, see: Pear, Vol. 2, p. 112; fig, Vol. 2, p. 145; raisins, Vol. 2, p. 81.

HEALTH COUNSELS

This Stewed Figs and Pears dessert can be highly recommended to those suffering from:

✓The **respiratory system,** due to the *expectorant* and *softening* effects of figs upon the bronchial tubes.

✓The **kidneys,** because of the *diuretic* action of pears, which helps with urine production and makes urine less dense.

✓The **intestine,** due to the combination of both fruits, which *regulates* the bowel **movement.**

NUTRITIONAL VALUE* per serving

Energy	266 kcal = 1,112 kj
Protein	2.22 g
Carbohydrates	58.2 g
Fiber	10.6 g
Total fat	*1.32 g*
Saturated fat	*0.156 g*
Cholesterol	—
Sodium	*5.00 mg*

1% 2% 4% 10% 20% 40% 100%

% Daily Value (based on a 2,000 calorie diet) provided by each serving of this dish

CALORIC PROPORTION*

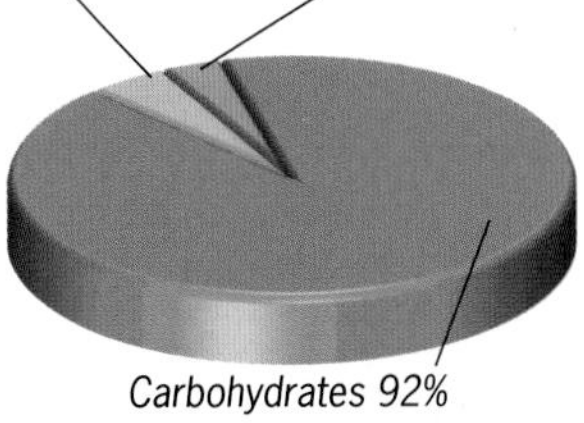

Percentage distribution of **calories for each nutrient**

Suggestions from the Chef

- The dish may be **sweetened** by adding sugar when boiling, or pouring molasses over it when serving.
- Sprinkle with **cinnamon** powder, or add whipped **cream** or **ice cream.** In this case, omit the syrup.

Gastroduodenal Ulcer

***Cinnamon** is easy to digest, opens the appetite, and stimulates the secretion of gastric juices. For this last reason, it is not advisable for those suffering from gastroduodenal ulcer (see Vol. 1, p. 340).*

* Additional ingredients not included.

49 Recipes for the Liver and the Gallbladder

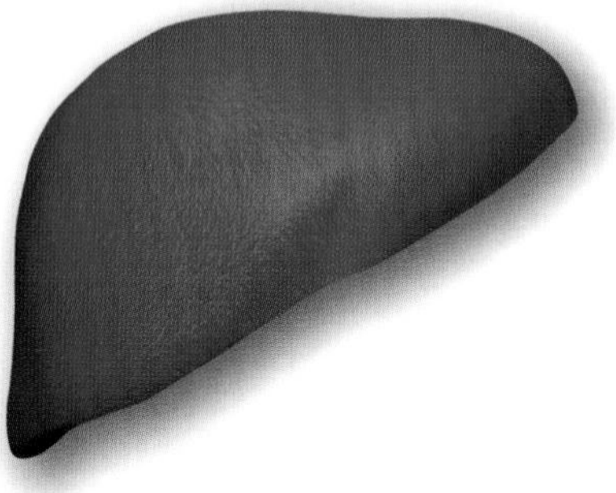

Chapter Summary

Recipes

Artichoke Soup 231
Belgian Endive Salad 230
Cardoons in Almond Sauce 232
Italian-style Artichokes 236
Rice with Artichokes 234
Tamarind Drink 237

A balanced and natural diet can help to keep the liver and the gallbladder in a healthy state.

Furthermore, there are certain foods such as those in this chapter's recipes, which particularly help the detoxification function of the liver. This process is among the most important for the organism's health.

THE LIVER carries out its multiple functions, **detoxification** being one of them, in a still and quiet manner. A balanced and natural diet is of utmost importance to keep this organ in optimal condition as well as to prevent possible disorders.

On the other hand, an unbalanced diet, with plenty of protein from flesh meat, shellfish, alcoholic beverages, drugs in general, certain medicines, along with chemical products, disturb the health of this important organ.

What Helps the Liver

There are certain foods that ***help*** the liver to carry out its cleansing function. Furthermore, some foods have the capacity to **strengthen** and **regenerate** this organ. **Artichokes, cardoons,** and **Belgian endives** are examples. That is why these ingredients are significant components in the recipes of this chapter.

The food that is the best friend of the liver is undoubtedly the artichoke. It is an ***authentic*** **medicine** for the liver. Hepatic patients are often recommended to take artichoke **extract,** as it contains **cynarin** (see Vol. 2, p. 179).

The artichoke or globe **artichoke** is a ***very versatile*** horticultural product. It can be used raw, steamed, baked, and as an ingredient in many dishes. Its looks and taste are unique and pleasant. Therefore, as often as possible, we should use ***natural*** artichokes *prepared in the* ***simplest*** *possible* ***way.***

Artichokes can be **frozen.** They may also be **canned,** although they lose their best properties in this way.

For example, women on **oral contraceptives** (the "pill"), whose estrogens need to be metabolized and excreted by the liver, will benefit from an ***abundant*** intake of **artichokes.**

What Helps the Gallbladder

The gallbladder stores **bile** secreted by the liver. This organ later empties its contents into the intestine in order to help in the digestion of fat.

Recipes in this chapter help to facilitate healthy functioning of the gallbladder. In addition, dishes made up of whole cereals and legumes prevent the development of biliary stones or gallstones, which is the most common disorder of this organ. These recipes are also recommended for those who have undergone gallbladder surgery.

Menus for the Liver

Hepatitis

Whole Bread

BREAKFAST

- "Sweet Cassava Salad" (Vol. 3, p. 218)
- "Whole Bread" Toast with "Tahini" with wheat germ (Vol. 3, p. 46; Vol. 1, p. 72; Vol. 2, p. 310)

Sweet Cassava Salad

LUNCH

- "Sweet Cassava Salad" (Vol. 3, p. 218)
- "Potato Stew" (Vol. 3, p. 190)
- "Stuffed Artichokes" (Vol. 3, p. 286)
- "Whole Bread" (Vol. 3, p. 46; Vol. 1, p. 72)
- "Refreshing Tea" (Vol. 3, p. 254)

Cardoons in Almond Sauce

SUPPER

- Onion, Watercress, and Carrot Salad (Vol. 2, pp. 132, 142, 25)
- "Cardoons in Almond Sauce" (Vol. 3, p. 232)

HEALTH COUNSELS

This menu is recommended in case of **hepatitis.** An inflamed liver needs a slow process in order to recover. This process requires a natural diet with *plenty* of ***vitamins*** and ***carbohydrates*** that is *free* from **meat,** especially fatty meat and **shellfish.**

Artichokes and cardoons, which are included in this menu, *facilitate* the *detoxifying* function of the liver.

Hepatopathy (Liver Disease)

BREAKFAST

- Grape Juice (Vol. 2, p. 78)
- Cherries and Loquats (Vol. 2, pp. 304, 298)
- Boiled Tapioca with "Almond Milk," sweetened with Honey (Vol. 1, pp. 108, 160; Vol. 3, p. 342)

Loquats

LUNCH

- "River Salad" (add lecithin) (Vol. 3, p. 206; Vol. 1, p. 89)
- "Rice with Artichokes" (Vol. 3, p. 234)
- "Onion and Pepper Pizza" (Vol. 3, p. 224)
- "Whole Bread" (Vol. 3, p. 46; Vol. 1, p. 72)
- Shredded Apple with Yogurt (Vol. 2, p. 229; Vol. 1, p. 202)

Rice with Artichokes

Grilled Vegetables

SUPPER

- "Grilled Vegetables" (Vol. 3, p. 189)
- shredded apple with yogurt (Vol. 2, p. 229; Vol. 1, p. 202)

HEALTH COUNSELS

This menu is especially recommended for those who have suffered or are currently suffering from hepatopathy (general liver disease). It helps *slow down* the development of **cirrhosis.** It may contribute to the *regeneration* of the liver after the impact of alcoholic beverages and other toxic substances.

It supplies ***simple carbohydrates***—such as those in grapes—necessary for and well tolerated by the liver. It also provides ***complex carbohydrates***—such as those in tapioca and rice. Vegetables included in the salad, as well as onions and fruits, also contribute to a healthy liver.

and the Gallbladder

Biliary Disorders

BREAKFAST

- Papaya (Vol. 2, p. 157)
- "Whole Bread" with "Hummus" (Vol. 3, pp. 46, 67; Vol. 1, p. 72)
- "Soy Milk" (Vol. 3, p. 305)

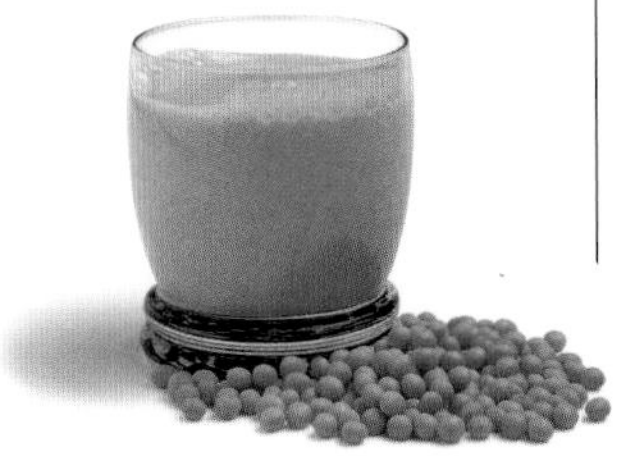

Soy Milk

LUNCH

- "Carrot and Apple Juice" (Vol. 3, p. 355)
- "Belgian Endive Salad" (Vol. 3, p. 230)
- "Italian-style Artichokes" (Vol. 3, p. 236)
- "Vegetable Hamburgers" (Vol. 3, p. 152)
- "Rye Bread" (Vol. 3, p. 194)

Vegetable Hamburgers

SUPPER

- Chicory, Onion, and Olive Salad (Vol. 2, pp. 176, 142, 165)
- "Artichoke Soup" (Vol. 3, p. 231)

Artichoke Soup

HEALTH COUNSELS

This *easy-to-digest* menu that is *low in* ***fat*** is ideal to avoid **gallstone colic** in those suffering from biliary stones in the gallbladder. Those suffering from **difficult digestion** caused by **gallbladder** *disorders,* and those who have undergone surgery, will also benefit from this menu.

Other Recipes for the Liver and the Gallbladder

SALADS

- "Spring Salad" (Vol. 3, p. 312)
- "Red and White Salad" (Vol. 3, p. 372)

Soups and Purées

- "Oat Soup" (Vol. 3, p. 147)
- "Cream of Onion" (Vol. 3, p. 220)

Main Courses

- "Sauerkraut and Carrots" (Vol. 3, p. 264)
- "Potato Stew" (Vol. 3, p. 221)

Breakfasts, Desserts, and Snacks

- "Oranges with Honey" (Vol. 3, p. 366)
- "Cereal Bars" (Vol. 3, p. 174)

Drinks

Freshly squeezed juices:

- Radish (Vol. 2, p. 181)

Infusions or decoctions:

- Artichoke (*EMP* p. 387)
- Boldo (*EMP* p. 390)
- Milk Thistle (*EMP* p. 395)
- Dandelion (*EMP* p. 397)
- Chicory (*EMP* p. 440)

- *See the recipe index at the beginning of this volume (Vol. 3, pp. 8-13).*
- *See also chapter 26, "Foods for the Liver and the Gallbladder" (Vol. 2, pp. 168-181).*

EMP = Encyclopedia of Medicinal Plants, Education and Health Library, Editorial Safeliz.

Preparation time: 00:15

Cooking time: - - - -

Belgian Endive Salad

INGREDIENTS (4 servings)

- 4 **Belgian endives** (witloofs)
- 200 g (≅ 7 oz) **radicchio**
- 1 **Welsh onion**
- 8 **radishes**
- 1 **apple**
- 50 g (≅ 1.75 oz) **green olives**
- 4 tablespoons of **brewer's yeast**

ADDITIONAL INGREDIENTS

- The juice of 1 **lemon**
- 2 tablespoons of olive **oil** (each tablespoon of oil adds around 120 kcal to the recipe, that is, 30 kcal per serving)
- Sea **salt** (see Vol. 3, p. 16)

PREPARATION

❶ Clean, wash, and chop the Belgian endives, the radicchio, the Welsh onion, and the radishes.
- Peel and chop the apple.

❷ Arrange the ingredients on dishes.
- Sprinkle 1 tablespoon of brewer's yeast on each dish and add salt.

❸ Dress at the time of serving.

Suggestions from the Chef

- **Endive** or **rhubarb,** which exert the same soothing effect upon the liver and the gallbladder, can be used to substitute Belgian endive.
- Any of the following ingredients may be **added** raw to the salad: chicory, dandelion, mint, artichoke hearts, or tender cardoon stems.

For more information about the ingredients, see: Belgian endive, Vol. 2, p. 175; radicchio, Vol. 2, p. 176; Welsh onion, Vol. 2, p. 144; radish, Vol. 2, p. 181; apple, Vol. 2, p. 229; olive, Vol. 2, p. 165; brewer's yeast, vol. 1, p. 358.

HEALTH COUNSELS

Belgian endives as well as radicchio contain active ingredients that help the liver to work well and make digestion easy. These ingredients are what cause the bitter taste. In addition, Welsh onions and radishes are *high* in ***sulfured essence*** that *quickens* the **detoxification** processes carried out by the liver. Therefore, Belgian Endive Salad is especially recommended for:

✓The **liver** and the **gallbladder.**

✓The **stomach,** due to its *invigorating* and *appetizing* effects.

✓The **respiratory system,** as radishes and Welsh onions *soften* the **bronchial phlegm** and help its *elimination* through expectoration.

✓**Slimming diets** as this dish contains few calories.

NUTRITIONAL VALUE* per serving

Energy	109 kcal = 454 kj
Protein	6.62 g
Carbohydrates	11.7 g
Fiber	9.24 g
Total fat	*1.83 g*
Saturated fat	*0.260 g*
Cholesterol	—
Sodium	*87.3 mg*

1% 2% 4% 10% 20% 40% 100%

% Daily Value (based on a 2,000 calorie diet) provided by each serving of this dish

CALORIC PROPORTION*

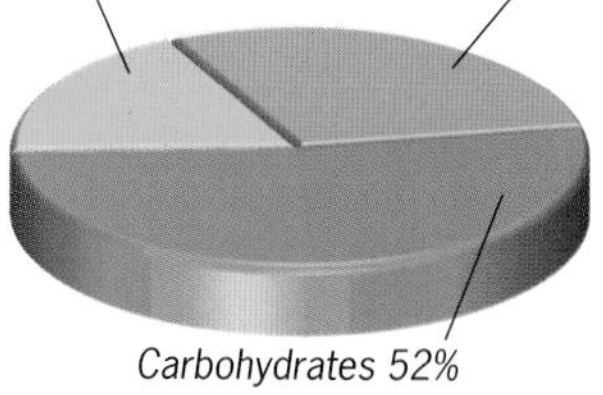

Percentage distribution of **calories for each nutrient**

* Additional ingredients not included.

Preparation time 00:15

Cooking time 00:25

Artichoke Soup

INGREDIENTS (4 servings)

- 1 kg (≅ 2 pounds) **artichokes**
- 2 teaspoons of **sesame**
- 1 liter (≅ 1 quart) of **water**

ADDITIONAL INGREDIENTS

- The juice of 1 **lemon**
- 2 tablespoons of olive **oil** (each tablespoon of oil adds around 120 kcal to the recipe, that is, 30 kcal per serving)
- Sea **salt** (see Vol. 3, p. 16)

PREPARATION

❶ Dispose of the stem, tips, and tougher artichoke leaves. Coat the artichokes with lemon juice to avoid darkening.
- Remove the inner down and slice.

❷ Heat the water and salt in a pot. When the water is boiling, add the artichokes, sesame, and oil.
- Boil for 20 minutes.

❸ Serve hot.

For more information about the ingredients, see: Artichoke, Vol. 2, p. 178; sesame, Vol. 1, p. 352; and the *Encyclopedia of Medicinal Plants:* Sesame, p. 611.

Suggestions from the Chef

At the time of serving the soup, sprinkle with fine chopped parsley.

HEALTH COUNSELS

This artichoke soup combines the preventive and healing properties of the artichoke with the *wealth* of ***vitamins*** and ***minerals*** *in sesame.* As it is easy to digest and is *low in* ***fat,*** it is good for those who wish to follow a simple and healthy diet. It is especially recommended for the following cases:

✓ **Cholelithiasis** (gallstones) and **alterations** in the **gallbladder emptying** process, as it regulates its function. Artichoke soup may be among the first foods taken after having had gallstone colic, or after gallbladder surgery (cholecystectomy). In these cases the added oil should be reduced.

✓ **Renal disorders,** such as colic, urine sediments, renal failure, and urinary infection.

✓ **Infarction** or **angina pectoris,** due to the artichoke's capacity to *reduce* **cholesterol** levels and to *improve* arterial **circulation.**

✓ **Obesity** or **diabetes.**

NUTRITIONAL VALUE* per serving

Energy	76 kcal = 317 kj
Protein	4.62 g
Carbohydrates	6.74 g
Fiber	7.10 g
Total fat	*1.68 g*
Saturated fat	*0.252 g*
Colesterol	—
Sodium	*118 mg*

1% 2% 4% 10% 20% 40% 100%

% Daily Value (based on a 2,000 calorie diet) provided by each serving of this dish

CALORIC PROPORTION*

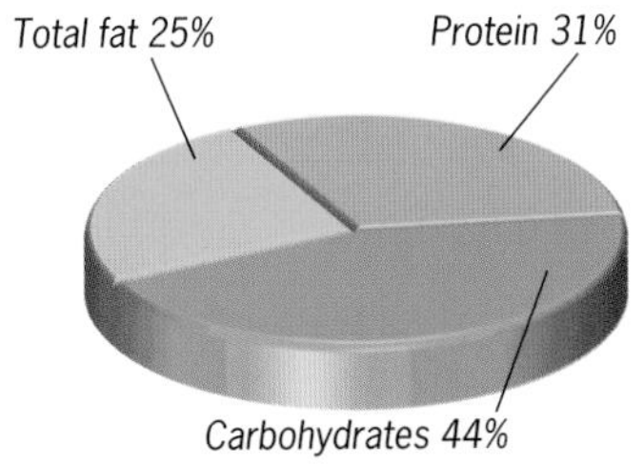

Percentage distribution of **calories for each nutrient**

* Additional ingredients not included.

Preparation time 00:30

Cooking time 0 1:30

Cardoons in Almond Sauce

INGREDIENTS (4 servings)

- 1 kg (≅ 2 pounds) **cardoons**
- 50 g (≅ 1.75 oz) raw blanched **almonds**
- 1 tablespoons of **whole flour**
- 3 **garlic** cloves
- 3 tablespoons of olive **oil**

ADDITIONAL INGREDIENTS

- **Parsley**
- The juice of one **lemon**
- Sea **salt** (see Vol. 3, p. 16)

HEALTHIER ALTERNATIVE: In order to lower the fat content, use a dressing made up of lemon, dietetic yeast, and a few drops of olive oil to season the cardoons instead of almond sauce.

For more information about the ingredients, see: Cardoons, Vol. 2, p. 177; almond, Vol. 2, p. 48; flour, Vol. 1, p. 68; garlic, Vol. 1, p. 338; oil, Vol. 1, p. 112; and the *Encyclopedia of Medicinal Plants:* Garlic, p. 230.

PREPARATION

❶ Cut the fleshy leaves of the cardoon near the bottom and remove the lengthwise outer threads using a knife. Throw the dried leaves out. In order to eliminate the down from the surface, which causes their bitter flavor, rub their surface (especially in the small leaves) with a brush or a piece of cloth.

- Wash in plenty of water and chop the stems into 3 or 4-cm chunks, including the central stem, as it is very tender and edible.
- Soak the cardoons in water with the lemon juice, to avoid the darkening of oxidation.

❷ Heat water in a pot. When boiling, add the cardoons. Add salt, and cook on a medium flame until the stems are tender. Thirty minutes are sufficient in the pressure cooker, while in a normal pot 50-60 minutes may be required.

- Drain and reserve the broth (if it is not too bitter).
- Grind the garlic, almonds, and parsley.
- Pour the oil in a frying pan. When it is hot, add the ground ingredients and the flour.
- When the flour becomes golden, add the broth (or simply water if the broth is too bitter). Stir constantly to avoid lumps until the sauce thickens.
- In a pot, place the cardoons together with the almond sauce. Simmer during 15 minutes.

❸ Serve hot.

Cut the fleshy leaves of the cardoon near the bottom.

Remove the lengthwise threads.

Once cleaned, chop the stems.

NUTRITIONAL VALUE*
per serving

Energy	228 kcal = 954 kj
Protein	4.52 g
Carbohydrates	10.7 g
Fiber	4.96 g
Total fat	*18.0 g*
Saturated fat	*2.17 g*
Cholesterol	—
Sodium	*164 mg*

1% 2% 4% 10% 20% 40% 100%

% Daily Value (based on a 2,000 calorie diet) provided by each serving of this dish

CALORIC PROPORTION*

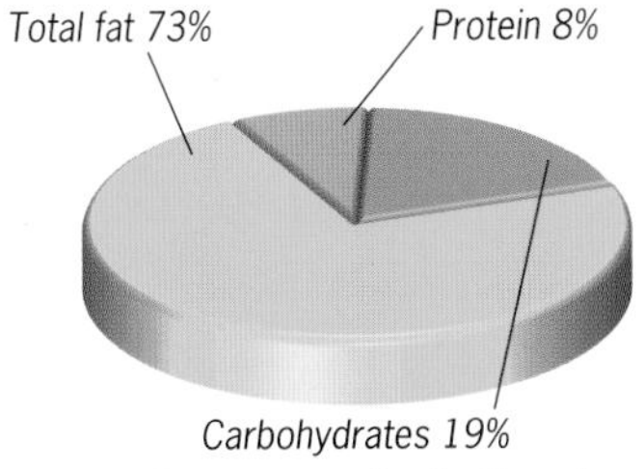

Percentage distribution of **calories for each nutrient**

* Additional ingredients not included.

HEALTH COUNSELS

Cardoons, like artichokes, contain ***cynarin.*** This substance stimulates liver function. One such function is that of *neutralizing* the **toxic elements** coming from outside the body and circulating in the bloodstream. Alcohol and certain food components are examples. At times, these toxic substances come from the organism itself. Metabolic waste is one example.

Aside from flavor, **almonds** supply ***protein, essential fatty acids, minerals*** (notably, ***calcium*** and ***phosphorus***), and ***vitamins,*** such as ***vitamin E.***

Therefore, this dish is especially beneficial for:

✓ The **liver,** particularly in case of hepatic **failure,** alcohol or pharmaceutical **intoxication, hepatitis,** and **cirrhosis.**

✓ The **gallbladder,** because cardoons produce **bile** that is *more fluid* and thereby *prevent* the formation of **gallstones.** In case of biliary disorders, it is recommended to reduce the amount of added oil.

✓ The **bones,** due to the *high content* of minerals, such as ***calcium*** and ***phosphorus*** from almonds.

✓ **Diabetes,** thanks to the gentle *hypoglycemic* (reduces blood sugar levels) action of cynarin in the cardoons and to the fact that they contain very *little* ***sugar*** and ***carbohydrates.***

Preparation time 00:30

Cooking time 00:40

Rice with Artichokes

INGREDIENTS (4 servings)

- 300 g (≅ 1 1/2 cups) **whole rice**
- 500 g (≅ 1 pound) **artichokes** (globe artichokes)
- 1 sweet **red pepper**
- 1 **tomato**
- 2 **garlic** cloves
- 3/4 liter (3/4 quart) of unsalted **vegetable broth**

ADDITIONAL INGREDIENTS

- The juice of one **lemon**
- **Parsley**
- 4 tablespoons of olive **oil** (each tablespoon of oil adds around 120 kcal to the recipe, that is, 30 kcal per serving)
- Sea **salt** (see Vol. 3, p. 16)

For more information about the ingredients, see: Rice, Vol. 2, p. 225; artichoke, Vol. 2, p. 178; pepper, Vol. 2, p. 198; tomato, Vol. 2, p. 275; garlic, Vol. 1, p. 338; and the *Encyclopedia of Medicinal Plants:* Garlic, p. 230.

PREPARATION

❶ Soak rice overnight in cold water or for 1 hour if hot water is used.

- Remove the tough outer leaves, tips and stems of the artichokes. Chop them lengthwise into 6 or more pieces per artichoke. Coat them with lemon juice to avoid darkening.
- Roast the pepper, peel it, remove its seeds, and cut into strips.
- Wash and crush the tomato.
- Peel and chop the garlic and parsley.

❷ Heat the oil in a frying pan, and sauté the artichokes. Set aside.

- In the same oil, sauté the pepper for a few minutes, add the tomato, and sauté for 5 additional minutes.
- Pour the vegetable broth (boiling) onto the sautéed ingredients. Add the rice (drained) and the salt.
- Boil rapidly for 10 minutes.
- Add the artichokes and the chopped garlic and parsley.
- Reduce the fire and simmer until the rice is cooked (dry and fluffy). Cover the pan if the broth is being absorbed too quickly.
- Turn off the stove and let the food rest for 5 minutes.

❸ Serve hot.

HEALTHIER ALTERNATIVE: Instead of sautéing the ingredients, steam them in a covered pot until the artichokes are half done. Add the vegetable broth at this time. Follow the recipe's directions from here.

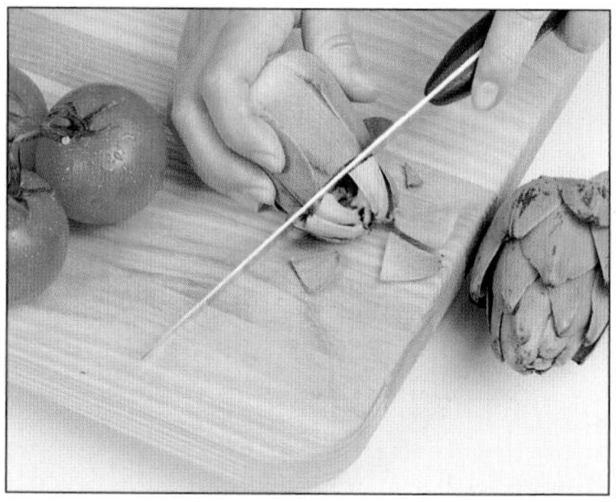

Cut off the tips and outer leaves of the artichoke.

Stir the vegetables for a few minutes.

Add the rice (previously drained) to the sautéed vegetables.

NUTRITIONAL VALUE*
per serving

Energy	319 kcal = 1,334 kj
Protein	8.40 g
Carbohydrates	61.0 g
Fiber	6.79 g
Total fat	*2.31 g*
Saturated fat	*0.453 g*
Cholesterol	—
Sodium	*67.0 mg*

1% 2% 4% 10% 20% 40% 100%

% Daily Value (based on a 2,000 calorie diet) provided by each serving of this dish

HEALTH COUNSELS

Artichokes are ideal to keep the liver in good condition. Combined with rice and the other ingredients included in this dish, we obtain a simple, nutritious, and healthy dish that is especially beneficial to those wishing to protect their:

✓ **Liver,** as artichokes help with the functions of this organ, especially its ability to *eliminate* **toxins** that circulate in the bloodstream. In addition, the ***carbohydrates*** from rice provide a good source of energy for the hepatic cells.

✓ **Arteries** and **heart** as ***cynarin*** in artichokes prevents **cholesterol** from attaching to the arteries. Also rice, especially if it is whole, helps to *control* levels of cholesterol. Peppers, tomatoes, and garlic used in this recipe *reduce* cholesterol levels and improve blood circulation.

✓ **Kidneys,** thanks to the *diuretic* action of artichokes that helps to produce urine, thus *eliminating* **toxins** circulating in the bloodstream.

✓ **Intestine,** due to the ***fiber*** contained in both artichokes and rice, especially if whole rice is used. This fiber *prevents* **constipation** and *facilitates* the function of the **large intestine.**

CALORIC PROPORTION*

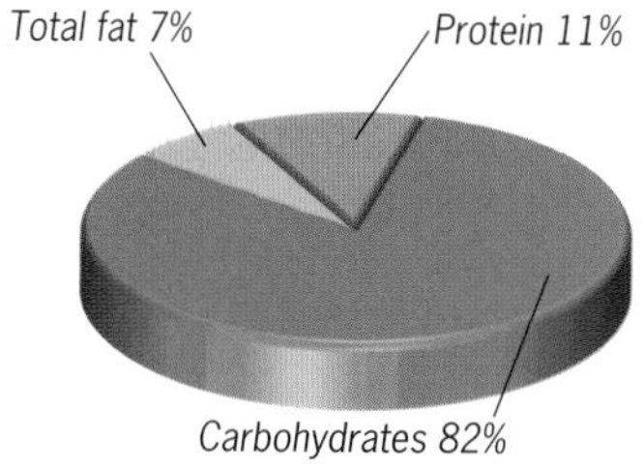

Percentage distribution of
calories for each nutrient

* Additional ingredients not included.

Preparation time 00:15

Cooking time 00:30

Italian-style Artichokes

INGREDIENTS (4 servings)

- 500 g (≅ 1 pound) **artichokes** (globe artichokes)
- 150 g (≅ 5.3 oz) **elbow macaroni** (pasta)
- 1 **onion**
- 1 **garlic** clove
- 1 liter (≅ 1 quart) of unsalted **vegetable broth**

ADDITIONAL INGREDIENTS

- 1 The juice of one **lemon**
- **Parsley**
- 4 tablespoons of olive **oil** (each tablespoon of oil adds around 120 kcal to the recipe, that is, 30 kcal per serving)
- Sea **salt** (see Vol. 3, p. 16)

PREPARATION

❶ Clean the artichokes in order to leave only the tenderest part –the heart. Chop them and coat them with lemon juice to avoid darkening.

- Peel and chop the onion and the garlic.
- In a mortar, grind the garlic and the parsley.

❷ Heat the oil in a pan and sauté the onion. When transparent, add the artichokes and sauté for 3 additional minutes.

- Add the vegetable broth. When boiling, add the elbow macaroni and the salt. Stir occasionally to avoid sticking.
- After 5 minutes, add the ground garlic and parsley.
- Boil until the pasta is *al dente* (firm to the bite).

❸ Serve hot.

HEALTHIER ALTERNATIVE: Instead of sautéing the ingredients, add them raw to the boiling vegetable broth.

For more information about the ingredients, see: Artichoke, Vol. 2, p. 178; pasta, Vol. 1, p. 74; onion, Vol. 2, p. 142; garlic, Vol. 1, p. 338; and the *Encyclopedia of Medicinal Plants:* Garlic, p. 230.

HEALTH COUNSELS

Pasta, when accompanied by artichoke, onion, garlic, and vegetable broth, is very well tolerated by those suffering from liver or gallbladder disorders. It is a nutritious, simple, and easy-to-digest dish, especially recommended to enhance the healthy functioning of:

✓ The **liver** and the **gallbladder,** thanks to the *protective* effect of artichokes.

✓ The **stomach** as it is well tolerated by those whose weak point is this organ.

✓ The **kidneys,** due to the *diuretic* effect of the artichokes and their ability to help *eliminate* **uric acid** through urine.

NUTRITIONAL VALUE* per serving

Energy	185 kcal = 773 kj
Protein	7.37 g
Carbohydrates	33.3 g
Fiber	4.98 g
Total fat	*0.754 g*
Saturated fat	*0.117 g*
Cholesterol	—
Sodium	*62.8 mg*

1% 2% 4% 10% 20% 40% 100%

% Daily Value (based on a 2,000 calorie diet) provided by each serving of this dish

CALORIC PROPORTION*

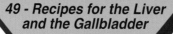

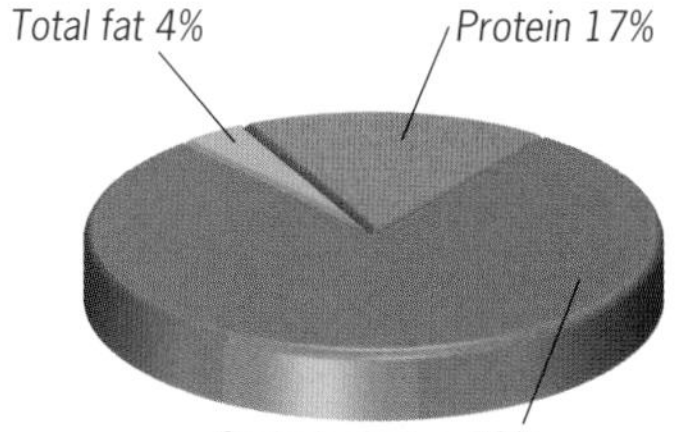

Percentage distribution of **calories for each nutrient**

* Additional ingredients not included.

Preparation time: 00:20

Cooking time: -- --

Tamarind Drink

INGREDIENTS (4 servings)

- 250 g (≅ 8.8 oz) **tamarind** (Indian date)
- 3 tablespoons of **honey**
- 1 liter of **water**

PREPARATION

❶Peel and wash the tamarinds.

❷Mix the pulp in a little water and blend with an electric blender.
- Add the remaining water and let rest for 5 minutes.
- Sieve and add honey. Stir to achieve a homogenous blend.
- Refrigerate.

❸Serve cold.

For more information about the ingredients, see: Tamarind, Vol. 1, p. 46; honey, Vol. 1, p. 160.

HEALTH COUNSELS

The pulp of the tamarind is the most used part. It has a pleasant sweet-and-sour flavor. Its medicinal properties make this drink appropriate for:

✓The **liver** and the **gallbladder,** as tamarind facilitates both **bile** *production* (*choleretic* action) as well as *elimination* (*cholagogue* action). Since this drink facilitates the hepatobiliary function, it is well suited for those suffering some degree of **hepatic failure,** or **biliary dyskinesia** (alterations of the gallbladder emptying process).

✓The **intestine,** as the tamarind's pulp is an effective and gentle *laxative.*

NUTRITIONAL VALUE per serving

Energy	132 kcal = 550 kj
Protein	0.931 g
Carbohydrates	33.4 g
Fiber	1.63 g
Total fat	*0.188 g*
Saturated fat	*0.085 g*
Cholesterol	—
Sodium	*9.50 mg*

1% 2% 4% 10% 20% 40% 100%

% Daily Value (based on a 2,000 calorie diet) provided by each serving of this drink

CALORIC PROPORTION

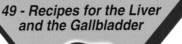

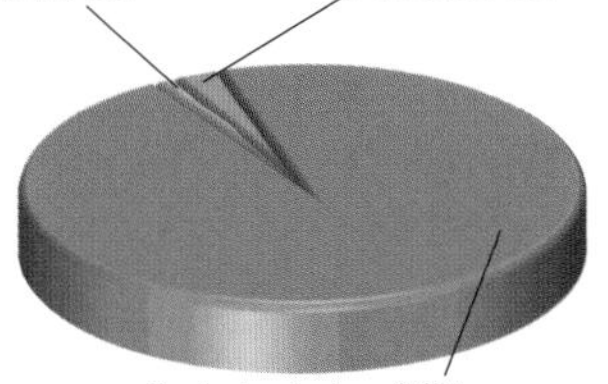

Percentage distribution of **calories for each nutrient**

50 RECIPES FOR THE STOMACH

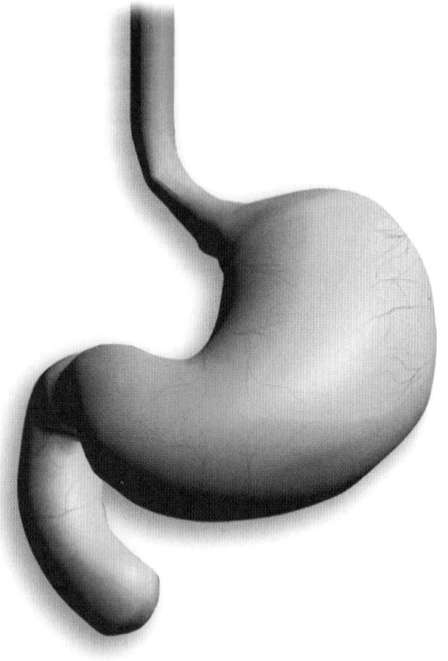

CHAPTER SUMMARY

RECIPES

Baked Potatoes 251
Chinese Salad 243
Christmas Red Cabbage 248
Cream of Banana 252
Cream of Zucchini 246
Crunchy Fennel 242
Pineapple Water 255
Potato Casserole 250
Potato Salad 245
Refreshing Tea 254
Sprouts Salad 244
Sweet Corn Platter 247
Tropical Fruit Salad 253

Within the process of food digestion, the stomach plays the fundamental role. Thus we see the necessity of eating foods that are "good for the stomach." These healthy recipes, as all others in the "ENCYCLOPEDIA OF FOODS AND THEIR HEALING POWER," not only provide a complete and balanced diet that makes us feel good, but they also provide a diet that does not overload the digestive system.

THE SIZE of the stomach varies greatly. It can shrink to the size of a large pear, but there are also cases where the stomach nearly reaches the pelvis. Consuming large amounts of food increases its volume.

Filling the stomach to its maximum at large meals can *change* its **functioning** as well as cause **obesity.**

The feeling of **complete fullness** that some persons look for when they eat ***is not healthy*** for the stomach or for the rest of the body. ***Ideally,*** after each meal we should *feel* that we ***could* continue eating** something more without making any special effort.

Rest for the Stomach

In the same way that the heart needs rest and takes its moments of repose between beats, our stomach also needs to enjoy periods of inactivity.

A ***very damaging*** but widespread habit is that of **eating continuously.** This happens, for example, to some housewives who do not work outside the home and who tend to eat continuously while they carry out their domestic chores; others outside or within the home indulge in continuous appetizers, snacks, sweets, cakes, or sandwiches throughout the day. These disorganized eating habits do not allow the stomach to rest except at night and such habits encourage obesity.

Taking care of health generally, and of the stomach in particular, does not only consist of giving the body nutritious food but in doing it in the right way.

Except in some specific cases, healthy adults can live on **two** main **meals a day**—one in the morning and the other at the beginning of the afternoon. If necessary, one can supplement these two meals with an early and light supper, primarily of fruit. In this way the stomach and all of the digestive system can enjoy a deserved **rest** and a chance to **recuperate.**

All the recipes given in this volume help to maintain a healthy stomach. Those in this chapter, however, are designed to take full advantage of the curative and preventive powers of certain foods especially favorable to the stomach (see Vol. 2, p. 182).

Menus for

Gastritis

Cherimoya or custard apple

BREAKFAST

- "Avocado Shake" (Vol. 3, p. 201)
- Oatmeal boiled with "Soy Milk" (Vol. 3, p. 305), sweetened with a little honey (Vol. 2, p. 41, Vol. 1, pp. 88, 160)
- Cherimoya or custard apple (Vol. 2, p. 59)

LUNCH

- Cabbage Juice (Vol. 2, p. 191)
- "Sprouts Salad" (Vol. 3, p. 244)
- "Cream of Pumpkin" (Vol. 3, p. 134)
- "Rice Pudding" (Vol. 3, p. 199)

Sprouts Salad

SUPPER

- "Chard with Potatoes and Pumpkin" (Vol. 3, p. 263)
- "Tropical Fruit Salad" (Vol. 3, p. 253)
- Licorice and Anise Tea (*EMP* pp. 308, 465)

Tropical Fruit Salad

HEALTH COUNSELS

This menu helps to protect the gastric system and helps the stomach to recuperate after suffering injury from alcoholic beverages, an abuse of ice cream or certain medicines, etc. It suits those with delicate stomachs or those who suffer from gastritis caused by eating or drinking too much.

Gastro-duodenal Ulcer

Mango

BREAKFAST

- Kiwi and Mango (Vol. 2, pp. 356, 341)
- Tapioca boiled in "Almond milk" (Vol. 3, p. 342) and sweetened with honey (if possible, with Manuka honey) (Vol. 2, p. 186)

LUNCH

- "Oriental Salad" (Vol. 3, p. 164)
- "Cream of Leeks" (Vol. 3, p. 262)
- "Baked Potatoes" (Vol. 3, p. 251)
- Natural Skim Yogurt (Vol. 1, p. 202)
- "Whole Bread" (Vol. 3, p. 46, Vol. 1, p. 72)

Baked Potatoes

SUPPER

- "Cabbage Soup" (Vol. 3, p. 375)
- "Baked Apples" (Vol. 3, p. 268)

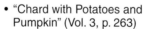

Baked Apples

HEALTH COUNSELS

These recipes represent a good example of an anti-ulcer menu because they help to neutralize the excess of acid and to heal the gastro-duodenal ulcer. Mangoes, tapioca, and potatoes act as antacids, while cabbage restores the stomach lining.

In spite of what some may say, an appropriate diet continues to be an important factor in the cure of the gastro-duodenal ulcer as well as helping to avoid relapses.

the Stomach

Dyspepsia

Papaya

BREAKFAST

- "Pineapple Water" (Vol.3, p. 255)
- Papaya (Vol. 2, p. 157)
- "Oatmeal" (Vol. 3, p. 154)

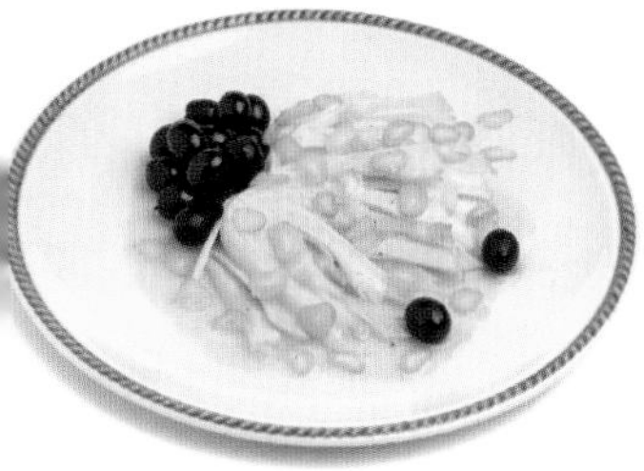

Crunchy Fennel

LUNCH

- "Carrot Juice and Tomato Juice" (Vol. 2, pp. 25, 275)
- "Crunchy Fennel" (Vol. 3, p. 242)
- "Potatoes with Peas" (Vol. 3, pp. 169)
- "Rye Bread" (Vol. 3, p. 194)
- "Aromatic Linden" (Vol. 3, p. 159)

SUPPER

- "Pomegranate Drink" (Vol. 3, p. 271)
- "Sweet Corn Platter" (Vol. 3, p. 247)

Pomegranate Drink

HEALTH COUNSELS

The ingredients of this menu help the digestion in the case of dyspepsia (slow digestion), as well as protecting the stomach. Pineapple and papaya contain digestive enzymes, and the oats in oatmeal soften the stomach and act as an anti-inflammatory. Delicate stomachs can also tolerate potatoes, peas, and fennel very well.

Other Recipes for the Stomach

SALADS

- "Cabbage Salad" (Vol. 3, p. 219)
- "Belgian Endive Salad" (Vol. 3, p. 230)
- "Chinese Salad" (Vol. 3, p. 243)

SOUPS AND PURÉES

- "Cream of Zucchini" (Vol. 3, p. 246)
- "Three-colored Purée" (Vol. 3, p. 377)
- "Vegetable Purée" (Vol. 3, p. 361)
- "Oats Soup" (Vol. 3, p. 147)
- "Cereal Soup" (Vol. 3, p. 314)

MAIN COURSES

- "Leek, Potato, and Pumpkin Stew" (Vol. 3, p. 281)
- "Christmas Red Cabbage" (Vol. 3, p. 248)
- "Potato Salad" (Vol. 3, p. 245)
- "Sautéed Soy Sprouts" (Vol. 3, p. 265)
- "Stuffed Peppers" (Vol. 3, p. 382)
- "Potato Casserole" (Vol. 3, p. 250)

BREAKFASTS, DESSERTS AND SNACKS

- "Peach Bavarian" (Vol. 3, p. 173)
- "Cream of Banana" (Vol. 3, p. 252)
- "Rice milk" (Vol. 3, p. 273)
- "Tiger Nut Horchata" (Vol. 3, p. 272)

DRINKS

- "Refreshing Tea" (Vol. 3, p. 254)

Freshly squeezed juice of:

- Pineapple (Vol. 2, p. 189)

Teas or herbal infusions of:

- Angelica (*EMP*, p. 426)
- Licorice (*EMP*, p. 308)
- German Camomile (*EMP*, p. 364)

- *See the recipe index at the beginning of this volume (Vol. 3, pp. 8-13).*
- *See also chapter 20, "Foods for Nervous System" (Vol. 2, pp. 30-51).*

EMP = Encyclopedia of Medicinal Plants, Edication and Health Library, Editorial Safeliz.

Preparation time: 00:15

Cooking time: - - - -

Crunchy Fennel

INGREDIENTS (4 servings)

- 400 g (≅ 14 oz) of **fennel** (bulb)
- 50 g (≅ 1.75 oz) of **black olives**

ADDITIONAL INGREDIENTS

- 2 teaspoons of **anise seeds**
- 1 **lemon** (juice)
- 2 tablespoons of olive **oil** (each tablespoon of oil adds around 120 kcal to the recipe, that is, 30 kcal per serving)
- Sea **salt** (see Vol. 3, p. 16)

PREPARATION

❶ Soak (soften) the anise seeds in the oil for several days.
- Cut the fennel in lengthwise slices and keep the small branches and leaves, if you have them, for decoration.

❷ Prepare a dressing with the lemon, salt, and olive oil.
- Serve on the plate along with the olives and add the dressing.

❸ Serve immediately.

For more information about these ingredients, see: Fennel, Vol. 2, p. 161; olive, Vol. 2, p. 165; and the *Encyclopedia of Medicinal Plants:* Fennel, Vol. 1, p. 360.

HEALTH COUNSELS

Cultivated fennel possesses a fleshy, aromatic bulb that is rather sweet. It can be eaten raw in a salad, as in our recipe, or it can be boiled; in any case, fennel provides a healthy option for:

✓The **stomach,** due to the *digestive* properties of its essence. Black olives, which *invigorate* the stomach and help the digestion, complement the beneficial effects of the fennel.

✓The **bowel,** because it *reduces* **intestinal** gas and works as a light but effective *laxative.* It is recommended particularly in the case of **flatulence** and constipation.

✓**Lactation,** because, in the same way as its equivalent in the wild, fennel performs a *galactogenous* action increasing the production of milk in lactating women.

NUTRITIONAL VALUE* per serving

Energy	**38 kcal = 160 kj**
Protein	**1.30 g**
Carbohydrates	**4.38 g**
Fiber	**3.30 g**
Total fat	***0.868 g***
Saturated fat	***0.088 g***
Cholesterol	—
Sodium	***107 mg***

1% 2% 4% 10% 20% 40% 100%

% Daily Value (based on a 2,000 calorie diet) provided by each serving of this dish

CALORIC PROPORTION*

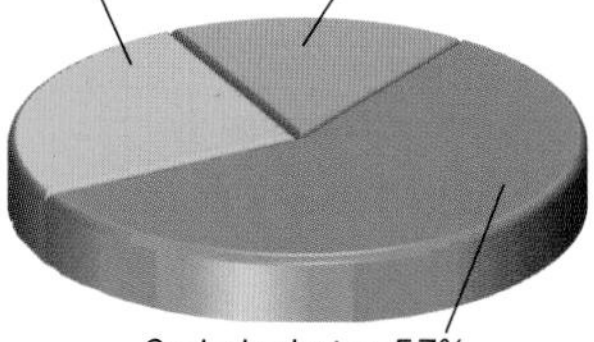

Percentage distribution of **calories for each nutrient**

*Additional ingredients are not included.

Preparation time 00:30 | Cooking time 00:05

Chinese salad

INGREDIENTS (4 servings)

- 1 **Chinese cabbage**
- 200 g (≅ 7 oz) of **meat analogs** (you can use commercialized brands or gluten; see Vol. 3, p. 52)
- 4 **Welsh onions**
- 85 g (≅ 3 oz) of **Chinese noodles**
- 25 g (≅ 1/4 cup) of sliced **almonds**
- 2 tablespoons of **sesame seeds**

ADDITIONAL INGREDIENTS

- 6 tablespoons of olive **oil** (each tablespoon of oil adds around 120 kcal to the recipe, that is, 30 kcal per serving)
- 1/2 cube of concentrated **vegetable stock** (without salt)
- 1 **lemon** (juice)
- 1 tablespoon of **sugar**

PREPARATION

❶ Wash and chop the cabbage and the onions very fine.

- Slice the meat analog and break up the dry noodles.

❷ Heat three tablespoons of oil in the frying pan and lightly fry the almonds and the meat analog.

- Remove from the flame and add the onions and the sesame seeds.
- Allow the ingredients to set in the pan until they cool.
- Place the cabbage in a salad bowl and add the dry noodles and the contents of the frying pan.
- Dress with a sweet and sour sauce. For the sauce, mix the rest of the oil with the concentrated vegetable stock, the juice from a lemon, and the sugar and beat it all together with the help of a fork.

❸ Serve immediately.

HEALTHIER ALTERNATIVE: Instead of frying the almonds and the meat analog, you can toast them in the oven or on the grill, or use them raw along with the rest of the ingredients. Those who wish to prevent obesity can reduce the amount of oil added.

For more information about the ingredients, see: Chinese cabbage, Vol. 2, p. 193; meat analogs, Vol. 1, p. 332; Welsh onion, Vol. 2, p. 144; pasta, Vol. 1, p. 74; almond, Vol. 2, p. 48; sesame, Vol. 1, p. 352; and the *Encyclopedia of Medicinal Plants:* Sesame, p. 611.

HEALTH COUNSELS

If well chewed, this salad strengthens the stomach while it provides proteins and other nutrients. It can be especially recommended for:

✓The **stomach,** because of the *anti-inflammatory* and *healing* properties of the cabbage in the case of an **ulcer.**

✓The **intestine,** due to the laxative effect of the ***fiber*** that helps to regulate the bowel movement.

✓The *prevention* of **cancer,** due to the *anticarcinogenic* action of the ***phytochemicals*** found in cabbage, sesame seeds, and soybeans (used in making meat analogs).

NUTRITIONAL VALUE* per serving

Nutrient	Amount
Energy	**329 kcal = 1,376 kj**
Protein	**15.3 g**
Carbohydrates	**28.1 g**
Fiber	**9.46 g**
Total fat	***16.0 g***
Saturated fat	***2.32 g***
Cholesterol	—
Sodium	***477 mg***

1% 2% 4% 10% 20% 40% 100%

% Daily Value (based on a 2,000 calorie diet) provided by each serving of this dish

CALORIC PROPORTION*

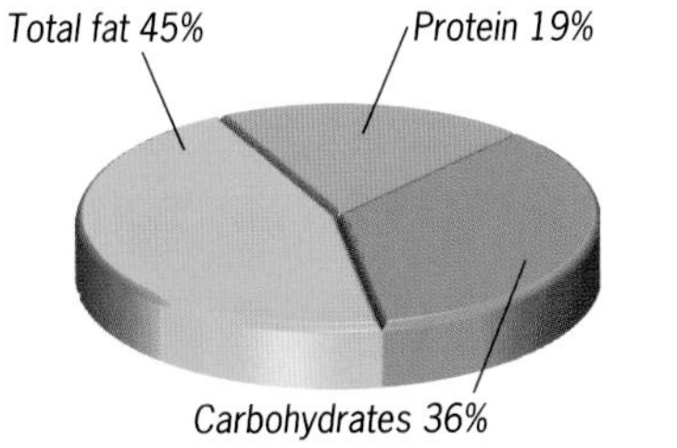

Percentage distribution of **calories for each nutrient**

*Additional ingredients are not included.

Preparation time 00:30

Cooking time 00:30

Sprouts Salad

INGREDIENTS (4 servings)

- 4 tablespoons of alfalfa and radish **sprouts** (germinated)
- 800 g (≅ 28 oz) of **potatoes**
- 1 sweet **red pepper**
- 150 g (≅ 5.3 oz) of tender **sweet corn**
- 1 or 2 cloves of **garlic**

ADDITIONAL INGREDIENTS

- 1/2 **lemon** (juice)
- **Sugar** (a pinch)
- 6 tablespoons of sunflower seed **oil** (each tablespoon of oil adds around 120 kcal to the recipe, that is, 30 kcal per serving)
- Sea **salt** (see Vol. 3, p. 16)

PREPARATION

❶Remove the seeds from the sweet pepper, wash, and chop.

- Mash the garlic with the salt in a mortar. Mix the mashed garlic and salt with the oil, the juice of the lemon, and the sugar.
- Wash the potatoes well.

❷Boil the potatoes with their skins.

- Let cool. Once cooled, peel and chop the potatoes.
- Add the sweet corn and the pepper.
- Add the dressing and allow the salad to set so that the vegetables can soak up the flavor.

❸Add the sprouts just before serving.

HEALTHIER ALTERNATIVE: To give the sweet flavor to the salad you can use honey instead of sugar.

For more information about the ingredients, see: Sprouts/germinated, Vol. 1, p. 86; potato, Vol. 2, p. 201; sweet pepper, Vol. 2, p. 198; corn, Vol. 2, p. 238; garlic, Vol. 1, p. 338; and the *Encyclopedia of Medicinal Plants:* Garlic, p. 230.

HEALTH COUNSELS

All raw salads have an invigorating effect on the stomach and the digestion. For this reason we recommend that you always begin the meal with a salad.

This salad of sprouts and potatoes combines the *digestive properties* of germinated sprouts and other vegetables with those of the potato. It is especially beneficial for:

✓The **stomach,** since the ***enzymes*** found in the sprouts *help* the **digestion** and *prevent* **flatulence** and a **bloated feeling** in the stomach. The potato also *soothes* and *protects* the stomach **lining.**

✓The **arteries** and the **heart,** because this dish is rich in ***antioxidant vitamins*** that *prevent* **arteriosclerosis.** It also contains little ***fat*** or ***cholesterol.*** Sunflower seed oil, recommended to dress the salad, is one of the *healthiest* oils *for the heart* along with olive oil.

NUTRITIONAL VALUE* per serving

Energy	183 kcal = 765 kj
Protein	5.67 g
Carbohydrates	36.2 g
Fiber	5.14 g
Total fat	*0.805 g*
Saturated fat	*0.137 g*
Cholesterol	—
Sodium	*17.6 mg*

1% 2% 4% 10% 20% 40% 100%

% Daily Value (based on a 2,000 calorie diet) provided by each serving of this dish

CALORIC PROPORTION*

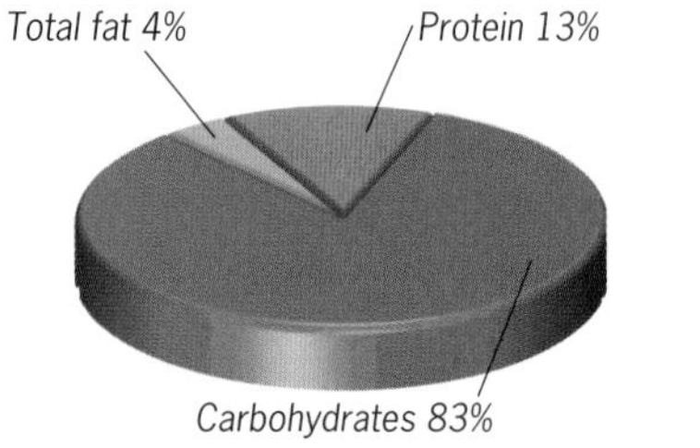

Percentage distribution of **calories for each nutrient**

*Additional ingredients are not included.

Preparation time 00:25

Cooking time 00:30

Potato Salad

INGREDIENTS (4 servings)

- 500 g (≅ 1 pound) of **potatoes**
- 250 g (≅ 8.8 oz) of **carrots**
- 100 g (≅ $^{2}/_{3}$ cup) of **peas**
- 100 g (≅ 1 cup) of **green beans**
- 2 baked **sweet peppers**
- 100 g (≅ 3.5 oz) of pitted **green olives**

ADDITIONAL INGREDIENTS

- 4 tablespoons of **soy mayonnaise** (Vol. 3, p. 58) (each tablespoon of this dressing adds 80 kcal, that is, around 20 kcal per serving)
- Sea **salt** (see Vol. 3, p. 16)

PREPARATION

❶ Peel, wash and cut the carrots.
- Remove the ends, wash, and cut the green beans.
- Wash the potatoes.
- Cut the pepper into thin slices.

❷ Boil the potatoes, without peeling them, in water with salt. Do the same with the carrots, peas, and green beans (separately, of course).
- Drain the potatoes and the vegetables.
- Peel and slice the potatoes.
- Mix the potatoes, the vegetables, the pepper, and the olives and put on the plate.

❸ Serve cold and topped with the mayonnaise dressing.

For more information about the ingredients, see: Potato, Vol. 2, p. 201; carrot, Vol. 2, p. 25; pea, Vol. 2, p. 73; green bean, Vol. 1, p. 109; sweet pepper, Vol. 2, p. 198; olive, Vol. 2, p. 165; and the *Encyclopedia of Medicinal Plants:* Green bean, p. 584.

HEALTH COUNSELS

This typical potato salad is a cold dish, and is especially welcome in summer. The combined action of the potato and the other vegetables make it a recommended dish for:

✓ The **stomach,** because of the *antacid* and *protective* properties that the potato and the carrot exercise on the **stomach lining.** The salad is better tolerated if soy milk mayonnaise is used instead of traditional mayonnaise made with egg. However, those who suffer from a delicate digestive system tolerate potato salad better if they simply dress it with a little olive or seed oil.

✓ The **arteries** and the **heart,** since this salad is made without egg and therefore has no ***cholesterol.*** Besides, the ***vitamins*** and ***antioxidant phytochemicas*** of carrots, green beans, peas, and sweet peppers help to maintain healthy arteries.

NUTRITIONAL VALUE* per serving

Energy	169 kcal = 705 kj
Protein	4.91 g
Carbohydrates	25.9 g
Fiber	6.82 g
Total fat	*3.06 g*
Saturated fat	*0.429 g*
Cholesterol	—
Sodium	*249 mg*

1% 2% 4% 10% 20% 40% 100%

% Daily Value (based on a 2,000 calorie diet) provided by each serving of this dish

CALORIC PROPORTION*

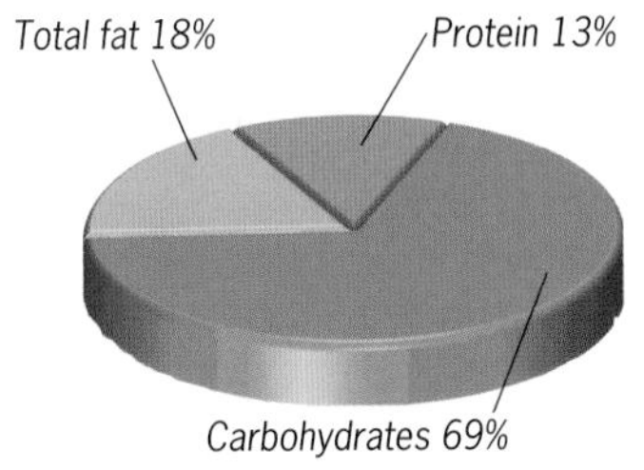

Percentage distribution of **calories for each nutrient**

*Additional ingredients are not included.

Preparation time 00:10

Cooking time 00:30

Cream of Zucchini

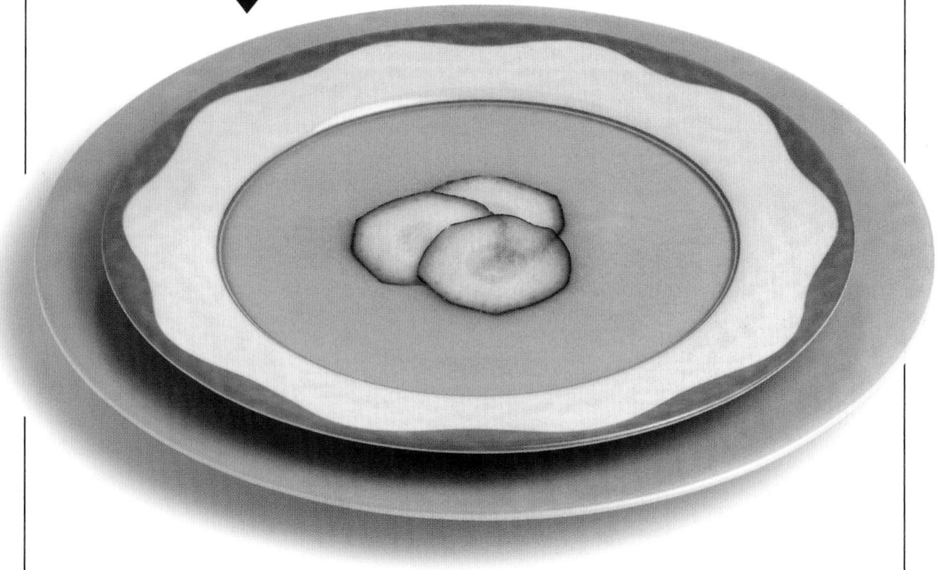

INGREDIENTS (4 servings)

- 1 kg (≅ 2 pounds) of **zucchini**
- 500 g (≅ 1 pound) of **white sauce** (Vol. 3, p. 59; made with non-dairy milk)
- 50 g (≅ 1.75 oz) of toasted **almonds**

ADDITIONAL INGREDIENTS

- Sea **salt** (see Vol. 3, p. 16)

PREPARATION

❶ Peel, wash, and cut the zucchini.
- Cut the almonds into pieces.

❷ Boil the zucchini in a little water with salt until tender.
- Prepare the white sauce.
- Blend the zucchini with the blender.
- Add the white sauce and mix well.

❸ Serve hot and decorated with slices of zucchini. The almonds are served on the side.

For more information about the ingredients, see: Zucchini, Vol. 2, p. 159; almond, Vol. 2, p. 48.

HEALTH COUNSELS

Zucchini, the main ingredient of this recipe, soothes the entire digestive tract. Combined with the white sauce and the almonds, it represents a tasty and healthy dish and is especially beneficial to:

✓The **stomach,** since it is easily digested. It is suitable for those who suffer from **dyspepsia** (indigestion), **gastritis,** or **gastro-duodenal ulcers.**

✓The **intestine,** since it soothes this organ. It is ideal for **irritable bowel syndrome** and during *recovery* from any **gastroenteritis.**

✓The **arteries** and the **heart,** for being a dish *low* in ***saturated fat*** and in ***sodium,*** especially if it is made with soy milk and without adding salt. Almonds provide **vitamin E** and help to *control* **cholesterol** levels.

NUTRITIONAL VALUE* per serving

Energy	248 kcal = 1,035 kj
Protein	8.48 g
Carbohydrates	9.94 g
Fiber	5.35 g
Total fat	*18.7 g*
Saturated fat	*2.24 g*
Cholesterol	—
Sodium	*20.6 mg*

1% 2% 4% 10% 20% 40% 100%

% Daily Value (based on a 2,000 calorie diet) provided by each serving of this dish

CALORIC PROPORTION*

Percentage distribution of **calories for each nutrient**

*Additional ingredients are not included.

Preparation time 00:10

Cooking time 00:30

Corn Platter

INGREDIENTS (4 servings)

- 500 g (≅ 1 pound) of tender **sweet corn**
- 500 g (≅ 1 pound) of **potatoes**
- 60 g (≅ 2 oz) of **green olives**
- 750 ml (≅ 3 cups) of **soy milk** (Vol. 3, p. 305)

ADDITIONAL INGREDIENTS

- 2 tablespoons of olive **oil** (each tablespoon of oil adds around 120 kcal to the recipe, that is, 30 kcal per serving)
- 1/2 teaspoon of **sweet paprika**
- Sea **salt** (see Vol. 3, p. 16)

PREPARATION

❶ Wash, peel, and cut the potatoes.

❷ Place the potatoes in a pot. Lightly fry them in the oil on a low fire.
- Add the milk and cook without covering.
- After 10 minutes, add the remaining ingredients; cover the pot and boil during 10 more minutes.

❸ Serve hot.

HEALTHIER ALTERNATIVE: Instead of frying the potatoes, boil them in the milk.

For more information about the ingredients, see: Sweet corn, Vol. 2, p. 238; potato, Vol. 2, p. 201; olive, Vol. 2, p. 165; soy milk, Vol. 1, p. 88.

HEALTH COUNSELS

Sweet corn, potatoes, and olives, which form a part of this recipe, are all products that *protect* and *stimulate* the **digestive functions.** They combine to provide a certain amount of ***protein*** and ***carbohydrates*** with very *little* ***fat.*** They also provide ***fiber, minerals,*** and ***vitamins.*** For these reasons, the corn platter is especially helpful to:

✓ The **stomach,** thanks to the *antacid* and *soothing* effects of the potato joined with the *protective* action of sweet corn on the **linings** of the digestive tract. Those who suffer from **poor digestion** or from **indigestion** of the stomach will benefit from the corn platter.

✓ The **intestine,** especially when **irritable bowel syndrome, intestinal gas,** or **constipation** are present.

NUTRITIONAL VALUE* per serving

Energy	257 kcal = 1,074 kj
Protein	11.3 g
Carbohydrates	38.0 g
Fiber	7.65 g
Total fat	*5.96 g*
Saturated fat	*0.761 g*
Cholesterol	—
Sodium	*113 mg*

1% 2% 4% 10% 20% 40% 100%

% Daily Value (based on a 2,000 calorie diet) provided by each serving of this dish

CALORIC PROPORTION*

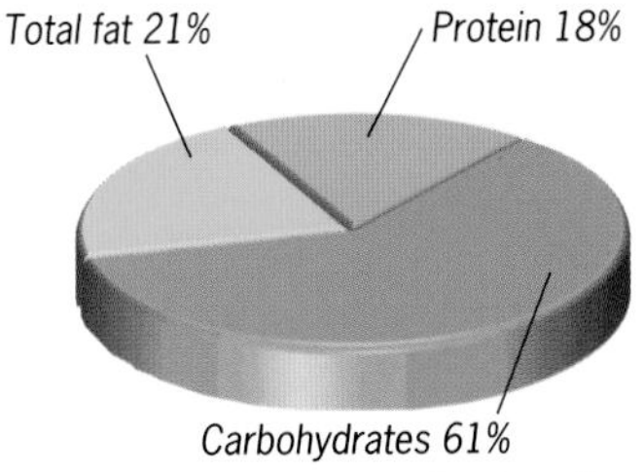

Percentage distribution of **calories for each nutrient**

*Additional ingredients are not included.

Preparation time 00:20

Cooking time 00:40

Christmas Red Cabbage

INGREDIENTS (4 servings)

- 1 kg (≅ 2 pounds) of **red cabbage**
- 250 g (≅ 8.8 oz) of **chestnuts**
- 2 **apples** (baking)
- 2 cloves of **garlic**

ADDITIONAL INGREDIENTS

- 4 tablespoons of olive **oil** (each tablespoon of oil adds around 120 kcal to the recipe, that is, 30 kcal per serving
- Sea salt (see Vol. 3, p. 16)

PREPARATION

❶ Wash and chop the red cabbage.
- Peel and chop the apples.
- Peel and chop the garlic.
- Make an incision in each chestnut. Scald the chestnuts in order to peel them.

❷ Boil the red cabbage in salted water until it is tender but still slightly crunchy.
- Boil the peeled chestnuts in a little salted water.
- Heat the oil in a pan; lightly fry the apples until they are slightly golden. Set them aside.
- In the same oil, fry the garlic until golden. Drain the red cabbage and the chestnuts and add them to the garlic. Continue to fry for 5 more minutes and add the apples; keep the pan on a very low fire for a few more minutes.

❸ Serve hot.

HEALTHIER ALTERNATIVE: Instead of frying the ingredients, bake them and sprinkle them with the oil and chopped garlic.

Wash and chop the red cabbage.

Fry the garlic until golden.

Cook for a few minutes over a low fire.

For more information about the ingredients, see: Red cabbage, Vol. 2, p. 193, chestnut, Vol. 2, p. 322; apple, Vol. 2, p. 229; garlic, Vol. 1, p. 338; and the *Encyclopedia of Medicinal Plants: Garlic,* p. 230.

Suggestions from the Chef

The dish can be decorated with a sliced, hard-boiled egg.

NUTRITIONAL VALUE*
per serving

Energy	**201 kcal = 841 kj**
Protein	**4.51 g**
Carbohydrates	**35.7 g**
Fiber	**10.1 g**
Total fat	***1.85 g***
Saturated fat	***0.307 g***
Cholesterol	—
Sodium	***27.7 mg***

1% 2% 4% 10% 20% 40% 100%

% Daily Value (based on a 2,000 calorie diet) provided by each serving of this dessert

HEALTH COUNSELS

Red cabbage is a type of cabbage that owes its peculiar purple color to the presence of some natural pigments called ***anthocyanins*** (see Vol. 2, p. 193). It shares the same *digestive* and *anticarcinogenic* properties of the common cabbage.

This recipe provides some ***protein*** and ***carbohydrates*** while having very *little* ***fat*** and *no* ***cholesterol.*** It gives needed nutrition and satisfies the palate without any risk of causing obesity. It is particularly recommended for:

✓The **stomach,** because of the *anti-inflammatory* properties of red cabbage and because the chestnuts have the capacity to *neutralize* the excess **acidity.** It helps in the case of **gastritis** and **gastroduodenal ulcers.**

✓The **intestine,** because the sulfurous and slightly sharp essence of all cabbage acts as a *natural regulator* for the intestinal flora. Those who suffer **dysbacteriosis** (alterations in the intestinal flora), **colitis,** and **diverticulosis** can benefit from Christmas Red Cabbage.

✓The **arteries** and the **heart,** because of the *low* ***sodium*** content of the dish—if one limits the addition of salt—and *low* ***fat,*** while it provides a rich source of ***potassium*** and ***fiber;*** all of which contributes to protecting the cardiovascular system.

✓The *prevention* of **cancer,** especially in the digestive tract (stomach, intestine and colon), thanks to the anticarcinogenic **phytochemicas** that may be found both in cabbage and garlic.

CALORIC PROPORTION*

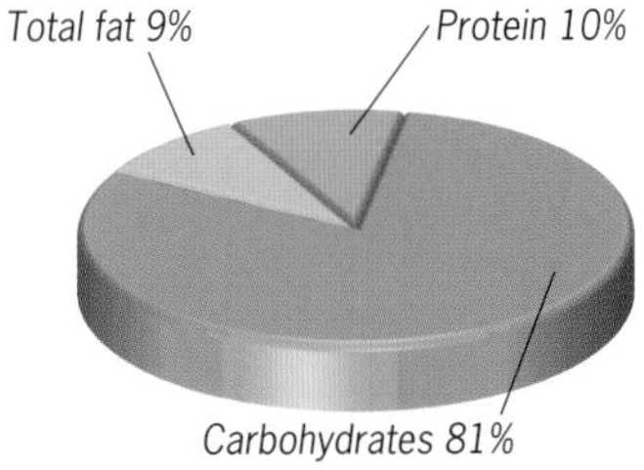

Percentage distribution of
calories for each nutrient

*Additional ingredients are not included.

Preparation time 00:15

Cooking time 00:30

Potato Casserole

INGREDIENTS (4 servings)

- 1 kg (≅ 2 pounds) of **potatoes**
- 2 **onions**
- 4 cloves of **garlic**
- 50 g (≅ 1.75 oz) of **green** and **black olives**
- 250 ml (≅ 1 cup) of **vegetable stock** (without salt)

ADDITIONAL INGREDIENTS

- **Parsley**
- 4 tablespoons of olive **oil** (each tablespoon of oil adds around 120 kcal to the recipe, that is, 30 kcal per serving
- Sea **salt** (see Vol. 3, p. 16)

PREPARATION

❶ Peel, wash, and cut the potatoes and the onions in round slices.

- Peel the garlic and chop the parsley; mash in a mortar along with the salt.
- Add the mashed garlic and parsley to the oil and the vegetable stock to form the sauce.

❷ Place the potatoes and onions in layers in an oven dish and pour the sauce over them.

- Cover with a lid and bake at 180°C until tender.

❸ Decorate with the olives and serve hot.

Suggestions from the Chef

You can also add sweet pepper and eggplant cut into lengthwise or round slices.

For more information about the ingredients, see: Potato, Vol. 2, p. 201; onion, Vol. 2, p. 142; garlic, Vol. 1, p. 338; olive, Vol. 2, p. 165; and the *Encyclopedia of Medicinal Plants:* Garlic, p. 230.

HEALTH COUNSELS

Those who know how to appreciate the natural flavors of healthy foods prepared with simplicity will enjoy this potato casserole. In addition, it is particularly good for:

✓The **stomach,** because of the potato's *protective* qualities as well as the *invigorating* effects of the onion, garlic, and olives. Those suffering from **slow digestion** or from **indigestion** can find relief with this dish.

✓Avoiding **acidification of the blood,** which is caused by certain metabolic disorders or by an inadequate diet. The potato, onion, and vegetable stock are *alkalinizers.*

✓To prevent **cancer.** The *anticarcinogenic* effects of onions and garlic have been thoroughly demonstrated, especially in the case of cancer of the stomach.

NUTRITIONAL VALUE* per serving

Energy	**203 kcal = 847 kj**
Protein	**5.44 g**
Carbohydrates	**39.9 g**
Fiber	**4.88 g**
Total fat	***1.02 g***
Saturated fat	***0.165 g***
Cholesterol	—
Sodium	***69.8 mg***

1% 2% 4% 10% 20% 40% 100%

% Daily Value (based on a 2,000 calorie diet) provided by each serving of this dish

CALORIC PROPORTION*

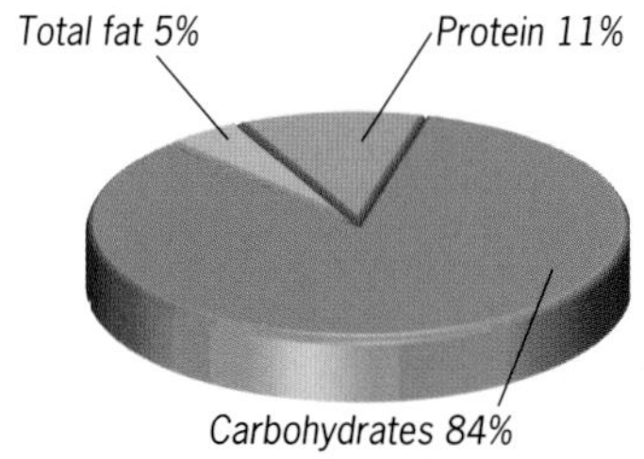

Percentage distribution of **calories for each nutrient**

*Additional ingredients are not included.

Preparation time 00:10

Cooking time 00:30

Baked Potatoes

INGREDIENTS (4 servings)

- 1 kg (≅ 2 pounds) of **potatoes**
- 2 cloves of **garlic**

ADDITIONAL INGREDIENTS

- **Parsley**
- 4 tablespoons of olive **oil** (each tablespoon of oil adds around 120 kcal to the recipe, that is, 30 kcal per serving)
- Sea salt (see Vol. 3, p. 16)

PREPARATION

❶ Wash the potatoes. Do not peel them.
- Cut them in half lengthwise and make lines running in the same direction on the flat surface with the point of a knife.
- Chop the garlic.

❷ Place the potatoes in a baking dish with the skin facing the bottom. Sprinkle with garlic and salt, and pour oil over them.
- Place the dish in an oven heated to 220°C. Leave until potatoes are golden.

❸ Decorate with parsley and, if you wish, with lettuce leaves. Serve immediately.

Suggestions from the Chef

- If you add half a glass of **water** to the baking dish, the potatoes will retain more **moisture.**
- You can also wrap them in aluminum foil and **bake, grill,** or **barbecue** them.
- They can be accompanied by a **salad** or by a side dish of **vegetables.**

HEALTH COUNSELS

Baking potatoes is one of the most tasty and healthy ways to eat them. In this way the tuber provides all its nutritional and preventive properties to:

✓ The **stomach,** with its *antacid* properties and its ability to be *easily digested.*

✓ The **heart** and the **arteries,** due to its high levels of **potassium** that helps to avoid **high blood pressure** and to protect the cardiovascular system.

✓ The **kidneys,** thanks to the fact that potatoes help to *eliminate* the **toxins** that circulate in the blood.

Obesity

*When you want to reduce the calories in your diet, do not eliminate the potato. Rather, reduce the **oils, fats,** and **gravies** that usually accompany it.*

For more information about the ingredients, see: Potato, Vol. 2, p. 201; garlic, Vol. 1, p. 338; and the *Encyclopedia of Medicinal Plants:* Garlic, p. 230.

NUTRITIONAL VALUE* per serving

Energy	162 kcal = 679 kj
Protein	4.33 g
Carbohydrates	33.7 g
Fiber	3.26 g
Total fat	*0.215 g*
Saturated fat	*0.055 g*
Cholesterol	—
Sodium	*12.5 mg*

1% 2% 4% 10% 20% 40% 100%

% Daily Value (based on a 2,000 calorie diet) provided by each serving of this dish

CALORIC PROPORTION*

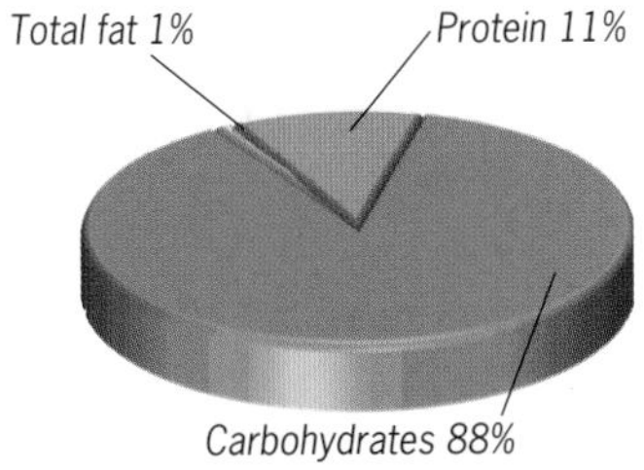

Percentage distribution of **calories for each nutrient**

*Additional ingredients are not included.

Preparation time: 00:10

Cooking time: 00:20

Cream of Banana

INGREDIENTS (4 servings)

- 1 **plantain** (cooking banana)
- 750 ml (≅ 3 cups) of skimmed **milk**
- 2 level tablespoons of **brown sugar** (raw)
- 750 ml (≅ 3 cups) of **water**

ADDITIONAL INGREDIENTS

- Sea **salt** (see Vol. 3, p. 16)

PREPARATION

❶ Peel the banana making sure that no parts of the peel remain.
- Cut the banana into chunks.
- Put the milk, water, sugar, and banana into a tall container and mix with the hand-held mixer.

❷ Put the mixture into a pot and cook on a low fire for 10-15 minutes; stir constantly with a wooden spoon so that it does not stick.

❸ Serve hot in soup bowls.

HEALTHIER ALTERNATIVE: Use non-dairy milk instead of cow's milk and honey instead of sugar.

For more information about the ingredients, see: Plantain, Vol. 2, p. 72; milk, Vol. 1, p. 182; brown sugar, Vol. 1, p. 170.

HEALTH COUNSELS

Cream of banana, a tasty and sweet dish, represents a dessert that can be enjoyed by those who are trying to care for their stomach. Unlike many other desserts, this dish has *very little* ***fat*** or ***cholesterol.*** It is especially good for:

✓ The **stomach,** because it is *easy to digest* and *neutralizes* excessive **gastric acidity.**

✓ The **intestine,** especially in cases of **intestinal diarrhea** or **celiac disease,** because the banana *soothes* the intestinal **lining** and is well tolerated.

✓ The **kidneys** and the **heart,** for its *low level* of ***sodium*** and *high level* of ***potassium.*** Those who suffer from **edema** (retention of fluid) and **high blood pressure** can especially benefit from this dish.

NUTRITIONAL VALUE* per serving

Nutrient	Amount
Energy	134 kcal = 562 kj
Protein	6.85 g
Carbohydrates	26.3 g
Fiber	0.805 g
Total fat	*0.467 g*
Saturated fat	*0.269 g*
Cholesterol	*3.38 mg*
Sodium	*101 mg*

1% 2% 4% 10% 20% 40% 100%

% Daily Value (based on a 2,000 calorie diet) provided by each serving of this dessert

CALORIC PROPORTION*

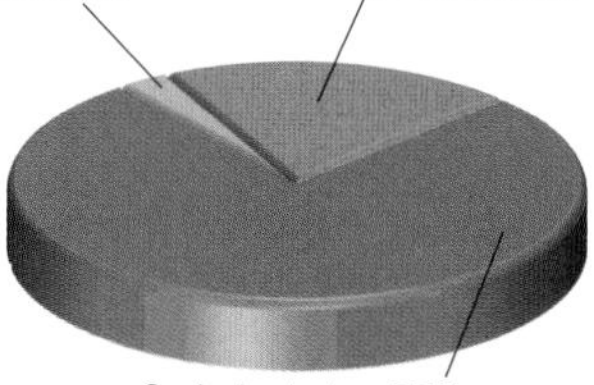

Percentage distribution of **calories for each nutrient**

*Additional ingredients are not included.

Preparation time 00:30

Cooking time - - - -

Tropical Fruit Salad

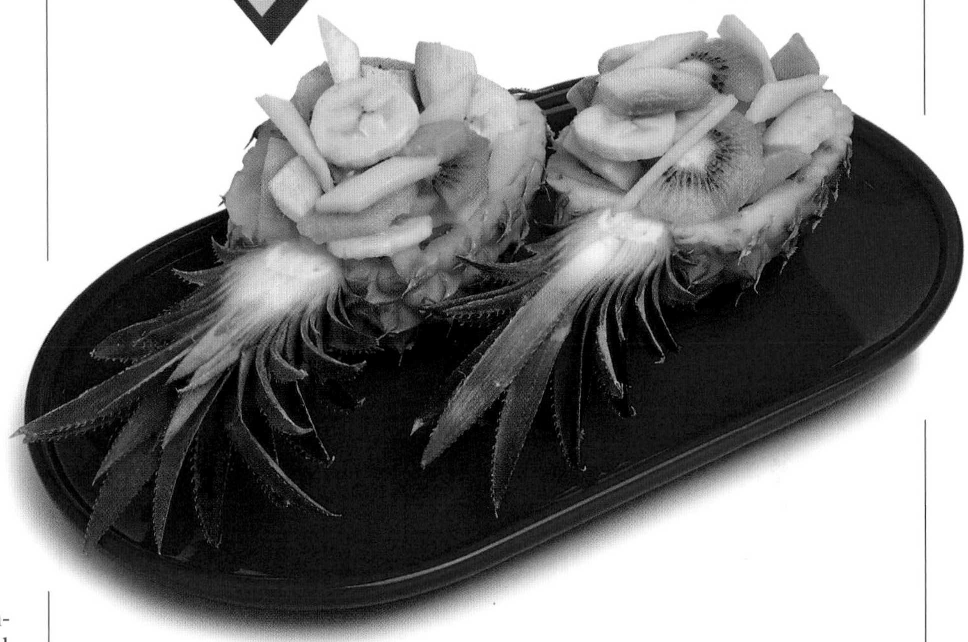

INGREDIENTS (4 servings)

- 2 small **pineapples**
- 2 **kiwis**
- 1 **mango**
- 1 **avocado**
- 2 **cherimoyas** (custard apples)
- 1 **banana**
- 1 small **papaya**

PREPARATION

❶Cut each pineapple in half lengthwise. Empty out the fruit, discard the hard central part and chop up the rest. Keep the juice obtained through the process.

- Peel and chop the banana and the kiwis (soak the banana in the pineapple juice to keep it from becoming brown).
- Peel the mango and the avocado and remove the central seed; chop both.
- Cut the papaya in half, empty out the seeds, peel, and chop it into pieces.
- Cut the cherimoyas in half, empty out the pulp with a spoon. Put the pulp through a sieve that does not allow the seeds to pass.

❷Mix all the chopped fruit in a bowl and then fill the empty pineapples with the mixture.

- Chill in the refrigerator for at least one hour.

❸Serve cold.

HEALTHIER ALTERNATIVE: To reduce the calories, use smaller pieces of fruit or reduce the amount.

For more information about the ingredients, see: Pineapple, Vol. 2, p. 189; kiwi, Vol. 2, p. 356; mango, Vol. 2, p. 341; avocado, Vol. 2, p. 108; cherimoya, Vol. 2, p. 59; banana, Vol. 2, p. 70; papaya, Vol. 2, p. 157.

HEALTH COUNSELS

In general, all fruit helps to produce good digestion and protects the stomach. This Tropical Fruit Salad serves as a delicious yet healthy dessert and is especially recommended for:

✓The **stomach,** because the pineapple *helps the digestion;* the avocado, papaya, and cherimoya *neutralize* excess **gastric acid;** and the mango and banana *soothe* and *protect* the inner **stomach lining.**

✓The **skin,** because fruit helps to *eliminate* **toxins** circulating in the blood that can cause **eczema.** In addition, these fruits are *high* in ***beta-carotene*** (provitamin A) that turns into vitamin A, necessary for healthy skin.

✓The **immune system,** since fruits fortify it by helping in its *fight* against **infection** and in the *prevention* of **cancer.**

✓The **heart** and the **arteries,** because of the ***antioxidant substances*** that prevent the deposit of **cholesterol** and **arteriosclerosis.**

NUTRITIONAL VALUE per serving

Energy	**447 kcal = 1,869 kj**
Protein	**5.13 g**
Carbohydrates	**88.3 g**
Fiber	**12.8 g**
Total fat	***8.02 g***
Saturated fat	***1.12 g***
Cholesterol	—
Sodium	***19.4 mg***

1% 2% 4% 10% 20% 40% 100%

% Daily Value (based on a 2,000 calorie diet) provided by each serving of this dessert

CALORIC PROPORTION

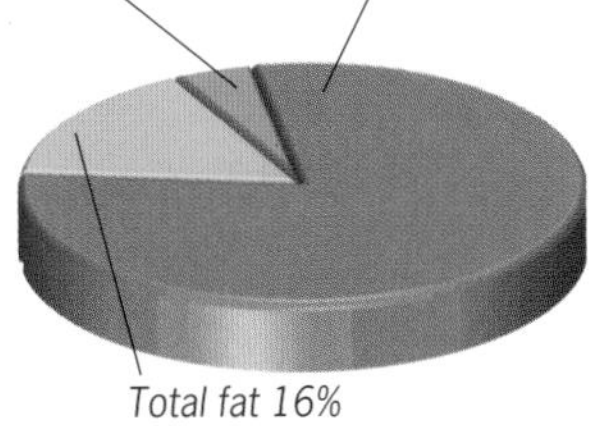

Percentage distribution of **calories for each nutrient**

Preparation time

- - - -

Cooking time

00:15

Refreshing Tea

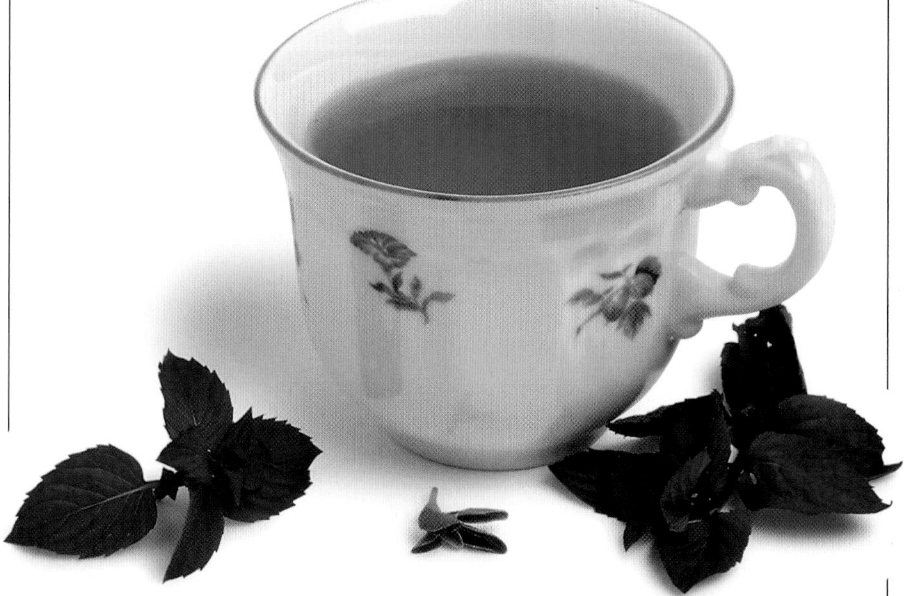

INGREDIENTS

- 1 tablespoon of **peppermint**
- 1 tablespoon of **linden**
- 1 tablespoon of ground **licorice**
- 1 tablespoon of **lemon verbena**
- $1^1/_2$ liters (≅ $1\ ^1/_2$ quarts) of **water**

PREPARATION

❶ Boil the water in a separate pot.
- Put the ingredients in a teapot and add the boiling water.

❷ Allow to steep for 15 minutes, strain and cool.

❸ Serve cold.

For more information about the ingredients, see: The *Encyclopedia of Medicinal Plants:* peppermint, p. 366; pennyroyal, p. 461; linden, p. 169; licorice, p. 308; lemon verbena, p. 459.

Suggestions from the Chef

- The herbal tea can be served with **ice** and a few drops of **lemon juice.**
- Although licorice sweetens this drink, those with a sweet tooth might prefer to add a little **honey.**

HEALTH COUNSELS

This delicious and refreshing herbal tea, gets its sweetness naturally from licorice and is good for:

✓The **stomach,** due to its *digestibility.* It also calms **acidity,** helps to relieve **indigestion,** fights **spasms** of the abdominal organs, and prevents **flatulence.** It represents the ideal ending or finishing touch for any meal, especially for those with delicate stomachs.

✓The **liver** and the **gallbladder,** because the plants in this drink enhance bile production and the emptying of the gallbladder.

✓The **nervous system,** since this herbal tea acts as a natural *relaxant* and *sedative.*

Peppermint

Preparation time: - - - -

Cooking time: 00:30

Pineapple Water

INGREDIENTS

- 1 **pineapple** (the rind)
- 2 liters (≅ 2 quarts) of **water**

PREPARATION

❶ Wash the rind of the pineapple well, cut it into pieces, and put it into a pot with cold water.

❷ Boil the rind in the water for 30 minutes.

• Remove the pineapple rind and allow the liquid to cool.

❸ Serve cold.

For more information about the ingredients, see: Pineapple, Vol. 2, p. 189.

HEALTH COUNSELS

This light and refreshing drink allows you to take advantage of the rind of the pineapple along with the rest of the fruit that tends to remain attached. It is good to drink this before meals (from half hour to 5 minutes before).

The pineapple water, obtained through cooking the pineapple rind, contains the same digestive properties of the pineapple along with the same combination of ***minerals*** and ***trace elements*** such as ***manganese, copper,*** and ***iron.*** It is especially recommended for:

✓ The **stomach,** because it helps the digestion.

✓ The **kidneys,** because of its mild *diuretic* properties.

Pineapple water contains enzymes such as bromelin that aid digestion and help to prevent indigestion.

Suggestions from the Chef

You can sweeten this drink with brown sugar, honey, or molasses (cane honey).

51

RECIPES FOR THE INTESTINE

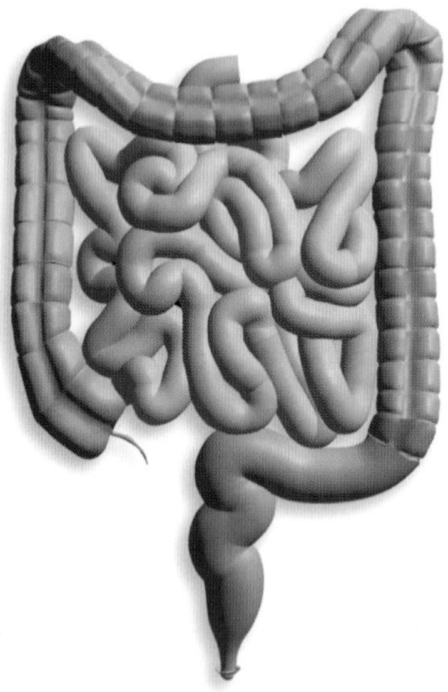

The human intestine—both small and large—normally reaches seven-and-a-half meters in length, which is four to five times the height of an average person. This great length gives evidence that our digestive tract is better designed for vegetable foods than for foods of animal origin, as is mentioned on this page. Recipes in this chapter contribute to prevent and cure constipation, diarrhea, and intestinal inflammation.

CHAPTER SUMMARY

RECIPES

Baked Apples 268
Chard with Potatoes and Pumpkin 263
Cream of Leeks 262
Mexican Salad 260
Persimmon Shake 270
Pomegranate Drink 271
Rice Milk 273
Sauerkraut and Carrots 264
Sautéed Soy Sprouts 265
Sweet Balls 269
Tabulé 261
Tiger Nut Horchata 272
Vegetable Rice 266

THE TWO first volumes of this ENCYCLOPEDIA OF FOODS AND THEIR HEALING POWER give the fundamental scientific reasons why many nutrition specialists recommend a vegetarian diet prepared in the simplest way (see especially Vol. 1, pp. 25, 37; Vol. 2, p. 388).

That is why the dishes and accompaniments in this third volume, HEALTHY RECIPES, are based on **vegetable** foods prepared in the **simplest** manner. **Vegetarian cuisine,** carried out in a systematic and balanced way, constitutes **the healthiest option.**

It has been demonstrated that a balanced **lacto-ovo vegetarian** diet does not necessarily lack any of the nutritional needs, even for children and adolescents in the peak of their development.

Furthermore, a vegetarian diet is the most appropriate for the way we are made physically.

When examining human **teeth,** it can be observed that they are not made to tear, as are those of carnivorous mammals. Our teeth contain flat molars capable of grinding grains and seeds.

We need to consider that the exceptionally long **intestine** of the human being makes it more like that of herbivorous animals and not like carnivores. This is an additional proof that a meat-based diet is not adequate for humans at any stage of their lives.

Carnivorous animals have proportionally a much shorter intestine than animals feeding on plant-based foods. This is because meat must pass quickly through the digestive tract so that the toxins inherent to meat (see Vol. 1, p. 300) as well as those produced by putrefaction are not absorbed by the blood of the eater.

In turn, vegetables travel slowly through the intestine giving it a chance to properly absorb the healthy properties contained within them.

Recipes in this chapter, apart from being prepared in a simple way, are especially designed to maintain and improve the functioning of the bowel.

Menus for

Laxative

Oatmeal

BREAKFAST
- "Avocado Shake" (Vol. 3, p. 201)
- "Oatmeal" (Vol. 3, p. 154)
- Oranges (Vol. 2, p. 360)

LUNCH
- "Asparagus Salad" (Vol. 3, p. 278)
- "Mixed Vegetables" (Vol. 3, p. 166)
- "Falafel Patties" (Vol. 3, p. 198)
- "Whole Bread" (Vol. 1, p. 72, Vol. 3, p. 46)
- "Aromatic Linden" (Vol. 3, p. 159)

Mixed Vegetables

Sauerkraut and Carrots

SUPPER
- "Tabulé" (Vol. 3, p. 261)
- "Sauerkraut and Carrots" (Vol. 3, p. 264)
- "Stewed Figs and Pears" (Vol. 3, p. 225)

HEALTH COUNSELS

This menu provides a mild laxative effect and supplies high levels of **fiber** in order to stimulate the bowel. It prevents **constipation** and helps to avoid further complications where constipation is habitually present.

Persons with **diverticulosis** or **hemorrhoids** may also benefit from this menu. Additionally, it can help to prevent **colon cancer.**

Astringent

Tiger Nut Horchata

BREAKFAST
- "Pomegranate Drink" (Vol. 3, pp. 271)
- "Rice Pudding" (Vol. 3, p. 199)
- "Tiger Nut Horchata" (Vol. 3, 272)

LUNCH
- "Seed Salad" (Vol. 3, p. 298)
- "Rice with Carrots" (Vol. 3, p. 133)
- "Sautéed Soy Sprouts" (Vol. 3, p. 265)
- "Baked Apples" (Vol. 3, p. 268)
- "Sweet Corn Drink" (Vol. 3 p. 293)

Sautéed Soy Sprouts

SUPPER
- "Chard with Potatoes and Pumpkin" (Vol. 3, p. 263)
- "Persimmon Shake" (Vol. 3, p. 270)
- "Rice milk" (Vol. 3, p. 273)

Chard with Potatoes and Pumpkin

HEALTH COUNSELS

This menu is astringent and helps to stop diarrhea in case of **gastroenteritis** or colitis. It can also be used by those suffering from **irritable bowel syndrome** or by those who tend to complain of **intestinal diarrhea.**

the Intestine

Gluten-Free

BREAKFAST
- "Oranges with Honey" (Vol. 3, p. 366)
- "Rice Crackers" (Vol. 3, p. 196)
- "Soy Milk" (Vol. 3, p. 305)

Oranges with Honey

Cream of Banana

LUNCH
- "Carrot and Apple Juice" (Vol. 3, p. 355)
- "Mexican Salad" (Vol. 3, p. 260)
- "Beans and Rice" (Vol. 3, p. 320)
- "Cream of Banana" (Vol. 3, p. 252)

SUPPER
- Tomato and Sweet Corn Salad (Vol. 2, pp. 275, 238)
- "Cream of Leeks" (Vol. 3, p. 262)
- "Sweet Balls" (Vol. 3, p. 269)

Cream of Leeks

HEALTH COUNSELS

A gluten-free diet is *prescriptive* **for celiac patients.** However, it is beneficial to *everyone* who suffers from intestinal problems. It is therefore recommended to those with **irritable bowel syndrome, intestinal fermentation,** and **Crohn's disease.**

Other Recipes for the Intestine

SALADS
- "Chinese Salad" (Vol. 3, p. 243)
- "Red and White Salad" (Vol. 3, p. 372)
- "Crunchy Fennel" (Vol. 3, p. 242)

SOUPS AND PURÉES
- "Three-colored Purée" (Vol. 3, p. 377)
- "Cereal Soup" (Vol. 3, p. 314)

MAIN COURSES
- "Vegetable Rice" (Vol. 3, p. 266)
- "Chickpea Stew" (Vol. 3, p. 148)
- "Autumn Cabbage" (Vol. 3, p. 376)
- "Stuffed Eggplant" (Vol. 3, p. 120)
- "Vegetable Pie" (Vol. 3, p. 104)
- "Spinach Lasagna" (Vol. 3, p. 108)
- "Vegetable Paella" (Vol. 3, p. 86)

BREAKFASTS, DESSERTS AND SNACKS
- "Granola" (Vol. 3, p. 156)

DRINKS
- "Watermelon Shake" (Vol. 3, p. 292)
- "Tamarind Drink" (Vol. 3, p. 237)

Teas or herbal infusions of:
- Star Anise (EMP, p. 455)
- Thyme (EMP, p. 769)
- German Camomile (EMP, p. 364)

- *See the recipe index at the beginning of this volume (Vol. 3, pp. 8-13).*
- *See also chapter 28, "Foods for the Intestine" (Vol. 2, pp. 206-241).*

EMP = Encyclopedia of Medicinal Plants, EDUCATION AND HEALTH LIBRARY, Editorial Safeliz.

Preparation time 00:20

Cooking time 00:20

Mexican Salad

INGREDIENTS (4 servings)

- 200 g (≅ 7 oz) of tender **sweet corn** (maize)
- 1 **red pepper**
- 1 **green pepper**
- 2 **carrots**
- 2 **tomatoes**
- 1 **cucumber**
- 1 head of **lettuce**
- 100 g (≅ 3.5 oz) **peas**
- 100 g (≅ 3.5 oz) **green** and **black olives**
- 1 tablespoon of **brewer's yeast**

ADDITIONAL INGREDIENTS

- **Parsley**
- The juice of $^1/_2$ **lemon**
- 4 tablespoons of olive **oil** (each tablespoon of oil adds around 120 kcal to the recipe, that is, 30 kcal per serving)
- Sea **salt** (see Vol. 3, p. 16)

PREPARATION

❶ Wash, peel, and chop the carrots and the cucumbers.
- Wash, remove the seeds, and chop the peppers in strips.
- Wash and chop the tomato.
- Wash the lettuce and set aside as whole leaves.
- Wash and chop the parsley.

❷ Boil peas in water and let them cool.
- Arrange all ingredients on each dish and sprinkle with salt.
- To prepare the dressing, add the chopped parsley and the lemon juice to the oil, and beat with a fork.

❸ Dress just before serving.

For more information about the ingredients, see: Corn, Vol. 2, p. 238; pepper, Vol. 2, p. 198; carrot, Vol. 2, p. 25; tomato, Vol. 2, p. 275; cucumber, Vol. 2, p. 339; lettuce, Vol. 2, p. 45; peas, Vol. 2, p. 73; olives, Vol. 2, p. 165; brewer's yeast, Vol. 1, p. 358.

HEALTH COUNSELS

This Mexican Salad, in addition to raw vegetables, includes corn (a grain) and peas (a legume). As any other salad, it is very healthy. It is rich in **vitamins** and other **antioxidant substances** that *protect* against **high cholesterol** levels and cancer. This salad is especially recommended for:

✓The **intestine,** due to the high **fiber** content of this vegetable combination, which stimulates bowel movement.

✓**Obesity,** as this dish, being low in **fat** and **calories** (especially if the added oil is reduced), produces a sense of *satiation.*

✓The **arteries** and the **heart,** because it contains antioxidants which *control* **arteriosclerosis.** In addition, all the above vegetables contribute to *reduce* **cholesterol** levels.

✓**Cancer** prevention, due to its high content in **vitamins** and **phytochemical** and **antioxidant elements.**

NUTRITIONAL VALUE* per serving

Energy	165 kcal = 688 kj
Protein	8.12 g
Carbohydrates	22.4 g
Fiber	9.02 g
Total fat	*2.78 g*
Saturated fat	*0.396 g*
Cholesterol	—
Sodium	*160 mg*

1% 2% 4% 10% 20% 40% 100%

% Daily Value (based on a 2,000 calorie diet) provided by each serving of this dish

CALORIC PROPORTION*

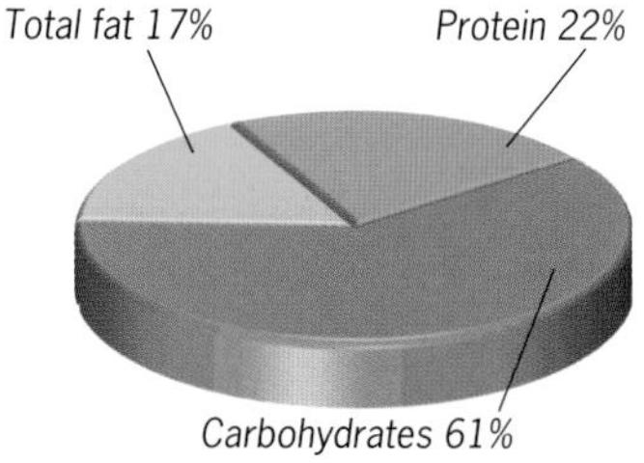

Percentage distribution of **calories for each nutrient**

*Additional ingredients are not included.

Preparation time	Cooking time
00:20	- - - -

Tabulé

INGREDIENTS (4 servings)

- 100 g (≅ 3.5 oz) of **bulgur wheat**
- 1 **onion**
- 2 **tomatoes**
- 1 **lettuce** core
- 1/2 liter (≅ 1/2 quart) of **water**

ADDITIONAL INGREDIENTS

- **Parsley**
- **Mint**
- The juice of 1/2 **lemon**
- 4 tablespoons of olive **oil** (each tablespoon of oil adds around 120 kcal to the recipe, that is, 30 kcal per serving)
- Sea **salt** (see Vol. 3, p. 16)

PREPARATION

❶ Pour the water in a pot until it boils. Remove from heat and immediately pour in the bulgur wheat. Let it soak for about 5 minutes. Wash with cold water; drain using a fine cloth; press it to let all the water out.
- Wash and chop the onion, the tomato, and the lettuce.
- Wash and chop the parsley and the mint.

❷ Mix the oil and lemon juice together with the vegetables and potherbs. Finally add the bulgur wheat.
- Cool in the refrigerator for 1 hour.

❸ Serve the tabulé cold.

Suggestions from the Chef

- **Bulgur wheat** is frequently used in the Middle East. It is a hard wheat grain that has been cracked and vaporized.
- **Tabulé** may also be prepared using **couscous** instead of bulgur wheat. Pepper and cucumber may be added. It is typical to use vinegar instead of lemon.

For more information about the ingredients, see: Wheat, Vol. 2, p. 306; onion, Vol. 2, p. 142; tomato, Vol. 2, p. 275; lettuce, Vol. 2, p. 45.

NUTRITIONAL VALUE* per serving

Nutrient	Per serving
Energy	**122 kcal = 512 kj**
Protein	**4.32 g**
Carbohydrates	**21.7 g**
Fiber	**5.37 g**
Total fat	***0.835 g***
Saturated fat	***0.14 g***
Cholesterol	—
Sodium	***12.8 mg***

1% 2% 4% 10% 20% 40% 100%

% Daily Value (based on a 2,000 calorie diet) provided by each serving of this dish

HEALTH COUNSELS

Tabulé is a salad that uses wheat as its base and a sour dressing such as lemon juice.

Wheat, together with the salad vegetables, contributes to the *healthy functioning* of the **bowel,** due to its high **fiber** content. Additionally, because of its low **fat** content and zero **cholesterol,** this dish is highly recommended for the **arteries** and the **heart.** It also helps to prevent **obesity.**

CALORIC PROPORTION*

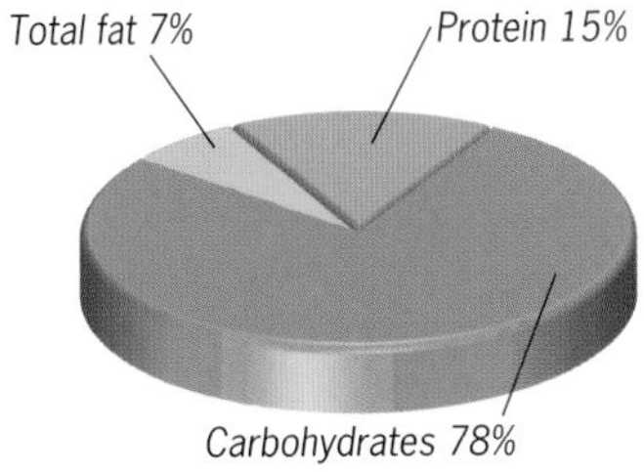

Percentage distribution of **calories for each nutrient**

*Additional ingredients are not included.

Preparation time 00:20

Cooking time 00:25

Cream of Leeks

INGREDIENTS (4 servings)

- 500 g (≅ 1 pound) of **leeks**
- 350 g (≅ 12 1/3 oz) of **potatoes**
- 1 1/4 liters (≅ 1 1/4 quarts) of **water**

ADDITIONAL INGREDIENTS

- 4 tablespoons of olive **oil** (each tablespoon of oil adds around 120 kcal to the recipe, that is, 30 kcal per serving)
- Sea **salt** (see Vol. 3, p. 16)

PREPARATION

❶ Peel, wash, and chop the leeks (see Vol. 3, p. 134) and the potatoes.

❷ Heat the oil in a pot and sauté leeks and potatoes with a pinch of salt.

- Add the water and let simmer for 15 minutes.
- Blend mixture with an electric blender.

❸ Serve hot.

HEALTHIER ALTERNATIVE: Instead of sautéing the ingredients, pour them directly in the hot water and boil for 20 minutes.

For more information about the ingredients, see: Leek, Vol. 2, p. 319; potato, Vol. 2, p. 201.

HEALTH COUNSELS

Leeks, *rich* in **celluloid fiber,** facilitate good intestinal functioning and stimulate bowel movement. Potatoes provide *a smooth protection* to the **digestive *lining.*** This fine-textured cream is easy to digest. The dish is especially beneficial to:

✓The **intestine,** because of the *invigorating* effect of leeks. The soft texture of this cream is easily digested, allowing the digestive system to rest.

✓The **stomach,** due to the *antacid* effect of potatoes.

✓The **kidneys,** as the *alkaline* effect of both leeks and potatoes favors the elimination of **waste substances** through the urine thus helping to keep the blood "clean."

NUTRITIONAL VALUE* per serving

Energy	93 kcal = 391 kj
Protein	2.39 g
Carbohydrates	19.2 g
Fiber	2.25 g
Total fat	*0.258 g*
Saturated fat	*0.043 g*
Cholesterol	—
Sodium	*16.7 mg*

1% 2% 4% 10% 20% 40% 100%

% Daily Value (based on a 2,000 calorie diet) provided by each serving of this dish

CALORIC PROPORTION*

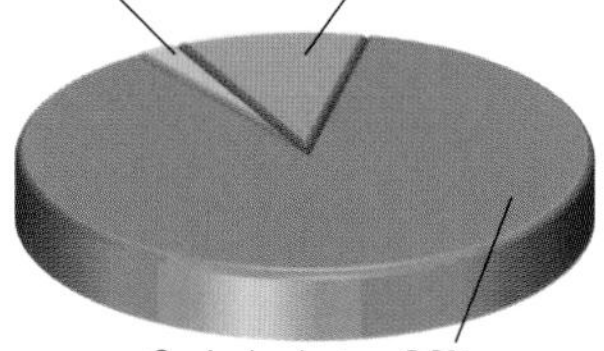

Percentage distribution of **calories for each nutrient**

*Additional ingredients are not included.

Preparation time 00:20

Cooking time 00:25

Chard with Potatoes and Pumpkin

INGREDIENTS (4 servings)

- 500 g (≅ 1 pound) of **chard**
- 500 g (≅ 1 pound) of **potatoes**
- 250 g (≅ 8.8 oz) of **pumpkin** (squash)

ADDITIONAL INGREDIENTS

- 4 tablespoons of olive **oil** (each tablespoon of oil adds around 120 kcal to the recipe, that is, 30 kcal per serving)
- Sea **salt** (see Vol. 3, p. 16)

PREPARATION

❶ Remove the lower fleshy part of the chard leaf and pull the fibers off.
- Wash and chop the chard leaves.
- Peel and chop the pumpkin and the potatoes.

❷ Bring 2 liters of water to boil in a large pot and add all the vegetables and salt.
- Cook on a medium stove for 20 minutes.
- Set aside the broth. It can be utilized in other recipes.

❸ Dress with raw oil and serve hot.

For more information about the ingredients, see: Chard, Vol. 2, p. 297; potato, Vol. 2, p. 201; pumpkin, Vol. 2, p. 97.

HEALTH COUNSELS

These vegetables combine very well both in flavor and in their preventive qualities. Together, they make a simple, yet balanced and healthy dish. This recipe supplies **carbohydrates** from the potatoes and the pumpkin. It also provides a small, but significant amount of **protein** from both potatoes and pumpkin. **Provitamin A** (beta-carotene) is also present in both chard and pumpkin. Finally, it contains ***minerals,*** particularly found in the chard. It is especially recommended for:

✓ The **intestine** and the **stomach,** because of the *soft* and *digestive* effects of all the ingredients. It is beneficial to those who suffer from **gastritis, ulcer,** and **colitis.** It also helps to prevent **constipation.**

✓ **Obesity** and its prevention, as this dish provides a *satisfying* effect much higher than would be expected from its calories. To keep a low calorie count, use very little oil in the dressing.

NUTRITIONAL VALUE* per serving

Energy	**116 kcal = 484 kj**
Protein	**4.85 g**
Carbohydrates	**19.7 g**
Fiber	**6.48 g**
Total fat	***0.225 g***
Saturated fat	***0.063 g***
Cholesterol	—
Sodium	***258 mg***

1% 2% 4% 10% 20% 40% 100%

% Daily Value (based on a 2,000 calorie diet) provided by each serving of this dish

CALORIC PROPORTION*

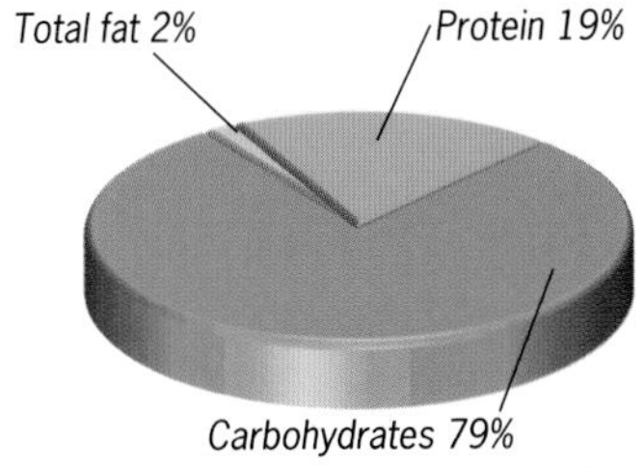

Percentage distribution of **calories for each nutrient**

*Additional ingredients are not included.

Preparation time 00:20 | Cooking time 00:30

Sauerkraut and Carrots

INGREDIENTS (4 servings)

- 500 g (≅ 1 pound) of **sauerkraut**
- 300 g (≅ 10.6 oz) of **carrots**
- 300 g (≅ 10.6 oz) of mushrooms
- 2 **onions**

ADDITIONAL INGREDIENTS

- 1 teaspoon of **juniper, cumin,** or **fennel seeds**
- **Potherbs** (thyme and parsley)
- 5 tablespoons of olive **oil** (each tablespoon of oil adds around 120 kcal to the recipe, that is, 30 kcal per serving)
- Sea **salt** (see Vol. 3, p. 16)

PREPARATION

❶Peel, and chop the onions and carrots.
- Wash and slice the mushrooms.
- Rinse the sauerkraut with water.

❷Heat 3 tablespoons of oil in a frying pan and sauté one onion.
- When the onion is transparent, add the sauerkraut, salt, and seeds.
- Let simmer on low heat for about 10 minutes, stirring occasionally.
- In another frying pan, heat the remaining oil and sauté the other chopped onion together with the mushrooms. Add salt and cook on a medium flame until the fluid given off by the mushrooms has evaporated.
- Boil the carrots in salted water until tender, but do not overcook.
- Drain and add to the sauerkraut; add the sautéed mushrooms and allow to simmer for an additional 5 minutes.

❸Serve hot. Sprinkle with washed and chopped parsley and thyme.

HEALTHIER ALTERNATIVE: Instead of sautéing the ingredients, steam them. The mushrooms may be roasted.

For more information about the ingredients, see: Sauerkraut, Vol. 2, p. 197; carrot, Vol. 2, p. 25; mushroom, Vol. 2, p. 294; onion, Vol. 2, p. 142.

HEALTH COUNSELS

The sauerkraut, or naturally fermented cabbage, is typical in Germany and other countries in Central Europe. Garnished with mushrooms and carrots, as suggested in this dish, sauerkraut *keeps* the **intestinal flora** in good condition. It also helps *fight* **constipation.** Additionally, it is believed that due to its high **lactic acid** content, sauerkraut helps prevent **arteriosclerosis** and **arthritis.**

Sauerkraut

*Not everything called sauerkraut is naturally fermented cabbage. In many cases, it is **industrially** produced with vinegar, sugar, and other additives, which is **not** so **healthy.***

NUTRITIONAL VALUE* per serving

Energy	101 kcal = 424 kj
Protein	4.19 g
Carbohydrates	15.0 g
Fiber	7.54 g
Total fat	*0.721 g*
Saturated fat	*0.124 g*
Cholesterol	—
Sodium	*857 mg*

1% 2% 4% 10% 20% 40% 100%

% Daily Value (based on a 2,000 calorie diet) provided by each serving of this dish

CALORIC PROPORTION*

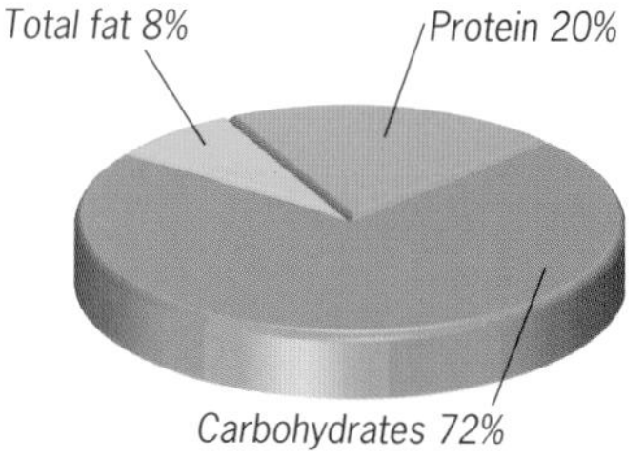

Percentage distribution of **calories for each nutrient**

*Additional ingredients are not included.

Preparation time 00:05

Cooking time 00:10

Sautéed Soy Sprouts

INGREDIENTS (4 servings)

- 500 g (≅ 1 pound) of **soy sprouts**
- 8 cloves of **garlic**

ADDITIONAL INGREDIENTS

- 3 tablespoons of **soy sauce** (each tablespoon of this sauce adds 857 mg of sodium to the recipe, that is, around 214 mg per serving; see Vol. 3, p.16)
- 3 tablespoons of olive **oil** (each tablespoon of oil adds around 120 kcal to the recipe, that is, 30 kcal per serving)

PREPARATION

❶ Peel the garlic cloves and cut in thin slices.

❷ Sauté the garlic with a few drops of oil in a clay pot.

• Add the soy sprouts and the soy sauce, stirring occasionally.

❸ Serve immediately while hot.

For more information about the ingredients, see: Soy beans, Vol. 2, p. 264, garlic, Vol. 1, p. 338; and the *Encyclopedia of Medicinal Plants:* garlic, p. 230.

HEALTH COUNSELS

Soybean sprouts are one of the most natural ways of eating this nutritious and healthy legume. Cooked and arranged as indicated in this recipe, they resemble the shape of elvers although they are much healthier.

Like any other sprout, soybean sprouts are *rich* in **enzymes,** which make **digestion** *easy* both for the stomach and the intestine. Additionally, they help to *regenerate* the **intestinal flora.** That is why these sprouts are light and easy to digest, as opposed to real elvers.

Soybean sprouts are also a good source of **protein, vitamins, minerals,** and **antioxidant substances,** which protect against **cholesterol** deposits in the arteries and against **cancer.**

NUTRITIONAL VALUE* per serving

Energy	**55 kcal = 231 kj**
Protein	**4.56 g**
Carbohydrates	**8.88 g**
Fiber	**2.50 g**
Total fat	***0.285 g***
Saturated fat	***0.068 g***
Cholesterol	—
Sodium	***9.54 mg***

1% 2% 4% 10% 20% 40% 100%

% Daily Value **(based on a 2,000 calorie diet)** provided by each serving of this dish

CALORIC PROPORTION*

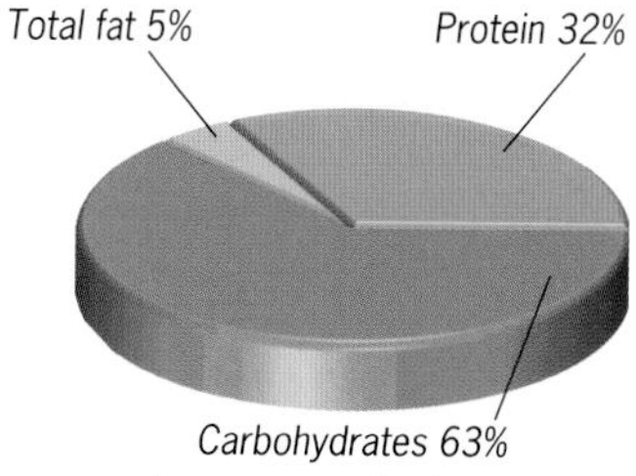

Percentage distribution of **calories for each nutrient**

*Additional ingredients are not included.

Preparation time 00:15

Cooking time 00:45

Vegetable Rice

INGREDIENTS (4 servings)

- 350 g (≅ 12.3 oz) of **whole grain rice**
- 1 **eggplant**
- 1 baked **red pepper** (bell pepper)
- 1 **tomato**
- 2 **garlic** cloves
- 750 ml (≅ 3 cups) of **vegetable broth** (without salt)

ADDITIONAL INGREDIENTS

- 8 tablespoons of olive **oil** (each tablespoon of oil adds around 120 kcal to the recipe, that is, 30 kcal per serving)
- Sea **salt** (see Vol. 3, p. 16)

Baked pepper

To bake the pepper, place it in a hot **oven** at maximum temperature until it is tender and the skin separates easily. Take it out of the oven and let it cool in a covered pot. Once it is completely cool, peel, cut it open and remove the seeds.

The pepper can also be **roasted** or **flamed** over an open fire. In these cases, the skin may become black, and washing may be necessary.

To **preserve** peppers, place them in a glass jar and boil in water for 40 minutes. For long preservation, freeze in a plastic container or plastic bag. It will be ready to use in this or any other recipe.

PREPARATION

❶ Soak the rice in cold water overnight or in hot water for one hour.
- Wash and chop the eggplant.
- Peel the red pepper and cut into strips.
- Wash and crush the tomato.
- Peel and chop the garlic.

❷ Heat the oil in a large, flat frying pan and sauté the pepper and the eggplant.
- Add the tomato after a few minutes and stir for two more minutes. Add the rice once it has been rinsed.
- Keep stirring and add the boiling broth.
- Add salt and stir. Simmer for about 5 more minutes.
- Add the chopped garlic and reduce heat enough for simmering until the rice is done—tender, loose, and dry.
- Remove from the stove and let set for 5 minutes.

❸ Serve hot.

HEALTHIER ALTERNATIVE: Instead of sautéing the ingredients, add them raw to the boiling vegetable broth.

For more information about the ingredients, see: Rice, Vol. 2, p. 225; eggplant, Vol. 2, p. 256; pepper, Vol. 2, p. 198; tomato, Vol. 2, p. 275; garlic, Vol. 1, p. 338; and the *Encyclopedia of Medicinal Plants:* garlic, p. 230.

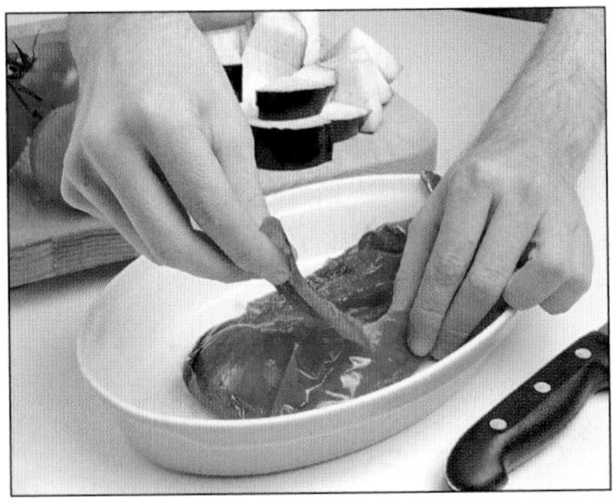

Peel the red pepper and cut into strips.

Sauté the pepper and the eggplant.

Add the rinsed rice.

NUTRITIONAL VALUE* per serving

Energy	358 kcal = 1,495 kj
Protein	8.15 g
Carbohydrates	70.1 g
Fiber	5.93 g
Total fat	*2.71 g*
Saturated fat	*0.526 g*
Cholesterol	—
Sodium	*11.2 mg*

1% 2% 4% 10% 20% 40% 100%

% Daily Value (based on a 2,000 calorie diet) provided by each serving of this dish

CALORIC PROPORTION*

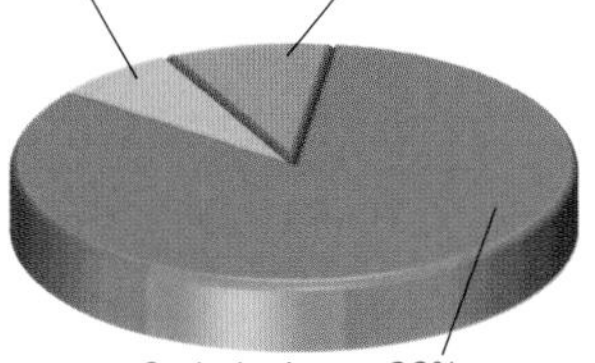

Percentage distribution of **calories for each nutrient**

HEALTH COUNSELS

Vegetable rice is one of the many healthy ways of cooking this universal grain. To the nutritional and preventive properties of rice, we should add those of peppers, eggplant, tomatoes, and garlic. The combination makes this dish especially beneficial for:

✓The **intestine,** due to the *regulating* action of rice upon the bowel **movement,** especially when this is whole grain rice. Peppers and eggplants supply **fiber,** which also facilitates defecation. In this way, the dish *prevents* illnesses associated with **constipation,** such as the formation of intestinal **diverticula, hemorrhoids,** and **cancer of the colon.**

✓The **liver** and the **gallbladder,** due to the action of the eggplant, which gently *actives* the emptying of the **gallbladder** and the *secretion* of **pancreatic juice.** This is why the dish is good for those with **long digestions** caused by bile disorders or insufficient pancreatic juice.

✓*Prevent* **cancer,** especially stomach and colon cancers, due to the *protective* action of ***fiber*** and ***beta-carotene*** (Provitamin A) in peppers. Eggplant and garlic also contain ***anticarcinogenic phytochemical elements.***

✓The **arteries** and the **heart,** due to the *low* ***sodium*** content of the dish—if one limits the addition of salt—and the *zero* level of ***cholesterol.*** Those who wish to maintain their heart and arteries in good condition, and prevent **hypertension** and **myocardial infarction,** should eat this dish frequently.

*Additional ingredients are not included.

Preparation time 00:15

Cooking time 00:20

Baked Apples

INGREDIENTS (4 servings)

- 4 **apples**
- 100 g (≅ 3.5 oz) of raw grated **almonds**
- 1 **banana**
- 2 tablespoons of **raisins,** preferably seedless

ADDITIONAL INGREDIENTS

- **Cinnamon** powder

PREPARATION

❶ Wash apples, remove their core and lay them on a baking tray.
- Set aside part of the almonds, banana, and raisins.
- Mash the banana and the almonds with a fork to form a consistent dough.
- Add the raisins to the dough.
- Fill the apples with the mixture.

❷ Bake in a 180°C oven until tender.

❸ Serve cold decorated with the remaining almonds, banana, and raisins.

For more information about the ingredients, see: Apple, Vol. 2, p. 229; almond, Vol. 2, p. 48; banana, Vol. 2, p. 70; raisins, Vol. 2, p. 81.

Suggestions from the Chef

Those with a sweet tooth may sweeten the almond paste and the banana with honey or sugar.

HEALTH COUNSELS

Apples are among the healthiest and most medicinal of fruits. Baked apples are particularly recommended for those who need to take special care of their large intestine. When combined with bananas, almonds, and raisins, it offers a delicious dessert that is especially recommended for:

✓The **intestine,** because of its *softening* and *regulating* effects. This apple dessert is always well tolerated by sensitive bowels and it is therefore recommended in cases of **slow digestion, flatulence,** and **colitis** of any kind. Due to its *regulatory effect,* it can be used in cases of **diarrhea** or **constipation.**

✓The **arteries** and the **heart,** because apples, bananas, and almonds prevent an excess of **cholesterol** and help to maintain healthy arteries.

NUTRITIONAL VALUE* per serving

Energy	275 kcal = 1,148 kj
Protein	5.68 g
Carbohydrates	30.4 g
Fiber	7.68 g
Total fat	*13.7 g*
Saturated fat	*1.38 g*
Cholesterol	—
Sodium	*6.87 mg*

1% 2% 4% 10% 20% 40% 100%

% Daily Value (based on a 2,000 calorie diet) provided by each serving of this dish

CALORIC PROPORTION*

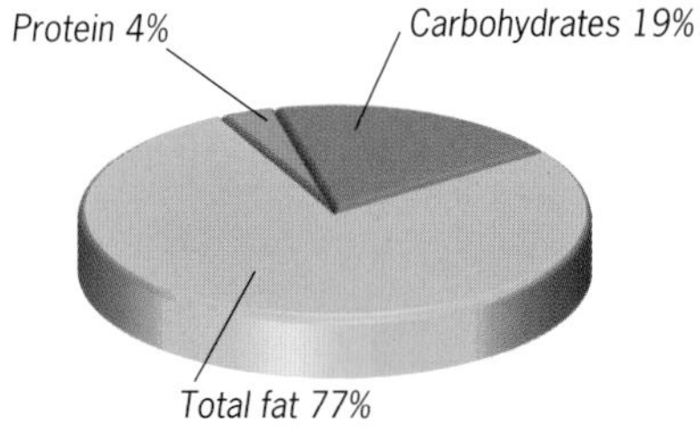

Percentage distribution of **calories for each nutrient**

*Additional ingredients are not included.

Preparation time 00:20

Cooking time - - - -

Sweet Balls

INGREDIENTS

- 50 g (≅ 1.75 oz) of **prunes**
- 50 g (≅ 1.75 oz) of dried **apricots**
- 50 g (≅ 1.75 oz) of dried **figs**
- 50 g (≅ 1.75 oz) of **raisins,** preferably seedless
- 100 g (≅ 3.5 oz) of grated **walnuts**
- 100 g (≅ 3.5 oz) of **honey**

PREPARATION

❶ Soak all dried fruits for 5 minutes in hot water. Drain.

- Chop all fruit very fine; add honey and half of the walnuts.

❷ Divide up the dough in small portions. With oil-coated hands, shape the portions into small balls.

- Roll the balls in the remaining grated walnuts.

❸ Let them dry on a tray for 2 or 3 days. Store in an airtight container. Use when ready.

For more information about the ingredients, see: Prunes, Vol. 2, p. 235; dried apricot, Vol. 2, p. 27; fig, Vol. 2, p. 145; raisins, Vol. 2, p. 81; walnut, Vol. 2, p. 64; honey, Vol. 1, p. 160.

HEALTH COUNSELS

The Sweet Balls, made with dried fruit, supply ***natural energy, vitamins,*** and ***minerals.*** Unlike sugar or refined products, these are rich in ***vitamins*** and ***minerals,*** which help in the combustion and utilization of natural sugars they contain, and that is why they are not harmful.

Besides supplying energy and sweetness, these sweet balls are beneficial to:

✓ The **intestine,** as all these dried fruits contain ***pectin*** (soluble ***fiber***) of gentle *laxative* effect, which contributes to the prevention and relief of **constipation.**

✓ **Children, athletes,** and **physical workers,** as each require a high-energy intake.

NUTRITIONAL VALUE per 100 g

Energy	**365 kcal = 1,526 kj**
Protein	**5.13 g**
Carbohydrates	**53.4 g**
Fiber	**5.28 g**
Total fat	***15.9 g***
Saturated fat	***1.46 g***
Cholesterol	—
Sodium	***10.1 mg***

1% 2% 4% 10% 20% 40% 100%

% Daily Value (based on a 2,000 calorie diet) provided by each 100 g of this dish

CALORIC PROPORTION

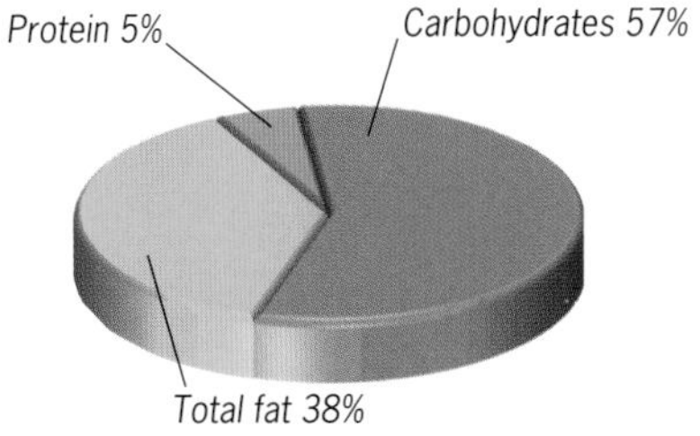

Percentage distribution of **calories for each nutrient**

Preparation time: 00:15
Cooking time: - - - -

Persimmon Shake

INGREDIENTS (4 servings)

- 4 **persimmons**
- 200 g (≅ 7 oz) of fresh **raspberries**
- 4 teaspoons of **brown sugar**
- The juice of one **lemon**

PREPARATION

❶ Cut the persimmons in halves and scoop out the pulp using a spoon. Remove the seeds, if there are any, and beat the pulp until it forms a homogenous paste.
- Place the paste in goblets.

❷ Put aside 4 raspberries, mash the rest with a fork and mix in the sugar and lemon juice.
- Lay this mixture on the persimmon paste.

❸ Serve immediately.

For more information about the ingredients, see: Persimmon, Vol. 2, p. 222; raspberry, Vol. 1, p. 49; sugar, Vol. 1, p. 170.

Suggestions from the Chef

This shake can be decorated with whipped **cream** and a whole raspberry on top.

HEALTH COUNSELS

Persimmons are *rich* in **tannin** (an astringent substance contained in certain plants), particularly when it is not too ripe. That is why a rough feeling is left in our mouths after eating a persimmon that is not quite ripe.

Tannin in persimmons, therefore, makes them *astringent.* At the same time, the ***pectin*** and ***mucilage*** contained within provide *softening* and *protecting* properties for the **intestinal *lining.***

Both persimmons and raspberries are a good source of ***vitamin A*** and ***C, folates,*** and various ***minerals.*** These combined ingredients offer a delicious shake which is highly beneficial to:

- ✓The **intestine,** especially in case of inflammation (**colitis**) and **irritable bowel syndrome.**
- ✓The **blood,** because of the ***iron*** content.
- ✓The **arteries,** because it *protects* against **arteriosclerosis.**
- ✓**Pregnant** women, for the *minerals* and *folates.*

NUTRITIONAL VALUE per serving

Energy	149 kcal = 623 kj
Protein	1.13 g
Carbohydrates	31.4 g
Fiber	7.40 g
Total fat	*0.484 g*
Saturated fat	*0.032 g*
Cholesterol	—
Sodium	*5.88 mg*

1% 2% 4% 10% 20% 40% 100%

% Daily Value **(based on a 2,000 calorie diet)** provided by each serving of this shake

CALORIC PROPORTION

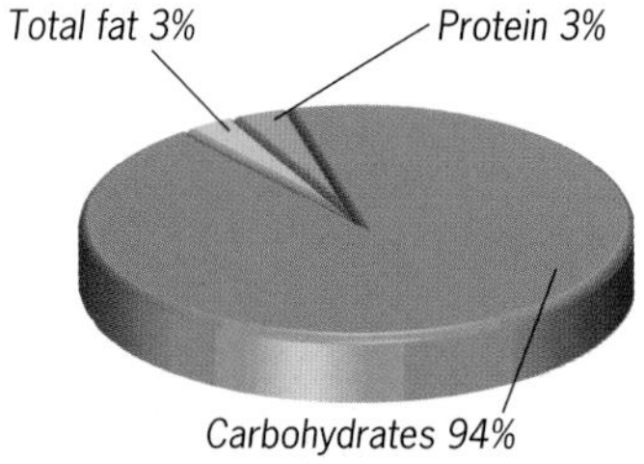

Percentage distribution of **calories for each nutrient**

Preparation time	Cooking time
00:30	- - - -

Pomegranate Drink

INGREDIENTS (4 servings)

- 1 kg (≅ 2 pounds) **pomegranates**
- 500 g (≅ 1 pound) of **pineapple**

PREPARATION

❶ Wash, peel and chop the pineapple (see Vol. 3, p. 255 on how to recycle the bark).
- Open the pomegranates and separate the grains (see Vol. 2, p. 237 for instructions on how to do it).

❷ Blend the fruit using a liquefier.
- Mix the juices well.

❸ Chill and serve immediately.

For more information about the ingredients, see: Pomegranate, Vol. 2, p. 236; pineapple, Vol. 2, p. 189.

Suggestions from the Chef

- If a liquefier is not available, blend the fruits and pass them through a colander.
- To make the process quicker, pomegranates may be squeezed with a **lemon squeezer.**

HEALTH COUNSELS

This mixture of pomegranate and pineapple juices makes a very pleasant and refreshing drink. In addition, the *medicinal properties* of both juices complement each other. The drink is especially beneficial to:

✓The **intestine,** due to the *anti-inflammatory* and slightly *astringent* properties of the pomegranate and to the *digestive* effects of the pineapple. It is especially appropriate for those who want to keep their bowel free from **flatulence** and **cramps.** This drink may be used in case of **gastroenteritis** or **colitis.**

✓The **stomach,** due to the *anti-inflammatory* and *digestive* effects of both fruits. This drink agrees very well with those suffering from **gastritis, upset stomach,** or **heartburn.**

NUTRITIONAL VALUE per serving

Energy	140 kcal = 587 kj
Protein	1.19 g
Carbohydrates	33.7 g
Fiber	0.250 g
Total fat	*0.121 g*
Saturated fat	*0.011 g*
Cholesterol	—
Sodium	*4.43 mg*

1% 2% 4% 10% 20% 40% 100%

% Daily Value (based on a 2,000 calorie diet) provided by each serving of this drink

CALORIC PROPORTION

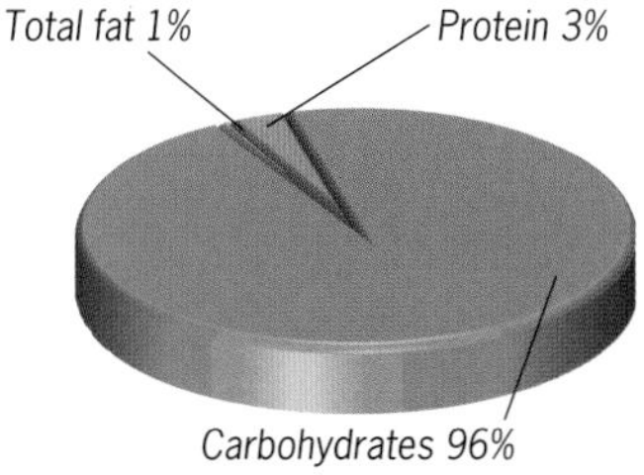

Percentage distribution of **calories for each nutrient**

Preparation time: 0 1:00 | Cooking time: - - - -

Tiger Nut Horchata

INGREDIENTS (4 servings)

- 160 g (≅ 5.6 oz) of dried **tiger nuts**
- $1^1/_8$ liters (≅ $1\ ^1/_8$ quarts) of **water**

ADDITIONAL INGREDIENTS

- The rind of one **lemon**

PREPARATION

❶ Sort the tiger nuts, making sure that the rotten ones and any other small objects are eliminated.
- Wash and soak them for 24 hours; change the water 2 or 3 times.
- Rinse and drain well.

❷ Grind tiger nuts with the lemon rind.
- Add half the water and let it set for 20 minutes. Pass through a fine cloth. Keep the liquid in a pitcher.
- Repeat the process with the remaining water and add to the pitcher.

❸ Serve cold.

For more information about the ingredients, see: Tiger nut, Vol. 2, p. 160; tiger nut horchata, Vol. 1, p. 369.

Suggestions from the Chef

Sweeten with brown sugar and add a cinnamon stick. In this way, the taste will be like the tiger nuts served in the Spanish horchata stands.

HEALTH COUNSELS

Tiger Nut Horchata is typical along the eastern coast of Spain, where it is consumed as a healthy and refreshing drink. This nutritious drink comes from a small root called "chufa" (tiger nut, earth almond). It supplies ***fiber, carbohydrates, protein, vitamin B_1*** and ***E,*** and ***minerals*** such as ***calcium, magnesium,*** and ***iron.***

Tiger Nut Horchata is highly beneficial to:

✓ The **intestine,** due to its smooth *astringent* effect and its ability to *slow down* intestinal **fermentation,** especially in case of **colitis.**

✓ The **stomach,** due to its *invigorating* effect on digestion.

NUTRITIONAL VALUE* per serving

Energy	148 kcal = 618 kj
Protein	2.32 g
Carbohydrates	15.1 g
Fiber	6.79 g
Total fat	*8.70 g*
Saturated fat	*1.04 g*
Cholesterol	—
Sodium	*2.90 g*

1% 2% 4% 10% 20% 40% 100%

% Daily Value (based on a 2,000 calorie diet) provided by each serving of this drink

CALORIC PROPORTION*

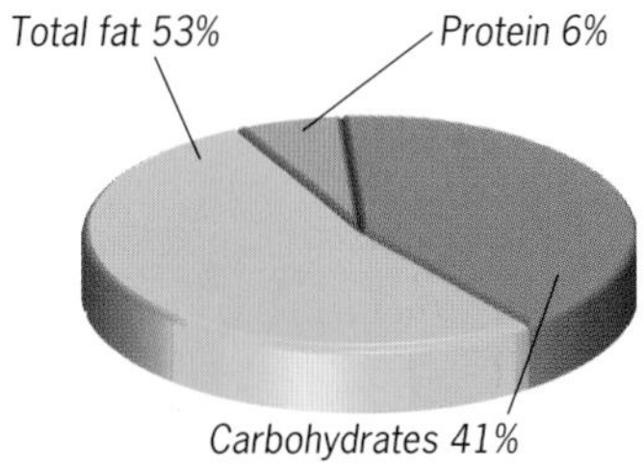

Percentage distribution of **calories for each nutrient**

*Additional ingredients are not included.

Preparation time 00:30

Cooking time 00:10

Rice Milk

INGREDIENTS (4 servings)

- 200 g (≅ 1 cup) of **rice**
- 1 tablespoon of **honey**
- 1 liter (≅ 1 quart) of **water**

ADDITIONAL INGREDIENTS

- 1 **cinnamon** stick
- The rind of 1 **lemon**

PREPARATION

❶Wash the rice.

❷Boil the water together with the lemon rind and the cinnamon stick for a few minutes.

- Pour this water on the rice and soak for 1 hour.
- Grind the rice with an electric blender until the mixture becomes milky.
- Sift to separate the solids (which can be utilized to prepare soups or hamburgers) from the liquid.
- Stir in the honey in order to sweeten the rice milk.

❸Serve cold (if warmed up, it becomes thick because of its high starch content).

For more information about the ingredients, see: Rice, Vol. 2, p. 225; honey, Vol. 1, p. 160.

HEALTH COUNSELS

Rice Milk can be used anytime as a refreshing and healthy drink. However, it is especially *useful* in case of **gastroenteritis** as it helps stop diarrhea.

Rice Milk supplies water and ***minerals*** (especially **potassium**) to replace the loss caused by diarrhea. It also has a *high* **starch** content, which produces an astringent effect.

Calcium

*Although this drink is called rice milk, its composition is **not** comparable to **cow's milk.** Rice milk contains **less calcium** and less **protein** than cow's milk, and it supplies **no amount of vitamin B_{12}.** However, it has other favorable and healthy properties (see photo captions, chapter 51).*

52 Recipes for the Urinary Tract

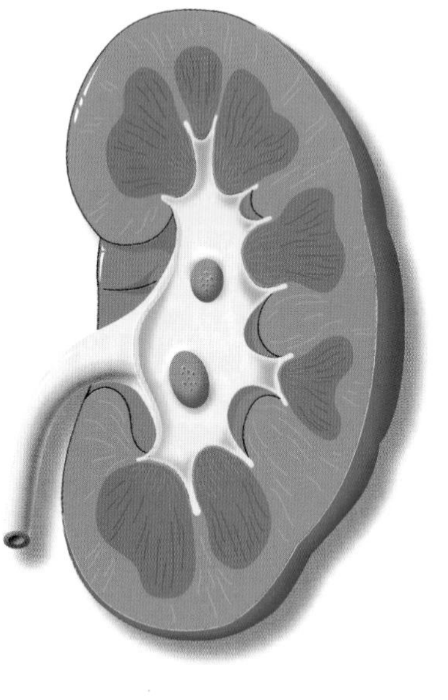

Chapter Summary

Recipes

Asparagus Fondant *284*
Asparagus Salad *278*
Celery Pie *290*
Eggplant Pie *289*
Fettuccini with Green Beans *283*
Garlic Eggplant *279*
Grecian Green Beans *288*
Hazelnut Milk *291*
Leek, Potato and Pumpkin Stew . . *281*
Rice with Cauliflower *282*
Stuffed Artichokes *286*
Sweet Corn Drink *293*
Vichyssoise *280*
Watermelon Shake *292*

The recipes in this chapter help to keep the kidneys healthy. This is so because most of the ingredients stimulate urine production. In order for these recipes to be most effective it is necessary to dress them sparingly.

THE INFLUENCE of diet upon the urinary system is manifested in various ways; these are outlined below:

- **General:** A natural and balanced diet favors well-functioning kidneys and urinary system.
- **Infections:** The female urinary system, especially the urinary bladder, is more prone to infections than that of males. Thus good hygiene and a diet high in vitamins and phytochemicals strengthen the immune system and protect it against cystitis and other forms of urinary infection (see Vol. 2, p. 349).
- **Prevention** of **stones:** There are **specific foods** and **medicinal plants** to prevent stone formation, as indicated in this ENCYCLOPEDIA OF FOODS AND THEIR HEALING POWER (see Vol. 2, p. 242) and the *Encyclopedia of Medicinal Plants* (*EMP*, p. 548).
- **Enhancement of renal functions:** The majority of plant-based foods, especially fruits and vegetables, enhance the work of the kidneys and produce a **diuretic** effect (increase the discharge of urine). On the contrary, foods of animal origin, such as eggs, fish and meat, do not favor the production of urine, and their protein increases the work of the kidneys. This is why it is recommended that, in cases of nephritis or renal inflammation, the patient reduce or eliminate the intake of these foods.

The ***excess*** of ***salt*** and of ***protein,*** typical of the western omnivorous diet, is a **major threat** to the health of kidneys. Both sodium and ***protein*** force the kidneys to carry an additional workload.

This is why the recipes contained in this chapter should satisfy the following two requirements:

- They should be **low** in ***sodium,*** which is easily achieved using unprocessed plant-based ingredients that contain *little* ***sodium*** and *much* ***potassium.*** This peculiar mineral proportion favors the production of urine. Of course, these dishes should be seasoned sparingly.
- They should keep a somewhat **lower** proportion of ***protein;*** this is achieved with plant-based foods, which generally have a lower concentration of protein. Besides, plant-based protein does not overwork renal functions.

Menus for

Diuretic

Watermelon Shake

BREAKFAST

- "Watermelon Shake" (Vol. 3, p. 292)
- Oranges (Vol. 2, p. 360)
- "Whole Bread" with "Chopped Tomato Sauce" (Vol. 3, pp. 46, 63)
- White Birch leaves and buds infusion (*EMP,* p. 568)

LUNCH

- "Asparagus Salad" (Vol. 3, p. 278)
- "Leek, Potato and Pumpkin Stew" (Vol. 3, p. 281)
- "Stuffed Artichokes" (Vol. 3, p. 286)
- Goldenrod infusion (*EMP,* p. 594)

Asparagus Salad

Grapes

SUPPER

- Grapes and pears (Vol. 2, pp. 78, 112)
- Wild Teasel decoction (*EMP,* p. 572)

HEALTH COUNSELS

This menu increases urine *production* and facilitates the *elimination* of waste substances. It is recommended when the **kidneys** need stimulation for extra urine production.

This menu helps the body to eliminate fluids and therefore offers *relief* to the *heart,* helping to avoid complications in case of **arterial hypertension (high-blood pressure)** and **heart failure.** To enhance its effect, reduce or completely eliminate salt from the diet.

Renal Lithiasis (Kidney Stones)

Pear

BREAKFAST

- Pineapple Juice (Vol. 2, p. 189)
- Pear (Vol. 2, p. 112)
- "Whole Bread" with "Mediterranean Tahini" (Vol. 3, pp. 46, 61)
- "Hazelnut Milk" (Vol. 3, p. 291)

LUNCH

- Celery, carrot, and onion salad dressed with lemon juice (Vol. 2, pp. 248, 25, 142, 124)
- "Grecian Green Beans" (Vol. 3, p. 288)
- "Garlic Eggplant" (Vol. 3, p. 279)
- Cashews (Vol. 2, p. 40)
- Saxifrage infusion (*EMP,* p. 591)

Garlic Eggplants

SUPPER

- "Celery Pie" (Vol. 3, p. 290)
- Peach (Vol. 2, p. 75)
- Winter Cherry decoction (*EMP,* p. 585)

Celery Pie

HEALTH COUNSELS

This menu can help to prevent **kidney stones** and those who may be prone to this problem. It helps *eliminate urinary sediments,* which may develop into stones.

the Urinary System

Urinary Infections

BREAKFAST

- European Cranberry juice (Vol. 2, p. 259)
- Melon (Vol. 2, p. 254)
- "Garlic Bread" (Vol. 3, p. 71)
- Pumpkin seeds (Vol. 2, p. 99)

Garlic Bread

Roasted Vegetables

LUNCH

- Fresh juice of borage leaves (Vol. 2, p. 358; *EMP*, p. 746)
- Nasturtium leaves, asparagus, onion, and garlic salad (Vol. 2, pp. 250, 142; Vol. 1, p. 338; *EMP*, p. 772)
- "Rice with Cauliflower" (Vol. 3, p. 282)
- "Roasted Vegetables" (Vol. 3, p. 384)
- "Sweet Corn Drink" (Vol. 3, p. 293)

SUPPER

- Loquats and apple (Vol. 2, pp. 298, 229)
- "Cream of Pumpkin" (Vol. 3, p. 134)
- Heather and Thyme infusion (*EMP*, p. 570, 769)

Cream of Pumpkin

HEALTH COUNSELS

The ingredients in this menu are known for their *preventive* effect on **urinary infections,** especially the European cranberries, onions, and garlic. **Chronic cystitis,** a condition affecting some women, can be prevented by these ingredients.

Other Recipes for the Urinary System

SALADS (always accompanied with garlic and lemon)

- "Violet Salad" (Vol. 3, p. 373)
- "Seed Salad" (Vol. 3, p. 298)
- "Cabbage Salad" (Vol. 3, p. 219)

SOUPS AND PURÉES

- "Artichoke Soup" (Vol. 3, p. 231)
- "Cream of Leeks" (Vol. 3, p. 262)

MAIN COURSES

- "Fettuccini with Green Beans" (Vol. 3, p. 283)
- "Vichyssoise" (Vol. 3, p. 280)
- "Asparagus Fondant" (Vol. 3, p. 284)
- "Eggplant Pie" (Vol. 3, p. 289)
- "Stuffed Kohlrabi" (Vol. 3, p. 337)
- "Baked Potatoes" (Vol. 3, p. 251)

BREAKFASTS, DESSERTS AND SNACKS

- "Winter Log" (Vol. 3, p. 340)
- "Stewed Figs and Pears" (Vol. 3, p. 225)

DRINKS

- "Carrot and Apple Juice" (Vol. 3, p. 355)
- "Melon and Orange Juice" (Vol. 3, p. 367)
- "Sangria (non-alcoholic)" (Vol. 3, p. 327)
- "Pomegranate Drink" (Vol. 3, p. 271)

Freshly squeezed juices:

- Lemon (Vol. 2, p. 124)
- Grapefruit juice (Vol. 2, p. 93)

Infusions or decoctions:

- Parsley (*EMP*, p. 583)

- *See the recipe index at the beginning of this volume (Vol. 3, pp. 8-13).*
- *See also chapter 29, "Foods for the Urinary System" (Vol. 2, pp. 242-259).*

EMP = Encyclopedia of Medicinal Plants, EDUCATION AND HEALTH LIBRARY, Editorial Safeliz.

Preparation time 00:20

Cooking time 00:20

Asparagus Salad

INGREDIENTS (4 servings)

- 500 g (≅ 1 pound) of **asparagus** (or a large can)
- 1/2 **pineapple**
- 1 **cucumber**
- 50 g (≅ 1.75 oz) of **capers**
- 12 **dates**
- 2 **celery** stalks

ADDITIONAL INGREDIENTS

- 4 tablespoons of olive **oil** (each tablespoon of oil adds around 120 kcal to the recipe, that is, 30 kcal per serving)
- **Chives**
- Sea **salt** (see Vol. 3, p. 16)

PREPARATION

❶ Cut off the tough section of the asparagus, peel skin if too fibrous, and wash.
- Wash the celery and remove the threads. Chop.
- Wash and slice cucumber.
- Peel the pineapple, cut the pulp and save the dripping juice.
- For the dressing, use the pineapple juice (if canned pineapple, use the juice of 1 lemon) with oil and salt.

❷ Boil the asparagus until tender (if they are raw).
- Arrange the ingredients on the plate.

❸ Dress when serving. Decorate with chives and, if desired, with olives.

For more information about the ingredients, see: Asparagus, Vol. 2, p. 250; pineapple, Vol. 2, p. 189; cucumber, Vol. 2, p. 339; caper, Vol. 1, p. 342; date, Vol. 2, p. 147; celery, Vol. 2, p. 248.

HEALTH COUNSELS

Due to the favorable action of asparagus on urinary production, this salad is especially beneficial for those wishing to keep their kidneys in good condition. The beneficial effect is strengthened by the presence of other ingredients such as cucumber and pineapple. Therefore, this Asparagus Salad is especially recommended for:

✓The **kidneys,** due to the *diuretic* effect of asparagus.

✓The **intestine,** because of the ***fiber*** contained in asparagus as well as in the other ingredients. This *regulates* the intestinal **tract** and *prevents* **constipation.**

Nephritis

*In case of kidney inflammation (nephritis), asparagus should be eaten **carefully** as it can exert a strong effect upon urine production.*

NUTRITIONAL VALUE* per serving

Energy	171 kcal = 715 kj
Protein	4.06 g
Carbohydrates	35.0 g
Fiber	6.18 g
Total fat	*1.45 g*
Saturated fat	*0.261 g*
Cholesterol	—
Sodium	*315 mg*

1% 2% 4% 10% 20% 40% 100%

% Daily Value (based on a 2,000 calorie diet) provided by each serving of this dish

CALORIC PROPORTION*

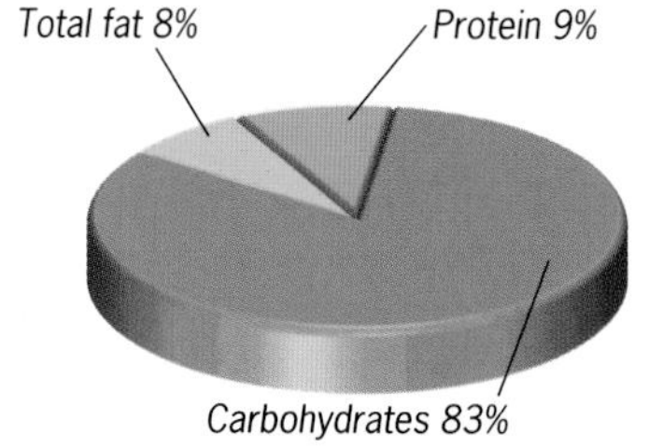

Percentage distribution of **calories for each nutrient**

*Additional ingredients are not included.

Preparation time: 00:15

Cooking time: - - - -

Garlic Eggplant

INGREDIENTS (4 servings)

- 1 large **eggplant**
- 2 **garlic** cloves

ADDITIONAL INGREDIENTS

- Fresh **parsley**
- The juice of 2 **lemons**
- 4 tablespoons of olive **oil** (each tablespoon of oil adds around 120 kcal to the recipe, that is, 30 kcal per serving)
- Sea **salt** (see Vol. 3, p. 16)

PREPARATION

❶ Peel and slice the eggplant.
- Peel the garlic, wash the parsley, and chop everything.

❷ Keep the eggplant soaking in the lemon juice and salt for 1 or 2 days in the refrigerator.
- Rinse the eggplant, scald it in boiling water and marinate it in a container, placing the slices in layers.
- Coat each layer with olive oil and finely chopped garlic and parsley.

❸ The best mixture of flavors is attained after 8 hours of being marinated. At that time, the eggplant can be eaten as an hors d'oeuvre or as a side dish.

Solanine

*The eggplant used in this dish should be **well ripened,** so that the alkaloid solanine may be **minimal,** or none.*

The process of scalding ripe eggplant will destroy any small amounts of solanine that may remain.

For more information about the ingredients, see: Eggplant, Vol. 2, p. 256; garlic, Vol. 1, p. 338; and the *Encyclopedia of Medicinal Plants:* Garlic, p. 230.

NUTRITIONAL VALUE*
per serving

Energy	**45 kcal = 190 kj**
Protein	**1.80 g**
Carbohydrates	**6.55 g**
Fiber	**4.00 g**
Total fat	***0.299 g***
Saturated fat	***0.056 g***
Cholesterol	—
Sodium	***5.24 mg***

1% 2% 4% 10% 20% 40% 100%

% Daily Value (based on a 2,000 calorie diet) provided by each serving of this dish

HEALTH COUNSELS

Eggplant stimulates urine production. This means it is recommended to those suffering from kidney **stones** or **high blood pressure.** Additionally, it also activates the digestive processes, which makes this recipe useful to those prone to *slow* or *heavy* **digestion.**

CALORIC PROPORTION*

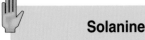

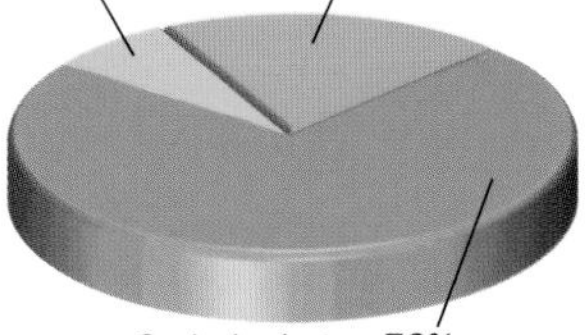

Percentage distribution of **calories for each nutrient**

*Additional ingredients are not included.

Vichyssoise

INGREDIENTS (4 servings)

- 500 g (≅ 1 pound) of **leeks**
- 500 g (≅ 1 pound) of **potatoes**
- 1 **onion**
- 1 **celery** stalk
- 2 skim, natural **yogurts**
- 750 ml (≅ 3 cups) of unsalted **vegetable broth**

ADDITIONAL INGREDIENTS

- The juice of 1 **lemon**
- 2 tablespoons of olive **oil** (each tablespoon of oil adds around 120 kcal to the recipe, that is, 30 kcal per serving)
- Sea **salt** (see Vol. 3, p. 16)

PREPARATION

❶ Peel, wash, and chop the vegetables.

❷ Heat the oil in a pot, and sauté the onions, leeks, and celery. When the vegetables are tender, add the potato, stir, and let simmer for 2 minutes.

- Add the vegetable broth and let simmer for 20 minutes.
- Let it cool. Blend with an electric blender. Add the yogurt, lemon juice, and salt.

❸ Serve cold and decorate with parsley or chives.

HEALTHIER ALTERNATIVE: Instead of sautéing the ingredients, pour them directly into the vegetable broth.

Suggestions from the Chef

This cream of leek soup of French origin can also be prepared with milk and cream.

Preparing it this way, however, increases its fat and cholesterol content.

For more information about the ingredients, see: Leek, Vol. 2, p. 319; potato, Vol. 2, p. 201; onion, Vol. 2, p. 142; celery, Vol. 2, p. 248; yogurt, Vol. 1, p. 201.

HEALTH COUNSELS

Leeks belong to the same botanical family as onions and garlic. Combined with potatoes, onions, and yogurt, they make a delicious and nutritious dish that is especially beneficial to:

✓ The **urinary system,** because of the *diuretic* and *cleansing* effects of leeks, which help eliminate waste substances such as **uric acid** circulating in the blood. Onions and potatoes also contribute to this function.

✓ The **musculoskeletal system,** since these ingredients favor the elimination of uric acid thus causing **joints** to work better. Additionally, yogurt supplies ***calcium,*** needed for the development and maintenance of healthy **bones.**

NUTRITIONAL VALUE* per serving

Energy	**170 kcal = 712 kj**
Protein	**7.21 g**
Carbohydrates	**31.9 g**
Fiber	**3.83 g**
Total fat	***0.495 g***
Saturated fat	***0.143 g***
Cholesterol	***1.13 mg***
Sodium	***89.2 mg***

1% 2% 4% 10% 20% 40% 100%

% Daily Value (based on a 2,000 calorie diet) provided by each serving of this dish

CALORIC PROPORTION*

Percentage distribution of **calories for each nutrient**

*Additional ingredients are not included.

Preparation time 00:20

Cooking time 00:25

Leek, Potato and Pumpkin Stew

INGREDIENTS (4 servings)

- 500 g (≅ 1 pound) of **leeks**
- 500 g (≅ 1 pound) of **potatoes**
- 250 g (≅ 8.8 oz) of **pumpkin** (squash)
- 1 1/2 liters (≅ 1 1/2 quarts) of **water**

ADDITIONAL INGREDIENTS

- 4 tablespoons of olive **oil** (each tablespoon of oil adds around 120 kcal to the recipe, that is, 30 kcal per serving)
- Sea **salt** (see Vol. 3, p. 16)

PREPARATION

❶ Peel, wash and chop the pumpkin and potatoes.
- Wash the leeks as indicated in Vol. 3, p. 134.
- Cut them in 2-3 cm cubes.

❷ Heat the water. When boiling, add vegetables and salt, and boil for an additional 20 minutes on a medium fire.

❸ Serve hot with broth. Dress with raw olive oil.

For more information about the ingredients, see: Leek, Vol. 2, p. 319; potato, Vol. 2, p. 201; pumpkin, Vol. 2, p. 97.

Suggestions from the Chef

Leek, Potato and Pumpkin Stew, like other vegetable dishes, may be dressed with **sautéed garlic.** Use 4 sliced garlic cloves, and sauté them in a frying pan with olive oil.

HEALTH COUNSELS

Properties contained in leeks, potatoes and pumpkin are excellent for the functioning of the kidneys and the cardiovascular system. These foods also have a ***low-sodium*** content, especially when they are lightly salted. An excess of sodium overloads the kidneys and produces **high-blood pressure.** Hence, this dish is especially recommended for:

✓The **kidneys,** as leeks *stimulate* **urine** production, and pumpkin and potatoes favor the *blood cleansing* action of these organs.

✓The **heart** and **arteries,** as this dish helps to *prevent* ***high-blood pressure,*** and the hardening and narrowing of the arteries known as **arteriosclerosis.** The fact that this dish supplies *very little* **fat** and *no* ***cholesterol*** means that it also helps to maintain a healthy heart.

✓The **stomach** and the **intestine,** as it *neutralizes excess acidity, facilitates digestion,* and *supplies* ***fiber*** which regulates **bowel movement.**

NUTRITIONAL VALUE* per serving

Energy	130 kcal = 544 kj
Protein	3.51 g
Carbohydrates	27.1 g
Fiber	2.98 g
Total fat	*0.338 g*
Saturated fat	*0.077 g*
Cholesterol	—
Sodium	*19.0 mg*

1% 2% 4% 10% 20% 40% 100%

% Daily Value (based on a 2,000 calorie diet) provided by each serving of this dish

CALORIC PROPORTION*

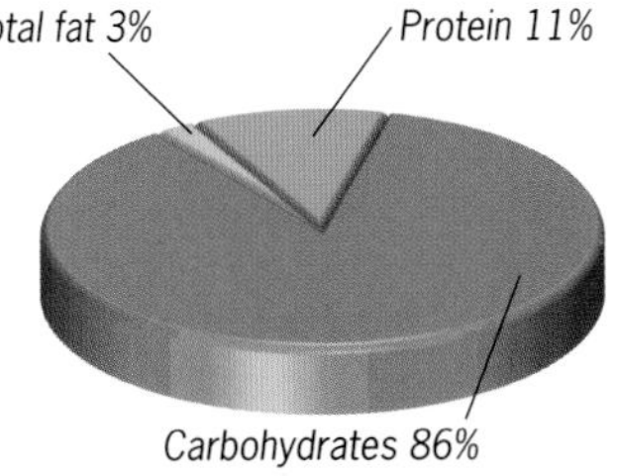

Percentage distribution of **calories for each nutrient**

*Additional ingredients are not included.

Preparation time 00:20 | Cooking time 00:45

Rice with Cauliflower

INGREDIENTS (4 servings)

- 300 g (≅ 1 1/2 cup) of **whole rice**
- 250 g (≅ 8.8 oz) of **cauliflower**
- 1/2 **sweet red pepper**
- 1 **tomato**
- 2 **garlic** cloves
- 750 ml (≅ 3 cups) of unsalted **vegetable broth**

ADDITIONAL INGREDIENTS

- **Parsley**
- **Saffron**
- 4 tablespoons of olive **oil** (each tablespoon of oil adds around 120 kcal to the recipe, that is, 30 kcal per serving)
- Sea salt (see Vol. 3, p. 16)

PREPARATION

❶ Soak the rice overnight in cold water or for 1 hour if hot water is used.

- Rinse and chop the cauliflower and the red pepper.
- Crush the tomato.
- Peel, chop, and pound the garlic and parsley using a mortar.

❷ Heat the oil in a large frying pan, and sauté the red pepper for 2 or 3 minutes. Add the cauliflower and then the tomato.

- When the liquid released by the sautéed vegetables has evaporated, add the rinsed rice and the boiling vegetable broth.
- Add salt and saffron. Boil at a high temperature for 5 to 10 minutes.
- Add the pounded garlic and parsley.
- Reduce the heat and simmer until the rice is done—tender, dry, and loose.
- Turn off the stove and let the dish stand for 5 minutes.

❸ Serve hot.

HEALTHIER ALTERNATIVE: Instead of sautéing the red peppers, cauliflower, and tomato, steam them for 10 minutes and then add the boiling vegetable broth and the rice.

For more information about the ingredients, see: Rice, Vol. 2, p. 225; cauliflower, Vol. 2, p. 154; pepper, Vol. 2, p. 198; tomato, Vol. 2, p. 275; garlic, Vol. 1, p. 338; and the *Encyclopedia of Medicinal Plants:* Garlic, p. 230.

HEALTH COUNSELS

Both rice and cauliflower have *low* **sodium** content, which helps the renal functioning. Additionally, they cause the blood to become more *alkaline* and this favors the elimination of **waste substances** circulating in the bloodstream. Most of these substances are acidic, such as the **uric acid.** For this reason, this dish is beneficial for:

✓The **kidneys,** since the dish stimulates their functioning and helps them to stay healthy.

✓The **arteries** and the **heart,** as it is a *very* ***low-sodium*** dish—especially if salt is not added—as well as low in ***fat,*** with *zero* ***cholesterol.*** Rice, especially whole rice, controls the cholesterol level in the blood, which protects the health of the arteries and the heart.

✓**Cancer** *prevention,* thanks to the ***fiber*** contained in rice and cauliflower, and to the ***anticarcinogenic phytochemicas*** of cauliflower.

NUTRITIONAL VALUE* per serving

Energy	**306 kcal = 1.278 kj**
Protein	**7.60 g**
Carbohydrates	**59.5 g**
Fiber	**4.99 g**
Total fat	***2.35 g***
Saturated fat	***0.451 g***
Cholesterol	**—**
Sodium	***27.0 mg***

1% 2% 4% 10% 20% 40% 100%

% Daily Value (based on a 2,000 calorie diet) provided by each serving of this dish

CALORIC PROPORTION*

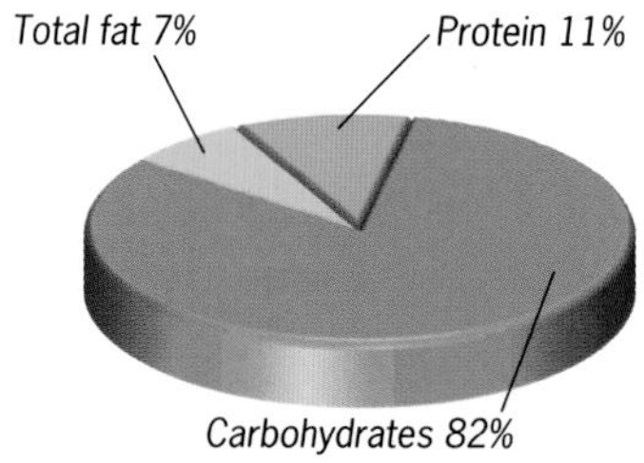

Percentage distribution of **calories for each nutrient**

*Additional ingredients are not included.

Preparation time 00:10

Cooking time 00:40

Fettuccini with Green Beans

INGREDIENTS (4 servings)

- 200 g (≅ 7 oz) of **fettuccini** (pasta)
- 250 g (≅ 8.8 oz) of green beans (string beans)
- 300 g (≅ 10.5 oz) of **Traditional Tomato Sauce** (Vol. 3, p. 62)
- 50 g (≅ 1.75 oz) of grated **mild cheese**

ADDITIONAL INGREDIENTS

- 2 tablespoons of olive **oil** (each tablespoon of oil adds around 120 kcal to the recipe, that is, 30 kcal per serving)
- Sea salt (see Vol. 3, p. 16)

PREPARATION

❶ Pull off the strings and cut off the ends of the beans. Wash and chop.

❷ Add the salt to half a liter of water and boil the green beans until tender but do not overcook. Rinse and put the broth aside.

- Add two cups of water to the broth and bring to a boil. Add the oil and the pasta.
- Boil until the pasta is *al dente* (firm to the bite) and rinse.
- Mix the fettuccini, green beans, and tomato sauce in an oven dish. Sprinkle grated cheese over the mixture and broil in the oven for 10-15 minutes.

❸ Serve hot.

HEALTHIER ALTERNATIVE: Instead of using cheese, try the "Grill without cheese" alternative (see Vol. 3, p. 73).

For more information about the ingredients, see: Pasta, Vol. 1, p. 74; green beans, Vol. 1, p. 109; tomato, Vol. 2, p. 275; fresh cheese, Vol. 1, p. 212; and the *Encyclopedia of Medicinal Plants:* green bean, p. 584.

HEALTH COUNSELS

Green beans are noted for their ***vitamins, minerals,*** and ***fiber,*** and for the ***active medicinal properties*** that help the kidneys and the heart to function better. However, they have a *low* level of ***carbohydrates*** and ***protein,*** which makes them combine well with pasta (rich in both nutrients). Tomatoes and cheese (or its corresponding substitute) add to the nutritious value of this dish, which is especially beneficial for:

✓ The **kidneys,** because of the *diuretic* effect of green beans which help to avoid the formation of kidney **stones** and of **edemas** (excess accumulation of serous fluid in tissue spaces).

✓ The **heart,** due to the *tonic* effect of green beans which helps increase the power of the heartbeat.

NUTRITIONAL VALUE* per serving

Energy	283 kcal = 1,181 kj
Protein	10.4 g
Carbohydrates	41.5 g
Fiber	4.04 g
Total fat	*6.83 g*
Saturated fat	*2.40 g*
Cholesterol	*5.75 mg*
Sodium	*58.2 mg*

1% 2% 4% 10% 20% 40% 100%

% Daily Value (based on a 2,000 calorie diet) provided by each serving of this dish

CALORIC PROPORTION*

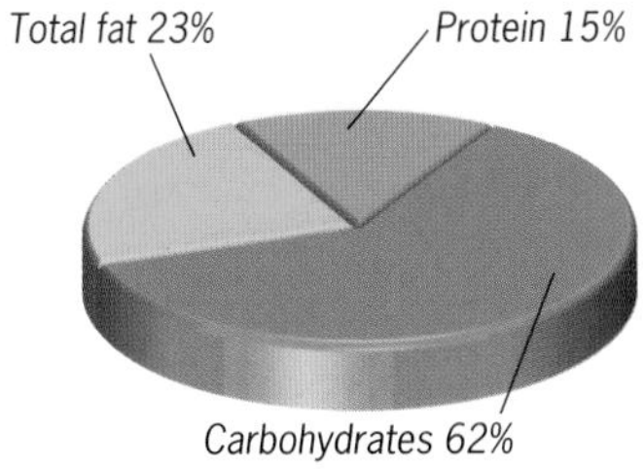

Percentage distribution of **calories for each nutrient**

*Additional ingredients are not included.

Preparation time 00:15

Cooking time 00:30

Asparagus Fondant

INGREDIENTS (4 servings)

- 500 g (≅ 1 pound) of **green asparagus**
- 400 g (≅ 14 oz) of long-grain parboiled **rice**
- 50 g (≅ 1.75 oz) of **quark cheese** (thick sour cream)
- 4 tablespoons of grated **cashews**
- 2 tablespoons of **brewer's yeast**

ADDITIONAL INGREDIENTS

- **Coriander**
- Sea **salt** (see Vol. 3, p. 16)

For more information about the ingredients, see: Asparagus, Vol. 2, p. 250; rice, Vol. 2, p. 225; quark cheese, Vol. 1, p. 213; cashew, Vol. 2, p. 40; brewer's yeast, Vol. 1, p. 358.

PREPARATION

❶ Peel the asparagus, remove the tough parts of the stems, and wash them.

- Tie up the asparagus using cooking thread.

❷ Bring to a boil a liter of water and place the asparagus bunch in the water in a vertical position. Cover the pot so that the asparagus tips may be steamed.

- When the stems are tender, remove from heat.
- Boil the rice (use twice the volume of water for each volume of rice). Boil rapidly for the first 5 minutes, and then simmer until the water has evaporated.
- To prepare the fondant, mix the cheese, the salt, the coriander, the brewer's yeast, and the grated cashews. Stir briskly with a fork.
- Cut the asparagus stems, blend them into purée and add them to the fondant.

❸ Serve in a plate the asparagus tips and the rice. Cover with the fondant.

HEALTHIER ALTERNATIVE: The fondant can be substituted by the "Alternative to Parmesan Cheese" (see Vol. 3, p. 73).

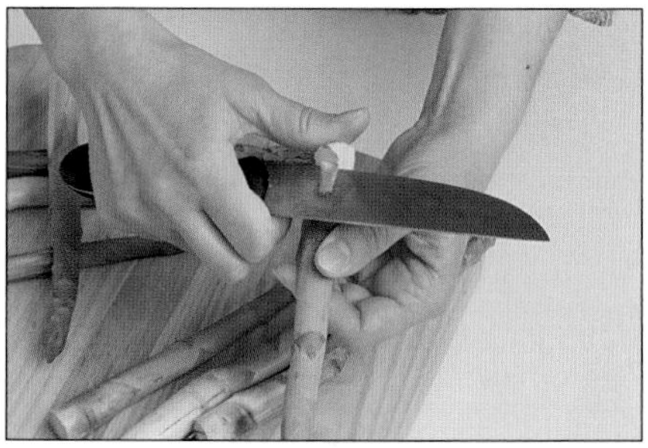

Remove the tough parts of the asparagus.

Tie up the asparagus using cooking thread.

Once the asparagus are boiled, set aside.

Mix the fondant ingredients.

Suggestions from the Chef

This dish can be decorated with **chopped, hard-boiled egg yolk.**

NUTRITIONAL VALUE*
per serving

Energy	472 kcal = 1,974 kj
Protein	14.0 g
Carbohydrates	85.1 g
Fiber	4.55 g
Total fat	*6.28 g*
Saturated fat	*1.39 g*
Cholesterol	*1.05 mg*
Sodium	*329 mg*

1% 2% 4% 10% 20% 40% 100%

% Daily Value (based on a 2,000 calorie diet) provided by each serving of this dish

HEALTH COUNSELS

This dish, with rice and asparagus as the base, is tasty and easy to digest. Its **cholesterol** content is *low,* and it becomes zero when the cheese is substituted with an alternative vegetarian sauce. It is especially beneficial to:

✓The **kidneys,** due to the *diuretic* action of asparagus.

✓The **stomach** and the **intestine,** as it is an *easily digested* dish. It is high in vegetable ***fiber,*** which exerts a *regulating* effect upon the ***intestinal functions.***

✓Control **obesity,** as this dish is a *satisfying,* low-calorie, nutritional dish due to the fiber contained in the asparagus.

Asparagine

Asparagine is an active substance contained in asparagus that is absorbed by the blood and quickly eliminated through the kidneys. This gives the urine a peculiar odor shortly after the consumption of asparagus.

CALORIC PROPORTION*

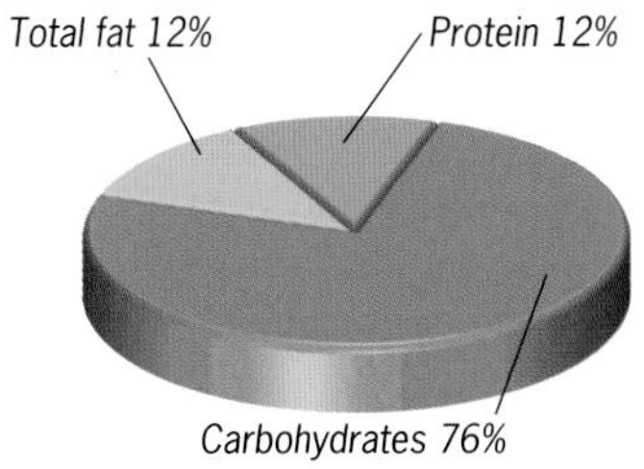

Percentage distribution of
calories for each nutrient

*Additional ingredients are not included.

Preparation time 00:20

Cooking time 00:40

Stuffed Artichokes

INGREDIENTS (4 servings)

- 8 artichokes (globe artichokes)
- 60 g (≅ 2 oz) of dehydrated **texturized vegetable soy protein**
- 1 **onion**
- 1 **garlic** clove
- 250 ml (≅ 1 cup) of **vegetable broth** (unsalted)

ADDITIONAL INGREDIENTS

- The juice of 1 **lemon**
- 1 tablespoon of **potherbs** (parsley, dill, marjoram)
- 3 tablespoons of olive **oil** (each tablespoon of oil adds around 120 kcal to the recipe, that is, 30 kcal per serving)
- Sea **salt** (see Vol. 3, p. 16)

PREPARATION

❶Soak the texturized vegetable soy protein in the vegetable broth.

- Peel and chop the onion and the garlic.
- Cut off the toughest outer leaves of the artichokes. Remove the tips. Wash and coat with lemon juice to avoid darkening.
- Cut each artichoke lengthwise into halves. Remove the inner fluff and place them in an oven dish.

❷Heat the oil in a pan, and sauté the onion. When it becomes transparent add the texturized vegetable protein and the potherbs. Stir and keep sautéing for 5 more minutes.

- Stuff the artichokes with the filling and bake in a 220°C oven until tender.
- Sprinkle with the chopped garlic a few minutes before removing from the oven.

❸Serve hot.

HEALTHIER ALTERNATIVE: Steam the ingredients instead of sautéing them.

Prepare the necessary ingredients.

Cut off the outer leaves of the artichokes.

Make the filling with onions, texturized vegetable soy protein, and aromatic leaves.

Suggestions from the Chef

- The filling can be enriched with tomato and red pepper sauce.
- It can be garnished with almond sauce (see Vol. 3, p. 232).

For more information about the ingredients, see: Artichoke, Vol. 2, p. 178; texturized vegetable soy protein, Vol. 1, p. 89; onion, Vol. 2, p. 142; garlic, Vol. 1, p. 338; and the *Encyclopedia of Medicinal Plants:* Garlic, p. 230.

NUTRITIONAL VALUE*
per serving

Energy	**200 kcal = 834 kj**
Protein	**34.7 g**
Carbohydrates	**9.82 g**
Fiber	**9.29 g**
Total fat	***1.52 g***
Saturated fat	***0.211 g***
Cholesterol	—
Sodium	***491 mg***

1% 2% 4% 10% 20% 40% 100%

% Daily Value (based on a 2,000 calorie diet) provided by each serving of this dish

HEALTH COUNSELS

Artichokes are not only beneficial to the liver, but also to the kidneys. Vegetable **protein,** supplied by the soybean in this recipe, taxes the kidneys' function less than animal protein. The vegetable broth is a good source of **minerals** and **trace elements.** As a whole, this is a tasty, nutritious recipe, especially recommended for:

- ✓The **urinary system,** due to the *diuretic* effect of artichokes, which contain **cynarin,** a property that facilitates the *cleansing* effect of the kidneys and allows for easy elimination of waste substances such as **urea.** Those suffering from **nephritis** (kidney inflammation), **nephrosis,** or **renal failure** may benefit from this recipe.
- ✓The **liver** and the **gallbladder,** because **cynarin** helps these two organs to function well.
- ✓The **arteries** and the **heart,** because both artichoke and soybeans help to *regulate* the levels of **cholesterol** in the blood. This *prevents* **arteriosclerosis** and *improves* **blood circulation.**

CALORIC PROPORTION*

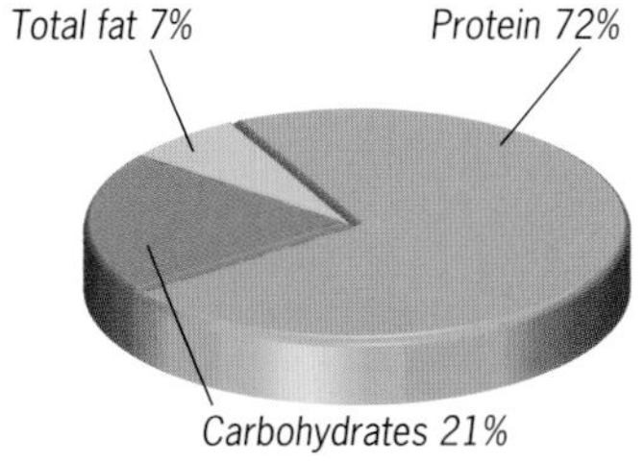

Percentage distribution of
calories for each nutrient

*Additional ingredients are not included.

Preparation time 00:10

Cooking time 00:40

Grecian Green Beans

INGREDIENTS (4 servings)

- 500 g (≅ 1 pound) of **green beans** (string beans)
- 500 g (≅ 1 pound) of **potatoes**
- 50 g (≅ 1.75 oz) of seedless **raisins**
- 50 g (≅ 1.75 oz) of raw peeled almonds
- 3 **garlic** cloves

ADDITIONAL INGREDIENTS

- 4 tablespoons of olive **oil** (each tablespoon of oil adds around 120 kcal to the recipe, that is, 30 kcal per serving)
- Sea **salt** (see Vol. 3, p. 16)

PREPARATION

❶ Peel, wash, and chop the potatoes.
- Cut off the tips and threads of the green beans. Chop them.

❷ Boil the green beans and the potatoes in plenty of water with salt for 20 minutes. Drain.
- Heat the oil in a frying pan, and sauté the garlic, almonds, and raisins. Add the potatoes and green beans and cook for an additional 20 minutes.

❸ Serve hot.

HEALTHIER ALTERNATIVE: Instead of sautéing the ingredients, place the green beans and potatoes in a baking dish, add oil, garlic, almonds, and raisins and bake at 220°C for 10 minutes.

For more information about the ingredients, see: Green bean, Vol. 1, p. 109; potato, Vol. 2, p. 201; raisins, Vol. 2, p. 81; almond, Vol. 2, p. 48; garlic, Vol. 1, p. 338; and the *Encyclopedia of Medicinal Plants:* green bean, p. 584; garlic, p. 230.

HEALTH COUNSELS

Green beans combine with potatoes very well and they are an ideal dish to maintain healthy kidneys. Adding almonds, raisins, and garlic enhances the nutritional value of this dish and its healing properties become especially good for:

✓ The **kidneys,** as green beans help to *eliminate* **waste substances.** Potatoes also increase the *cleansing* function of the kidneys. Potatoes and green beans are especially beneficial to those suffering from high **uric acid** or those predisposed to the formation of **kidney stones.**

✓ **Arteries** and **heart,** as this is a *low* ***fat*** and *low* ***sodium***—if less salt is added—dish and it does not contain *any* ***cholesterol.*** All these favor good circulation. Additionally, green beans *stimulate* the heart, and almonds supply ***essential fatty acids*** and ***vitamins from the B group*** which are essential for the proper function of the heart.

NUTRITIONAL VALUE* per serving

Energy	231 kcal = 966 kj
Protein	7.21 g
Carbohydrates	32.1 g
Fiber	7.73 g
Total fat	*6.85 g*
Saturated fat	*0.700 g*
Cholesterol	—
Sodium	*18.4 mg*

1% 2% 4% 10% 20% 40% 100%

% Daily Value (based on a 2,000 calorie diet) provided by each serving of this dish

CALORIC PROPORTION*

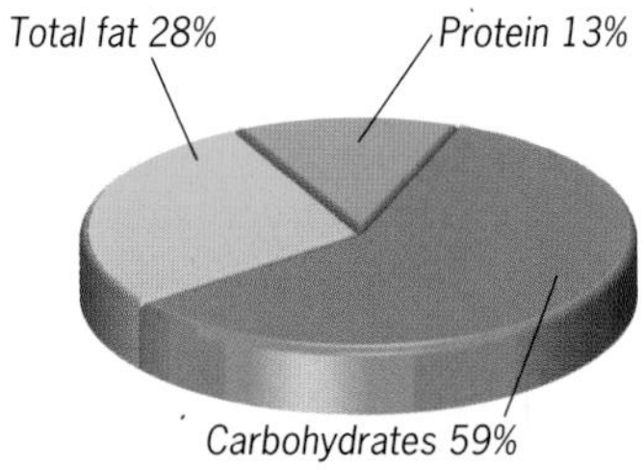

Percentage distribution of **calories for each nutrient**

*Additional ingredients are not included.

Preparation time 00:05

Cooking time 01:00

Eggplant Pie

INGREDIENTS

- 2 **eggplant**
- 2 sweet **red peppers**
- 2 **onions**
- 2 **tomatoes**
- 2 **garlic** cloves
- **Vegetable Pie dough** (Vol. 3, p. 104; to add color, mix in 2 tablespoons of paprika)
- 4 tablespoons of olive **oil**

ADDITIONAL INGREDIENTS

- Sea **salt** (see Vol. 3, p. 16)

PREPARATION

❶ Peel and chop the garlic and mix it with oil and salt.

❷ Bake the eggplants, the sweet red peppers, the onions, and the tomatoes (see Vol. 3, p. 384).

- Peel and cut the baked vegetables into strips. Add oil and garlic, and stir. Cover the tray with half the pie dough, arrange the vegetable filling, and cover with the remaining dough.
- Bake the pie as indicated in Vol. 3, p. 104.

❸ It can be eaten warm or cold.

For more information about the ingredients, see: Eggplant, Vol. 2, p. 256; pepper, Vol. 2, p. 198; onion, Vol. 2, p. 142; tomato, Vol. 2, p. 275; garlic, Vol. 1, p. 338; and the *Encyclopedia of Medicinal Plants:* Garlic, p. 230.

Suggestions from the Chef

This is an excellent dish to be taken when traveling or on an excursion because it can be eaten cold.

HEALTH COUNSELS

The Eggplant Pie contains vegetables such as eggplant, peppers, onions, and tomatoes that have an *alkaline* effect on the body and facilitate the *cleansing* function of the kidneys. Additionally, this is a recipe *high* in **vitamins** and **antioxidant phytochemicals,** which *protect* against **arteriosclerosis, cancer,** and **premature aging.** Therefore, this recipe is especially beneficial to:

✓ The **urinary system,** due to the *diuretic* action of eggplant and to the *alkaline* effect of the remaining vegetables, which help in the *cleansing* function of the kidneys. It is highly recommended to keep blood "clean" and maintain healthy kidneys.

✓ The **arteries** and the **heart,** due to the ***antioxidants*** contained in these vegetables, which *prevent* the formation of **cholesterol** deposits in the arteries.

✓ **Cancer** prevention, for its high content in *protective* elements.

NUTRITIONAL VALUE* per 100 g

Energy	173 kcal = 723 kj
Protein	2.72 g
Carbohydrates	15.6 g
Fiber	1.87 g
Total fat	*10.6 g*
Saturated fat	*1.44 g*
Cholesterol	—
Sodium	*4.05 mg*

1% 2% 4% 10% 20% 40% 100%

% Daily Value (based on a 2,000 calorie diet) provided by each serving of this dish

CALORIC PROPORTION*

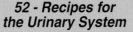

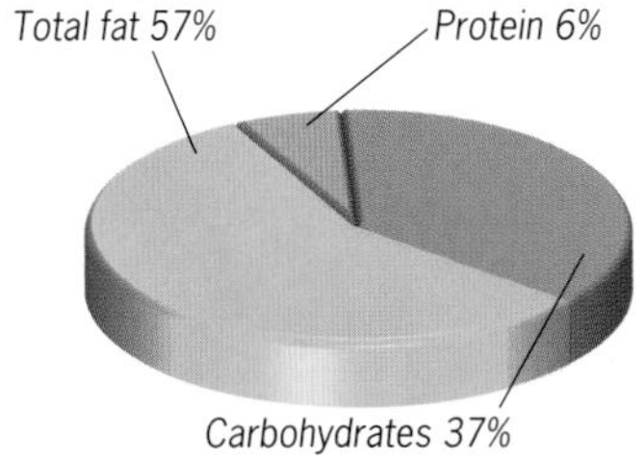

Percentage distribution of
calories for each nutrient

*Additional ingredients are not included.

Preparation time 00:20 | Cooking time 01:00

Celery Pie

INGREDIENTS

- 400 g (≅ 14 oz) of **celery**
- 300 g (≅ 10.6 oz) of **cauliflower**
- 300 g of (≅ 10.6 oz) **chestnuts** (they can be substituted for potatoes)
- 1 **onion**
- 50 g (≅ 2/3 cup) of **peas**
- 4 tablespoons of **hazelnut butter** (Vol. 3, p. 65)
- **Vegetable pie dough** (Vol. 3, p. 104; use half of the ingredients in this dish)

ADDITIONAL INGREDIENTS

- **Coriander**
- **Soy sauce** (tamari or miso) (each tablespoon of this sauce adds 857 mg of sodium to the recipe, that is, around 214 mg of sodium per serving; see Vol. 3, p. 16)
- **Mashed potatoes**

PREPARATION

❶ Peel and chop the onion.
- Wash and chop the cauliflower and the celery.

❷ Roll the pie dough over an oven dish and bake it at 220°C until golden.
- Boil and peel the chestnuts.
- In a separate pot boil cauliflower, celery, onions, and peas.
- Blend all vegetables in the form of a purée; add the soy sauce and pour the mixture over the pie dough.
- Using a fork, make some grooves on the surface for decoration. Bake in a hot oven at a high temperature for 10 minutes.
- Grill for a few more minutes until the surface is golden.

❸ Serve hot, decorated with thick mashed potatoes.

For more information about the ingredients, see: Celery, Vol. 2, p. 248; cauliflower, Vol. 2, p. 154; chestnut, Vol. 2, p. 322; onion, Vol. 2, p. 142; peas, Vol. 2, p. 73; hazelnut, Vol. 2, p. 252.

HEALTH COUNSELS

Celery Pie is prepared with ingredients that are especially beneficial to the kidneys, particularly celery. All stimulate **urine** *production* and the *elimination* of **toxic substances.**

For this reason, this celery pie is recommended to those suffering from **kidney stones,** high **uric acid,** urinary **sediments** or **fluid retention** (edema).

Pregnancy

*It is not advisable for **pregnant** women to eat celery during the first three months of gestation, as it can stimulate **uterine contractions,** and increase the risk of miscarriage.*

NUTRITIONAL VALUE* per 100 g

Nutrient	Value
Energy	150 kcal = 628 kj
Protein	3.21 g
Carbohydrates	18.1 g
Fiber	3.30 g
Total fat	*6.14 g*
Saturated fat	*0.729 g*
Cholesterol	—
Sodium	*29.6 mg*

1% 2% 4% 10% 20% 40% 100%

% Daily Value (based on a 2,000 calorie diet) provided by each 100 g of this dish

CALORIC PROPORTION*

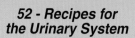

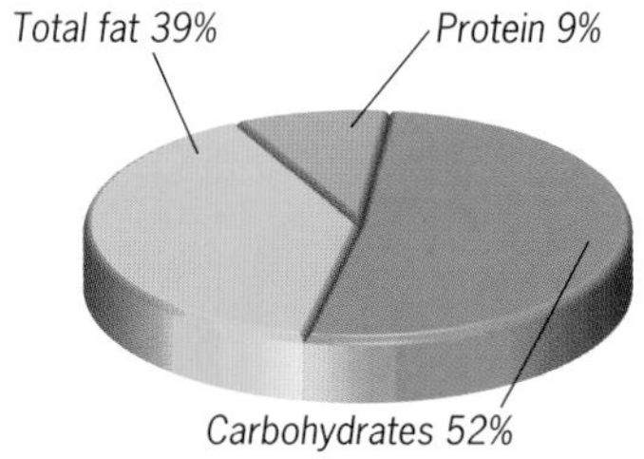

Percentage distribution of **calories for each nutrient**

*Additional ingredients are not included.

Preparation time: 00:15

Cooking time: - - - -

Hazelnut Milk

INGREDIENTS (4 servings)

- 4 tablespoons of **hazelnut butter** (Vol. 3, p. 65)
- 1 liter of **water**

PREPARATION

❶ Place the water and the hazelnut butter (Vol. 3, p. 65) in a pitcher-like container.

❷ Beat with a hand blender until the mixture is smooth.

- If hazelnut butter sediments are to be eliminated, pass through a cloth.

❸ Serve hot or cold.

For more information about the ingredients, see: Hazelnut, Vol. 2, p. 252.

NUTRITIONAL VALUE per serving

Energy	126 kcal = 528 kj
Protein	2.61 g
Carbohydrates	1.84 g
Fiber	1.22 g
Total fat	*12.5 g*
Saturated fat	*0.921 g*
Cholesterol	—
Sodium	*0.600 mg*

1% 2% 4% 10% 20% 40% 100%

% Daily Value (**based on a 2,000 calorie diet**) provided by each serving of this drink

HEALTH COUNSELS

Hazelnut Milk is a refreshing and nutritious drink, which shares the preventive properties of this nut. For this reason, it is beneficial to:

✓ The **kidneys,** because it *prevents* the formation of **stones.** This is why the drink is appropriate for those suffering from renal colic.

✓ **Diabetes,** since this drink, in spite of its significant energy contribution, supplies *few* ***carbohydrates*** provided no sugar is added.

CALORIC PROPORTION

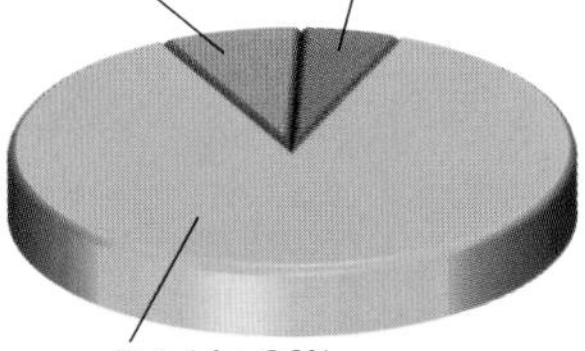

Percentage distribution of
calories for each nutrient

Suggestions from the Chef

This drink may be sweetened using brown sugar or honey.

Preparation time: 00:15

Cooking time: ----

Watermelon Shake

INGREDIENTS (4 servings)

- 1 **watermelon** (1 kg pulp)

PREPARATION

❶ Cut and gather the pulp.

❷ Blend the pulp, including the seeds.
- Sift in order to catch the seed remains.

❸ Serve cold.

For more information about the ingredients, see: Watermelon, Vol. 2, p. 251.

Watermelon Cure

In order to carry out a watermelon cure, it is ideal to combine this shake with the fruit itself.

*The **seeds** are also edible and their nutritional value is comparable to that of nuts.*

HEALTH COUNSELS

Watermelon is one of the most refreshing fruits. Besides its supply of **vitamins** and **minerals,** it significantly *stimulates* the kidneys to produce **urine.** This makes it recommended for:

✓The **kidneys** and the **urinary tract,** due to its *diuretic* action, which is superior to that of melon. It is helpful to those suffering from **kidney stones,** both to help eliminate them in the case of renal **colic** and to prevent their formation.

✓The **intestine,** due to its *laxative* action.

✓The control of **obesity,** due to its *satisfying* effect and the *low* level of *calories.*

NUTRITIONAL VALUE per serving

Energy	80 kcal = 334 kj
Protein	1.55 g
Carbohydrates	16.7 g
Fiber	1.25 g
Total fat	*1.08 g*
Saturated fat	*0.120 g*
Cholesterol	—
Sodium	*5.00 mg*

1% 2% 4% 10% 20% 40% 100%

% Daily Value (based on a 2,000 calorie diet) provided by each serving of this shake

CALORIC PROPORTION

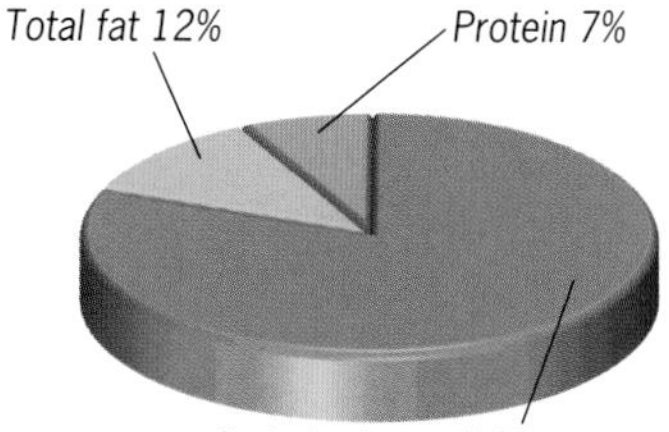

Percentage distribution of **calories for each nutrient**

Preparation time

00:10

Cooking time

00:25

Sweet Corn Drink

INGREDIENTS (4 servings)

- 100 g (≅ 3.5 oz) of sweet **corn**
- 3 teaspoons of **honey**
- 1 liter (≅ 1 quart) of **water**
- 2 **lemons**

PREPARATION

❶ Squeeze the lemons and set aside the juice.
- Wash the lemon rind and the corn.

❷ Boil the corn and lemon rind until tender.
- Drain and reserve the corn for a different recipe.

❸ Serve cold or hot. Add the lemon juice and honey immediately before drinking.

For more information about the ingredients, see: Corn, Vol. 2, p. 238; honey, Vol. 1, p. 160; lemon, Vol. 2, p. 124; and the *Encyclopedia of Medicinal Plants:* corn, p. 599.

HEALTH COUNSELS

Sweet Corn Drink may be considered as a corn and lemon rind decoction. Besides being aromatic and refreshing, it provides the kidneys and the digestive system with the beneficial properties of corn. It is especially recommended for:

✓The **kidneys,** as it contributes to urine production (*diuretic* effect) and the elimination of the wastes that circulate in the bloodstream (*blood cleansing* effect). Those suffering from **renal failure,** excess of **uric acid, kidney stones,** and **urinary infections,** would greatly benefit from this corn drink.

✓The **circulatory system** and the **heart,** as it helps to prevent **high-blood pressure** and **edema** (accumulation of serous fluid in tissue spaces)

✓The **intestine,** due to the *soothing* effect of corn in case of **dyspepsia, irritable bowel syndrome,** and **colitis.**

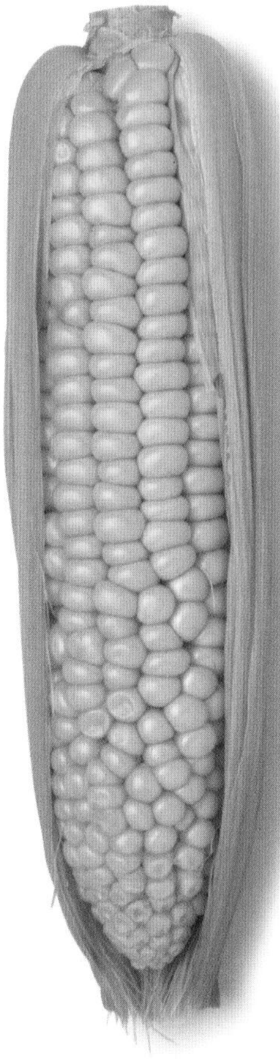

Suggestions from the Chef

If this drink seems too acid to the taste, reduce the amount of lemon juice.

53 Recipes for The Reproductive System

Chapter Summary

Recipes

Sardinian Adzuki 302
Seed Salad 298
Sesame Crepes 304
Soy Milk 305
Stuffed Tomatoes 300
Tofu Salad 299
Vegetarian Tamales 301

The reproductive functions of men and women may be enhanced in a natural way by the recipes in this chapter. In addition, these recipes contribute to the prevention of breast cancer and prostate cancer, which are among the most frequent forms of cancer in our days.

Out of all the ingredients in these recipes, the **soybean** is the most notable for its effective action upon the reproductive system: It prevents and relieves the symptoms of **menopause,** favors the hormonal balance, is an excellent nutritional source for **pregnant** women, and *protects against* **breast cancer** and **prostate cancer.** This is due to its outstanding combination of protein, essential fatty acids, vitamins, minerals, and phytochemical elements such as ***isoflavones*** (see Vol. 2, p. 267).

Cholesterol is one of the greatest enemies of male sexual potency, as it settles in the arteries and impedes the free flow of blood into the penis. This makes the erection mechanism difficult.

Foods included in this chapter's recipes do not contain any cholesterol and help to reduce its level in the blood. This helps to preserve male sexual potency.

Additionally, soy-based products contain vegetable hormones or phytoestrogens such as isoflavones. These natural substances promote the hormonal balance, especially in women. This produces an invigorating effect upon sexual life.

THE FOLLOWING is a statement from Dr. Isidro Aguilar in Vol. 1, p. 36 of his *Encyclopedia of Health and Education for the Family,* which is part of this EDUCATION AND HEALTH LIBRARY:

"The lifestyle and the particular means of nutrition significantly influence the conservation of all the human potentials. For example, the prestigious medical magazine "The Lancet" has recently published the results of a study directed by Doctor Tina Kold Jeusen of the Rigshospital of Copenhagen (Denmark), where it is shown that men who eat ecologically cultivated food produce 43% more spermatozoids than the normal population. This significant increase does not seem, according to this study, to be due only to the eating of food not treated with pesticides, but also to the healthier lifestyle, in all aspects, which is carried out by those who eat natural products."

The Prostate Gland

Tomatoes are also prescriptive in recipes for the male reproductive system, due to the presence of ***lycopene*** (see Vol. 2, p. 276). This is a carotene-based substance that gives tomatoes their red color, and serves as an antioxidant and a protector of the prostate gland.

In addition to soybeans, tomatoes, and other lifestyle-related habits, the following are also beneficial in keeping the prostate (see Vol. 2, p. 262) healthy, even in old age: zinc, magnesium, bee pollen, fiber, and two essential fatty acids—linoleic and linolenic acids. On the other hand, it is advisable to eliminate:

- **Coffee,** as the essential oils that produce its aroma irritate the urinary ducts and the prostate.
- **Tobacco, alcohol, vinegar, salty foods, sausages,** and **hot spices** such as chile or hot pepper.

Menus for

Menopause

Apples

BREAKFAST

- Freshly squeezed orange juice with wheat germ (Vol. 2, pp. 360, 310)
- Apples (Vol. 2, p. 229)
- "Rice Pudding" (Vol. 3, p. 199)
- Evening primrose oil (*EMP*, p. 237)

LUNCH

- Lemon and grapefruit juice (Vol. 2, p. 124, 93)
- "Tofu Salad" (Vol. 3, p. 299)
- "Soybean Stew" (Vol. 3, p. 381)
- "Whole bread" (Vol. 3, p. 46; Vol. 1, p. 72)
- "Infusion of Mugwort" (*EMP*, p. 624)

Lemon and grapefruit juice

Cashew Stew

SUPPER

- "Cashew Stew" (Vol. 3, p. 150)
- Feijoa, kiwi, or orange (Vol. 2, pp. 263, 356, 360)

HEALTH COUNSELS

This menu supplies ***phytoestrogens*** (vegetable hormones)—enhancers of hormonal balance—which are contained in tofu and soybeans. Additionally, it supplies **vitamin E** from wheat germ, and essential fatty acids from evening primrose oil. Consequently, it is recommended to women approaching **menopause,** in order to alleviate the typical discomforts of this stage. It is also appropriate for young women with **dysmenorrhea** (painful period).

Sexual Impotence

BREAKFAST

- Cleansing broth and lemon juice (Vol. 1, p. 369; Vol. 2, p. 124)
- Apricots (Vol. 2, p. 26)
- "Cereal Bars" (Vol. 3, p. 174)
- "Soy Milk" (Vol. 3, p. 305)

Cereal Bars

LUNCH

- Carrot juice (Vol. 2, p. 25)
- "Seed Salad" (Vol. 3, p. 298)
- "Mung Bean Stew" (Vol. 3, p. 315)
- Walnuts (Vol. 2, p. 64)
- "Whole Bread" (Vol. 3, p. 46; Vol. 1, p. 72)
- Ginseng (*EMP*, p. 608)

Mung Bean Stew

SUPPER

- "Soy Croquettes" (Vol. 3, p. 326)
- "Sesame Crepes" (Vol. 3, p. 304)
- Infusion of Damiana (*EMP*, p. 613)

Soy Croquettes

HEALTH COUNSELS

This is a very healthy menu that, due to its *high content* in ***vitamin A*** and ***vitamin E,*** as well as in ***zinc*** and other ***trace minerals,*** offers a *stimulating* effect upon sexuality. The ***phytoestrogens*** contained in soybeans contribute to hormonal balance.

It is advisable in the case of low sexual **desire** both in men and women. It contributes to prevent and cure male sexual **impotence.**

the Reproductive System

Prostate maladies

Soy Milk

BREAKFAST

- Soaked prunes (Vol. 2, p. 235)
- "Soy Milk" (Vol. 3, p. 305)
- Toasted "Whole Bread" with sugarcane syrup and pumpkin, sesame, and sunflower seeds sprinkled on top (Vol. 3, p. 46; Vol. 2, p. 99; Vol. 1, pp. 72, 352)

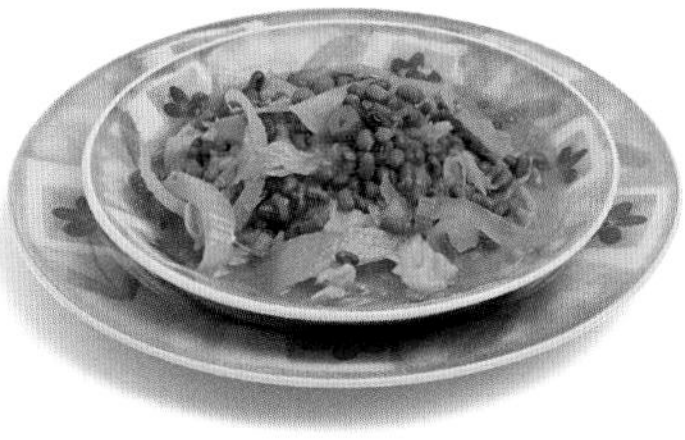

Sardinian Adzuki

LUNCH

- "Stuffed Tomatoes" (Vol. 3, p. 300)
- "Sardinian Adzuki" (Vol. 3, pp. 302)
- "Rye Bread" (Vol. 3, p. 194)
- Bearberry infusion (*EMP,* p. 564)

SUPPER

- Tomato and onion salad (Vol. 2, pp. 275, 142)
- "Stuffed Peppers" (Vol. 3, p. 382)
- Echinacea infusion (*EMP,* p. 755)

Stuffed Peppers

HEALTH COUNSELS

This menu is especially designed for men who wish to use dietary measures to prevent **prostate** problems. The soybeans, other seeds, and tomatoes supply active ingredients to avoid prostatic **hypertrophy** (excessive growth of the prostate gland).

Prunes fight constipation, a condition that can worsen the urinary problems caused by prostate hypertrophy.

Other Recipes for the Reproductive System

SALADS

- "Sprouts Salad" (Vol. 3, p. 244)
- "Chickpea Salad" (Vol. 3, p. 186)
- "Mexican Salad" (Vol. 3, p. 260)

SOUPS AND PURÉES

- "Cereal Soup" (Vol. 3, p. 314)
- "Oat Soup" (Vol. 3, p. 147)

MAIN COURSES

- "Chinese Noodles" (Vol. 3, p. 316)
- "Borage and Potatoes" (Vol. 3, p. 362)
- "Vegetable Turnovers" (Vol. 3, p. 106)
- "Vegetarian Tamales" (Vol. 3, p. 301)
- "Rice Hamburgers" (Vol. 3, p. 170)

BREAKFASTS, DESSERTS AND SNACKS

- "Tofu and Herbs Spread" (Vol. 3, p. 66)
- "Granola" (Vol. 3, p. 156)
- "Muesli" (Vol. 3, p. 175)
- "Lentil Spread" (Vol. 3, p. 67)

DRINKS

- "Vegetable Juice" (Vol. 3, p. 385)
- "Melon and Orange Juice" (Vol. 3, p. 367)

Freshly squeezed juices:

- Cabbage (Vol. 2, p. 191)
- Tomato (Vol. 2, p. 275)

- *See the recipe index at the beginning of this volume (Vol. 3, pp. 8-13).*
- *See also chapter 30, "Foods for the Reproductive System" (Vol. 2, pp. 260-277).*

EMP = Encyclopedia of Medicinal Plants, Education and Health Library, Editorial Safeliz.

Preparation time 00:30

Cooking time - - - -

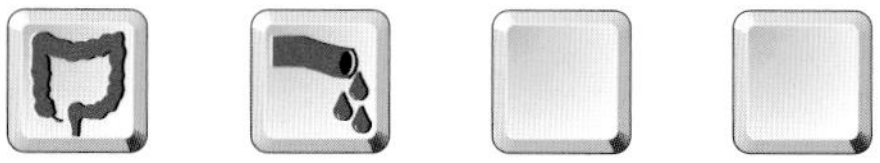

Seed Salad

INGREDIENTS (4 servings)

- 100 g (≅ 3.5 oz) of **alfalfa** sprouts
- 1 **endive**
- 100 g (≅ 3.5 oz) of shelled **walnuts**
- 2 **carrots**
- 2 **apples**
- 1 **Welsh onion**
- 1 **celery** stalk
- 1 tablespoon of roasted **sesame**
- 2 tablespoons of shelled **sunflower seeds**
- 1 tablespoon of **brewer's yeast**

ADDITIONAL INGREDIENTS

- **Basil**
- The juice of 1/2 lemon
- 4 tablespoons of olive **oil** (each tablespoon of oil adds around 120 kcal to the recipe, that is, 30 kcal per serving)
- Sea **salt** (see Vol. 3, p. 16)

PREPARATION

❶ Wash and chop the endive and the celery stalk.

- Peel, wash, and chop the carrots and Welsh onions.
- Peel, core, and slice the apples.
- Arrange the vegetables, apples, basil, chopped walnuts, and alfalfa sprouts on plates.

❷ For the dressing, grind in a mortar the sesame and sunflower seeds together with the salt; add brewer's yeast, oil, and lemon juice.

❸ Dress when serving.

HEALTHIER ALTERNATIVE: One or two tablespoons of wheat germ may be added to each plate (see Vol. 2, p. 310).

For more information about the ingredients, see: Alfalfa, Vol. 2, p 130; endive, Vol. 2, p.176; walnut, Vol. 2, p. 64; carrot, Vol. 2, p. 25; apple, Vol. 2, p. 229; Welsh onion, Vol. 2, p.144; celery, Vol. 2, p. 248; sesame, Vol. 1, p. 352; sunflower seeds, Vol. 2, p. 105; brewer's yeast, Vol. 1, p. 358; and the *Encyclopedia of Medicinal Plants:* sesame, p. 611.

HEALTH COUNSELS

This salad offers a wealth in both sprouted seeds (alfalfa) and non-sprouted seeds (walnuts). Both, with the accompanying vegetables, supply nutrients and elements especially beneficial to:

✓ The **reproductive organs,** because these seeds are high in ***essential fatty acids,*** such as ***linoleic acid*** (necessary for the synthesis of prostaglandins). These are substances that intervene in several organic functions, including those associated with the reproductive system. Seeds also supply ***vitamin E***—the so-called reproduction vitamin.

✓ The **intestine,** because of the ***enzymes*** supplied by the alfalfa sprouts and the raw vegetables that *facilitate* the **digestive process.**

✓ The **blood,** due to the presence of ***iron*** and other ***minerals*** that are necessary for blood production.

NUTRITIONAL VALUE* per serving

Energy	303 kcal = 1,267 kj
Protein	8.96 g
Carbohydrates	19.4 g
Fiber	8.69 g
Total fat	*20.3 g*
Saturated fat	*2.00 g*
Cholesterol	—
Sodium	*59.2 mg*

1% 2% 4% 10% 20% 40% 100%

% Daily Value (based on a 2,000 calorie diet) provided by each serving of this dish

CALORIC PROPORTION*

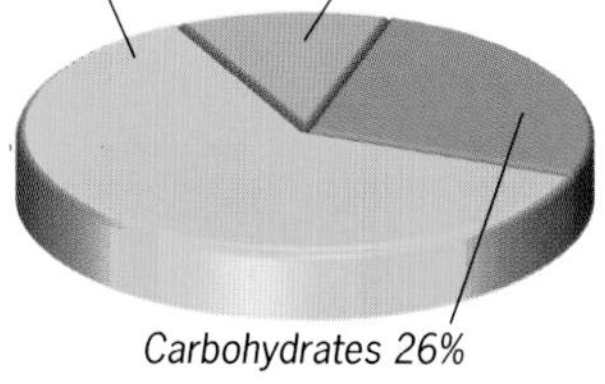

Percentage distribution of **calories for each nutrient**

*Additional ingredients are not included.

Preparation time 00:30 | Cooking time 00:10

Tofu Salad

INGREDIENTS (4 servings)

- 400 g (≅ 14 oz) of **tofu** (soybean curd)
- 200 g (≅ 7 oz) of **carrots**
- 1 **lettuce** core
- 1 **cucumber**
- 1 Welsh **onion**
- 1 **celery** stalk

ADDITIONAL INGREDIENTS

- 3 tablespoons of **soy sauce** (each tablespoon of this sauce adds 857 mg of sodium to the recipe, that is, around 214 mg per serving; see Vol. 3, p. 16)
- The juice of 1 **lemon**
- 1 teaspoon of **honey**
- 1 teaspoon of sesame **oil** (each tablespoon of oil adds around 120 kcal to the recipe, that is, 30 kcal per serving)

PREPARATION

❶Peel, wash, and slice the Welsh onion in fine rings.

- Wash the celery stalk and chop fine.
- Cut the cucumber lengthwise into two halves, remove the seeds, and cut into thin, long strips.
- Peel the carrots and cut them into thin, long strips.
- Separate the leaves of the lettuce core and wash them.
- Prepare the dressing by mixing the soy sauce, lemon juice, sesame seed oil, and honey.
- Cut tofu into large cubes.

❷Soak the tofu in warm water until it floats. Remove from the water and allow to cool. Using your hands, pull to pieces and marinate in the dressing for a few minutes.

❸Arrange the leaves of lettuce in a soup bowl and add the vegetables and the dressed tofu.

HEALTHIER ALTERNATIVE: In order to lower the sodium intake, use only lemon juice and oil as dressing and omit salt.

For more information about the ingredients, see: Tofu, Vol. 1, p. 88; carrot, Vol. 2, p. 25; lettuce, Vol. 2, p. 45; cucumber, Vol. 2, p. 339; Welsh onion, Vol. 2, p. 144; celery, Vol. 2, p. 248.

HEALTH COUNSELS

Tofu is to soy milk as cheese is to cow's milk. It is *rich* in ***protein, calcium,*** and other ***minerals.*** Its taste is neutral and it can easily absorb the taste of the corresponding dressing. Whether raw or cooked, its consistency is juicy and pleasant. From the culinary point of view, this makes tofu quite versatile.

Tofu can advantageously substitute cheese and provide benefits in the area of health. It contains *zero* ***cholesterol*** as well as ***isoflavones*** (see Vol. 1, p. 411) in greater proportion than any other soy product. Tofu Salad is especially recommended for:

✓The **reproductive organs,** due to the favorable effect of isoflavones.

✓The **musculoskeletal system,** as it *prevents* **osteoporosis.**

✓The **arteries,** as it *reduces* **cholesterol.**

NUTRITIONAL VALUE* per serving

Energy	**117 kcal = 490 kj**
Protein	**9.84 g**
Carbohydrates	**6.88 g**
Fiber	**4.08 g**
Total fat	***5.09 g***
Saturated fat	***0.748 g***
Cholesterol	—
Sodium	***52.4 mg***

1% 2% 4% 10% 20% 40% 100%

% Daily Value (based on a 2,000 calorie diet) provided by each serving of this dish

CALORIC PROPORTION*

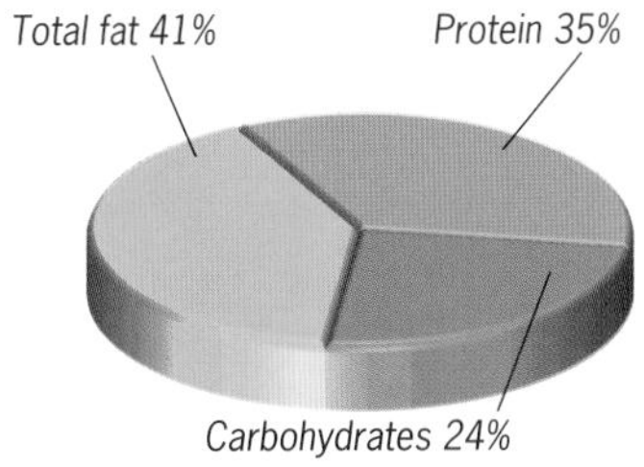

Percentage distribution of **calories for each nutrient**

*Additional ingredients are not included.

Preparation time 00:15 | Cooking time 00:20

Stuffed Tomatoes

INGREDIENTS (4 servings)

- 4 **tomatoes**
- 100 g (≅ 2/3 oz) of **peas**
- 1 **onion**
- 1 **cucumber**
- 1 head of **lettuce**
- 50 g (≅ 1.75 oz) of **green olives**

ADDITIONAL INGREDIENTS

- 4 tablespoons of olive **oil** (each tablespoon of oil adds around 120 kcal to the recipe, that is, 30 kcal per serving)
- The juice of 1 **lemon**
- Sea **salt** (see Vol. 3, p. 16)

PREPARATION

❶ Wash and chop the head of lettuce. Peel and chop the cucumber and the onion.
- Wash the tomatoes, remove their tops, empty and chop the pulp.

❷ Boil the peas in salted water. Rinse and let cool.
- Mix vegetables and olives.
- Add oil, lemon juice, and salt.
- Stuff the tomatoes with the mixture.

❸ Serve cold.

For more information about the ingredients, see: Tomato, Vol. 2, p. 275; pea, Vol. 2, p. 73; onion, Vol. 2, p. 142; cucumber, Vol. 2, p. 339; lettuce, Vol. 2, p. 45; olive, Vol. 2, p. 165.

HEALTH COUNSELS

Raw tomatoes, stuffed with vegetables and peas, form a very healthy dish *high* in ***vitamins*** and ***antioxidant phytochemicals***—for example, ***vitamin C,*** and ***lycopene*** in tomatoes, and ***flavonoids*** in onions. This dish is beneficial to the entire organism, and especially to:

✓ The **reproductive** organs, and particularly the **prostate gland,** due to the *preventive* action of tomatoes against **cancer** and the **hypertrophy** of this gland. The other vegetables included in this recipe *reinforce* the tomato's antioxidant and *preventive* effects.

✓ The **arteries** and the **heart,** because this recipe supplies ***antioxidant substances,*** which *avoid* **cholesterol** deposits in the arteries and favor blood **circulation.**

✓ **Cancer** *prevention,* especially that of **prostate, stomach, colon,** and **breast.**

NUTRITIONAL VALUE* per serving

Energy	106 kcal = 441 kj
Protein	5.52 g
Carbohydrates	13.6 g
Fiber	6.46 g
Total fat	*1.75 g*
Saturated fat	*0.246 g*
Cholesterol	—
Sodium	*84.1 mg*

1% 2% 4% 10% 20% 40% 100%

% **Daily Value** (based on a 2,000 calorie diet) provided by each serving of this dish

CALORIC PROPORTION*

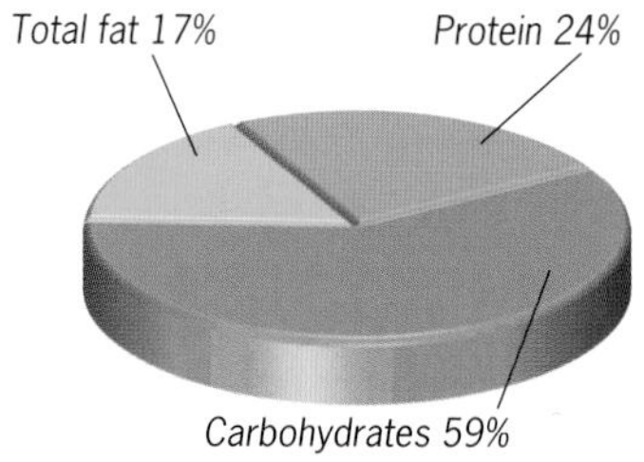

Percentage distribution of **calories for each nutrient**

*Additional ingredients are not included.

Preparation time 00:20

Cooking time 02:30

Vegetarian Tamales

INGREDIENTS (6 servings)

- 150 g (≅ 5.3 oz) of black **beans**
- 150 g (≅ 5.3 oz) of shelled, toasted **pumpkin** (squash) **seeds**
- 1 **chayote** (vegetable pear)
- 1 **zucchini** (courgette)
- $^{1}/_{2}$ kg (≅ 1 pound) of **cornmeal**
- 2 liters (≅ 2 quarts) of **water**

ADDITIONAL INGREDIENTS

- 6 tablespoons of olive **oil** (each tablespoon of oil adds around 120 kcal to the recipe, that is, 30 kcal per serving)
- **Coriander**
- 4 **banana** or **corn** leaves
- Sea **salt** (see Vol. 3, p. 16)

PREPARATION

❶ Soak beans overnight.
- Chop the chayote, the zucchini, and the coriander.
- Mix the oil, salt, and cornmeal to form dough. As the dough is being formed, add one-half cup of water little by little, until the dough may be rolled without tearing.

❷ Boil the beans in salted water until tender. Rinse.
- Grate the pumpkin seeds with a little water. Mix with beans, chayote, zucchini, and coriander to prepare the filling.
- Spread a portion of the corn dough over each banana/corn leaf. Place a tablespoon of filling on each center and roll. Wrap in the leaf and tie with cooking thread.
- Place the wrapped tamales in a pot with plenty of water and boil for 1 hour.

❸ Serve hot.

For more information about the ingredients, see: Bean (common bean), Vol. 2, p. 343; pumpkin seeds, Vol. 2, p. 99; chayote, Vol. 1, p. 107; zucchini, Vol. 2, p. 159; flour, Vol. 1, p. 69.

HEALTH COUNSELS

Vegetarian Tamales are Hispanic-American in origin. Among the many advantages of this dish is the combination of ***protein*** from a cereal (corn) with protein from a legume (beans). This produces a ***high-quality biological protein.*** The dish is especially beneficial for:

✓ The **reproductive organs,** especially the **prostate gland.** This is due to the pumpkin seeds that *slow down* the **excessive growth** of this gland.

✓ **Pregnant** women, due to **protein, iron, folates,** and other essential nutrients contained in this dish.

✓ The **skin,** because of the bean's *high content* in ***niacin,*** which *prevents* **pellagra** and *maintains* a healthy **complexion.**

NUTRITIONAL VALUE* per serving

Energy	**479 kcal = 2,001 kj**
Protein	**14.4 g**
Carbohydrates	**61.7 g**
Fiber	**15.0 g**
Total fat	***15.1 g***
Saturated fat	***2.71 g***
Cholesterol	—
Sodium	***13.3 mg***

1% 2% 4% 10% 20% 40% 100%

% Daily Value **(based on a 2,000 calorie diet)** provided by each serving of this dish

CALORIC PROPORTION*

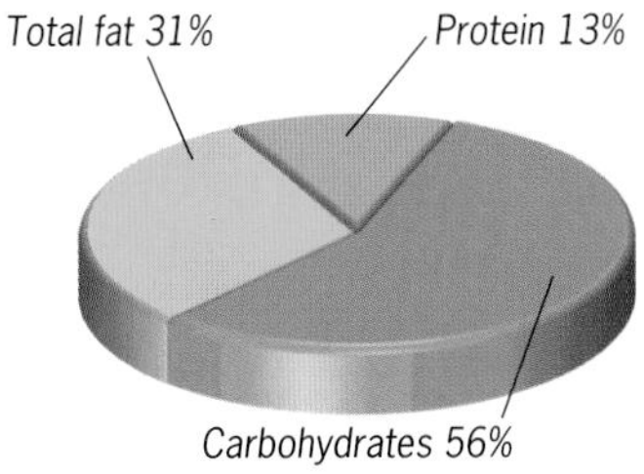

Percentage distribution of **calories for each nutrient**

*Additional ingredients are not included.

Preparation time 00:20

Cooking time 01:00

Sardinian Adzuki

INGREDIENTS (4 servings)

- 300 g (≅ 10.6 oz) of **adzuki**
- 500 g (≅ 1 pound) of **cabbage**
- 1 **fennel** bulb
- 1 **onion**
- 160 g (≅ 5.6 oz) of **Traditional Tomato Sauce** (Vol. 3, p. 62)
- 2 **garlic** cloves
- $1^1/_2$ liters (≅ $1\,^1/_2$ quarts) of **water**

ADDITIONAL INGREDIENTS

- 1 **laurel** leaf
- Sea **salt** (see Vol. 3, p. 16)

PREPARATION

❶ Clean the adzuki of possible impurities and soak overnight.
- Clean and cut the cabbage and fennel into strips.
- Chop the onion.
- Peel and chop the garlic.

❷ Boil the adzuki in water at a high temperature for 10 minutes.
- Add vegetables and laurel leaf and reduce to medium heat.
- Add salt and, 15 minutes later, add the chopped garlic and the tomato sauce. Boil until the adzuki is tender.

❸ Serve hot.

HEALTHIER ALTERNATIVE: Instead of tomato sauce, add raw, crushed tomato and olive oil while the adzuki is boiling.

Have all the necessary ingredients ready.

Prepare the tomato sauce according to the directions.

Add the clean, chopped vegetables to the pot.

For more information about the ingredients, see: Adzuki, Vol. 2, p. 266; cabbage, Vol. 2, p. 191; fennel, Vol. 2, p. 161; onion, Vol. 2, p. 142; tomato, Vol. 2, p. 275; garlic, Vol. 1, p. 338; and the *Encyclopedia of Medicinal Plants:* Garlic, p. 230.

NUTRITIONAL VALUE*
per serving

Energy	**347 kcal = 1,451 kj**
Protein	**18.6 g**
Carbohydrates	**50.9 g**
Fiber	**15.5 g**
Total fat	***2.73 g***
Saturated fat	***0.448 g***
Cholesterol	—
Sodium	***51.3 mg***

1% 2% 4% 10% 20% 40% 100%

% Daily Value (based on a 2,000 calorie diet)
provided by each serving of this dish

HEALTH COUNSELS

Adzuki, also known as red soybean, is a very nutritious legume that is *high* in protein, ***B_1*** and ***B_6 vitamins, folates,*** and ***minerals,*** especially ***iron.*** Its composition and properties are similar to those of the common soybean, although it contains *less* ***fat*** and *more* ***carbohydrates*** than soybeans.

This adzuki dish can fill a large part of the nutritional needs of any person—child, sportsman, or pregnant woman. Its healthy effects are especially notable in the following cases:

✓Men who are prone to suffer from **prostate cancer,** due to the *preventive* action of ***isoflavones*** which are present in all types of soybeans. In addition to being able to prevent cancer, this legume specifically *prevents* ***adenoma*** (hypertrophy) of the prostate.

✓Women suffering from **menopause,** because of the effects of ***isoflavones,*** which are vegetable hormones similar to estrogens (see Vol. 2, p. 268). They soothe the symptoms of menopause, *prevent* ***osteoporosis,*** and *protect* against ***breast cancer.***

✓**Pregnant** women, due to the *wealth* of ***folates, iron,*** and ***protein*** contained in this legume.

✓Persons suffering from other types of **cancer** or who are at high risk, thanks to the *anticarcinogenic* effect of most ingredients in this recipe—adzuki, cabbage, onion, and garlic.

✓**Athletes** as well as other persons carrying out **hard physical work,** due to the ***energy*** and the nutrients supplied.

CALORIC PROPORTION*

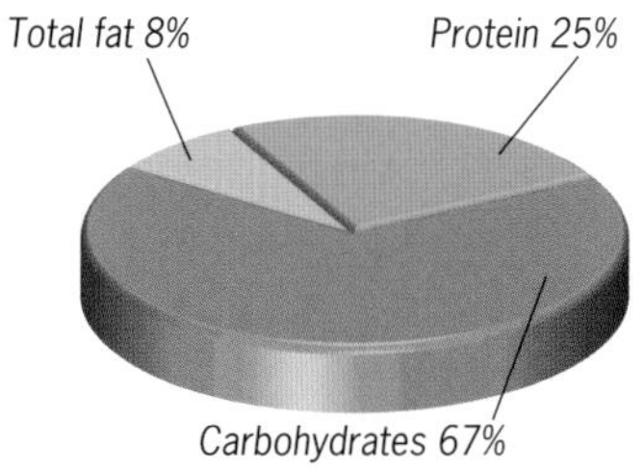

Percentage distribution of
calories for each nutrient

*Additional ingredients are not included.

Preparation time 00:05 | Cooking time 00:20

Sesame Crepes

INGREDIENTS (4 servings)

- **Crepe** batter (Vol. 3, p. 42)
- 4 tablespoons of **sesame seeds**
- 4 **bananas**
- 5 tablespoons of maple **syrup** (or molasses, or honey)

ADDITIONAL INGREDIENTS

- The juice of one **lemon**

PREPARATION

❶ Peel bananas, slice them and coat them with the lemon juice.
- Add 1 tablespoon of maple syrup to the crepe batter.

❷ In a non-stick frying pan, heat a few drops of oil and add 1 tablespoon of sesame seeds. Pour one-fourth of the batter over the sesame.
- Turn over to obtain a golden crepe on both sides.
- Repeat three times to obtain four crepes.
- Arrange each crepe in a dish with the banana slices, and pour over it a tablespoon of maple syrup (molasses or honey).

❸ Serve immediately.

For more information about the ingredients, see: Sesame, Vol. 1, p. 352, banana, Vol. 2, p. 70; maple syrup, Vol. 1, p. 174; and the *Encyclopedia of Medicinal Plants:* sesame, p. 611.

HEALTH COUNSELS

These Sesame crepes, filled with banana and covered with maple syrup make a healthy and delicious dessert for both the young and the grownups. They are especially recommended for:

✓ The **reproductive organs,** thanks to *nutritional* and *invigorating* properties of sesame, which improve the sexual as well as reproductive functions.

✓ The **nervous system,** due to the *balancing* effect of sesame—rich in ***B*** and ***E vitamins*** and ***trace minerals.*** Maple syrup or molasses enhances the effect.

NUTRITIONAL VALUE* per serving

Energy	307 kcal = 1,285 kj
Protein	6.11 g
Carbohydrates	45.6 g
Fiber	3.46 g
Total fat	*10.9 g*
Saturated fat	*1.75 g*
Cholesterol	*42.5 mg*
Sodium	*24.8 mg*

1% 2% 4% 10% 20% 40% 100%

% Daily Value (based on a 2,000 calorie diet) provided by each serving of this dessert

CALORIC PROPORTION*

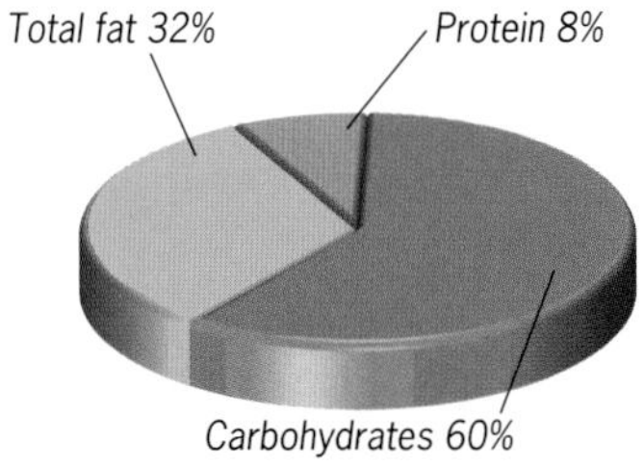

Percentage distribution of **calories for each nutrient**

*Additional ingredients are not included.

Preparation time 00:10

Cooking time 00:40

Soy Milk

INGREDIENTS (4 servings)

- 100 g (≅ 3.5 oz) of **white soybeans**
- $1^1/_2$ (≅ $1\ ^1/_2$ quarts) liters of **water**

ADDITIONAL INGREDIENTS

- 1 **cinnamon** stick

PREPARATION

❶ Wash soybeans, and soak overnight.
- Soak soybeans and grind them with an electric blender adding the $1^1/_2$ liters of water.

❷ Boil the water with soybeans and cinnamon for 30 minutes.
- Stir frequently and watch out to avoid spilling.
- Pass through cheesecloth to separate the solids.

❸ Serve cold or hot.

For more information about the ingredients, see: Soybean, Vol. 2, p. 264, soy milk, Vol. 1, p. 88.

Suggestions from the Chef

- If desired, this drink may be sweetened with honey or molasses.
- If more diluted milk is wanted, add a little more water.

HEALTH COUNSELS

Soy milk possesses comparable nutritional value to that of cow's milk but with several advantages: Soy milk does *not* contain ***casein*** (a milk protein that stimulates the production of cholesterol); it *lacks* ***lactose,*** the characteristic sugar of milk which produces digestive intolerance; finally, it contains *zero* ***cholesterol.***

One of the most notable advantages of soy milk is its content of ***isoflavones,*** a kind of vegetable hormone that *protects* against **osteoporosis, arteriosclerosis,** and certain types of **cancer** (see Vol. 2, pp. 373-377). That is why soy milk is especially beneficial for:

✓The **reproductive system,** due to the ***isoflavones,*** which soothe the discomforts of menopause and protect against **breast** and **prostate cancers.**

✓The **heart** and the **arteries,** as it helps control the level of **cholesterol** in the blood.

✓The **intestine,** as this drink is a good substitute for cow's milk, if intolerance exists.

NUTRITIONAL VALUE* per serving

Energy	83 kcal = 345 kj
Protein	6.88 g
Carbohydrates	1.28 g
Fiber	3.25 g
Total fat	*4.78 g*
Saturated fat	*0.535 g*
Cholesterol	—
Sodium	*30.0 mg*

1% 2% 4% 10% 20% 40% 100%

% Daily Value (based on a 2,000 calorie diet) provided by each serving of this drink

CALORIC PROPORTION*

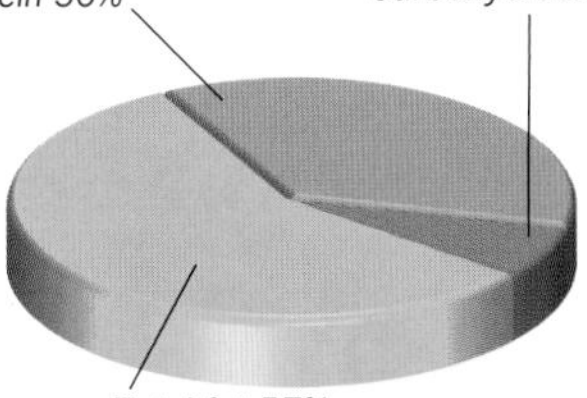

Percentage distribution of **calories for each nutrient**

*Additional ingredients are not included.

54 RECIPES FOR METABOLISM

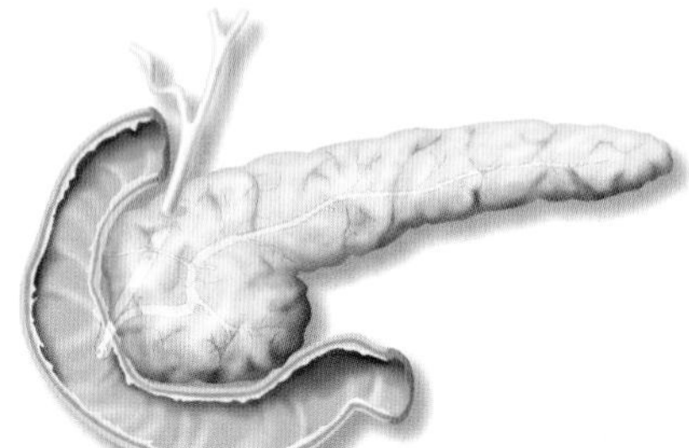

CHAPTER SUMMARY

RECIPES

Beans and Rice 320
Cereal Soup 314
Chinese Noodles 316
Couscous with Vegetables 322
Cream of Mushroom 313
Kombú Paella 318
Lentil Stew 321
Mung Bean Stew 315
Portuguese Beans 324
Sangria (non-alcoholic) 327
Soy Croquettes 326
Spring Salad 312

As a general statement, it can be said that the metabolism is a set of biochemical reactions produced by the organism thus allowing the assimilation of food so that the body can grow and carry out its vital functions. In a sense, any food taken affects the metabolism. However, the recipes included in this chapter affect in a direct way one or more metabolic processes or phases.

METABOLISM affects health and lifestyle; on the other hand, it is also certain that lifestyle affects the metabolic processes. And one of the *determinant* factors of **lifestyle** and **quality of life** is **diet.**

Diabetics are an evident example. They live their lives conditioned by this metabolic disease which forces them to follow a number of habits and steps, especially when their diabetes is dependent upon insulin. All diabetics know that when they control their diet in an exacting and consistent manner, their quality of life can be practically equal to those whose metabolism works perfectly.

The same thing can be said of people in good health. Their diet may cause their metabolism to function optimally or to prematurely deteriorate.

Basal Metabolic Rate

If we wish to maintain our ideal weight, we must bear in mind a basic principle. Living organisms consume energy even under absolute rest. In order to function, all organs need energy provided by food.

The amount of energy used up by someone in complete rest, just by being alive, is called the **basal metabolic rate.** For the average **male** of 73 kg (≅ 161 lb)this rate is ***1,742 kcal/day*** (*7,315 kj/day*). The rate for a **woman** of 63 kg (≅ 139 lb) is ***1,440 kcal/day*** (*6,672 kj/day*).

Therefore, all calories above the basal metabolic rate should be "burned" by daily activities (Vol. 3, p. 311).

It is evident that there may be significant differences between persons with the same physical activity. But it is certain and clear that if we take in a greater amount of energy than our organism consumes, our bodies will store it as adipose tissue (fat).

As said before, with a **vegetarian diet** it is *easier* to ***maintain*** our **weight** (see Vol. 2, p. 280) and ***avoid overtaxing*** the **metabolic functions** (**anabolism**—synthesis or construction phase and **catabolism**—elimination phase).

Menus for

Diabetes

Hazelnut Milk

BREAKFAST

- "Rye Bread" with "Guacamole" (Vol. 3, pp. 194, 67
- "Hazelnut Milk" (Vol. 3, p. 291)

LUNCH

- "Spring Salad" (Vol. 3, p. 312)
- "Couscous with Vegetables" (Vol. 3, p. 322)
- "Vegetable Hamburgers" (Vol. 3, p. 152)
- "Infusion of Burdock" (*EMP,* p. 697)

Couscous with Vegetables

Cream of Mushroom

SUPPER

- "Cream of Mushroom" (Vol. 3, p. 313)
- Apple (Vol. 2, p. 229)

HEALTH COUNSELS

This menu is especially designed for **diabetics.** Most of its ***carbohydrates*** are ***complex in nature*** (rye, couscous), because they are best tolerated in case of diabetes.

It supplies some ***proteins,*** *zero* ***cholesterol,*** and *almost no* **saturated fat,** which prevents arteriosclerosis—a very frequent complication of diabetes.

Diabetes

Peanut Butter

BREAKFAST

- Pear and Mango (Vol. 2, pp. 112, 341)
- "Rye Bread" with "Peanut Butter" (Vol. 3, pp. 194, 65)
- "Soy Milk" (Vol. 3, p. 305)

LUNCH

- "Red and White Salad" (Vol. 3, p. 372)
- "Soybean Stew" (Vol. 3, p. 381)
- "Spring Rolls" (Vol. 3, p. 102)
- Artichoke Leaves Infusion (*EMP,* p. 387)

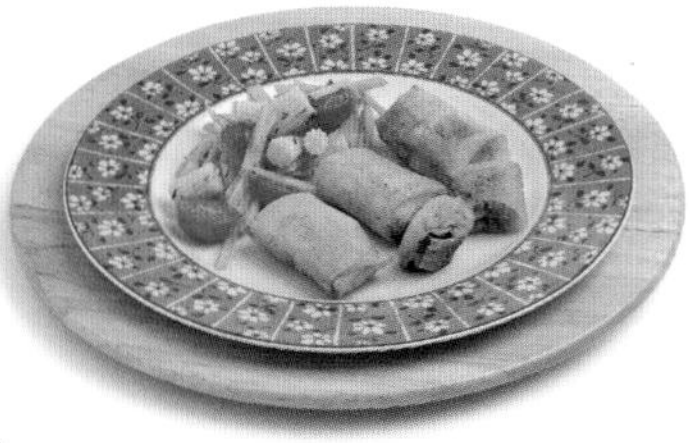

Spring Rolls

Cereal Soup

SUPPER

- Avocado, Onion, and Celery Salad (Vol. 2, pp. 108, 142, 248)
- "Cereal Soup" (Vol. 3, p. 314)

HEALTH COUNSELS

This menu, based on whole-grain cereals, legumes, and vegetables, is appropriate for **diabetics.** These ingredients are easily tolerated by diabetics, as they do *not* produce *sudden increases* of the **glucose** (sugar) **level** in the blood.

Just as the previous menu, this one prevents arteriosclerosis and helps to increase the diabetics' quality of life.

Metabolism (1)

Cleansing

BREAKFAST

- Freshly squeezed Orange Juice (Vol. 2, p. 360)
- Strawberries and/or Cherries (Vol. 2, pp. 103, 304)
- Boiled Chestnuts (Vol. 2, p. 322)
- "Almond Milk" (Vol. 3, p. 342)

Almond Milk

Sangria

LUNCH

- "Sangria" (non-alcoholic) (Vol. 3, p. 327)
- "Stuffed Tomatoes" (Vol. 3, p. 300)
- "Spanish Bouillon" (Vol. 3, p. 332)
- "Garlic Eggplant" (Vol. 3, p. 279)

SUPPER

- Cleansing Broth with Lemon Juice (Vol. 1, p. 369; Vol. 2, p. 124)
- "Boiled Vegetables" (Vol. 3, p. 223)
- Apple (Vol. 2, p. 229)

Cleansing Broth

HEALTH COUNSELS

This is a **cleansing** and **alkalinizing** menu, which avoids blood acidification. It is recommended to those following a **cleansing cure** in order to free their blood from impurities. It is also recommended to those suffering from any degree of **intoxication** due to highly processed foods or a diet rich in meat and shellfish, and those suffering from chronic disorders such as **gout, rheumatism, allergies,** or **arteriosclerosis.**

High-calorie

3,000 kcal (calories) approximately

BREAKFAST

- "Avocado Shake" (Vol. 3, p. 201)
- 100 g of "Granola" (Vol. 3, p. 156)
- "Almond Milk" (Vol. 3, p. 342)

Granola

Pinto Beans

LUNCH

- "Seed Salad" (Vol. 3, p. 298)
- "Pinto Beans" (Vol. 3, p. 353)
- "Oranges with Honey" (Vol. 3, p. 366)
- 100 g of "Whole Bread" (Vol. 3, p. 46; Vol. 1, p. 72)

SUPPER

- "Cream of Zucchini" (Vol. 3, p. 246)
- "Tropical Fruit Salad" (Vol. 3, p. 253)

Tropical Fruit Salad

HEALTH COUNSELS

This high-calorie menu is recommended to those carrying out **moderate** or **intensive physical exercise** and, therefore, needing significant levels of energy.

In addition to being *rich* in **calories,** this menu is relatively *poor* in **fat,** and serves as a blood tonic. It does not overtax the body, as would meat and meat-related foods.

If you decide to use **oil,** remember that each tablespoon adds about 133 kcal (calories).

Menus for

Slimming

1,000 kcal (calories) approximately

Whole bread

BREAKFAST

- 100 g (≅ 3.5 oz) of Orange (Vol. 2, p. 254)
- 100 g (≅ 3.5 oz) of Melon (Vol. 2, p. 360
- 50 g (≅ 1.75 oz) of "Whole Bread" (Vol. 3, p. 46; Vol. 1, p. 72)
- 50 g (≅ 1.75 oz) of tofu (Vol. 1, p. 88)

LUNCH

- 1 dose of Fucus (Sea Ware) in decoction or powder (*EMP,* p. 650), fifteen minutes before the beginning of the meal.
- "River Salad" (Vol. 3, p. 206)
- "Soybean Stew" (Vol. 3, p. 381)
- 1 Apple (Vol. 2, p. 229)
- 50 g (≅ 1.75 oz) of "Whole Bread" (Vol. 3, p. 46; Vol. 1, p. 72)

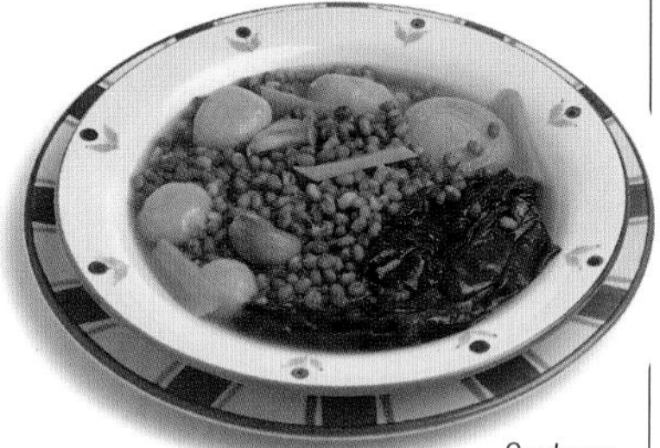

Soybean Stew

Borage and Potatoes

SUPPER

- "Zucchini Salad" (Vol. 3, p. 185)
- "Borage and Potatoes" (Vol. 3, p. 362)
- Dry Asparagus Root Infusion (*EMP,* p. 649)

HEALTH COUNSELS

This is a **slimming** menu with 1,000 kcal, and is *low* in **fat** and serves as a **blood tonic** (it cleans the blood). Since 1,000 kcal is a level of energy under the basal metabolic rate (see Vol. 3, p. 306), users of this or other similar menus, should follow it **under medical supervision.**

If you decide to use **oil,** remember that each tablespoon adds about 133 kcal (calories).

Anti-obesity

1,500 kcal (calories) approximately

Hazelnut Butter

BREAKFAST

- "Watermelon Shake" (Vol. 3, p. 292)
- 100 g (≅ 1.75 oz) of "Whole Bread" (Vol. 3, p. 46; Vol. 1, p. 72)
- 2 tablespoons of "Hazelnut Butter" (Vol. 3, p. 65)

LUNCH

- 1 dose of Fucus (Sea Ware) in decoction or powder (*EMP,* p. 650), fifteen minutes before the beginning of the meal.
- "Violet Salad" (Vol. 3, p. 373)
- "Kombú Paella" (Vol. 3, p. 318)
- 1 Banana (Vol. 2, p. 70)

Kombú Paella

Grilled Vegetables

SUPPER

- "Grilled Vegetables" (Vol. 3, p. 189)
- 1 Pear (Vol. 2, p. 112)
- 100 g (≅ 1.75 oz) of "Whole Bread" (Vol. 3, p. 46; Vol. 1, p. 72)

HEALTH COUNSELS

This **anti-obesity** menu is *more moderate* than that of 1,000 kcal (calories) as it supplies about 1,500 kcal (calories). This amount of energy *surpasses slightly* that of the basal metabolic rate for an average-weight woman.

This means that, with the energy supplied by this menu, the body can carry on its vital functions during twenty-four hours. However, any additional physical exercise will be realized using body reserves stored as fat, and weight will be lost.

If you decide to use **oil,** remember that each tablespoon adds about 133 kcal (calories).

Metabolism (and 2)

How many calories are needed?

Throughout the entire life span, the body consumes energy continuously. At least, our bodies burn **one kcal each minute.**

According to the table below, it is easy to figure out the minimal amount of energy required for each twenty-four-hour period. This is known as the **basal metabolic rate** (see Vol. 3, p. 306). To this number of calories, the exercise done needs to be added:

Daily Needs in Calories = Minimal Needs (Basal Metabolic Rate) + Needs According to Exercise Done

Taking in the necessary calories is important to avoid overweight. For each **9 kcal** (calories) taken and not burned, there is an *increase of* **one gram of body fat.**

Women

Minimal caloric needs for an average female of 63 kg of weight:

1 kcal/min. x 60 min. x 24 hours = 1,440 kcal/24 hours

If, for example, she practices light swimming for one hour a day, the following number of calories should be *added:*

(5-1) kcal/min. x 60 min. = 240 kcal

Men

Minimal caloric needs for a male of 63 kg of weight:

1.1 kcal/min. x 60 min. x 24 hours = 1,584 kcal/24 hours

For a male of 73 kg of weight, which is considered average, the *minimal* caloric needs should be increased in 10% (1% per each kg of weight above 63):

1,584 + 10% = 1,742 kcal

If this man plays soccer for one hour a day, for example, the following number of calories should be *added:*

(8.8-1.1) kcal/min. x 60 min. = 462 kcal

Calories burned per minute in various activities

These amounts correspond to a weight of 63 kg (kilos) (140 pounds), for both men and women. Each kilo of weight above 63 increases the minimal needs at rest (Basal Metabolic Rate) by 1%. For example, a woman of 83 kg will need 20% more calories, thus her caloric consumption at rest would be 1.2 kcal/minute.

Activity	kcal/min. women	kcal/min. men
Absolute rest (minimal needs)	1	1.1
Write or study while sitting	1.5	1.65
Walk, cook, carry out light manual work	3	3.3
Walk briskly or play ping-pong, vacuum	4	4.4
Jog, light swimming	5	5.5
Play tennis, go up stairs	6	6.6
Cut logs using a hand saw, cycle at 20 km/h	7	7.7
Dig the ground, play soccer	8	8.8
Run at about 10 km/h, play basketball	9	9.9
Swim energetically	10	11

Preparation time 00:15

Cooking time 00:30

Spring Salad

INGREDIENTS (4 servings)

- 500 g (≅ 1 pound) of **tomatoes**
- 500 g (≅ 1 pound) of **potatoes**
- 400 g (≅ 14 oz) of **green beans** (string beans)
- 150 g of **peas**
- 1 **onion**
- 1 **carrot**
- 1 **garlic** clove

ADDITIONAL INGREDIENTS

- **Parsley**
- **Oregano**
- 3 tablespoons of olive **oil** (each tablespoon of oil adds around 120 kcal to the recipe, that is, 30 kcal per serving)
- Sea **salt** (see Vol. 3, p. 16)

PREPARATION

❶ Peel and chop the onion and the carrot.
- Wash and chop the tomatoes.
- Cut off the tips of the green beans, separate the strings, wash the beans and chop them.
- Peel and chop the garlic clove.

❷ Boil the potatoes leaving the skin on.
- In a different pot, boil the peas and the green beans. Drain.
- Place all the ingredients in a salad bowl and dress with the herbs, oil, and salt.

❸ Serve cold.

For more information about the ingredients, see: Tomato, Vol. 2, p. 275; potato, Vol. 2, p. 201; green bean, Vol. 1, p. 109; pea, Vol. 2, p. 73; onion, Vol. 2, p. 142; carrot, Vol. 2, p. 25; garlic, Vol. 1, p. 338; and the *Encyclopedia of Medicinal Plants:* Green bean, p. 584; garlic, p. 230.

Suggestions from the Chef

It can be accompanied by "Soy Mayonnaise" (see Vol. 3, p. 58).

HEALTH COUNSELS

This salad combines boiled vegetables, such as green beans and potatoes, with raw vegetables, such as tomatoes. This makes it more tolerable by those who suffer from dental deficiencies. As all salads, this is a very healthy dish, especially beneficial for:

✓ The **metabolism,** as it supplies ***minerals, trace minerals,*** and ***vitamins,*** all necessary for **growth.** Besides, all the ingredients contained in this Spring Salad are *alkalinizing* and cause the *elimination* of **uric acid** and other wastes contained in blood.

✓ **Diabetes,** because green beans have certain *anti-diabetic* effects and *prevent* **excess glucose** (sugar) in the blood. Besides, peas and potatoes are well tolerated by diabetics, thanks to their *high content* in **fiber.**

✓ The **arteries** and the **heart,** due to the ***antioxidants*** contained in vegetables.

NUTRITIONAL VALUE* per serving

Energy	195 kcal = 813 kj
Protein	8.03 g
Carbohydrates	33.1 g
Fiber	9.40 g
Total fat	*0.723 g*
Saturated fat	*0.130 g*
Cholesterol	—
Sodium	*39.7 mg*

1% 2% 4% 10% 20% 40% 100%

% **Daily Value** (based on a 2,000 calorie diet) provided by each serving of this dish

CALORIC PROPORTION*

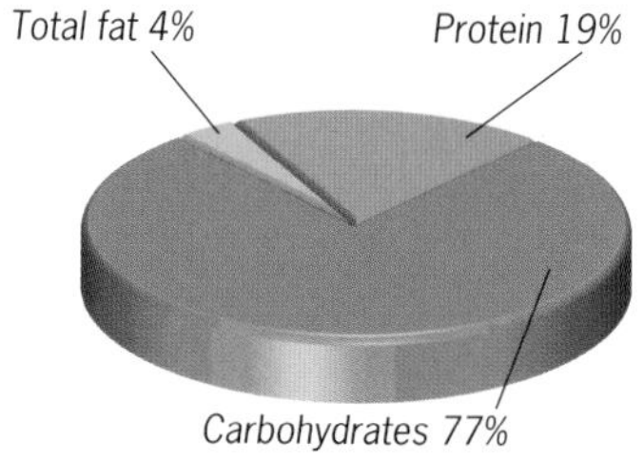

Percentage distribution of **calories for each nutrient**

*Additional ingredients are not included.

Preparation time 00:15

Cooking time 00:30

Cream of Mushroom

INGREDIENTS (4 servings)

- 300 g (≅ 10.6 oz) of **mushrooms**
- 1 **onion**
- 2 tablespoons of **whole-wheat flour**
- 1/2 liter (≅ 1/2 quart) of **"Soy Milk"** (Vol. 3, p. 305)
- 1/2 liter (≅ 1/2 quart) of **vegetable broth** (unsalted)

ADDITIONAL INGREDIENTS

- **Parsley**
- 3 tablespoons of olive **oil** (each tablespoon of oil adds around 120 kcal to the recipe, that is, 30 kcal per serving)
- Sea **salt** (see Vol. 3, p. 16)

PREPARATION

❶ Clean, wash and chop the mushrooms.
- Peel and chop the onion.

❷ Heat the oil in a pot, and sauté the onion until it looks transparent.
- Add mushrooms and salt.
- Once the fluids of the mushrooms have evaporated, add the flour. When it turns golden, add the soy milk and a little vegetable broth. Stir until thick.
- Blend with an electric blender, add the rest of the vegetable broth and simmer for an additional 10 minutes.

❸ Serve hot and decorated with parsley.

Suggestions from the Chef

- A **creamy touch** can be added by adding milk or cream.
- Other creams can be made using other kinds of mushrooms (like milky cup mushroom).

For more information about the ingredients, see: Mushroom, Vol. 2, p. 294; onion, Vol. 2, p. 142; flour, Vol. 1, p. 68; soy milk, Vol. 1, p. 88.

HEALTHIER ALTERNATIVE: Instead of sautéing the mushrooms and the onion, boil them in the vegetable broth; in the mean time, roast the flour slightly, add the soy milk, bring to a boil, and add the previously boiled ingredients. Keep simmering until mushrooms and vegetables are tender. Blend the mixture.

NUTRITIONAL VALUE* per serving

Energy	87 kcal = 362 kj
Protein	5.73 g
Carbohydrates	8.16 g
Fiber	3.59 g
Total fat	*2.78 g*
Saturated fat	*0.325 g*
Cholesterol	—
Sodium	*18.6 mg*

1% 2% 4% 10% 20% 40% 100%

% Daily Value (based on a 2,000 calorie diet) provided by each serving of this dish

HEALTH COUNSELS

Mushrooms supply a certain amount of ***protein*** and very little ***fat*** or ***carbohydrates.*** This dish is especially recommended in case of:

✓**Diabetes,** as mushrooms *hardly increase* the **glucose** (sugar) level in the blood and are thus well tolerated by diabetics.

✓**Obesity,** since apart from supplying *few* **calories,** this dish leaves the person with a notable sense of *satisfaction.*

CALORIC PROPORTION*

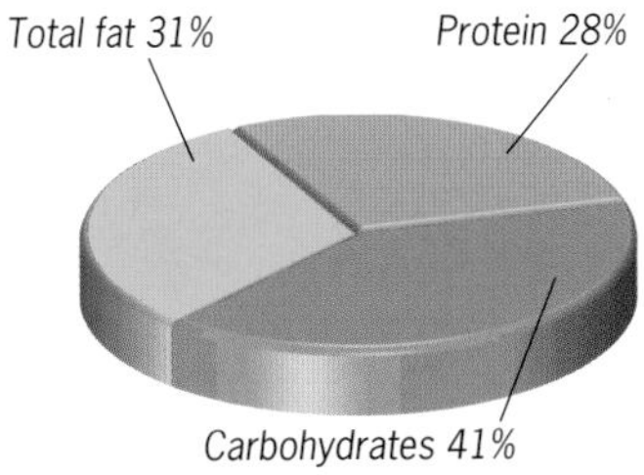

Percentage distribution of **calories for each nutrient**

*Additional ingredients are not included.

Preparation time 00:10

Cooking time 00:25

Cereal Soup

INGREDIENTS (4 servings)

- 150 g (≅ 5.3 oz) of assorted **rolled cereal**
- 1 **carrot**
- 1 **onion**
- 1 **leek**
- 1 **tomato**
- $1^1/_2$ liters (≅ $1\ ^1/_2$ quarts) of unsalted **vegetable broth**

ADDITIONAL INGREDIENTS

- **Basil** (sweet basil)
- 2 tablespoons of olive **oil** (each tablespoon of oil adds around 120 kcal to the recipe, that is, 30 kcal per serving)
- Sea **salt** (see Vol. 3, p. 16)

PREPARATION

❶ Peel, wash, and chop the carrot, the onion, and the leek.
- Mash the tomato.

❷ Heat the vegetable broth in a pot. At the point of boiling, add the vegetables, oil, basil, rolled cereal, and salt.
- Boil for 20 minutes.

❸ Serve hot.

For more information about the ingredients, see: Rolled cereal, Vol. 1, p. 67; carrot, Vol. 2, p. 25; onion, Vol. 2, p. 142; leek, Vol. 2, p. 319; tomato, Vol. 2, p. 275.

Suggestions from the Chef

The onion may be sautéed.

HEALTH COUNSELS

Rolled (flaked) cereals are obtained by precooking the various whole grains. This process makes them slightly more digestible. Grains form the basic staple for human beings. Prepared in this way and combined with several vegetables they are very healthy, due to both their nutritional value and their ability to prevent many illnesses that especially affect industrialized countries:

✓ **Diabetes,** because of the *regulating* action of whole cereals upon the **glucose** (sugar) level in the blood.

✓ Diseases resulting from **arteriosclerosis,** like coronary conditions (particularly myocardial infarction), and stroke.

✓ **Gastritis** and **constipation,** due to the *digestive* and *regulating* effects of the cereal upon the intestine.

NUTRITIONAL VALUE* per serving

Energy	187 kcal = 783 kj
Protein	6.23 g
Carbohydrates	32.6 g
Fiber	6.92 g
Total fat	*1.56 g*
Saturated fat	*0.376 g*
Cholesterol	—
Sodium	*22.6 mg*

1% 2% 4% 10% 20% 40% 100%

% **Daily Value** (based on a 2,000 calorie diet) provided by each serving of this dish

CALORIC PROPORTION*

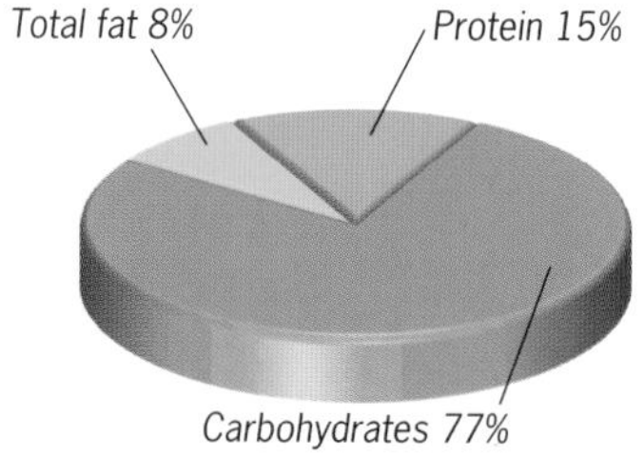

Percentage distribution of **calories for each nutrient**

*Additional ingredients are not included.

Preparation time 00:20 | Cooking time 00:40

Mung Bean Stew

INGREDIENTS (4 servings)

- 200 g (≅ 7 oz) of **mung beans**
- 250 g (≅ 8.8 oz) of **chard**
- 1 **carrot**
- 1 **onion**
- 1 **potato**
- 3 **garlic** cloves
- $1^1/_2$ liters (≅ $1\ ^1/_2$ quarts) of **water** or unsalted **vegetable broth**

ADDITIONAL INGREDIENTS

- 2 tablespoons of olive **oil** (each tablespoon of oil adds around 120 kcal to the recipe, that is, 30 kcal per serving)
- Sea **salt** (see Vol. 3, p. 16)

PREPARATION

❶ Eliminate possible impurities in mung beans and wash them.
- Wash and chop the vegetables.
- Peel and chop each garlic clove in 3 or 4 pieces (or else, add them whole after having removed the outer hull).

❷ Pour the mung beans in water or vegetable broth and bring to a boil.
- Boil 15 minutes on a high flame and add the vegetables, the garlic, the oil, and the salt.
- Simmer for an additional 20 minutes.

❸ Serve hot with broth.

For more information about the ingredients, see: Mung bean, Vol. 2, p. 266; chard, Vol. 2, p. 297; carrot, Vol. 2, p. 25; onion, Vol. 2, p. 142; potato, Vol. 2, p. 201; garlic, Vol. 1, p. 338; and the *Encyclopedia of Medicinal Plants:* Garlic, p. 230.

HEALTH COUNSELS

Mung beans are also called **green soybeans.** Their make-up is similar to that of ordinary soybeans, but with a *lesser* amount of fat. It is a very nutritious legume, especially recommended for:

✓ The **metabolism,** due to its supply of ***high quality biological nutrients.*** These contribute to the **body growth,** to the maintenance of **organs** and **tissue,** and to **energy** production. It is a dish well tolerated by diabetics.

✓ The **reproductive organs,** thanks to the **phytoestrogens** contained in soybeans, which prevent **prostate cancer** and **breast cancer.** They also counterbalance the undesirable effect of natural hormones (see Vol. 2, p. 268).

✓ The **arteries** and the **heart,** as soybeans *regulate* **cholesterol** levels and *prevent* **arteriosclerosis.**

NUTRITIONAL VALUE* per serving

Energy	147 kcal = 613 kj
Protein	9.37 g
Carbohydrates	15.5 g
Fiber	6.53 g
Total fat	*3.61 g*
Saturated fat	*0.430 g*
Cholesterol	—
Sodium	*146 mg*

1% 2% 4% 10% 20% 40% 100%

% Daily Value (based on a 2,000 calorie diet) provided by each serving of this dish

CALORIC PROPORTION*

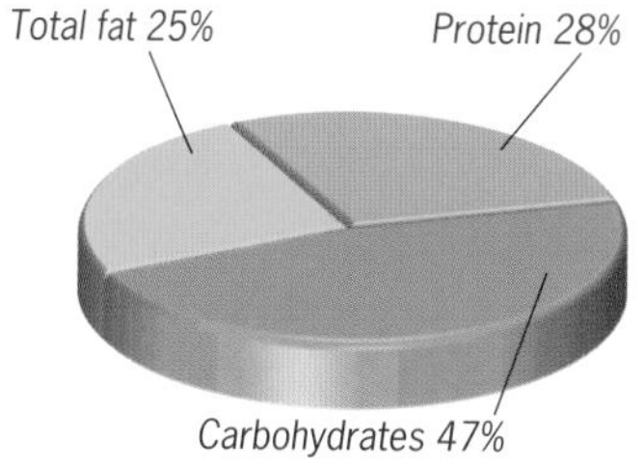

Percentage distribution of **calories for each nutrient**

*Additional ingredients are not included.

Chinese Noodles

INGREDIENTS (4 servings)

- 400 g (≅ 14 oz) of **soy noodles**
- 25 g (≅ 1 oz) of aromatic dried **mushrooms**
- 100 g (≅ 3.5 oz) of sliced **bamboo shoots**
- 1 **Welsh onion**
- 1 **carrot**
- 1 **celery** stalk
- 50 g (≅ 1/3 cup) of **peas**
- 50 g (≅ 1.75 oz) of sweet **red peppers**
- 1 tablespoon of **whole flour**
- 1 liter (≅ 1 quart) of unsalted **vegetable broth**

ADDITIONAL INGREDIENTS

- 3 tablespoons of **soy sauce** (each tablespoon of sauce adds 857 mg of sodium to the recipe, that is, around 214 mg per serving; see Vol. 3, p. 16)
- 1 tablespoon of **sesame oil** and 4 tablespoons of olive **oil** (each tablespoon of oil adds around 120 kcal to the recipe, that is, 30 kcal per serving)
- **Ginger** (ginger root)

For more information about the ingredients, see: Soybean, Vol. 2, p. 264; eastern mushrooms, Vol. 1, p. 151; bamboo shoots, Vol. 1, p. 108; Welsh onion, Vol. 2, p. 144; carrot, Vol. 2, p. 25; celery, Vol. 2, p. 248; pea, Vol. 2, p. 73; pepper, Vol. 2, p. 198; flour, Vol. 1, p. 68.

PREPARATION

❶ Soak the dried mushrooms in the warm vegetable broth for 15 minutes. Drain and chop.
- Peel, wash, and chop the Welsh onion into slices.
- Peel, wash, and chop the carrots and celery in very fine strips.
- Peel the pepper, remove the seeds and cut into fine strips.

❷ Heat the olive oil in a pot, and sauté the vegetables, the bamboo, and the mushrooms.
- Add the vegetable broth. When it starts boiling, add whole flour previously dissolved in a little cold water. Add the rest of the ingredients.
- Boil for 5 to 10 minutes.
- Remove the ginger.

❸ Serve hot.

HEALTHIER ALTERNATIVE: Instead of sautéing, add the raw ingredients to the boiling vegetable broth.

Prepare the necessary ingredients.

Sauté the vegetables, the bamboo shoots and the mushrooms.

Pour the vegetable broth and add the flour.

NUTRITIONAL VALUE*
per serving

Energy	**419 kcal = 1,753 kj**
Protein	**3.34 g**
Carbohydrates	**97.1 g**
Fiber	**4.32 g**
Total fat	***0.475 g***
Saturated fat	***0.099 g***
Cholesterol	**—**
Sodium	***46.5 mg***

1% 2% 4% 10% 20% 40% 100%

% Daily Value (based on a 2,000 calorie diet)
provided by each serving of this dish

HEALTH COUNSELS

Chinese noodles, made from soybeans, are little known in western countries. However, they are commonly used in many Asian regions, where they are a staple food. The use of this dish is especially beneficial for:

✓The **metabolism,** as ***proteins*** and ***other nutrients*** contained in this dish stimulate *growth* during the stages of **development.** The high proportion of carbohydrates contained in this recipe helps the proteins to be used for physical development, instead of being burned to produce energy. Additionally, mushrooms have an *anti-diabetic* effect, helping this dish to be well tolerated by **diabetic patients.**

✓**Cancer** *prevention,* thanks to the prophylactic action of soybeans, especially on **breast** and **prostate** cancers.

✓The **musculoskeletal system** as soybeans *help increase* ***calcium*** deposits in the bones, thus protecting against **osteoporosis.** This makes the dish very appropriate for women before and after **menopause.**

CALORIC PROPORTION*

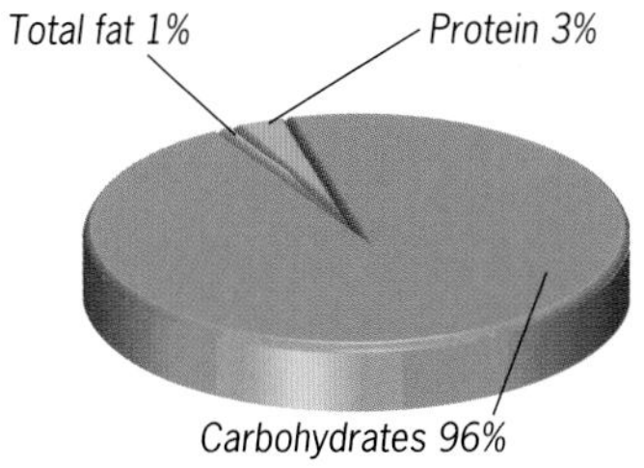

Percentage distribution of
calories for each nutrient

*Additional ingredients are not included.

Kombú Paella

INGREDIENTS (6 servings)

- 400 g (≅ 2 cups) of **whole rice**
- 160 g (≅ 5.6 oz) of **peas**
- 100 g (≅ 3.5 oz) of **kombú seaweed**
- 120 g (≅ 4.2 oz) of **tofu**
- 2 **onions**
- 4 **turnips**
- 2 **garlic** cloves
- 1 liter (≅ 1 quart) of **water** or unsalted **vegetable broth**

ADDITIONAL INGREDIENTS

- A few **saffron** threads
- One **laurel** leaf
- **Thyme**
- 4 tablespoons of olive **oil** (each tablespoon of oil adds around 120 kcal to the recipe, that is, 30 kcal per serving)
- 2 tablespoons of **soy sauce** (each tablespoon of sauce adds 857 mg of sodium to the recipe, that is, around 214 mg per serving; see Vol. 3, p. 16)
- Sea **salt** (see Vol. 3, p. 16)

PREPARATION

❶Soak rice in cold water overnight or in hot water for 1 hour.
- Cut the tofu into cubes.
- Cut the seaweed into strips, wash, and soak in water.
- Peel onions and slice them into rings.
- Peel turnips and cut them into small cubes.
- Grind in a mortar the garlic, salt, saffron, and thyme.

❷Heat the oil in a large, flat frying pan with handles and sauté the onions and the turnips until they are tender.
- Add the rice, laurel, and the mixture from the mortar. Stir and add the hot water. Boil on a medium flame for 20 minutes.
- After 10 minutes of boiling, add the peas and the seaweed.
- Keep it boiling until the water has evaporated and the rice grains are tender and fluffy.
- Place the tofu in a pot, and add soy sauce and a little water. Simmer for a few minutes so that it absorbs flavor.

❸Serve the paella garnished with sauce and tofu.

Prepare the ingredients.

Add the vegetable broth to the sautéed ingredients.

Add the rice and sauté briefly.

Soak tofu in soy sauce diluted in water.

Hyperthyroidism

Patients suffering from hyperthyroidism are recommended to abstain from this dish, due to the iodine content of seaweed.

For more information about the ingredients, see: Rice, Vol. 2, p. 225; pea, Vol. 2, p. 73; seaweed, Vol. 1, p. 134; tofu, Vol. 1, p. 88; onion, Vol. 2, p. 142; turnip, Vol. 2, p. 320; garlic, Vol. 1, p. 338; and the *Encyclopedia of Medicinal Plants:* Garlic, p. 230.

HEALTHIER ALTERNATIVE: Instead of sautéing the ingredients, add them raw to the boiling water or vegetable broth.

NUTRITIONAL VALUE*
per serving

Energy	327 kcal = 1,367 kj
Protein	10.5 g
Carbohydrates	59.3 g
Fiber	6.53 g
Total fat	*3.09 g*
Saturated fat	*0.561 g*
Cholesterol	—
Sodium	*79.4 mg*

1% 2% 4% 10% 20% 40% 100%

% Daily Value (based on a 2,000 calorie diet) provided by each serving of this dish

HEALTH COUNSELS

To the advantages of whole rice, peas, and tofu, the specific properties of kombú seaweed (see Vol. 1, p. 134) must be added. Kombú is the name given to a mixture of dried seaweed, pressed in sheets and very much appreciated in oriental cuisine. The seaweed in this dish supplies a pleasant taste that reminds one of fish. This dish is nutritious and healthy, especially for:

- ✓The **metabolism,** due to its *high quality* ***protein*** and *balanced* ***calories.***
- ✓Combating **obesity,** due to the *satisfying* effect of **fiber** contained in the whole rice as well as the ***alginate*** in seaweed which increases in volume inside the stomach. This dish nourishes at the same time that it eases the sense of hunger, thus reducing calorie intake and combating obesity.
- ✓The **thyroid gland,** due to the ***iodine*** contained in seaweed, which is necessary for the correct functioning of this endocrine gland.
- ✓The **arteries** and the **heart,** as the ingredients of this dish avoid increases in **cholesterol.** The **fiber** from rice, peas, and seaweed as well as the ***protein*** from soybeans contained in tofu serve as good protection against coronary disease and other forms of **arteriosclerosis.**

CALORIC PROPORTION*

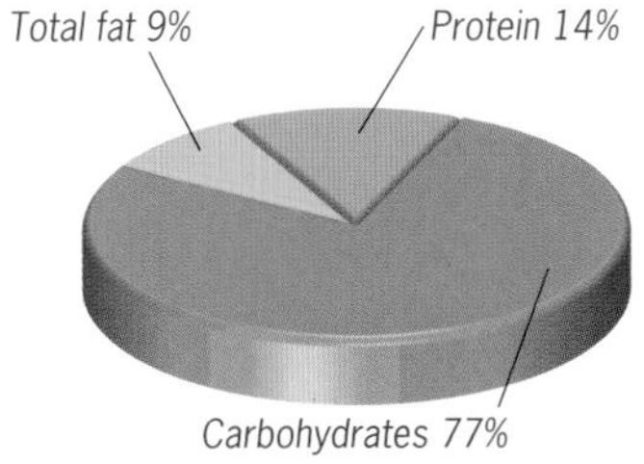

Percentage distribution of
calories for each nutrient

*Additional ingredients are not included.

Preparation time 00:20

Cooking time 02:00

Beans and Rice

INGREDIENTS (4 servings)

- 200 g (≅ 1 cup) of **whole rice**
- 250 g (≅ 8.8 cups) **cabbage**
- 100 g (≅ 3.5 oz) of **red beans**
- 1 **tomato**
- 2 **garlic** cloves
- 750 ml (≅ 3 cups) of **water**

ADDITIONAL INGREDIENTS

- **Thyme, sage,** and **parsley**
- 4 tablespoons of olive **oil** (each tablespoon of oil adds around 120 kcal to the recipe, that is, 30 kcal per serving)
- Sea **salt** (see Vol. 3, p. 16)

PREPARATION

❶ Soak the beans and the rice separately overnight or for one hour if hot water is used.
- Cut the cabbage in fine and long strips.
- Peel and chop the garlic.
- Wash and chop the parsley.
- Wash and crush the tomato.
- Wash the sage and the thyme.

❷ Boil the beans in plenty of water on a low flame.
- After one hour of boiling, set at medium heat and little by little add the remaining ingredients while maintaining constant boiling—tomato, cabbage, rice, sage, thyme, oil, salt, garlic, and parsley. Simmer until all water has been evaporated.
- Remove from heat and let stand for 10 minutes.

❸ Serve hot.

Suggestions from the Chef

If a **pressure pot** is used, put all the ingredients in the pot at the beginning and cook for 45 minutes. In a **fast cooker,** 25 or 30 minutes will suffice.

For more information about the ingredients, see: Rice, Vol. 2, p. 225; cabbage, Vol. 2, p. 191; bean, Vol. 2, p. 343; tomato, Vol. 2, p. 275; garlic, Vol. 1, p. 338; and the *Encyclopedia of Medicinal Plants:* Garlic, p. 230.

HEALTH COUNSELS

The legume-cereal combination, such as beans and rice, supplies *high-quality **protein*** that is well assimilated by our bodies. This nutritious dish is highly beneficial for:

✓ The **metabolism,** especially in times of **growth, pregnancy, lactation,** and **convalescence** due to weakening diseases.

✓ The **diabetic** diet, as the ***complex carbohydrates*** found in rice and beans are well tolerated and do not cause significant increases in glucose (sugar) levels.

✓ The **intestine,** due to the *invigorating* effect of ***fiber*** for cases of light constipation. As it does not contain gluten, this dish is appropriate for **celiac patients.**

✓ The **arteries** and the **heart,** since rice and beans *reduce* **cholesterol** levels.

NUTRITIONAL VALUE* per serving

Energy	240 kcal = 1,003 kj
Protein	6.98 g
Carbohydrates	44.9 g
Fiber	4.98 g
Total fat	*1.90 g*
Saturated fat	*0.363 g*
Cholesterol	—
Sodium	*20.3 mg*

1% 2% 4% 10% 20% 40% 100%

% Daily Value (based on a 2,000 calorie diet) provided by each serving of this dish

CALORIC PROPORTION*

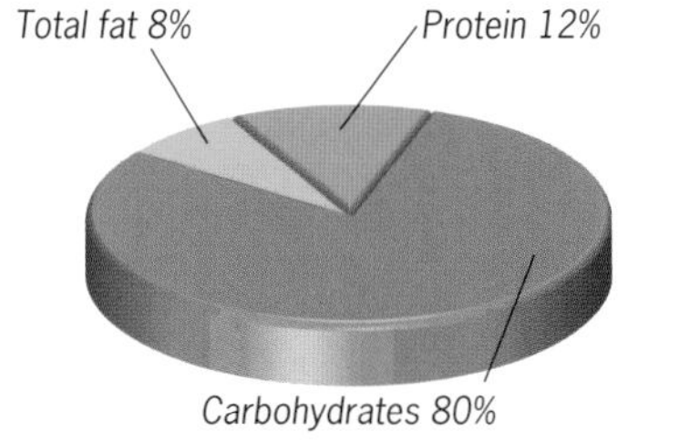

Percentage distribution of **calories for each nutrient**

*Additional ingredients are not included.

Preparation time 00:05

Cooking time 00:45

Lentil Stew

INGREDIENTS (4 servings)

- 250 g (≅ 8.8 oz) of **lentils**
- 1 **onion**
- 1 **garlic** bulb
- 1 **tomato**

ADDITIONAL INGREDIENTS

- **Potherbs** (rosemary, thyme, parsley...)
- 1 **laurel** leaf
- 3 tablespoons of olive **oil** (each tablespoon of oil adds around 120 kcal to the recipe, that is, 30 kcal per serving)
- Sea **salt** (see Vol. 3, p. 16)

PREPARATION

❶ Soak lentils overnight or for 1 hour if hot water is used.
- Peel the onion and cut it in half.
- Peel the outer husk of the garlic bulb without peeling the cloves completely.
- Wash and crush the tomato.

❷ In a pot, pour the water and add the salt. Add all ingredients and boil on a high flame.
- When the boiling point is reached, reduce heat to the minimum and simmer until lentils are tender (approximately 30 minutes).

❸ Serve hot.

For more information about the ingredients, see: Lentil, Vol. 2, p. 127; onion, Vol. 2, p. 142; garlic, Vol. 1, p. 338; tomato, Vol. 2, p. 275; and the *Encyclopedia of Medicinal Plants:* Garlic, p. 230.

HEALTH COUNSELS

In general, legumes are highly nutritious, and in one form or another, they should not be missing from our weekly menu. Lentils, cooked in a simple manner, as shown in this recipe, are healthy for everyone and are especially recommended for:

✓ The **metabolism,** thanks to their balanced composition and nutritional value. This facilitates good metabolic assimilation for the *production* and *maintenance* of body **tissue.**

✓ **Diabetes,** as lentils are well tolerated by those suffering from this disease.

✓ The **blood,** due to their *high* ***iron*** content as well as ***other nutrients*** necessary for blood formation.

✓ **Pregnancy, lactation,** and **growth** periods as they supply ***protein, iron,*** and ***folates,*** all very necessary in these stages.

NUTRITIONAL VALUE* per serving

Energy	254 kcal = 1,061 kj
Protein	19.2 g
Carbohydrates	24.7 g
Fiber	8.79 g
Total fat	*0.885 g*
Saturated fat	*0.127 g*
Cholesterol	—
Sodium	*13.9 mg*

1% 2% 4% 10% 20% 40% 100%

% Daily Value (based on a 2,000 calorie diet) provided by each serving of this dish

CALORIC PROPORTION*

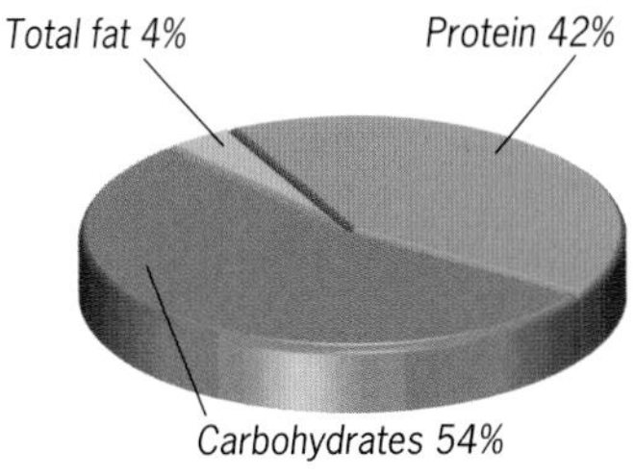

Percentage distribution of **calories for each nutrient**

*Additional ingredients are not included.

Preparation time 00:20

Cooking time 01:45

Couscous with Vegetables

INGREDIENTS (4 servings)

- 200 g (≅ 7 oz) of **chickpeas**
- 300 g (≅ 10.6 oz) of **couscous** semolina
- 2 **tomatoes**
- 2 **turnips**
- 2 **carrots**
- 1 **onion**
- 1 **potato**
- 1 **zucchini** (courgette)
- 2 **celery** stalks
- 2 **garlic** cloves

ADDITIONAL INGREDIENTS

- 1 teaspoon of **paprika**
- 1 teaspoon of **spices** (turmeric, cinnamon, cumin...)
- 5 tablespoons of olive **oil** (each tablespoon of oil adds around 120 kcal to the recipe, that is, 30 kcal per serving)
- Sea **salt** (see Vol. 3, p. 16)

PREPARATION

❶Soak the chickpeas overnight in cold water or for one and a half hours in hot water.

- Peel and chop the zucchini, the potato, the onion, the garlic, the turnips, and the carrots. Mash the tomatoes.

❷Heat 3 liters of water in a pot; add the salt and chickpeas.

- Soak couscous in lukewarm water and salt. Use an equal volume of water and couscous.
- When the chickpeas are tender (40 to 60 minutes) add vegetables little by little so that the mixture continues to boil at medium heat.
- Place a steaming basket over the chickpeas and steam the couscous 15 minutes (or boil it in water for 5 minutes). Stir occasionally to avoid packing.

❸Serve, arranging couscous, chickpeas, and vegetables separately.

Prepare the necessary ingredients.

Soak the couscous in salted lukewarm water.

Suggestions from the Chef

Couscous may also be cooked separately—boiled for about 5 minutes or cooked in the microwave for 4 minutes at maximum power.

For more information about the ingredients, see: Chickpea, Vol. 2, p. 91; semolina, Vol. 1, p. 69; tomato, Vol. 2, p. 275; turnip, Vol. 2, p. 320; carrot, Vol. 2, p. 25; onion, Vol. 2, p. 142; tomato, Vol. 2, p. 275; potato, Vol. 2, p. 201; zucchini, Vol. 2, p. 159; celery, Vol. 2, p. 248; garlic, Vol. 1, p. 338; and the *Encyclopedia of Medicinal Plants:* Garlic, p. 230.

Add the vegetables to the pot where the chickpeas are boiling.

NUTRITIONAL VALUE*
per serving

Energy	586 kcal = 2,451 kj
Protein	23.5 g
Carbohydrates	97.2 g
Fiber	18.9 g
Total fat	*4.24 g*
Saturated fat	*0.522 g*
Cholesterol	—
Sodium	*137 mg*

1% 2% 4% 10% 20% 40% 100%

% Daily Value (based on a 2,000 calorie diet)
provided by each serving of this dish

HEALTH COUNSELS

Couscous is durum wheat semolina that, combined with chickpeas and various vegetables, makes a very nutritious meal. The cereal and legume combination offered in this recipe supplies a ***complete protein*** wherein all amino acids are found in the right proportion. The various vegetables garnishing this dish enhance its nutritional value and its healthful qualities upon:

✓ The **metabolism,** especially during the stages of **growth** (childhood and adolescence), **pregnancy, lactation,** and **convalescence** of weakening diseases, as well as in any case of additional nutritional needs.

✓ **Diabetes,** because it contains ***complex carbohydrates,*** which do not cause significant increases in glucose (sugar) levels.

✓ The **intestine,** due to the ***fiber*** supplied by all the ingredients that make up this dish. Fiber is necessary for the proper functioning of the bowel and it has been demonstrated that it *prevents* **cancer of the colon.**

✓ The **arteries** and the **heart,** as ***fiber*** contributes to *reduce* the **cholesterol** level and to *prevent* **arteriosclerosis.** Vegetables supply ***vitamins*** and ***antioxidant phytochemicas*** that avoid cholesterol being deposited on the artery walls thus causing deterioration.

CALORIC PROPORTION*

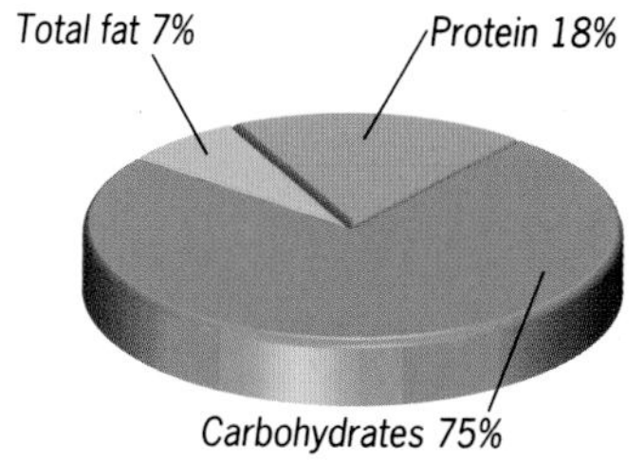

Percentage distribution of
calories for each nutrient

*Additional ingredients are not included.

Preparation time 00:20

Cooking time 01:15

Portuguese Beans

INGREDIENTS (4 servings)

- 250 g (≅ 8.8 oz) of **beans**
- 6 **cabbage** leaves
- 750 g (≅ 22 oz) of **potatoes**
- 4 slices of **cornbread**

ADDITIONAL INGREDIENTS

- 1 tablespoon of olive **oil** (each tablespoon of oil adds around 120 kcal to the recipe, that is, 30 kcal per serving)
- Sea **salt** (see Vol. 3, p. 16)

PREPARATION

❶ Soak the beans overnight in cold water or for 1 hour if hot water is used.

- Peel, wash, and slice the potatoes.
- Wash and chop the cabbage.

❷ Boil the beans in plenty of water with salt until they are tender. Drain.

- In a separate pot, boil the potatoes and the cabbage in salted water and one tablespoon of oil.
- Drain the vegetables (set aside the broth) and add the beans.
- Place the bread slices in a deep clay dish and pour in the hot broth.
- Lay the beans and vegetables over the bread.

❸ Serve hot and dress with a little oil.

Peel, wash, and chop the vegetables.

Boil beans and vegetables separately.

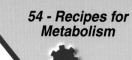

Soak the bread slices with the vegetable broth.

Suggestions from the Chef

For homemade cornbread, follow the "Rye Bread" recipe (Vol. 3, p. 194) using **corn flour** instead of rye flour.

For more information about the ingredients, see: bean, Vol. 2, p. 343; cabbage, Vol. 2, p. 191; potato, Vol. 2, p. 201; corn flour, Vol. 1, p. 69.

NUTRITIONAL VALUE*
per serving

Energy	428 kcal = 1,790 kj
Protein	20.1 g
Carbohydrates	70.0 g
Fiber	16.3 g
Total fat	*1.77 g*
Saturated fat	*0.326 g*
Cholesterol	—
Sodium	*28.4 mg*

1% 2% 4% 10% 20% 40% 100%

% Daily Value (based on a 2,000 calorie diet) provided by each serving of this dish

HEALTH COUNSELS

Portuguese Beans are another example of an appropriate combination of legumes, grains, and vegetables. These three types of healthy foods complement each other, thus forming a very nutritious dish, especially recommended for:

- ✓ The **metabolism,** because of the ***complete protein*** obtained through the combination of ingredients in this dish. Protein, together with the ***energy*** supplied by these Portuguese Beans, contributes to the good functioning of the organic metabolic processes.
- ✓ The **diabetic** diet as the ***carbohydrates*** obtained in this dish are of a ***complex*** nature. This avoids sudden increases in glucose (sugar) levels, and makes this dish *well tolerated* by diabetic patients.
- ✓ The **skin,** as the **niacin** from beans is necessary to maintain it in good health and helping in the regeneration of the dermis cells.
- ✓ The **arteries** and the **heart,** since this is a *low fat* and *low-**sodium***—if little salt is added—dish. It is ***cholesterol****-free* and helps to reduce the levels of this substance in the blood. All this contributes to *prevent* **arteriosclerosis** and *improve* arterial blood circulation.

CALORIC PROPORTION*

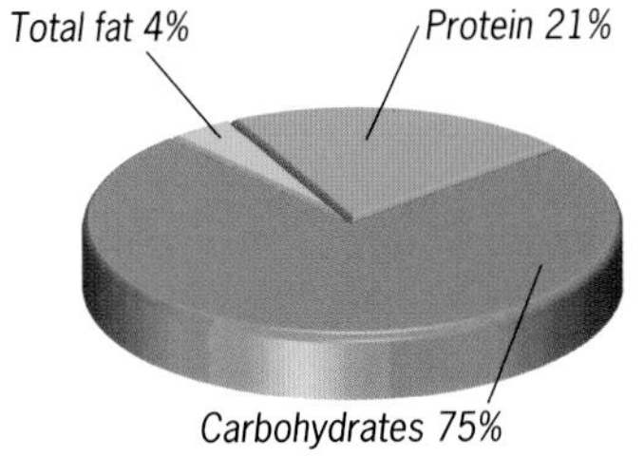

Percentage distribution of
calories for each nutrient

*Additional ingredients are not included.

Preparation time 00:15 | Cooking time 00:40

Soy Croquettes

INGREDIENTS (4 servings)

- 300 g (≅ 5.3 oz) of boiled white **soybeans**
- 1 **onion**
- 1 **tomato**
- 50 g (≅ 1 cup) of **whole flour**
- 250 ml (≅ 1 cup) of soy milk (Vol. 3, p. 305)
- 1 **egg**
- 30 g (≅ 2/3 cup) of **bread crumbs**

ADDITIONAL INGREDIENTS

- 2 tablespoons of olive **oil** (each tablespoon of oil adds around 120 kcal to the recipe, that is, 30 kcal per serving)
- Sea **salt** (see Vol. 3, p. 16)

PREPARATION

❶Peel, wash and chop the onion and the tomato.
- Mash the soybeans to form a thick purée.

❷Heat the oil in a frying pan, and sauté the onion until it turns transparent.
- Add the flour and stir for 2 minutes. Add the soy milk (cold), tomato, and salt. Stir until it becomes thick.
- Remove from heat and add the soybean purée mixing it well. Let cool.
- When the mixture is thoroughly cool, take portions with a tablespoon and shape into croquettes.
- Beat the egg.
- Roll each croquette in egg and then in breadcrumbs. Bake at 220°C until golden throughout.

❸Serve hot. They may be garnished with watercress.

HEALTHIER ALTERNATIVE: Instead of sautéing the onion, steam it and lightly toast the flour. Mix with the cold milk and heat until it thickens. Follow the recipe until it is time to roll the croquettes—this can be done without egg (see Vol. 3, p. 76).

For more information about the ingredients, see: Soybean, Vol. 2, p. 264; onion, Vol. 2, p. 142; tomato, Vol. 2, p. 275; whole flour, Vol. 1, p. 68; soy milk, Vol. 1, p. 88; bread, Vol. 1, p. 70; egg, Vol. 1, p. 218.

HEALTH COUNSELS

These Soy Croquettes supply a well-balanced proportion of nutrients. Its *high-quality* ***protein*** is easily digested by the organism. This makes the recipe especially beneficial to:

✓The **metabolism,** when there is a high nutritional demand. This is the case with **children, adolescents, pregnant women, convalescent** patients, and those carrying out **intense physical exercise.**

✓The **reproductive organs,** as the ***phytoestrogens*** in soybeans protect against **breast** and **prostate** cancers and help to prevent the inconveniences of **menopause.**

NUTRITIONAL VALUE* per serving

Energy	**452 kcal = 1,888 kj**
Protein	**34.5 g**
Carbohydrates	**33.3 g**
Fiber	**10.7 g**
Total fat	***18.5 g***
Saturated fat	***2.93 g***
Cholesterol	***63.8 mg***
Sodium	***34.5 mg***

1% 2% 4% 10% 20% 40% 100%

% Daily Value (based on a 2,000 calorie diet) provided by each serving of this dish

CALORIC PROPORTION*

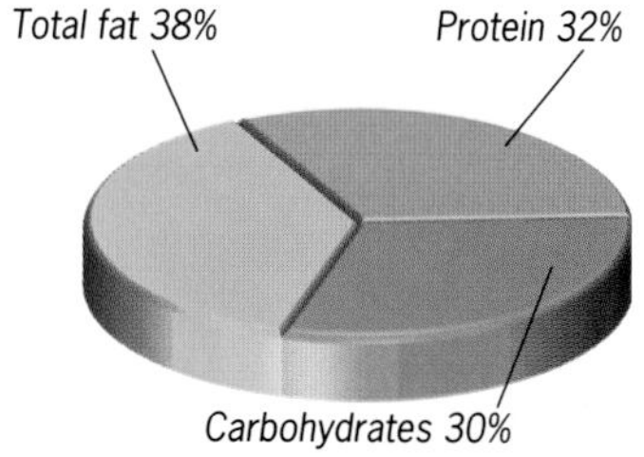

Percentage distribution of **calories for each nutrient**

*Additional ingredients are not included.

Preparation time
00: 10

Cooking time
-- --

Sangria (non-alcoholic)

INGREDIENTS (4 servings)
- 1 liter (≅ 1 quart) of **red grape juice**
- 1/2 liter (≅ 1/2 quart) of **lemon soft drink**
- 1 **peach**
- 1 **apple**
- 1 **lemon**
- 1 **cinnamon** stick

PREPARATION

❶ Cut peach and apple in small cubes.
- Wash and slice lemon. Do not peel.

❷ Pour the grape juice and the lemon soft drink in a pitcher.
- Add the diced fruit and the cinnamon stick.
- Chill in the refrigerator for 2 or 3 hours.

❸ Serve the sangria very cold, with the fruit pieces and ice.

HEALTHIER ALTERNATIVE: Instead of lemon soft drink, use the juice of two lemons and 1/2 liter of water.

For more information about the ingredients, see: Grape, Vol. 2, p. 78; peach, Vol. 2, p. 75; apple, Vol. 2, p. 229; lemon, Vol. 2, p. 124; cinnamon, Vol. 1, p. 340; and the *Encyclopedia of Medicinal Plants:* Cinnamon, Vol. 2, p. 442.

HEALTH COUNSELS

Sangria is a refreshing and nutritious drink. Prepared following the directions of this recipe, it has the advantage of being *non-**alcoholic*** and, at the same time, supplies ***sugars*** and ***vitamins*** from the fruit that transmits a *nutritious* and *invigorating* effect. Sangria is good for the whole body, especially during the summer season; but it is especially beneficial to:

✓ The **metabolism** as it is supplies energy in an easily digested form of sugar. It helps *alleviate* **tiredness** and the state of **fatigue** typical in hot climates. Furthermore, this drink exerts a positive *alkalinizing* action, which facilitates the *elimination* of **acid residuals** coming from the metabolism, such as **uric acid.**

✓ The **heart** and the **arteries,** as grapes, peaches, and all fruits in general contain ***vitamins, antioxidants,*** and other substances that *protect* against **arteriosclerosis.**

✓ The **kidneys,** due to the *diuretic* effect of fruit and fruit juice.

Suggestions from the Chef

Sangria may take a large variety of fruits. Try to prepare it with pear, sweet orange (with rind), mango, etc.

55 RECIPES FOR THE MUSCULOSKELETAL SYSTEM

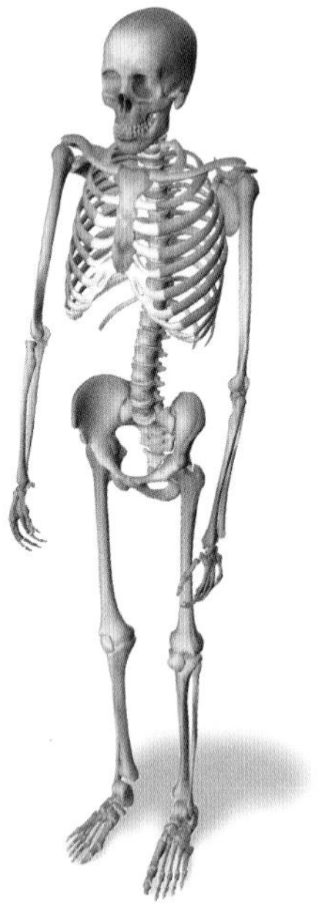

CHAPTER SUMMARY

RECIPES

Almond Milk 342
Broccoli Bake 336
Coconut Balls 339
Coconut Milk 343
Fettuccini with Green Sauce 335
Garden Pasta 334
Leek Pie 338
Potatoes and Almonds 333
Spanish Bouillon 332
Stuffed Kohlrabi 337
Winter Log 340

More than two thousand years ago, the Greek athletes, even though in a merely empirical way and at times quite wrong, knew that their success depended upon their diet in a great measure.

Today, professional and amateur athletes know that in order to attain top achievement, an adequate diet is as important as good physical fitness.

This chapter's recipes include a number of ingredients that contribute to prevent osteoporosis and rheumatic illnesses.

THE PHENOMENAL development that sports medicine has undergone over the past years is due to the great social and economical repercussion sports—both professional and amateur—today.

And one of the basic facets of **sports medicine** is **nutrition.** All elite sportsmen follow a well planned diet.

A great change

Until recently, most sports experts still recommended the consumption of large amounts of animal foods, especially meat.

This is perhaps a reminiscence from pre-scientific medicine. According to such a view, the consumption of animal muscle—basically meat—should "produce" good muscles.

Today, mass media have publicized the fact that some of the Olympic champions are vegetarian and that the majority reduce to the minimum or eliminate meat intake during the days preceding the games.

It is also known that bicycle race champions basically follow a vegetarian diet in order to meet the maximum demands of this extremely hard competition. They follow a high carbohydrate diet (cereals, pasta, and potatoes) with a moderate proportion of protein and fat.

At times, the diet prescribed to team players by some of the best-known soccer coaches is the topic of conversation. These coaches are convinced that the achievement of their players improves when they follow a vegetarian diet.

Of course, what is good to the musculoskeletal system—**bones and muscles**—of these sports stars, must also be good for everybody.

Maximum physical and mental **achievement** is obtained through a diet that is based on vegetable products prepared in the most natural and simplest way.

Practically all the recipes presented in this third volume meet these two conditions. And the recipes of this chapter include some of the ingredients that may benefit our bones and muscles to the maximum, as demonstrated scientifically.

Menus for

Osteoporosis

Cherimoya and Orange Shake

BREAKFAST

- "Cherimoya and Orange Shake" (Vol. 3, p. 178)
- "Whole Bread" with "Almond Butter" and molasses (Vol. 3, pp. 46, 65; Vol. 1, p. 175)

LUNCH

- "Tofu Salad" (Vol. 3, p. 299)
- "Spanish Bouillon" (Vol. 3, p. 332)
- "Broccoli Bake" (Vol. 3, p. 336)
- "Whole Bread" (Vol. 3, p. 46)
- Horsetail infusion (*EMP*, p. 704)

Spanish Bouillon

Seed Salad

SUPPER

- "Seed Salad" (Vol. 3, p. 298)
- "Cabbage Soup" (Vol. 3, p. 375)
- Natural skimmed yogurt (Vol. 1, p. 201)

HEALTH COUNSELS

This is a **mineral restorative** menu that supplies all minerals required by the organism to keep bones in good health. It is therefore especially recommended for **osteoporosis, rickets,** and **osteomalacia,** as well as in the *recovery* from **bone fractures.** Cherimoya, orange, broccoli, tofu, cabbage, and yogurt are all good sources of ***calcium*** and other ***minerals.***

Arthritis

BREAKFAST

- Black currant juice (Vol. 2, p. 329)
- Melon or watermelon (Vol. 2, pp. 254, 251)
- "Oatmeal" (Vol. 3, p. 154)
- "Coconut Milk" (Vol. 3, p. 343)

Watermelon

LUNCH

- Nettle juice (*EMP*, p. 278)
- Raw leek, soybean sprout, walnut, and wheat germ salad (Vol. 2, pp. 319, 266, 64; Vol. 1, p. 127)
- "Millet Croquettes" (Vol. 3, p. 111)
- "Leek Pie" (Vol. 3, p. 338)
- "Whole Bread" (Vol. 3, p. 46)

Millet Croquettes

Stuffed Kohlrabi

SUPPER

- "Stuffed Kohlrabi" (Vol. 3, p. 337)
- "Rye Bread" with "Chestnut Butter" (Vol. 3, pp. 194, 65)
- Apple (Vol. 2, p. 229)
- Devil's claw infusion or extract (*EMP*, p. 670)

HEALTH COUNSELS

This menu has a *very low* ***purine*** content. Purine is a **uric acid**-forming substance. Thus this dish is recommended in case of **uric arthritis.** It is also appropriate for those suffering from **rheumatoid arthritis** and other forms of joint rheumatism.

the Musculoskeletal System

Athletes

BREAKFAST

- "Tropical Shake" (Vol. 3, p. 158)
- "Bircher-muesli" (Vol. 3, p. 175)
- "Coconut Balls" (Vol. 3, p. 339)

Coconut Balls

LUNCH

- "Chinese Salad" (Vol. 3, p. 243)
- "Garden Pasta" (Vol. 3, p. 334)
- "Nut Hamburgers" (Vol. 3, p. 171)
- "Winter Log" (Vol. 3, p. 340)
- "Rye Bread" (Vol. 3, p. 194)
- Ginseng root powder or extract (*EMP,* p. 608)

Nut Hamburgers

SUPPER

- Raw coconut (Vol. 2, p. 325)
- "Potatoes and Almonds" (Vol. 3, p. 333), add 1 tablespoon of sesame (*EMP,* p. 611)

Potatoes and Almonds

HEALTH COUNSELS

Those who practice **sports** or **intense physical exercise** and require a significant caloric intake to keep their muscles in tune as well as the rest of their musculoskeletal system can obtain benefits from this menu. Most of its *calories* come from ***complex carbohydrates,*** which are assimilated slowly and make up the best energy source for sportsmen and sportswomen.

Other Recipes for the Musculoskeletal System

SALADS

- Sprouts, especially alfalfa sprouts (Vol. 1, p. 87; Vol. 2, p. 131)

SOUPS AND PURÉES

- "Vichyssoise" (Vol. 3, p. 280)
- "Cream of Leeks" (Vol. 3, p. 262)
- "Cereal Soup" (Vol. 3, p. 314)

MAIN COURSES

- "Turnip Greens and Potatoes" (Vol. 3, p. 208)
- "Cardoons in Almond Sauce" (Vol. 3, p. 232)
- "Fettuccini with Green Sauce" (Vol. 3, p. 335)
- "Vegetable Cannelloni" (Vol. 3, p. 98)
- "Mexican Meat Analogs" (Vol. 3, p. 88)
- "Vegetable Turnovers" (Vol. 3, p. 106)

BREAKFASTS, DESSERTS AND SNACKS

- "Rice Crackers" (Vol. 3, p. 200)
- "Almond Cookies" (Vol. 3, p. 155)
- "Sweet Balls" (Vol. 3, 269)
- "Granola" (Vol. 3, 156)
- "Cereal Bars" (Vol. 3, p. 175)

DRINKS

- "Soy Milk" (Vol. 3, p. 355)
- "Almond Milk" (Vol. 3, p. 342)

Freshly squeezed juices:

- Cabbage (Vol. 2, p. 191)
- Lemon (Vol. 2, p. 124)

Infusions or decoctions:

- Lavender (*EMP*, p. 161)
- Black Alder (*EMP*, p. 487)
- Meadow-sweet (*EMP,* 667)

- *See the recipe index at the beginning of this volume (Vol. 3, pp. 8-13).*
- *See also chapter 32, "Foods for the Musculoskeletal System" (Vol. 2, pp. 312-329).*

EMP = Encyclopedia of Medicinal Plants, Education and Health Library, Editorial Safeliz.

Preparation time 00:20

Cooking time 00:30

Spanish Bouillon

INGREDIENTS (4 servings)

- 500 g (≅ 1 pound) of **turnip greens** (turnip leaves)
- 500 g (≅ 1 pound) of **potatoes**
- 1 **onion**
- 1 liter of **vegetable broth** (unsalted)

ADDITIONAL INGREDIENTS

- 2 tablespoons of olive **oil** (each tablespoon of oil adds around 120 kcal to the recipe, that is, 30 kcal per serving)
- Sea **salt** (see Vol. 3, p. 16)

PREPARATION

❶ Wash and chop the turnip greens.
- Peel and chop the potatoes and the onion.

❷ Heat the vegetable broth in a pot. At boiling point, add chopped onions, turnip greens, potatoes, and salt.
- Boil for 20 minutes, then add oil. Let simmer for an additional 2 or 3 minutes.

❸ Serve hot.

Suggestions from the Chef

- When the turnip greens are not quite tender, this vegetable may be strong to those not used to the taste. To counteract it, add **carrot** to the stew.
- Another alternative consists of changing the boiling water twice, although this process causes a loss of minerals and vitamins.

For more information about the ingredients, see: Turnip leaves, Vol. 2, p. 321; potato, Vol. 2, p. 201; onion, Vol. 2, p. 142.

HEALTH COUNSELS

Turnip greens are the leaves of certain variety of turnips, and are traditionally eaten in Galicia (Spain). They are much more nutritious than the turnip itself. They have a *very high* ***calcium*** content (190 mg/100 g), even greater than milk (120 mg/100 g). Additionally, they supply other minerals, such as ***iron,*** as well as ***vitamins*** such as ***A*** and ***C,*** apart from ***folates.*** All this makes this stew highly recommended for:

✓ The **musculoskeletal system,** as it helps *prevent* **osteoporosis, rickets,** and **osteomalacia.**

✓ The **metabolism,** due to its *alkalinizing* and *cleansing* actions (it facilitates the elimination of wastes through the urine).

✓ The **blood,** due to its ***iron*** content as well as other *antianemic* properties found in this food.

NUTRITIONAL VALUE* per serving

Energy	127 kcal = 531 kj
Protein	4.38 g
Carbohydrates	22.1 g
Fiber	6.28 g
Total fat	*0.535 g*
Saturated fat	*0.123 g*
Cholesterol	—
Sodium	*57.1 mg*

1% 2% 4% 10% 20% 40% 100%

% Daily Value (based on a 2,000 calorie diet) provided by each serving of this dish

CALORIC PROPORTION*

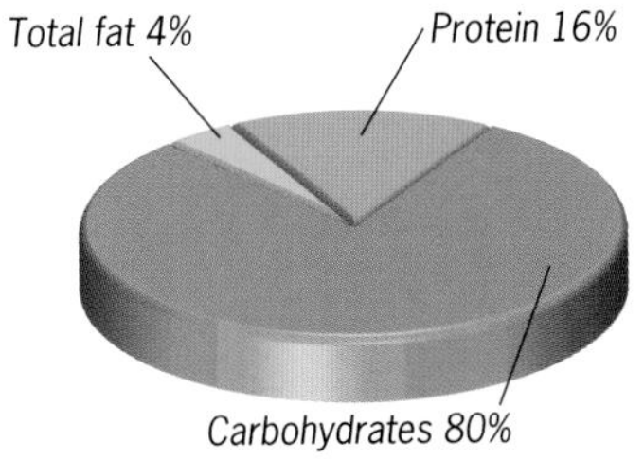

Percentage distribution of **calories for each nutrient**

*Additional ingredients are not included.

Preparation time 00:20

Cooking time 00:30

Potatoes and Almonds

INGREDIENTS (4 servings)

- 1 kg (≅ 2 pounds) of **potatoes**
- 50 g (≅ 1.75 oz) of raw blanched **almonds**
- 2 **garlic** cloves
- 1 liter of **vegetable broth** (unsalted)

ADDITIONAL INGREDIENTS

- 8 tablespoons of olive **oil** (each tablespoon of oil adds around 120 kcal to the recipe, that is, 30 kcal per serving)
- **Saffron**
- **Parsley**
- Sea **salt** (see Vol. 3, p. 16)

PREPARATION

❶ Peel, wash and chop the potatoes.
- Peel and chop the garlic.

❷ Heat oil in a pot and roast the almonds until golden.
- Remove almonds from pot and keep it with oil on the fire.
- In this oil, sauté the potatoes with a lid on. Stir occasionally.
- In a mortar, grind saffron, garlic, and parsley with a little salt.
- Mix the mortar content in a little vegetable broth and add it to the potatoes. Add the rest of the broth until the potatoes are covered. Simmer.
- Grind the almonds in a mortar. When potatoes are almost done (about 15 minutes boiling), add the almonds and simmer for an additional 5 minutes.

❸ Serve hot.

HEALTHIER ALTERNATIVE: Instead of roasting the almonds and sautéing the potatoes, use toasted almonds and boil the potatoes from raw in the vegetable broth, adding the other ingredients at the same time.

For more information about the ingredients, see: Potato, Vol. 2, p. 201; almond, Vol. 2, p. 48; garlic, Vol. 1, p. 338 and the *Encyclopedia of Medicinal Plants:* Garlic, p. 230.

HEALTH COUNSELS

Potatoes are a good source of ***complex carbohydrates,*** which supply energy to the musculoskeletal system. Both almonds and vegetable broth constitute a good source of ***calcium*** and ***other minerals*** necessary for healthy bones. Therefore, this tasty and nutritious potato dish is especially recommended for:

✓The **musculoskeletal system,** due to its *energy* content and its *mineral restorative* action upon the skeleton.

✓The **stomach** and **intestine,** due to the *softening* effect of potatoes.

✓Times of **growth, convalescence, pregnancy, lactation,** and **malnutrition,** as well as any time when an additional supply of energy and minerals is required.

NUTRITIONAL VALUE* per serving

Energy	236 kcal = 987 kj
Protein	6.82 g
Carbohydrates	34.9 g
Fiber	4.63 g
Total fat	*6.74 g*
Saturated fat	*0.673 g*
Cholesterol	—
Sodium	*13.9 mg*

1% 2% 4% 10% 20% 40% 100%

% Daily Value (based on a 2,000 calorie diet) provided by each serving of this dish

CALORIC PROPORTION*

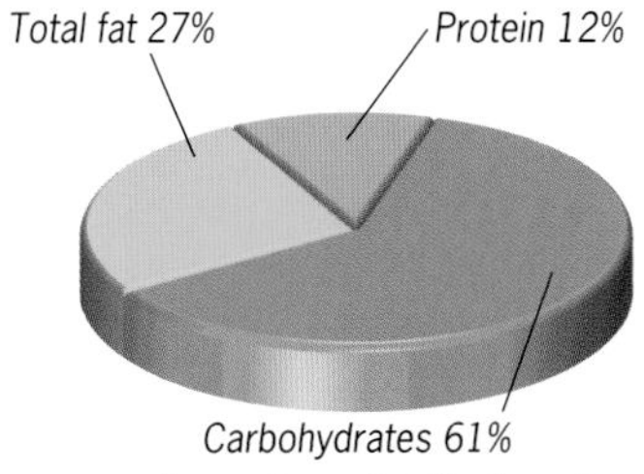

Percentage distribution of **calories for each nutrient**

*Additional ingredients are not included.

Preparation time 00:20

Cooking time 00:45

Garden Pasta

INGREDIENTS (4 servings)

- 250 g (≅ 8.8 oz) of **macaroni**
- 150 g (≅ 5.3 oz) of **green beans**
- 150 g (≅ 1 cup) of **peas**
- 250 g (≅ 8.8 oz) of **carrots**
- 1 sweet **green pepper**
- 2 **tomatoes**
- 1 **onion**

ADDITIONAL INGREDIENTS

- 4 tablespoons of olive **oil** (each tablespoon of oil adds around 120 kcal to the recipe, that is, 30 kcal per serving)
- Sea **salt** (see Vol. 3, p. 16)

PREPARATION

❶ Wash and chop the green beans and carrots.

- Peel the onion and chop it fine. Wash the pepper and cut it into strips.
- Wash, peel, and crush the tomatoes.

❷ Boil the green beans, the carrots, and the peas in a liter of salted water for 20 minutes or until tender. Drain and set aside.

- Boil macaroni for 15 minutes in a liter of salted water. Drain when *al dente* (firm to the bite).
- Heat the oil in a frying pan, and sauté the onion and the pepper.
- When golden, add the crushed tomato and sauté for an additional 5 minutes.
- Add the cooked vegetables and salt. Cook on low fire for 10 minutes with the lid on.
- Mix with macaroni.

❸ Serve hot or cold as a salad.

HEALTHIER ALTERNATIVE: Instead of sautéing the onion and the pepper, boil or steam; add the crushed tomato and follow the rest of the recipe.

For more information about the ingredients, see: Macaroni (pasta), Vol. 1, p. 74; green bean, Vol. 1, p.109; pea, Vol. 2, p. 73; carrot, Vol. 2, p. 25; pepper, Vol. 2, p. 198; tomato, Vol. 2, p. 275; and the *Encyclopedia of Medicinal Plants:* green bean, p. 584.

HEALTH COUNSELS

The ingredients in this dish supply energy from wheat that can be easily assimilated. The combination of pasta and vegetables is especially recommended for:

✓ The **musculoskeletal system,** because pasta nutrients supply a very appropriate fuel so that **muscles** may be contracted with energy, as sportsmen very well know. In addition, the vegetables garnishing the pasta have an *alkalinizing* effect, which favors the *absorption* and *fixation* of ***calcium*** in the ***bones.***

✓ The **arteries** and the **heart,** as this is a *very low-**fat**, low-**sodium*** (if salt is not added), and ***cholesterol**-free* dish.

✓ **Cancer** *prevention,* due to ***antioxidants,*** which are anticarcinogenic substances, contained in the vegetables.

NUTRITIONAL VALUE* per serving

Energy	340 kcal = 1,421 kj
Protein	12.7 g
Carbohydrates	61.4 g
Fiber	8.55 g
Total fat	*1.72 g*
Saturated fat	*0.255 g*
Cholesterol	—
Sodium	*40.7 mg*

1% 2% 4% 10% 20% 40% 100%

% Daily Value (based on a 2,000 calorie diet) provided by each serving of this dish

CALORIC PROPORTION*

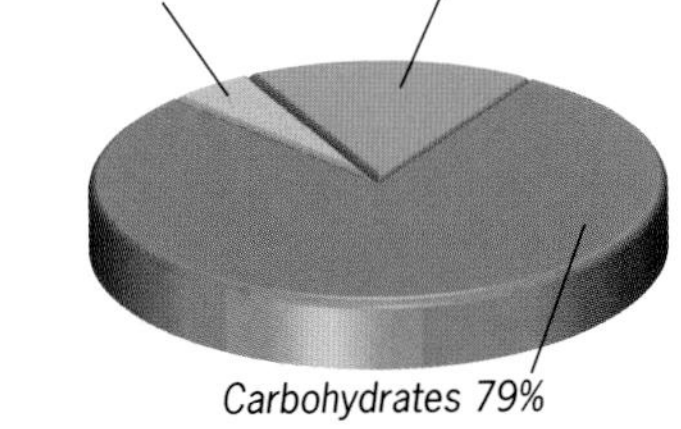

Percentage distribution of **calories for each nutrient**

*Additional ingredients are not included.

Preparation time 00:10

Cooking time 00:20

Fettuccini with Green Sauce

INGREDIENTS (4 servings)

- 400 g (≅ 14 oz) of **fettuccini**
- 100 g (≅ 3.5 oz) of raw blanched **almonds**

ADDITIONAL INGREDIENTS

- **Green sauce** (Vol. 3, p. 64) (each tablespoon of this sauce adds 41 kcal to the recipe, that is, around 10 kcal per serving)
- Sea **salt** (see Vol. 3, p. 16)

PREPARATION

❶ Prepare the green sauce as directed.
• Chop the almonds.

❷ Boil the pasta in plenty of water with salt. Drain when *al dente* (firm to the bite).
• Arrange the fettuccini in a serving dish and cover with the green sauce and the chopped almonds.

❸ Serve hot.

For more information about the ingredients, see: Pasta, Vol. 1, p. 74; almond, Vol. 2, p. 48.

Suggestions from the Chef

- Sprinkle with grated **cheese** or use the "Alternative to Parmesan Cheese" (see p. 73).
- Lightly **toast** the almonds.

NUTRITIONAL VALUE* per serving

Energy	518 kcal = 2,166 kj
Protein	17.8 g
Carbohydrates	74.7 g
Fiber	5.13 g
Total fat	*14.6 g*
Saturated fat	*1.46 g*
Cholesterol	—
Sodium	*9.75 mg*

1% 2% 4% 10% 20% 40% 100%

% Daily Value (based on a 2,000 calorie diet) provided by each serving of this dish

HEALTH COUNSELS

Pasta, a basic ingredient of this dish, is a good source of ***complex carbohydrates.*** These supply energy to the muscles and the musculoskeletal system. Additionally, almonds supply ***calcium, phosphorus,*** and other ***minerals*** which are necessary for the bones to reach the right degree of hardness. Therefore, fettuccini with green sauce is especially recommended for:

✓The **musculoskeletal system,** as this dish supplies ***energy*** for motion and ***minerals*** for healthy bones.

✓The **arteries** and the **heart,** as this is a ***cholesterol****-free* dish with *very little* ***sodium*** (if salt is not added); thus, it helps to *prevent* **arteriosclerosis.**

CALORIC PROPORTION*

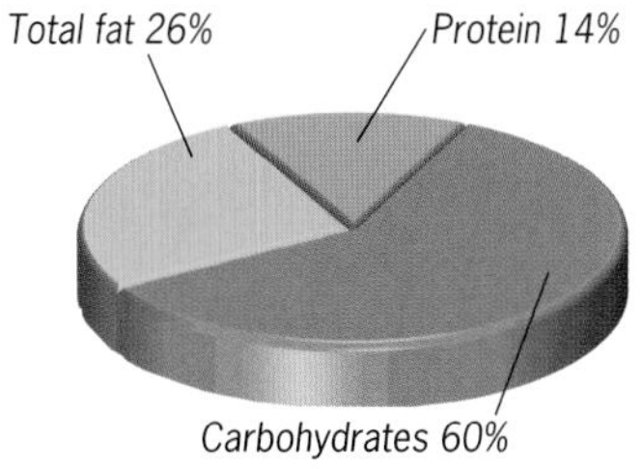

Percentage distribution of **calories for each nutrient**

*Additional ingredients are not included.

Preparation time 00:20

Cooking time 00:30

Broccoli Bake

INGREDIENTS (4 servings)

- 1 kg (≅ 2 pounds) of **broccoli**
- 4 tomatoes
- 100 g (≅ 3.5 oz) of raw blanched **almonds**
- 500 g (≅ 1 pound) of **Béchamel sauce** (Vol. 3, p. 59)

ADDITIONAL INGREDIENTS

- 1 tablespoon of olive **oil** (each tablespoon of oil adds around 120 kcal to the recipe, that is, 30 kcal per serving)
- **Parsley**
- **Chives**
- Sea **salt** (see Vol. 3, p. 16)

PREPARATION

❶ Wash tomatoes and cut into thick slices.
- Toast and chop the almonds.
- Wash and chop chives and parsley.
- Clean the broccoli and separate it into small branches.

❷ Boil the broccoli in salted water for 3 minutes.
- Brush a baking dish with oil and add the broccoli and the tomato. Bake for 20 minutes at 180°C.
- Prepare a traditional white sauce.
- Arrange vegetables in a serving dish and pour the white sauce and almonds the top.

❸ Serve garnished with parsley and chives.

For more information about the ingredients, see: Broccoli, Vol. 2, p. 63; tomato, Vol. 2, p. 275; almond, Vol. 2, p. 48.

HEALTH COUNSELS

This casserole is a very healthy dish, *high* in ***vitamins*** and ***minerals*** of *antioxidant* effect. At the same time, it contributes to the *prevention* of several diseases, including **cancer.** This recipe is especially appropriate for:

✓ The **musculoskeletal system,** as it is *high* in ***calcium*** from almonds and broccoli. Those wishing to avoid **osteoporosis,** as well as **pregnant** and **lactating** women will particularly benefit from this dish.

✓ The **arteries** and the **heart,** due to the *preventive* effect of tomatoes, broccoli, and almonds, which *reduce* **cholesterol** and *avoid* **arteriosclerosis.**

✓ **Cancer** *prevention,* thanks to the *protective* effect of broccoli and tomatoes, especially against **digestive system** and **prostate cancers.**

NUTRITIONAL VALUE* per serving

Energy	405 kcal = 1,694 kj
Protein	17.8 g
Carbohydrates	20.4 g
Fiber	14.0 g
Total fat	*26.5 g*
Saturated fat	*3.03 g*
Cholesterol	—
Sodium	*101 mg*

1% 2% 4% 10% 20% 40% 100%

% Daily Value (based on a 2,000 calorie diet) provided by each serving of this dish

CALORIC PROPORTION*

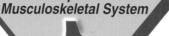

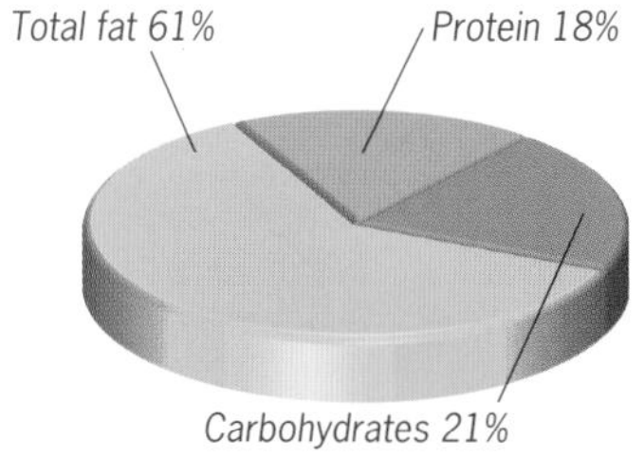

Percentage distribution of **calories for each nutrient**

*Additional ingredients are not included.

Preparation time 00:20

Cooking time 01:30

Stuffed Kohlrabi

INGREDIENTS (4 servings)

- 4 **kohlrabies** or **turnips**
- 150 g (≅ 5.3 oz) of **leeks**
- 1 sweet **yellow pepper**
- 30 g (≅ 1 oz) of polished **millet**
- 250 g (≅ 1 cup) of **white sauce** (Vol. 3, p. 59)

ADDITIONAL INGREDIENTS

- 3 tablespoons of olive **oil** (each tablespoon of oil adds around 120 kcal to the recipe, that is, 30 kcal per serving)
- **Parsley**
- Sea **salt** (see Vol. 3, p. 16)

PREPARATION

❶ Wash the vegetables.
- Chop the pepper in strips and the leeks in slices.

❷ Boil the kohlrabies in salted water for 30 minutes and save the water.
- Hollow out the kohlrabies. Chop and reserve the inside.
- Boil the millet in the broth from kohlrabies, and let rest for 20 minutes.
- Heat oil in a frying pan, and sauté the leeks and the pepper. When they become tender, add the millet and the chopped kohlrabi.
- Stuff the kohlrabies with the mixture.
- Prepare the traditional white sauce and pour over the stuffed kohlrabies.
- Bake for 10 minutes at 200°C.

❸ Serve garnished with parsley.

HEALTHIER ALTERNATIVE: Instead of sautéing the leeks and the pepper, they may be steamed.

For more information about the ingredients, see: Kohlrabi, Vol. 2, p. 193; leek, Vol. 2, p. 319; pepper, Vol. 2, p. 198; millet, Vol. 1, p. 76.

HEALTH COUNSELS

The kohlrabi stuffed with millet and leek is a dish quite *high* in ***energy, vitamins,*** and ***minerals,*** apart from being easily digested. It is especially recommended for:

✓ The **musculoskeletal system,** because of the *cleansing* effect of kohlrabies and leeks, which help *eliminate* ***uric acid.*** Thus, this dish *prevents* the accumulation of uric acid in the joints, the cause of **gout.**

✓ The **kidneys,** due to the *alkalizing* and *cleansing* effects of kohlrabies and leeks. They stimulate **urine** *production* as well as *elimination* of **waste substances.**

NUTRITIONAL VALUE* per serving

Energy	163 kcal = 683 kj
Protein	5.62 g
Carbohydrates	15.9 g
Fiber	7.52 g
Total fat	*6.58 g*
Saturated fat	*0.945 g*
Cholesterol	—
Sodium	*37.0 mg*

1% 2% 4% 10% 20% 40% 100%

% Daily Value (based on a 2,000 calorie diet) provided by each serving of this dish

CALORIC PROPORTION*

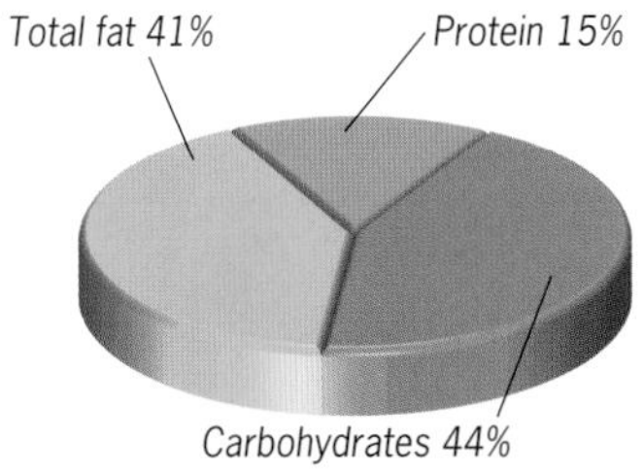

Percentage distribution of **calories for each nutrient**

*Additional ingredients are not included.

Preparation time 00:15

Cooking time 00:45

Leek Pie

INGREDIENTS

- **Pie crust** base (Vol. 3, p. 43)
- 500 g (≅ 1 pound) of **leeks**
- 100 g (≅ 3.5 oz) of grated tender **cheese**
- 1 **onion**
- 1 tablespoon of **whole flour**
- 2 **garlic** cloves
- 3 tablespoons of olive **oil**

ADDITIONAL INGREDIENTS

- **Oregano**
- Sea **salt** (see Vol. 3, p. 16)

PREPARATION

❶Peel and chop the onion and the garlic.

- Trim, wash, and cut the leeks into strips (see Vol. 3, p. 134).

❷Boil leeks in salted water. Drain.

- Prepare the piecrust, roll it over an oven dish and bake it. Remove before it gets brown.
- Heat oil in a frying pan, and sauté the onions. When they become transparent, add leeks and garlic.
- After 2 minutes, add the flour and stir. When the mixture becomes golden, add half a cup of leek broth and keep stirring to avoid lumps. Add salt, oregano, and half of the cheese. Stir and remove from heat.
- Pour this dough over the piecrust. Cover with the remaining cheese and bake for an additional 20 minutes until the cheese is melted.

❸It can be served cold or hot.

HEALTHIER ALTERNATIVE: Steam the ingredients instead of sautéing them. The flour may also be excluded and even cheese may be substituted by the "Alternative to Cheese Sauce" (see Vol. 3, p. 73).

For more information about the ingredients, see: Leek, Vol. 2, p. 319, cheese, Vol. 1, p. 212; onion, Vol. 2, p. 142; flour, Vol. 1, p. 68; garlic, Vol. 1, p. 338; oil, Vol. 1, p. 118; and the *Encyclopedia of Medicinal Plants:* Garlic, p. 230.

HEALTH COUNSELS

Leeks and onions, with their *alkalinizing* and *cleansing* effect, help to *eliminate* **uric acid,** which makes joints swollen. Thus, this pie is recommended:

✓To improve the condition of the **musculoskeletal system** of those suffering from **gout** or **uric arthritis.**

✓To facilitate the *cleansing* of the **respiratory mucosa** in case of **sinusitis, pharyngitis,** and **bronchitis,** due to the expectorant effect of leeks and onions.

✓To *prevent* **constipation,** for its content in vegetable ***fiber,*** especially as it is prepared with whole flour.

NUTRITIONAL VALUE* per 100 g

Energy	265 kcal = 1,106 kj
Protein	6.66 g
Carbohydrates	19.5 g
Fiber	3.80 g
Total fat	*17.1 g*
Saturated fat	*4.04 g*
Cholesterol	*28.7 mg*
Sodium	*49.8 mg*

1% 2% 4% 10% 20% 40% 100%

% Daily Value (based on a 2,000 calorie diet) provided by each 100 g of this dish

CALORIC PROPORTION*

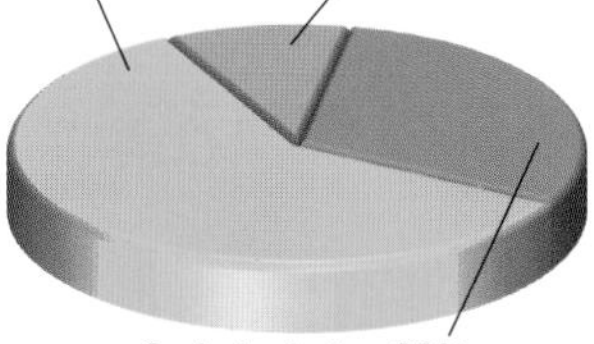

Percentage distribution of **calories for each nutrient**

*Additional ingredients are not included.

Preparation time 00:10 | Cooking time 00:25

Coconut Balls

INGREDIENTS

- 150 g (≅ 5.3 oz) of shredded **coconut**
- 150 g (≅ 5.3 oz) of rolled **oats**
- 50 g (≅ 1.75 oz) of **carrots**
- 50 g (≅ 1.75 oz) of seedless **grapes**
- 1/2 liter (≅ 1/2 quart) of **hazelnut milk** (Vol. 3 p. 291)
- 50 g (≅ 1.75 oz) of **brown sugar**

ADDITIONAL INGREDIENTS

- 1 **cinnamon** stick

PREPARATION

❶ Peel and shred the carrot.

❷ Boil hazelnut milk, carrot, rolled oats, grapes, sugar, and cinnamon stick in a pot.

- Stir constantly until a thick paste is obtained.
- Remove the cinnamon stick and let cool.
- Mix in one third of the shredded coconut.
- Shape into small balls and coat them with the remaining shredded coconut.

❸ Store balls in a cool place until it is time to use them.

For more information about the ingredients, see: Coconut, Vol. 2, p. 325; oats, Vol. 2, p. 41; carrot, Vol. 2, p. 25; grape, Vol. 2, p. 78; hazelnut, Vol. 2, p. 252; brown sugar, Vol. 1, p. 170.

HEALTH COUNSELS

Coconut contains ***phosphorus, calcium,*** and ***magnesium,*** and it contributes to the restoration of minerals in the skeleton. Oats as well as the remaining ingredients supply ***vitamins,*** especially of the ***B*** complex. Aside from being a healthy and high-energy dessert, these coconut balls are beneficial to:

✓ The **musculoskeletal system,** especially during the stages of **growth,** as there is a particular need of ***calcium*** and ***energy.*** It is also recommended in case of **osteoporosis** and **decalcification.**

✓ The **nervous system,** because of the *sedative* effect of oats.

✓ The **metabolism,** when there is an increased energy demand—**pregnancy, lactation, physical strain,** and **sports.**

NUTRITIONAL VALUE* per 100 g

Energy	195 kcal = 817 kj
Protein	3.70 g
Carbohydrates	26.5 g
Fiber	4.25 g
Total fat	*7.72 g*
Saturated fat	*4.40 g*
Cholesterol	—
Sodium	*11.6 mg*

1% 2% 4% 10% 20% 40% 100%

% Daily Value (based on a 2,000 calorie diet) provided by each 100 g of this dessert

CALORIC PROPORTION*

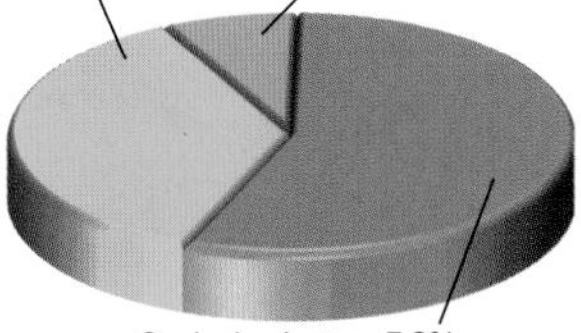

Percentage distribution of **calories for each nutrient**

*Additional ingredients are not included.

Preparation time

0 1:00

Cooking time

- - - -

Winter Log

INGREDIENTS

- 100 g (≅ 1.75 oz) of boiled peeled **chestnuts**
- 80 g (≅ 2.8 oz) of **tofu**
- 80 g (≅ 2.8 oz) of ground **almonds**
- 200 g (≅ 7 oz) of ground **hazelnuts**
- 150 g (≅ 5.3 oz) of **brown sugar**
- 4 **whole bread** slices
- 100 g (≅ 3.5 oz) of **carob flour**
- 200 g (≅ 7 oz) of **quark cheese**

PREPARATION

❶ Mix chestnuts, tofu, almonds, 3/4 of ground hazelnuts, 100 g of sugar, and the bread slices to form a firm, sticky dough. Divide it into two parts.

❷ With one of the parts, shape into a cylinder to be the inner part of the log.

- To the other part, add the carob flour. Spread the mixture over aluminum foil forming a rectangle the same lengt as the previous cylinder and wide enough to cover it almost entirely (this will become the log's "bark").
- Over the second dough (the dark one), place the cylinder (the light dough) and wrap it without removing the aluminum foil, leaving the log's edges uncovered.
- Place the log in an oblong pan and keep it in the refrigerator for 4 or 5 hours.
- Beat the quark cheese together with the hazelnuts and the remaining sugar to form icing.

❸ Empty the log from the pan, remove the aluminum foil and serve. Place the log on a serving tray and cover it with the icing.

Prepare the necessary ingredients.

Shape the log using aluminum foil.

Prepare the icing with cheese, sugar, and ground hazelnuts.

Prepare a carob flour icing for decoration.

Suggestions from the Chef

- To decorate, place aluminum foil in a frying pan on low fire. Add 60 g of **fondant chocolate.** As it melts, spread the chocolate over the aluminum foil with a wooden spatula to form a thin layer. Let it cool. Once hardened, cut into irregular strips and arrange them over the icing along the log.
- The melted chocolate can also be poured over the back of ivy leaves and may be separated once the chocolate is cold and hard.
- Carob flour may be substituted by **low-fat cocoa powder.**
- Both the outer layer and the mixture used for the log's core are delicious as **crepe's filling** (see Vol. 3, p. 42).

For more information about the ingredients, see: Chestnut, Vol. 2, p. 322; tofu, Vol. 1, p. 88; almond, Vol. 2, p. 48; hazelnut, Vol. 2, p. 252; sugar, Vol. 1, p. 170; bread, Vol. 1, p. 70; carob, Vol. 1, p. 46; cheese, Vol. 1, p. 213.

Chestnut

*Chestnuts are high in **complex carbohydrates** which, in order to be well digested, require adequate **mastication** and **insalivation.** This is the case for both raw and cooked chestnuts.*

HEALTH COUNSELS

This nutritious dessert makes up a "main dish" by itself. It supplies a considerable amount of ***energy, protein,*** and ***minerals*** and barely *any* ***cholesterol.*** Its use is especially beneficial to:

✓ The **musculoskeletal system** due to its supply of energy, vitamins, and minerals that *contribute* to the **bone and muscle development,** especially at the time of **growth,** when **sports** are practiced, and under **intense physical work.** Nuts and tofu make of this dessert a good source of ***calcium*** and ***minerals*** for the bones.

✓ The **metabolism** and the **kidneys,** due to the *alkalinizing* effect of chestnuts that *neutralizes* the **acidosis** caused by illness.

✓ **Pregnancy** and **lactation,** due to the ***energy, protein, minerals,*** and other nutrients supplied by this dessert. Additionally, chestnuts and almonds have a *galactogenous* effect (they stimulate the secretion of milk).

NUTRITIONAL VALUE per 100 g

Energy	316 kcal = 1,323 kj
Protein	9.18 g
Carbohydrates	30.2 g
Fiber	7.59 g
Total fat	*18.0 g*
Saturated fat	*1.74 g*
Cholesterol	*1.66 mg*
Sodium	*92.0 mg*

1% 2% 4% 10% 20% 40% 100%

% Daily Value (based on a 2,000 calorie diet) provided by each 100 g of this dessert

CALORIC PROPORTION

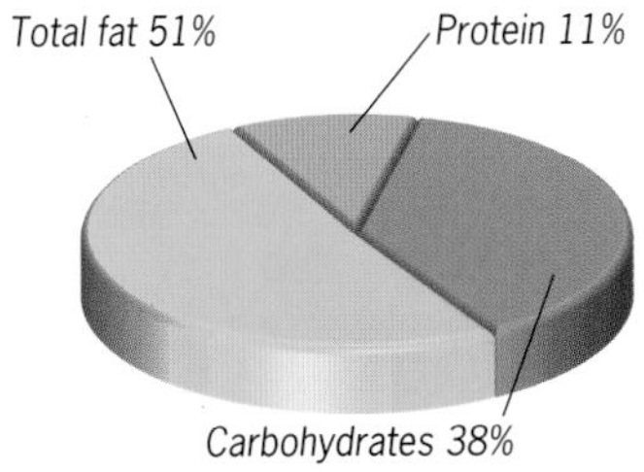

Percentage distribution of **calories for each nutrient**

Preparation time 01:15

Cooking time ----

Almond Milk

INGREDIENTS (4 servings)

- 250 g (≅ 8.8 oz) of raw **almonds**
- 1 liter of **water**

PREPARATION

❶ To peel the almonds, scald them in boiling water for 5 minutes.

❷ Once peeled, soak them overnight. Drain and chop them (reserve the soaking water).

- Place the chopped almonds in a deep container and add 3 cups of the soaking water. Let rest for half an hour.
- Sieve using a fine cloth and reserve this milk in a jar.
- Repeat the previous step with the almond meal left in the cloth using the remaining soaking water.

❸ Stir well and keep in the refrigerator until it is time to use.

For more information about the ingredients, see: Almond, Vol. 2, p. 48.

Suggestions from the Chef

- Sprinkle with a little **cinnamon** powder and sweeten.
- If less thick milk is desired, pour an additional half a cup of water.

HEALTH COUNSELS

This almond-based drink, made through a simple and natural process, is similar to cow's milk as far as ***protein*** and ***minerals,*** including ***calcium,*** are concerned. Besides, it retains a good portion of the nutritional and preventive properties of almonds, and it is easily digested by children and old people who may have problems to digest almonds. This drink is especially recommended for:

✓ The **musculoskeletal system,** due to the high content in calcium and other minerals necessary for the *formation* and *maintenance* of bones.

✓ The **skin,** when **eczema** and **cutaneous rash** appear due to allergies and intolerance to cow's milk.

✓ The **arteries** and the **heart** because the ***unsaturated fatty acids*** as well as the ***vitamin E*** contained in almonds contribute to *reduce* ***cholesterol.***

✓ **Pregnancy** and **lactation,** as almonds stimulate the secretion of milk.

NUTRITIONAL VALUE per serving

Energy	69 kcal = 287 kj
Protein	6.23 g
Carbohydrates	3.56 g
Fiber	1.36 g
Total fat	*3.26 g*
Saturated fat	*0.309 g*
Cholesterol	—
Sodium	*6.19 mg*

1% 2% 4% 10% 20% 40% 100%

% Daily Value (based on a 2,000 calorie diet) provided by each serving of this drink

CALORIC PROPORTION

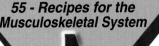

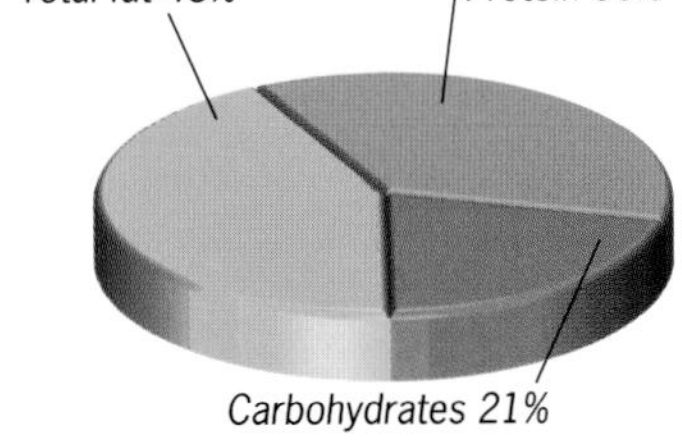

Percentage distribution of **calories for each nutrient**

Preparation time 00:30

Cooking time - - - -

Coconut Milk

INGREDIENTS (4 servings)

- 1 **coconut** (250 g of pulp)
- 1 liter (≅ 1 quart) of **water**

PREPARATION

❶ Husk, wash, and finely chop the coconut. Soak it overnight in the liter of water.

❷ Drain the coconut (keep the soaking water), blend in an electric blender, and let it soak in the previous water for 20 minutes.

- Sieve using a cloth and drain the coconut milk well.

❸ Serve cold.

For more information about the ingredients, see: Coconut, Vol. 2, p. 325.

Suggestions from the Chef

- Alternatively, 600 g of **shredded coconut** and one liter of lukewarm water may be used to obtain 1 liter of coconut milk—Soak for 15 minutes and sieve using a fine cloth. The whitish liquid obtained is the coconut milk.
- If less concentrated milk is desired, add a little water.

HEALTH COUNSELS

Coconuts supply ***calcium, phosphorus,*** and ***magnesium.*** They also act as a ***mineral restorative*** agent. Coconut milk retains a good portion of this fruit's properties, without the need of mastication. Its use is beneficial for:

✓The **musculoskeletal system,** especially to *prevent* illnesses such as **arthritis** and **osteoporosis.**

✓The **skin** and its **attachments,** as minerals contained in coconuts keep them healthy. **Dry skin, weak hair,** and **frail nails** improve with the use of coconut milk.

NUTRITIONAL VALUE per serving

Energy	**32 kcal = 135 kj**
Protein	**1.04 g**
Carbohydrates	**2.34 g**
Fiber	**1.13 g**
Total fat	***2.09 g***
Saturated fat	***1.86 g***
Cholesterol	—
Sodium	***11.3 mg***

1% 2% 4% 10% 20% 40% 100%

% Daily Value (based on a 2,000 calorie diet) provided by each serving of this drink

CALORIC PROPORTION

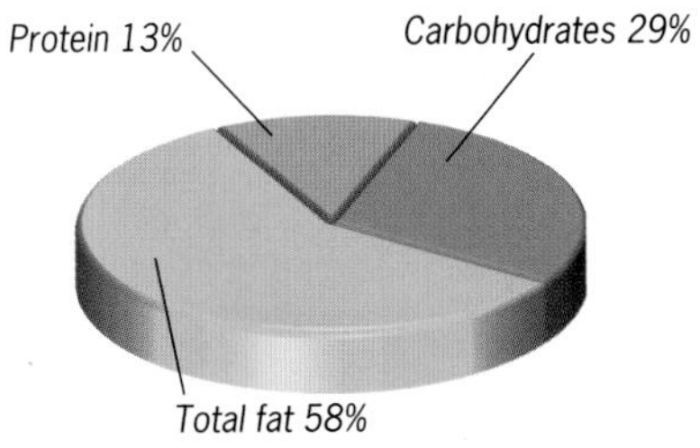

Percentage distribution of **calories for each nutrient**

56 RECIPES FOR THE SKIN

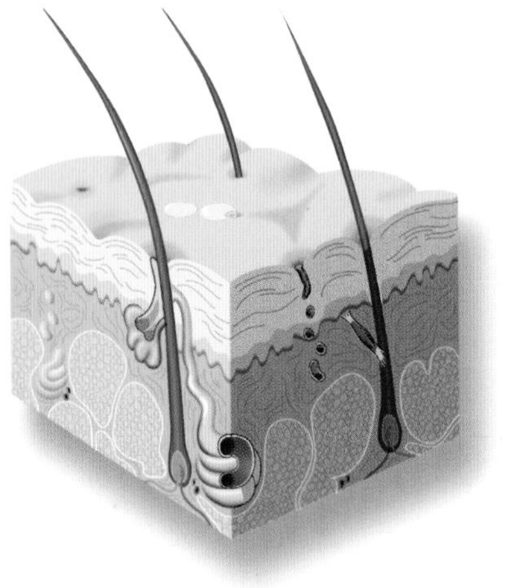

CHAPTER SUMMARY

RECIPES

Andalusian Asparagus *349*
Beans with Spinach *352*
Carrot and Apple Juice *355*
Cream of Asparagus *350*
Cream of Avocado *351*
Filled Cucumbers *348*
Mango Custard *354*
Pinto Beans *353*

Our skin, a surface of over two square meters in adults, protects us from infections and injuries; additionally, it also maintains the necessary moisture and temperature inside our bodies.

Furthermore, the skin is the organ that shows, clearly and immediately, various illness signs.

Hence everybody's desire and need to maintain a beautiful skin, which is to say, a truly healthy skin. Diet is undoubtedly the most influential factor in skin health.

THE MOST important factor to keep our **skin** and its attached structures in top condition is not beauty products but rather correct hygiene and a balanced diet. Skin is much more than a wrapper to the body. It is a **protecting** and **excreting** organ.

Skin, hair, and nails

Skin is made up of two main layers, from the outer to the inner layer:

- **Epidermis.** Cells in this layer divide constantly and move toward the surface where they flatten, die, and are transformed into a substance called **keratin,** which is eventually eliminated in the shape of almost invisible scales.
  Each cell in the innermost layer of the epidermis takes about three to four weeks to reach the outer part.
- **Dermis.** Inner layer that remains firmly attached to the epidermis. The dermis is made up of bundles of protein fibers (**collagen**) and of elastic fibers. It is here where the **sweat, sebaceous,** and **apocrine** (located in armpits, breasts, and groins; they produce odor and are considered a sex characteristic) glands are located. Additionally, **hair follicles, blood vessels,** and **nerve terminals** are found in the dermis.

Both hair and nails are specialized formations of **keratin:**

- **Nails** develop through living skin cells, even though nails themselves are dead tissue.
- **Hair** (down, fuzz) develops from the pilose follicle cells.

Adequate feeding

To keep skin, hair, and nails in good condition, it is necessary to follow a **balanced diet,** especially in regards to **protein, vitamins, minerals** (iron), and **essential fatty acids.** Besides, diet should be ***free*** from:

- **Intoxicating** substances, such as alcohol.
- Foods containing **waste substances** that must be eliminated through the skin, causing eczema, such as shellfish, sausages, and variety meats.
- **Chemical substances** that cause allergies, such as artificial coloring, certain preservatives, and additives.

The recipes presented in this chapter meet all the above requirements. Additionally, they include ingredients, such as **cucumber, avocado,** and **mango** that nourish, protect, and make skin more beautiful.

Menus for

Acne

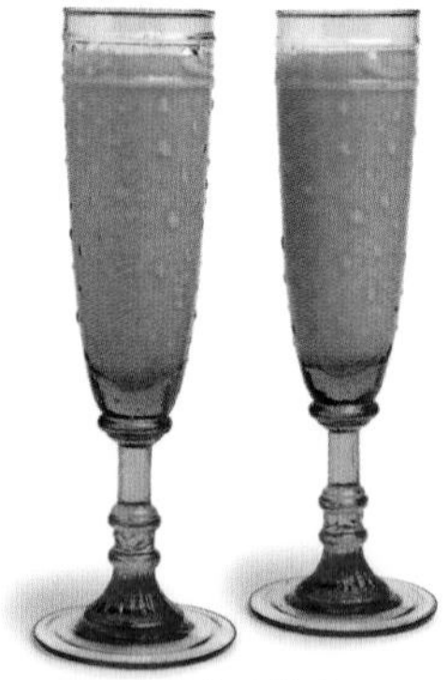

Apricot Shake

BREAKFAST

- "Apricot Shake" (Vol. 3, p. 141)
- Muesli (Vol. 3, p. 174)
- "Soy Milk" (Vol. 3, p. 305)
- Evening primrose oil pills (*EMP*, p. 238)

Carrot Juice

LUNCH

- Freshly liquefied carrot juice (Vol. 2, p. 25)
- Tofu, avocado, tomato, spinach, and onion salad with sesame and brewer's yeast (Vol. 1, pp. 88, 352, 358; Vol. 2, pp. 108, 275, 28, 142)
- "Cream of Asparagus" (Vol. 3, p. 350)
- "Whole bread" with "Peanut Butter" (Vol. 1 p. 72; Vol. 3 pp. 46, 65)
- Milfoil flowers and burdock root infusion (*EMP*, pp. 691, 697)

Tofu and Herbs Spread

SUPPER

- Freshly squeezed orange juice with wheat germ (Vol. 2, p. 360, 310)
- "Rye Bread" toast with "Tofu and Herbs Spread" (Vol. 3, p. 194, 66)

HEALTH COUNSELS

This is a highly recommended menu in case of **acne,** as it supplies ***vitamin A*** (from apricots, carrots, and spinach), ***vitamin C*** (from tomatoes and oranges), and ***vitamin E*** (from wheat germ), which protect the skin cells. It also contains ***phytoestrogens*** (from soy milk and tofu) that enhance hormonal balance, ***trace minerals*** (from brewer's yeast and wheat germ), and cleansing vegetables such as asparagus.

Dermatitis and Allergies

Tropical Fruit Salad

BREAKFAST

- Aloe gel or juice first thing in the morning (*EMP*, p. 694)
- "Tropical Fruit Salad" (Vol. 3, p. 253)
- "Rice Crackers" with "Mediterranean Tahini" (Vol. 3, pp. 196, 61)
- "Soy Milk" (Vol. 3, p. 305)

LUNCH

- "Almond Milk" (Vol. 3, p. 342)
- "Spinach Salad" (Vol. 3, p. 132)
- "Portuguese Beans" (Vol. 3, p. 324)
- Dried apricots (Vol. 2, p. 27)
- "Whole Bread" (Vol. 1, p. 72; Vol. 3, p. 46)

Spinach Salad

SUPPER

- "Cream of Avocado" (Vol. 3, p. 351)
- "Mango Custard" (Vol. 3, p. 354)

Mango Custard

HEALTH COUNSELS

This menu is especially designed for **dermatitis** or **eczema,** as it is free from the products and substances that frequently cause these disorders. Furthermore, rice, soybeans, avocados, and mangoes exert a *softening* and *protecting* action upon the skin.

the Skin

Skin Beauty

BREAKFAST

- Mango (Vol. 2, p. 341)
- "Whole Bread" toast with "Hazelnut Butter" (Vol. 1, p. 72; Vol. 3, pp. 46, 65)
- "Coconut Milk" (Vol. 3, p. 343)

Coconut Milk

LUNCH

- "Filled Cucumbers" (Vol. 3, p. 348)
- "Pinto Beans" (Vol. 3, p. 353)
- Natural skimmed yogurt with molasses, wheat germ, walnuts, and raisins (Vol. 1, pp. 202, 175; Vol. 2, pp. 310, 64, 78)
- "Whole Bread" (Vol. 1, p. 72; Vol. 3, p. 46)

Pinto Beans

SUPPER

- "Carrot and Apple Juice" (Vol. 3, p. 355)
- "Chard with Potatoes and Pumpkin" (Vol. 3, p. 263)
- Brewer's yeast (Vol. 1, p. 358)

Chard with Potatoes and Pumpkin

HEALTH COUNSELS

Skin and **hair beauty,** as well healthy **nails,** are enhanced through this menu, due to its content in ***provitamin A*** (mango, carrot, chard), ***minerals*** (coconut, molasses, brewer's yeast, wheat germ), and ***essential fatty acids*** (hazelnuts, walnuts).

Other Recipes for the Skin

SALADS

- "Mexican Salad" (Vol. 3, p. 260)
- "Chickpea Salad" (Vol. 3, p. 186)
- "Asparagus Salad" (Vol. 3, p. 278)

SOUPS AND PURÉES

- "Cereal Soup" (Vol. 3, p. 314)
- "Three-colored Purée" (Vol. 3, p. 377)
- "Vegetable Purée" (Vol. 3, p. 361)

MAIN COURSES

- "Andalusian Asparagus" (Vol. 3, p. 349)
- "Beans and Spinach" (Vol. 3, p. 352)
- "Rice with Carrots" (Vol. 3, p. 133)
- "Vegetarian Tamale" (Vol. 3, p. 301)
- "Stuffed Peppers" (Vol. 3, p. 382)
- "Carrot Croquettes" (Vol. 3, p. 112)

BREAKFASTS, DESSERTS AND SNACKS

- "Carrot Cake" (Vol. 3, p. 125)
- Whole cereals (Vol. 1, p. 65)
- Breads prepared with whole grains (Vol. 1, 72)

DRINKS

Freshly squeezed juices:

- Cucumber (Vol. 2, p. 339)
- Spinach (Vol. 2, p. 28)
- Mango (Vol. 2, p. 341)

Infusions, decoctions or other uses of:

- Pansy (*EMP,* p. 735)
- Dandelion (*EMP,* p. 397)
- White birch (*EMP,* p. 568)

- *See the recipe index at the beginning of this volume (Vol. 3, pp. 8-13).*
- *See also chapter 33, "Foods for the Skin" (Vol. 2, pp. 330-347).*

EMP = Encyclopedia of Medicinal Plants, Edication and Health Library, Editorial Safeliz.

Preparation time 00:15

Cooking time 00:15

Filled Cucumbers

INGREDIENTS (4 servings)

- 2 **cucumbers**
- 300 g (≅ 10.6 oz) of **spinach**
- 100 g (≅ 3.5 oz) of sweet **corn**
- 100 g (≅ 3.5 oz) of **quark cheese**
- 50 g (≅ 1.75 oz) of **fava beans** (broad beans)

ADDITIONAL INGREDIENTS

- 8 **basil** leaves
- **Parsley**
- The juice of 1/2 **lemon**
- 6 tablespoons of olive **oil** (each tablespoon of oil adds around 120 kcal to the recipe, that is, 30 kcal per serving)
- Sea salt (see Vol. 3, p. 16)

PREPARATION

❶Cut the cucumbers lengthwise and empty them.
- Chop the extracted pulp.
- Wash the spinach.

❷Steam the spinach for 5 minutes. Cool down and chop.
- Combine the cheese, the lemon juice, the oil, and the salt.
- Add the spinach, the fava beans, the cucumber pulp, the basil, and the parsley to the cheese mixture.
- Fill the cucumbers.
- Sprinkle corn kernels to decorate.

❸Serve cold.

HEALTHIER ALTERNATIVE: Instead of using cheese, soy mayonnaise (see Vol. 3, p. 58) may be used.

For more information about the ingredients, see: Cucumber, Vol. 2, p. 339; spinach, Vol. 2, p. 28; fava bean, Vol. 2, p. 137; cheese, Vol. 1, p. 213; corn, Vol.2, p. 238.

HEALTH COUNSELS

This salad has an informal, somewhat exotic, look. As any other salad made up of raw vegetables, it is light and healthy, and especially beneficial to:

✓The **skin,** due to the *hydrating effect* of cucumbers and the other vegetables. ***Minerals*** supplied by this salad, such as ***sulfur,*** from cucumbers and ***iron,*** from spinach, *help to maintain* skin, **nails,** and **hair** in good health. This recipe is recommended for those wishing to keep their skin smooth and avoid nails and hair becoming frail.

✓The **blood,** thanks to **iron** in spinach and fava beans, which *prevents* **anemia.**

✓The **vision,** due to ***carotenoids*** in spinach, as well as other ***antioxidants*** found in the vegetables, which protect the retina and avoid its deterioration.

NUTRITIONAL VALUE* per serving

Energy	**82 kcal = 345 kj**
Protein	**7.78 g**
Carbohydrates	**8.49 g**
Fiber	**4.03 g**
Total fat	***1.25 g***
Saturated fat	***0.444 g***
Cholesterol	***2.10 mg***
Sodium	***173 mg***

1% 2% 4% 10% 20% 40% 100%

% Daily Value (based on a 2,000 calorie diet) provided by each serving of this dish

CALORIC PROPORTION*

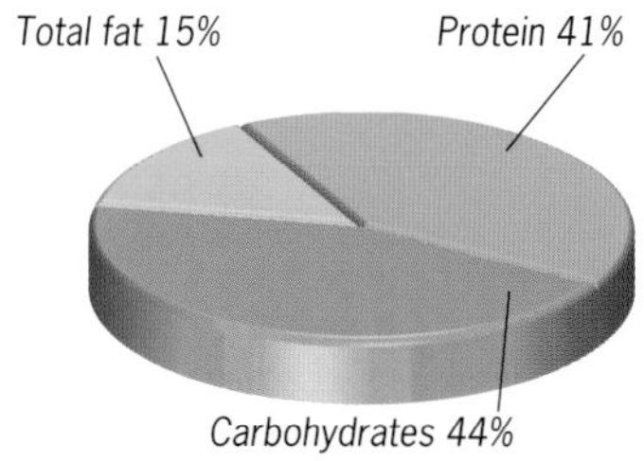

Percentage distribution of **calories for each nutrient**

*Additional ingredients are not included.

Preparation time 00:15

Cooking time 00:30

Andalusian Asparagus

INGREDIENTS (4 servings)

- 750 g (≅ 26.5 oz) of **green asparagus**
- 2 slices of **whole bread**
- 1 tablespoon of **whole flour**
- 2 **garlic** cloves

ADDITIONAL INGREDIENTS

- **Parsley**
- **Saffron**
- 1/2 a teaspoon of sweet **paprika**
- The juice of one **lemon**
- 3 tablespoons of olive **oil** (each tablespoon of oil adds around 120 kcal to the recipe, that is, 30 kcal per serving)
- Sea **salt** (see Vol. 3, p. 16)

PREPARATION

❶Wash the asparagus, discard the woody stems and peel if necessary.

- Chop the asparagus into medium chunks.
- Peel the garlic.

❷Boil the asparagus in a pot with a little water and salt.

- In a frying pot, sauté the garlic and the bread.
- In a mortar, grind the sautéed mixture together with the other garlic (raw), the paprika and the parsley. Add to the asparagus pot.
- In the oil left on the frying pan, toast the flour and add it to the pot.
- Stir, keeping a low flame until the sauce thickens.

❸Serve hot.

HEALTHIER ALTERNATIVE: Instead of sautéing the garlic and bread, bake them and toast the flour without oil.

For more information about the ingredients, see: Asparagus, Vol. 2, p. 250; whole bread, Vol. 1, p. 72; flour, Vol. 1, p. 68; garlic, Vol. 1, p. 338 and the *Encyclopedia of Medicinal Plants:* Garlic, p. 230.

HEALTH COUNSELS

This is a tasty and unique way to prepare healthy asparagus. The recipe is highly recommended for:

✓The **skin,** due to the *cleansing* and *detoxifying* effect of asparagus. They help *eliminate* **toxic residues** via the uterine excreted through the metabolism. In this way, they do not accumulate in the skin where they may cause dermatosis and eczema.

✓The **intestine,** due to its ***fiber*** content which *prevents* **constipation.**

✓The **urinary system,** due to the *diuretic* effect of asparagus .

✓**Slimming** diets, as asparagus, posses a *satisfying* effect and supply very *few* **calories.**

NUTRITIONAL VALUE* per serving

Energy	**76 kcal = 318 kj**
Protein	**4.95 g**
Carbohydrates	**10.8 g**
Fiber	**4.18 g**
Total fat	***0.868 g***
Saturated fat	***0.190 g***
Cholesterol	—
Sodium	***4.07 mg***

1% 2% 4% 10% 20% 40% 100%

% Daily Value (based on a 2,000 calorie diet) provided by each serving of this dish

CALORIC PROPORTION*

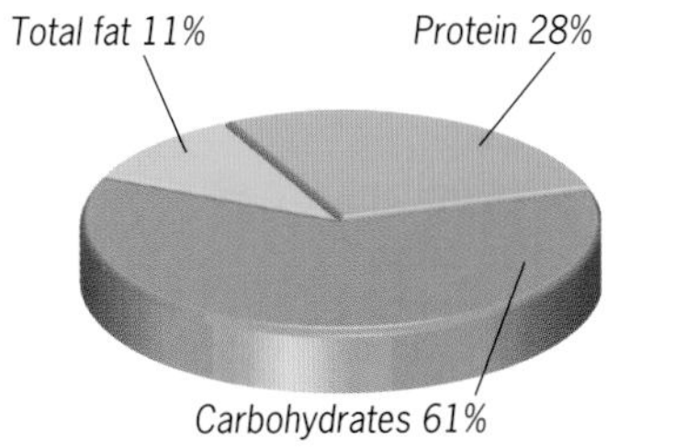

Percentage distribution of **calories for each nutrient**

*Additional ingredients are not included.

Preparation time 00:10

Cooking time 00:30

Cream of Asparagus

INGREDIENTS (4 servings)

- 500 g (≅ 1 pound) of **asparagus**
- 500 g (≅ 1 pound) of **Béchamel sauce** (Vol. 3, p. 59)

ADDITIONAL INGREDIENTS

- **Mint**
- Sea **salt** (see Vol. 3, p. 16)

PREPARATION

❶ Peel, wash, and chop the asparagus in small pieces.

❷ Boil the asparagus in a pot with a liter of water and salt.

- Blend the asparagus with an electric blender and pass through a grinder to sieve them well.
- Prepare the white sauce.
- Add this sauce to the asparagus puré and mix thoroughly.

❸ Serve hot, garnished with mint.

For more information about the ingredients, see: Asparagus, Vol. 2, p. 250.

Suggestions from the Chef

Natural-style canned asparagus may be used.

HEALTH COUNSELS

Asparagus are more nutritious than is commonly believed. They contain ***fiber, complex-B vitamins, folates, provitamin A*** (beta-carotene), and ***vitamins C*** and ***E.*** Besides, they are *high* in ***minerals*** and ***trace elements.*** This Cream of Asparagus, as described here, is light and easy to digest, and it is beneficial to:

✓ The **skin,** due to the *cleansing* effect of asparagus, which helps to eliminate waste substances circulating in the blood and causing skin rash. That is why this dish is recommended in case of eczema or dermatitis. Furthermore, asparagus contain the necessary minerals to keep skin, **nails,** and **hair** in good health.

✓ The **kidneys,** as they stimulate urine production.

NUTRITIONAL VALUE* per serving

Energy	164 kcal = 685 kj
Protein	5.67 g
Carbohydrates	6.18 g
Fiber	3.09 g
Total fat	*12.5 g*
Saturated fat	*1.70 g*
Cholesterol	—
Sodium	*282 mg*

1% 2% 4% 10% 20% 40% 100%

% Daily Value **(based on a 2,000 calorie diet)** provided by each serving of this dish

CALORIC PROPORTION*

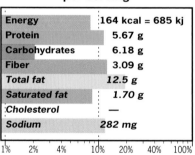

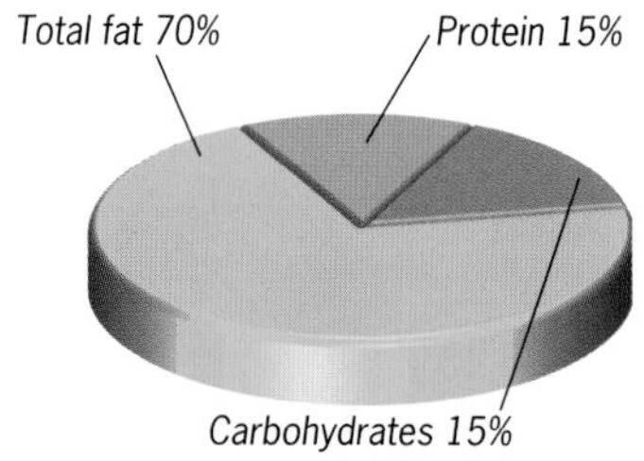

Percentage distribution of **calories for each nutrient**

*Additional ingredients are not included.

Preparation time 00:20 | Cooking time 00:25

Cream of Avocado

INGREDIENTS (4 servings)

- 2 **avocados**
- 1 **lettuce**
- 200 g (≅ 7 oz) of **spring onions**
- 4 toasts of dextrin-free **whole bread**
- 1 liter (≅ 1 quart) of unsalted **vegetable broth**

ADDITIONAL INGREDIENTS

- **Spearmint**
- 2 tablespoons of olive **oil** (each tablespoon of oil adds around 120 kcal to the recipe, that is, 30 kcal per serving)
- Sea **salt** (see Vol. 3, p. 16)

PREPARATION

❶ Peel and chop the spring onions.
- Wash and chop the lettuce.
- Peel, stone, and chop the avocados.
- Wash and chop the spearmint leaves.

❷ Heat oil in a pot, and sauté the onion and lettuce.
- Add the avocados, stir a little, and pour the vegetable broth. Boil for 10 minutes. Blend using an electric blender and add the spearmint.

❸ Serve cold, placing a slice of toast on each dish.

HEALTHIER ALTERNATIVE: Steam the spring onions and lettuce instead of sautéing them.

For more information about the ingredients, see: Avocado, Vol. 2, p. 108; lettuce, Vol. 2, p. 45; Onion, Vol. 2, p. 144; whole bread, Vol. 1, p. 72.

HEALTH COUNSELS

Avocados are high in ***fatty acids, vitamin E, iron*** and other necessary nutrients to preserve healthy skin. Combined with onion, vegetable broth, and whole bread, it makes a nutritious and healthy dish, which is easy to digest and especially recommended for:

✓The **skin,** due to the nutrients in avocados that protect the skin. **Dry skin, eczema,** and other skin disorders improve with the use of this recipe.

✓The **nervous system,** as ***vitamins*** and ***fatty acids*** supplied by avocados are necessary for the good functioning of neurons. This dish is beneficial in case of **nervousness, irritability** and nervous **depression.**

✓The diet for **diabetics,** as both avocados and onions *prevent* **high glucose** (sugar) in the blood.

NUTRITIONAL VALUE* per serving

Energy	190 kcal = 794 kj
Protein	5.17 g
Carbohydrates	12.0 g
Fiber	6.17 g
Total fat	*12.4 g*
Saturated fat	*2.01 g*
Cholesterol	—
Sodium	*22.9 mg*

1% 2% 4% 10% 20% 40% 100%

% Daily Value (based on a 2,000 calorie diet) provided by each serving of this dish

CALORIC PROPORTION*

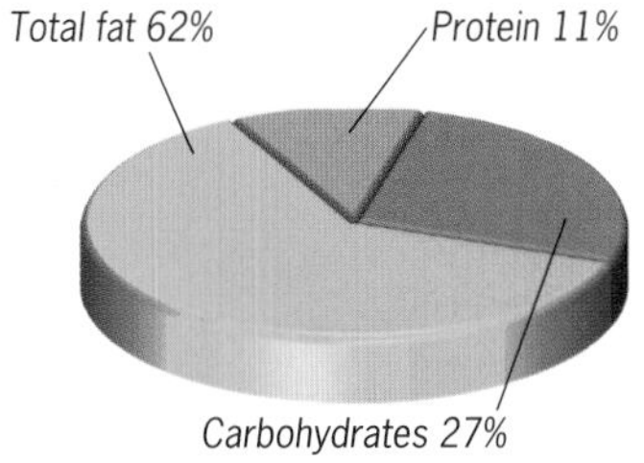

Percentage distribution of **calories for each nutrient**

*Additional ingredients are not included.

Preparation time 00:20

Cooking time 01:30

Beans and Spinach

INGREDIENTS (4 servings)

- 300 g (≅ 10.6 oz) of common **beans**
- 400 g (≅ 14 oz) of **spinach**
- 2 large **carrots** (or else 10-12 small ones)
- 1 **onion**
- 4 **garlic** cloves

ADDITIONAL INGREDIENTS

- **Thyme**
- 5 tablespoons of olive **oil** (each tablespoon of oil adds around 120 kcal to the recipe, that is, 30 kcal per serving)
- Sea **salt** (see Vol. 3, p. 16)

PREPARATION

❶ Soak beans overnight in cold water or for one hour if hot water is used.

- Peel and chop the onions and garlic.
- Wash and chop the spinach.
- Peel, wash, and chop (if large-size) the carrots.

❷ Boil the beans in plenty of water with salt.

- Heat the oil in a frying pan, and sauté the onion, garlic, and spinach.
- Add the sautéed mixture to the beans and carrots after having boiled for one hour.
- Shake the pot gently to mix all the ingredients and allow the broth to thicken. Do not stir with a spoon so as not to mash the beans.
- Keep simmering until the beans are tender.

❸ Serve hot or cold, thick or soupy, according to taste.

HEALTHIER ALTERNATIVE: Instead of sautéing the onion, garlic, and spinach, add them raw.

For more information about the ingredients, see: Bean, Vol. 2, p. 343; spinach, Vol. 2, p. 28; carrot, Vol. 2, p. 25; onion, Vol. 2, p. 142; garlic, Vol. 1, p. 338; and the *Encyclopedia of Medicinal Plants:* Garlic, p. 230.

HEALTH COUNSELS

This dish, like any other legume dish, is *very high* in essential nutrients, such as ***protein*** and ***iron.***

Additionally, beans are a good source of ***niacin*** and of ***pantothenic acid,*** two fundamental nutritional ingredients for the good health of skin. Iron as well as ***carotenoids*** from spinach also contribute to the beauty and smoothness of skin. Therefore, this dish is especially beneficial to:

✓The **skin,** especially in case of **dryness, atrophy, eczema,** and frail **nails.**

✓The **blood,** as it contributes to *prevent* and *treat* **anemia.**

✓The **arteries,** as it *reduces* **cholesterol** levels, and *avoids* **arteriosclerosis.**

✓The **metabolism,** particularly during **growth** stages, **intense physical activity** and **sports.**

NUTRITIONAL VALUE* per serving

Nutrient	Amount
Energy	327 kcal = 1,368 kj
Protein	22.0 g
Carbohydrates	44.4 g
Fiber	17.2 g
Total fat	*1.22 g*
Saturated fat	*0.258 g*
Cholesterol	—
Sodium	*119 mg*

1% 2% 4% 10% 20% 40% 100%

% Daily Value (based on a 2,000 calorie diet) provided by each serving of this dish

CALORIC PROPORTION*

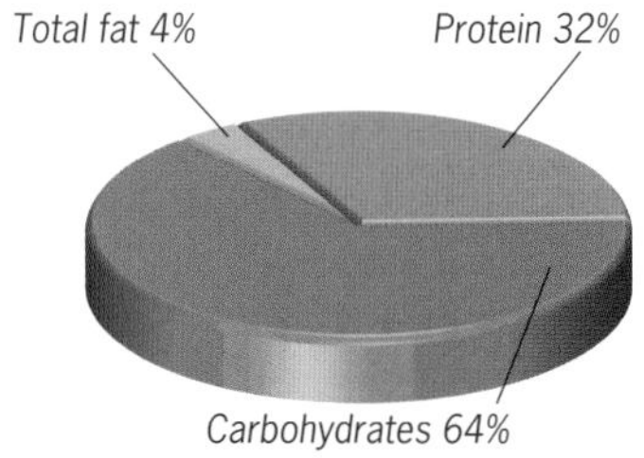

Percentage distribution of **calories for each nutrient**

*Additional ingredients are not included.

Preparation time 00:10 | Cooking time 01:30

Pinto Beans

INGREDIENTS (4 servings)

- 400 g (≅ 14 oz) of **pinto beans**
- 250 g (≅ 8.8 oz) of **pumpk** (squash)
- 2 **carrots**
- 1 **tomato**
- 1 **onion**
- 1 dry **sweet pepper**
- 1 **garlic** bulb

ADDITIONAL INGREDIENTS

- 2 **laurel** leaves
- 1/2 teaspoon of **sweet paprika**
- 3 tablespoons of olive **oil** (each tablespoon of oil adds around 120 kcal to the recipe, that is, 30 kcal per serving)
- Sea **salt** (see Vol. 3, p. 16)

PREPARATION

❶Soak beans overnight in cold water or for one hour if hot water is used.
- Peel, wash, and chop the pumpkin, carrots, and tomato.
- Peel the garlic and the onions. Do not chop them.

❷Drain and rinse the beans. Heat a pot with water and salt, and add the beans. At boiling point, reduce heat and simmer.
- When the beans begin to soften, add the vegetables, laurel leaves, sweet pepper, paprika, and oil.
- To avoid the beans being crushed, do not stir with a spoon, but rather shake the pot gently, holding onto the handles.

❸Serve hot.

For more information about the ingredients, see: Bean, Vol. 2, p. 343; pumpkin, Vol. 2, p. 97; carrot, Vol. 2, p. 25; tomato, Vol. 2, p. 275; onion, Vol. 2, p. 142; pepper, Vol. 2, p. 198; garlic, Vol. 1, p. 338; and the *Encyclopedia of Medicinal Plants:* Garlic, p. 230.

HEALTH COUNSELS

This is a highly nutritious dish, recommended to those wishing to follow a simple and healthy diet. Its use benefits the entire body, and especially:

✓The **skin,** thanks to the beans' ***niacin*** and ***pantothenic acid,*** as well as the ***beta-carotene*** found in pumpkin, carrots, and other vegetables. All these improve the health of the skin, and prevent **eczema, dry skin,** skin **atrophy, chapping,** and other skin maladies.

✓The **arteries** and the **heart,** as beans' ***fiber*** *reduces* **cholesterol.** Besides, the ***beta-carotene*** supplied by pumpkins and the other vegetables *avoids* **arteriosclerosis.**

✓The **blood,** in case of **anemia,** thanks to the *high-**iron*** content of beans.

NUTRITIONAL VALUE* per serving

Energy	**428 kcal = 1,787 kj**
Protein	**26.6 g**
Carbohydrates	**61.5 g**
Fiber	**19.8 g**
Total fat	***1.60 g***
Saturated fat	***0.435 g***
Cholesterol	—
Sodium	***40.9 mg***

1% 2% 4% 10% 20% 40% 100%

% Daily Value (based on a 2,000 calorie diet) provided by each serving of this dish

CALORIC PROPORTION*

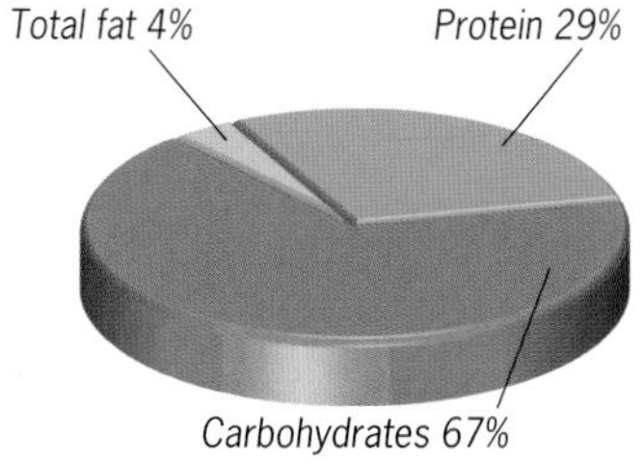

Percentage distribution of
calories for each nutrient

*Additional ingredients are not included.

Preparation time 00:10 | Cooking time 00:30

Mango Custard

INGREDIENTS (4 servings)

- 3 **mangoes**
- 1/2 liter (≅ 1/2 quart) of **soy milk** (Vol. 3, p. 305)
- 1 tablespoon of **brown sugar**
- 6 heaped tablespoons of **agar-agar** flakes (12 g)

ADDITIONAL INGREDIENTS

- 1/2 teaspoon of **ginger** powder

PREPARATION

❶ Peel and chop two mangoes.
- Gather the pulp and excess mango juice into a container.
- Add the ginger.

❷ Heat the soy milk and the sugar.
- When the milk is hot, add the agar-agar and stir until completely dissolved.
- Combine with the chopped mango.
- Put a mold under cold water. Fill it in with the mango mixture.
- Cool in the refrigerator overnight so that it sets.

❸ Empty at the time of serving. Decorate with thin mango slices around the custard.

Suggestions from the Chef

- Instead of agar-agar, use cornstarch or **rice flour.** These products thicken when heated and add consistency to the custard.
- Caramelize the mold bottom with molasses.

For more information about the ingredients, see: Mango, Vol. 2, p. 341; soy milk, Vol. 1, p. 88; agar-agar, Vol. 1, p. 130; brown sugar, Vol. 1, p. 170.

HEALTH COUNSELS

Mango is the fresh fruit with highest content of ***provitamin A.*** It also contains ***vitamins E, B1, B2, B6,*** and ***niacin.*** Combined with soy milk, as shown in this recipe, makes up a very healthy dessert that, unlike others, is low in ***saturated fat*** and is ***cholesterol-free.*** It is especially recommended for:

✓The **skin,** due to its high content in vitamins—especially A—which contributes to *avoid* **premature aging,** as well as skin **dryness, eczema,** and skin **inflammation.**

✓**Vision,** due to the *protecting* effect of vitamin A upon the eyes.

✓**Myocardial infarction** and **cancer** *prevention,* due to mangoes' *antioxidant* effect, and soybeans' *protecting action,* which avoid both illnesses.

NUTRITIONAL VALUE* per serving

Energy	196 kcal = 818 kj
Protein	4.68 g
Carbohydrates	37.1 g
Fiber	5.57 g
Total fat	*2.95 g*
Saturated fat	*0.405 g*
Cholesterol	—
Sodium	*23.4 mg*

1% 2% 4% 10% 20% 40% 100%

% Daily Value (based on a 2,000 calorie diet) provided by each serving of this dessert

CALORIC PROPORTION*

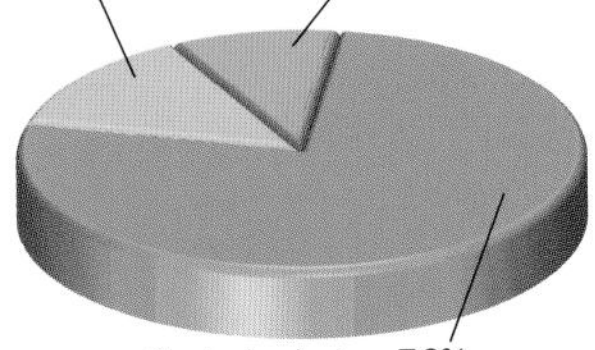

Percentage distribution of **calories for each nutrient**

*Additional ingredients are not included.

Preparation time: 00:20

Cooking time: - - - -

Carrot and Apple Juice

INGREDIENTS (4 servings)

- 500 g (≅ 1 pound) of **carrots**
- 500 g (≅ 1 pound) of **apples**
- A few drops of **lemon** juice

PREPARATION

❶ Wash, peel and chop the apples and the carrots.

❷ Liquify and add the lemon juice.
- Mix the juices well.

❸ Serve cold immediately.

For more information about the ingredients, see: Apple, Vol. 2, p. 229; carrot, Vol. 2, p. 25; lemon, Vol. 2, p. 124.

HEALTH COUNSELS

Apple, carrot, and lemon juices combine quite well and offer a drink full of preventive and healing qualities. Its use benefits the entire body, but more especially:

✓The **skin,** because apples detoxify the intestine and *remove* the *cause* of **eczema** and other skin **disorders.** Carrots supply a good amount of ***beta-carotene*** (provitamin A) which turns into vitamin A, and protects the skin. This drink is ideal to maintain a beautiful and shiny complexion, and to fight **dry skin** and skin **atrophy.**

✓The **intestine,** due to the *detoxifying* effect of apples and carrots, which *fight* **fermentation,** *protect* the intestinal **flora,** and *avoid* **constipation.**

✓The **liver,** as both carrots and apples *soften* the **bile** and favor the *detoxifying* function of this organ.

NUTRITIONAL VALUE per serving

Energy	**77 kcal = 322 kj**
Protein	**0.773 g**
Carbohydrates	**17.9 g**
Fiber	**0.700 g**
Total fat	***0.223 g***
Saturated fat	***0.039 g***
Cholesterol	**—**
Sodium	***24.8 mg***

1% 2% 4% 10% 20% 40% 100%

% Daily Value (based on a 2,000 calorie diet) provided by each serving of this drink

CALORIC PROPORTION

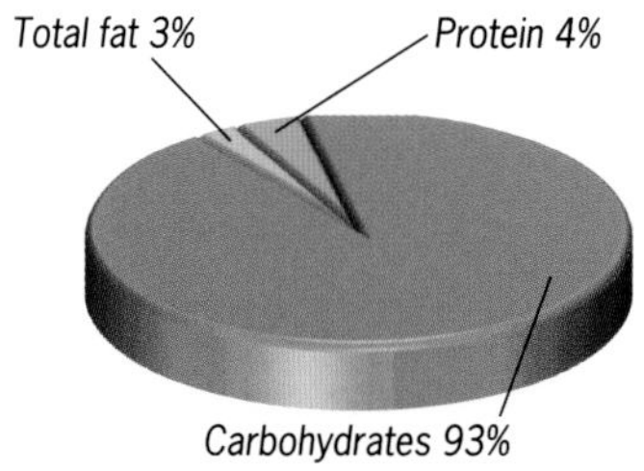

Percentage distribution of **calories for each nutrient**

57 RECIPES FOR THE INFECTIONS

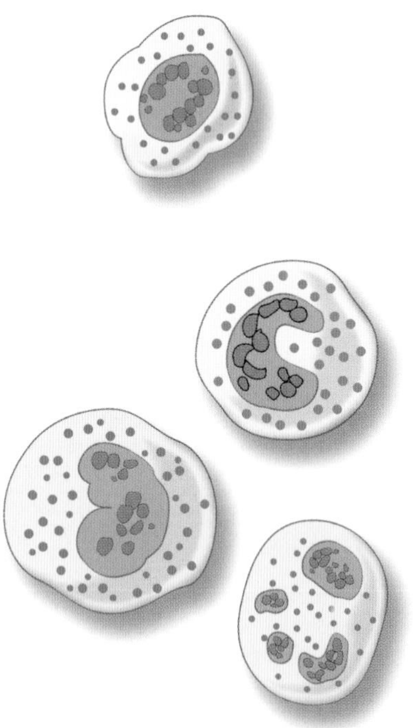

Suffering from an infection does not need to be an obstacle to enjoy healthy and tasty recipes that, at the same time, help the body to fight germs.

The good condition of anti-infectious defenses greatly depends upon a natural diet that is high in antioxidant substances of plant origin.

CHAPTER SUMMARY

RECIPES

Andalusian Gazpacho . . . . *.360*
Baked Tomatoes . . . . *.364*
Borage and Potatoes . . . . *.362*
Melon and Orange Juice . . . . *.367*
Oranges with Honey . . . . *.266*
Vegetable Purée . . . . *.361*

THOSE SUFFERING from an **infection** or running a **fever** do not need to deprive themselves of well-prepared, delicious dishes. However, these should be very light and healthy recipes that meet the following conditions:

- Contain a ***high*** *proportion* of **water:** In case of fever, it is necessary to supply a greater amount of fluid in order to compensate for the dehydrating effect of **sweating.** Fluids are also necessary in order to enhance **urine** production, and thus facilitate the elimination of the multiple waste substances excreted as a result of the infection.
- **Easy-to-digest** and ***low-fat.*** In the **acute phase,** it is also recommended that they be *low* in ***protein*** and in ***calories,*** that is, very light.
- Contain **natural antibiotics** among their ingredients (see Vol. 2, p. 351), such as **garlic** and **onion.** These substances contribute to destroy germs, which do not develop resistance to them.
- Contain ingredients that enhance defenses (**immunostimulants**). **Vegetables,** and especially **tomatoes** (part of the make-up of several recipes in this chapter), as well as **oranges,** *stimulate* the production of **antibodies,** due to their *antioxidant* action and to their content in ***vitamin A*** and ***vitamin C.***

Recipes included in this chapter's menus as well as the specific recipes presented in detail meet most of these conditions. In general, **salads** made up of **raw vegetables** also meet these requirements and are adequate for those suffering from an infectious disease.

However, in the case of infections that **weaken** the person, salad mastication becomes more difficult. This is also the case for **children** and the **elderly.** Therefore, in all these cases **gazpacho** is recommended. This is a typical dish that belongs to the Mediterranean diet. It is an authentic "salad purée," a refreshing and healthy dish high in vitamins, (see Vol. 1, p. 102; Vol. 3, p. 360). Considering that garlic counts among the ingredients, and occasionally onion, gazpacho also includes anti-infectious properties.

Once the **acute phase** *is over,* it is good to add more caloric and substancial dishes to the diet. These should be high in vitamins and substances that stimulate anti-infectious defense mechanisms. Most recipes in the fourth part of this encyclopedia fulfill this role (see Vol. 3, p. 126).

Menus for

Fever

Barley water

BREAKFAST

- Barley water (Vol. 2, p. 163)
- Freshly squeezed "Melon and Orange Juice" (Vol. 3, p. 367)

Borage and Potatoes

LUNCH

- Cleansing broth with lemon juice half an hour before lunch (Vol. 1, p. 369; Vol. 2, p. 124)
- "Borage with Potatoes" (Vol. 3, p. 362)
- "Whole Bread" (Vol. 1, p. 72; Vol. 3, p. 46)
- Plain skimmed yogurt (Vol. 1, p. 202)

Apple

SUPPER

- Barberry and white willow infusion (*EMP,* pp. 384, 676)
- Baked apple or shredded raw apple (Vol. 2, p. 229)
- "Oranges with Honey" (Vol. 3, p. 366)

HEALTH COUNSELS

This is a very convenient menu in case of **fever,** as it is *high* in ***water*** and ***mineral salts,*** as well as being light and very easy to digest. Borage cleans the blood and stimulates sweating, which helps fight fever.

Low Defenses

Hummus

BREAKFAST

- Acerola or tangerine (Vol. 2, pp. 367, 359)
- "Whole Bread" with "Hummus" (Vol. 1, p. 72; Vol. 3, p. 67)
- "Hazelnut Milk" lightly sweetened with molasses and wheat germ (Vol. 3, p. 291; Vol. 1, p. 175; Vol. 2, p. 310)

LUNCH

- Gentian and sea buckthorn (*EMP,* pp. 452, 758)
- "Andalusian Gazpacho" (Vol. 3, p. 360)
- "Vegetable Purée" with alfalfa sprouts (Vol. 3, p. 361; Vol. 1, p. 86)
- "Baked Tomatoes" (Vol. 3, p. 364)
- "Whole Bread" (Vol. 1, p. 72, Vol. 3, p. 46)

Andalusian Gazpacho

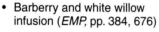

Tomato Juice

SUPPER

- Tomato juice (Vol. 2, p. 275)
- "Rye Bread" toasts with "Tahini" (Vol. 3, pp. 194, 61)

HEALTH COUNSELS

This is an ideal menu for cases with ***low defenses,*** since acerolas, tangerines, gazpacho (raw vegetables and greens purée), and tomatoes have *immunostimulant* properties. Molasses and sesame (within tahini) supply trace minerals, such as ***zinc*** and ***selenium,*** which increase defenses.

the Infections

General Infections

BREAKFAST

- Black elder and bramble infusion (*EMP*, pp. 767, 541)
- Kiwis (Vol. 2, p. 356)
- "Oatmeal" (Vol. 3, p. 154)

Oatmeal

Autumn Rice

LUNCH

- Alfalfa juice or capsules (*EMP*, p. 269)
- Tomato, onion, and garlic salad (Vol. 2, pp. 275, 142; Vol. 1, p. 338)
- "Autumn Rice" with pumpkin seeds (Vol. 3, p. 168; Vol. 1, p. 58)
- "Rye Bread" (Vol. 3, p. 194)
- "Persimmon Shake" (Vol. 3, p. 270)

SUPPER

- "Apricot Shake" (Vol. 3, p. 141)
- "Party Melon" (Vol. 3, p. 176)

Party Melon

HEALTH COUNSELS

The ingredients in this menu are notable for their *cleansing*—such as black elder, alfalfa, and melon—, *defense stimulant*—such as kiwi and garlic—, *antibiotic*—garlic and onion—, and *membrane protecting*—apricot—properties. This is why this menu is useful in any type of **infection.**

Other Recipes for Infections

SALADS

- "Seed Salad" (Vol. 3, p. 298)
- "Spinach Salad" (Vol. 3, p. 132)
- "Mexican Salad" (Vol. 3, p. 260)

SOUPS AND PURÉES

- "Cream of Onion" (Vol. 3, p. 220)
- "Cereal Soup" (Vol. 3, p. 314)
- "Garlic Soup" (Vol. 3, p. 374)

MAIN COURSES

- "Potato Stew" (Vol. 3, p. 221)
- "Tomato and Vegetable Stew" (Vol. 3, p. 212)
- "Rice with Cauliflower" (Vol. 3, p. 282)
- "Sautéed Marinated Gluten" (Vol. 3, p. 91)
- "Onion and Pepper Pizza" (Vol. 3, p. 224)

BREAKFASTS, DESSERTS AND SNACKS

- "Tropical Fruit Salad" (Vol. 3, p. 253)
- "Bircher-Muesli" (Vol. 3, p. 175)

DRINKS

- "Cherimoya and Orange Shake" (Vol. 3, p. 178)
- "Vegetable Juice" (Vol. 3, p. 385)

Freshly squeezed juices:

- Celery and tomato (Vol. 2, pp. 248, 275)
- Orange, lemon, and grapefruit (Vol. 2, pp. 360, 124, 93)
- Carrot (Vol. 2, p. 25)
- Melon (Vol. 2, p. 254)

Infusions:

- Thyme (EMP, p. 769)
- Nasturtium (EMP, p. 772)
- Aloe (gel or juice) (EMP, p. 694)

- *See the recipe index at the beginning of this volume (Vol. 3, pp. 8-13).*
- *See also chapter 34, "Foods for the Skin" (Vol. 2, pp. 348-367).*

EMP = Encyclopedia of Medicinal Plants, EDICATION AND HEALTH LIBRARY, Editorial Safeliz.

Preparation time: 00:30

Cooking time: - - - -

Andalusian Gazpacho

INGREDIENTS (4 servings)

- 750 g (≅ 26.5 oz) of **tomatoes**
- 1 **sweet pepper**
- 1 **cucumber**
- 2 **garlic** cloves
- 250 ml (≅ 1 cup) of **water**
- 4 tablespoons of olive **oil**

ADDITIONAL INGREDIENTS

- Sea **salt** (see Vol. 3, p. 16)

PREPARATION

❶ Wash, peel, and chop the vegetables and the garlic.

❷ In a blender container, place the vegetables, garlic, and water and blend well. Add the oil and the salt and blend a little more.

• Sieve the gazpacho to eliminate the vegetable skins.

❸ Serve very cold.

For more information about the ingredients, see: Tomato, Vol. 2, p. 275; pepper, Vol. 2, p. 198; cucumber, Vol. 2, p. 339; garlic, Vol. 1, p. 338; olive oil, Vol. 1, p. 118; and the *Encyclopedia of Medicinal Plants:* Garlic, p. 230.

Suggestions from the Chef

Traditionally, and according to the local customs, the following may be added to gazpacho:

- A bit of vinegar or lemon juice;
- Bread (80 g), soaked in water;
- Very small cubes of cucumber, green pepper, onion, tomato, or bread;
- Water and/or ice.

HEALTH COUNSELS

All the ingredients of gazpacho, and especially tomatoes and garlic have a *stimulant* effect upon the **immune system.** Consequently, this recipe, apart from being refreshing and *high* in ***antioxidant vitamins,*** is good for ill and healthy individuals and is particularly beneficial for the prevention and treatment of:

✓ Any kind of **infectious disease,** as it helps the body to fight against infections.

✓ **AIDS** and **cancer,** as gazpacho is very high in antioxidant substances that *protect* the **cells** and *build* organic **defenses.**

✓ **Arteries** and **heart** diseases, such as **arteriosclerosis, thrombosis,** and **myocardial infarction.**

NUTRITIONAL VALUE* per serving

Energy	192 kcal = 803 kj
Protein	2.87 g
Carbohydrates	10.0 g
Fiber	2.76 g
Total fat	15.5 g
Saturated fat	2.10 g
Cholesterol	—
Sodium	26.0 mg

1% 2% 4% 10% 20% 40% 100%

% Daily Value (based on a 2,000 calorie diet) provided by each serving of this dish

CALORIC PROPORTION*

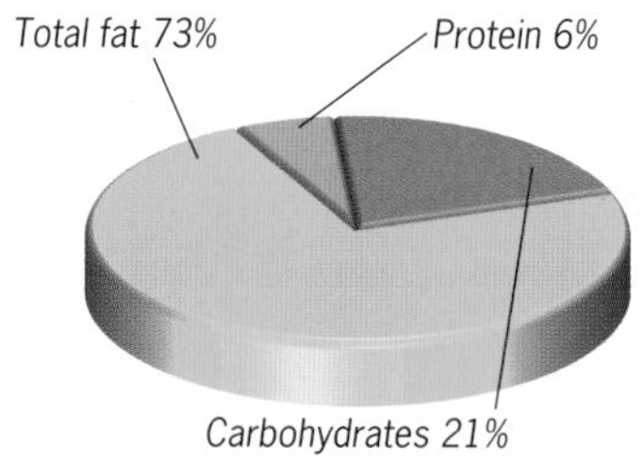

Percentage distribution of **calories for each nutrient**

*Additional ingredients are not included.

Preparation time 00:20
Cooking time 00:30

Vegetable Purée

INGREDIENTS (4 servings)

- 300 g (≅ 10.6 oz) of **potatoes**
- 250 g (≅ 8.8 oz) of **green beans**
- 250 g (≅ 8.8 oz) of **carrots**
- 1 **leek**
- 1 **tomato**
- 1 **celery** stalk
- 1 **turnip**
- 1 sweet **green pepper**
- 2 **garlic** cloves
- 1$^1/_2$ liters (≅ 1 $^1/_2$ quarts) of water

ADDITIONAL INGREDIENTS

- 3 tablespoons of olive **oil** (each tablespoon of oil adds around 120 kcal to the recipe, that is, 30 kcal per serving)
- Sea **salt** (see Vol. 3, p. 16)

PREPARATION

❶ Peel, wash, and chop all the ingredients.

❷ Heat water in a pot. At boiling point, add the ingredients.
- Keep boiling for 20 minutes until all vegetables are tender.
- Add the raw oil.
- Using an electric blender, blend to obtain a smooth purée.

❸ Serve hot and enjoy immediately.

For more information about the ingredients, see: Potatoes, Vol. 2, p. 201; green bean, Vol. 1, p. 109; carrot, Vol. 2, p. 25; leek, Vol. 2, p. 319; tomato, Vol. 2, p. 275; celery, Vol. 2, p. 248; turnip, Vol. 2, p. 320; pepper, Vol. 2, p. 198; garlic, Vol. 1, p. 338 and the *Encyclopedia of Medicinal Plants:* Green bean, p. 584; garlic, p. 230.

HEALTH COUNSELS

Vegetables, when cooked and reduced to a purée, constitute one of the **easiest** foods to **digest.** That is why it is among the *first* to be included in the **infant's diet.**

Apart from nutrients, this dish supplies important substances to fight **infections,** such as ***antioxidants*** (***vitamin C*** and ***beta-carotene***), ***minerals,*** and ***phytochemicals.*** All these stimulate the production of defenses.

The *cleansing* and *alkalinizing* effects og vegetables help to *neutralize* and *eliminate* **waste substances** excreted when fighting microorganisms.

In addition to being beneficial to prevent and cure infections, this dish is also good for the **stomach, intestine,** and **heart.**

NUTRITIONAL VALUE* per serving

Energy	145 kcal = 608 kj
Protein	4.73 g
Carbohydrates	26.2 g
Fiber	7.28 g
Total fat	*0.629 g*
Saturated fat	*0.106 g*
Cholesterol	—
Sodium	*83.4 mg*

1% 2% 4% 10% 20% 40% 100%

% Daily Value (based on a 2,000 calorie diet) provided by each serving of this dish

CALORIC PROPORTION*

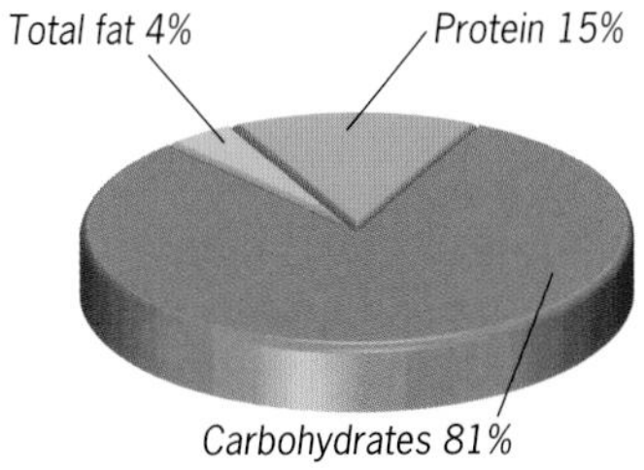

Percentage distribution of **calories for each nutrient**

*Additional ingredients are not included.

Preparation time 00:20

Cooking time 00:30

Borage and Potatoes

INGREDIENTS (4 servings)

- 1 kg (≅ 2 pounds) of **borage**
- 500 g (≅ 1 pound) of **potatoes**
- 2 liters (≅ 2 quarts) of **water**

ADDITIONAL INGREDIENTS

- 4 tablespoons of olive **oil** (each tablespoon of oil adds around 120 kcal to the recipe, that is, 30 kcal per serving)
- Sea **salt** (see Vol. 3, p. 16)

For more information about the ingredients, see: Borage, Vol. 2, p. 358; potato, Vol. 2, p. 201.

PREPARATION

❶Prepare the borage, peeling and washing the thick stems. Brush the tender ones to eliminate any soil.
- Chop the stems and tender leaves into pieces.
- Peel, wash and chop the potatoes.

❷Heat two liters of water in a pot. At boiling point, add the potatoes and the salt.
- Bring to a boil again and add half of the borage.
- Repeat again adding the remaining borage. This is to avoid interrupting the boiling process and to attain a uniform color.
- Boil at a medium heat for 20 minutes.
- Drain the borage and the potatoes.

❸Serve hot, dressing with raw olive oil.

Prepare the necessary ingredients.

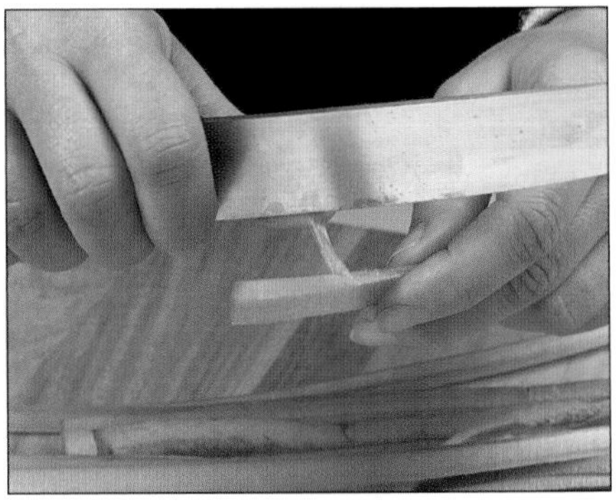

Peel the thickest borage's stems.

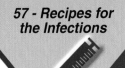

Chop the tender stems and borage's leaves.

Suggestions from the Chef

- Use the most **tender** borage stems. These are those harvested in winter, during **cold** weather.
- The dish may be **enriched** by adding boiled carrot or pumpkin.

Obesity

In case of obesity, and to reduce even further the caloric content of this dish (or any other), dress with just a few drops of lemon juice or with salt-free soy sauce extract.

NUTRITIONAL VALUE*
per serving

Energy	**111 kcal = 462 kj**
Protein	**4.77 g**
Carbohydrates	**21.0 g**
Fiber	**7.15 g**
Total fat	***1.15 g***
Saturated fat	***0.281 g***
Cholesterol	**—**
Sodium	***126 mg***

1% 2% 4% 10% 20% 40% 100%

% Daily Value (based on a 2,000 calorie diet)
provided by each serving of this dish

HEALTH COUNSELS

This borage dish has many healthy properties, especially due to that vegetable:

✓Softens the respiratory **membrane,** and *facilitates* **expectoration,**

✓Has significant *diuretic* and *cleansing* effects,

✓Contains *few* ***calories,*** and

✓Is *easy* to ***digest.***

Its use, therefore, is especially recommended for:

✓**Infectious** diseases in general, especially those of **viral origin,** such as **influenza.**

✓**Respiratory infections,** with or without fever, such as **colds, pharyngitis,** and bronchial **catarrh.**

✓**Kidney** diseases, including renal **stones.**

✓**Obesity,** as it contributes relatively *few* ***calories,*** even though it is quite *satisfying.*

CALORIC PROPORTION*

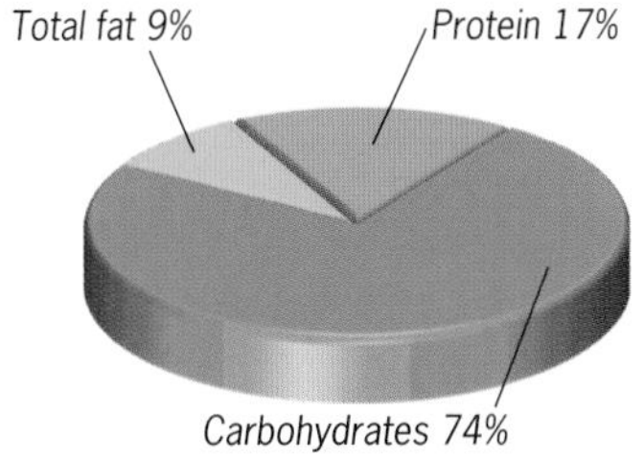

Percentage distribution of
calories for each nutrient

*Additional ingredients are not included.

Baked Tomatoes

INGREDIENTS (4 servings)

- 4 **tomatoes**
- 200 g (≅ 7 oz) of **corn**
- 60 g (≅ 2 oz) of **Texturized soy protein** (dried)
- 1 **onion**
- 2 **garlic** cloves
- 250 ml (≅ 1 cup) of unsalted **vegetable broth**
- 1 sweet **red pepper**

ADDITIONAL INGREDIENTS

- 1 teaspoon of **potherbs** (dill, tarragon, basil...)
- 2 tablespoons of olive **oil** (each tablespoon of oil adds around 120 kcal to the recipe, that is, 30 kcal per serving)
- Sea **salt** (see Vol. 3, p. 16)

PREPARATION

❶Soak the texturized soy protein in the vegetable broth for 30 minutes.
- Peel and chop the onion and garlic.
- Wash the tomatoes. Remove their upper parts and empty them. Reserve the pulp.
- Wash and chop the pepper.

❷Heat oil in a frying pan and sauté the onion. When it is transparent, add the potherbs, corn, texturized soy protein, and pepper. Cook on a low flame for 10 minutes.
- Add the tomato pulp and keep cooking for an additional 5 minutes.
- Stuff the tomatoes with the mixture and sprinkle with the garlic.
- Bake the stuffed tomatoes until they are tender.

❸Serve hot.

HEALTHIER ALTERNATIVE: Steam the onion or cook it in its own juices, instead of sautéing it.

Prepare the necessary ingredients.

Peel and chop the onion and garlic.

Suggestions from the Chef

Baked tomatoes may also be stuffed with other grains, such as rice or couscous, together with various vegetables and even nuts.

For more information about the ingredients, see: Tomato, Vol. 2, p. 275; corn, Vol. 2, p. 238; texturized soy protein, Vol. 1, p. 89; onion, Vol. 2, p. 142; garlic, Vol. 1, p. 338; and the *Encyclopedia of Medicinal Plants:* Garlic, p. 230.

Sauté all the ingredients for a few minutes in order to prepare the filling.

NUTRITIONAL VALUE* per serving

Energy	168 kcal = 700 kj
Protein	17.0 g
Carbohydrates	21.1 g
Fiber	5.65 g
Total fat	*1.62 g*
Saturated fat	*0.230 g*
Cholesterol	—
Sodium	*186 mg*

1% 2% 4% 10% 20% 40% 100%

% Daily Value (based on a 2,000 calorie diet) provided by each serving of this dish

HEALTH COUNSELS

Baked tomatoes, prepared as indicated here, make up a balanced and nutritious dish which supplies many necessary substances for the *production* of **defenses** against infections—***proteins, vitamins, minerals,*** and ***trace elements.*** It is therefore a nutritious and healthy recipe, which is especially beneficial for:

✓The **immune system,** when it is necessary to increase *production* of **antibodies** in order to *prevent* various kinds of **infections,** or to fight them.

✓**Cancer** *prevention,* as foods enhancing the function of the immune system will also contribute to prevent cancer. Furthermore, this recipe contains specific substances with proven *anticarcinogenic* agents, such as ***lycopene*** from tomatoes and ***phytoestrogens*** from soybeans.

✓The **arteries,** as this dish does *not* contain ***cholesterol*** and it is *low* in ***sodium***—if salt is omitted—and in ***fat,*** which eases blood circulation through the arteries.

✓The **metabolism,** as it supplies the necessary nutrients for **growth,** such as ***protein*** in soybeans and ***beta-carotene*** (provitamin A) in corn.

CALORIC PROPORTION*

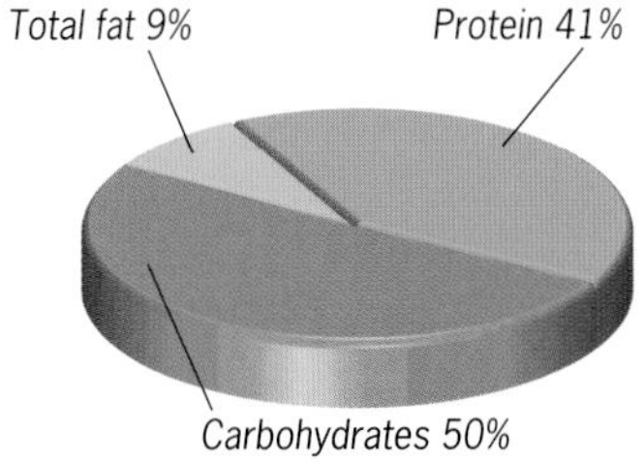

Percentage distribution of
calories for each nutrient

*Additional ingredients are not included.

Preparation time: 00:25

Cooking time: - - - -

Oranges with Honey

INGREDIENTS (6 servings)

- 1 kg (≅ 2 pounds) of **oranges**
- 100 g (≅ 1 cup) of shelled **walnuts**
- 4 tablespoons of **honey**

PREPARATION

❶ Peel and slice the oranges. Gather the extra juice.

❷ Mix in the orange juice with the walnuts and honey.

- Arrange the orange slices in goblets.
- Add the honey-walnut-juice mixture.

❸ Use immediately.

For more information about the ingredients, see: Orange, Vol. 2, p. 360; walnut, Vol. 2, p. 64; honey, Vol. 1, p. 160.

Suggestions from the Chef

It may also be topped with plain yogurt, quark cheese, or even whipped cream for those with a sweet tooth.

HEALTH COUNSELS

The ingredients of this dessert are very effective to fight **infections** because:

✓ **Honey** contains ***natural antibiotic substances;***

✓ **Oranges** are *high* in ***vitamin C*** and ***flavonoids,*** which stimulate the production of anti-infectious defenses; and

✓ **Walnuts** are *high* in ***protein, essential fatty acids, zinc*** and other ***trace minerals,*** all necessary for the good functioning of the **immune system.**

Therefore, this nutritious and delicious dessert is especially recommended for:

✓ **Infections,** especially those of **respiratory** type; this is for both the *prevention* and *acute phases.*

✓ **Cancer** *prevention.*

✓ At times of excessive energy demand, such as **growth** stages, **pregnancy,** and **lactation.**

NUTRITIONAL VALUE per serving

Energy	220 kcal = 921 kj
Protein	3.69 g
Carbohydrates	28.4 g
Fiber	4.03 g
Total fat	*10.5 g*
Saturated fat	*0.951 g*
Cholesterol	—
Sodium	*2.33 mg*

1% 2% 4% 10% 20% 40% 100%

% Daily Value (based on a 2,000 calorie diet) provided by each serving of this dessert

CALORIC PROPORTION

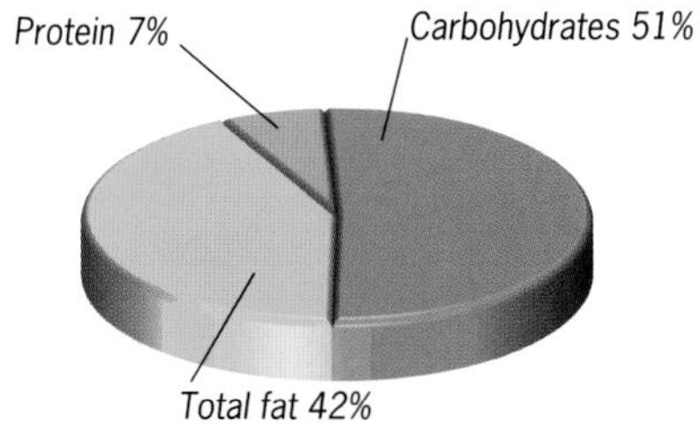

Percentage distribution of **calories for each nutrient**

Preparation time: 00:15

Cooking time: -- --

Melon and Orange Juice

INGREDIENTS (4 servings)

- 1 kg (≅ 2 pounds) of **melon**
- 1 kg (≅ 2 pounds) of **oranges**

PREPARATION

❶ Peel and chop the fruit.

❷ Process the fruit through a liquidizer. (If a liquidizer is not available, squeeze the oranges, add the melon chunks and use an ordinary electric blender).

❸ Serve cold.

For more information about the ingredients, see: Melon, Vol. 2, p. 254; orange, Vol. 2, p. 360.

Suggestions from the Chef

- In order to take full advantage of this drink's properties, use **immediately after preparing** it, and do not eat other food at the time.
- Drink it as an **appetizer,** at least half an hour before a meal. This helps the digestion of food and the drink is best assimilated.

HEALTH COUNSELS

This drink combines the *anti-infectious* qualities of oranges with the *refreshing* and *cleansing* effects of melon. Like all juices, it supplies ***vitamins, minerals,*** and ***phytochemicals*** that promote and revitalize health throughout the body. It is especially beneficial for:

✓ **Infections,** due to its *preventive* properties as well as to its refreshing and hydrating actions, in case of fever. It is an *ideal* juice for any patient suffering from an infection, whether light or severe, acute or chronic.

✓ The **urinary system,** thanks to its *diuretic* effect. It is good for urinary infections, such as **urethritis, cystitis,** or **pyelonephritis.**

✓ **Vision,** as it is *high* in ***carotenoids*** and ***antioxidant substances,*** which *protect* the **retina.**

✓ **Cancer** *prevention.*

NUTRITIONAL VALUE per serving

Energy	84 kcal = 352 kj
Protein	1.65 g
Carbohydrates	19.0 g
Fiber	0.382 g
Total fat	*0.242 g*
Saturated fat	*0.031 g*
Cholesterol	—
Sodium	*15.5 mg*

1% 2% 4% 10% 20% 40% 100%

% Daily Value (based on a 2,000 calorie diet) provided by each serving of this drink

CALORIC PROPORTION

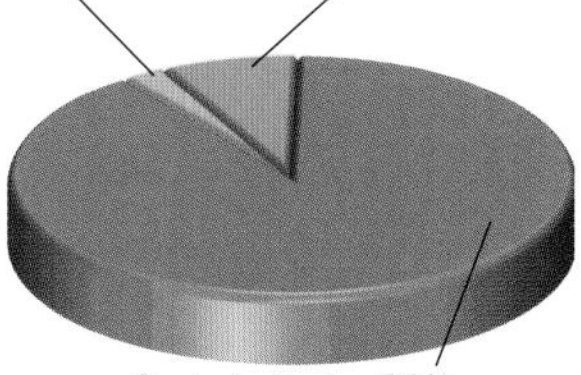

Percentage distribution of **calories for each nutrient**

58 RECIPES FOR CANCER PREVENTION

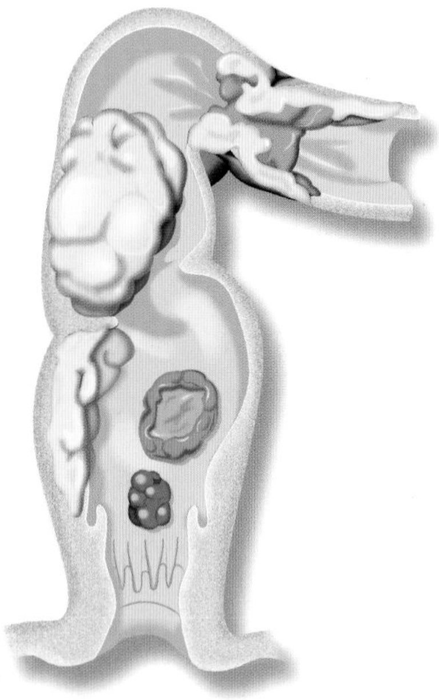

CHAPTER SUMMARY

RECIPES

Autumn Cabbage *376*
Cabbage Soup *375*
Cabbage Varieties *378*
Garlic Soup *374*
Red and White Salad *372*
Rice Salad *380*
Roasted Vegetables *384*
Soybean Stew *381*
Stuffed Peppers *382*
Three-colored Purée *377*
Vegetable Juice *385*
Violet Salad *373*

Each recipe in this chapter contains, among the ingredients, one or more foods of proven effectiveness in the prevention of cancer.

They are therefore recommended to those who are at risk of suffering from any type of cancer, and also to those who have already been diagnosed and are in a treatment phase.

IT WAS NOT UNTIL well into the last third of the 20th century that official medicine recognized that an inadequate diet is a decisive factor in the onset of various types of cancer.

In 1995, the European Union Cancer Specialists Commission published the European Code against Cancer, which later became popularly known as the **European Decalogue Against Cancer.** This is the actual summarized version:

1. Do not smoke. Smokers, stop as quickly as possible and do not smoke in the presence of others. If you do not smoke, do not try it.
2. If you drink alcohol, whether beer, wine or spirits, moderate your consumption.
3. Increase your daily intake of vegetables and fresh fruits. Eat cereals with a high fibre content frequently.
4. Avoid becoming overweight, increase physical activity and limit intake of fatty foods.
5. Avoid excessive exposure to the sun and avoid sunburn especially in children.
6. Apply strictly regulations aimed at preventing any exposure to known cancer-causing substances. Follow all health and safety instructions on substances which may cause cancer.
7. See your doctor if you notice a lump, a sore which does not heal (including in the mouth), a mole which changes in shape, size or colour, or any abnormal bleeding.
8. See your doctor if you have problems such as a persistent cough, persistent hoarseness, a change in bowel or urinary habits or unexplained weight loss.
9. For women: Have a cervical smear regularly. Participate in organised screening programmes for cervical cancer.
10. For women: Check your breasts regularly. Participate in organised mammographic screening programmes if you are over 50.

This commission predicted that in five years, "if these European 'Ten Commandments' were respected, there would be a significant reduction in deaths due to cancer in the European Union, which [...] could come close to 15%."

It should be noted that at least ***three*** of these **"commandments"** are related to dietary habits. It is therefore natural that in the ENCYCLOPEDIA OF FOODS AND THEIR POWER, we devote a good number of pages to this matter (see Vol. 2, p. 368).

It should also be borne in mind that the foods that are capable of protecting us against cancer are not limited to those included as ingredients in this chapter. On the other hand, some **dietary products** are carcinogenic (see Vol. 2, p. 372).

Menus to

Digestive Cancer (Mouth, Stomach, Colon)

Pineapple

BREAKFAST

- Freshly squeezed orange juice with wheat germ (Vol. 2, pp. 360, 310)
- "Rye Bread" with rubbed tomato and garlic (Vol. 3, p. 194; Vol. 2, p. 275; Vol. 1, p. 338; *EMP,* p. 230)
- Pineapple (Vol. 2, p. 189)

LUNCH

- Cabbage juice (Vol. 2, p. 191)
- "Violet Salad" (Vol. 3, p. 373)
- "Cream of Pumpkin" (Vol. 3, p. 134)
- "Stuffed Peppers" (Vol. 3, p. 382)
- "Whole Bread" (Vol. 1, p. 72; Vol. 3, p. 46)

Stuffed Peppers

SUPPER

- "Garlic Soup" (Vol. 3, p. 374)
- "Tropical Fruit Salad" (Vol. 3, p. 253)

Garlic Soup

HEALTH COUNSELS

This menu appropriately combines foods *high* in ***antioxidants,*** such as oranges and peppers, as well as garlic and several types of cabbages. All of them exert an *anticarcinogenic* effect, and especially *prevent* **mouth cancer, esophagus cancer, stomach cancer,** and **cancer of the colon.**

Breast Cancer and Prostate Cancer

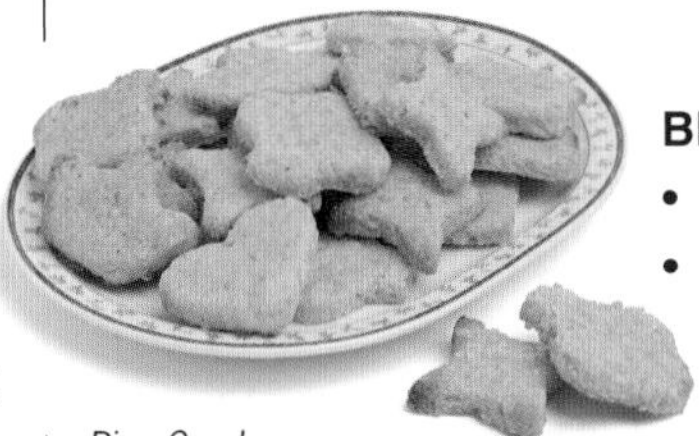

Rice Crackers

BREAKFAST

- Kiwi (Vol. 2, p. 356)
- Mango (Vol. 2, p. 341)
- "Rice Crackers" with "Tahini" (Vol. 3, p. 196, 61)
- "Soy Milk" (Vol. 3, p. 305)

LUNCH

- "Andalusian Gazpacho" (Vol. 3, p. 360)
- "Soybean Stew" (Vol. 3, p. 381)
- "Roasted Vegetables" (Vol. 3, p. 384)
- "Spinach Shake" (Vol. 3, p. 140)
- "Whole Bread" (Vol. 1,p. 72, Vol. 3, p. 46)

Roasted Vegetables

SUPPER

- "Melon and Orange Juice" with a tablespoon of wheat germ (Vol. 3, p. 367, Vol. 2, p. 310)
- "Rye Bread" toast with "Tofu and Herbs Spread" (Vol. 3,pp. 194, 66)

Tofu and Herbs Spreads

HEALTH COUNSELS

This menu is especially recommended to *prevent* **breast cancer** and **prostate cancer.** This is because it includes several soybean products, which have been found to protect against cancer of the reproductive organs.

Tomato, kiwi, and mango also contribute to the *anticarcinogenic* effect of this menu.

Prevent Cancer

Other Types of Cancer

BREAKFAST

- "Oranges with Honey" (Vol.3, p. 366)
- "Cereal Bars" (Vol. 3, p. 174)
- "Soy Milk" (Vol. 3, p. 305)

Cereal Bars

Red and White Salad

LUNCH

- Carrot juice and tomato juice (Vol. 2, pp. 275, 25)
- "Red and White Salad" (Vol. 3, p. 372)
- "Cabbage Varieties" (Vol. 3, p. 378)
- "Rice Hamburgers" (Vol. 3, p. 170)
- "Rye Bread" (Vol. 3, p. 194)

SUPPER

- Tomato and onion salad (Vol. 2, p. 275, 142)
- "Three-colored Purée" (Vol. 3, p. 377)

Three-colored Purée

HEALTH COUNSELS

The ingredients of this menu are outstanding for their *proved* **anticarcinogenic** effect, especially soybeans, broccoli, carrots, tomatoes, and onions. It is highly recommended to *reinforce* the **defenses** of those under *high risk* of suffering any type of cancer.

Other Recipes to Prevent Cancer

SALADS

- "Rainbow Salad" (Vol. 3, p. 184)
- "Stuffed Tomatoes" (Vol. 3, p. 300)
- "Spinach Salad" (Vol. 3, p. 132)
- "Rice Salad" (Vol. 3, p. 380)

SOUPS AND PURÉES

- "Cabbage Soup" (Vol. 3, p. 375)
- "Cream of Onion" (Vol. 3, p. 220)

MAIN COURSES

- "Sardinian Adzuki" (Vol. 3, p. 302)
- "Vegetable Rice" (Vol. 3, p. 266)
- "Christmas Red Cabbage" (Vol. 3, p. 248)
- "Autumn Cabbage" (Vol. 3, p. 376)
- "Broccoli Bake" (Vol. 3, p. 336)
- "Chinese Noodles" (Vol. 3, p. 316)
- "Soy Hamburgers" (Vol. 3, p. 117)

BREAKFASTS, DESSERTS AND SNACKS

- "Party Melon" (Vol. 3, p. 176)
- "Mango Custard" (Vol. 3, p. 354)
- "Fruit Salad" (Vol. 3, p. 200)

DRINKS

- "Vegetable Juice" (Vol. 3, p. 385)
- "Carrot and Apple Juice" (Vol. 3, p. 355)
- Cleansing broth (Vol. 1, p. 369)

Freshly squeezed juice of:

- Red beet (Vol. 2, p. 122)
- Carrot (Vol. 2, p. 25)
- Lemon and grapefruit (Vol. 2, pp. 93, 124)
- Tomato (Vol. 2, p. 275)
- Onion and celery (Vol. 2, pp. 142, 148)

- *See the recipe index at the beginning of this volume (Vol. 3, pp. 8-13).*
- *See also chapter 35, "Foods and Cancer" (Vol. 2, pp. 368-377).*

EMP = Encyclopedia of Medicinal Plants, EDUCATION AND HEALTH LIBRARY, Editorial Safeliz.

Preparation time: 00:15
Cooking time: - - - -

Red and White Salad

INGREDIENTS (4 servings)

- 150 g (≅ 5.3 oz) of **cauliflower**
- 150 g (≅ 5.3 oz) of **cabbage** (from the core)
- 1 **Belgian endive**
- 1 boiled **red beet**
- 2 **tomatoes**
- 1 sweet **red pepper**
- 4 **radishes**

ADDITIONAL INGREDIENTS

- The juice of one **lemon**
- 4 tablespoons of olive **oil** (each tablespoon of oil adds around 120 kcal to the recipe, that is, 30 kcal per serving)
- Sea **salt** (see Vol. 3, p. 16)

PREPARATION

❶ Wash and finely chop the cabbage.
- Wash the cauliflower, remove the darkened parts if necessary and break apart into small florets.
- Wash and chop the tomato and the pepper.
- Wash the Belgian endive and separate the leaves.
- Wash and slice the radishes.

❷ Arrange the endive leaves on each of the plates as well as the other vegetables.
- Dress with the salt, oil, and lemon juice.

❸ Serve immediately.

Suggestions from the Chef

Cabbage may be substituted by naturally fermented **sauerkraut.**

For more information about these ingredients, see: Cauliflower, Vol. 2, p. 154; cabbage, Vol. 2, p. 191; Belgian endive, Vol. 2, p. 175; beet, Vol. 2, p. 122; tomato, Vol. 2, p. 275; pepper, Vol. 2, p. 198; radish, Vol. 2, p. 181.

HEALTH COUNSELS

Vegetables included in this salad have in common a high content of: ***vitamins, minerals, trace minerals,*** and ***phytochemicals.*** Most of these vegetables have been *proved* to exert a *preventive* action upon various types of **cancer,** especially cabbage, cauliflower, beet, and tomato. Combined, these vegetables make up a very healthy salad. Its use is highly recommended to:

✓ *Prevent* **cancer** in general, and particularly the following types of cancer: **esophagus, stomach, intestine, pancreas, lung, prostate,** and **breast.**

✓ Avoid **constipation.**

✓ Fight **obesity, high blood pressure,** and **arteriosclerosis.**

✓ **Diabetic's** diet, as it *hardly* contains ***sugars*** and several of these vegetables possess a *hypoglycemic* effect.

NUTRITIONAL VALUE* per serving

Energy	74 kcal = 308 kj
Protein	3.70 g
Carbohydrates	10.3 g
Fiber	5.83 g
Total fat	*0.636 g*
Saturated fat	*0.084 g*
Cholesterol	—
Sodium	*62.7 mg*

1% 2% 4% 10% 20% 40% 100%

% Daily Value (based on a 2,000 calorie diet) provided by each serving of this dish

CALORIC PROPORTION*

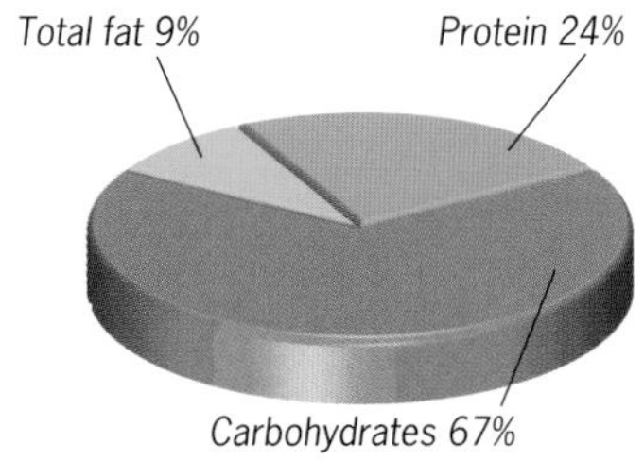

Percentage distribution of **calories for each nutrient**

*Additional ingredients are not included.

Preparation time 00:15 Cooking time 00:30

Violet Salad

INGREDIENTS (4 servings)

- 250 g (≅ 8.8 oz) of **red cabbage**
- 250 g (≅ 8.8 oz) of **beets**
- 200 g (≅ 7 oz) of **mushrooms**
- 2 **celery** stalks
- 2 **artichokes**
- 100 g (≅ 3.5 oz) of **black olives**

ADDITIONAL INGREDIENTS

- 4 tablespoons of olive **oil** (each tablespoon of oil adds around 120 kcal to the recipe, that is, 30 kcal per serving)
- The juice of 2 **lemons**
- Sea **salt** (see Vol. 3, p. 16)

PREPARATION

❶ Wash well and slice the mushrooms. Coat them with some of the lemon juice.
- Wash the artichokes and discard the outer leaves, the stem and the leaf tips. Slice in very thin slices. Coat with lemon juice (do not use it all).
- Select the red cabbage core (most tender part), wash it and chop it into thin sticks.
- Wash the celery and slice into thin strips.

❷ Boil the whole beet, stems included, until it is tender. Let it cool, peel, eliminate the stems, and slice it.
- Scald the mushrooms for 5 minutes.
- Arrange all the ingredients in a salad bowl, add the black olives, and dress with the remaining lemon juice plus oil.

❸ Serve immediately.

For more information about the ingredients, see: Red cabbage, Vol. 2, p. 193; beet, Vol. 2, p. 122; mushroom, Vol. 2, p. 294; celery, Vol. 2, p. 248; artichoke, Vol. 2, p. 178; olive, Vol. 2, p. 165.

HEALTH COUNSELS

Red cabbage, beet, and black olives have in common a **high content** in certain ***phytochemicals*** called ***anthocianins*** (see Vol. 1, p. 411). These are natural pigments that give the dark blue, black-blue, or reddish colors to these vegetables. They are extremely healthy due to their *intense antioxidant* effect that helps them *protect* our **cells** from **cancer** and *early aging.*

Celery, artichoke, and lemon are also *antioxidants* and *cleansing* foods that contribute to *eliminate* **toxic substances,** at times **carcinogenic,** that penetrate our body. This salad is, therefore, a highly recommended dish to *prevent* **cancer, obesity, arteriosclerosis,** and **diabetes.**

NUTRITIONAL VALUE* per serving

Energy	90 kcal = 378 kj
Protein	4.16 g
Carbohydrates	11.0 g
Fiber	6.52 g
Total fat	*1.86 g*
Saturated fat	*0.263 g*
Cholesterol	—
Sodium	*242 mg*

1% 2% 4% 10% 20% 40% 100%

% Daily Value (based on a 2,000 calorie diet) provided by each serving of this dish

CALORIC PROPORTION*

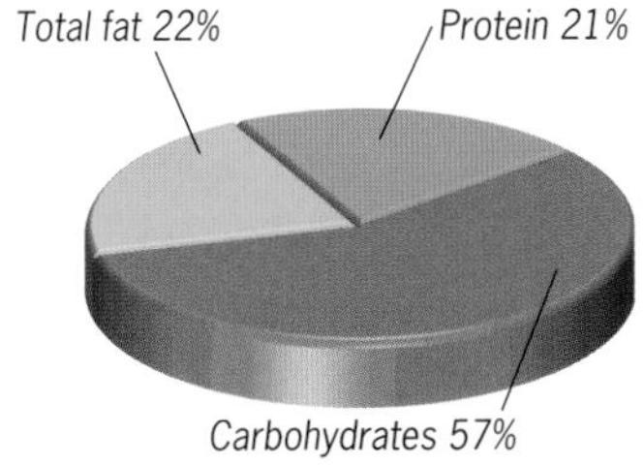

Percentage distribution of **calories for each nutrient**

*Additional ingredients are not included.

Preparation time 00:05

Cooking time 00:20

Garlic Soup

INGREDIENTS (4 servings)

- 1 **garlic** bulb
- 150 g (≅ 5.3 oz) of dried **whole bread**
- 1 **tomato**
- 1 liter (≅ 1 quart) of unsalted **vegetable broth**

ADDITIONAL INGREDIENTS

- 5 tablespoons of olive **oil** (each tablespoon of oil adds around 120 kcal to the recipe, that is, 30 kcal per serving)
- 1/2 teaspoon of sweet **paprika** (or a dried pepper)
- Sea **salt** (see Vol. 3, p. 16)

PREPARATION

❶ Separate the garlic cloves and, without removing the individual husk, crack them or make a cut in each of them.
- Slice the bread thinly.
- Peel and crush the tomato.

❷ Heat the oil in a pot and sauté the garlic. When they become golden, add the bread and stir. Add the paprika, tomato, vegetable broth, and salt.
- Boil for 10 minutes.

❸ Serve hot.

HEALTHIER ALTERNATIVE: Instead of sautéing the ingredients, add them raw to the boiling vegetable broth.

Suggestions from the Chef

This classic dish of the **Mediterranean cuisine** may vary in their ingredients depending on geographical location. For example, onion, red, or green peppers may be added.

For more information about the ingredients, see: Garlic, Vol. 1, p. 338; bread, Vol. 1, p. 72; tomato, Vol. 2, p. 275; and the *Encyclopedia of Medicinal Plants:* Garlic, p. 230.

HEALTH COUNSELS

Garlic is one of the ***most effective*** foods in cancer prevention. Its ***sulfur essence*** *stimulates* the body cells in charge of protecting us from cancer. Furthermore, garlic is able to neutralize ***nitrosamines*** and other carcinogenic substances that may be found in meat products (see Vol. 1, p. 270).

Therefore, this humble but nutritious and tasty soup brings about significant healthy benefits, especially for:

✓**Cancer** *prevention* in general, and particularly **stomach, colon,** and **breast** cancers. Whole bread and tomato enhance garlic's *anticarcinogenic* action.

✓The **respiratory system,** due to garlic's *balsamic* and *expectorant* effects.

✓The **arteries,** as it helps to *control* the level of **cholesterol.**

NUTRITIONAL VALUE* per serving

Energy	**121 kcal = 504 kj**
Protein	**4.83 g**
Carbohydrates	**20.2 g**
Fiber	**3.39 g**
Total fat	***1.65 g***
Saturated fat	***0.377 g***
Cholesterol	—
Sodium	***8.42 mg***

1% 2% 4% 10% 20% 40% 100%

% Daily Value (based on a 2,000 calorie diet) provided by each serving of this dish

CALORIC PROPORTION*

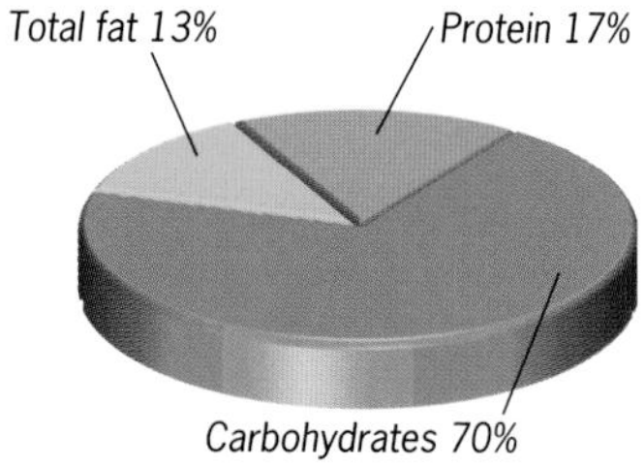

Percentage distribution of **calories for each nutrient**

*Additional ingredients are not included.

Preparation time 00:05

Cooking time 00:30

Cabbage Soup

INGREDIENTS (4 servings)

- 500 g (≅ 1 pound) of **cabbage**
- 100 g (≅ 3.5 oz) of **whole rice**
- 1 **onion**
- 1 liter (≅ 1 quart) of unsalted **vegetable broth**

ADDITIONAL INGREDIENTS

- 1/2 teaspoon of sweet **paprika**
- 3 tablespoons of olive **oil** (each tablespoon of oil adds around 120 kcal to the recipe, that is, 30 kcal per serving)
- Sea **salt** (see Vol. 3, p. 16)

PREPARATION

❶ Wash the cabbage.
- Peel and chop the onion.
- Crush the whole rice with an electric blender.

❷ Heat oil in a pot and sauté the onion.
- Add the cabbage and a little salt.
- After 2 or 3 minutes, add the crushed rice. Stir. Add paprika.
- Pour the vegetable broth. Boil on a medium flame for 20 minutes.

❸ Serve hot.

HEALTHIER ALTERNATIVE: Instead of sautéing the ingredients, add them raw to the boiling vegetable broth.

HEALTH COUNSELS

This simple, but nutritious and tasty cabbage soup is prepared using ingredients, such as cabbage and whole rice, endowed with healthy properties. Therefore, it is especially beneficial for:

✓ **Cancer** *prevention,* thanks to the sulfurated ***phytochemicals*** found in cabbage. These *stop* the development of certain **tumors** (see Vol. 2, p. 196). Onion, whole rice, and oil that accompany the cabbage, also contribute to this recipe's cancer-preventive effect.

✓ The **stomach,** due to cabbage's *soothing* properties.

✓ The **intestine,** thanks to the *laxative* effect of ***fiber.***

✓ The **musculoskeletal system** as ***calcium*** and other minerals supplied by cabbage and vegetable broth, contribute to *prevention* of **osteoporosis.**

NUTRITIONAL VALUE* per serving

Energy	136 kcal = 568 kj
Protein	4.11 g
Carbohydrates	24.7 g
Fiber	4.40 g
Total fat	*1.07 g*
Saturated fat	*0.185 g*
Cholesterol	—
Sodium	*24.6 mg*

1% 2% 4% 10% 20% 40% 100%

% Daily Value (based on a 2,000 calorie diet) provided by each serving of this dish

CALORIC PROPORTION*

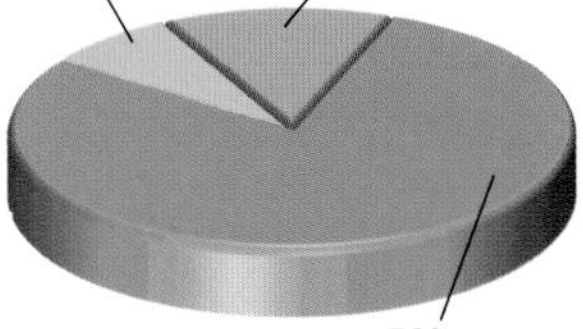

Percentage distribution of **calories for each nutrient**

*Additional ingredients are not included.

For more information about the ingredients, see: Cabbage, Vol. 2, p. 191; rice, Vol. 2, p. 225; onion, Vol. 2, p. 142.

Preparation time 00:25

Cooking time 00:50

Autumn Cabbage

INGREDIENTS (4 servings)

- 600 g (≅ 21 oz) of **cabbage**
- 400 g (≅ 14 oz) of **mushrooms**
- 400 g (≅ 14 oz) of **potatoes**
- 2 **onions**
- 12 pitted **prunes**
- 40 g (≅ 1.4 oz) of **brewer's yeast**
- 1 liter (≅ 1 quart) of unsalted **vegetable broth**

ADDITIONAL INGREDIENTS

- 4 tablespoons of walnut **oil** (each tablespoon of oil adds around 120 kcal to the recipe, that is, 30 kcal per serving)
- **Coriander**
- **Juniper berries**
- Sea **salt** (see Vol. 3, p. 16)

PREPARATION

❶ Peel and chop the onions.
- Wash the cabbage and chop it in fine strips.
- Peel, wash, and chop the potatoes.
- Wash the mushrooms.
- Wash and chop the coriander.

❷ Place the onions, cabbage, mushrooms, potatoes, prunes, coriander, and juniper berries in a pot. Cover with the vegetable broth and add salt.
- Simmer covered for 45 minutes.

❸ Serve hot.

For more information about the ingredients, see: Cabbage, Vol. 2, p. 191; mushroom, Vol. 1, p. 152; potato, Vol. 2, p. 201; onion, Vol. 2, p. 142; prune, Vol. 2, p. 235; brewer's yeast, Vol. 1, p. 358.

HEALTH COUNSELS

This cabbage dish supplies a wide variety of nutrients: ***Protein*** from mushrooms; ***carbohydrates*** from potatoes; and ***minerals*** coming from cabbage, onion, and brewer's yeast. At the same time, this dish adequately combines several foods known to be able to prevent cancer, such as cabbage and onion. It is good for everyone as a nutritious and healthy dish, but it is especially recommended for:

✓**Cancer** *prevention,* for the *high content* of ***protective phytochemicals*** found in cabbage and onion, whose effect continues even after being cooked. Prunes also contribute to prevent cancer of the colon, and to *fight* **constipation.**

✓The **stomach,** due to *scarring* effects of cabbage and *antacid* and *softening* actions of the potato.

✓The **intestine,** due to its *high-**fiber*** content, and to the gentle *laxative* effect of prunes.

NUTRITIONAL VALUE* per serving

Energy	289 kcal = 1,207 kj
Protein	11.6 g
Carbohydrates	52.8 g
Fiber	12.5 g
Total fat	*1.68 g*
Saturated fat	*0.218 g*
Cholesterol	—
Sodium	*44.5 mg*

1% 2% 4% 10% 20% 40% 100%

% Daily Value (based on a 2,000 calorie diet) provided by each serving of this dish

CALORIC PROPORTION*

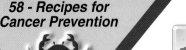

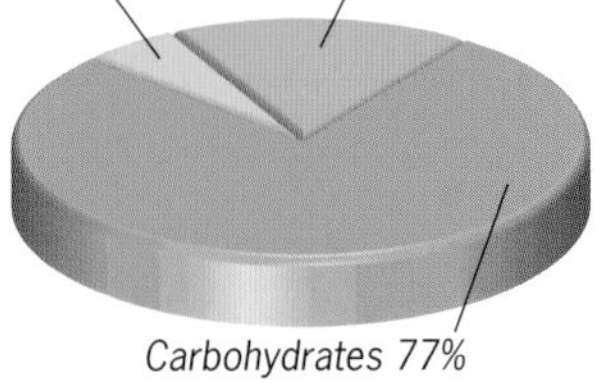

Percentage distribution of **calories for each nutrient**

*Additional ingredients are not included.

Preparation time 00:10

Cooking time 00:40

Three-colored Purée

INGREDIENTS (4 servings)

- 300 g (≅ 10.6 oz) of **potatoes**
- 150 g (≅ 5.3 oz) of **carrots**
- 120 g (≅ 4.2 oz) of roasted **chestnuts**
- 120 g (≅ 4.2 oz) of **broccoli**
- 150 g (≅ 5.3 oz) of boiled **red beet**
- 20 g (≅ 1/5 cup) of ground **almonds**
- 20 g (≅ 1/4 cup) of ground **hazelnuts**
- 40 g (≅ 1.4 oz) of **brewer's yeast**

ADDITIONAL INGREDIENTS

- **Parsley**
- 4 tablespoons of olive **oil** (each tablespoon of oil adds around 120 kcal to the recipe, that is, 30 kcal per serving)

PREPARATION

❶ Wash the carrots and the potatoes.

- Wash the broccoli and separate into florets.

❷ Boil the potatoes and the carrots.

- Add the broccoli florets after 10 minutes of boiling. Keep boiling until the potatoes are done.
- After they have cooled down, peel carrots and potatoes.
- Prepare the purées separately: For the first one, combine half of the potatoes with the carrots and almonds; for the second one, the other half of the potatoes, the red beets, and oil; for the third one, the chestnuts, broccoli, and hazelnuts.

❸ Add brewer's yeast and salt to each purée.

For more information about the ingredients, see: Potato, Vol. 2, p. 201; carrot, Vol. 2, p. 25; chestnut, Vol. 2, p. 322; broccoli, Vol. 2, p. 63; red beet, Vol. 2, p. 122; almond, Vol. 2, p. 48; hazelnut, Vol. 2, p. 252; brewer's yeast, Vol. 1, p. 358.

HEALTH COUNSELS

This purée is nutritious and high in anticarcinogenic substances, found especially in carrots, broccoli, and red beets. Because of its purée form, it is ideal for those with mastication difficulties (such as children or the elderly) or digestive problems (such as those suffering from the stomach). It is especially beneficial for:

✓ **Cancer** *prevention,* due to its ***phytochemicals*** and ***antioxidant vitamins*** from vegetables and nuts. The abundant ***fiber*** contained in this dish *facilitates* **bowel movement,** which helps in the *protective* action against cancer.

✓ The **stomach** and the **intestine,** due to its *antacid* effect, its easy digestion, and its gentle *laxative* action.

✓ The **arteries** and the **heart,** as it *reduces* the level of **cholesterol.**

NUTRITIONAL VALUE* per serving

Energy	236 kcal = 987 kj
Protein	9.26 g
Carbohydrates	28.5 g
Fiber	9.17 g
Total fat	*7.11 g*
Saturated fat	*0.705 g*
Cholesterol	—
Sodium	*60.6 mg*

1% 2% 4% 10% 20% 40% 100%

% Daily Value (based on a 2,000 calorie diet) provided by each serving of this dish

CALORIC PROPORTION*

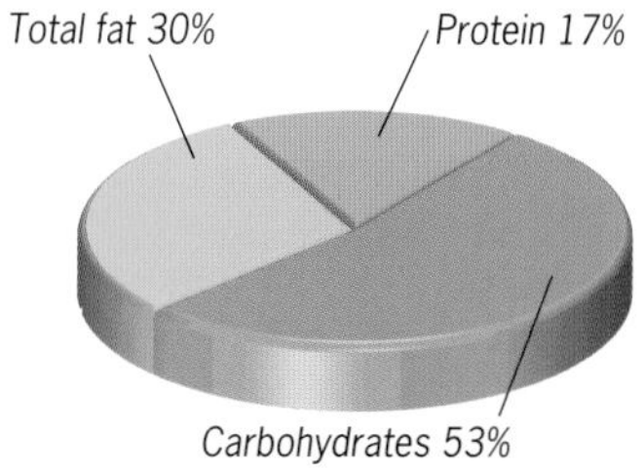

Percentage distribution of **calories for each nutrient**

*Additional ingredients are not included.

Preparation time 00:20

Cooking time 00:25

Cabbage Varieties

INGREDIENTS (4 servings)

- 500 g (≅ 1 pound) of **cabbage** or **Brussels sprouts** or **cauliflower** or **broccoli**
- 500 g (≅ 1 pound) of **potatoes**
- 250 g (≅ 8.8 oz) of **carrot** or **pumpkin** (squash)

ADDITIONAL INGREDIENTS

- 4 tablespoons of olive **oil** (each tablespoon of oil adds around 120 kcal to the recipe, that is, 30 kcal per serving)
- Sea **salt** (see Vol. 3, p. 16)

PREPARATION

❶ Wash and chop the selected cabbage.

- Peel, wash, and chop the potatoes and the carrots (or pumpkin).

❷ Boil water with salt and add the vegetables.

- Boil for 20 minutes. Drain. Reserve the broth for a different recipe.

❸ Serve hot and dress with the raw oil and salt.

Cauliflower

*It is advisable to avoid cauliflower in case of **cholelithiasis** (stones in the gallbladder), as it may cause **dyspepsia** (heavy digestion).*

*Due to its **high** content in cellulose **fiber,** it may produce intestinal **flatulence** in prone persons. Although they may be inconvenient, intestinal gases are of no health risk.*

For more information about the ingredients, see: Brussels sprouts, Vol. 2, p. 192, cabbage, Vol. 2, p. 191; cauliflower, Vol. 2, p. 154; broccoli, Vol. 2, p. 63; potato, Vol. 2, p. 201; carrot, Vol. 2, p. 25; pumpkin, Vol. 2, p. 97.

Suggestions from the Chef

These boiled dishes may be accompanied by other vegetables, and even tender legumes, such as peas. In such cases, the dish resembles "Mixed Vegetables" (see Vol. 3, p. 166).

NUTRITIONAL VALUE* per serving

Energy	144 kcal = 601 kj
Protein	5.77 g
Carbohydrates	25.0 g
Fiber	7.10 g
Total fat	*0.572 g*
Saturated fat	*0.101 g*
Cholesterol	—
Sodium	*59.1 mg*

1% 2% 4% 10% 20% 40% 100%

% Daily Value (based on a 2,000 calorie diet) provided by each serving of this dish

HEALTH COUNSELS

These boiled cabbages, Brussels sprouts, cauliflower, and broccoli, are simple to prepare, tasty, and healthy.

All these vegetables belong to the cruciferous botanical family (see Vol. 1, p. 106), as well as turnips, watercress, and radish. These plants share in common the content of a sulfur essence, slightly spicy, made up of phytochemicals (see Vol. 1, p. 106; Vol. 2, p. 194) able to prevent the cells' carcinogenic degeneration, among other properties. This makes these dishes especially recommended to prevent:

✓ **Cancer** in general. ***Carotene*** from carrots and pumpkin also contribute to the same.

✓ **Stomach disorders,** such as **acidity** and **gastritis,** due to the *healing* action of cabbage and the *antacid* and *soothing* effect of potatoes.

✓ **Constipation** and **intestinal diverticulosis,** thanks to the *high-**fiber*** content of these dishes.

CALORIC PROPORTION*

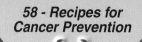

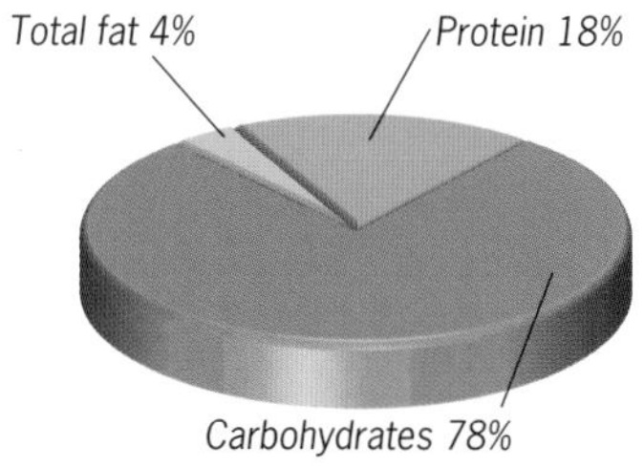

Percentage distribution of **calories for each nutrient**

*Additional ingredients are not included.

Boiled Broccoli

Boiled Brussels Sprouts

Boiled Cauliflower

Boiled Cabbage

Preparation time 00:20

Cooking time 00:40

Rice Salad

INGREDIENTS (4 servings)

- 200 g (≅ 7 oz) of **whole rice**
- 100 g (≅ 3.5 oz) of **green beans**
- 100 g (≅ 3.5 oz) of **peas**
- 2 **carrots**
- 1 sweet **red pepper** (baked)
- 1 **onion**
- 50 g (≅ 1.75 oz) of pitted **olives**

ADDITIONAL INGREDIENTS

- 2 tablespoons of olive **oil** (each tablespoon of oil adds around 120 kcal to the recipe, that is, 30 kcal per serving)
- Sea **salt** (see Vol. 3, p. 16)

PREPARATION

❶ Soak the rice for one hour in hot water or overnight if cold water is used.
- Remove the threads, chop, and wash the green beans.
- Peel and chop the carrot.
- Cut the pepper into strips.
- Peel and chop the onion.

❷ Boil the green beans, peas, and carrots in salted water. Drain.
- Boil the rice for 30 minutes. Drain.
- Heat the oil in a frying pan and sauté the onion. When it becomes transparent, add the rice and vegetables and stir for a few moments. Remove from the fire and let cool.

❸ Arrange in a serving dish and decorate with the olives and the red pepper strips.

Suggestions from the Chef

Garnish with mayonnaise sauce (see Vol. 3, p. 58).

For more information about the ingredients, see: Rice, Vol. 2, p. 225; green bean, Vol. 1, p. 109; pea, Vol. 2, p. 73; carrot, Vol. 2, p. 25; pepper, Vol. 2, p. 198; onion, Vol. 2, p. 142; olive, Vol. 2, p. 165; and the *Encyclopedia of Medicinal Plants;* Green bean, p. 584.

HEALTH COUNSELS

Vegetables in this dish supply ***vitamins,*** and ***phytochemicals*** that possess an *antioxidant effect.* It has been proven that protecting substances from vegetables and whole cereals in this salad can *neutralize,* at least partially, the action of **contaminants** that *promote* **cancer.** Due to this fact and to the general healthy benefits that this salad's nutritious ingredients have, it is recommendable for:

✓ **Cancer** *prevention,* and particularly cancer of the **digestive tract.**

✓ *Prevention* of **high blood pressure, arteriosclerosis,** and **coronary** disease, due to the *diuretic* effect from the vegetables and to the **cholesterol**-*regulating* effect of whole rice.

HEALTHIER ALTERNATIVE: Instead of sautéing the onion, boil it with the vegetables and dress everything with raw oil.

NUTRITIONAL VALUE* per serving

Energy	**265 kcal = 1,110 kj**
Protein	**6.80 g**
Carbohydrates	**47.2 g**
Fiber	**6.84 g**
Total fat	***3.01 g***
Saturated fat	***0.501 g***
Cholesterol	—
Sodium	***133 mg***

1% 2% 4% 10% 20% 40% 100%

% Daily Value (based on a 2,000 calorie diet) provided by each serving of this dish

CALORIC PROPORTION*

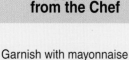

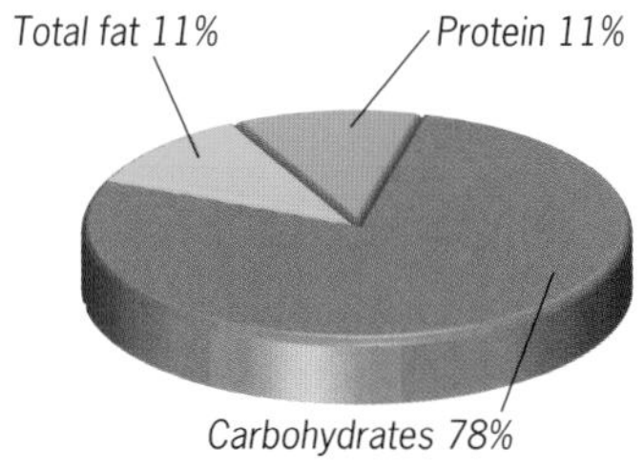

Percentage distribution of
calories for each nutrient

*Additional ingredients are not included.

Preparation time	Cooking time
00:15	02:00

Soybean Stew

INGREDIENTS (4 servings)

- 300 g (≅ 10.6 oz) of **white soybeans**
- 250 g (≅ 8.8 oz) of **chard**
- 200 g (≅ 7 oz) of skinless **pumpkin** (squash)
- 1 **onion**
- 1 **garlic** clove
- 40 g (≅ 1.4 oz) of **wheat germ**

ADDITIONAL INGREDIENTS

- 4 tablespoons of olive **oil** (each tablespoon of oil adds around 120 kcal to the recipe, that is, 30 kcal per serving)
- Sea **salt** (see Vol. 3, p. 16)

PREPARATION

❶ Soak the soybeans overnight in cold water or for one hour if hot water is used.
- Wash, peel, and chop the vegetables.
- Peel and chop the garlic and onion.

❷ Boil the soybeans in salted water until they are tender (1 hour in the pressure cooker).

❸ Serve hot. Sprinkle a tablespoon of wheat germ on each dish.

For more information about the ingredients, see: Soybean, Vol. 2, p. 264; chard, Vol. 2, p. 297; pumpkin, Vol. 2, p. 97; onion, Vol. 2, p. 142; garlic, Vol. 1, p. 338; wheat germ, Vol. 2, p. 310; and the *Encyclopedia of Medicinal Plants:* Garlic, p. 230.

Suggestions from the Chef

If a **thicker** stew is desired, boil a whole potato. Once it is tender, mash it and add it to the mixture. Boil the stew for a few additional minutes.

HEALTH COUNSELS

White soybean or common soybean is sometimes called a "superlegume," due to its dense concentration of nutrients. It has *more* ***fat*** and *fewer* ***carbohydrates*** than other similar legumes, such as mung beans or adzuki beans. Hence, it is *higher* in ***calories*** and with a *more creamy* consistency than the other legumes.

Soy is *very high* in ***protein, B-complex vitamins,*** and ***minerals,*** such as ***iron, calcium,*** and anticarcinogenic ***phytochemicals*** called ***isoflavones.*** This dish, one of the highest nutritional concentration presented in this encyclopedia, is especially recommended for:

✓ **Cancer** *prevention,* particularly that of **prostate, breast,** and **colon.** The isoflavones in soybeans are greatly responsible for this effect, together with pumpkin's ***carotene.***

✓ **Growth** periods, **pregnancy, lactation,** and **sports.**

✓ **Menstruation** disorders, **menopause** symptoms, and **osteoporosis** *prevention.*

✓ Diet for **diabetics.**

NUTRITIONAL VALUE* per serving

Energy	389 kcal = 1,628 kj
Protein	31.8 g
Carbohydrates	25.7 g
Fiber	11.6 g
Total fat	*16.1 g*
Saturated fat	*2.37 g*
Cholesterol	—
Sodium	*130 mg*

1% 2% 4% 10% 20% 40% 100%

% Daily Value (based on a 2,000 calorie diet) provided by each serving of this dish

CALORIC PROPORTION*

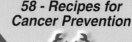

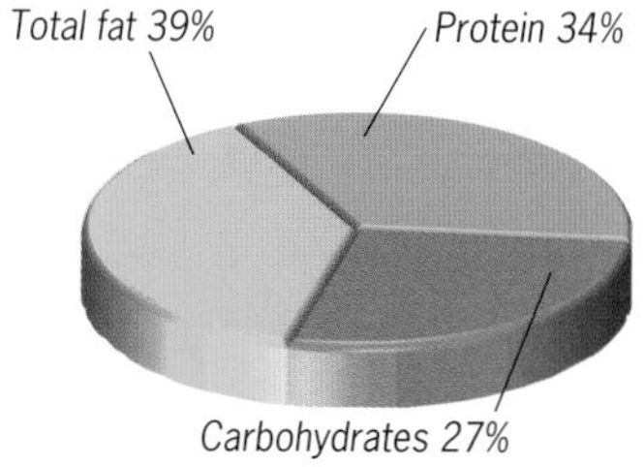

Percentage distribution of **calories for each nutrient**

*Additional ingredients are not included.

Stuffed Peppers

INGREDIENTS (4 servings)

- 4 sweet **red peppers**
- 300 g (≅ 10.6 oz) of **tofu** (soybean curd)
- 100 g (≅ 1/2 cup) of **whole rice**
- 2 **tomatoes**
- 3 **garlic** cloves
- 200 g (≅ 7 oz) of **Almond Cream Sauce** (Vol. 3, p. 64)

ADDITIONAL INGREDIENTS

- **Basil**
- 3 tablespoons of olive **oil** (each tablespoon of oil adds around 120 kcal to the recipe, that is, 30 kcal per serving)
- 1 teaspoon of sweet **paprika**
- Sea **salt** (see Vol. 3, p. 16)

For more information about the ingredients, see: Pepper, Vol. 2, p. 198; tofu, Vol. 1, p. 88; rice, Vol. 2, p. 225; tomato, Vol. 2, p. 275; garlic, Vol. 1, p. 338; and the Encyclopedia of Medicinal Plants: Garlic, p. 230.

PREPARATION

❶ Soak the rice for one hour in very hot water or overnight if cold water is used.
- Peel and chop the garlic.
- Chop the tomato into cubes.
- Freeze the tofu overnight (this process changes the texture). Thaw, drain, and chop in small cubes.

❷ Boil the rice in salted water for 30 minutes. Drain if necessary.
- Bake the whole peppers. Let them cool down. Peel them.
- Heat the oil in a frying pan and sauté the garlic. Before it gets golden, add paprika. Stir and add the tofu, basil, and salt.
- Sauté on a low flame for 5 minutes. Add tomato. Allow an additional 5 minutes and add the rice, stirring and keeping on the heat for a few more minutes.
- Stuff the peppers with the mixture. Seal them with a toothpick.
- Arrange the stuffed peppers on a casserole. Pour the Almond Cream Sauce over them, and bake for 10 minutes.

❸ Serve hot.

HEALTHIER ALTERNATIVE: Instead of sautéing the ingredients, cook them in their own juices in an anti-adherent pot.

Chop tofu and tomatoes.

Once the garlic is sautéed, add the tofu to the frying pan.

Stuff the peppers with the sauté.

Suggestions from the Chef

Stuffed Peppers may be served with **other sauces** such as Cucumber and Yogurt (see Vol. 3, p. 61) or White Sauces (Vol. 3, p. 59), or else may be served cold in summer with a mayonnaise sauce (Vol. 3, p. 58).

NUTRITIONAL VALUE*
per serving

Energy	308 kcal = 1,286 kj
Protein	11.3 g
Carbohydrates	37.1 g
Fiber	8.57 g
Total fat	*10.4 g*
Saturated fat	*1.40 g*
Cholesterol	—
Sodium	*22.4 mg*

1% 2% 4% 10% 20% 40% 100%

% Daily Value (based on a 2,000 calorie diet) provided by each serving of this dish

HEALTH COUNSELS

Stuffed Peppers are a nutritious and well-balanced dish, as far as nutritional composition is concerned. From the viewpoint of health, one of the most relevant features of this dish is that all the ingredients are *effective* in cancer prevention:

- ✓ Sweet **paprika,** because of its content in ***vitamin A,*** and ***C,*** and *antioxidant* **flavonoids.**
- ✓ **Whole rice,** for its ***fiber*** content, which prevents **cancer** of the **colon** and **breast cancer.**
- ✓ **Tomatoes,** as they supply ***lycopene,*** which *prevents* **prostate cancer.**
- ✓ **Tofu** for being *high* in ***isoflavones*** which *prevent* **prostate** and **breast cancers.**
- ✓ **Garlic** and olive **oil,** both endowed with *anticarcinogenic* effects.

For all these reasons, this dish is particularly recommended for:

- ✓ **Cancer** *prevention* in general, and specifically that of **stomach, colon, breast,** and **prostate.** Those at risk of suffering from any of these types of cancer, or those who have been diagnosed as having any of these, should include this dish in their diet.
- ✓ The **stomach,** due to the *appetizing* effect of sweet paprika, especially useful in case of **lack of appetite** and of **gastric atony.**
- ✓ The **intestine,** due to the *laxative* action of the plant ***fiber*** coming from rice and from the other vegetables.
- ✓ The **reproductive system,** due to the *regulating* effect of tofu upon **menstruation.**

CALORIC PROPORTION*

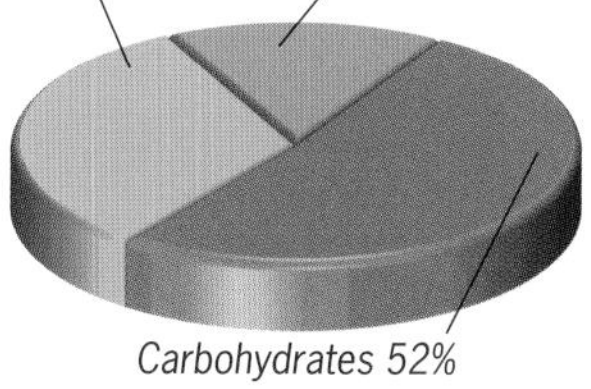

Percentage distribution of
calories for each nutrient

*Additional ingredients are not included.

Preparation time 00:15

Cooking time 01:15

Roasted Vegetables

INGREDIENTS (4 servings)

- 4 **eggplant**
- 2 sweet **red peppers**
- 2 **tomatoes**
- 2 **onions**
- 2 **garlic** cloves

ADDITIONAL INGREDIENTS

- **Parsley**
- 4 tablespoons of olive **oil** (each tablespoon of oil adds around 120 kcal to the recipe, that is, 30 kcal per serving)
- Sea **salt** (see Vol. 3, p. 16)

PREPARATION

❶ Wash all the vegetables.
- Peel and chop the garlic.

❷ Grill-roast the vegetables according to the following lengths:
- Onions, 1 hour;
- Eggplant, 45 minutes;
- Peppers, 30 minutes;
- Tomatoes, 15 minutes;
- Let them cool. Peel and chop into large chunks.
- In a deep platter, mix in all vegetables and add oil, salt, and chopped garlic.

❸ Serve and sprinkle with parsley.

For more information about the ingredients, see: Eggplant, Vol. 2, p. 256; pepper, Vol. 2, p. 198; tomato, Vol. 2, p. 275; onion, Vol. 2, p. 142; garlic, Vol. 1, p. 338; and the *Encyclopedia of Medicinal Plants:* Garlic, p. 230.

Suggestions from the Chef

The vegetables can also be roasted in the **oven.**

HEALTH COUNSELS

These roasted vegetables have among the ingredients three vegetables from the Solanaceae botanical family (see Vol. 1, p. 111)—pepper, eggplant, and tomato. They are *high* in ***carotenoids*** (vegetable red pigments similar to carrot's carotene), ***flavonoids,*** and ***vitamin C,*** all ***antioxidants*** that *neutralize* the action of **carcinogenic substances.**

This roast is very healthy, not only for its ingredients, but also for the way of preparation (oven). Vegetables processed in this way are better tolerated by delicate stomachs. This dish is especially recommended for the prevention of:

✓ **Cancer,** thanks to the *protecting* actions of the ingredients, including onion, garlic, and olive oil.

✓ **Arteriosclerosis,** arterial **thrombosis,** and **coronary disease,** as all the vegetables keep the arteries in good condition and *improve* blood **circulation.**

✓ **Constipation,** due to the *high* ***fiber*** *content.*

NUTRITIONAL VALUE* per serving

Energy	144 kcal = 600 kj
Protein	5.34 g
Carbohydrates	22.3 g
Fiber	10.8 g
Total fat	*1.09 g*
Saturated fat	*0.180 g*
Cholesterol	—
Sodium	*21.5 mg*

1% 2% 4% 10% 20% 40% 100%

% Daily Value (based on a 2,000 calorie diet) provided by each serving of this dish

CALORIC PROPORTION*

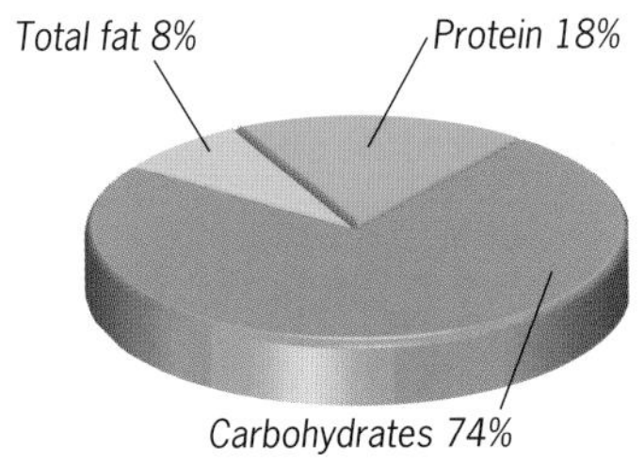

Percentage distribution of **calories for each nutrient**

*Additional ingredients are not included.

Preparation time 00:15 | Cooking time - - - -

Vegetable Juice

INGREDIENTS (4 servings)

- 500 g (≅ 1 pound) of **carrots**
- 500 g (≅ 1 pound) of **tomatoes**
- 1 **cucumber**

PREPARATION

❶ Wash and chop the carrots and tomatoes.
- Peel and chop the cucumber.

❷ Process the vegetables through the electric liquidizer and mix the juices well.

❸ Serve cold immediately.

For more information about the ingredients, see: Carrot, Vol. 2, p. 25; tomato, Vol. 2, p. 275; cucumber, Vol. 2, p. 339.

Suggestions from the Chef

Try to add a few **tamari** (soy sauce) drops, a bit of lemon juice, or a pinch of salt.

HEALTH COUNSELS

Carrots and tomatoes have in common their intense color—orange in one and bright red in the other. In both vegetables, the color is due to their *high* content in ***plant pigments.*** Notable examples of these substances are ***beta-carotene*** (provitamin A) in carrots and ***lycopene*** in tomatoes.

Unlike artificial food coloring, usually dangerous for our health, plant pigments are highly beneficial. One of their most notable qualities is to *protect* the **cells** against carcinogenic substances, thus avoiding cancer development.

Therefore, this colored juice is especially recommended for:

✓ **Cancer** *prevention,* especially that of **digestive organs, lung,** and **prostate.**

✓ *Prevention* of **arteriosclerosis.**

✓ The *strengthening* of our body's **anti-infectious defenses.**

NUTRITIONAL VALUE per serving

Energy	**52 kcal = 216 kj**
Protein	**1.70 g**
Carbohydrates	**11.1 g**
Fiber	**1.05 g**
Total fat	***0.182 g***
Saturated fat	***0.030 g***
Cholesterol	—
Sodium	***30.6 mg***

1% 2% 4% 10% 20% 40% 100%

% Daily Value (based on a 2,000 calorie diet) provided by each serving of this drink

CALORIC PROPORTION

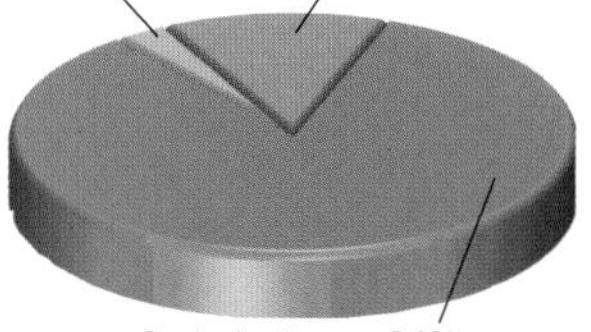

Percentage distribution of **calories for each nutrient**

AVERAGE WEIGHT PER FRUIT AND VEGETABLE PIECE

According to the USDA Nutrient Data Laboratory, Agricultural Research Service. http://www.nal.usda.gov/fnic/foodcomp/

Avocado

Medium: 201 g

1 cup, pureed: 230 g;
1 cup, sliced: 146 g

Prune

Medium: 8.4 g

1 cup, pitted: 170 g

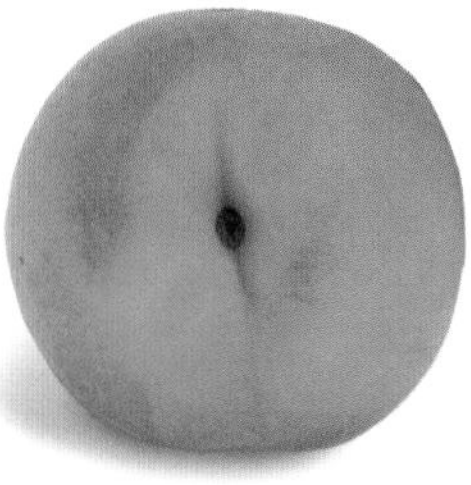

Peach

Small: 79 g; medium: 98 g;
large: 157 g

1 cup, sliced: 170 g

Radish

1 large: 9 g; 1 medium: 4.5 g;
1 small: 2 g

1 cup, sliced: 116 g

Belgian endive

Medium: 53 g;
1 cup: 90 g

Lemon

Medium: 108 g

Pear

Large: 209 g;
Medium: 166 g; Small: 139 g

1 cup, sliced: 165 g

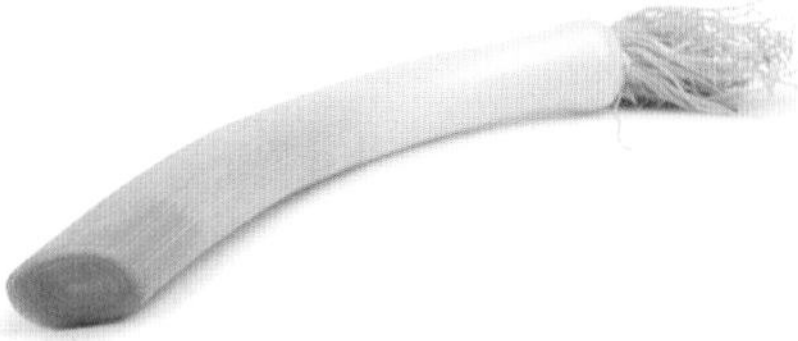

Leek

Medium: 89 g

1 cup: 89 g

Papaya

Large: 380 g;
Medium: 304 g; Small: 152 g

1 cup, cubes: 140 g;
1 cup, mashed: 230 g

Pineapple

Medium: 472 g

1 slice: 84 g; 1 slice, thin: 56 g;
1 cup, diced: 155 g

Red beet

Medium: 82 g

1 cup: 136 g

Cucumber

Large: 280 g; Medium: 201 g;
Small: 158 g

1 cup, sliced: 119 g

Mango

Medium (without refuse): 207 g

1 cup, sliced: 165 g

Tangerine

Large: 98 g; Medium: 84 g;
Small: 70 g

1 cup, sections: 195 g

Date

Medium: 8.3 g

1 cup, pitted, chopped: 178 g

Kiwi

Large (without skin): 91 g;
Medium (without skin): 76 g

1 cup: 177

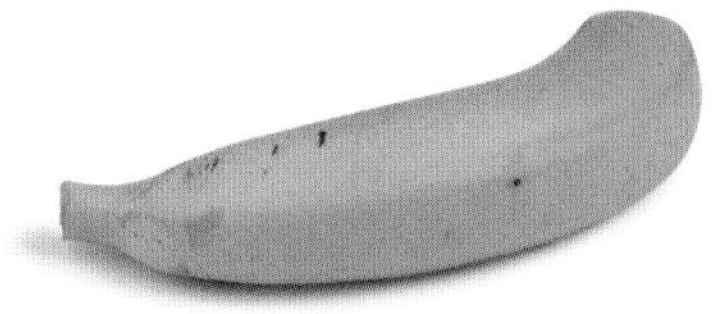

Banana
Extra large: 152 g; Large: 136 g;
Medium: 118 g; Small: 101 g
1 cup, mashed: 225 g;
1 cup, sliced: 150 g

Artichoke
Large: 162 g;
Medium: 128 g

Eggplant
Medium, unpeeled: 548 g;
Medium, peeled: 458 g

Tomato
Large: 182 g;
Medium: 123 g; Small: 91 g
1 cup: 180 g;
1 slice or wedge: 20 g

Onion
Large: 150 g; Medium: 110 g; Small: 70 g
1 cup, chopped: 160 g;
1 cup, sliced: 115 g

Zucchini
Large: 323 g; Medium: 196 g; Small: 118 g
1 cup, chopped: 124 g;
1 cup, sliced: 113 g

Carrot
Large: 72 g; Medium: 61 g; Small: 50 g
1 cup, chopped: 128 g;
1 cup, grated: 110 g;
1 cup, strips or slices: 122 g

Apple
Large: 212 g; Medium: 138 g; Small: 106 g
1 cup, chopped: 125 g; 1 cup, sliced: 110 g

Red pepper
Large: 164 g; medium: 119 g; small: 74 g
1 cup, chopped: 149 g; 1 cup, sliced: 92 g

Potato
Large: 369 g; Medium: 213 g;
Small: 170 g
1 cup, diced: 150

Orange
Large: 300 g;
Medium: 159 g;
Small: 120 g

Green pepper
Large: 164 g; medium: 119 g; small: 74 g
1 cup, chopped: 149 g; 1 cup, sliced: 92 g

Usual Volumes and Weights in the Kitchen

According to the USDA Nutrient Data Laboratory, Agricultural Research Service. http://www.nal.usda.gov/fnic/foodcomp/

Weight of each product in grams

Product	Teaspoon	Tablespoon	Cup
Water Water-based liquids	 Teaspoon: 5 ml weight: 5 g	 Tablespoon: 15 ml weight: 15 g	 Cup: 240 ml weight: 240 g
Rolled oats	 Teaspoon: 1.6 g	 Tablespoon: 5 g	 Cup: 181 g
Brown Sugar	 Teaspoon: 4.5 g	 Tablespoon: 14 g	 Cup: 220 g
Whole Rice	 Teaspoon: 3.75 g	 Tablespoon: 11.9 g	 Cup: 190 g
Whole Flour	 Teaspoon: 2.5 g	 Tablespoon: 7.5 g	 Cup: 120 g
Oil	 Teaspoon: 4.5 g	 Tablespoon: 13.5 g	 Cup: 216 g

MEASUREMENT EQUIVALENCIES

See Vol. 2, p. 417 all the measurement units used in this Encyclopedia.

1 tablespoon (tbsp) = 3 teaspoons (tsp)
1/16 cup (c) = 1 tablespoon
1/8 cup = 2 tablespoons
1/6 cup = 2 tablespoons + 2 teaspoons
1/4 cup = 4 tablespoons
1/3 cup = 5 tablespoons + 1 teaspoon
3/8 cup = 6 tablespoons
1/2 cup = 8 tablespoons
2/3 cup = 10 tablespoons + 2 teaspoons
3/4 cup = 12 tablespoons
1 cup = 48 teaspoons
1 cup = 48 tablespoons 8 fluid ounces (fl oz) = 1 cup
1 pint (pt) = 2 cups
1 quart (qt) = 2 pints
4 cups = 1 quart
1 gallon = 4 quarts
16 ounces (oz) = 1 pound (lb)

USA Measurement System

1 **Gallon** = 3.7854 **l** (liters)
1 **Pound** = 453.592 **g** (grams)
1 **Ounce** = 28.349 **g** (grams)
1 **Inch** = 2.54 **cm** (centimeters)
1 **Pint** USA = 473.2 **ml** (milliliters)

Temperature units

To convert Fahrenheit degrees (°F) into centigrade or Celsius (°C):

- Subtract 32
- Multiply 5
- Divide by 9

according to the formula:

$$°C = \frac{5 \times (°F - 32)}{9}$$

To convert centigrade or Celsius (°C) into Fahrenheit (F):

- Multiply by 9
- Divide by 5
- Add 32

according to the formula:

$$°F = \frac{°C \times 9}{5} + 32$$

To Convert...		Multiply by...
cm (centimeters)	into **inches**	0.3937
gallons USA	into **liters**	3.7854
g (grams)	into **ounces**	0.0353
g (grams)	into **pounds**	0.0022
kcal (calories)	into **kj** (kilojoules)	4.18
kj (joules)	into **kcal** (calories)	0.2392
kg (kilos / kilograms)	into **pounds**	2.2046
kg (kilos / kilograms)	into **ounces**	35.27
pounds	into **kg** (kilos / kilograms)	0.4536
pounds	into **g** (grams)	453.592
l (liters)	into **gallons** USA	0.2642
l (liters)	into **pints** USA	2.1133
l (liters)	into fluid **ounces**	33.814
ml (milliliters)	into fluid **ounces**	0.0338
ml (milliliters)	into **pints** USA	0.0021
ml (milliliters)	into cubic **inches**	0.061
ounces	into **g** (grams)	28.349
ounces	into **kg** (kilos / kilograms)	0.0284
fluid ounces	into **liters**	0.0296
fluid ounces	into **ml** (milliliters)	29.57
pints USA	into **l** (liters)	0.4732
pints USA	into **ml** (milliliters)	473.2
inches	into **cm** (centimeters)	2.54
cubic inches	into **ml** (milliliters = **c.c.** = **cm**^{3})	16.387

A few Celsius-Fahrenheit equivalencies

°C	°F
–10	14
–5	23
0	**32**
5	41
10	50
15	59
20	68
25	77
30	86
35	95
37,8	**100**
40	104
45	113
50	122
60	140
70	158
80	176
90	194
100	**212**

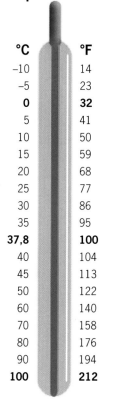

English Synonyms and Equivalents

Of the main food products used in this volume of Healthy Recipes

See also the General Aplphabetical Index in Vol. 2 p. 425.
Synonyms of culinary herbs used in the recipes of this volume may be found in the Encyclopedia of Medicinal Plants, *p. 786.*

Adlay = Teargrass, Job's tears, Adlay millet
African spinach = Amaranth
Alfalfa = Lucerne, Sativa
Alkekengy = Winter cherry
Alligator pear = Avocado
Amaranth = Pigweed, African spinach, Redroot
Amaranth greens = Amaranthus spinach, Callaloo, Chinese spinach
Ambarella = Jew plum, Golden apple
American elderberry = Sweet elder, Eastern elderberry
Ananás = Pineapple
Andean lupin = Lupine
Angle luffa = Sponge gourd
Anona = Cherimoya
Apricock = Apricot
Arrowroot = Maranta
Artichoke = Globe artichoke
Arugula = Rocket, Rugula, Rucola
Asparagus cowpea = Yard-long bean
Aubergine = Eggplant
Australian nut = Macadamia
Avocado = Alligator pear, Zuttano, Fuerte

Babaco = Chamburo
Bahri date = Dates
Balsam pear = Bitter melon
Bambara groundnut = Congo goober, Ground pea
Baobab = Monkey bread
Barbary fig = Prickly pear
Barbary pear = Prickly pear
Barberry = California barberry, Oregon grape, Holly-leave barberry
Barley = Malt
Beechwheat = Buckwheat
Belgian endive = Witloof, French endive
Belimbing = Carambola
Bell pepper = Pepper
Bengal gram = Chickpea
Bengal grass = Millet
Benoil tree = Moringa nut
Bilimbi = Carambola
Bitter orange = Seville orange
Black salsify = Scorzonera
Blackberry = Bramble berry
Black-cap = Raspberry
Blackthorn plum = Sloeberry
Bladder cherry = Winter cherry
Borassus palm = Palmyra palm
Bramble berry = Blackberry
Brazil nuts = Creamnuts, Paranuts
Brazilian cherry = Pitanga
Breadfruit = Breadnut, Sukun
Brier hip = Dog rose, Wild brier, Rose hip, Eglantine gall
Brinjal = Eggplant
Broad bean = Fava bean
Broccoli = Asparagus broccoli, Calabrese, Italian asparagus
Broomcorn = Sorghum
Buckwheat = Beechwheat, Saracen corn, Sarrazin, Saracen corn
Buddha's hand = Chayote

Cactus pear = Prickly pear
Cajan = Pigeon pea
Calabaza = Squash
Calabrese = Broccoli
California barberry = Barberry
Calvance pea = Chickpea
Callaloo = Amaranth greens
Camore = Sweet potato
Cape gooseberry = Gooseberry, Groundcherry
Carambola = Belimbing, Bilimbi, Star apple, Five-angled fruit, Star fruit
Caraunda = Karanda
Cassava = Manioc, Yuca
Caucasian persimmon = Date plum
Cayenne pineapple = Pineapple
Ceci = Chickpea
Civet-cat fruit = Durian
Clover radish = Radish
Clusterbean = Guar
Cobnut = Hazelnut
Coconut = Cokernut
Cocoplum = Icaco [plum]
Cocoyam = Malanga
Cokernut = Coconut
Common persimmon = Persimmon
Congo goober = Bambara groundnut
Corn = Sweet corn, Maize
Cornsalad = Lamb's lettuce
Cos = Lettuce
Costa Rican guava = Wild guava
Courge = Squash
Courgette = Zucchini
Coyote melon = Squash
Creamnuts = Brazil nuts
Cuban spinach = Purslane
Curuba = Banana passion fruit
Cush-cush yam = Sweet yam
Custard apple = Cherimoya
Cut-eye bean = Jack bean
Chamburo = Babaco
Chard = Swiss chard, Seakale-beet, Leaf beet, Sea kale chard
Chayote = Vegetable pear, Mirliton, Buddha's hand, Christophene
Cherimoya = Custard apple, Anona, Sherbet-fruit
Chick pea = Chickpea, Garbanzo bean
Chickpea = Ceci, Garbanzo [bean], Bengal gram, Calvance pea, Chick pea, Dwarf pea, Gram pea, Yellow gram
Chinese apple = Pomegranate
Chinese date = Jujube, Jujube
Chinese fig = Persimmon
Chinese gooseberry = Kiwi
Chinese hazel = Hazelnut
Chinese jujube = Jujube
Chinese okra = Sponge gourd
Chinese rhubarb = Rhubarb
Chinese spinach = Amaranth greens
Christophene = Chayote
Chufa = Tiger nut

Dalima = Pomegranate
Dasheen = Taro
Date plum = Caucasian persimmon
Dog rose = Brier hip
Duku = Langsat
Durian = Civet-cat fruit, Lahong, Tutong
Dwarf pea = Chickpea

Earth almond = Tiger nut
Earthnut = Peanut
Eastern elderberry = American elderberry
Eggplant = Guinea squash, Aubergine, Brinjal
Eglantine gall = Brier hip
Elephant apple = Quince

Fava bean = Horse-bean, Field-bean, Tick-bean, Broad bean, Windsor bean
Feijoa = Pineapple guava, Guavasteen
Fennel = Finnocchio, Sweet, anise, Roman fennel, Sweet fennel, Florence, Finocchio, Sweet anise
Field-bean = Fava bean
Filbert = Hazelnut
Finocchio = Fennel
Five-angled fruit = Carambola
Fly agaric = Amanita muscaria
Fuerte = Avocado

Garbanzo bean = Chick pea
Garden peas = Peas
Genipa = Honeyberry, Limoncillo, Akee, Spanish lime, Mamoncillo
Glasswort = Marsh samphire
Globe artichoke = Artichoke
Golden apple = Ambarella
Golden zucchini = Zucchini
Gombo = Okra
Goober [pea] = Peanut
Goodluckplant = Lucky clover
Gooseberry = Cape gooseberry
Goosefoot = Quinoa
Gourd = Squash
Grain sorghum = Sorghum
Gram pea = Chickpea
Granadilla = Passion fruit
Grapefruit = Shaddock, Marsh grapefruit
Grass-pea = Lathyrus pea
Great millet = Sorghum
Green bean = String bean, Fresh bean, Snap bean, Peas
Green pepper = Pepper
Greengage = Plum
Grenade = Pomegranate
Ground pea = Bambara groundnut
Groundcherry = Cape gooseberry
Groundnut = Peanut
Guar = Clusterbean
Guava = Guayaba, Goyave, Guyaba, Mountain guava
Guavasteen = Feijoa
Guayaba = Guava
Guinea squash = Eggplant
Gungo pea = Pigeon pea
Guyaba = Guava

Hazelnut = Filbert, Turkish filbert, American hazelnut, European hazel, Cobnut, Chinese hazel
Heart of palm = Swamp cabbage
Honeyberry = Genipa
Horsebean = Jack bean
Huckleberry = Bilberry
Hyacinth bean = Lablab

Icaco [plum] = Cocoplum
Ice-cream bean = Guama
Imbu = Umbu
Inca wheat = Quinoa
Indian fig = Prickly pear
Indian jujube = Jujube
Indian mulberry = Malay custard apple, Morinda
Indian nut = Pine nuts
Indian pear = Prickly pear
Indian yam = Sweet yam
Irish potato = Potato
Italian squash = Zucchini

Jack bean = Horsebean, Cut-eye bean, Sword bean
Jackfruit = Nagka
Jambos = Rose apple
Japanese medlar = Loquat
Japanese plum = Loquat
Java apple = Makopa, Jambos, Wax-apple
Jerusalem artichoke = Sunchoke
Jew plum = Ambarella
Jícama = Mexican potato, Yam bean
Job's tears = Adlay
Jubilee = Watermelon

Jujube = Chinese date, Chinese jujube, Red date, Indian jujube, Chinese date
Juneberry = Serviceberry

Kaki fruit = Persimmon
Kiwi = Chinese gooseberry, Yang tao
Kumara = Sweet potato

Lablab = Hyacinth bean, Bonavist bean
Lady's finger = Okra
Lahong = Durian
Lamb's lettuce = Cornsalad, Mâche
Langsat = Duku, Lanzone
Lanzone = Langsat
Lathyrus pea = Grass-pea, Chickling vetch
Leaf beet = Chard
Lettuce = Celtuce, Cos, Garden, lettuce, Romaine lettuce
Loquat = Tanaka, Japanese medlar, Japanese plum
Lovegrass = Teff
Lucerne = Alfalfa
Lucky clover = Goodluckplant
Luffa = Angled loofah, Ridged loofah, Silk gourd
Lychi = Litchi

Macadamia = Australian nut, Queensland nut
Mâche = Lamb's lettuce
Maize = Corn
Malanga = Tannia, Yautia, Cocoyam
Malay custard apple = Indian mulberry
Malt = Barley
Mamey apple = Mamey
Mammey sapote = Mamey
Mamoncillo = Genipa
Mandarin orange = Tangerine
Mani = Peanut
Manioc = Cassava
Man-kay = Mango
Maranta = Arrowroot
Marsh grapefruit = Grapefruit
Marsh samphire = Glasswort, Sea salicomia, Samphire
Melon = Muskmelon, Sweet, melon, Muskmelon, Sweet melon
Melon fruit = Papaya
Melon pear = Pepino
Mexican apple = White sapote
Mexican potato = Jícama
Millet = Bengal grass
Miner's lettuce = Purslane
Mirliton = Chayote
Monkey bread = Baobab
Morinda = Indian mulberry
Moringa nut = Benoil tree
Muskmelon = Melon

Nagka = Jackfruit
Nana = Pineapple
Night-blooming cereus = Queen of the night, Night-flowering cactus
Noblecane = Sugarcane
Nopal = Prickly pear

Oca = Ulluco
Ochro = Okra
Okra = Gombo, Lady's finger, Quiabo, Vendakai
Oregon grape = Barberry
Oyster plant = Salsify

Palmyra palm = Borassus palm
Papaw = Papaya
Papaya = Pawpaw, Melon fruit
Papayuela = Wild papaya
Paprika = Pepper
Paranuts = Brazil nuts
Passion fruit = Granadilla, Wild water melon
Pawpaw = Papaya
Peach = Persian apple
Peach palm = Pejebaye
Peanut = Mani, Groundnut, Earthnut, Goober [pea], Runner peanut, Spanish peanut
Pecan = Carya pecan
Pejebaye = Peach palm
Pepper = Sweet pepper, Bell pepper, Green pepper, Paprika
Persian apple = Peach
Persimmon = Kaki fruit, Sharon fruit, Chinese fig, Common persimmon, Kaki fruit, Sharon fruit
Pieplant = Rhubarb
Pigeon pea = Cajan, Gungo pea
Pigweed = Amaranth
Pine kernel = Pine nuts
Pine nuts = Pine kernel, Indian, nut, Nut pine
Pineapple = Cayenne pineapple, Nana, Ananás
Pineapple guava = Feijoa
Pineapple quince = Quince
Pitanga = Brazilian cherry, Surinam cherry, Petanga
Plum = Greengage, Prune
Pomegranate = Dalima, Chinese apple, Grenade
Potato = White, potato, Irish potato
Prickly pear = Barbary fig, Barbary pear, Cactus pear, Indian fig, Tuna fig, Indian pear, Nopal
Prune = Plum
Pumpkin = Squash
Purple raspberry = Raspberry
Purslane = Cuban spinach, Miner's lettuce

Queensland nut = Macadamia
Quiabo = Okra
Quince = Elephant apple, Pineapple quince
Quinoa = Goosefoot, Inca wheat

Radicchio = Red-leaf chicory
Radish = Clover radish
Raspberry = Black-cap, Purple raspberry, Thimbleberry
Red date = Jujube
Red mombin = Spanish plum
Red-leaf chicory = Radicchio
Redroot = Amaranth
Red-stemmed cardoon = Cardoon
Rhubarb = Pieplant, Chinese rhubarb
Ricotta = Whey, cheese

Ridged loofah = Luffa
Rocket = Arugula
Romaine lettuce [Green] = Lettuce
Roman fennel = Fennel
Rose apple = Jambu, Wax-apple
Rose hip = Brier hip
Rucola = Arugula
Rugula = Arugula
Runner peanut = Peanut

Salsify = Oyster plant, Vegetable oyster
Samphire = Marsh samphire
Saracen corn = Buckwheat
Sativa = Alfalfa
Scorzonera = Black salsify, Black oyster-plant, Viper-grass
Scurvy grass = Spoonwort
Sea kale chard = Chard
Sea salicomia = Marsh samphire
Seakale-beet = Chard
Serviceberry = Juneberry, Sorbapple, Shadblow, Shadbush
Seville orange = Sour orange, Bitter orange
Shadblow = Serviceberry
Shadbush = Serviceberry
Shaddock = Grapefruit
Shallot = White shallot
Sharon fruit = Persimmon
Silk gourd = Luffa
Sloeberry = Blackthorn plum
Snap bean = Green bean
Sorbapple = Serviceberry
Sorghum = Broomcorn, Grain sorghum, Great millet, grass
Sour grass = Sorrel
Sour orange = Seville orange
Spanish cardoon = Cardoon
Spanish lime = Genipa
Spanish peanut = Peanut
Spanish plum = Red mombin
Special bean = Asparagus
Sponge gourd = Angle luffa, Loofah, Vegetable sponge, Chinese okra
Spoonwort = Scurvy grass
Squash = Pumpkin, Courge, Calabaza, Coyote melon, Gourd
Squash blossoms = Pumpkin flowers
Star apple = Carambola
Star fruit = Carambola
String bean = Green bean
Sudan grass = Sorghum
Sugarcane = Noblecane, White sugar
Sukun = Breadfruit
Sunchoke = Jerusalem artichoke
Surinam cherry = Pitanga
Swamp cabbage = Heart of palm
Sweet anise = Fennel
Sweet bell pepper = Pepper
Sweet corn = Corn
Sweet elder = American **elderberry**
Sweet fennel = Fennel
Sweet melon = Melon
Sweet potato = Batata, Camore, Kumara
Sweet yam = Cush-cush yam, Indian yam

Sweet anise = Fennel
Swiss chard = Chard
Sword bean = Jack bean

Tamarillo = Tomato tree
Tanaka = Loquat
Tangerine = Mandarin orange
Tannia = Malanga
Taro = Tarrow, Dasheen
Tarrow = Taro
Teargrass = Adlay
Teff = Lovegrass, Toff
Thimbleberry = Raspberry
Tick-bean = Fava bean
Tiger nut = Chufa, Earth almond, Chufa, Earth almond
Toff = Teff
Tomato tree = Tamarillo
Tuber nigrum = Black truffle
Tuna fig = Prickly pear
Turkish filbert = Hazelnut
Tutong = Durian

Ulluco = Oca
Umbu = Imbu

Vegetable marrow = Zucchini
Vegetable oyster = Salsify
Vegetable pear = Chayote
Vendakai = Okra
Viper-grass = Scorzonera

Walnut = Persian walnut, Heartnut
Watermelon = Jubilee, Java apple
Whey cheese = Ricotta
White potato = Potato
White sapote = Mexican apple, Zapote
White shallot = Shallot
White sugar = Sugarcane
White asparagus = Asparagus
Whortleberry = Bilberry
Wild brier = Brier hip
Wild guava = Costa Rican guava
Wild papaya = Papayuela
Wild water melon = Passion fruit
Windsor bean = Fava bean
Winter cherry = Alkekengy, Bladder cherry
Witloof = Belgian endive

Yam bean = Jícama
Yang tao = Kiwi
Yard-long bean = Asparagus bean, Asparagus cowpea
Yautia = Malanga
Yellow gram = Chickpea
Yuca = Cassava

Zapote = White sapote
Zucchini = Courgette, Vegetable marrow, Golden zucchini, Italian squash
Zuttano = Avocado

Recipe Index by Ingredients

*See the main **English synonyms** in Vol. 3, pp. 390-391.*

Adzuki
Sardinian Adzuki, 3/302

Alfalfa Sprouts
Sprouts Salad, 3/244
Seed Salad, 3/298

Almond
Broccoli Bake, 3/336
Cardoons in Almond Sauce, 3/232
Rice Crackers, 3/196
Cream of Zucchini, 3/246
Almond Croquettes, 3/151
Chinese Salad, 3/243
Fettuccini with Green Sauce, 3/335
Almond Cookies, 3/155
Nut Hamburgers, 3/171
Vegetable Hamburgers, 3/152
Grecian Green Beans, 3/288
Almond Milk, 3/342
Baked Apples, 3/268
Potatoes and Almonds, 3/333
Three-colored Purée, 3/377
Almond Soup, 3/146
Winter Log, 3/340
Vegetable Cannelloni, 3/98

Almond Milk
Tropical Shake, 3/158
Avocado Shake, 3/201

Apple
Avocado Shake, 3/201
Baked Apples, 3/268
Belgian Endive Salad, 3/230
Bircher-Muesli, 3/175
Cabbage Salad, 3/219
Carrot and Apple Juice, 3/355
Christmas Red Cabbage, 3/248
Fruit Salad, 3/200
Sangria (non-alcoholic), 3/327
Seed Salad, 3/298

Apricot
Apricot Shake, 3/141

Artichoke
Artichoke Cannelloni, 3/100
Artichoke Soup, 3/231
Italian-style Artichokes, 3/236
Mixed Vegetables, 3/166
Potato Stew, 3/190
Rice with Artichokes, 3/234
Stuffed Artichokes, 3/286
Vegetable Paella, 3/86
Violet Salad, 3/373

Asparagus
Andalusian Asparagus, 3/349
Asparagus Fondant, 3/284
Asparagus Salad, 3/278
Cream of Asparagus, 3/350
Grilled Vegetables, 3/189

Avocado
Stuffed Avocados, 3/207
Avocado Shake, 3/201
Cream of Avocado, 3/351
Pasta Bow Salad, 3/165
Tropical Fruit Salad, 3/253

Bamboo Shoots
Chinese Noodles, 3/316

Banana
Apricot Shake, 3/141
Baked Apples, 3/268
Banana Shake, 3/179
Banana Soup, 3/188
Bircher-Muesli, 3/175
Fruit Salad, 3/200
Party Melon, 3/176
Sesame Crepes, 3/304
Tropical Fruit Salad, 3/253
Tropical Shake, 3/158

Bean
Beans and Rice, 3/320
Beans with Spinach, 3/352
Pinto Beans, 3/353
Portuguese Beans, 3/324
Vegetarian Tamale, 3/301

Beet/Red Beet
Sweet Cassava Salad, 3/218
Violet Salad, 3/373
Red and White Salad, 3/372
Three-colored Purée, 3/377

Belgian Endive
Belgian Endive Salad, 3/230
River Salad, 3/206
Red and White Salad, 3/372

Borage
Borage and Potatoes, 3/362

Bread/Bread Crumbs
Almond Croquettes, 3/151
Andalusian Asparagus, 3/349
Carrot Croquettes, 3/112
'Cordon Bleu' Eggplant, 3/121
Cream of Avocado, 3/351
Garlic Soup, 3/374
Millet Croquettes, 3/111
Nut Hamburgers, 3/171
Nut Loaf, 3/94
Rice Crackers, 3/196
Rice Hamburgers, 3/170
Soy Croquettes, 3/326
Soy Hamburgers, 3/117
Spinach Croquettes, 3/213
Vegetable Hamburgers, 3/152
Vegetarian Sausages and Drumsticks, 3/92
Winter Log, 3/340

Brewer´s Yeast
Asparagus Fondant, 3/284
Autumn Cabbage, 3/376
Belgian Endive Salad, 3/230
Mexican Salad, 3/260
Nut Hamburgers, 3/171
Seed Salad, 3/298
Three-colored Purée, 3/377

Broccoli
Broccoli Bake, 3/336
Cabbage Varieties, 3/378
Three-colored Purée, 3/377

Brussels Sprouts
Cabbage Varieties, 3/378

Cabbage
Autumn Cabbage, 3/376
Beans and Rice, 3/320
Cabbage Rolls, 3/101
Cabbage Salad, 3/219
Cabbage Soup, 3/375
Cabbage Varieties, 3/378
Celery Pie, 3/290
Chickpea Stew, 3/148
Chinese Salad, 3/243
Portuguese Beans, 3/324
Red and White Salad, 3/372
Sardinian Adzuki, 3/302
Sauerkraut and Carrots, 3/264
Spinach Salad, 3/132
Stuffed Kohlrabi, 3/337
Three-colored Purée, 3/377

Caper
Stuffed Avocados, 3/207
Mexican Meat Analogs, 3/88
Asparagus Salad, 3/278

Cardoon
Cardoons in Almond Sauce, 3/232

Carrot
Beans with Spinach, 3/352
Boiled Marinated Gluten, 3/90
Boiled Vegetables, 3/223
Cabbage Varieties, 3/378
Carrot and Apple Juice, 3/355
Carrot Cake, 3/125
Carrot Croquettes, 3/112
Catalonian Fava Beans, 3/209
Cereal Soup, 3/314
Chickpea Salad, 3/186
Chickpea Stew, 3/148
Chinese Noodles, 3/316
Chinese Stir-Fry, 3/116
Coconut Balls, 3/339
Couscous with Vegetables, 3/322
Garden Pasta, 3/334
Lentils and Rice, 3/211
Mexican Salad, 3/260
Mixed Vegetables, 3/166
Mung Bean Stew, 3/315
Nut Loaf, 3/94
Pasta Bows with Chickpeas, 3/149
Pinto Beans, 3/353
Potato Salad, 3/245
Potatoes and Mushrooms, 3/83
Quinoa Risotto, 3/136
Rainbow Salad, 3/184
Rice Salad, 3/380
Rice with Carrots, 3/133
Sauerkraut and Carrots, 3/264
Seed Salad, 3/298
Spinach Salad, 3/132
Spring Rolls, 3/102
Spring Salad, 3/312
Sweet Cassava Salad, 3/218
Three-colored Purée, 3/377
Tofu Salad, 3/299
Vegetable Hamburgers, 3/152
Vegetable Juice, 3/385
Vegetable Pie, 3/104
Vegetable Purée, 3/361

Cashew
Asparagus Fondant, 3/284
Cashew Stew, 3/150

Cauliflower
Rice with Cauliflower, 3/282
Cabbage Varieties, 3/378
Red and White Salad, 3/372
Celery Pie, 3/290

Celery
Asparagus Salad, 3/278
Celery Pie, 3/290
Chickpea Salad, 3/186
Chickpea Stew, 3/148
Chinese Noodles, 3/316
Couscous with Vegetables, 3/322
Pasta Bows with Chickpeas, 3/149
Seed Salad, 3/298
Stuffed Avocados, 3/207
Tofu Salad, 3/299
Vegetable Purée, 3/361
Vichyssoise, 3/280
Violet Salad, 3/373

Cereals
Cereal Soup, 3/314

Chard
Chard with Potatoes and Pumpkin, 3/263
Chickpea Stew, 3/148
Vegetable Pie, 3/104
Pasta with Chard, 3/82
Soybean Stew, 3/381
Mung Bean Stew, 3/315

Chayote
Vegetarian Tamale, 3/301

Cheese
Artichoke Cannelloni, 3/100
Asparagus Fondant, 3/284
Banana Casserole, 3/124
'Cordon Bleu' Eggplant, 3/121
Fettuccini with Green Beans, 3/283
Filled Cucumbers, 3/348
Italian-style Macaroni, 3/84
Leek Pie, 3/338
Mushroom Lasagna, 3/110
Nut Loaf, 3/94
Spinach Lasagna, 3/108
Vegetable Cannelloni, 3/98
Winter Log, 3/340

Cherimoya
Cherimoya and Orange Shake, 3/178

Tropical Fruit Salad, 3/253

Chestnut

Celery Pie, 3/290
Christmas Red Cabbage, 3/248
Three-colored Purée, 3/377
Winter Log, 3/340

Chickpea

Chickpea Stew, 3/148
Couscous with Vegetables, 3/322
Chickpea Salad, 3/186
Falafel Patties, 3/198
Pasta Bows with Chickpeas, 3/149

Chinese Cabbage

Chinese Salad, 3/243

Coconut

Cereal Bars, 3/174
Bircher-Muesli, 3/175
Coconut Balls, 3/339
Almond Cookies, 3/155
Coconut Milk, 3/343

Corn

Baked Tomatoes, 3/364
Corn Platter, 3/247
Filled Cucumbers, 3/348
Mexican Salad, 3/260
Rainbow Salad, 3/184
Sprouts Salad, 3/244
Stuffed Avocados, 3/207
Sweet Corn Drink, 3/293

Corn Flour

Chinese Stir-Fry, 3/116
Pasta with Chard, 3/82
Rice Hamburgers, 3/170
Soy Hamburgers, 3/117
Vegetarian Tamale, 3/301

Cornbread

Portuguese Beans, 3/324

Couscous

Couscous with Vegetables, 3/322

Cucumber

Andalusian Gazpacho, 3/360
Asparagus Salad, 3/278
Chickpea Salad, 3/186
Filled Cucumbers, 3/348
Mexican Salad, 3/260
Stuffed Tomatoes, 3/300
Tofu Salad, 3/299
Vegetable Juice, 3/385

Date

Asparagus Salad, 3/278

Dried Apricot

Cereal Bars, 3/174
Bircher-Muesli, 3/175
Sweet Balls, 3/269

Dry Fig

Cereal Bars, 3/174
Bircher-Muesli, 3/175
Sweet Balls, 3/269

Egg

Almond Croquettes, 3/151
Banana Casserole, 3/124
Carrot Cake, 3/125
Carrot Croquettes, 3/112
'Cordon Bleu' Eggplant, 3/121
Millet Croquettes, 3/111
Mushroom and Young Garlic Scramble Eggs, 3/119
Mushroom Lasagna, 3/110
Nut Loaf, 3/94
Oat Medallions, 3/122
Pasta with Chard, 3/82
Rice Crackers, 3/196
Soy Croquettes, 3/326
Soy Hamburgers, 3/117
Spanish Omelet, 3/114
Spinach Croquettes, 3/213
Spring Rolls, 3/102
Stuffed Eggs, 3/118
Vegetarian Sausages and Drumsticks, 3/92

Eggplant

Boiled Marinated Gluten, 3/90
'Cordon Bleu' Eggplant, 3/121
Eggplant Pie, 3/289
Garlic Eggplant, 3/279
Grilled Vegetables, 3/189
Roasted Vegetables, 3/384
Stuffed Eggplant, 3/120
Stuffed Eggs, 3/118
Tomato and Vegetable Stew, 3/212
Vegetable Cannelloni, 3/98
Vegetable Rice, 3/266

Endive

Seed Salad, 3/298

Fava Beans

Catalonian Fava Beans, 3/209
Filled Cucumbers, 3/348
Mixed Vegetables, 3/166

Fennel

Sardinian Adzuki, 3/302
Crunchy Fennel, 3/242

Fig

Stewed Figs and Pears, 3/225

Garlic

Alioli, 3/58
Andalusian Asparagus, 3/349
Andalusian Gazpacho, 3/360
Artichoke Cannelloni, 3/100
Autumn Rice, 3/168
Baked Potatoes, 3/251
Baked Tomatoes, 3/364
Banana Soup, 3/188
Beans and Rice, 3/320
Beans and Spinach, 3/352
Boiled Marinated Gluten, 3/90
Cabbage Rolls, 3/101
Cardoons in Almond Sauce, 3/232
Chickpea Stew, 3/148
Chinese Stir-Fry, 3/116
Christmas Red Cabbage, 3/248
'Cordon Bleu' Eggplant, 3/121
Couscous with Vegetables, 3/322
Eggplant Pie, 3/289
Falafel Patties, 3/198
Fufú/Mangú, 3/172
Garlic Eggplant, 3/279
Garlic Soup, 3/374
Grecian Green Beans, 3/288
Grilled Vegetables, 3/189
Italian-style Artichokes, 3/236
Kombú Paella, 3/318
Leek Pie, 3/338
Lentil Stew, 3/321
Mangú/Fufú, 3/172
Mexican Meat Analogs, 3/88
Mixed Vegetables, 3/166
Mung Bean Stew, 3/315
Mushroom Lasagna, 3/110
Nut Hamburgers, 3/171
Nut Loaf, 3/94
Oat Soup, 3/147
Oriental Salad, 3/164
Oven Potatoes, 3/250
Pasta Bows and Mushrooms, 3/85
Pasta Bows with Chickpeas, 3/149
Pasta with Chard, 3/82
Pinto Beans, 3/353
Potato Stew, 3/190
Potatoes and Almonds, 3/333
Potatoes and Mushrooms, 3/83
Potatoes and Spinach, 3/138
Potatoes with Peas, 3/169
Quinoa Risotto, 3/136
Rice Hamburgers, 3/170
Rice with Artichokes, 3/234
Rice with Carrots, 3/133
Rice with Cauliflower, 3/282
Rice with Pumpkin, 3/193
Rice with Spinach, 3/192
Roasted Vegetables, 3/384
Sardinian Adzuki, 3/302
Sautéed Marinated Gluten, 3/91
Sautéed Soy Sprouts, 3/265
Soy Hamburgers, 3/117
Soybean Stew, 3/381
Spinach Lasagna, 3/108
Spring Salad, 3/312
Sprouts Salad, 3/244
Stuffed Artichokes, 3/286
Stuffed Peppers, 3/382
Tomato and Vegetable Stew, 3/212
Vegetable Hamburgers, 3/152
Vegetable Paella, 3/86
Vegetable Purée, 3/361
Vegetable Rice, 3/266
Vegetarian Sausages and Drumsticks, 3/92
Zucchini Salad, 3/185

German Camomile

Refreshing Tea, 3/254

Gluten

Boiled Marinated Gluten, 3/90
Cabbage Rolls, 3/101
Chinese Stir-Fry, 3/116
Hot Marinated Gluten, 3/89
Sautéed Marinated Gluten, 3/91
Spinach Lasagna, 3/108
Vegetarian Sausages and Drumsticks, 3/92

Grape

Coconut Balls, 3/339

Grape Juice

Sangria (non-alcoholic), 3/327
Aromatic Linden, 3/159

Green Bean

Chickpea Stew, 3/148
Fettuccini with Green Beans, 3/283
Garden Pasta, 3/334
Grecian Green Beans, 3/288
Mixed Vegetables, 3/166
Pasta Bow Salad, 3/165
Potato Salad, 3/245
Rice Salad, 3/380
Spring Salad, 3/312
Vegetable Paella, 3/86
Vegetable Pie, 3/104
Vegetable Purée, 3/361

Hazelnut

Bircher-Muesli, 3/175
Cereal Bars, 3/174
Oat Soup, 3/147
Three-colored Purée, 3/377
Winter Log, 3/340

Hazelnut Milk

Apricot Shake, 3/141
Coconut Balls, 3/339

Honey

Cereal Bars, 3/174
Avocado Shake, 3/201
Apricot Shake, 3/141
Spinach Shake, 3/140
Peach Bavarian, 3/173
Sweet Corn Drink, 3/293
Bircher-Muesli, 3/175
Sweet Balls, 3/270
Strawberry Delight, 3/177
Oranges with Honey, 3/366
Tamarind Drink, 3/237

Kiwi

Tropical Fruit Salad, 3/253

Kohlrabi

Stuffed Kohlrabi, 3/337

Leek

Cereal Soup, 3/314
Chickpea Stew, 3/148
Cream of Leeks, 3/262
Cream of Pumpkin, 3/134
Leek Pie, 3/338
Leek, Potato, and Pumpkin Stew, 3/281
Leeks with Mayonnaise, 3/222
Stuffed Kohlrabi, 3/337
Vegetable Purée, 3/361
Vichyssoise, 3/280

Lemon

Bircher-Muesli, 3/175
Oat Medallions, 3/122
Peach Bavarian, 3/173
Sangria (non-alcoholic), 3/327
Sweet Corn Drink, 3/293

Lentil

Lentil Stew, 3/321
Lentils and Rice, 3/211

Lettuce

Chickpea Salad, 3/186
Cream of Avocado, 3/351
Mexican Salad, 3/260
Oriental Salad, 3/164

Stuffed Tomatoes, 3/300
Tabulé, 3/261
Tofu Salad, 3/299
Zucchini Salad, 3/185

Licorice

Refreshing Tea, 3/254

Lima Bean

Vegetable Paella, 3/86

Linden

Refreshing Tea, 3/254
Aromatic Linden, 3/159

Mango

Mango Custard, 3/354
Tropical Fruit Salad, 3/253

Melon

Melon and Orange Juice, 3/367
Party Melon, 3/176

Milk

Banana Casserole, 3/124
Banana Soup, 3/188
Carrot Croquettes, 3/112
Cream of Banana, 3/252
Millet Croquettes, 3/111
Oat Medallions, 3/122
Spinach Croquettes, 3/213

Millet

Peach Bavarian, 3/173
Stuffed Kohlrabi, 3/337
Millet Croquettes, 3/111

Molasses

Almond Cookies, 3/155
Banana Shake, 3/179

Mung Bean

Mung Bean Stew, 3/315

Mushroom

Cashew Stew, 3/150
Cream of Mushroom, 3/313
Mushroom Lasagna, 3/110
Oriental Salad, 3/164
Sauerkraut and Carrot, 3/264
Vegetable Paella, 3/86
Violet Salad, 3/373

Mushrooms

Autumn Cabbage, 3/376
Chinese Noodles, 3/316
Chinese Stir-Fry, 3/116
Mushroom and Young Garlic Scrambled Eggs, 3/119
Mushroom Lasagna, 3/110
Pasta Bows and Mushrooms, 3/85
Potatoes and Mushrooms, 3/83
Vegetable Cannelloni, 3/98
Vegetable Pie, 3/104

Olives

Banana Casserole, 3/124
Belgian Endive Salad, 3/230
Cashew Stew, 3/150
Corn Platter, 3/247
Crunchy Fennel, 3/242
Lentils and Rice, 3/211
Mexican Meat Analogs, 3/88
Mexican Salad, 3/260
Oven Potatoes, 3/250
Potato Salad, 3/245
Rainbow Salad, 3/184
Rice Salad, 3/380
Stuffed Avocados, 3/207
Stuffed Tomatoes, 3/300
Vegetable Turnovers, 3/106
Violet Salad, 3/373

Onion

Almond Croquettes, 3/151
Almond Soup, 3/146
Artichoke Cannelloni, 3/100
Autumn Cabbage, 3/376
Baked Tomatoes, 3/364
Banana Casserole, 3/124
Banana Soup, 3/188
Beans with Spinach, 3/352
Boiled Marinated Gluten, 3/90
Boiled Vegetables, 3/223
Cabbage Rolls, 3/101
Cabbage Soup, 3/375
Carrot Croquettes, 3/112
Cashew Stew, 3/150
Catalonian Fava Beans, 3/209
Celery Pie, 3/290
Cereal Soup, 3/314
Chickpea Stew, 3/148
Couscous with Vegetables, 3/322
Cream of Mushroom, 3/313
Cream of Onion, 3/220
Eggplant Pie, 3/289
Fufú, 3/172
Garden Pasta, 3/334
Grilled Vegetables, 3/189
Hot Marinated Gluten, 3/89
Italian-style Artichokes, 3/236
Italian-style Macaroni, 3/84
Kombú Paella, 3/318
Leek Pie, 3/338
Lentil Stew, 3/321
Lentils and Rice, 3/211
Mangú, 3/172
Mexican Meat Analogs, 3/88
Millet Croquettes, 3/111
Mixed Vegetables, 3/166
Mung Bean Stew, 3/315
Mushroom Lasagna, 3/110
Nut Hamburgers, 3/171
Nut Loaf, 3/94
Onion and Pepper Pizza, 3/224
Onion Sausages, 3/96
Oven Potatoes, 3/250
Pasta Bows with Chickpeas, 3/149
Pinto Beans, 3/353
Potato Stew, 3/190
Potato Stew, 3/221
Potatoes and Mushrooms, 3/83
Potatoes with Peas, 3/169
Quinoa Risotto, 3/136
Rice Salad, 3/380
Rice with Carrot, 3/133
Rice with Pumpkin, 3/193
Roasted Vegetables, 3/384
Sardinian Adzuki, 3/302
Sauerkraut and Carrots, 3/264
Sautéed Marinated Gluten, 3/91
Soy Croquettes, 3/326
Soy Hamburgers, 3/117
Soybean Stew, 3/381
Spanish Bouillon, 3/332
Spanish Omelet, 3/114
Spinach Croquettes, 3/213
Spring Rolls, 3/102
Spring Salad, 3/312
Stuffed Artichokes, 3/286
Stuffed Eggplant, 3/120
Stuffed Tomatoes, 3/300
Tabulé, 3/261
Tomato and Vegetable Stew, 3/212
Vegetable Cannelloni, 3/98
Vegetable Hamburgers, 3/152
Vegetable Pie, 3/104
Vegetable Turnovers, 3/106
Vichyssoise, 3/280

Orange

Aromatic Linden, 3/159
Banana Shake, 3/179
Cherimoya and Orange Shake, 3/178
Fruit Salad, 3/200
Melon and Orange Juice, 3/367
Oranges with Honey, 3/366
Party Melon, 3/176
Peach Bavarian, 3/173

Papaya

Tropical Fruit Salad, 3/253

Pasta

Italian-style Artichokes, 3/236
Artichoke Cannelloni, 3/100
Vegetable Cannelloni, 3/98
Pasta Bow Salad, 3/165
Spaghetti with Spinach, 3/210
Pasta Bows with Chickpeas, 3/149
Pasta Bows with Mushrooms, 3/85
Fettuccini with Green Beans, 3/283
Fettuccini with Green Sauce, 3/335
Spinach Lasagna, 3/108
Mushroom Lasagna, 3/110
Italian-style Macaroni, 3/84
Garden Pasta, 3/334
Pasta with Chard, 3/82

Pea

Boiled Vegetables, 3/223
Celery Pie, 3/290
Chinese Noodles, 3/316
Garden Pasta, 3/334
Kombú Paella, 3/318
Mexican Salad, 3/260
Mixed Vegetables, 3/166
Mushroom Lasagna, 3/110
Pasta Bow Salad, 3/156
Potato Salad, 3/245
Potato Stew, 3/190
Potatoes with Peas, 3/169
Rice Salad, 3/380
Spring Salad, 3/312
Stuffed Tomatoes, 3/300
Vegetable Paella, 3/86

Peach

Fruit Salad, 3/200
Peach Bavarian, 3/173
Sangria (non-alcoholic), 3/327

Peanut

Granola, 3/156

Pear

Stewed Figs and Pears, 3/225
Fruit Salad, 3/200

Pepper

Rice with Artichoke, 3/234
Andalusian Gazpacho, 3/360
Baked Tomatoes, 3/364
Banana Casserole, 3/124
Boiled Marinated Gluten, 3/90
Catalonian Fava Beans, 3/209
Chickpea Salad, 3/186
Chickpea Stew, 3/148
Chinese Noodles, 3/316
Eggplant Pie, 3/289
Garden Pasta, 3/334
Grilled Vegetables, 3/189
Hot Marinated Gluten, 3/89
Lentils and Rice, 3/211
Mexican Meat Analogs, 3/88
Mexican Salad, 3/260
Onion and Pepper Pizza, 3/224
Pinto Beans, 3/353
Potato Salad, 3/245
Potato Stew, 3/190
Potatoes and Mushrooms, 3/83
Red and White Salad, 3/372
Rice Salad, 3/380
Rice with Cauliflower, 3/282
Rice with Pumpkin, 3/193
Roasted Vegetables, 3/384
Sautéed Marinated Gluten, 3/91
Spinach Croquettes, 3/213
Sprouts Salad, 3/244
Stuffed Kohlrabi, 3/337
Stuffed Peppers, 3/382
Tomato and Vegetable Stew, 3/212
Vegetable Paella, 3/86
Vegetable Pie, 3/104
Vegetable Purée, 3/361
Vegetable Rice, 3/266
Vegetable Turnovers, 3/106

Persimmon

Persimmon Shake, 3/270

Pine Nut

Autumn Rice, 3/168
Artichoke Cannelloni, 3/100
Vegetable Cannelloni, 3/98
Spinach Croquettes, 3/213
Spaghetti with Spinach, 3/210
Potatoes and Spinach, 3/138
Onion Sausages, 3/96

Pineapple

Asparagus Salad, 3/278
Fruit Salad, 3/200
Pineapple Water, 3/255
Pomegranate Drink, 3/271
Tropical Fruit Salad, 3/253

Plantain

Banana Casserole, 3/124
Banana Soup, 3/188
Cream of Banana, 3/252
Fufú, 3/172
Mangú, 3/172
Peppermint Refreshing Tea, 3/254

Pomegranate

Pomegranate Drink, 3/271

Potato
Autumn Cabbage, 3/376
Baked Potatoes, 3/251
Boiled Vegetables, 3/223
Borage and Potatoes, 3/362
Cabbage Varieties, 3/378
Chard with Potatoes and Pumpkin, 3/263
Corn Platter, 3/247
Couscous with Vegetables, 3/322
Cream of Leeks, 3/262
Cream of Pumpkin, 3/134
Grecian Green Salad, 3/288
Leek, Potato, and Pumpkin Stew, 3/281
Mexican Meat Analogs, 3/88
Mixed Vegetables, 3/166
Mung Bean Stew, 3/315
Oven Potatoes, 3/250
Portuguese Beans, 3/324
Potato Salad, 3/245
Potato Stew, 3/190
Potato Stew, 3/221
Potatoes and Almonds, 3/333
Potatoes and Mushrooms, 3/83
Potatoes and Spinach, 3/138
Potatoes with Peas, 3/169
Spanish Bouillon, 3/332
Spanish Omelet, 3/114
Spring Salad, 3/312
Sprouts Salad, 3/244
Three-colored Purée, 3/377
Turnip Greens and Potatoes, 3/208
Vegetable Purée, 3/361
Vichyssoise, 3/280

Prune
Autumn Cabbage, 3/376
Oatmeal, 3/154
Sweet Balls, 3/269

Pumpkin
Cabbage Varieties, 3/378
Chard with Potatoes and Pumpkin, 3/263
Cream of Pumpkin, 3/134
Leek, Potato, and Pumpkin Stew, 3/281
Pinto Beans, 3/353
Rice with Pumpkin, 3/193
Soybean Stew, 3/381
Spinach Salad, 3/132
Turnip Greens and Potatoes, 3/208

Pumpkin Seed
Vegetarian Tamale, 3/301

Quinoa
Quinoa Risotto, 3/136

Radicchio
Belgian Endive Salad, 3/230

Radish
Belgian Endive Salad, 3/230
Red and White Salad, 3/372
Spinach Salad, 3/132
Sweet Cassava Salad, 3/218

Raisins
Baked Apples, 3/268
Bircher-Muesli, 3/175
Cereal Bars, 3/174
Grecian Green Beans, 3/288
Party Melon, 3/176
Party Melon, 3/176
Stewed Figs and Pears, 3/225
Sweet Balls, 3/269

Raspberry
Persimmon Shake, 3/270
Party Melon, 3/176

Red Cabbage
Christmas Red Cabbage, 3/248
Rainbow Salad, 3/184
Violet Salad, 3/373

Rice
Almond Soup, 3/146
Asparagus Fondant, 3/284
Autumn Rice, 3/168
Beans and Rice, 3/320
Cabbage Rolls, 3/101
Cabbage Soup, 3/375
Kombú Paella, 3/318
Lentils and Rice, 3/211
Oriental Salad, 3/164
Rice Crackers, 3/196
Rice Hamburgers, 3/170
Rice Milk, 3/273
Rice Pudding, 3/199
Rice Salad, 3/380
Rice with Artichokes, 3/234
Rice with Carrots, 3/133
Rice with Cauliflower, 3/282
Rice with Pumpkin, 3/193
Rice with Spinach, 3/192
Stuffed Peppers, 3/382
Vegetable Paella, 3/86
Vegetable Rice, 3/266

Rice Flour
Peach Bavarian, 3/173

Rolled Oats
Almond Croquettes, 3/351
Bircher-Muesli, 3/175
Cereal Bars, 3/174
Coconut Balls, 3/339
Granola, 3/156
Oat Medallions, 3/122
Oat Soup, 3/147
Oatmeal, 3/154
Vegetable Hamburgers, 3/152

Rye Flour
Rye Bread, 3/194

Seaweed
Kombú Paella, 3/318

Sesame Seed
Almond Cookies, 3/155
Artichoke Soup. 3/231
Cereal Bars, 3/174
Chinese Salad, 3/243
Seed Salad, 3/298
Sesame Crepes, 3/304
Spinach Salad, 3/132

Soy Milk
Almond Croquettes, 3/151
Bircher-Muesli, 3/175
Cashew Stew, 3/150
Corn Platter, 3/247
Cream of Mushroom, 3/313
Mango Custard, 3/354
Peach Bavarian, 3/173
Rice Pudding, 3/199
Soy Croquettes, 3/326

Soy Noodles
Chinese Noodles, 3/316

Soybean
Soy Croquettes, 3/326
Soy Milk, 3/305
Soybean Stew, 3/381

Soybean Sprouts
Chinese Stir-Fry, 3/116
Oriental Salad, 3/164
Sautéed Soy Sprouts, 3/265
Spring Rolls, 3/102

Spearmint
Refreshing Tea, 3/254

Spinach
Beans with Spinach, 3/352
Filled Cucumbers, 3/348
Potatoes and Spinach, 3/138
Rice with Spinach, 3/192
River Salad, 3/206
Spaghetti with Spinach, 3/210
Spinach Croquettes, 3/213
Spinach Lasagna, 3/108
Spinach Salad, 3/132
Spinach Shake, 3/140

Strawberry
Fruit Salad, 3/200
Party Melon, 3/176
Strawberry Delight, 3/177

Sunflower Seed
Seed Salad, 3/298
Spinach Salad, 3/132
Strawberry Delight, 3/177

Sweet Cassava
Sweet Cassava Salad, 3/218

Tamarind
Tamarind Drink, 3/237

Tangerine
Party Melon, 3/176

Textured Soy Protein
Baked Tomatoes, 3/364
Mexican Meat Analogs, 3/88
Soy Hamburgers, 3/117
Spring Rolls, 3/102
Stuffed Artichokes, 3/286

Tiger Nut
Tiger Nut Horchata, 3/272

Tofu
Kombú Paella, 3/318
Rice Hamburgers, 3/170
Stuffed Peppers, 3/382
Tofu Salad, 3/299
Vegetable Turnovers, 3/106
Winter Log, 3/340

Tomato
Andalusian Gazpacho, 3/360
Baked Tomatoes, 3/364
Beans and Rice, 3/320
Broccoli Bake, 3/336
Catalonian Fava Beans, 3/209
Cereal Soup, 3/314
Chickpea Salad, 3/186
Chickpea Stew, 3/148
Couscous with Vegetables, 3/322
Eggplant Pie, 3/289
Garden Pasta, 3/334
Garlic Soup, 3/374
Grilled Vegetables, 3/189
Italian-style Macaroni, 3/84
Lentil Stew, 3/321
Lentils and Rice, 3/211
Mexican Meat Analogs, 3/88
Mexican Salad, 3/260
Mushroom Lasagna, 3/110
Onion and Pepper Pizza, 3/224
Pasta Bows with Chickpeas, 3/149
Pinto Beans, 3/353
Potatoes and Mushrooms, 3/83
Rainbow Salad, 3/184
Red and White Salad, 3/372
Rice with Artichokes, 3/234
Rice with Cauliflower, 3/282
Rice with Pumpkin, 3/193
Roasted Vegetables, 3/384
Sautéed Marinated Gluten, 3/91
Soy Croquettes, 3/326
Spinach Lasagna, 3/108
Spring Salad, 3/312
Stuffed Eggplant, 3/120
Stuffed Peppers, 3/382
Stuffed Tomatoes, 3/300
Tabulé, 3/261
Tomato and Vegetable Stew, 3/212
Vegetable Hamburgers, 3/152
Vegetable Juice, 3/385
Vegetable Paella, 3/86
Vegetable Pie, 3/104
Vegetable Purée, 3/361
Vegetable Rice, 3/266

Turnip
Couscous with Vegetables, 3/322
Kombú Paella, 3/318
Stuffed Kohlrabi, 3/337
Vegetable Purée, 3/361

Turnip Greens
Spanish Bouillon, 3/332
Turnip Greens and Potatoes, 3/208

Vegetarian Meat Analog
Stuffed Eggplant, 3/120
Chinese Salad, 3/243
Spinach Lasagna, 3/108
Banana Casserole, 3/124
Italian-style Macaroni, 3/84
Vegetable Cannelloni, 3/98

Walnut
Autumn Rice, 3/168
Bircher-Muesli, 3/175
Cabbage Rolls, 3/101
Cereal Bars, 3/174
Granola, 3/156
Nut Loaf, 3/94
Oranges with Honey, 3/366
Rice Hamburgers, 3/170

Seed Salad, 3/298
Spaghetti with Spinach, 3/210
Spinach Lasagna, 3/108
Strawberry Delight, 3/177
Sweet Balls, 3/269

Watercress
Rainbow Salad, 3/184
River Salad, 3/206

Watermelon
Watermelon Shake, 3/292

Welsh Onion
Belgian Endive Salad, 3/230
Cabbage Salad, 3/219
Chinese Noodles, 3/316
Chinese Salad, 3/243
Cream of Avocado, 3/351
Oriental Salad, 3/164
Seed Salad, 3/298
Stuffed Avocados, 3/207
Sweet Cassava Salad, 3/218
Tofu Salad, 3/299

Wheat
Tabulé, 3/261
Almond Cookies, 3/155

Wheat Flour
Almond Cookies, 3/155
Almond Croquettes, 3/151
Andalusian Asparagus, 3/349
Banana Soup, 3/188
Cardoons in Almond Sauce, 3/232
Carrot Cake, 3/125
Carrot Croquettes, 3/112
Cashew Stew, 3/150
Chinese Noodles, 3/316
Chinese Stir-Fry, 3/116
'Cordon Bleu' Eggplant, 3/121
Cream of Mushroom, 3/313
Leek Pie, 3/338
Millet Croquettes, 3/111
Nut Hamburgers, 3/171
Oat Medallions, 3/122
Peach Bavarian, 3/173
Rice Crackers, 3/196
Rye Bread, 3/194
Soy Croquettes, 3/326
Spinach Croquettes, 3/213
Spring Rolls, 3/102
Vegetable Hamburgers, 3/152
Vegetarian Sausages and Drumsticks, 3/92

Wheat Germ
Spinach Salad, 3/132
Granola, 3/156
Vegetable Hamburgers, 3/152
Soybean Stew, 3/381

Yam
Yam with Tomato, 3/191

Yogurt
Spinach Shake, 3/140
Vichyssoise, 3/280
Yogurt Mayonnaise, 3/58

Young Garlic
Mushroom and Young Garlic Scrambled Eggs, 3/119

Zucchini
Almond Soup, 3/146
Couscous with Vegetables, 3/322
Cream of Zucchini, 3/246
Grilled Vegetables, 3/189
Pasta Bows with Chickpeas, 3/149
Spring Rolls, 3/102
Tomato and Vegetable Stew, 3/212
Vegetable Hamburgers, 3/152
Vegetarian Tamale, 3/301
Zucchini Salad, 3/185

RECIPE INDEX BY COURSE

Base Recipes
Crepes, 3/42
Fresh Italian Pasta, 3/48
Marinated Gluten with Vegetables, 3/53
Marinated Gluten, 3/52
Mexican Corn Tortillas, 3/44
Mexican Wheat Tortillas, 3/45
Pie Crust, 3/43

Breads
Almond Cookies, 3/155
Arabian Pocket Bread, 3/47
Baked Apples, 3/268
Carrot Cake, 3/125
Coconut Balls, 3/339
Cream of Banana, 3/252

Breakfasts (see also Desserts)
Almond Cookies, 3/155
Almond Milk, 3/342
Apricot Shake, 3/141
Avocado Shake, 3/201
Baked Apples, 3/268
Banana Shake, 3/179
Bircher-Muesli, 3/175
Carrot and Apple Juice, 3/355
Carrot Cake, 3/125
Cereal Bars, 3/174
Cherimoya and Orange Shake, 3/178
Chufa Milk, 3/272
Coconut Balls, 3/339
Coconut Milk, 3/343
Cream of Banana, 3/252
Fruit Salad, 3/200
Garlic Bread, 3/71
Granola, 3/156
Hazelnut Milk, 3/291
Mango Custard, 3/354
Melon and Orange Juice, 3/367
Muffins (without egg), 3/77
Oatmeal, 3/154
Oranges with Honey, 3/366
Party Melon, 3/176
Peach Bavarian, 3/173
Persimmon Shake, 3/270
Pomegranate Drink, 3/271
Rice Crackers, 3/196
Rice Milk, 3/273
Rice Pudding, 3/199
Sesame Crepes, 3/304
Soy Milk, 3/305
Spinach Shake, 3/140
Stewed Figs and Pears, 3/225
Strawberry Delight, 3/177
Sweet Balls, 3/269
Sweet Corn Drink, 3/293
Sweet Walnut Rolls, 3/77
Tamarind Drink, 3/237
Tomato and Garlic Bread, 3/71
Tropical Fruit Salad, 3/253
Tropical Shake, 3/158
Watermelon Shake, 3/292
Winter Log, 3/340

Butters and Spreads
Almond Butter, 3/65
Chestnut Butter, 3/65
Guacamole, 3/67
Hazelnut Butter, 3/65
Hot Vegetable Paté, 3/66
Hummus, 3/67
Lentil Spread, 3/67
Lupine Spread, 3/66
Mushroom Spread, 3/66
Olive Spread (Vegetarian Caviar), 3/67
Peanut Butter, 3/65
Tofu and Herbs Spread, 3/66
Walnut Butter, 3/65

Desserts (see also Breakfasts)
Fruit Salad, 3/200
Mango Custard, 3/354
Muffins (without egg), 3/77
Oranges with Honey, 3/366
Party Melon, 3/176
Peach Bavarian, 3/173
Rice Crackers, 3/196
Rice Pudding, 3/199
Rye Bread, 3/194
Sesame Crepes, 3/304
Stewed Figs and Pears, 3/225
Strawberry Delight, 3/177
Sweet Balls, 3/269
Sweet Walnut Rolls (without egg), 3/77
Tropical Fruit Salad, 3/253
Whole Bread, 3/46
Winter Log, 3/340

Drinks and Shakes
Almond Milk, 3/342
Andalusian Gazpacho, 3/360
Apricot Shake, 3/141
Aromatic Linden, 3/159
Avocado Shake, 3/201
Banana Shake, 3/179
Carrot and Apple Juice, 3/355
Cherimoya and Orange Shake, 3/178
Coconut Milk, 3/343
Hazelnut Milk, 3/291
Melon and Orange Juice, 3/367
Persimmon Shake, 3/270
Pineapple Water, 3/255
Pomegranate Drink, 3/271
Refreshing Tea, 3/254
Rice Milk, 3/273
Sangria (non-alcoholic), 3/327
Soy Milk, 3/305
Spinach Shake, 3/140
Sweet Corn Drink, 3/293
Tamarind Drink, 3/237
Tiger Nut Horchata, 3/272
Tropical Shake, 3/158
Vegetable Juice, 3/385
Watermelon Shake, 3/292

First Courses and Entrées
'Cordon Bleu' Eggplant, 3/121
Almond Croquettes, 3/151
Almond Soup, 3/146

Andalusian Asparagus, 3/349
Artichoke Cannelloni, 3/100
Artichoke Soup, 3/231
Asparagus Fondant, 3/284
Autumn Cabbage, 3/376
Autumn Rice, 3/168
Baked Potatoes, 3/251
Baked Tomatoes, 3/364
Banana Casserole, 3/124
Banana Soup, 3/188
Beans and Rice, 3/320
Beans with Spinach, 3/352
Boiled Marinated Gluten, 3/90
Boiled Vegetables, 3/223
Borage and Potatoes, 3/362
Broccoli Bake, 3/336
Cabbage Rolls, 3/101
Cabbage Soup, 3/375
Cabbage Varieties, 3/378
Cardoons in Almond Sauce, 3/232
Carrot Croquettes, 3/112
Cashew Stew, 3/150
Catalonian Fava Beans, 3/209
Celery Pie, 3/290
Cereal Soup, 3/314
Chard with Potatoes and Pumpkin, 3/263
Chickpea Stew, 3/148
Chinese Noodles, 3/316
Chinese Stir-Fry, 3/116
Christmas Red Cabbage, 3/248
Corn Platter, 3/247
Couscous with Vegetables, 3/322
Cream of Asparagus, 3/350
Cream of Avocado, 3/351
Cream of Leeks, 3/262
Cream of Mushroom, 3/313
Cream of Onion, 3/220
Cream of Pumpkin, 3/134
Cream of Zucchini, 3/246
Eggplant Pie, 3/289
Falafel Patties, 3/198
Fettuccini with Green Beans, 3/283
Fettuccini with Green Sauce, 3/335
Fufú, 3/172
Garden Pasta, 3/334
Garlic Eggplants, 3/279
Garlic Soup, 3/374
Grecian Green Beans, 3/288
Grilled Vegetables, 3/189
Hot Marinated Gluten, 3/89
Italian-style Artichokes, 3/236
Italian-style Macaroni, 3/84
Kombú Paella, 3/318
Leek Pie, 3/338
Leek, Potato, and Pumpkin Stew, 3/281
Lentil Stew, 3/321
Lentils and Rice, 3/211
Mangú, 3/172
Mexican Meat Analogs, 3/88
Millet Croquettes, 3/111
Mixed Vegetables, 3/166
Mung Bean Stew, 3/315
Mushroom and Young Garlic Scrambled Eggs, 3/119
Mushroom Lasagna, 3/110
Nut Hamburgers, 3/171
Nut Loaf, 3/94
Oat Medallions, 3/122
Oat Soup, 3/147
Onion and Pepper Pizza, 3/224
Onion Sausages, 3/96
Oven Potatoes, 3/250
Pasta Bows and Mushrooms, 3/85
Pasta Bows with Chickpeas, 3/149
Pasta with Chard, 3/82
Pinto Beans, 3/353
Portuguese Beans, 3/324
Potato Salad, 3/245
Potato Stew, 3/190
Potato Stew, 3/221
Potatoes and Almonds, 3/333
Potatoes and Mushrooms, 3/83
Potatoes and Spinach, 3/138
Potatoes with Peas, 3/169
Quesadillas, 3/70
Quinoa Risotto, 3/136
Rice Hamburgers, 3/170
Rice Salad, 3/380
Rice with Artichokes, 3/234
Rice with Carrots, 3/133
Rice with Cauliflower, 3/282
Rice with Pumpkin, 3/193
Rice with Spinach, 3/192
Roasted Vegetables, 3/384
Sardinian Adzuki, 3/302
Sauerkraut and Carrots, 3/264
Sautéed Marinated Gluten, 3/91
Sautéed Soy Sprouts, 3/265
Soy Croquettes, 3/226
Soy Hamburgers, 3/117
Soybean Stew, 3/381
Spaghetti with Spinach, 3/210
Spanish Bouillon, 3/332
Spanish Omelet (without egg), 3/76
Spanish Omelet, 3/114
Spinach Croquettes, 3/213
Spinach Lasagna, 3/108
Spring Rolls, 3/102
Stuffed Artichokes, 3/286
Stuffed Eggplant, 3/120
Stuffed Eggs, 3/118
Stuffed Kohlrabi, 3/337
Stuffed Peppers, 3/382
Tacos, 3/70
Three-colored Purée, 3/377
Tomato and Vegetable Stew, 3/212
Turnip Greens and Potatoes, 3/208
Vegetable Cannelloni, 3/98
Vegetable Paella, 3/86
Vegetable Pie, 3/104
Vegetable Purée, 3/361
Vegetable Rice, 3/266
Vegetable Turnovers, 3/106
Vegetable Hamburgers, 3/152
Vegetarian Sausages and Drumsticks, 3/92
Vegetarian Tamale, 3/301
Vichyssoise, 3/280
Yam with Tomato, 3/191

Salads

Andalusian Gazpacho, 3/360
Asparagus Salad, 3/278
Belgian Endive Salad, 3/230
Cabbage Salad, 3/219
Chickpea Salad, 3/186
Chinese Salad, 3/243
Crunchy Fennel, 3/242
Filled Cucumbers, 3/348
Leeks with Mayonnaise, 3/222
Mexican Salad, 3/260
Oriental Salad, 3/164
Pasta Bow Salad, 3/165
Potato Salad, 3/245
Rainbow Salad, 3/184
Red and White Salad, 3/372
Rice Salad, 3/380
River Salad, 3/206
Seed Salad, 3/298
Spinach Salad, 3/132
Spring Salad, 3/312
Sprouts Salad, 3/244
Stuffed Avocados, 3/207
Stuffed Tomatoes, 3/300
Sweet Cassava Salad, 3/218
Tabulé, 3/261
Tofu Salad, 3/299
Vegetable Juice, 3/385
Violet Salad, 3/373
Zucchini Salad, 3/185

Sauces

Alioli, 3/58
Almond Cream Sauce, 3/64
Alternative to Cheese Sauce, 3/73
Alternative to Parmesan Cheese, 3/73
Andalusian Dressing, 3/57
Beet Dressing, 3/57
Bolognese Sauce, 3/60
Chopped Tomato Sauce, 3/63
Cucumber and Yogurt, 3/61
Green Sauce, 3/64
Herb Sauce, 3/60
Iranian Dressing, 3/57
Lemon Vinaigrette, 3/56
Mediterranean Sauce, 3/61
Mushroom Sauce, 3/64
Natural Tomato Sauce, 3/63
Orange Sauce, 3/61
Oregano Vinaigrette, 3/56
Pesto Sauce, 3/60
Radish Dressing, 3/57
Red Tomato Sauce, 3/63
Seasoned White Sauce, 3/59
Sesame Sauce, 3/60
Soy Mayonnaise, 3/58
Soy Sweet-and-Sour Sauce, 3/56
Sweet-and-Sour Sauce from Seeds, 3/56
Tahini, 3/61
Tomato Specialty Sauce, 3/62
Traditional Tomato Sauce, 3/62
Vegetable Mayonnaise, 3/58
Vegetable Sauce, 3/64
White Sauce from Vegetable Stock, 3/59
White Sauce with Onion, 3/59
White Sauce, 3/59
Yogurt Mayonnaise, 3/58

Snacks, canapés, sandwiches, and subs

Artichoke Canapés, 3/69
Asparagus and Egg Canapés, 3/69
Banana Kebabs, 3/75
Canoes, 3/72
Celery Kebabs, 3/75
Cheese and Red Pepper Canapés, 3/68
Cheese Balls, 3/72
Cucumber and Onion Canapés, 3/68
Curried Rice Canapés, 3/69
Fresh Cheese Kebabs, 3/75
Garden "Fish", 3/72
Garlic Bread, 3/71
Guacamole, 3/67
Lettuce and Heart of Palm Canapés, 3/68
Mushroom Canapés, 3/69
Mushroom Kebabs, 3/74
Quesadillas, 3/70
Rice Crackers, 3/196
Soy or Meat Analog Kebabs, 3/74
Spanish Omelet (without egg), 3/76
Spanish Omelet, 3/114
Sweet-and-Sour Kebab, 3/75
Taco Salad, 3/70
Tacos, 3/70
Tofu Kebabs, 3/74
Tomato and Garlic Bread, 3/71
Tropical Salad Rolls, 3/71
Vegetarian Sausage Kebabs, 3/74
Zucchini Canapés, 3/68

INDEX OF RECIPES

Alioli, 3/58
Almond Butter, 3/65
Almond Cookies, 3/155
Almond Cream Sauce, 3/64
Almond Croquettes, 3/151
Almond Milk, 3/342
Almond Soup, 3/146
Alternative to Cheese Sauce, 3/73
Alternative to Parmesan Cheese, 3/73
Andalusian Asparagus, 3/349
Andalusian Dressing, 3/57
Andalusian Gazpacho, 3/360
Apricot Shake, 3/141
Arabian Pocket Bread, 3/47
Aromatic Linden, 3/159
Artichoke Canapés, 3/69
Artichoke Cannelloni, 3/100
Artichoke Soup, 3/231
Asparagus and Egg Canapés, 3/69
Asparagus Fondant, 3/284
Asparagus Salad, 3/278
'Au gratin' without Cheese, 3/73
Autumn Cabbage, 3/376
Autumn Rice, 3/168
Avocado Shake, 3/201

Baked Apples, 3/268
Baked Potatoes, 3/251
Baked Tomatoes, 3/364
Banana Casserole, 3/124
Banana Kebabs, 3/75
Banana Shake, 3/179
Banana Soup, 3/188
Batter (without egg), 3/76
Beans and Rice, 3/320
Beans with Spinach, 3/352
Beet Dressing, 3/57
Belgian Endive Salad, 3/230
Bircher-Muesli, 3/175
Boiled Marinated Gluten, 3/90
Boiled Vegetables, 3/223
Bolognese Sauce, 3/60
Borage with Potatoes, 3/362
Broccoli Bake, 3/336

Cabbage Rolls, 3/101
Cabbage Salad, 3/219
Cabbage Soup, 3/375
Cabbage Varieties, 3/378
Canoes, 3/72
Cardoons in Almond Sauce, 3/232
Carrot and Apple Juice, 3/355
Carrot Cake, 3/125
Carrot Croquettes, 3/112
Cashew Stew, 3/150
Catalonian Fava Beans, 3/209
Celery Kebabs, 3/75
Celery Pie, 3/290
Cereal Bars, 3/174
Cereal Soup, 3/314
Chard with Potatoes and Pumpkin, 3/263
Cheese and Red Pepper Canapés, 3/68
Cheese Balls, 3/72
Cherimoya and Orange Shake, 3/178
Chestnut Butter, 3/65
Chickpea Salad, 3/186
Chickpea Stew, 3/148
Chinese Noodles, 3/316
Chinese Salad, 3/243
Chinese Stir-Fry, 3/116
Chopped Tomato Sauce, 3/63
Christmas Red Cabbage, 3/248
Coconut Balls, 3/339
Coconut Milk, 3/343
'Cordon Bleu' Eggplant, 3/121
Corn Platter, 3/247
Couscous with Vegetables, 3/322
Cream of Asparagus, 3/350
Cream of Avocado, 3/351
Cream of Banana, 3/252
Cream of Leeks, 3/262
Cream of Mushroom, 3/313
Cream of Onion, 3/220
Cream of Pumpkin, 3/134
Cream of Zucchini, 3/246
Crepes, 3/42
Crunchy Fennel, 3/242
Cucumber and Onion Canapés, 3/68
Cucumber and Yogurt Sauce, 3/61
Curried Rice Canapés, 3/69

Eggplant Pie, 3/289

Falafel Patties, 3/198
Fettuccini with Green Beans, 3/283
Fettuccini with Green Sauce, 3/335
Filled Cucumbers, 3/348
Fresh Cheese Kebabs, 3/75
Fresh Italian Pasta, 3/48
Fruit Salad, 3/200
Fufú, 3/172

Garden "Fish", 3/72
Garden Pasta, 3/334
Garlic Bread, 3/71
Garlic Eggplant, 3/279
Garlic Soup, 3/374
Gluten, 3/52
Granola, 3/156
Grecian Green Beans, 3/288
Green Mayonnaise, 3/58
Green Sauce, 3/64
Grilled Vegetables, 3/189
Guacamole, 3/67

Hazelnut Butter, 3/65
Hazelnut Milk, 3/291
Herb Sauce, 3/60
Hot Marinated Gluten, 3/89
Hot Vegetable Paté, 3/66
Hummus, 3/67

Iranian Dressing, 3/57
Italian-Style Artichokes, 3/236
Italian-style Macaroni, 3/84

Kombú Paella, 3/318

Leek Pie, 3/338
Leek, Potato, and Pumpkin Stew, 3/281
Leeks with Mayonnaise, 3/222
Lemon Vinaigrette, 3/56
Lentil Spread, 3/67
Lentil Stew, 3/321
Lentils and Rice, 3/211
Lettuce and Hearts of Palm Canapés, 3/68
Lupine Spread, 3/66

Mango Custard, 3/354
Mangú, 3/172
Marinated Gluten with Vegetables, 3/53
Mediterranean Sauce, 3/61
Melon and Orange Juice, 3/367
Mexican Corn Tortillas, 3/44
Mexican Meat Analogs, 3/88
Mexican Salad, 3/260
Mexican Wheat Tortillas, 3/45
Millet Croquettes, 3/111
Mixed Vegetables, 3/166
Muffins (without egg), 3/77
Mung Bean Stew, 3/315
Mushroom and Young Garlic Scrambled Eggs, 3/119
Mushroom Canapés, 3/69
Mushroom Kebabs, 3/74
Mushroom Lasagna, 3/110
Mushroom Sauce, 3/64
Mushroom Spread, 3/66

Natural Tomato Sauce, 3/63
Nut Hamburgers, 3/171
Nut Loaf, 3/94

Oat Medallions, 3/122
Oat Soup, 3/147

Oatmeal, 3/154
Olive Spread, 3/67
Onion and Pepper Pizza, 3/224
Onion Sausages, 3/96
Orange Sauce, 3/61
Oranges with Honey, 3/366
Oregano Vinaigrette, 3/56
Oriental Salad, 3/164
Oven Potatoes, 3/250

Party Melon, 3/176
Pasta Bow Salad, 3/165
Pasta Bows and Mushrooms, 3/85
Pasta Bows with Chickpeas, 3/149
Pasta with Chard, 3/82
Peach Bavarian, 3/173
Peanut Butter, 3/65
Persimmon Shake, 3/270
Pesto Sauce, 3/60
Pie Crust, 3/43
Pineapple Water, 3/255
Pinto Beans, 3/353
Pomegranate Drink, 3/271
Portuguese Beans, 3/324
Potato Salad, 3/245
Potato Stew, 3/190
Potato Stew, 3/221
Potatoes and Almonds, 3/333
Potatoes and Mushrooms, 3/83
Potatoes and Spinach, 3/138
Potatoes with Peas, 3/169

Quesadillas, 3/70
Quinoa Risotto, 3/136

Radish Dressing, 3/57
Rainbow Salad, 3/184
Red and White Salad, 3/372
Red Tomato Sauce, 3/63
Refreshing Tea, 3/254
Rice Crackers, 3/196
Rice Hamburgers, 3/170
Rice Milk, 3/273
Rice Pudding, 3/199
Rice Salad, 3/380
Rice with Artichokes, 3/234
Rice with Carrots, 3/133
Rice with Cauliflower, 3/282
Rice with Pumpkin, 3/193
Rice with Spinach, 3/192
River Salad, 3/206
Roasted Vegetables, 3/384
Rye Bread, 3/194

Sangria (non-alcoholic), 3/327
Sardinian Adzuki, 3/302
Sauerkraut and Carrot, 3/264
Sautéed Marinated Gluten, 3/91
Sautéed Soy Sprouts, 3/265
Seasoned White Sauce, 3/59
Seed Salad, 3/298
Sesame Crepes, 3/304
Sesame Sauce, 3/60
Soy Croquettes, 3/326
Soy Hamburgers, 3/117
Soy Mayonnaise, 3/58
Soy Milk, 3/305
Soy or Meat Analogs Kebabs, 3/74
Soy Sweet-and-Sour Sauce, 3/56
Soybean Stew, 3/381
Spaghetti with Spinach, 3/210
Spanish Bouillon, 3/332
Spanish Omelet (without egg), 3/76
Spanish Omelet, 3/114
Spinach Croquettes, 3/213
Spinach Lasagna, 3/108
Spinach Salad, 3/132
Spinach Shake, 3/140
Spring Rolls, 3/102
Spring Salad, 3/312
Sprouts Salad, 3/244
Stewed Figs and Pears, 3/225
Strawberry Delight, 3/177
Stuffed Artichokes, 3/286
Stuffed Avocados, 3/207
Stuffed Eggplant, 3/120
Stuffed Eggs, 3/118
Stuffed Kohlrabi, 3/337
Stuffed Peppers, 3/382
Stuffed Tomatoes, 3/300
Sweet Balls, 3/269
Sweet Cassava Salad, 3/218
Sweet Corn Drink, 3/293
Sweet Walnut Rolls (without egg), 3/77
Sweet-and-Sour Kebabs, 3/75
Sweet-and-Sour Sauce from Seeds, 3/56

Tabulé, 3/261
Taco Salad, 3/70
Tacos, 3/70
Tahini, 3/61
Tamarind Drink, 3/237
Three-colored Purée, 3/377
Tiger Nut Horchata, 3/272
Tofu and Herbs Spread, 3/66
Tofu Kebabs, 3/74
Tofu Salad, 3/299
Tomato and Garlic Bread, 3/71
Tomato and Vegetable Stew, 3/212
Tomato Specialty Sauce, 3/62
Traditional Tomato Sauce, 3/62
Tropical Fruit Salad, 3/253
Tropical Salad Rolls, 3/71
Tropical Shake, 3/158
Turnip Greens and Potatoes, 3/208

Vegetable Hamburgers, 3/152
Vegetable Juice, 3/385
Vegetable Mayonnaise, 3/58
Vegetable Paella, 3/86
Vegetable Pie, 3/104
Vegetable Purée, 3/361
Vegetable Rice, 3/266
Vegetable Sauce, 3/64
Vegetable Turnovers, 3/106
Vegetables Cannelloni, 3/98
Vegetarian Sausage Kebabs, 3/74
Vegetarian Sausages and Drumsticks, 3/92
Vegetarian Tamale, 3/301
Vichyssoise, 3/280
Violet Salad, 3/373

Walnut Butter, 3/65
Watermelon Shake, 3/292
White Sauce from Vegetable Stock, 3/59
White Sauce with Onion, 3/59
White Sauce, 3/59
Whole Bread, 3/46
Winter Log, 3/340

Yam with Tomato, 3/191
Yogurt Mayonnaise, 3/58

Zucchini Canapés, 3/68
Zucchini Salad, 3/185

Source of Illustrations

Corel Stock Photo Library: 311.

Digital stock: 79, 161, 203, 239, 345, 357, 369.

Life Art: 128, 160, 202, 214, 226, 238, 256, 328.

PhotoDisc: 22.

Stockbyte: 129, 181, 215, 227, 295, 305, 329.

■ ■ ■

All **photographs, charts, graphs, and drawings** not included in the above list have been carried out by the **Safeliz Publishers Team** (see p. 4).